Consumer and Commercial Statutes

Consumer and Commercial Statutes

First edition

Compiled by Paul Dobson LLB, Barrister

Principal lecturer in law at the Polytechnic of North London

© Longman Group UK Ltd 1989

ISBN 0 85121 5173

Published by
Longman Group UK Limited
21–27 Lamb's Conduit Street, London WC1N 3NJ

Associated Offices
Australia, Hong Kong, Malaysia, Singapore, USA

All rights reserved. No part of this publication may be reproduced, stored in a retrieval system, or transmitted, in any form or by any means, electronic, mechanical, photocopying, recording or otherwise, without prior written permission of the copyright owner, or a licence permitting restricted copying issued by the Copyright Licensing Agency Ltd, 33–34 Alfred Place, London WC1E 7DP.

A CIP catalogue record for this book is available from the British Library.

Typeset by Kerrypress Ltd, Luton.
Printed by Bookcraft (Bath) Ltd.

Contents

Statutes

Bills of Lading Act 1855	1
Bills of Sale Act 1878	2
Bankers' Books Evidence Act 1879, section 9	10
Bills of Sale Act (1878) Amendment Act 1882	11
Bills of Exchange Act 1882	17
Factors Act 1889	51
Bills of Sale Act 1890	56
Law of Distress Amendment Act 1908	57
Auctions (Bidding Agreements) Act 1927	62
Cheques Act 1957	64
Trading Representations (Disabled Persons) Act 1958	67
Mock Auctions Act 1961	69
Hire Purchase Act 1964, Part III	71
Trading Stamps Act 1964	75
Misrepresentation Act 1967	81
Trade Descriptions Act 1968	83
Auctions (Bidding Agreements) Act 1969	100
Administration of Justice Act 1970, section 40	103
Unsolicited Goods & Services Acts 1971 and 1975	104
Supply of Goods (Implied Terms) Act 1973	109
Fair Trading Act 1973	115
Powers of Criminal Courts Act 1973, sections 35 to 38	148
Consumer Credit Act 1974	152
Torts (Interference with Goods) Act 1977	275
Unfair Contract Terms Act 1977	286
Estate Agents Act 1979	304
Sale of Goods Act 1979	337
Magistrates' Courts Act 1980, section 40	365
Supreme Court Act 1981, section 138	366
Supply of Goods and Services Act 1982	367
County Courts Act 1984, sections 99 and 103	378
Data Protection Act 1984	380
Law Reform (Miscellaneous Provisions) (Scotland) Act 1985, section 10	383
Minors' Contracts Act 1987	384
Consumer Protection Act 1987	386
Consumer Arbitration Agreements Act 1988	438

Statutory Instruments

Mail Order Transactions 1976	443
Consumer Transactions (Restrictions on Statements) Order 1976	445
Business Advertisements (Disclosure) Order 1977	449
Consumer Protection (Cancellation of Contracts Concluded away from Business Premises) Regulations 1987	450
Control of Misleading Advertisements Regulations 1988	458

Bills of Lading Act 1855
Chapter 111

An Act to amend the Law relating to Bills of Lading　　　[14 August 1855]

Whereas, by the custom of merchants, a bill of lading of goods being transferable by endorsement, the property in the goods may thereby pass to the endorsee, but nevertheless all rights in respect of the contract contained in the bill of lading continue in the original shipper or owner; and it is expedient that such rights should pass with the property: And whereas it frequently happens that the goods in respect of which bills of lading purport to be signed have not been laden on board, and it is proper that such bills of lading in the hands of a bona fide holder for value should not be questioned by the master or other person signing the same on the ground of the goods not having been laden as aforesaid:

1. Rights under bills of lading to vest in consignee or endorsee

Every consignee of goods named in a bill of lading, and every endorsee of a bill of lading, to whom the property in the goods therein mentioned shall pass upon or by reason of such consignment or endorsement, shall have transferred to and vested in him all rights of suit, and be subject to the same liabilities in respect of such goods as if the contract contained in the bill of lading had been made with himself.

2. Not to affect right of stoppage in transitu or claims for freight

Nothing herein contained shall prejudice or affect any right of stoppage in transitu, or any right to claim freight against the original shipper or owner, or any liability of the consignee or endorsee by reason or in consequence of his being such consignee or endorsee, or of his receipt of the goods by reason or in consequence of such consignment or endorsement.

3. Bill of lading in hands of consignee, etc, conclusive evidence of shipment as against master, etc—Proviso

Every bill of lading in the hands of a consignee or endorsee for valuable consideration, representing goods to have been shipped on board a vessel, shall be conclusive evidence of such shipment as against the master or other person signing the same, notwithstanding that such goods or some part thereof may not have been so shipped, unless such holder of the bill of lading shall have had actual notice at the time of receiving the same that the goods had not been in fact laden on board; Provided, that the master or other person so signing may exonerate himself in respect of such misrepresentation by showing that it was caused without any default on his part, and wholly by the fraud of the shipper, or of the holder, or some person under whom the holder claims.

Bills of Sale Act 1878
Chapter 31

ARRANGEMENT OF SECTIONS

Section
1. Short title
2. Commencement
3. Application
4. Interpretation of terms
5. Application of Act to trade machinery
6. Certain instruments giving powers of distress to be subject to this Act
7. Fixtures or growing crops not to be deemed separately assigned when the land passes by the same instrument

* * *

9. Avoidance of certain duplicate bills of sale
10. Mode of registering bills of sale
11. Renewal of registration
12. Form of register
13. The registrar
14. Rectification of register
15. Entry of satisfaction
16. Copies may be taken, etc.
17. Affidavits

* * *

19. Collection of fees under 38 & 39 Vict c 77, s 26

* * *

21. Rules
22. Time for registration
23. As to bills of sale and under repealed Acts
24. Extent to Act

SCHEDULES

An Act to consolidate and amend the Law for preventing Frauds upon Creditors by secret Bills of Sale of Personal Chattels

[22nd July 1878]

[*This Act should be read subject to the provisions of the Bills of Sale* (1878) *Amendment Act* 1882.]

Bills of Sale Act 1878

1. Short title

This Act may be cited for all purposes as the Bills of Sale Act 1878.

2. Commencement

... on the first day of January one thousand eight hundred and seventy-nine is in this Act referred to as the commencement of this Act.

[*The words omitted were repealed by the Statute Law Revision Act* 1894.]

3. Application

This Act shall apply to every bill of sale executed on or after the first day of January one thousand eight hundred and seventy-nine (whether the same be absolute, or subject or not subject to any trust) whereby the holder or grantee has power, either with or without notice, and either immediately or at any future time, to seize or take possession of any personal chattels comprised in or made subject to such bill of sale.

4. Interpretation of terms

In this Act the following words and expressions shall have the meanings in this section assigned to them respectively, unless there be something in the subject or context repugnant to such construction; (that is to say),

> The expression 'bill of sale' shall include bills of sale, assignments, transfers, declarations of trust without transfer, inventories of goods with receipt thereto attached, or receipts for purchase moneys of goods, and other assurances of personal chattels, and also powers of attorney, authorities, or licenses to take possession of personal chattels as security for any debt, and also any agreement, whether intended or not to be followed by the execution of any other instrument by which a right in equity to any personal chattels, or to any charge or security thereon, shall be conferred, but shall not include the following documents; that is to say, assignments for the benefit of the creditors of the person making or giving the same, marriage settlements, transfers or assignments of any ship or vessel or any share thereof, transfers of goods in the ordinary course of business of any trade or calling, bills of sale of goods in foreign parts or at sea, bills of lading, India warrants, warehouse-keepers' certificates, warrants or orders for the delivery of goods, or any other documents used in the ordinary course of business as proof of the possession or control of goods, or authorising or purporting to authorise, either by indorsement or by delivery, the possessor of such document to transfer or receive goods thereby represented:

> The expression 'personal chattels' shall mean goods, furniture and other articles capable of complete transfer by delivery, and (when separately assigned or charged) fixtures and growing crops, but shall not include chattel interests in real estate, nor fixtures (except trade machinery as hereinafter defined), when assigned together with a freehold or leasehold interest in any land or building to which they are affixed, nor growing crops when assigned together with any interest in the land on which they grow, nor shares or interests in the stock, funds, or securities of any government, or in the capital or property of incorporated or joint stock companies, nor choses in action, nor any stock or produce upon any farm or lands which by virtue of any covenant or agreement or

Bills of Sale Act 1878

of the custom of the country ought not to be removed from any farm where the same are at the time of making or giving of such bill of sale:

Personal chattels shall be deemed to be in the 'apparent possession' of the person making or giving a bill of sale, so long as they remain or are in or upon any house, mill, warehouse, building, works, yard, land, or other premises occupied by him, or are used and enjoyed by him in any place whatsoever, notwithstanding that formal possession thereof may have been taken by or given to any other person:

'Prescribed' means prescribed by rules made under the provisions of this Act.

5. Application of Act to trade machinery

From and after the commencement of this Act trade machinery shall, for the purposes of this Act, be deemed to be personal chattels, and any mode of disposition of trade machinery by the owner thereof which would be a bill of sale as to any other personal chattels shall be deemed to be a bill of sale within the meaning of this Act.

For the purposes of this Act—

'Trade machinery' means the machinery used in or attached to any factory or workshop;

   1st Exclusive of the fixed motive-powers, such as the water-wheels and steam-engines, and the steam-boilers, donkey-engines, and other fixed appurtenances of the said motive-powers; and

   2nd Exclusive of the fixed power machinery, such as the shafts, wheels, drums, and their fixed appurtenances, which transmit the action of the motive-powers to the other machinery, fixed and loose; and,

   3rd Exclusive of the pipes for steam gas and water in the factory or workshop.

   The machinery or effects excluded by this section from the definition of trade machinery shall not be deemed to be personal chattels within the meaning of this Act.

'Factory or workshop' means any premises on which any manual labour is exercised by way of trade, or for purposes of gain, in or incidental to the following purposes or any of them; that is to say,

(*a*) In or incidental to the making any article or part of an article; or

(*b*) In or incidental to the altering, repairing, ornamenting, finishing of any article; or

(*c*) In or incidental to the adapting for sale any article.

6. Certain instruments giving powers of distress to be subject to this Act

Every attornment instrument or agreement, not being a mining lease, whereby a power of distress is given or agreed to be given by any person to any other person by way of security for any present future or contingent debt or advance, and whereby any rent is reserved or made payable as a mode of providing for the payment of interest on such debt or advance, or otherwise for the purpose of such security only, shall be deemed to be a bill of sale, within the meaning of this Act, of any personal chattels which may be seized or taken under such power of distress.

Provided, that nothing in this section shall extend to any mortgage of any estate or interest in any land tenement or hereditament which the mortgagee, being in possession, shall have demised to the mortgagor as his tenant at a fair and reasonable rent.

7. Fixtures or growing crops not to be deemed separately assigned when the land passes by the same instrument

No fixtures or growing crops shall be deemed, under this Act, to be separately assigned or charged by reason only that they are assigned by separate words, or that power is given to sever them from the land or building to which they are affixed, or from the land on which they grow, without otherwise taking possession of or dealing with such land or building, or land, if by the same instrument any freehold or leasehold interest in the land or building to which such fixtures are affixed, or in the land on which such crops grow, is also conveyed or assigned to the same persons or person.

The same rule of constructon shall be applied to all deeds or instruments, including fixtures or growing crops, executed before the commencement of this Act, and then subsisting and in force, in all questions arising under any bankruptcy liquidation assignment for the benefit of creditors, or execution of any process of any court, which shall take place or be issued after the commencement of this Act.

[*Section 8 was repealed by the Bills of Sale Act* (1878) *Amendment Act* 1882, *sections* 3 *and* 15 *in respect of bills of sale given by way of security for the payment of money.*]

9. Avoidance of certain duplicate bills of sale

Where a subsequent bill of sale is executed within or on the expiration of seven days after the execution of a prior unregistered bill of sale, and comprises all or any part of the personal chattels comprised in such prior bill of sale, then, if such subsequent bill of sale is given as a security for the same debt as is secured by the prior bill of sale, or for any part of such debt, it shall, to the extent to which it is a security for the same debt or part thereof, and so far as respects the personal chattels or part thereof comprised in the prior bill, be absolutely void, unless it is proved to the satisfaction of the court having cognizance of the case that the subsequent bill of sale was bona fide given for the purpose of correcting some material error in the prior bill of sale, and not for the purpose of evading this Act.

10. Mode of registering bills of sale

A bill of sale shall be attested and registered under this Act in the following manner:

* * *

(2) Such bill, with every schedule or inventory thereto annexed or therein referred to, and also a true copy of such bill and of every such schedule or inventory, and of every attestation of the execution of such bill of sale, together with an affidavit of the time of such bill of sale being made or given, and of its due execution and attestation, and a description of the residence and occupation of the person making or giving the same (or in case the same is made or given by any person under or in the execution of any process, then a description of the residence and occupation of the person against whom such process issued), and of every attesting witness to such bill of sale, shall be presenting to and the said copy and affidavit shall be filed with the registrar within seven clear days after the making or giving of such bill of sale, in like manner as a warrant of attorney in any personal action given by a trader is not by law required to be filed:

(3) If the bill of sale is made or given subject to any defeasance or condition, or declaration of trust not contained in the body thereof, such defeasance, condition, or declaration shall be deemed to be part of the bill, and shall be written on the same paper or parchment therewith before the registration, and shall be truly set forth in the copy filed under this Act therewith and as part thereof, otherwise the registration shall be void.

In case two or more bills of sale are given, comprising in whole or in part any of the same chattels, they shall have priority in the order of the date of their registration respectively as regards such chattels.

A transfer of assignment of a registered bill of sale need not be registered.

[*Subsection (1) was repealed by the Bills of Sale Act* (1878) *Amendment Act* 1882, *sections* 3 *and* 10, *in respect of bills of sale given by way of security for the payment of money. This section should be read subject to the Administration of Justice Act* 1925, *section* 23(2), *which provides:—*

(2) Section ten of the Bills of Sale Act, 1878, shall have effect as though it required the presentation to the registrar on the registration of a bill of sale, in addition to the copy of the bill of sale mentioned in paragraph (2) of that section, of such number of copies of the bill and every schedule and inventory annexed thereto as the registrar may deem to be necessary for the purpose of carrying out the requirements of the said section eleven as amended by this section.]

11. Renewal of registration

The registration of a bill of sale, whether executed before or after the commencement of this Act, must be renewed once at least every five years, and if a period of five years elapses from the registration or renewed registration of a bill of sale without a renewal or further renewal (as the case may be), the registration shall become void.

The renewal of a registration shall be effected by filing with the registrar an affidavit stating the date of the bill of sale and of the last registration thereof, and the names, residence, and occupations of the parties thereto as stated therein, and that the bill of sale is still a subsisting security.

Every such affidavit may be in the form set forth in the Schedule (A) to this Act annexed.

Bills of Sale Act 1878

A renewal of registration shall not become necessary by reason only of a transfer or assignment of a bill of sale.

12. Form of register

The registrar shall keep a book (in this Act called 'the register') for the purposes of this Act, and shall, upon the filing of any bill of sale or copy under this Act, enter therein in the form set forth in the second schedule (B) to this Act annexed, or in any other prescribed form, the name, residence and occupation of the person by whom the bill was made or given (or in case the same was made or given by any person under or in the execution of process, then the name, residence and occupation of the person against whom such process was issued, and also the name of the person or persons to whom or in whose favour the bill was given), and the other particulars shown in the said schedule or to be prescribed under this Act, and shall number all such bills registered in each year consecutively, according to the respective dates of their registration.

Upon the registration of any affidavit of renewal the like entry shall be made, with the addition of the date and number of the last previous entry relating to the same bill, and the bill of sale or copy originally filed shall be thereupon marked with the number affixed to such affidavit of renewal.

The register shall also keep an index of the names of the grantors of registered bills of sale with reference to entries in the register of the bills of sale given by each such grantor.

Such index shall be arranged in divisions corresponding with the letters of the alphabet, so that all grantors whose surnames begin with the same letter (and no others) shall be comprised in one division, but the arrangement within each such division need not be strictly alphabetical.

13. The registrar

The masters of the Supreme Court of Judicature attached to the Queen's Bench Division of the High Court of Justice, or such other officers as may for the time being be assigned for this purpose under the provisions of the Supreme Court of Judicature Acts, 1873 and 1875, shall be the registrar for the purposes of this Act, and any one of the said masters may perform all or any of the duties of the registrar.

14. Rectification of register

Any judge of the High Court of Justice on being satisfied that the omission to register a bill of sale or an affidavit or renewal thereof within the time prescribed by this Act, or the omission or mis-statement of the name, residence or occupation of any person, was accidental or due to inadvertence, may in his discretion order such omission or mis-statement to be rectified by the insertion in the register of the true name, residence or occupation, or by extending the time for such registration on such terms and conditions (if any) as to security, notice by advertisement or otherwise, or as to any other matter, as he thinks fit to direct.

15. Entry of satisfaction

Subject to and in accordance with any rules to be made under and for the purposes of this Act, the registrar may order a memorandum of satisfaction

Bills of Sale Act 1878

to be written upon any registered copy of a bill of sale, upon the prescribed evidence being given that the debt (if any) for which such bill of sale was made or given has been satisfied or discharged.

16. Copies may be taken, etc.

Any person shall be entitled to have an office copy or extract of any registered bill of sale, and affidavit of execution filed therewith, or copy thereof, and of any affidavit filed therewith, if any, or registered affidavit of renewal, upon paying for the same at the like rate as for office copies of judgments of the High Court of Justice, and any copy of a registered bill of sale, and affidavit purporting to be an office copy thereof, shall in all courts, and before all arbitrators or other persons, be admitted as prima facie evidence thereof, and of the fact and date of registration as shown thereon. . . .

[*The words omitted were repealed by the Bills of Sale Act (1878) Amendment Act 1882, section 16.*]

17. Affidavits

Every affidavit required by or for the purposes of this Act may be sworn before a master of any division of the High Court of Justice, or before any commissioner empowered to take affidavits in the Supreme Court of Judicature . . . .

[*The words omitted were repealed by the Perjury Act 1911, section 17 and schedule.*]

[*Section 18 was repealed by the Statute Law Revision Act 1950.*]

19. Collection of fees under 38 & 39 Vict c 77 s 26

Section twenty-six of the Supreme Court of Judicature Act, 1875, and any enactments for the time being in force amending or substituted for that section, shall apply to fees under this Act, and an order under that section may, if need be, be made in relation to such fees accordingly.

[*See the Supreme Court Fees Order 1980 (S.I. 1980 No. 821), items 21 and 24.*]

[*Section 20 was repealed by the Bills of Sale Act (1878) Amendment Act 1882, sections 3 and 15, in respect of bills of sale given by way of security for the payment of money.*]

21. Rules

Rules for the purposes of this Act may be made and altered from time to time by the like persons and in the like manner in which rules and regulations may be made under and for the purposes of the Supreme Court of Judicature Acts, 1873 and 1875.

[*See Rules of the Supreme Court, Order 95.*]

22. Time for registration

When the time for registering a bill of sale expires on a Sunday, or other day on which the registrar's office is closed, the registration shall be valid if made on the next following day on which the office is open.

Bills of Sale Act 1878

23. As to bills of sale and under repealed Acts

... Provided that (except as is herein expressly mentioned with respect to construction and with respect to renewal of registration) nothing in this Act shall affect any bill of sale executed before the commencement of this Act, and as regards bills of sale so executed the Acts hereby repealed shall continue in force.

Any renewal after the commencement of this Act of the registration of a bill of sale executed before the commencement of this Act, and registered under the Acts hereby repealed, shall be made under this Act in the same manner as the renewal of a registration made under this Act.

[*The words omitted were repealed by the Statute Law Revision Act 1894.*]

24. Extent of Act

This Act shall not extend to Scotland or to Ireland.

SCHEDULES

Schedule A

I [*A.B.*] of do swear that a bill of sale, bearing date the day of 18 [*insert the date of the bill*], and made between [*insert the names and descriptions of the parties in the original bill of sale*] and which said bill of sale [*or,* and a copy of which said bill of sale, *as the case may be*] was registered on the day of 18 [*insert date of registration*], is still a subsisting security.

Sworn, &c.

Schedule B

Satisfaction entered.	No.	By whom given (or against whom process issued).			To whom given.	Nature of Instrument.	Date.	Date of Registration.	Date of Registration of affidavit of renewal.
		Name	Residence.	Occupation.					

Bankers' Books Evidence Act 1879
Chapter 11

9. Interpretation of 'bank', 'banker' and 'bankers' books'

(1) In this Act the expresssions 'bank' and 'banker' mean—
   [(*a*) an institution authorised under the Banking Act 1987 or a municipal bank within the meaning of that Act;]
   [(*aa*) a building society (within the meaning of the Building Societies Act 1986);]
   [(*b*)...]
   (*c*) the National Savings Bank; and
   (*d*) the Post Office, in the exercise of its powers to provide banking services.

(2) Expressions in this Act relating to 'bankers' books' include ledgers, day books, cash books, account books and other records used in the ordinary business of the bank, whether those records are in written form or are kept on microfilm, magnetic tape or any other form of mechanical or electronic data retrieval mechanism.

[*This section appears here as substituted by the Banking Act 1979, section 51(1) and Schedule 6, paragraph 1. Amendments since then, denoted by square brackets, were made as follows: subsection (1)(a) was substituted by the Banking Act 1987, section 108(1) and Schedule 6, paragraph 1; subsection (1)(aa) was inserted by the Building Societies Act 1986, section 120 and Schedule 18, paragraph 1; subsection (1)(b) was repealed by the Trustee Savings Bank Act 1985, sections 4(3) and 7(3) and Schedule 4.*]

Bills of Sale Act (1878) Amendment Act 1882
Chapter 43

ARRANGEMENT OF SECTIONS

Section
1. Short title
2. Commencement of Act
3. Construction of Act
4. Bill of sale to have schedule of property attached thereto
5. Bill of sale not to affect after-acquired property
6. Exception as to certain things
7. Bill of sale with power to seize except in certain events to be void
7A. Defaults under consumer credit agreements
8. Bill of sale to be void unless attested and registered
9. Form of bill of sale
10. Attestation
11. Local registration of contents of bills of sale
12. Bill of sale under £30 to be void
13. Chattels not to be removed or sold
14. Bill of sale not to protect chattels against poor and parochial rates
15. Repeal of part of Bills of Sale Act, 1878
16. Inspection of registered bills of sale
17. Debentures to which Act not to apply
18. Extent of Act

SCHEDULE

An Act to amend the Bills of Sale Act, 1878

[18th August 1882]

1. Short title

This Act may be cited for all purposes as the Bills of Sale Act (1878) Amendment Act, 1882; and this Act and the Bills of Sale Act, 1878, may be cited together as the Bills of Sale Acts, 1878 and 1882.

2. Commencement of Act

This Act shall come into operation on the first day of November one thousand eight hundred and eighty-two, which date is hereinafter referred to as the commencement of this Act.

3. Construction of Act

The Bills of Sale Act, 1878, is hereinafter referred to as 'the principal Act,' and this Act shall, so far as is consistent with the tenor thereof, be construed as one with the principal Act; but unless the context otherwise requires shall not apply to any bill of sale duly registered before the commencement of this Act so long as the registration thereof is not avoided by non-renewal or otherwise.

The expression 'bill of sale,' and other expressions in this Act, have the same

Bills of Sale Act (1878) Amendment Act 1882

meaning as in the principal Act, except as to bills of sale or other documents mentioned in section four of the principal Act, which may be given otherwise than by way of security for the payment of money, to which last-mentioned bills of sale and other documents this Act shall not apply.

4. Bill of sale to have schedule of property attached thereto

Every bill of sale shall have annexed thereto or written thereon a schedule containing an inventory of the personal chattels comprised in the bill of sale; and such bill of sale, save as hereinafter mentioned, shall have effect only in respect of the personal chattels specifically described in the said schedule; and shall be void, except as against the grantor, in respect of any personal chattels not so specifically described.

5. Bill of sale not to affect after-acquired property

Save as hereinafter mentioned, a bill of sale shall be void, except as against the grantor, in respect of any personal chattels specifically described in the schedule thereto of which the grantor was not the true owner at the time of the execution of the bill of sale.

6. Exception as to certain things

Nothing contained in the foregoing sections of this Act shall render a bill of sale void in respect of any of the following things; (that is to say,)

(1) Any growing crops separately assigned or charged where such crops were actually growing at the time when the bill of sale was executed.

(2) Any fixtures separately assigned or charged, and any plant, or trade machinery where such fixtures, plant, or trade machinery are used in, attached to, or brought upon any land, farm, factory, workshop, shop, house, warehouse, or other place in substitution for any of the like fixtures, plant, or trade machinery specifically described in the schedule to such bill of sale.

7. Bill of sale with power to seize except in certain events to be void

Personal chattels assigned under a bill of sale shall not be liable to be seized or taken possession of by the grantee for any other than the following causes:—

(1) If the grantor shall make default in payment of the sum or sums of money thereby secured at the time therein provided for payment, or in the performance of any covenant or agreement contained in the bill of sale and necessary for maintaining the security;

(2) If the grantor shall become a bankrupt, or suffer the said goods or any of them to be distrained for rent, rates, or taxes;

(3) If the grantor shall fraudulently either remove or suffer the said goods, or any of them, to be removed from the premises;

(4) If the grantor shall not, without reasonable excuse, upon demand in writing by the grantee, produce to him his last receipts for rent, rates, and taxes;

(5) If execution shall have been levied against the goods of the grantor under any judgment at law;

Provided that the grantor may within five days from the seizure of taking possession of any chattels on account of any of the above-mentioned causes, apply to High Court, or to a judge thereof in chambers, and such court or judge, if satisfied that by payment of money or otherwise the said cause of seizure no longer exists, may restrain the grantee from removing or selling the said chattels, or may make such other order as may seem just.

7A. Defaults under consumer credit agreements

(1) Paragraph (1) of section 7 of this Act does not apply to a default relating to a bill of sale given by way of security for the payment of money under a regulated agreement to which section 87(1) of the Consumer Credit Act 1974 applies—

(*a*) unless the restriction imposed by section 88(2) of that Act has ceased to apply to the bill of sale; or
(*b*) if, by virtue of section 89 of that Act, the default is to be treated as not having occurred.

(2) Where paragraph (1) of section 7 of this Act does apply in relation to a bill of sale such as is mentioned in subsection (1) of this section, the proviso to that section shall have effect with the substitution of 'county court' for 'High Court'.

[*Section 7A was inserted by the Consumer Credit Act* 1974, *section* 192(3)(a), *and Schedule* 4, *Part I, paragraph* 1.]

8. Bill of sale to be void unless attested and registered

Every bill of sale shall be duly attested, and shall be registered under the principal Act within seven clear days after the execution thereof, or if it is executed in any place out of England then within seven clear days after the time at which it would in the ordinary course of post arrive in England if posted immediately after the execution thereof; and shall truly set forth the consideration for which it was given; otherwise such bill of sale shall be void in respect of the personal chattels comprised therein.

9. Form of bill of sale

A bill of sale made or given by way of security for the payment of money by the grantor thereof shall be void unless made in accordance with the form in the schedule to this Act annexed.

[*This section should be read subject to the Bills of Sale Act* 1890, *section* 1 *as amended by the Bills of Sale Act* 1891, *which provides*:—

1. An instrument charging or creating any security on or declaring trusts of imported goods given or executed at any time prior to their deposit in a warehouse, factory, or store, or to their being reshipped for export, or delivered to a purchaser not being the person giving or executing such instrument, shall not be deemed a bill of sale within the meaning of the Bills of Sale Acts 1878 and 1882.]

10. Attestation

The execution of every bill of sale by the grantor shall be attested by one or more credible witness or witnesses, not being a party or parties thereto . . .

[*The words omitted were repealed by the Statute Law Revision Act* 1898]

11. Local registration of contents of bills of sale

Where the affidavit (which under section ten of the principal Act is required to accompany a bill of sale when presented for registration) describes the residence of the person making or giving the same or of the person against whom the process is issued to be in some place outside [the London insolvency district] or where the bill of sales describes the chattels enumerated therein as being in some place outside [the London insolvency district], the registrar under the principal Act shall forthwith and within three clear days after registration in the principal registry, and in accordance with the prescribed directions, transmit an abstract in the prescribed form of the contents of such bill of sale to the county court registrar in whose district such places are situate, and if such places are in the districts of different registrars to each such registrar.

Every abstract so transmitted shall be filed, kept, and indexed by the registrar of the county court in the prescribed manner, and any person may search, inspect, make extracts from, and obtain copies of the abstract so registered in the like manner and upon the like terms as to payment or otherwise as near as may be as in the case of bills of sale registered by the registrar under the principal Act.

[*The words in square brackets were substituted by the Insolvency Act 1985, Schedule 8.*]

[*This section should be read subject to the Administration of Justice Act* 1925, *section* 23(1) *which provides:*—

23.—(1) Section eleven of the Bills of Sale Act (1878) Amendment Act, 1882 (which makes provision for the local registration of the contents of bills of sale), shall have effect as if it required the registrar of bills of sale to transmit to county court registrar's copies of the bills instead of abstracts of the contents of the bills, and references in that section to the abstract transmitted and the abstract registered shall be construed accordingly.]

12. Bill of sale under £30 to be void

Every bill of sale made or given in consideration of any sum under thirty pounds shall be void.

13. Chattels not to be removed or sold

All personal chattels seized or of which possession is taken . . . under or by virtue of any bill of sale (whether registered before or after the commencement of this Act), shall remain on the premises where they were so seized or so taken possession of, and shall not be removed or sold until after the expiration of five clear days from the day they were so seized or so taken possession of.

[*The words omitted were repealed by the Statute Law Revision Act* 1898.]

14. Bill of sale not to protect chattels against poor and parochial rates

A bill of sale to which this Act applies shall be no protection in respect of personal chattels included in such bill of sale which but for such bill of sale would have been liable to distress under a warrant for the recovery of taxes and poor and other parochial rates.

Bills of Sale Act (1878) Amendment Act 1882

15. Repeal of part of Bills of Sale Act 1878

... all ... enactments contained in the principal Act which are inconsistent with this Act are repealed . . . .

[*The words omitted were repealed by the Statute Law Revision Act 1898.*]

16. Inspection of registered bills of sale

... any person shall be entitled at all reasonable times to search the register, on payment of a fee of one shilling, or such other fee as may be prescribed, and subject to such regulations as may be prescribed, and shall be entitled at all reasonable times to inspect, examine, and make extracts from any and every registered bill of sale without being required to make a written application, or to specify any particulars in reference thereto, upon payment of one shilling for each bill of sale inspected, and such payment shall be made by a judicature stamp. Provided that the said extracts shall be limited to the dates of execution, registration, renewal of registration, and satisfaction, to the names, addresses, and occupations of the parties, to the amount of the consideration, and to any further prescribed particulars.

[*The words omitted were repealed by the Statute Law Registion Act 1898.*]

17. Debentures to which Act not to apply

Nothing in this Act shall apply to any debentures issued by any mortgage, loan, or other incorporated company, and secured upon the capital stock or goods, chattels, and effects of such company.

18. Extent of Act

This Act shall not extend to Scotland or Ireland.

SCHEDULE

FORM OF BILL OF SALE

This Indenture made the   day of   between *A.B.* of   of the one part, and *C.D.* of   of the other part, witnesseth that in consideration of the sum of £   now paid to *A.B.* by *C.D.*, the receipt of which the said *A.B.* hereby acknowledges [*or whatever else the consideration may be*], he the said *A.B.* doth hereby assign unto *C.D.*, his executors, administrators, and assigns, all and singular the several chattels and things specifically described in the schedule hereto annexed by way of security for the payment of the sum of £   , and interest thereon at the rate of   per cent per annum [*or whatever else may be the rate*]. And the said *A.B.* doth further agree and declare that he will duly pay to the said *C.D.* the principal sum aforesaid, together with the interest then due, by equal   payments of £   on the   day of   [*or whatever else may be the stipulated times or time of payment*]. And the said *A.B.* doth also agree with the said *C.D.* that he will [*here insert terms as to insurance, payment of rent, or otherwise, which the parties may agree to for the maintenance or defeasance of the security*].

Bills of Sale Act (1878) Amendment Act 1882

Provided always, that the chattels hereby assigned shall not be liable to seizure or to be taken possession of by the said *C.D.* for any cause other than those specified in section seven of the Bills of Sale Act (1878) Amendment Act 1882.

In witness, &c.

Signed and sealed by the said *A.B.* in the presence of me *E.F.* [*add witness's name, address, and description*].

Bills of Exchange Act 1882
Chapter 61

ARRANGEMENT OF SECTIONS

PART I

PRELIMINARY

Section
1. Short title
2. Interpretation of terms

PART II

BILLS OF EXCHANGE

Form and Interpretation

3. Bill of exchange defined
4. Inland and foreign bills
5. Effect where different parties to bill are the same person
6. Address to drawee
7. Certainty required as to payee
8. What bills are negotiable
9. Sum payable
10. Bill payable on demand
11. Bill payable at a future time
12. Omission of date in bill payable after date
13. Ante-dating and post-dating
14. Computation of time of payment
15. Case of need
16. Optional stipulations by drawer or indorser
17. Definition and requisites of acceptance
18. Time for acceptance
19. General and qualified acceptances
20. Inchoate instruments
21. Delivery

Capacity and Authority of Parties

22. Capacity of parties
23. Signature essential to liability
24. Forged or unauthorised signature
25. Procuration signatures
26. Person signing as agent or in representative capacity

The Consideration for a Bill

27. Value, and holder for value
28. Accommodation bill or party

Bills of Exchange Act 1882

Section
29. Holder in due course
30. Presumption of value and good faith

Negotiation of Bills

31. Negotiation of bill
32. Requisites of a valid indorsement
33. Conditional indorsement
34. Indorsement in blank and special indorsement
35. Restrictive indorsement
36. Negotiation of overdue or dishonoured bill
37. Negotiation of bill to party already liable thereon
38. Rights of the holder

General duties of the Holder

39. When presentment for acceptance is necessary
40. Time for presenting bill payable after sight
41. Rules as to presentment for acceptance, and excuses for non-presentment
42. Non-acceptance
43. Dishonour by non-acceptance and its consequences.
44. Duties as to qualified acceptances
45. Rules as to presentment for payment
46. Excuses for delay or non-presentment for payment
47. Dishonour by non-payment
48. Notice of dishonour and effect of non-notice
49. Rules as to notice of dishonour
50. Excuses for non-notice and delay
51. Noting or protest of bill
52. Duties of holder as regards drawee or acceptor

Liabilities of Parties

53. Funds in hands of drawee
54. Liability of acceptor
55. Liability of drawer or indorser
56. Stranger signing bill liable as indorser
57. Measure of damages against parties to dishonoured bill
58. Transferor by delivery and transferee

Discharge of Bill

59. Payment in due course
60. Banker paying demand draft whereon indorsement is forged
61. Acceptor the holder at maturity
62. Express waiver
63. Cancellation
64. Alteration of bill

Acceptance and Payment for Honour

65. Acceptance for honour supra protest
66. Liability of acceptor for honour
67. Presentment to acceptor for honour

Section
68. Payment for honour supra protest

Lost Instruments

69. Holder's right to duplicate of lost bill
70. Action on lost bill

Bill in a Set

71. Rules as to sets

Conflict of Laws

72. Rules where laws conflict

PART III

Cheques on a Banker

73. Cheque defined
74. Presentment of cheque for payment
75. Revocation of banker's authority

Crossed Cheques

76. General and special crossings defined
77. Crossing by drawer or after issue
78. Crossing a material part of cheque
79. Duties of banker as to crossed cheques
80. Protection to banker and drawer where cheque is crossed
81. Effect of crossing on holder

* * *

PART IV

Promissory Notes

83. Promissory note defined
84. Delivery necessary
85. Joint and several notes
86. Note payable on demand
87. Presentment of note for payment
88. Liability of maker
89. Application of Part II to notes

PART V

Supplementary

90. Good faith
91. Signature
92. Computation of time
93. When noting equivalent to protest
94. Protest when notary not accessible

Section
95. Dividend warrants may be crossed

* * *

97. Savings
98. Saving of summary diligence in Scotland
99. Construction with other Acts, &c
100. Parole evidence allowed in certain judicial proceedings in Scotland

SCHEDULE I—Form

An Act to codify the law relating to Bills of Exchange, Cheques, and Promissory Notes.

[18th August 1882]

PART I

PRELIMINARY

1. Short title

This Act may be cited as the Bills of Exchange Act, 1882.

2. Interpretation of terms

In this Act, unless the context otherwise requires,—

'Acceptance' means an acceptance completed by delivery or notification.
'Action' includes counter-claim and set off.
'Banker' includes a body of persons whether incorporated or not who carry on the business of banking.
'Bankrupt' includes any person whose estate is vested in a trustee or assignee under the law for the time being in force relating to bankruptcy.
'Bearer' means the person in possession of a bill or note which is payable to bearer.
'Bill' means bill of exchange, and 'note' means promissory note.
'Delivery' means transfer of possession, actual or constructive, from one person to another.
'Holder' means the payee or indorsee of a bill or note who is in possession of it, or the bearer thereof.
'Indorsement' means an indorsement completed by delivery.
'Issue' means the first delivery of a bill or note, complete in form to a person who takes it as a holder.
'Person' includes a body of persons whether incorporated or not.
'Value' means valuable consideration.
'Written' includes printed, and 'writing' includes print.

Bills of Exchange Act 1882

PART II

BILLS OF EXCHANGE

Form and Interpretation

3. Bill of exchange defined

(1) A bill of exchange is an unconditional order in writing, addressed by one person to another, signed by the person giving it, requiring the person to whom it is addressed to pay on demand or at a fixed or determinable future time a sum certain in money to or to the order of a specified person, or to bearer.

(2) An instrument which does not comply with these conditions, or which orders any act to be done in addition to the payment of money, is not a bill of exchange.

(3) An order to pay out of a particular fund is not unconditional within the meaning of this section; but an unqualified order to pay, coupled with (*a*) an indication of a particular fund out of which the drawee is to reimburse himself or a particular account to be debited with the amount, or (*b*) a statement of the transaction which gives rise to the bill, is unconditional.

(4) A bill is not invalid by reason—

(*a*) That it is not dated;
(*b*) That it does not specify the value given, or that any value has been given therefor;
(*c*) That it does not specify the place where it is drawn or the place where it is payable.

[*Section 3 should be read subject to the Decimal Currency Act* 1969, *section 2, which provides*:—

2.—(1) A bill of exchange or promissory note drawn or made on or after the appointed day shall be invalid if the sum payable is an amount of money wholly or partly in shillings or pence.

(2) A bill of exchange or promissory note for an amount wholly or partly in shillings or pence dated 15th February 1971 or later shall be deemed to have been drawn or made before 15th February 1971 if it bears a certificate in writing by a banker that it was so drawn or made.].

4. Inland and foreign bills

(1) An inland bill is a bill which is or on the face of it purports to be (*a*) both drawn and payable within the British Islands, or (*b*) drawn within the British Islands upon some person resident therein. Any other bill is a foreign bill.

For the purposes of this Act 'British Islands' means any part of the United Kingdom of Great Britain and Ireland, the islands of Man, Guernsey, Jersey, Alderney, and Sark, and the islands adjacent to any of them being part of the dominions of Her Majesty.

(2) Unless the contrary appear on the face of the bill the holder may treat it as an inland bill.

Bills of Exchange Act 1882

5. Effect where different parties to bill are the same person

(1) A bill may be drawn payable to, or to the order of, the drawer; or it may be drawn payable to, or to the order of, the drawee.

(2) Where in a bill drawer and drawee are the same person, or where the drawee is a fictitious person or a person not having capacity to contract, the holder may treat the instrument, at his option, either as a bill of exchange or as a promissory note.

6. Address to drawee

(1) The drawee must be named or otherwise indicated in a bill with reasonable certainty.

(2) A bill may be addressed to two or more drawees whether they are partners or not, but an order addressed to two drawees in the alternative or to two or more drawees in succession is not a bill of exchange.

7. Certainty required as to payee

(1) Where a bill is not payable to bearer, the payee must be named or otherwise indicated therein with reasonable certainty.

(2) A bill may be made payable to two or more payees jointly, or it may be made payable in the alternative to one of two, or one or some of several payees. A bill may also be made payable to the holder of an office for the time being.

(3) Where the payee is a fictitious or non-existing person the bill may be treated as payable to bearer.

8. What bills are negotiable

(1) When a bill contains words prohibiting transfer, or indicating an intention that it should not be transferable, it is valid as between the parties thereto, but is not negotiable.

(2) A negotiable bill may be payable either to order or to bearer.

(3) A bill is payable to bearer which is expressed to be so payable, or on which the only or last indorsement is an indorsement in blank.

(4) A bill is payable to order which is expressed to be so payable, or which is expressed to be payable to a particular person, and does not contain words prohibiting transfer or indicating an intention that it should not be transferable.

(5) Where a bill, either originally or by indorsement, is expressed to be payable to the order of a specified person, and not to him or his order, it is nevertheless payable to him or his order at his option.

9. Sum payable

(1) The sum payable by a bill is a sum certain within the meaning of this Act, although it is required to be paid—

    (*a*) With interest.
    (*b*) By stated instalments.
    (*c*) By stated instalments, with a provision that upon default in payment of any instalment the whole shall become due.

(*d*) According to an indicated rate of exchange or according to a rate of exchange to be ascertained as directed by the bill.

(2) Where the sum payable is expressed in words and also in figures, and there is a discrepancy between the two, the sum denoted by the words is the amount payable.

(3) Where a bill is expressed to be payable with interest, unless the instrument otherwise provides, interest runs from the date of the bill, and if the bill is undated from the issue thereof.

10. Bill payable on demand

(1) A bill is payable on demand—

(*a*) Which is expressed to be payable on demand, or at sight, or on presentation; or
(*b*) In which no time for payment is expressed.

(2) Where a bill is accepted or indorsed when it is overdue, it shall, as regards the acceptor who so accepts, or any indorser who so indorses it, be deemed a bill payable on demand.

11. Bill payable at a future time

A bill is payable at a determinable future time within the meaning of this Act which is expressed to be payable—

(1) At a fixed period after date or sight.

(2) On or at a fixed period after the occurrence of a specified event which is certain to happen, though the time of happening may be uncertain.

An instrument expressed to be payable on a contingency is not a bill, and the happening of the event does not cure the defect.

12. Omission of date in bill payable after date

Where a bill expressed to be payable at a fixed period after date is issued undated, or where the acceptance of a bill payable at a fixed period after sight is undated, any holder may insert therein the true date of issue or acceptance, and the bill shall be payable accordingly.

Provided that (1) where the holder in good faith and by mistake inserts a wrong date, and (2) in every case where a wrong date is inserted, if the bill subsequently comes into the hands of a holder in due course the bill shall not be avoided thereby, but shall operate and be payable as if the date so inserted had been the true date.

13. Ante-dating and post-dating

(1) Where a bill or an acceptance or any indorsement on a bill is dated, the date shall, unless the contrary be proved, be deemed to be the true date of the drawing, acceptance, or indorsement, as the case may be.

(2) A bill is not invalid by reason only that it is ante-dated or post-dated, or that it bears date on a Sunday.

14. Computation of time of payment

(1) The bill is due and payable in all cases on the last day of the time of payment as fixed by the bill or, if that is a non-business day, on the succeeding business day.

(2) Where a bill is payable at a fixed period after date, after sight, or after the happening of a specified event, the time of payment is determined by excluding the day from which the time is to begin to run and by including the day of payment.

(3) Where a bill is payable at a fixed period after sight, the time begins to run from the date of the acceptance if the bill be accepted, and from the date of noting or protest if the bill be noted or protested for non-acceptance, or for non-delivery.

(4) The term 'month' in a bill means calendar month.

[*Subsection* (1) *was substituted by the Banking and Financial Dealings Act* 1971, *section* 3(2).]

15. Case of need

The drawer of a bill and any indorser may insert therein the name of a person to whom the holder may resort in case of need, that is to say, in case the bill is dishonoured by non-acceptance or non-payment. Such person is called the referee in case of need. It is in the option of the holder to resort to the referee in case of need or not as he may think fit.

16. Optional stipulations by drawer or indorser

The drawer of a bill, and any indorser, may insert therein an express stipulation—

(1) Negativing or limiting his own liability to the holder:

(2) Waiving as regards himself some or all of the holder's duties.

17. Definition and requisites of acceptance

(1) The acceptance of a bill is the signification by the drawee of his assent to the order of the drawer.

(2) An acceptance is invalid unless it complies with the following conditions, namely:

    (*a*) It must be written on the bill and be signed by the drawee. The mere signature of the drawee without additional words is sufficient.

    (*b*) It must not express that the drawee will perform his promise by any other means than the payment of money.

18. Time for acceptance

A bill may be accepted—

(1) before it has been signed by the drawer, or while otherwise incomplete:

(2) When it is overdue, or after it has been dishonoured by a previous refusal to accept, or by non-payment:

(3) When a bill payable after sight is dishonoured by non-acceptance, and

the drawee subsequently accepts it, the holder, in the absence of any different agreement, is entitled to have the bill accepted as of the date of first presentment to the drawee for acceptance.

19. General and qualified acceptances

(1) An acceptance is either (*a*) general or (*b*) qualified.

(2) A general acceptance assents without qualification to the order of the drawer. A qualified acceptance in express terms varies the effect of the bill as drawn.
In particular an acceptance is qualified which is—

- (*a*) conditional, that is to say, which makes payment by the acceptor dependent on the fulfilment of a condition therein stated;
- (*b*) partial, that is to say, an acceptance to pay part only of the amount for which the bill is drawn;
- (*c*) local, that is to say, an acceptance to pay only at a particular specified place;

An acceptance to pay at a particular place is a general acceptance, unless it expressly states that the bill is to be paid there only and not elsewhere:

- (*d*) qualified as to time;
- (*e*) the acceptance of some one or more of the drawees, but not of all.

20. Inchoate instruments

(1) Where a simple signature on a blank [stamped] paper is delivered by the signer in order that it may be converted into a bill, it operates as a prima facie authority to fill it up as a complete bill of any amount [the stamp will cover], using the signature for that of the drawer, or the acceptor, or an indorser; and, in like manner, when a bill is wanting in any material particular, the person in possession of it has a prima facie authority to fill up the omission in any way he thinks fit.

(2) In order that any such instrument when completed may be enforceable against any person who became a party thereto prior to its completion, it must be filled up within a reasonable time, and strictly in accordance with the authority given. Reasonable time for this purpose is a question of fact.
Provided that if any such instrument after completion is negotiated to a holder in due course it shall be valid and effectual for all purposes in his hands, and he may enforce it as if it had been filled up within a reasonable time and strictly in accordance with the authority given.

[*The words in square brackets were repealed, except as respects Northern Ireland, by the Finance Act* 1970, *Section* 36(8) *and Schedule* 8.]

21. Delivery

(1) Every contract on a bill, whether it be the drawer's, the acceptor's or an indorser's, is incomplete and revocable, until delivery of the instrument in order to give effect thereto.
Provided that where an acceptance is written on a bill, and the drawee gives notice to or according to the directions of the person entitled to the bill that he has accepted it, the acceptance then becomes complete and irrevocable.

Bills of Exchange Act 1882

(2) As between immediate parties, and as regards a remote party other than a holder in due course, the delivery—

(*a*) in order to be effectual must be made either by or under the authority of the party drawing, accepting, or indorsing, as the case may be;

(*b*) may be shown to have been conditional or for a special purpose only, and not for the purpose of transferring the property in the bill.

But if the bill in the hands of a holder in due course a valid delivery of the bill by all parties prior to him so as to make them liable to him is conclusively presumed.

(3) Where a bill is no longer in the possession of a party who has signed it as drawer, acceptor, or indorser, a valid and unconditional delivery by him is presumed until the contrary is proved.

Capacity and Authority of Parties

22. Capacity of parties

(1) Capacity to incur liability as a party to a bill is co-extensive with capacity to contract.

Provided that nothing in this section shall enable a corporation to make itself liable as drawer, acceptor, or indorser of a bill unless it is competent to it so to do under the law for the time being in force relating to corporations.

(2) Where a bill is drawn or indorsed by an infant, minor, or corporation having no capacity or power to incur liability on a bill, the drawing or endorsement entitled the holder to receive payment of the bill, and to enforce it against any other party thereto.

23. Signature essential to liability

No person is liable as drawer, indorser, or acceptor of a bill who has not signed it as such: Provided that

(1) Where a person signs a bill in a trade or assumed name, he is liable thereon as if he had signed it in his own name;

(2) The signature of the name of a firm is equivalent to the signature by the person so signing of the names of all persons liable as partners in that firm.

24. Forged or unauthorised signature

Subject to the provisions of this Act, where a signature on a bill is forged or placed thereon without the authority of the person whose signature it purports to be, the forged or unauthorised signature is wholly inoperative, and no right to retain the bill or to give a discharge therefor or to enforce payment thereof against any party thereto can be acquired through or under that signature, unless the party against who it is sought to retain or enforce payment of the bill is precluded from setting up the forgery or want of authority.

Provided that nothing in this section shall affect the ratification of an unauthorised signature not amounting to a forgery.

25. Procuration signatures

A signature by procuration operates as notice that the agent has but a limited authority to sign, and the principal is only bound by such signature if the agent in so signing was acting within the actual limits of his authority.

26. Person signing as agent or in representative capacity

(1) Where a person signs a bill as drawer, indorser, or acceptor, and adds words to his signature, indicating that he signs for or on behalf of a principal, or in a representative character, he is not personally liable thereon; but the mere addition to his signature of words describing him as an agent, or as filling a representative character, does not exempt him from personal liability.

(2) In determining whether a signature on a bill is that of the principal or that of the agent by whose hand it is written, the construction most favourable to the validity of the instrument shall be adopted.

The Consideration for a Bill

27. Value and holder for value

(1) Valuable consideration for a bill may be constituted by,—

(*a*) Any consideration sufficient to support a simple contract;
(*b*) An antecedent debt or liability. Such a debt or liability is deemed valuable consideration whether the bill is payable on demand or at a future time.

(2) Where value has at any time been given for a bill the holder is deemed to be a holder for value as regard the acceptor and all parties to the bill who became parties prior to such time.

(3) Where the holder of a bill has a lien on it, arising either from contract or by implication of law, he is deemed to be a holder for value to the extent of the sum for which he has a lien.

28. Accommodation bill or party

(1) An accommodation party to a bill is a person who has signed a bill as drawer, acceptor, or indorser, without receiving value therefor, and for the purpose of lending his name to some other person.

(2) An accommodation party is liable on the bill to a holder for value; and it is immaterial whether, when such holder took the bill, he knew such party to be an accommodation party or not.

29. Holder in due course

(1) A holder in due course is a holder who has taken a bill, complete and regular on the fact of it, under the following conditions; namely,

(*a*) That he became the holder of it before it was overdue, and without notice that it had been previously dishonoured, if such was the fact;
(*b*) That he took the bill in good faith and for value, and that at the time the bill was negotiated to him he had no notice of any defect in the title of the person who negotiated it.

(2) In particular the title of a person who negotiated a bill is defective within the meaning of this Act when he obtained the bill, or the acceptance thereof, by fraud, duress, or force and fear, or other unlawful means, or for an illegal consideration, or when he negotiates it in breach of faith, or under such circumstances as amount to a fraud.

Bills of Exchange Act 1882

(3) A holder (whether for value or not), who derives his title to a bill through a holder in due course, and who is not himself a party to any fraud or illegality affecting it, has all the rights of that holder in due course as regard the acceptor and all parties to the bill prior to that holder.

30. Presumption of value and good faith

(1) Every party whose signature appears on a bill is prima facie deemed to have become a party thereto for value.

(2) Every holder of a bill is prima facie deemed to be a holder in due course; but if in an action on a bill it is admitted or proved that the acceptance, issue, or subsequent negotiation of the bill is affected with fraud, duress, or force and fear, or illegality, the burden of proof is shifted, and unless and until the holder proves that, subsequent to the alleged fraud or illegality, value has in good faith been given for the bill.

Negotiation of Bills

31. Negotiation of bill

(1) A bill is negotiated when it is transferred from one person to another in such a manner as to constitute the transferee the holder of the bill.

(2) A bill payable to bearer is negotiated by delivery.

(3) A bill payable to order is negotiated by the indorsement of the holder completed by delivery.

(4) Where the holder of a bill payable to his order transfers it for value without indorsing it, the transfer gives the transferee such title as the transferor had in the bill, and the transferee in addition acquires the right to have indorsement of the transferor.

(5) Where any person is under obligation to indorse a bill in a representative capacity, he may indorse the bill in such terms as to negative personal liability.

32. Requisites of a valid endorsement

An indorsement in order to operate as a negotiation must comply with the following conditions, namely:—

(1) It must be written on the bill itself and be signed by the indorser. The simple signature of the indorser on the bill, without additional words, is sufficient.

An endorsement written on an allonge, or on a 'copy' of a bill issued or negotiated in a country where 'copies' are recognised, is deemed to be written on the bill itself.

(2) It must be an indorsement of the entire bill. A partial indorsement, that is to say, an indorsement which purports to transfer to the indorsee a party only of the amount payable, or which purports to transfer the bill or two or more indorsees severally, does not operate as a negotiation of the bill.

(3) Where a bill is payable to the order of two or more payees or indorsees who are not partners all must endorse, unless the one indorsing has authority to indorse for the others.

(4) Where, in a bill payable to order, the payee or indorsee is wrongly

designated, or his name is mis-spelt, he may indorse the bill as therein described, adding, if he think fit, his proper signature.

(5) Where there are two or more indorsements on a bill, each indorsement is deemed to have been made in the order in which it appears on the bill, until the contrary is proved.

(6) An indorsement may be made in blank or special. It may also contain terms making it restrictive.

33. Conditional indorsement

Where a bill purports to be indorsed conditionally, the condition may be disregarded by the payer, and payment to the indorsee is valid whether the condition has been fulfilled or not.

34. Indorsement in blank and special indorsement

(1) An indorsement in blank specifies no indorsee, and a bill so indorsed becomes payable to bearer.

(2) A special indorsement specifies the person to whom, or to whose order, the bill is to be payable.

(3) The provisions of this Act relating to a payee apply with the necessary modifications to an indorsee under a special indorsement.

(4) When a bill has been indorsed in blank, any holder may convert the blank indorsement into a special indorsement by writing above the indorser's signature a direction to pay the bill to or to the order of himself or some other person.

35. Restrictive indorsement

(1) An indorsement is restrictive which prohibits the further negotiation of the bill or which expresses that it is a mere authority to deal with the bill as thereby directed and not a transfer of the ownership thereof, as, for example, if a bill be indorsed 'Pay D. only,' or 'Pay D. for the account of X.,' or 'Pay D. or order for collection.'

(2) A restrictive indorsement gives the indorsee the right to receive payment of the bill and to sue any party thereto that his indorser could have sued, but gives him no power to transfer his rights as indorsee unless it expressly authorise him to do so.

(3) Where a restrictive indorsement authorises further transfer, all subsequent indorsees take the bill with the same rights and subject to the same liabilities as the first indorsee under the restrictive indorsement.

36. Negotiation of overdue or dishonoured bill

(1) Where a bill is negotiable in its origin it continues to be negotiable until it has been (a) restrictively indorsed or (b) discharged by payment or otherwise.

(2) Where an overdue bill is negotiated, it can only be negotiated subject to any defect of title affecting it at its maturity, and thenceforward no person who takes it can acquire or give a better title than that which the person from whom he took it had.

(3) A bill payable on demand is deemed to be overdue within the meaning

and for the purposes, of this section, when it appears on the face of it to have been in circulation for an unreasonable length of time. What is an unreasonable length of time for this purpose is a question of fact.

(4) Except where an indorsement bears date after the maturity of the bill, every negotiation is prima facie deemed to have been effected before the bill was overdue.

(5) Where a bill which is not overdue has been dishonoured any person who takes it with notice of the dishonour takes it subject to any defect of title attaching thereto at the time of dishonour, but nothing in this subsection shall affect the rights of a holder in due course.

37. Negotiation of bill to party already liable thereon

Where a bill is negotiated back to the drawer, or to a prior indorser or to the acceptor, such party may, subject to the provisions of this Act, re-issue and further negotiate the bill, but he is not entitled to enforce payment of the bill against any intervening party to whom he was previously liable.

38. Rights of the holder

The rights and powers of the holder of a bill are as follows:—

(1) He may sue on the bill in his own name;

(2) Where he is a holder in due course, he holds the bill free from any defect of title of prior parties, as well as from mere personal defences available to prior parties among themselves, and may enforce payment against all parties liable on the bill;

(3) Where his title is defective (*a*) if he negotiates the bill to a holder in due course, that holder obtains a good and complete title to the bill, and (*b*) if he obtains payment of the bill the person who pays him in due course gets a valid discharge for the bill.

General duties of the Holder

39. When presentment for acceptance is necessary

(1) Where a bill is payable after sight, presentment for acceptance is necessary in order to fix the maturity of the instrument.

(2) Where a bill expressly stipulates that it shall be presented for acceptance, or where a bill is drawn payable elsewhere than at the residence or place of business of the drawee it must be presented for acceptance before it can be presented for payment.

(3) In no other case is presentment for acceptance necessary in order to render liable any party to the bill.

(4) Where the holder of a bill, drawn payable elsewhere than at the place of business or residence of the drawee, has not time, with the exercise of reasonable diligence, to present the bill for acceptance before presenting it for payment on the day that it falls due, the delay caused by presenting the bill for acceptance before presenting it for payment is excused, and does not discharge the drawer and indorsers.

Bills of Exchange Act 1882

40. Time for presenting bill payable after sight

(1) Subject to the provisions of this Act, when a bill payable after sight is negotiated, the holder must either present it for acceptance or negotiate it within a reasonable time.

(2) If he do not do so, the drawer and all indorsers prior to that holder are discharged.

(3) In determining what is a reasonable time within the meaning of this section, regard shall be had to the nature of the bill, the usage of trade with respect to similar bills, and the facts of the particular case.

41. Rules as to presentment for acceptance, and excuses for non-presentment

(1) A bill is duly presented for acceptance which is presented in accordance with the following rules:—

- (*a*) The presentment must be made by or on behalf of the holder to the drawee or to some person authorised to accept or refuse acceptance on his behalf at a reasonable hour on a business day and before the bill is overdue:
- (*b*) Where a bill is addressed to two or more drawees, who are not partners, presentment must be made to them all, unless one has authority to accept for all, then presentment may be made to him only;
- (*c*) Where the drawee is dead presentment may be made to his personal representative;
- (*d*) Where the drawee is bankrupt, presentment may be made to him or to his trustee;
- (*e*) Where authorised by agreement or usage, a presentment through the post office is sufficient.

(2) Presentment in accordance with these rules is excused, and a bill may be treated as dishonoured by non-acceptance—

- (*a*) Where the drawee is dead or bankrupt, or is a fictitious person or a person not having capacity to contract by bill;
- (*b*) Where, after the exercise of reasonable diligence, such presentment cannot be effected;
- (*c*) Where although the presentment has been irregular, acceptance has been refused on some other ground.

(3) The fact that the holder has reason to believe that the bill, on presentment, will be dishonoured, does not excuse presentment.

42. Non-acceptance

(1) When a bill is duly presented for acceptance and is not accepted within the customary time, the person presenting it must treat it as dishonoured by non-acceptance. If he do not, the holder shall lose his right of recourse against the drawer and indorsers.

43. Dishonour by non-acceptance and its consequences

(1) A bill is dishonoured by non-acceptance—

- (*a*) when it is duly presented for acceptance, and such an acceptance as is prescribed by this Act is refused or cannot be obtained; or (*b*) when presentment for acceptance is excused and the bill is not accepted.

(2) Subject to the provisions of this Act when a bill is dishonoured by non-acceptance, an immediate right of recourse against the drawer and indorsers accrues to the holder, and no presentment for payment is necessary.

44. Duties as to qualified acceptances

(1) The holder of a bill may refuse to take a qualified acceptance, and if he does not obtain an unqualified acceptance may treat the bill as dishonoured by non-acceptance.

(2) Where a qualified acceptance is taken, and the drawer or an indorser has not expressly or impliedly authorised the holder to take a qualified acceptance, or does not subsequently assent thereto, such drawer or indorser is discharged from his liability on the bill.

The provisions of this subsection do not apply to a partial acceptance, whereof due notice has been given. Where a foreign bill has been accepted as to part, it must be protested as to the balance.

(3) When the drawer or indorser of a bill receives notice of a qualified acceptance, and does not within a reasonable time express his dissent to the holder he shall be deemed to have assented thereto.

45. Rules as to presentment for payment

Subject to the provisions of this Act a bill must be duly presented for payment. If it be not so presented the drawer and indorsers shall be discharged.

A bill is duly presented for payment which is presented in accordance with the following rules:—

(1) Where the bill is not payable on demand, presentment must be made on the day it falls due.

(2) Where the bill is payable on demand, then, subject to the provisions of this Act, presentment must be made within a reasonable time after its issue in order to render the drawer liable, and within a reasonable time after its indorsement, in order to render the indorser liable.

In determining what is a reasonable time, regard shall be had to the nature of the bill, the usage of trade with regard to similar bills, and the facts of the particular case.

(3) Presentment must be made by the holder or by some person authorised to receive payment on his behalf at a reasonable hour on a business day, at the proper place as hereinafter defined, either to the person designated by the bill as payer, or to some person authorised to pay or refuse payment on his behalf if with the exercise of reasonable diligence such person can there be found.

(4) A bill is presented at the proper place:—

(*a*) Where place of payment is specified in the bill and the bill is there presented.
(*b*) Where no place of payment is specified, but the address of the drawee or acceptor is given in the bill, and the bill is there presented.
(*c*) Where no place of payment is specified and no address given,

Bills of Exchange Act 1882

and the bill is presented at the drawee's or acceptor's place of business if known, and if not, at his ordinary residence if known.

(*d*) In any other case if presented to the drawee or acceptor wherever he can be found, or if presented at his last known place of business or residence.

(5) Where a bill is presented at the proper place, and after the exercise of reasonable diligence no person authorised to pay or refuse payment can be found there, no further presentment to the drawee or acceptor is required.

(6) Where a bill is drawn upon, or accepted by two or more persons who are not partners, and no place of payment is specified, presentment must be made to them all.

(7) Where the drawee or acceptor of a bill is dead, and no place of payment is specified, presentment must be made to a personal representative, if such there be, and with the exercise of reasonable diligence he can be found.

(8) Where authorised by agreement or usage a presentment through the post office is sufficient.

46. Excuses for delay or non-presentment for payment

(1) Delay in making presentment for payment is excused when the delay is caused by circumstances beyond the control of the holder, and not imputable to his default, misconduct, or negligence. When the cause of delay ceases to operate presentment must be made with reasonable diligence.

(2) Presentment for payment is dispensed with,—

(*a*) Where, after the exercise of reasonable diligence presentment, as required by this Act, cannot be effected.
The fact that the holder has reason to believe that the bill will, on presentment, be dishonoured, does not dispense with the necessity for presentment.
(*b*) Where the drawee is a fictitious person.
(*c*) As regards the drawer where the drawee or acceptor is not bound, as between himself and the drawer, to accept or pay the bill, and the drawer has no reason to believe that the bill would be paid if presented.
(*d*) As regards an indorser, where the bill was accepted or made for the accommodation of that indorser, and he has no reason to expect that the bill would be paid if presented.
(*e*) By waiver of presentment, express or implied.

47. Dishonour by non-payment

(1) A bill is dishonoured by non-payment (*a*) when it is duly presented for payment and payment is refused or cannot be obtained, or (*b*) when presentment is excused and the bill is overdue and unpaid.

(2) Subject to the provisions of this Act, when a bill is dishonoured by non-payment, an immediate right or recourse against the drawer and indorsers accrues to the holder.

Bills of Exchange Act 1882

48. Notice of dishonour and effect of non-notice

Subject to the provisions of this Act, when a bill has been dishonoured by non-acceptance or by non-payment, notice of dishonour must be given to the drawer and each indorser, and any drawer or indorser to whom such notice is not given is discharged; Provided that—

(1) Where a bill is dishonoured by non-acceptance, and notice of dishonour is not given, the rights of a holder in due course subsequent to the omission, shall not be prejudiced by the omission.

(2) Where a bill is dishonoured by non-acceptance and due notice of dishonour is given, it shall not be necessary to give notice of a subsequent dishonour by non-payment unless the bill shall in the meantime have been accepted.

49. Rules as to notice of dishonour

Notice of dishonour in order to be valid and effectual must be given in accordance with the following rules:—

(1) The notice must be given by or on behalf of the holder, or by or on behalf of an indorser who, at the time of giving it, is himself liable on the bill.

(2) Notice of dishonour may be given by an agent either in his own name, or in the name of any party entitled to give notice whether that party be his principal or not.

(3) Where the notice is given by or on behalf of the holder, it ensures for the benefit of all subsequent holders and all prior indorsers who have a right of recourse against the party to whom it is given.

(4) Where notice is given by or on behalf of an indorser entitled to give notice as hereinbefore provided, it ensures for the benefit of the holder and all indorsers subsequent to the party to whom notice is given.

(5) The notice may be given in writing or by personal communication, and may be given in any terms which sufficiently identify the bill, and intimate that the bill has been dishonoured by non-acceptance or non-payment.

(6) The return of a dishonoured bill to the drawer or an indorser is, in point of form, deemed a sufficient notice of dishonour.

(7) A written notice need not be signed, and an insufficient written notice may be supplemented and validated by verbal communication. A misdescription of the bill shall not vitiate the notice unless the party to whom the notice is given is in fact misled thereby.

(8) Where notice of dishonour is required to be given to any person, it may be given either to the party himself, or to his agent in that behalf.

(9) Where the drawer or indorser is dead, and the party giving notice knows it, the notice must be given to a personal representative if such there be, and with the exercise of reasonable diligence he can be found.

(10) Where the drawer or indorser is bankrupt, notice may be given either to the party himself or to the trustee.

(11) Where there are two or more drawers or indorsers who are not partners,

Bills of Exchange Act 1882

notice must be given to each of them, unless one of them has authority to receive such notice for the others.

(12) The notice may be given as soon as the bill is dishonoured and must be given within a reasonable time thereafter.

In the absence of special circumstances notice is not deemed to have been given within a reasonable time, unless—

>   (*a*) where the person giving and the person to receive notice reside in the same place, the notice is given or sent off in time to reach the latter on the day after the dishonour of the bill.
>
>   (*b*) where the person giving and the person to receive notice reside in different places, the notice is sent off on the day after the dishonour of the bill, if there be a post at a convenient hour on that day, and if there be no such post on that day then by the next post thereafter.

(13) Where a bill when dishonoured is in the hands of an agent, he may either himself give notice to the parties liable on the bill, or he may give notice to his principal. If he gives notice to his principal, he must do so within the same time as if he were the holder, and the principal upon receipt of such notice has himself the same time for giving notice as if the agent had been an independent holder.

(14) Where a party to a bill receives due notice of dishonour, he has after the receipt of such notice the same period of time for giving notice to antecedent parties that the holder has after the dishonour.

(15) Where a notice of dishonour is duly addressed and posted, the sender is deemed to have given due notice of dishonour, notwithstanding any miscarriage by the post office.

50. Excuses for non-notice and delay

(1) Delay in giving notice of dishonour is excused where the delay is caused by circumstances beyond the control of the party giving notice, and not imputable to his default, misconduct, or negligence. When the cause of delay ceases to operate the notice must be given with reasonable diligence.

(2) Notice of dishonour is dispensed with—

>   (*a*) When, after the exercise of reasonable diligence, notice as required by this Act cannot be given to or does not reach the drawer or indorser sought to be charged:
>
>   (*b*) By waiver express or implied. Notice of dishonour may be waived before the time of giving notice has arrived, or after the omission to give due notice:
>
>   (*c*) As regards the drawer in the following cases, namely, (1) where drawer and drawee are the same person, (2) where the drawee is a fictitious person or a person not having capacity to contract, (3) where the drawer is the person to whom the bill is presented for payment, (4) where the drawee or acceptor is as between himself and the drawer under no obligation to accept or pay the bill, (5) where the drawer has countermanded payment:
>
>   (*d*) As regards the indorser in the following cases, namely, (1) where the drawee is a fictitious person or a person not having capacity to contract and the indorser was aware of the fact at the time he indorsed the bill, (2) where the indorser is the person to whom the bill is presented

Bills of Exchange Act 1882

for payment, (3) where the bill was accepted or made for his accommodation.

51. Noting or protest of bill

(1) Where an inland bill has been dishonoured it may, if the holder think fit, be noted for non-acceptance or non-payment, as the case may be; but it shall not be necessary to note or protest any such bill in order to preserve the recourse against the drawer or indorser.

(2) Where a foreign bill, appearing on the face of it to be such, has been dishonoured by non-acceptance it must be duly protested for non-acceptance, and where such a bill, which has not been previously dishonoured by non-acceptance, is dishonoured by non-payment it must be duly protested for non-payment. If it be not so protested the drawer and indorsers are discharged. Where a bill does not appear on the face of it to be a foreign bill, protest thereof in case of dishonour is unnecessary.

(3) A bill which has been protested for non-acceptance may be subsequently protested for non-payment.

(4) Subject to the provisions of this Act, when a bill is noted or protested, [it may be noted on the day of its dishonour and must be noted not later than the next succeeding business day]. When a bill has been duly noted, the protest may be subsequently extended as of the date of the noting.

(5) Where the acceptor of a bill becomes bankrupt or insolvent or suspends payment before it matures, the holder may cause the bill to be protested for better security against the drawer and indorsers.

(6) A bill must be protested at the place where it is dishonoured: Provided that—

(*a*) When a bill is presented through the post office, and returned by post dishonoured, it may be protested at the place to which it is returned and on the day of its return if received during business hours, and if not received during business hours, then not later than the next business day:

(*b*) When a bill drawn payable at the place of business or residence of some person other than the drawee, has been dishonoured by non-acceptance, it must be protested for non-payment at the place where it is expressed to be payable, and no further presentment for payment to, or demand on, the drawee is necessary.

(7) A protest must contain a copy of the bill, and must be signed by the notary making it, and must specify—

(*a*) The person at whose request the bill is protested;
(*b*) The place and date of protest, the cause or reason for protesting the bill, the demand made, and the answer given, if any, or the fact that the drawee or acceptor could not be found.

(8) Where a bill is lost or destroyed, or is wrongly detained from the person entitled to hold it, protest may be made on a copy or written particulars thereof.

(9) Protest is dispensed with by any circumstance which would dispense with notice of dishonour. Delay in noting or protesting is excused when the delay is caused by circumstances beyond the control of the holder, and not imputable

to his default, misconduct, or negligence. When the cause of delay ceases to operate the bill must be noted or protested with reasonable diligence.

[*The words in square brackets were substituted by the Bills of Exchange (Time of Noting) Act, 1917, section 1.*]

52. Duties of holder as regards drawee or acceptor

(1) When a bill is accepted generally presentment for payment is not necessary in order to render the acceptor liable.

(2) When by the terms of a qualified acceptance presentment for payment is required, the acceptor, in the absence of an express stipulation to that effect, is not discharged by the omission to present the bill for payment on the day that it matures.

(3) In order to render the acceptor of a bill liable it is not necessary to protest it, or that notice of dishonour should be given to him.

(4) Where the holder of a bill presents it for payment, he shall exhibit the bill to the person from whom he demands payment, and when a bill is paid the holder shall forthwith deliver it up to the party paying it.

Liabilities of Parties

53. Funds in hands of drawee

(1) A bill, of itself, does not operate as an assignment of funds in the hands of the drawee available for the payment thereof, and the drawee of a bill who does not accept as required by this Act is not liable on the instrument. This subsection shall not extend to Scotland.

(2) [Subject to section 75A of this Act] in Scotland, where the drawee of a bill has in his hands funds available for the payment thereof, the bill operates as an assignment of the sum for which it is drawn in favour of the holder, from the time when the bill is presented to the drawee.

[*The words in square brackets were inserted by the Law Reform (Miscellaneous Provisions) (Scotland) Act 1985.*]

54. Liability of acceptor

The acceptor of a bill, by accepting it—

(1) Engages that he will pay it according to the tenor of his acceptance;

(2) Is precluded from denying to a holder in due course:
    (*a*) The existence of the drawer, the genuineness of his signature, and his capacity and authority to draw the bill;
    (*b*) In the case of a bill payable to drawer's order, the then capacity of the drawer to indorse, but not the genuineness or validity of his indorsement;
    (*c*) In the case of a bill payable to the order of a third person, the existence of the payee and his then capacity to indorse, but not the genuineness or validity of his indorsement.

55. Liability of drawer or indorser

(1) The drawer of a bill by drawing it—

(*a*) Engages that on due presentment it shall be accepted and paid according to its tenor, and that if it be dishonoured he will compensate the holder or any indorser who is compelled to pay it, provided that the requisite proceedings on dishonour be duly taken;

(*b*) Is precluded from denying to a holder in due course the existence of the payee and his then capacity to indorse.

(2) The indorser of a bill by indorsing it—

(*a*) Engages that on due presentment it shall be accepted and paid according to its tenor, and that if it be dishonoured he will compensate the holder or a subsequent indorser who is compelled to pay it, provided that the requisite proceedings on dishonour be duly taken;

(*b*) Is precluded from denying to a holder in due course the genuineness and regularity in all respects of the drawer's signature and all previous indorsements;

(*c*) Is precluded from denying to his immediate or a subsequent indorsee that the bill was at the time of his indorsement a valid and subsisting bill, and that he had then a good title thereto.

56. Stranger signing bill liable as indorser

Where a person signs a bill otherwise than as drawer or acceptor, he thereby incurs the liabilities of an indorser to a holder in due course.

57. Measure of damages against parties to dishonoured bill

Where a bill is dishonoured, the measure of damages, which shall be deemed to be liquidated damages, shall be as follows:

(1) The holder may recover from any party liable on the bill, and the drawer who has been compelled to pay the bill may recover from the acceptor, and an indorser who has been compelled to pay the bill may recover from the acceptor or from the drawer, or from a prior indorser—

(*a*) The amount of the bill;

(*b*) Interest thereon from the time of presentment for payment if the bill is payable on demand, and from the maturity of the bill in any other case;

(*c*) The expenses of noting, or, when protest is necessary, and the protest has been extended, the expenses of protest.

[*Subsection (2) was repealed by the Administration of Justice Act 1977, sections 4, 32(4), and Schedule 5, except in relation to bills drawn before 29th August 1977.*]

(3) Where by this Act interest may be recovered as damages, such interest may, if justice require it, be withheld wholly or in part, and where a bill is expressed to be payable with interest at a given rate, interest as damages may or may not be given at the same rate as interest proper.

58. Transferor by delivery and transferee

(1) Where the holder of a bill payable to bearer negotiates it by delivery without indorsing it, he is called a 'transferor by delivery'.

(2) A transferor by delivery is not liable on the instrument.

(3) A transferor by delivery who negotiates a bill thereby warrants to his

immediate transferee being a holder for value that the bill is what it purports to be, that he has a right to transfer it, and that at the time of transfer he is not aware of any fact which renders it valueless.

Discharge of Bill

59. Payment in due course

(1) A bill is discharged by payment in due course by or on behalf of the drawee or acceptor.

'Payment in due course' means payment made at or after the maturity of the bill to the holder thereof in good faith and without notice that his title to the bill is defective.

(2) Subject to the provisions hereinafter contained, when a bill is paid by the drawer or an indorser it is not discharged; but

> (*a*) Where a bill payable to, or to the order of, a third party is paid by the drawer, the drawer may enforce payment thereof against the acceptor, but may not re-issue the bill.
> (*b*) Where a bill is paid by an indorser, or where a bill payable to drawer's order is paid by the drawer, the party paying it is remitted to his former rights as regards the acceptor or antecedent parties, and he may, if he thinks fit, strike out his own and subsequent indorsements, and again negotiate the bill.

(3) Where an accommodation bill is paid in due course by the party accommodated the bill is discharged.

60. Banker paying demand draft whereon indorsement is forged

When a bill payable to order on demand is drawn on a banker, and the banker on whom it is drawn pays the bill in good faith and in the ordinary course of business, it is not incumbent on the banker to show that the indorsement of the payee or any subsequent indorsement was made by or under the authority of the person whose indorsement it purports to be, and the banker is deemed to have paid the bill in due course, although such indorsement has been forged or made without authority.

61. Acceptor the holder at maturity

When the acceptor of a bill is or becomes the holder of it at or after its maturity, in his own right, the bill is discharged.

62. Express waiver

(1) When the holder of a bill at or after its maturity absolutely and unconditionally renounces his rights against the acceptor the bill is discharged.

The renunciation must be in writing, unless the bill is delivered up to the acceptor.

(2) The liabilities of any party to a bill may in like manner be renounced by the holder before, at, or after its maturity; but nothing in this section shall affect the rights of a holder in due course without notice of the renunciation.

Bills of Exchange Act 1882

63. Cancellation

(1) Where a bill is intentionally cancelled by the holder or his agent, and the cancellation is apparent thereon, the bill is discharged.

(2) In like manner any party liable on a bill may be discharged by the intentional cancellation of his signature by the holder or his agent. In such cases any indorser who would have had a right of recourse against the party whose signature is cancelled, is also discharged.

(3) A cancellation made unintentionally, or under a mistake, or without the authority of the holder is inoperative; but where a bill or any signature thereon appears to have been cancelled the burden of proof lies on the party who alleges that the cancellation was made unintentionally, or under a mistake, or without authority.

64. Alteration of bill

(1) Where a bill or acceptance is materially altered without the assent of all parties liable on the bill, the bill is avoided except as against a party who has himself made, authorised, or assented to the alteration, and subsequent indorsers.

Provided that,

Where a bill has been materially altered, but the alteration is not apparent, and the bill is in the hands of a holder in due course, such holder may avail himself of the bill as if it had not been altered, and may enforce payment of it according to its original tenor.

(2) In particular the following alterations are material, namely, any alteration of the date, the sum payable, the time of payment, the place of payment, and, where a bill has been accepted generally, the addition of a place of payment without the acceptor's assent.

[*This section should be read subject to the Decimal Currency Act 1969, Section 3, which provides:—*

    3.—(1) On and after the appointed day any reference to an amount of money in the old currency contained in an instrument to which this section applies shall, in so far as it refers to an amount in shillings or pence, be read as referring to the corresponding amount in the new currency calculated in accordance with the provisions of Schedule 1 to this Act.

    (2) If a reference to an amount of money in the old currency contained in an instrument to which this section applies is altered so as to make it read as it would otherwise fall to be read in accordance with subsection (1) of this section, the alteration shall not affect the validity of the instrument and, in the case of a bill of exchange or promissory note, shall not be treated as a material alteration for the purposes of section 64 of the Bills of Exchange Act 1882.]

Acceptance and Payment for Honour

65. Acceptance for honour supra protest

(1) Where a bill of exchange has been protested for dishonour by non-acceptance, or protested for better security, and is not overdue, any person, not being a party already liable thereon, may, with the consent of the holder,

intervene and accept the bill supra protest, for the honour of any party liable thereon, or for the honour of the person for whose account the bill is drawn.

(2) A bill may be accepted for honour for part only of the sum for which it is drawn.

(3) An acceptance for honour supra protest in order to be valid must—

    (*a*) be written on the bill, and indicate that it is an acceptance for honour;
    (*b*) be signed by the acceptor for honour.

(4) Where an acceptance for honour does not expressly state for whose honour it is made, it is deemed to be an acceptance for the honour of the drawer.

(5) Where a bill payable after sight is accepted for honour, its maturity is calculated from the date of the noting for non-acceptance, and not from the date of the acceptance for honour.

66. Liability of acceptor for honour

(1) The acceptor for honour of a bill by accepting it engages that he will, on due presentment, pay the bill according to the tenor of his acceptance, if it is not paid by the drawee, provided it has been duly presented for payment, and protested for non-payment, and that he receives notice of these facts.

(2) The acceptor for honour is liable to the holder and to all parties to the bill subsequent to the party for whose honour he has accepted.

67. Presentment to acceptor for honour

(1) Where a dishonoured bill has been accepted for honour supra protest, or contains a reference in case of need, it must be protested for non-payment before it is presented for payment to the acceptor for honour, or referee in case of need.

(2) Where the address of the acceptor for honour is in the same place where the bill is protested for non-payment, the bill must be presented to him not later than the day following its maturity; and where the address of the acceptor for honour is in some place other than the place where it was protested for non-payment, the bill must be forwarded not later than the day following its maturity for presentment to him.

(3) Delay in presentment or non-presentment is excused by any circumstance which would excuse delay in presentment for payment or non-presentment for payment.

(4) When a bill of exchange is dishonoured by the acceptor for honour it must be protested for non-payment by him.

68. Payment for honour supra protest

(1) Where a bill has been protested for non-payment, any person may intervene and pay it supra protest for the honour of any party liable thereon, or for the honour of the person for whose account the bill is drawn.

(2) Where two or more persons offer to pay a bill for the honour of different parties, the person whose payment will discharge most parties to the bill shall have the preference.

Bills of Exchange Act 1882

(3) Payment for honour supra protest, in order to operate as such and not as a mere voluntary payment, must be attested by a notarial act of honour which may be appended to the protest or form an extension of it.

(4) The notarial act of honour must be founded on a declaration made by the payer for honour, or his agent in that behalf, declaring his intention to pay the bill for honour, and for whose honour he pays.

(5) Where a bill has been paid for honour, all parties subsequent to the party for whose honour it is paid are discharged, but the payer for honour is subrogated for, and succeeds to both the rights and duties of, the holder as regards the party for whose honour he pays, and all parties liable to that party.

(6) The payer for honour on paying to the holder the amount of the bill and the notarial expenses incidental to its dishonour is entitled to receive both the bill itself and the protest. If the holder does not on demand deliver them up he shall be liable to the payer for honour in damages.

(7) Where the holder of a bill refuses to receive payment supra protest he shall lose his right of recourse against any party who would have been discharged by such payment.

Lost Instruments

69. Holder's right to duplicate of lost bill

Where a bill has been lost before it is overdue, the person who was the holder of it may apply to the drawer to give him another bill of the same tenor, giving security to the drawer if required to indemnify him against all persons whatever in case the bill alleged to have been lost shall be found again.

If the drawer on request as aforesaid refuses to give such duplicate bill, he may be compelled to do so.

70. Action on lost bill

In any action or proceeding upon a bill, the court or a judge may order that the loss of the instrument shall not be set up, provided an indemnity be given to the satisfaction of the court or judge against the claims of any other person upon the instrument in question.

[*Section 70 is repealed in relation to Northern Ireland by the Judicature (Northern Ireland) Act 1978, section 122.*]

Bill in a Set

71. Rules as to sets

Where a bill is drawn in a set, each part of the set being numbered, and containing a reference to the other parts, the whole of the parts constitute one bill.

(2) Where the holder of a set indorses two or more parts to different persons, he is liable on every such part, and every indorser subsequent to him is liable on the part he has himself indorsed as if the said parts were separate bills.

(3) Where two or more parts of a set are negotiated to different holders in due course, the holder whose title first accrues is as between such holders deemed

the true owner of the bill; but nothing in this subsection shall affect the rights of a person who in due course accepts or pays the part first presented to him.

(4) The acceptance may be written on any part, and it must be written on one part only.

If the drawee accepts more than one part, and such accepted parts get into the hands of different holders in due course, he is liable on every such part as if it were a separate bill.

(5) When the acceptor of a bill drawn in a set pays it without requiring the part bearing his acceptance to be delivered up to him, and that part at maturity is outstanding in the hands of a holder in due course, he is liable to the holder thereof.

(6) Subject to the preceding rules, where any one part of a bill drawn in a set is discharged by payment or otherwise, the whole bill is discharged.

Conflict of Laws

72. Rules where laws conflict

Where a bill drawn in one country is negotiated, accepted, or payable in another, the rights, duties, and liabilities of the parties thereto are determined as follows:

(1) The validity of a bill as regards requisites in form is determined by the law of the place of issue, and the validity as regards requisites in form of the supervening contracts, such as acceptance, or indorsement, or acceptance supra protest, is determined by the law of the place where such contract was made.

Provided that—

(*a*) Where a bill is issued out of the United Kingdom it is not invalid by reason only that it is not stamped in accordance with the law of the place of issue;

(*b*) Where a bill, issued out of the United Kingdom, conforms, as regards requisites in form, to the law of the United Kingdom, it may, for the purpose of enforcing payment thereof, be treated as valid as between all persons who negotiate, hold, or become parties to it in the United Kingdom.

(2) Subject to the provisions of this Act, the interpretation of the drawing, indorsement, acceptance, or acceptance supra protest of a bill, is determined by the law of the place where such contract is made.

Provided that where an inland bill is indorsed in a foreign country the indorsement shall as regards the payer be interpreted according to the law of the United Kingdom.

(3) The duties of the holder with respect to presentment for acceptance or payment and the necessity for or sufficiency of a protest or notice of dishonour, or otherwise, are determined by the law of the place where the act is done or the bill is dishonoured.

[*Subsection (4) was repealed by the Administration of Justice Act 1977, sections 4, 32(4) and Schedule 5, except in relation to bills drawn before 29th August 1977.*]

Bills of Exchange Act 1882

(5) Where a bill is drawn in one country and is payable in another, the due date thereof is determined according to the law of the place where it is payable.

PART III

CHEQUES ON A BANKER

73. Cheque defined

A cheque is a bill of exchange drawn on a banker payable on demand.

Except as otherwise provided in this Part, the provisions of this Act applicable to a bill of exchange payable on demand apply to a cheque.

74. Presentment of cheque for payment

Subject to the provisions of this Act—

(1) Where a cheque is not presented for payment within a reasonable time of its issue, and the drawer or the person on whose account it is drawn had the right at the time of such presentment as between him and the banker to have the cheque paid and suffers actual damage through the delay, he is discharged to the extent of such damage, that is to say, to the extent to which such drawer or person is a creditor of such banker to a larger amount than he would have been had such cheque been paid.

(2) In determining what is a reasonable time regard shall be had to the nature of the instrument, the usage of trade and of bankers, and the facts of the particular case.

(3) The holder of such cheque as to which such drawer or person is discharged shall be a creditor, in lieu of such drawer or person, of such banker to the extent of such discharge, and entitled to recover the amount from him.

75. Revocation of banker's authority

The duty and authority of a banker to pay a cheque drawn on him by his customer are determined by—

(1) Countermand of payment:
(2) Notice of the customer's death.

[**75A.**

(1) On the countermand of payment of a cheque, the banker shall be treated as having no funds available for payment of the cheque.

(2) This section applies to Scotland only.]

[*Section 75A was inserted by the Law Reform (Miscellaneous Provisions) (Scotland) Act 1985, section 11.*]

Crossed Cheques

76. General and special crossings defined

(1) Where a cheque bears across its face an addition of—

Bills of Exchange Act 1882

(a) The words 'and company' or any abbreviation thereof between two parallel transverse lines, either with or without the words 'not negotiable'; or

(b) Two parallel transverse lines simply, either with or without the words 'not negotiable';

that addition constitutes a crossing, and the cheque is crossed generally.

(2) Where a cheque bears across its face an addition of the name of a banker, either with or without the words 'not negotiable,' that addition constitutes a crossing, and the cheque is crossed specially and to that banker.

77. Crossing by drawer or after issue

(1) A cheque may be crossed generally or specially by the drawer.

(2) Where a cheque is uncrossed, the holder may cross it generally or specially.

(3) Where a cheque is crossed generally the holder may cross it specially.

(4) Where a cheque is crossed generally or specially, the holder may add the words 'not negotiable.'

(5) Where a cheque is crossed specially, the banker to whom it is crossed may again cross it specially to another banker for collection.

(6) Where an uncrossed cheque, or a cheque crossed generally, is sent to a banker for collection, he may cross it specially to himself.

78. Crossing a material part of cheque

A crossing authorised by this Act is a material part of the cheque; it shall not be lawful for any person to obliterate or, except as authorised by this Act, to add to or alter the crossing.

79. Duties of banker as to crossed cheques

(1) Where a cheque is crossed specially to more than one banker except when crossed to an agent for collection being a banker, the banker on whom it is drawn shall refuse payment thereof.

(2) Where the banker on whom a cheque is drawn which is so crossed nevertheless pays the same, or pays a cheque crossed generally otherwise than to a banker, or if crossed specially otherwise than to the banker to whom it is crossed, or his agent for collection being a banker, he is liable to the true owner of the cheque for any loss he may sustain owing to the cheque having been so paid.

Provided that where a cheque is presented for payment which does not at the time of presentment appear to be crossed, or to have had a crossing which has been obliterated, or to have been added to or altered otherwise than as authorised by this Act, the banker paying the cheque in good faith and without negligence shall not be responsible or incur any liability, nor shall the payment be questioned by reason of the cheque having been crossed, or of the crossing having been obliterated or having been added to or altered otherwise than as authorised by this Act, and of payment having been made otherwise than to a banker or to the banker to whom the cheque is or was crossed, or to his agent for collection being a banker, as the case may be.

80. Protection to banker and drawer where cheque is crossed

Where the banker, on whom a crossed cheque is drawn, in good faith and without negligence pays it, if crossed generally, to a banker, and if crossed specially, to the banker to whom it is crossed, or his agent for collection being a banker, the banker paying the cheque, and, if the cheque has come into the hands of the payee, the drawer, shall respectively be entitled to the same rights and be placed in the same position as if payment of the cheque had been made to the true owner thereof.

81. Effect of crossing on holder

Where a person takes a crossed cheque which bears on it the words 'not negotiable', he shall not have and shall not be capable of giving a better title to the cheque than that which the person from whom he took it had.

[Section 82 was repealed by the Cheques Act 1957, section 6(3) and Schedule.]

PART IV

Promissory Notes

83. Promissory note defined

(1) A promissory note is an unconditional promise in writing made by one person to another signed by the maker, engaging to pay, on demand or at a fixed or determinable future time, a sum certain in money, to, or to the order of, a specified person or to bearer.

(2) An instrument in the form of a note payable to maker's order is not a note within the meaning of this section unless and until it is endorsed by the maker.

(3) A note is not invalid by reason only that it contains also a pledge of collateral security with authority to sell or dispose thereof.

(4) A note which is, or on the face of it purports to be, both made and payable within the British Islands is an inland note. Any other note is a foreign note.

84. Delivery necessary

A promissory note is inchoate and incomplete until delivery thereof to the payee or bearer.

85. Joint and several notes

(1) A promissory note may be made by two or more makers, and they may be liable thereon jointly, or jointly and severally according to its tenor.

(2) Where a note runs 'I promise to pay' and is signed by two or more persons it is deemed to be their joint and several note.

86. Note payable on demand

(1) Where a note payable on demand has been indorsed, it must be presented for payment within a reasonable time of the indorsement. If it be not so presented the indorser is discharged.

Bills of Exchange Act 1882

(2) In determining what is a reasonable time, regard shall be had to the nature of the instrument, the usage of trade, and the facts of the particular case.

(3) Where a note payable on demand is negotiated, it is not deemed to be overdue, for the purpose of affecting the holder with defects of title of which he had no notice, by reason that it appears that a reasonable time for presenting it for payment has elapsed since its issue.

87. Presentment of note for payment

(1) Where a promissory note is in the body of it made payable at a particular place, it must be presented for payment at that place in order to render the maker liable. In any other case, presentment for payment is not necessary in order to render the maker liable.

(2) Presentment for payment is necessary in order to render the indorser of a note liable.

(3) Where a note is in the body of it made payable at a particular place, presentment at that place is necessary in order to render an indorser liable; but when a place of payment is indicated by way of memorandum only, presentment at that place is sufficient to render the indorser liable, but a presentment to the maker elsewhere, if sufficient in other respects, shall also suffice.

88. Liability of maker

The maker of a promissory note by making it—

(1) Engages that he will pay it according to its tenor;

(2) Is precluded from denying to a holder in due course the existence of the payee and his then capacity to indorse.

89. Application of Part II to notes

(1) Subject to the provisions in this Part and, except as by this section provided, the provisions of this Act relating to bills of exchange apply, with the necessary modifications, to promissory notes.

(2) In applying those provisions the maker of a note shall be deemed to correspond with the acceptor of a bill, and the first indorser of a note shall be deemed to correspond with the drawer of an accepted bill payable to drawer's order.

(3) The following provisions as to bills do not apply to notes; namely, provisions relating to—

    (*a*) Presentment for acceptance;
    (*b*) Acceptance;
    (*c*) Acceptance supra protest;
    (*d*) Bills in a set.

(4) Where a foreign note is dishonoured, protest thereof is unnecessary.

PART V

SUPPLEMENTARY

90. Good faith

A thing is deemed to be done in good faith, within the meaning of this Act, where it is in fact done honestly, whether it is done negligently or not.

91. Signature

(1) Where, by this Act, any instrument or writing is required to be signed by any person, it is not necessary that he should sign it with his own hand, but it is sufficient if his signature is written thereon by some other person by or under his authority.

(2) In the case of a corporation, where by this Act, any instrument or writing is required to be signed, it is sufficient if the instrument or writing be sealed with the corporate seal.

But nothing in this section shall be construed as requiring the bill or note of a corporation to be under seal.

92. Computation of time

Where, by this Act, the time limited for doing any act or thing is less than three days, in reckoning time, non-business days are excluded.

'Non-business days' for the purposes of this Act mean—

(*a*) Sunday, Good Friday, Christmas Day:
(*b*) A bank holiday under [the Banking and Financial Dealings Act 1971]:
(*c*) A day appointed by Royal proclamation as a public fast or thanksgiving day.
[[(*d*) a day declared by an order under section 2 of the Banking and Financial Dealings Act 1971 to be a non-business day.]]

Any other day is a business day.

[*The words in square brackets were substituted, and the words in double square brackets inserted, by the Banking and Financial Dealings Act 1971, section 4(4).*]

93. When noting equivalent to protest

For the purposes of this Act, where a bill or note is required to be protested within a specified time or before some further proceeding is taken, it is sufficient that the bill has been noted for protest before the expiration of the specified time or the taking of the proceeding; and the formal protest may be extended at any time thereafter as of the date of the noting.

94. Protest when notary not accessible

Where a dishonoured bill or note is authorised or required to be protested, and the services of a notary cannot be obtained at the place where the bill is dishonoured, any householder or substantial resident of the place may, in the presence of two witnesses, give a certificate, signed by them, attesting the dishonour of the bill, and the certificate shall in all respects operate as if it were a formal protest of the bill.

The form given in Schedule 1 to this Act may be used with necessary modifications, and if used shall be sufficient.

95. Dividend warrants may be crossed

The provisions of this Act as to crossed cheques shall apply to a warrant for payment of dividend.

[*Section 96 was repealed by the Statute Law Revision Act* 1898.]

97. Savings

(1) The rules in bankruptcy relating to bills of exchange, promissory notes, and cheques, shall continue to apply thereto notwithstanding anything in this Act contained.

(2) The rules of common law including the law merchant, save in so far as they are inconsistent with the express provisions of this Act, shall continue to apply to bills of exchange, promissory notes, and cheques.

(3) Nothing in this Act or in any repeal effected thereby shall affect—

- (*a*) . . . any law or enactment for the time being in force relating to the revenue:
- (*b*) The provisions of the Companies Act, 1862, or Acts amending it, or any Act relating to joint stock banks or companies:
- (*c*) The provisions of any Act relating to or confirming the privileges of the Bank of England or the Bank of Ireland respectively:
- (*d*) The validity of any usage relating to dividend warrants or the indorsements thereof.

[*The words omitted were repealed by the Statute Law Revision Act* 1898]

98. Saving of summary diligence in Scotland

Nothing in this Act or in any repeal effected thereby shall extend or restrict, or in any way alter or affect the law and practice in Scotland in regard to summary diligence.

99. Construction with other Acts, &c

Where any Act or document refers to any enactment repealed by this Act, the Act or document shall be construed, and shall operate, as if it referred to the corresponding provisions of this Act.

100. Parole evidence allowed in certain judicial proceedings in Scotland

In any judicial proceeding in Scotland, any fact relating to a bill of exchange, bank cheque, or promissory note, which is relevant to any question of liability thereon, may be proved by parole evidence: Provided that this enactment shall not in any way affect the existing law and practice whereby the party who is, according to the tenor of any bill of exchange, bank cheque, or promissory note, debtor to the holder in the amount thereof, may be required, as a condition of obtaining a sist of diligence, or suspension of a charge, or threatened charge, to make such consignation, or to find such caution as the court or judge before whom the cause is depending may require . . .

[*The words omitted were repealed by the Prescription and Limitation (Scotland) Act* 1973, *section* 16(3), *and Schedule* 5, *Part I.*]

SCHEDULES

First Schedule

Form of protest which may be used when the services of a notary cannot be obtained.

Know all men that I, *A.B.* [householder], of   in the county of   in the United Kingdom, at the request of *C.D.*, there being no notary public available, did on the   day of   1888 at   demand payment [*or* acceptance] of the bill of exchange hereunder written, from *E.F.*, to which demand he made answer [state answer, if any] wherefore I now, in the presence of *G.H.* and *J.K.* do protest the said bill of exchange.

          (Signed)   *A.B.*
                            G.H.   Witnesses.
                            J.K.

N.B.—The bill itself should be annexed, or a copy of the bill and all that is written thereon should be underwritten.

[*Schedule* 2 *was repealed by the Statute Law Revision Act* 1898.]

Factors Act 1889

Factors Act 1889
Chapter 45

ARRANGEMENT OF SECTIONS

Preliminary

Section
1. Definitions

Dispositions by Mercantile Agents

2. Powers of mercantile agent with respect to disposition of goods
3. Effect of pledges of documents of title
4. Pledge for antecedent debt
5. Rights acquired by exchange of goods or documents
6. Agreements through clerks, &c
7. Provisions as to consignors and consignees

Dispositions by Sellers and Buyers of Goods

8. Disposition by seller remaining in possession
9. Disposition by buyer obtaining possession
10. Effect of transfer of documents on vendor's lien or right of stoppage in transitu

Supplemental

11. Mode of transferring documents
12. Saving for rights of true owner
13. Saving for common law powers of agent

* * *

16. Extent of Act
17. Short title

* * *

An Act to amend and consolidate the Factors Acts

[26th August 1889]

Preliminary

1. Definitions

For the purposes of this Act—

(1) The expression 'mercantile agent' shall mean a mercantile agent having in the customary course of his business as such agent authority either to sell goods, or to consign goods for the purpose of sale, or to buy goods, or to raise money on the security of goods:

(2) A person shall be deemed to be in possession of goods or of the documents

of title to goods, where the goods or documents are in his actual custody or are held by any other person subject to his control or for him or on his behalf:

(3) The expression 'goods' shall include wares and merchandise:

(4) The expression 'document of title' shall include any bill of lading, dock warrant, warehouse-keeper's certificate, and warrant or order for the delivery of goods, and any other document used in the ordinary course of business as proof of the possession or control of goods, or authorising or purporting to authorise, either by endorsement or by delivery, the possessor of the document to transfer or receive goods thereby represented:

(5) The expression 'pledge' shall include any contract, pledging, or giving a lien or security on, goods, whether in consideration of an original advance or of any further or continuing advance or of any pecuniary liability:

(6) The expression 'person' shall include any body of persons corporate or unincorporate.

Dispositions by Mercantile Agents

2. Powers of mercantile agent with respect to disposition of goods

(1) Where a mercantile agent is, with the consent of the owner, in possession of goods or of the documents of title to goods, any sale, pledge, or other disposition of the goods, made by him when acting in the ordinary course of business of a mercantile agent, shall, subject to the provisions of this Act, be as valid as if he were expressly authorised by the owner of the goods to make the same; provided that the person taking under the disposition acts in good faith, and has not at the time of the disposition notice that the person making the disposition has not authority to make the same.

(2) Where a mercantile agent has, with the consent of the owner, been in possession of goods or of the documents of title to goods, any sale, pledge, or other disposition, which would have been valid if the consent had continued, shall be valid notwithstanding the determination of the consent: provided that the person taking under the disposition has not at the time thereof notice that the consent has been determined.

(3) Where a mercantile agent has obtained possession of any documents of title to goods by reason of his being or having been, with the consent of the owner, in possession of the goods represented thereby, or of any other documents of title to the goods, his possession of the first-mentioned documents shall, for the purposes of this Act, be deemed to be with the consent of the owner.

(4) For the purposes of this Act the consent of the owner shall be presumed in the absence of evidence to the contrary.

3. Effect of pledges of documents of title

A pledge of the documents of title to goods shall be deemed to be a pledge of the goods.

4. Pledge for antecedent debt

Where a mercantile agent pledges goods as security for a debt or liability due from the pledgor to the pledgee before the time of the pledge, the pledgee shall acquire no further right to the goods than could have been enforced by the pledgor at the time of the pledge.

5. Rights acquired by exchange of goods or documents

The consideration necessary for the validity of a sale, pledge, or other disposition, of goods, in pursuance of this Act, may be either a payment in cash, or the delivery or transfer of other goods, or of a document of title to goods, or of a negotiable security, or any other valuable consideration; but where goods are pledged by a mercantile agent in consideration of the delivery or transfer of other goods, or of a document of title to goods, or of a negotiable security, the pledgee shall acquire no right or interest in the goods so pledged in excess of the value of the goods, documents, or security when so delivered or transferred in exchange.

6. Agreements through clerks, etc.

For the purposes of this Act an agreement made with a mercantile agent through a clerk or other person authorised in the ordinary course of business to make contracts of sale or pledge on his behalf shall be deemed to be an agreement with the agent.

7. Provisions as to consignors and consignees

(1) Where the owner of goods has given possession of the goods to another person for the purpose of consignment or sale, or has shipped the goods in the name of another person, and the consignee of the goods has not had notice that such person is not the owner of the goods, the consignee shall, in respect of advances made to or for the use of such person, have the same lien on the goods as if such person were the owner of the goods, and may transfer any such lien to another person.

(2) Nothing in this section shall limit or affect the validity of any sale, pledge, or disposition, by a mercantile agent.

Dispositions by Sellers and Buyers of Goods

8. Disposition by seller remaining in possession

Where a person, having sold goods, continues, or is, in possession of the goods or of the documents of title to the goods, the delivery or transfer by that person, or by a mercantile agent acting for him, of the goods or documents of title under any sale, pledge, or other disposition thereof, or under any agreement for sale, pledge, or other disposition thereof, to any person receiving the same in good faith and without notice of the previous sale, shall have the same effect as if the person making the delivery or transfer were expressly authorised by the owner of the goods to make the same.

9. Disposition by buyer obtaining possession

Where a person, having bought or agreed to buy goods, obtains with the consent of the seller possession of the goods or the documents of title to the goods, the delivery or transfer, by that person or by a mercantile agent acting

Factors Act 1889

for him, of the goods or documents of title, under any sale, pledge, or other disposition thereof, or under any agreement for sale, pledge, or other disposition thereof, to any person receiving the same in good faith and without notice of any lien or other right of the original seller in respect of the goods, shall have the same effect as if the person making the delivery or transfer were a mercantile agent in possession of the goods or documents of title with the consent of the owner.

[For the purposes of this section—
  (i) the buyer under a conditional sale agreement shall be deemed not to be a person who has bought or agreed to buy goods, and
  (ii) 'conditional sale agreement' means an agreement for the sale of goods which is a consumer credit agreement within the meaning of the Consumer Credit Act 1974 under which the purchase price or part of it is payable by instalments, and the property in the goods is to remain in the seller (notwithstanding that the buyer is to be in possession of the goods) until such conditions as to the payment of instalments or otherwise as may be specified in the agreement are fulfilled.]

[*The words in square brackets were inserted by the Consumer Credit Act 1974, section 192(3)(a), and Schedule 4, Part I, paragraph 2.*]

10. Effect of transfer of documents on vendor's lien or right of stoppage in transitu

Where a document of title to goods has been lawfully transferred to a person as a buyer or owner of the goods, and that person transfers the document to a person who takes the document in good faith and for valuable consideration, the last-mentioned transfer shall have the same effect for defeating any vendor's lien or right of stoppage in transitu as the transfer of a bill of lading has for defeating the right of stoppage in transitu.

Supplemental

11. Mode of transferring documents

For the purposes of this Act, the transfer of a document may be by endorsement, or, where the document is by custom or by its express terms transferable by delivery, or makes the goods deliverable to bearer, then by delivery.

12. Saving for rights of true owner

(1) Nothing in this Act shall authorise an agent to exceed or depart from his authority as between himself and his principal, or exempt him from any liability, civil or criminal, for so doing.

(2) Nothing in this Act shall prevent the owner of goods from recovering the goods from an agent or his trustee in bankruptcy at any time before the sale or pledge thereof, or shall prevent the owner of goods pledged by an agent from having the right to redeem the goods at any time before the sale thereof, on satisfying the claim for which the goods were pledged, and paying to the agent, if by him required, any money in respect of which the agent would by law be entitled to retain the goods or the documents of title thereto, or any of them, by way of lien as against the owner, or from recovering from any person with whom the goods have been pledged any balance of money remaining in his hands as the produce of the sale of the goods after deducting the amount of his lien.

Factors Act 1889

(3) Nothing in this Act shall prevent the owner of goods sold by an agent from recovering from the buyer the price agreed to be paid for the same, or any part of that price, subject to any right of set off on the part of the buyer against the agent.

13. Saving for common law powers of agent

The provisions of this Act shall be construed in amplification and not in derogation of the powers exercisable by an agent independently of this Act.

[*Sections 14 and 15 were repealed by the Statute Law Revision Act 1908.*]

16. Extent of Act

This Act shall not extend to Scotland.

[*See Factors (Scotland) Act 1890.*]

17. Short title

This Act may be cited as the Factors Act, 1889.

[*The Schedule was repealed by the Statute Law Revision Act 1908.*]

Bills of Sale Act 1890
Chapter 53

An act to exempt certain letters of hypothecation from the operation of the Bills of Sale Act 1882. [10th August 1890]

1. Exemption of letters of hypothecation of imported goods from 41 & 42 Vict c 31, and 45 & 46 Vict c 43, s 9

[An instrument charging or creating any security on or declaring trusts of imported goods given or executed at any time prior to their deposit in a warehouse, factory, or store, or to their being reshipped for export, or delivered to a purchaser not being the person giving or executing such instrument, shall not be deemed a bill of sale within the meaning of the Bills of Sale Acts, 1878 and 1882.]

[*Section 1 was substituted by the Bills of Sale Act* 1891, *section* 1.]

2. Saving of 46 & 47 Vict c 52, s 44

Nothing in this Act shall affect the operation of section forty-four of the Bankruptcy Act, 1883, in respect of any goods comprised in any such instrument as is hereinbefore described, if such goods would but for this Act be goods within the meaning of subsection three of that section.

3. Short title

This Act may be cited as the Bills of Sale Act, 1890.

Law of Distress Amendment Act 1908
Chapter 53

ARRANGEMENT OF SECTIONS
Section
1. Under tenant or lodger, if distress levied, to make declaration that immediate tenant has no property in goods distrained
2. Penalty
3. Payments by under tenant or lodger to superior landlord
4. Exclusion of certain goods
[4A. Hire-purchase etc. agreements]
5. Exclusion of certain under tenants
6. To avoid distress

* * *

8. Repeal of 34 & 35 Vict. c 79
9. Definitions
10. Act not to extend to Scotland
11. Short title

An Act to amend the Law as regards a Landlord's right of Distress for Rent.
[21st December 1908]

1. Under tenant or lodger, if distress levied, to make declaration that immediate tenant has no property in goods distrained

If any superior landlord shall levy, or authorise to be levied, a distress on any furniture, goods, or chattels of—

(a) any under tenant liable to pay by equal instalments not less often than every actual or customary quarter of a year a rent which would return in any whole year the full annual value of the premises or of such part thereof as is comprised in the under tenancy, or

(b) any lodger, or

(c) any other person whatsoever not being a tenant of the premises or of any part thereof, and not having any beneficial interest in any tenancy of the premises or of any part thereof,

for arrears of rent due to such superior landlord by his immediate tenant, such under tenant, lodger, or other person aforesaid may serve such superior landlord, or the bailiff or other agent employed by him to levy such distress, with a declaration in writing made by such under tenant, lodger, or other person aforesaid, setting forth that such immediate tenant has no right of property or beneficial interest in the furniture, goods, or chattels so distrained or threatened to be distrained upon, and that such furniture, goods, or chattels are the property or in the lawful possession of such under tenant, lodger, or other person aforesaid, and are not goods or livestock to which this Act is expressed not to apply; and also, in the case of an under tenant or lodger, setting forth the amount of rent (if any) then due to his immediate landlord, and the times at which

Law of Distress Amendment Act 1908

future instalments of rent will become due, and the amount thereof, and containing an undertaking to pay to the superior landlord any rent so due or to become due to his immediate landlord, until the arrears of rent in respect of which the distress was levied or authorised to be levied have been paid off and to such declaration shall be annexed a correct inventory, subscribed by the under tenant, lodger, or other person aforesaid, of the furniture, goods, and chattels referred to in the declaration . . .

[*The words omitted were repealed by the Perjury Act* 1911, *section* 17 *and Schedule.*]

2. Penalty

If any superior landlord, or any bailiff or other agent employed by him, shall, after being served with the before-mentioned declaration and inventory, and in the case of an under tenant or lodger after such undertaking as aforesaid has been given, and the amount of rent (if any) then due has been paid or tendered in accordance with that undertaking, levy or proceed with a distress on the furniture, goods, or chattels of the under tenant, lodger, or other person aforesaid, such superior landlord, bailiff, or other agent shall be deemed guilty of an illegal distress, and the under tenant, lodger, or other person aforesaid, may apply to a justice of the peace for an order for the restoration to him of such goods, and such application shall be heard before a stipendiary magistrate, or before two justices in places where there is no stipendiary magistrate, and such magistrate or justices shall inquire into the truth of such declaration and inventory, and shall make such order for the recovery of the goods or otherwise as to him or them may seem just, and the superior landlord shall also be liable to an action at law at the suit of the under tenant, lodger, or other person aforesaid, in which action the truth of the declaration and inventory may likewise be inquired into.

3. Payments by under tenant or lodger to superior landlord

For the purposes of the recovery of any sums payable by an under tenant or lodger to a superior landlord under such an undertaking as aforesaid, or under a notice served in accordance with section six of this Act, the under tenant or lodger shall be deemed to be the immediate tenant of the superior landlord, and the sums payable shall be deemed to be rent; but, where the under tenant or lodger has, in pursuance of any such undertaking or notice as aforesaid, paid any sums to the superior landlord, he may deduct the amount thereof from any rent due or which may become due from him to his immediate landlord, and any person (other than the tenant for whose rent the distress is levied or authorised to be levied) from whose rent a deduction has been made in respect of such a payment may make the like deductions from any rent due or which may become due from him to his immediate landlord.

4. Exclusion of certain goods

This Act shall not apply—

(1) to goods belonging to the husband or wife of the tenant whose rent is in arrear, nor to goods comprised in any . . . settlement made by such tenant, nor to goods in the possession, order, or disposition of such tenant by the consent and permission of the true owner under such circumstances that such tenant is the reputed owner thereof, nor

Law of Distress Amendment Act 1908

to any [agisted livestock within the meaning of section 18 of the Agricultural Holdings Act 1986 to which that section] applies;

(2) (*a*) to goods of a partner of the immediate tenant; (*b*) to goods (not being goods of a lodger) upon premises where any trade or business is carried on in which both the immediate tenant and the under tenant have an interest; (*c*) to goods (not being goods of a lodger) on premises used as offices or warehouses where the owner of the goods neglects for one calendar month after notice (which shall be given in like manner as a notice to quit) to remove the goods and vacate the premises; (*d*) to goods belonging to and in the offices of any company or corporation on premises the immediate tenant whereof is a director or officer, or in the employment of such company or corporation:

Provided that it shall be competent for a stipendiary magistrate, or where there is no stipendiary magistrate for two justices, upon application by the superior landlord or any under tenant or other such person as aforesaid, upon hearing the parties to determine whether any goods are in fact goods covered by subsection (2) of this section.

[*The words omitted were repealed by the Consumer Credit Act 1974, section 192(3)(b) and Schedule 5, Part I. The words in square brackets in subsection (1) were substituted by the Agricultural Holdings Act 1986, section 100 and Schedule 14.*]

4A. [Hire purchase etc. agreements

(1) Goods—

(*a*) bailed under a hire-purchase agreement or a consumer hire agreement, or
(*b*) agreed to be sold under a conditional sale agreement,

are, where the relevant agreement has not been terminated, excluded from the application of this Act except during the period between the service of a default notice under the Consumer Credit Act 1974 in respect of the goods and the date on which the notice expires or is earlier complied with.

(2) Goods comprised in a bill of sale are excluded from the application of this Act except, during the period between service of a default notice under the Consumer Credit Act 1974 in respect of goods subject to a regulated agreement under which a bill of sale is given by way of security and the date on which the notice expires or is earlier complied with.

(3) In this section—

'conditional sale agreement' means an agreement for the sale of goods under which the purchase price or part of it is payable by instalments, and the property in the goods is to remain in the seller (notwithstanding that the buyer is to be in possession of the goods) until such conditions as to the payment of instalments or otherwise as may be specified in the agreement are fulfilled;

'consumer hire agreement' has the meaning given by section 15 of the Consumer Credit Act 1974;

'hire-purchase agreement' means an agreement, other than a conditional sale agreement, under which—

(*a*) goods are bailed in return for periodical payments by the person to whom they are bailed, and
(*b*) the property in the goods will pass to that person if the terms of the agreement are complied with and one or more of the following occurs—
  (i) the exercise of an option to purchase by that person,
  (ii) the doing of any other specified act by any party to the agreement,
  (iii) the happening of any other specified event; and

'regulated agreement' has the meaning given by section 189(1) of the Consumer Credit Act 1974.]

[*Section 4A was inserted by the Consumer Credit Act* 1974, *section* 192(3)(*a*) *and Schedule* 4, *Part I, paragraph* 5.]

5. Exclusion of certain under tenants

This Act shall not apply to any under tenant where the under tenancy has been created in breach of any covenant or agreement in writing between the landlord and his immediate tenant, or where the under tenancy has been created under a lease existing at the date of the passing of this Act contrary to the wish of the landlord in that behalf, expressed in writing and delivered at the premises within a reasonable time after the circumstances have come or with due diligence would have come, to his knowledge.

6. To avoid distress

In cases where the rent of the immediate tenant of the superior landlord is in arrear it shall be lawful for such superior landlord to serve upon any under tenant or lodger a notice (by registered post addressed to such under tenant or lodger upon the premises) stating the amount of such arrears of rent, and requiring all future payments of rent, whether the same has already accrued due or not, by such under tenant or lodger to be made direct to the superior landlord giving such notice until such arrears shall have been duly paid, and such notice shall operate to transfer to the superior landlord the right to recover, receive, and give a discharge for such rent.

[*Section 7 was repealed by the Statute Law Revision Act* 1927.]

8. Repeal of 34 & 35 Vict c 79

The Lodgers' Goods Protection Act 1871, shall wherever and so far as this Act applies, be repealed . . .

[*The words omitted were repealed by the Statute Law Revision Act* 1927.]

9. Definitions

In this Act the words 'superior landlord' shall be deemed to include a landlord in cases where the goods seized are not those of an under tenant or lodger; and the words 'tenant' and 'under tenant' do not include a lodger.

10. Act not to extend to Scotland

This Act shall not extend to Scotland and shall only apply in Ireland to a rent issuing out of lands or tenements situate wholly within the boundaries of a municipality or of a township having town commissioners.

11. Short title

This Act may be cited as the Law of Distress Amendment Act 1908.

Auctions (Bidding Agreements) Act 1927
Chapter 12

An Act to render illegal certain agreements and transactions affecting bidding at auctions. [29th July 1927.]

1. Certain bidding agreements to be illegal

(1) If any dealer agrees to give, or gives, or offers any gift or consideration to any other person as an inducement or reward for abstaining, or for having abstained, from bidding at a sale by auction either generally or for any particular lot, or if any person agrees to accept, or accepts, or attempts to obtain from any dealer any such gift or consideration as aforesaid, he shall be guilty of an offence under this Act, and shall be liable on summary conviction to a fine not exceeding one hundred pounds, or to a term of imprisonment for any period not exceeding six months, or to both such fine and such imprisonment:

Provided that, where it is proved that a dealer has previously to an auction entered into an agreement in writing with one or more persons to purchase goods at the auction bona fide on a joint account and has before the goods were purchased at the auction deposited a copy of the agreement with the auctioneer, such an agreement shall not be treated as an agreement made in contravention of this section.

(2) For the purposes of this section the expression 'dealer' means a person who in the normal course of his business attends sales by auction for the purpose of purchasing goods with a view to reselling them.

(3) In England and Wales a prosecution for an offence under this section shall not be instituted without the consent of the Attorney-General or the Solicitor-General.

2. Right of vendors to treat certain sales as fraudulent

Any sale at an auction, with respect to which any such agreement or transaction as aforesaid has been made or effected, and which has been the subject of a prosecution and conviction, may, as against a purchaser who has been a party to such agreement or transaction, be treated by the vendor as a sale induced by fraud:

Provided that a notice or intimation by the vendor to the auctioneer that he intends to exercise such power in relation to any sale at the auction shall not affect the obligation of the auctioneer to deliver the goods to the purchaser.

3. Copy of Act to be exhibited at sale

The particulars which under section seven of the Auctioneers Act 1845, are required to be affixed or suspended in some conspicuous part of the room or place where the auction is held shall include a copy of this Act, and that section shall have effect accordingly.

Auctions (Bidding Agreements) Act 1927

4. Short title, commencement and extent

(1) This Act may be cited as the Auctions (Bidding Agreements) Act 1927, and shall come into operation on the first day of January, nineteen hundred and twenty-eight.

(2) This Act shall not extend to Northern Ireland.

Cheques Act, 1957
Chapter 36

ARRANGEMENT OF SECTIONS

Section
1. Protection of bankers paying unindorsed or irregularly indorsed cheques, &c.
2. Rights of bankers collecting cheques not indorsed by holders.
3. Unindorsed cheques as evidence of payment.
4. Protection of bankers collecting payment of cheques, &c.
5. Application of certain provisions of Bills of Exchange Act, 1882, to instruments not being bills of exchange.
6. Construction, saving and repeal.
7. Provisions as to Northern Ireland.
8. Short title and commencement.

SCHEDULE—Enactments repealed.

An Act to amend the law relating to cheques and certain other instruments.
[17th July, 1957]

1. Protection of bankers paying unindorsed or irregularly indorsed cheques, &c.

(1) Where a banker in good faith and in the ordinary course of business pays a cheque drawn on him which is not indorsed or is irregularly indorsed, he does not, in doing so, incur any liability by reason only of the absence of, or irregularity in, indorsement, and he is deemed to have paid it in due course.

(2) Where a banker in good faith and in the ordinary course of business pays any such instrument as the following, namely,—

(a) a document issued by a customer of his which, though not a bill of exchange, is intended to enable a person to obtain payment from him of the sum mentioned in the document;

(b) a draft payable on demand drawn by him upon himself, whether payable at the head office or some other office of his bank;

he does not, in doing so, incur any liability by reason only of the absence of, or irregularity in, indorsement, and the payment discharges the instrument.

2. Rights of bankers collecting cheques not indorsed by holders

A banker who gives value for, or has a lien on, a cheque payable to order which the holder delivers to him for collection without indorsing it, has such (if any) rights as he would have had if, upon delivery, the holder had indorsed it in blank.

3. Unindorsed cheques as evidence of payment

An unindorsed cheque which appears to have been paid by the banker on whom it is drawn is evidence of the receipt by the payee of the sum payable by the cheque.

4. Protection of bankers collecting payment of cheques, &c

(1) Where a banker, in good faith and without negligence,—

  (a) receives payment for a customer of an instrument to which this section applies; or
  (b) having credited a customer's account with the amount of such an instrument, receives payment thereof for himself;

and the customer has no title, or a defective title, to the instrument, the banker does not incur any liability to the true owner of the instrument by reason only of having received payment thereof.

(2) This section applies to the following instruments, namely,—

  (a) cheques;
  (b) any document issued by a customer of a banker which, though not a bill of exchange, is intended to enable a person to obtain payment from that banker of the sum mentioned in the document;
  (c) any document issued by a public officer which is intended to enable a person to obtain payment from the Paymaster General or the Queen's and Lord Treasurer's Remembrancer of the sum mentioned in the document but is not a bill of exchange;
  (d) any draft payable on demand drawn by a banker upon himself, whether payable at the head office or some other office of his bank.

(3) A banker is not to be treated for the purposes of this section as having been negligent by reason only of his failure to concern himself with absence of, or irregularity in, indorsement of an instrument.

5. Application of certain provisions of Bills of Exchange Act, 1882, to instruments not being bills of exchange

The provisions of the Bills of Exchange Act, 1882, relating to crossed cheques shall, so far as applicable, have effect in relation to instruments (other than cheques) to which the last foregoing section applies as they have effect in relation to cheques.

6. Construction, saving and repeal

(1) This Act shall be construed as one with the Bills of Exchange Act, 1882.

(2) The foregoing provisions of this Act do not make negotiable any instrument which, apart from them, is not negotiable.

(3) *(This subsection was repealed by the Statute Law (Repeals) Act 1974.)*

7. Provisions as to Northern Ireland

This Act extends to Northern Ireland, [. . .] *(The words omitted were repealed by the Northern Ireland Constitution Act 1973.)*

8. Short title and commencement

(1) This Act may be cited as the Cheques Act, 1957.

(2) This Act shall come into operation at the expiration of a period of three months beginning with the day on which it is passed.

Schedule

(This was repealed by the Statute Law (Repeals) Act 1974.)

Trading Representations (Disabled Persons) Act 1958
Chapter 49

An Act to control the making of representations by traders with respect to the employment or assistance of blind or other disabled persons in connection with the production, preparation, packing or sale of goods, and for purposes connected therewith. [23rd July, 1958]

(*The Act is reproduced here as amended by the Trading Representations (Disabled Persons) (Amendment) Act 1972, the amendments being indicated by square brackets.*)

1. Sale of goods advertised as made by, or sold for, benefit of blind or otherwise disabled persons

(1) It shall not be lawful, in selling [any goods or exchanging any article or thing for any other article or thing] or soliciting orders for goods of any description in the course of a business carried on by any person, for any representation that, or implying that, blind or otherwise disabled persons, or any description of such persons,—

- (*a*) are employed in the production, preparation or packing of the goods, [article or thing] or,
- (*b*) benefit (otherwise than as users of the goods, [article or thing]) from the sale of the goods [or the exchange of the article or thing] or the carrying on of the business,

to be made in the course of visits from house to house, or by post or by telephone; [. . .] and any person who contravenes this subsection shall be liable—

- (i) on summary conviction, to a fine not exceeding [the prescribed sum]; and
- (ii) on conviction on indictment, to a fine or imprisonment for a term not exceeding two years or both.]

(*The reference to the prescribed sum was substituted by the Magistrates' Courts Act 1980.*)

(2) The foregoing subsection shall not apply where the business is being carried on—

- (*a*) by a local authority, or
- (*b*) by any fund, institution, association or undertaking which is registered or exempted from registration under the War Charities Act 1940 or that Act as extended by section forty-one of the National Assistance Act 1948, or
- (*c*) by a company, association or body providing facilities under section fifteen of the Disabled Persons (Employment) Act 1944 in pursuance of arrangements under subsection (2) of that section, or
- (*d*) by any body of persons exempted by the Secretary of State for Employment (hereinafter referred to as 'the Secretary of State') from

Trading Representations (Disabled Persons) Act 1958

the operation of the foregoing subsection, being a body appearing to the Secretary of State to be carrying on business without profit to its members,

or where the person carrying on the business is substantially disabled and all goods, [articles or things] with respect to which the representation is made were [produced by his own labour].

(3) In England or Wales a local authority may institute proceedings for an offence under this section.

(4) Where an offence under this section which has been committed by a body corporate is proved to have been committed with the consent or connivance of, or to be attributable to any neglect on the part of, any director, manager, secretary or other similar officer of the body corporate, or any person purporting to act in any such capacity, he as well as the body corporate shall be deemed to be guilty of that offence and shall be liable to be proceeded against and punished accordingly.

(5) In this section 'house' includes a place of business, and 'local authority' means [. . .] the council of a county [other than a metropolitan county, or of a district or London borough] or the Common Council of the City of London, or, in Scotland, a [regional islands or district] council.

(*The words omitted from subsection 5 were repealed by the Local Government Act 1985. The other amendments were made respectively by the Local Government Act 1972 and the Local Government (Scotland) Act 1973.*)

2–3. (*Sections 2 and 3 were repealed by the Trading Representations (Disabled Persons) Amendment Act 1972.*)

4. Interpretation of references to disablement

(1) The references in subsection (1) of section one of this Act to blind or otherwise disabled persons are references to persons under any disability, whether physical or mental, attributable to illness, injury, imperfect development or congenital deformity.

(2) The references in this Act to substantially disabled persons are references to persons substantially handicapped, whether permanently or not, by any such disability as aforesaid.

5. Short title and extent

(1) This Act may be cited as the Trading Representations (Disabled Persons) Act, 1958.

(2) This Act shall not extend to Northern Ireland.

Mock Auctions Act 1961
Chapter 47

An Act to prohibit certain practices in relation to sales purporting to be sales by auction. [27th July, 1961]

1. Penalties for promoting or conducting mock auctions

(1) It shall be an offence to promote or conduct, or to assist in the conduct of, a mock auction at which one or more lots to which this Act applies are offered for sale.

(2) Any person guilty of an offence under this Act shall be liable—

   (*a*) on summary conviction to a fine not exceeding one hundred pounds, or to imprisonment for a term not exceeding three months, or to both such a fine and such imprisonment;
   (*b*) on conviction on indictment, to a fine not exceeding one thousand pounds or to imprisonment for a term not exceeding two years, or to both such a fine and such imprisonment.

(3) Subject to the following provisions of this section, for the purposes of this Act a sale of goods by way of competitive bidding shall be taken to be a mock auction if, but only if, during the course of the sale—

   (*a*) any lot to which this Act applies is sold to a person bidding for it, and either it is sold to him at a price lower than the amount of his highest bid for that lot, or part of the price at which it is sold to him is repaid or credited to him or is stated to be so repaid or credited, or
   (*b*) the right to bid for any lot to which this Act applies is restricted, or is stated to be restricted, to persons who have bought or agreed to buy one or more articles, or
   (*c*) any articles are given away or offered as gifts.

(4) A sale of goods shall not be taken to be a mock auction by virtue of paragraph (*a*) of the last preceding subsection, if it is proved that the reduction in price, or the repayment or credit, as the case may be,—

   (*a*) was on account of a defect discovered after the highest bid in question had been made, being a defect of which the person conducting the sale was unaware when that bid was made, or
   (*b*) was on account of damage sustained after that bid was made.

2. Offences by bodies corporate

Where an offence punishable under this Act which has been committed by a body corporate is proved to have been committed with the consent or connivance or to be attributable to any neglect on the part of any director, manager, secretary or other similar officer of the body corporate or any person purporting to act in such capacity, he, as well as the body corporate, shall be deemed to be guilty of that offence and shall be liable to be proceeded against and punished accordingly.

3. Interpretation

(1) In this Act 'sale of goods by way of competitive bidding' means any sale of goods at which the persons present, or some of them, are invited to buy articles by way of competitive bidding, and 'competitive bidding' includes any mode of sale whereby prospective purchasers may be enabled to compete for the purchase of articles, whether by way of increasing bids or by the offer of articles to be bid for at successively decreasing prices or otherwise.

(2) In this Act 'lot to which this Act applies' means a lot consisting of or including one or more prescribed articles; and 'prescribed articles' means any plate, plated articles, linen, china, glass, books, pictures, prints, furniture, jewellery, articles of household or personal use or ornament or any musical or scientific instrument or apparatus.

(3) In this Act 'stated', in relation to a sale of goods by way of competitive bidding, means stated by or on behalf of the person conducting the sale, by an announcement made to the persons for the time being present at the sale.

(4) For the purposes of this Act any bid stated to have been made at a sale of goods by way of competitive bidding shall be conclusively presumed to have been made, and to have been a bid of the amount stated; and any reference in this Act to the sale of a lot to a person who has made a bid for it includes a reference to a purported sale thereof to a person stated to have bid for it, whether that person exists or not.

(5) For the purposes of this Act anything done in or about the place where a sale of goods by way of competitive bidding is held, if done in connection with the sale, shall be taken to be done during the course of the sale, whether it is done at the time when any articles are being sold or offered for sale by way of competitive bidding or before or after any such time.

(6) Subject to the provisions of section thirty-three of the Interpretation Act, 1889 (which relates to offences under two or more laws), nothing in this Act shall derogate from any right of action or other remedy (whether civil or criminal) in proceedings instituted otherwise than under this Act.

4. Short title, commencement, and extent

(1) This Act may be cited as the Mock Auctions Act, 1961.

(2) This Act shall come into operation at the expiration of a period of one month beginning with the date on which it is passed.

(3) This Act shall not extend to Northern Ireland.

Hire Purchase Act 1964
Chapter 29

Part III

Title to Motor Vehicles on Hire-Purchase or Conditional Sale

(*Part III is reproduced here as re-enacted by the consumer Credit Act 1974, Schedule 4.*)

27. Protection of purchasers in motor vehicles

(1) This section applies where a motor vehicle has been bailed or (in Scotland) hired under a hire-purchase agreement, or has been agreed to be sold under a conditional sale agreement, and, before the property in the vehicle has become vested in the debtor, he disposes of the vehicle to another person.

(2) Where the disposition referred to in subsection (1) above is to a private purchaser, and he is a purchaser of the motor vehicle in good faith without notice of the hire-purchase or conditional sale agreement (the 'relevant agreement') that disposition shall have effect as if the creditor's title to the vehicle has been vested in the debtor immediately before that disposition.

(3) Where the person to whom the disposition referred to in subsection (1) above is made (the 'original purchaser') is a trade or finance purchaser, then if the person who is the first private purchaser of the motor vehicle after that disposition (the 'first private purchaser') is a purchaser of the vehicle in good faith without notice of the relevant agreement, the disposition of the vehicle to the first private purchaser shall have effect as if the title of the creditor to the vehicle had been vested in the debtor immediately before he disposed of it to the original purchaser.

(4) Where, in a case within subsection (3) above—

(*a*) the disposition by which the first private purchaser becomes a purchaser of the motor vehicle in good faith without notice of the relevant agreement is itself a bailment or hiring under a hire-purchase agreement, and
(*b*) the person who is the creditor in relation to that agreement disposes of the vehicle to the first private purchaser, or a person claiming under him, by transferring to him the property in the vehicle in pursuance of a provision in the agreement in that behalf,

the disposition referred to in paragraph (*b*) above (whether or not the person to whom it is made is a purchaser in good faith without notice of the relevant agreement) shall as well as the disposition referred to in paragraph (*a*) above, have effect as mentioned in subsection (3) above.

(5) The preceding provisions of this section apply—

(*a*) notwithstanding anything in [section 21 of the Sale of Goods Act 1979] (sale of goods by a person not the owner), but
(*b*) without prejudice to the provisions of the Factors Acts (as defined by [section 61(1) of the said Act of 1979]) or of any other enactment enabling

Hire Purchase Act 1964

the apparent owner of goods to dispose of them as if he were the true owner.

(The words in square brackets were substituted by the Sale of Goods Act 1979, section 63 and Schedule 2.)

(6) Nothing in this section shall exonerate the debtor from any liability (whether criminal or civil) to which he would be subject apart from this section; and, in a case where the debtor disposes of the motor vehicle to a trade or finance purchaser, nothing in this section shall exonerate—

   (*a*) that trade or finance purchaser, or
   (*b*) any other trade or finance purchaser who becomes a purchaser of the vehicle and is not a person claiming under the first private purchaser,

from any liability (whether criminal or civil) to which he would be subject apart from this section.

28. Presumptions relating to dealings with motor vehicles

(1) Where in any proceedings (whether criminal or civil) relating to a motor vehicle it is proved—

   (*a*) that the vehicle was bailed or (in Scotland) hired under a hire-purchase agreement, or was agreed to be sold under a conditional sale agreement and
   (*b*) that a person (whether a party to the proceedings or not) became a private purchaser of the vehicle in good faith without notice of the hire-purchase or conditional sale agreement (the 'relevant agreement'),

this section shall have effect for the purposes of the operation of section 27 of this Act in relation to those proceedings.

(2) It shall be presumed for those purposes, unless the contrary is proved, that the disposition of the vehicle to the person referred to in subsection (1)(*b*) above (the 'relevant purchaser') was made by the debtor.

(3) If it is proved that that disposition was not made by the debtor, then it shall be presumed for those purposes, unless the contrary is proved—

   (*a*) that the debtor disposed of the vehicle to a private purchaser purchasing in good faith without notice of the relevant agreement, and
   (*b*) that the relevant purchaser is or was a person claiming under the person to whom the debtor so disposed of the vehicle.

(4) If it is proved that the disposition of the vehicle to the relevant purchaser was not made by the debtor, and that the person to whom the debtor disposed of the vehicle (the 'original purchaser') was a trade or finance purchaser, then it shall be presumed for those purposes, unless the contrary is proved.

   (*a*) that the person who, after the disposition of the vehicle to the original purchaser, first became a private purchaser of the vehicle was a purchaser in good faith without notice of the relevant agreement, and
   (*b*) that the relevant purchaser is or was a person claiming under the original purchaser.

(5) Without prejudice to any other method of proof, where in any proceedings a party thereto admits a fact, that fact shall, for the purposes of this section, be taken as against him to be proved in relation to those proceedings.

Hire Purchase Act 1964

29. Interpretation of Part III.

(1) In this Part of this Act—

'conditional sale agreement' means an agreement for the sale of goods under which the purchase price or part of it is payable by instalments, and the property in the goods is to remain in the seller (notwithstanding that the buyer is to be in possession of the goods) until such conditions as to the payment of instalments or otherwise as may be specified in the agreement are fulfilled;

'creditor' means the person by whom goods are bailed or (in Scotland) hired under a hire-purchase agreement or as the case may be, the seller under a conditional sale agreement, or the person to whom his rights and duties have passed by assignment or operation of law;

'disposition' means any sale or contract of sale (including a conditional sale agreement), any bailment or (in Scotland) hiring under a hire-purchase agreement and any transfer of the property in goods in pursuance of a provision in that behalf contained in a hire-purchase agreement, and includes any transaction purporting to be a disposition (as so defined), and dispose of shall be construed accordingly;

'hire-purchase agreement' means an agreement, other than a conditional sale agreement, under which—

(*a*) goods are bailed or (in Scotland) hired in return for periodical payments by the person to whom they are bailed or hired, and

(*b*) the property in the goods will pass to that person if the terms of the agreement are complied with and one or more of the following occurs—

(i) the exercise of an option to purchase by that person,

(ii) the doing of any other specified act by any party to the agreement,

(iii) the happening of any other specified events; and

'motor vehicle' means a mechanically propelled vehicle intended or adapted for use on roads to which the public has access.

(2) In this Part of this Act 'trade or finance purchaser' means a purchaser who, at the time of the disposition made to him, carries on a business which consists, wholly or partly,—

(*a*) of purchasing motor vehicles for the purpose of offering or exposing them for sale, or

(*b*) of providing finance by purchasing motor vehicles for the purpose of bailing or (in Scotland) hiring them under hire-purchase agreements or agreeing to sell them under conditional sale agreements,

and 'private purchaser' means a purchaser who, at the time of the disposition made to him, does not carry on any such business.

(3) For the purposes of this Part of this Act a person becomes a purchaser of a motor vehicle if, and at the time when, a disposition of the vehicle is made to him; and a person shall be taken to be a purchaser of a motor vehicle without notice of a hire-purchase agreement or conditional sale agreement if, at the time of the disposition made to him, he has no actual notice that the vehicle is or was the subject of any such agreement.

(4) In this Part of this Act the 'debtor' in relation to a motor vehicle which has been bailed or hired under a hire-purchase agreement, or, as the case may be, agreed to be sold under a conditional sale agreement, means the person

Hire Purchase Act 1964

who at the material time (whether the agreement has before that time been terminated or not) either—

(*a*) is the person to whom the vehicle is bailed or hired under that agreement, or

(*b*) is, in relation to the agreement, the buyer,

including a person who at that time is, by virtue of section 130(4) of the Consumer Credit Act 1974 treated as a bailee or (in Scotland) a custodier of the vehicle.

(5) In this Part of this Act any reference to the title of the creditor to a motor vehicle which has been bailed or (in Scotland) hired under a hire-purchase agreement, or agreed to be sold under a conditional sale agreement, and is disposed of by the debtor, is a reference to such title (if any) to the vehicle as, immediately before that disposition, was vested in the person who then was the creditor in relation to the agreement.

Trading Stamps Act 1964
Chapter 71

An Act to make provision with respect to trading stamps, including provision for regulating the issue, use and redemption of trading stamps; to provide for regulating the business of issuing and redeeming trading stamps; and for purposes connected with the matters aforesaid. [31st July 1964.]

1. Restrictions on persons who may carry on business as promoters of trading stamp schemes

(1) No person other than a company or an industrial and provident society shall carry on business as the promoter of a trading stamp scheme.

(2) (*Subsection (2) was repealed by the Companies Act 1967.*)

(3) If a person carried on business in contravention of subsection (1) of this section he shall be liable—

(*a*) on conviction on indictment to a fine of any amount, and
(*b*) on summary conviction to a fine not exceeding one hundred pounds.

(4) In this and the next following section—
'company' means a company formed and registered under the [Companies Act 1985] or an existing company within the meaning of that Act, and 'private company' has the same meaning as in that Act;
'industrial and provident society' means a society registered under the Industrial and Provident Societies Act 1965.

2. Statements required on face of trading stamps

[(1) No person shall after the coming into force of this section issue any trading stamp, or cause any trading stamp to be issued, or deliver any trading stamp to any person in connection with the sale of any goods, the bailment or (in Scotland) the hiring of any goods under a hire-purchase agreement or the performance of any services, unless such trading stamp bears on its face in clear and legible characters a value expressed in or by reference to current coin of the realm.]

(*Subsection (1) was substituted by the Consumer Credit Act 1974.*)

(2) As from the coming into force of this section it shall be the duty of a company or industrial and provident society carrying on business as the promoter of a trading stamp scheme to secure that all trading stamps issued under the scheme bear on their face in clear and legible characters—

(*a*) in case of a company, either the name of the company or a business name registered in respect of the company under the Registration of Business Names Act 1916;
(*b*) in the case of industrial and provident society, the name of the society.

(3) A person guilty of a contravention of subsection (1) of this section or of a failure to comply with subsection (2) of this section shall on summary conviction be liable to a fine not exceeding—

(*a*) in the case of an offence by a promoter of a trading stamp scheme, one hundred pounds, and
(*b*) in the case of an offence by some other person, twenty pounds.

3. Redemption of trading stamps for cash

(1) If the holder of any number of redeemable trading stamps which have an aggregate cash value of not less than five shillings so requests, the promoter of the trading stamp scheme shall redeem them by paying over their aggregate cash value.

(2) The holder may exercise his right under the foregoing subsection—

(*a*) by presenting the stamps at any reasonable time at the promoter's registered office, or
(*b*) by sending the stamps by post to that office with sufficient instructions as to the manner in which the cash value is to be paid over,

or in any other manner afforded by the promoter.

(3) The obligation under this section in the case of an aggregate cash value which includes a fraction of a new penny shall be arrived at by taking the sum to the nearest new penny below the aggregate cash value.

[(4) In this section 'redeemable trading stamps' means trading stamps delivered after the coming into force of this section in accordance with a trading stamp scheme on or in connection with either—

(*a*) the purchase of any goods,
(*b*) the bailment or (in Scotland) the hiring of any goods under a hire-purchase agreement, or
(*c*) the obtaining of any services for money,

and 'the holder', in relation to such a trading stamp, means the person to whom it was so delivered or any person who holds it without notice of any defect in title.]

(*Subsection (4) was substituted by the Consumer Credit Act 1974.*)

(5) Subject to the following subsection this section shall also apply to trading stamps so delivered before the date of the coming into force of this section if a cash value is stated on their face.

(6) This section shall not apply—

(*a*) to trading stamps which have been so delivered before the date of the coming into force of this section and which show on their face that they were so delivered before that date, or
(*b*) to trading stamps which have been so delivered not later than six months after the passing of this Act and which show on their face, instead of any reference to any kind of value to the holder, a value indicating the sum paid on the purchase or other transaction in connection with which they were delivered or some other value which, having regard to the terms of the trading stamp scheme, it would be unreasonable to take as their value for the purposes of redemption under this section.

(7) Any agreement under which the rights conferred by this section on holders of redeemable trading stamps are surrendered or modified shall be void.

Trading Stamps Act 1964

[4. Warranties to be implied on redemption of trading stamps or goods

(1) In every redemption of trading stamps for goods, notwithstanding any terms to the contrary on which the redemption is made, there is—

   (*a*) an implied warranty on the part of the promoter of the trading stamp scheme that he has a right to give the goods in exchange;

   (*b*) an implied warranty that the goods are free from any charge or encumbrance not disclosed or known to the person obtaining the goods before, or at the time of, redemption and that that person will enjoy quiet possession of the goods except so far as it may be disturbed by the owner or other person entitled to the benefit of any charge or encumbrance so disclosed or known;

   (*c*) an implied warranty that the goods are of merchantable quality, except that there is no such warranty—

   (i) as regards defects specifically drawn to the attention of the person obtaining the goods before or at the time of redemption; or

   (ii) if that person examines the goods before or at the time of redemption, as regards defects which that examination ought to reveal.

(2) Goods of any kind are of merchantable quality within the meaning of this section if they are quality within the meaning of this section if they are as fit for the purpose or purposes for which goods of that kind are commonly bought as it is reasonable to expect having regard to any description applied to them and all the other relevant circumstances.

(3) In the application of this section to Scotland for any reference to a warranty there shall be substituted a reference to a stipulation.]

(*Section 4 was substituted by the Supply of Goods (Implied Terms) Act 1973, section 16.*)

5. Catalogues and stamp books to include name and address of promoter

(1) Every catalogue published by or on behalf of the promoter of a trading stamp scheme which indicates (whether by reference to a stated number of filled stamp books or otherwise) the number of trading stamps required to obtain anything described in the catalogue, and every stamp book published by or on behalf of the promoter of such a scheme, shall contain a prominent statement of the name of the promoter and the address of the promoter's registered office.

(2) If the promoter of a trading stamp scheme publishes, issues or distributes a catalogue or stamp book which fails to comply with any of the requirements of this section, he shall be liable on summary conviction to a fine not exceeding one hundred pounds.

6. Advertisements referring to value of trading stamps

(1) It shall be unlawful for the promoter of a trading stamp scheme, or for any person carrying on a trade or business in which a trading stamp scheme is operated, after the coming into force of this section to issue or publish, or cause to be issued or published, an advertisement in any medium which conveys, or purports to convey, the cash value of any trading stamps—

   (*a*) by means of a statement which associates the worth of any trading stamps with what the holder pays or may pay to obtain them, or (*b*) in terms which are misleading or deceptive.

(2) A person contravening this section shall be liable on summary conviction to a fine not exceeding fifty pounds.

(3) For the purposes of this section an advertisement issued by way of display or exhibition in a public place shall be treated as issued on every day on which it is so displayed or exhibited, but in proceedings brought by virtue of this subsection in a case where the display or exhibition began before the date of the coming into force of this section, it shall be a defence to show that the defendant had taken all reasonable steps to secure that the display or exhibition was terminated before the date.

7. Display of information in shops

(1) In the case of every shop in which a trading stamp scheme is operated—

- (*a*) there shall be kept posted a notice stating the cash value of the trading stamps issued under the scheme and giving such particulars as will enable customers readily to ascertain the number of trading stamps, if any, to which they are entitled on any purchase or other transaction, and
- (*b*) if any current catalogue has been published for the trading stamp scheme by or on behalf of the promoter, a copy of that catalogue shall be kept where it can be conveniently consulted by customers.

(2) A notice under this section shall be posted in such characters and in such a position as to be conveniently read by customers.

(3) If without reasonable excuse any of the foregoing provisions of this section are not complied with in the case of any shop, the occupier or other person having control of the shop shall be liable on summary conviction to a fine not exceeding twenty pounds.

(4) If any person pulls down any notice posted in pursuance of this section, he shall be liable on summary conviction to a fine not exceeding twenty pounds.

(5) In this section 'current catalogue' means any such catalogue as is described in section 5(1) of this Act, being a catalogue which has not been superseded or withdrawn.

8. Offences committed by corporations

Where any offence under this Act committed by a corporation is proved to have been committed with the consent or connivance of any director, manager, secretary or other officer of the corporation, he, as well as the corporation, shall be deemed to be guilty of that offence and shall be liable to be proceeded against and punished accordingly.

9. Venue in summary proceedings

Summary proceedings against a person for an offence under this Act may be taken before the court having jurisdiction in the place where that person is for the time being or, in the case of a body corporate, for the time being has a place of business.

Trading Stamps Act 1964

10. Interpretation

(1) In this Act, unless the context otherwise requires, the following expressions have the meanings hereby assigned to them respectively, that is to say—

'cash value' means, in relation to any trading stamp, the value stated on such stamp;

['conditional sale agreement' means an agreement for the sale of goods under which the purchase price or part of it is payable by instalments, and the property in the goods is to remain in the seller (notwithstanding that the buyer is to be in possession of the goods) until such conditions as to the payment of instalments or otherwise as may be specified in the agreement are fulfilled;]

'corporation' means any body corporate, whether incorporated in Great Britain or elsewhere;

'goods' includes vehicles, vessels, aircraft and animals, and generally includes articles and property of any description;

['hire-purchase agreement' means an agreement, other than a conditional sale agreement, under which—

(a) goods are bailed or (in Scotland) hired in return for periodical payments by the person to whom they are bailed or hired, and
(b) the property in the goods will pass to that person if the terms of the agreement are complied with and one or more of the following occurs—

(i) the exercise of an option to purchase by that person,
(ii) the doing of any other specified act by any party to the agreement,
(iii) the happening of any other specified event;]

[. . .]

'to redeem' means, in relation to any trading stamps, to exchange such stamps (whether by delivering up the stamps or by suffering the same to be cancelled or otherwise howsoever) for money or for goods or for any other benefit, allowance, concession or advantage (but not including the service or repair by the seller or manufacturer of the goods upon or in connection with the purchase of which the stamps are delivered or the replacement of such goods if defective); and the expressions 'redeemable' and 'redemption' shall be construed accordingly;

'shop' includes any premises, and any vehicle, stall or place other than premises, on or in which any retail trade or business is carried on;

'stamp' means any stamp, coupon, voucher, token or similar device, whether adhesive or not, other than lawful money of the realm;

'stamp book' means a book or similar article in or to which it is intended that trading stamps shall be affixed;

['trading stamp' means a stamp which is, or is intended to be, delivered to any person on or in connection with either—

(i) the purchase of any goods, or
(ii) the bailment or (in Scotland) the hiring of any goods under a hire-purchase agreement,

(other than the purchase of a newspaper or other periodical of which the stamp forms part or in which it is contained) and is, or is intended to be, redeemable (whether singly or together with other such stamps) by that or some other person:

Provided that a stamp shall not be deemed to be a trading stamp if—

(a) it is delivered or is intended to be delivered to a person (in this definition called 'the purchaser') on or in connection with the purchaser, or the bailment or (in Scotland) the hiring to him of any goods, and

(b) it is intended to be, and is not, redeemable from any person other than—

  (i) the person (in this definition called 'the seller') from whom the purchaser purchased those goods, or whom bailed or hired those goods to him, or

  (ii) any person from whom the seller (whether directly or indirectly) acquired those goods, and

(c) in the case where a business is carried on by six or more retail establishments, the stamp is one of a kind obtainable at no more than six of those retail establishments and not obtainable by the public elsewhere, and the arrangements under which it is redeemable are entirely separate from arrangements under which any other stamps, whether trading stamps or not, are redeemable.

and references in this definition to the purchase of goods include references to the obtaining of services for money;]

'trading stamp scheme' means any arrangements for making trading stamps available for use in shops or elsewhere, together with arrangements for their redemption, and 'promoter,' in relation to a trading stamp scheme, includes, in a case where a person carrying on a retail trade or business assumes responsibility for the redemption of trading stamps, that person.

(2) For the purposes of this Act, a person shall be deemed to be a director of a corporation if he occupies in relation thereto the position of a director, by whatever name called, or is a person in accordance with whose directions or instructions the directors of the corporation or any of them act;

Provided that a person shall not, by reason only that the directors of a corporation act on advice given by him in a professional capacity, be taken to be a person in accordance with whose directions or instructions those directors act.

(*The amendments in square brackets were made by the Consumer Credit Act 1974.*)

11. Short title, extent and commencement

(1) This Act may be cited as the Trading Stamps Act 1964.

(2) This Act shall not extend to Northern Ireland.

(3) Section 1 of this Act shall come into force at the expiration of a period of six months beginning with the date of the passing of this Act, and sections 2 to 7 of this Act shall come into force at the expiration of a period of twelve months beginning with that date.

Misrepresentation Act 1967
Chapter 7

An Act to amend the law relating to innocent misrepresentations and to amend sections 11 and 35 of the Sale of Goods Act 1893. [22nd March 1967]

1. Removal of certain bars to rescission for innocent misrepresentation

Where a person has entered into a contract after a misrepresentation has been made to him, and—

(a) the misrepresentation has become a term of the contract; or
(b) the contract has been performed;

or both, then, if otherwise he would be entitled to rescind the contract without alleging fraud, he shall be so entitled, subject to the provisions of this Act, notwithstanding the matters mentioned in paragraphs (a) and (b) of this section.

2. Damages for misrepresentation

(1) Where a person has entered into a contract after a misrepresentation has been made to him by another party thereto and as a result thereof he has suffered loss, then, if the person making the misrepresentation would be liable to damages in respect thereof had the misrepresentation been made fraudulently, that person shall be so liable notwithstanding that the misrepresentation was not made fraudulently, unless he proves that he had reasonable ground to believe and did believe up to the time the contract was made that the facts represented were true.

(2) Where a person has entered into a contract after a misrepresentation has been made to him otherwise than fraudulently, and he would be entitled, by reason of the misrepresentation, to rescind the contract, then, if it is claimed, in any proceedings arising out of the contract, that the contract ought to be or has been rescinded, the court or arbitrator may declare the contract subsisting and award damages in lieu of rescission, if of opinion that it would be equitable to do so, having regard to the nature of the misrepresentation and the loss that would be caused by it if the contract were upheld, as well as to the loss that rescission would cause to the other party.

(3) Damages may be awarded against a person under subsection (2) of this section whether or not he is liable to damages under subsection (1) thereof, but where he is so liable any award under the said subsection (2) shall be taken into account in assessing his liability under the said subsection (1).

3. Avoidance of provision excluding liability for misrepresentation

If any [contract] contains a [term] which would exclude or restrict—

(a) any liability to which a party to a contract may be subject by reason of any misrepresentation made by him before the contract was made; or (*b*) any remedy available to another party to the contract by reason of such a misrepresentation;

[that term shall be of no effect except in so far as it satisfies the requirement of reasonableness as stated in section 11(1) of the Unfair Contract Terms Act 1977; and it is for those claiming that the term satisfies that requirement to show that it does.]

[*The words in square brackets were substituted by the Unfair Contract Terms Act 1977, section 8.*]

[*Section 4 was repealed by the Sale of Goods Act 1979, section 63(2) and Schedule 3.*]

5. Saving for past transactions

Nothing in this Act shall apply in relation to any misrepresentation or contract of sale which is made before the commencement of this Act.

6. Short title commencement and extent

(1) This Act may be cited as the Misrepresentation Act 1967.

(2) This Act shall come into operation at the expiration of the period of one month beginning with the date on which it is passed.

(3) This Act . . . does not extend to Scotland.

(4) This Act does not extend to Northern Ireland.

[*The words in subsection (3) were repealed by the Sale of Goods Act 1979, section 63(2) and Schedule 3.*]

Trade Descriptions Act 1968
Chapter 29

Prohibition of false trade descriptions

1. Prohibition of false trade descriptions

(1) Any person who, in the course of a trade or business,—

- (*a*) applies a false trade description to any goods; or
- (*b*) supplies or offers to supply any goods to which a false trade description is applied;

shall, subject to the provisions of this Act, be guilty of an offence.

(2) Sections 2 to 6 of this Act shall have effect for the purposes of this section and for the interpretation of expressions used in this section, wherever they occur in this Act.

2. Trade description

(1) A trade description is an indication, direct or indirect, and by whatever means given, of any of the following matters with respect to any goods or parts of goods, that is to say—

- (*a*) quantity, size or gauge;
- (*b*) method of manufacture, production, processing or reconditioning;
- (*c*) composition;
- (*d*) fitness for purpose, strength, performance, behaviour or accuracy;
- (*e*) any physical characteristics not included in the preceding paragraphs;
- (*f*) testing by any person and results thereof;
- (*g*) approval by any person or conformity with a type approved by any person;
- (*h*) place or date of manufacture, production, processing or reconditioning;
- (*i*) person by whom manufactured, produced, processed or reconditioned;
- (*j*) other history, including previous ownership or use.

(2) The matters specified in subsection (1) of this section shall be taken—

- (*a*) in relation to any animal, to include sex, breed or cross, fertility and soundness;
- (*b*) in relation to any semen, to include the identity and characteristics of the animal from which it was taken and measure of dilution.

(3) In this section 'quantity' includes length, width, height, area, volume, capacity, weight and number.

(4) Notwithstanding anything in the preceding provisions of this section, the following shall be deemed not to be trade descriptions, that is to say, any description or mark applied in pursuance of—

- (*a*) (*Subsection (a) was repealed by the European Communities Act 1972.*);
- (*b*) section 2 of the Agricultural Produce (Grading and Marking) Act 1928 (as amended by the Agricultural Produce (Grading and Marking)

Amendment Act 1931) or any corresponding enactment of the Parliament of Northern Ireland;
(c) the Plant Varieties and Seeds Act 1964;
(d) the Agriculture and Horticulture Act 1964 [or any Community grading rules within the meaning of that Act];
(e) the Seeds Act (Northern Ireland) 1965;
(f) the Horticulture Act (Northern Ireland) 1966;
(g) [the Consumer Protection Act 1987];

[any statement made in respect of, or mark applied to, any material in pursuance of Part IV of the Agriculture Act 1970, any name or expression to which a meaning has been assigned under section 70 of that Act when applied to any material in the circumstances specified in that section] any mark prescribed by a system of classification compiled under section 5 of the Agriculture Act 1967 [and any designation, mark or description applied in pursuance of a scheme brought into force under section 6(1) or an order made under section 25(1) of the Agriculture Act 1970].

(The words in square brackets in subsection (4)(d) were added by the European Communities Act 1972. Subsection (4)(g) was substituted by the Consumer Protection Act 1987. The words in square brackets following subsection 4(g) were added by the Agriculture Act 1970.)

(5) Notwithstanding anything in the preceding provisions of this section,

(a) where provision is made under the [Food Act 1984], the Food and Drugs (Scotland) Act 1956 or the Food and Drugs Act (Northern Ireland) 1958 [or the Consumer Protection Act 1987] prohibiting the application of a description except to goods in the case of which the requirements specified in that provision are complied with, that description, when applied to such goods, shall be deemed not to be a trade description.

[(b) where by virtue of any provision made under Part V of the Medicines Act 1968 (or made under any provisions of the said Part V as applied by an order made under section 104 or section 105 of that Act) anything which, in accordance with this Act, constitutes the application of a trade description to goods is subject to any requirements or restrictions imposed by that provision, when applied to goods in circumstances to which those requirements or restrictions are applicable, shall be deemed not to be a trade description.]

(The words in square brackets in subsection (5)(a) were substituted by the Food Act 1984. Subsection (5)(b) will be added by, when it is brought into force, paragraph 16 of Schedule 5 to the Medicines Act 1968.)

3. False trade description

(1) A false trade description is a trade description which is false to a material degree.

(2) A trade description which, though not false, is misleading, that is to say, likely to be taken for such an indication of any of the matters specified in section 2 of this Act as would be false to a material degree, shall be deemed to be a false trade description.

(3) Anything which, though not a trade description, is likely to be taken for an indication of any of those matters and, as such an indication, would be false to a material degree, shall be deemed to be false trade description.

(4) A false indication, or anything likely to be taken as an indication which would be false, that any goods comply with a standard specified or recognised by any person or implied by the approval of any person shall be deemed to be a false trade description, if there is no such person or no standard so specified, recognised or implied.

4. Applying a trade description to goods

(1) A person applies a trade description to goods if he—
  (a) affixes or annexes it to or in any manner marks it on or incorporates it with—
    (i) the goods themselves, or
    (ii) anything in, on or with which the goods are supplied; or
  (b) places the goods in, on or with anything which the trade description has been affixed or annexed to, marked on or incorporated with, or places any such thing with the goods; or
  (c) uses the trade description in any manner likely to be taken as referring to the goods.

(2) An oral statement may amount to the use of a trade description.

(3) Where goods are supplied in pursuance of a request in which a trade description is used and the circumstances are such as to make it reasonable to infer that the goods are supplied as goods corresponding to that trade description, the person supplying the goods shall be deemed to have applied that trade description to the goods.

5. Trade descriptions used in advertisements

(1) The following provisions of this section shall have effect where in an advertisement a trade description is used in relation to any class of goods.

(2) The trade description shall be taken as referring to all goods of the class, whether or not in existence at the time the advertisement is published—
  (a) for the purpose of determining whether an offence has been committed under paragraph (a) of section 1(1) of this Act; and
  (b) where goods of the class are supplied or offered to be supplied by a person publishing or displaying the advertisement, also for the purpose of determining whether an offence has been committed under paragraph (b) of the said section 1(1).

(3) In determining for the purposes of this section whether any goods are of a class to which a trade description used in an advertisement relates regard shall be had not only to the form and content of the advertisement but also to the time, place, manner and frequency of its publication and all other matters making it likely or unlikely that a person to whom the goods are supplied would think of the goods as belonging to the class in relation to which the trade description is used in the advertisement.

6. Offer to supply

A person exposing goods for supply or having goods in his possession for supply shall be deemed to offer to supply them.

Power to define terms and to require display, etc. of information

7. Definition orders

Where it appears to the Board of Trade—

(*a*) that it would be in the interest of persons to whom any goods are supplied; or
(*b*) that it would be in the interest of persons by whom any goods are exported and would not be contrary to the interest of persons to whom such goods are supplied in the United Kingdom;

that any expressions used in relation to the goods should be understood as having definite meanings, the Board may by order assign such meanings either—

(i) to those expressions when used in the course of a trade or business as, or as part of, a trade description applied to the goods; or
(ii) to those expressions when so used in such circumstances as may be specified in the order;

and where such a meaning is so assigned to an expression it shall be deemed for the purposes of this Act to have that meaning when used as mentioned in paragraph (i) or, as the case may be, paragraph (ii) of this section.

8. Marking orders

(1) Where it appears to the Board of Trade necessary or expedient in the interest of persons to whom any goods are supplied that the goods should be marked with or accompanied by any information (whether or not amounting to or including a trade description) or instruction relating to the goods, the Board may, subject to the provisions of this Act, by order impose requirements for securing that the goods are so marked or accompanied, and regulate or prohibit the supply of goods with respect to which the requirements are not complied with; and the requirements may extend to the form and manner in which the information or instruction is to be given.

(2) Where an order under this section is in force with respect to goods of any description, any person who, in the course of any trade or business, supplies or offers to supply goods of that description in contravention of the order shall, subject to the provisions of this Act, be guilty of an offence.

(3) An order under this section may make different provision for different circumstances and may, in the case of goods supplied in circumstances where the information or instruction required by the order would not be conveyed until after delivery, require the whole or part thereof to be also displayed near the goods.

9. Information etc. to be given in advertisements

(1) Where it appears to the Board of Trade necessary or expedient in the interest of persons to whom any goods are to be supplied that any description of advertisements of the goods should contain or refer to any information (whether or not amounting to or including a trade description) relating to the goods the Board may, subject to the provisions of this Act, by order impose requirements as to the inclusion of that information, or of an indication of the means by which it may be obtained, in such description of advertisements of the goods as may be specified in the order.

Trade Descriptions Act 1968

(2) An order under this section may specify the form and manner in which any such information or indication is to be included in advertisements of any description and may make different provisions for different circumstances.

(3) Where an advertisement of any goods to be supplied in the course of any trade or business fails to comply with any requirement imposed under this section, any person who publishes the advertisement shall, subject to the provisions of this Act, be guilty of an offence.

10. Provisions supplementary to sections 8 and 9

(1) A requirement imposed by an order under section 8 or section 9 of this Act in relation to any goods shall not be confined to goods manufactured or produced in any one country or any one of a number of countries or to goods manufactured or produced outside any one or more countries, unless—

- (*a*) it is imposed with respect to a description of goods in the case of which the Board of Trade are satisfied that the interest of persons in the United Kingdom to whom goods of that description are supplied will be sufficiently protected if the requirement is so confined; and
- (*b*) the Board of Trade are satisfied that the order is compatible with the international obligations of the United Kingdom.

(2) Where any requirements with respect to any goods are for the time being imposed by such an order and the Board of Trade are satisfied, on the representation of persons appearing to the Board to have a substantial interest in the matter, that greater hardship would be caused to such persons if the requirements continued to apply than is justified by the interest of persons to whom such goods are supplied, the power of the Board to relax or discontinue the requirements by a further order may be exercised without the consultation and notice required by section 38(3) of this Act.

Mis-statements other than false trade descriptions

11. False or misleading indications as to price of goods

(*This section was repealed by the Consumer Protection Act 1987.*)

12. False representations as to royal approval or award, etc

(1) If any person, in the course of any trade or business, gives, by whatever means, any false indication, direct or indirect, that any goods or services supplied by him or any methods adopted by him are or are of a kind supplied to or approved by Her Majesty or any member of the Royal Family, he shall, subject to the provisions of this Act, be guilty of an offence.

(2) If any person, in the course of any trade or business, uses, without the authority of Her Majesty, any device or emblem signifying the Queen's Award to Industry or anything so nearly resembling such a device or emblem as to be likely to deceive, he shall, subject to the provisions of this Act, be guilty of an offence.

13. False representations as to supply of goods or services

If any person, in the course of any trade or business, gives, by whatever means, any false indication, direct or indirect, that any goods or services supplied by him are of a kind supplied to any person he shall, subject to the provisions of this Act, be guilty of an offence.

14. False or misleading statements as to services etc

(1) It shall be an offence for any person in the course of any trade or business—

(*a*) to make a statement which he knows to be false; or
(*b*) recklessly to make a statement which is false;

as to any of the following matters, that is to say,—

(i) the provision in the course of any trade or business of any services, accommodation or facilities;
(ii) the nature of any services, accommodation or facilities provided in the course of any trade or business;
(iii) the time at which, manner in which or persons by whom any services, accommodation or facilities are so provided;
(iv) the examination, approval or evaluation by any person of any services, accommodation or facilities so provided; or
(v) the location or amenities of any accommodation so provided.

(2) For the purposes of this section

(*a*) anything (whether or not a statement as to any of the matters specified in the preceding subsection) likely to be taken for such a statement as to any of those matters as would be false shall be deemed to be a false statement as to that matter; and
(*b*) a statement made regardless of whether it is true or false shall be deemed to be made recklessly, whether or not the person making it had reasons for believing that it might be false.

(3) In relation to any services consisting of or including the application of any treatment or process or the carrying out of any repair, the matters specified in subsection (1) of this section shall be taken to include the effect of the treatment, process or repair.

(4) In this section 'false' means false to a material degree and 'services' does not include anything done under a contract of service.

15. Orders defining terms for purposes of section 14

Where it appears to the Board of Trade that it would be in the interest of persons for whom any services, accommodation or facilities are provided in the course of any trade or business that any expressions used with respect thereto should be understood as having definite meanings, the Board may by order assign such meanings to those expressions when used as, or as part of, such statements as are mentioned in section 14 of this Act with respect to those services, accommodation or facilities; and where such a meaning is so assigned to an expression it shall be deemed for the purposes of this Act to have that meaning when so used.

Prohibition of importation of certain goods

16. Prohibition of importation of goods bearing false indication of origin

Where a false trade description is applied to any goods outside the United Kingdom and the false indication, or one of the false indications, given, or likely to be taken as given, thereby is an indication of the place of manufacture, production, processing or reconditioning of the goods or any part thereof, the goods shall not be imported into the United Kingdom.

17. Restriction on importation of goods bearing infringing trade marks

(*This section inserts section 64A into the Trade Marks Act 1938.*)

Provisions as to offences

18. Penalty for offences

A person guilty of an offence under this Act for which no other penalty is specified shall be liable—

- (*a*) on summary conviction, to a fine not exceeding four hundred pounds; and
- (*b*) on conviction on indictment, to a fine or imprisonment for a term not exceeding two years or both.

19. Time-limit for prosecutions

(1) No prosecution for an offence under this Act shall be commenced after the expiration of three years from the commission of the offence or one year from its discovery by the prosecutor, whichever is the earlier.

(2) Notwithstanding anything in [section 127(1) of the Magistrates' Courts Act 1980], a magistrates' court may try an information for an offence under this Act if the information was laid at any time within twelve months from the commission of the offence.

(*The words in square brackets were substituted by the Magistrates' Courts Act 1980.*)

(3) Notwithstanding anything in section 23 of the Summary Jurisdiction (Scotland) Act 1954 (limitation of time for proceedings in statutory offences) summary proceedings in Scotland for an offence under this section may be commenced at any time within twelve months from the time when the offence was committed, and subsection (2) of the said section 23 shall apply for the purposes of this subsection as it applies for the purposes of that section.

(4) Subsections (2) and (3) of this section do not apply where—

- (*a*) the offence was committed by the making of an oral statement; or
- (*b*) the offence was one of supplying goods to which a false trade description is applied, and the trade description was applied by an oral statement; or
- (*c*) the offence was one where a false trade description is deemed to have been applied to goods by virtue of section 4(3) of this Act and the goods were supplied in pursuance of an oral request.

20. Offences by corporations

(1) Where an offence under this Act which has been committed by a body corporate is proved to have been committed with the consent and connivance of, or to be attributable to any neglect on the part of, any director, manager, secretary or other similar officer of the body corporate, or any person who was purporting to act in any such capacity, he as well as the body corporate

shall be guilty of that offence and shall be liable to be proceeded against and punished accordingly.

(2) In this section 'director,' in relation to any body corporate established by or under any enactment for the purpose of carrying on under national ownership any industry or part of an industry or undertaking, being a body corporate whose affairs are managed by the members thereof, means a member of that body corporate.

21. Accessories to offences committed abroad

(1) Any person who, in the United Kingdom, assists in or induces the commission in any other country of an act in respect of goods which, if the act were committed in the United Kingdom, would be an offence under section 1 of this Act shall be guilty of an offence, except as provided by subsection (2) of this section, but only if either—

- (*a*) the false trade description concerned is an indication (or anything likely to be taken as an indication) that the goods or any part thereof were manufactured, produced, processed or reconditioned in the United Kingdom; or
- (*b*) the false trade description concerned—
    - (i) consists of or comprises an expression (or anything likely to be taken as an expression) to which a meaning is assigned by an order made by virtue of section 7(*b*) of this Act, and
    - (ii) where that meaning is so assigned only in circumstances specified in the order, the trade description is used in those circumstances.

(2) A person shall not be guilty of an offence under subsection (1) of this section if, by virtue of section 32 of this Act, the act, though committed in the United Kingdom, would not be an offence under section 1 of this Act had the goods been intended for despatch to the other country.

(3) Any person who, in the United Kingdom, assists in or induces the commission outside the United Kingdom of an act which, if committed in the United Kingdom, would be an offence under section 12 of this Act shall be guilty of an offence.

22. Restrictions on institution of proceedings and admission of evidence

(1) Where any act or omission constitutes both an offence under this Act and an offence under any provision contained in or having effect by virtue of Part IV of the [Weights and Measures Act 1985] or [Part V of the Weights and Measures (Northern Ireland) Order 1981]—

- (*a*) proceedings for the offence shall not be instituted under this Act, except by virtue of section 23 thereof, without the service of such a notice as is required by [subsection (3) of section 83 of the said Act of 1985] or, as the case may be, [paragraph (3) of Article 46 of the said Order of 1981] nor after the expiration of the period mentioned in paragraph (*c*) of that subsection [or, as the case may be, that paragraph] and
- (*b*) [sections 35, 36 and 37(1) and (2) of the said Act of 1985] or, as the case may be, of [Article 24 of the said Order of 1981], shall, with the necessary modifications, apply as if the offence under this Act were an offence under Part IV of that Act [or, as the case may be, Part V of that Order,] or any instrument made thereunder.

(*The words in square brackets are amendments made, respectively, by the enactments referred to in those brackets.*)

(2) Where any act or omission constitutes both an offence under this Act and an offence under the food and drugs laws, evidence on behalf of the prosecution concerning any sample procured for analysis shall not be admissible in proceedings for the offence under this Act unless the relevant provisions of those laws have been complied with.

In this subsection 'the foods and drugs laws' means the [Food Act 1984], the Food and Drugs (Scotland) Act 1956, the Food and Drugs Act (Northern Ireland) 1958 and [or the Medicines Act 1968] any instrument made thereunder and 'the relevant provisions' means—

- (*a*) in relation to the [said Act of 1980, sections 80 and 84] and Part I of Schedule 7;
- (*b*) in relation to the said Act of 1956, sections 30 and 33; and
- (*c*) in relation to the said Act of 1958, sections 35 and 38; [and
- (*d*) in relation to the said Act of 1968, so much of Schedule 3 to that Act as is applicable to the circumstances in which the sample was procured;]

or any provision replacing any of the said provisions by virtue of [section 118 or 119 of the said Act of 1984], section 56 [or 56A] of the said Act of 1956, or section 68 of the said Act of 1958 [or paragraph 27 of Schedule 3 to the said Act of 1968].

(*The amendments in square brackets were made, respectively, by the statutes referred to in those brackets. The amendments relating to the Medicines Act 1968 will not come into effect until the relevant commencement order is made under that Act.*)

(3) The Board of Trade may by order provide that in proceedings for an offence under this Act in relation to such goods as may be specified in the order (other than proceedings for an offence falling within the preceding provisions of this section) evidence on behalf of the prosecution concerning any sample procured for analysis shall not be admissible unless the sample has been dealt with in such manner as may be specified in the order.

23. Offences due to fault of other person

Where the commission by any person of an offence under this Act is due to the act or default of some other person that other person shall be guilty of the offence, and a person may be charged with and convicted of the offence by virtue of this section whether or not proceedings are taken against the first-mentioned person.

Defences

24. Defence of mistake, accident, etc

(1) In any proceedings for an offence under this Act it shall, subject to subsection (2) of this section, be a defence for the person charged to prove—

- (*a*) that the commission of the offence was due to a mistake or to reliance on information supplied to him or to the act or default of another person, an accident or some other cause beyond his control; and
- (*b*) that he took all reasonable precautions and exercised all due diligence

to avoid the commission of such an offence by himself or any person under his control.

(2) If in any case the defence provided by the last foregoing subsection involves the allegation that the commission of the offence was due to the act or default of another person or to reliance on information supplied by another person, the person charged shall not, without leave of the court, be entitled to rely on that defence unless, within a period ending seven clear days before the hearing, he has served on the prosecutor a notice in writing giving such information identifying or assisting in the identification of that other person as was then in his possession.

(3) In any proceedings for an offence under this Act of supplying or offering to supply goods to which a false trade description is applied it shall be a defence for the person charged to prove that he did not know, and could not with reasonable diligence have ascertained, that the goods did not conform to the description or that the description had been applied to the goods.

25. Innocent publication of advertisement

In proceedings for an offence under this Act committed by the publication of an advertisement it shall be a defence for the person charged to prove that he is a person whose business it is to publish or arrange for the publication of advertisements and that he received the advertisement for publication in the ordinary course of business and did not know and had no reason to suspect that its publication would amount to an offence under this Act.

Enforcement

26. Enforcing authorities

(1) It shall be the duty of every local weights and measures authority to enforce within their area the provisions of this Act and of any order made under this Act. [. . .]

(*The square brackets indicate words repealed by the Weights and Measures Act 1985.*)

(2) Every local weights and measures authority shall, whenever the Board of Trade so direct, make to the Board a report on the exercise of their functions under this Act in such form and containing such particulars as the Board may direct.

(3)–(4) (*Subsections (3) and (4) were repealed by the Local Government, Planning and Land Act 1980.*)

(5) Nothing in this section shall be taken as authorising a local weights and measures authority in Scotland to institute proceedings for an offence.

27. Power to make test purchases

A local weights and measures authority shall have power to make, or to authorise any of their officers to make on their behalf, such purchases of goods, and to authorise any of their officers to secure the provision of such services, accommodation or facilities, as may appear expedient for the purposes of determining whether or not the provisions of this Act and any order made thereunder are being complied with.

28. Power to enter premises and inspect and seize goods and documents

(1) A duly authorised officer of a local weights and measures authority or of a Government department may, at all reasonable hours and on production, if required, of his credentials, exercise the following powers, that is to say,—

- (a) he may, for the purpose of ascertaining whether any offence under this Act has been committed, inspect any goods and enter any premises other than premises used only as a dwelling;
- (b) if he has reasonable cause to suspect that an offence under this Act has been committed, he may, for the purpose of ascertaining whether it has been committed, require any person carrying on a trade or business or employed in connection with a trade or business to produce any books or documents relating to the trade or business and may take copies of, or of any entry in, any such book or document;
- (c) if he has reasonable cause to believe that an offence under this Act has been committed, he may seize and detain any goods for the purpose of ascertaining, by testing or otherwise, whether the offence has been committed;
- (d) he may seize and detain any goods or documents which he has reason to believe may be required as evidence in proceedings for an offence under this Act;
- (e) he may, for the purpose of exercising his powers under this subsection to seize goods, but only if and to the extent that it is reasonably necessary in order to secure that the provisions of this Act and of any order made thereunder are duly observed, require any person having authority to do so to break open any container or open any vending machine and, if that person does not comply with the requirement, he may do so himself.

(2) An officer seizing any goods or documents in the exercise of his powers under this section shall inform the person from whom they are seized and, in the case of goods seized from a vending machine, the person whose name and address are stated on the machine as being the proprietor's or, if no name and address are so stated, the occupier of the premises on which the machine stands or to which it is affixed.

(3) If a justice of the peace, on sworn information in writing—

- (a) is satisfied that there is reasonable grounds to believe either—
  - (i) that any goods, books or documents which a duly authorised officer has power under this section to inspect are on any premises and that their inspection is likely to disclose evidence of the commission of an offence under this Act; or
  - (ii) that any offence under this Act has been, is being or is about to be committed on any premises; and
- (b) is also satisfied either—
  - (i) that admission to the premises has been or is likely to be refused and that notice of intention to apply for a warrant under this subsection has been given to the occupier; or
  - (ii) that an application for admission, or the giving of such a notice, would defeat the object of the entry or that the premises are unoccupied or that the occupier is temporarily absent and it might defeat the object of the entry to await his return;

the justice may by warrant under his hand, which shall continue in force for a period of one month, authorise an officer of a local weights and measures authority or of a Government department to enter the premises, if need be by force.

In the application of this subsection to Scotland, 'justice of the peace' shall be construed as including a sheriff and a magistrate.

(4) An officer entering any premises by virtue of this section may take with him such other persons and such equipment as may appear to him necessary; and on leaving any premises which he has entered by virtue of a warrant under the preceding subsection he shall, if the premises are unoccupied or the occupier is temporarily absent, leave them effectively secured against trespassers as he found them.

(5) If any person discloses to any person—

(*a*) any information with respect to any manufacturing process or trade secret obtained by him in premises which he has entered by virtue of this section; or
(*b*) any information obtained by him in pursuance of this Act;

he shall be guilty of an offence unless the disclosure was made in or for the purpose of the performance by him or any other person of functions under this Act.

[(5A) Subsection (5) of this section does not apply to disclosure for a purpose specified in [section 38(2)(a), (b) or (c) of the Consumer Protection Act 1987.]]

(*Subsection (5A) was added by the Consumer Credit Act 1974 and amended by the Consumer Protection Act 1987.*)

(6) If any person who is not a duly authorised officer of a local weights and measures authority or of a Government department purports to act as such under this section he shall be guilty of an offence.

(7) Nothing in this section shall be taken to compel the production by a solicitor of a document containing a privileged communication made by or to him in that capacity or to authorise the taking of possession of any such document which is in his possession.

29. Obstruction of authorised officers

(1) Any person who—

(*a*) wilfully obstructs an officer of a local weights and measures authority or of a Government department acting in pursuance of this Act; or
(*b*) wilfully fails to comply with any requirement properly made to him by such an officer under section 28 of this Act; or
(*c*) without reasonable cause fails to give such an officer so acting any other assistance or information which he may reasonably require of him for the purpose of the performance of his functions under this Act,

shall be guilty of an offence and liable, on summary conviction, to a fine not exceeding fifty pounds.

(2) If any person, in giving any such information as is mentioned in the preceding subsection, makes any statement which he knows to be false, he shall be guilty of an offence.

Trade Descriptions Act 1968

(3) Nothing in this section shall be construed as requiring a person to answer any question or give any information if to do so might incriminate him.

30. Notice of test and intended prosecution

(1) Where any goods seized or purchased by an officer in pursuance of this Act are submitted to a test, then—

    (*a*) if the goods were seized, the officer shall inform the person mentioned in section 28(2) of this Act of the result of the test;

    (*b*) if the goods were purchased and the test leads to the institution of proceedings for an offence under this Act, the officer shall inform the person from whom the goods were purchased, or, in the case of goods sold through a vending machine, the person mentioned in section 28(2) of this Act, of the result of the test;

and shall, where as a result of the test proceedings for an offence under this Act are instituted against any person, allow him to have the goods tested on his behalf if it is reasonably practicable to do so.

(2) (*Subsections (2) to (4) were repealed by the Fair Trading Act 1973.*)

31. Evidence by certificate

(1) The Board of Trade may by regulations provide that certificates issued by such persons as may be specified by the regulations in relation to such matters as may be so specified shall, subject to the provisions of this section, be received in evidence of those matters in any proceedings under this Act.

(2) Such a certificate shall not be received in evidence—

    (*a*) unless the party against whom it is to be given in evidence has been served with a copy thereof not less than seven days before the hearing; or

    (*b*) if that party has, not less than three days before the hearing, served on the other party a notice requiring the attendance of the person issuing the certificate.

(3) In any proceedings under this Act in Scotland, a certificate received in evidence by virtue of this section or, where the attendance of a person issuing a certificate is required under subsection (2)(*b*) of this section, the evidence of that person, shall be sufficient evidence of the matters stated in the certificate.

(4) For the purposes of this section any document purporting to be such a certificate as is mentioned in this section shall be deemed to be such a certificate unless the contrary is shown.

(5) Regulations under this section shall be made by statutory instrument which shall be subject to annulment in pursuance of a resolution of either House of Parliament.

Miscellaneous and supplemental.

32. Power to exempt goods sold for export, etc

(1) In relation to goods which are intended—

    (*a*) for despatch to a destination outside the United Kingdom and any designated country within the meaning of [section 24(2)(*b*) of the Weights and Measures Act 1985] or section 15(5)(*b*) of the Weights and Measures Act (Northern Ireland) 1967; or

(*b*) for use as stores within the meaning of the [Customs and Excise Management Act 1979] in a ship or aircraft on a voyage or flight to an eventual destination outside the United Kingdom; or

(*c*) for use by Her Majesty's forces or by a visiting force within the meaning of any of the provisions of Part I of the Visiting Forces Act 1952; or

[(*d*) for industrial use within the meaning of the Weights and Measures Act 1985 or for constructional use];

section 1 of this Act shall apply as if there were omitted from the matters included in section 2(1) of this Act those specified in paragraph (*a*) thereof; and, if the Board of Trade by order specify any other of those matters for the purposes of this section with respect to any description of goods, the said section 1 shall apply, in relation to goods of that description which are intended for despatch to a destination outside the United Kingdom and such country (if any) as may be specified in the order, as if the matters so specified were also omitted from those included in the said section 2(1).

(*The words in square brackets were substituted by the Weights and Measures Act 1985 and the Customs and Excise Management Act 1979.*)

[(2) In this section 'constructional use', in relation to any goods, means the use of those goods in constructional work (or, if the goods are explosives within the meaning of the Explosives Acts 1875 and 1923, in mining, quarrying or demolition work) in the course of the carrying on of a business.]

(*Subsection (2) was added by the Weights and Measures Act 1985.*)

33. Compensation for loss, etc. of goods seized under s. 28

(1) Where, in the exercise of his powers under section 28 of this Act, an officer of a local weights and measures authority or of a Government department seizes and detains any goods and their owner suffers loss by reason thereof or by reason that the goods, during the detention, are lost or damaged or deteriorate, then, unless the owner is convicted of an offence under this Act committed in relation to the goods, the authority or department shall be liable to compensate him for the loss so suffered.

(2) Any disputed question as to the right to or the amount of any compensation payable under this section shall be determined by arbitration and, in Scotland, by a single arbiter appointed, failing agreement between the parties, by the sheriff.

34. Trade marks containing trade descriptions

The fact that a trade description is a trade mark, or part of a trade mark, within the meaning of the Trade Marks Act 1938 does not prevent it from being a false trade description when applied to any goods, except where the following conditions are satisfied, that is to say—

(*a*) that it could have been lawfully applied to the goods if this Act had not been passed; and

(*b*) that on the day this Act is passed the trade mark either is registered under the Trade Marks Act 1938 or is in use to indicate a connection in the course of trade between such goods and the proprietor of the trade mark; and

(c) that the trade mark as applied is used to indicate such a connection between the goods and the proprietor of the trade mark or a person registered under section 28 of the Trade Marks Act 1938 as a registered user of the trade mark; and

(d) that the person who is the proprietor of the trade mark is the same person as, or a successor in title of, the proprietor on the day this Act is passed.

35. Saving for civil rights

A contract for the supply of any goods shall not be void or unenforceable by reason only of a contravention of any provision of this Act.

36. Country of origin

(1) For the purposes of this Act goods shall be deemed to have been manufactured or produced in the country in which they last underwent a treatment or process resulting in a substantial change.

(2) The Board of Trade may by order specify—

(a) in relation to any description of goods, what treatment or process is to be regarded for the purposes of this section as resulting or not resulting in a substantial change;

(b) in relation to any description of goods different parts of which were manufactured or produced in different countries, or of goods assembled in a country different from that in which their parts were manufactured or produced, in which of those countries the goods are to be regarded for the purposes of this Act as having been manufactured or produced.

37. Market research experiments

(1) In this section 'market research experiment' means any activities conducted for the purpose of ascertaining the opinion of persons (in this section referred to as 'participants') of—

(a) any goods; or
(b) anything in, on or with which the goods are supplied; or
(c) the appearance or any other characteristic of the goods or of any such thing; or
(d) the name or description under which the goods are supplied.

(2) This section applies to any market research experiment with respect to which the following conditions are satisfied, that is to say,—

(a) that any participant to whom any goods are supplied in the course of the experiment is informed, at or before the time at which they are supplied to him, that they are supplied for such a purpose as is mentioned in subsection (1) of this section, and

(b) that no consideration in money or money's worth is given by a participant for the goods or any goods supplied to him for comparison.

(3) Neither section 1 nor section 8 of this Act shall apply in relation to goods supplied or offered to be supplied, whether to a participant or any other person, in the course of a market research experiment to which this section applies.

Trade Descriptions Act 1968

38. Orders

(1) Any power to make an order under the preceding provisions of this Act shall be exercisable by statutory instrument, which shall be subject to annulment in pursuance of a resolution of either House of Parliament, and includes power to vary or revoke such an order by a subsequent order.

(2) Any order under the preceding provisions of this Act which relates to any agricultural, horticultural or fishery produce, whether processed or not, food, feeding stuffs or ingredients of food or feeding stuffs, fertilisers or any goods used as pesticides or for similar purposes shall be made by the Board of Trade acting jointly with the following Ministers, that is to say, if the order extends to England and Wales, the Minister of Agriculture, Fisheries and Food, and if it extends to Scotland or Northern Ireland, the Secretary of State concerned.

(3) The following provisions shall apply to the making of an order under section 7, 8, 9, 15 or 36 of this Act, except in the case mentioned in section 10(2) thereof, that is to say—

(*a*) before making the order the Board of Trade shall consult with such organisations as appear to them to be representative of interests substantially affected by it and shall publish, in such manner as the Board think appropriate, notice of their intention to make the order and of the place where copies of the proposed order may be obtained; and

(*b*) the order shall not be made until the expiration of a period of twenty-eight days from the publication of the notice and may then be made with such modifications (if any) as the Board of Trade think appropriate having regard to any representations received by them.

39. Interpretation

(1) The following provisions shall have effect, in addition to sections 2 to 6 of this Act, for the interpretation in this Act of expressions used therein, that is to say—

'advertisement' includes a catalogue, a circular and a price list;
'goods' includes ships and aircraft, things attached to land and growing crops;
'premises' includes any place and any stall, vehicle, ship or aircraft; and
'ship' includes any boat and any other description of vessel used in navigation.

(2) For the purposes of this Act, a trade description or statement published in any newspaper, book or periodical or in any film or sound or television broadcast [or in a programme included in a cable programme service] shall not be deemed to be a trade description applied or statement made in the course of a trade or business unless it is or forms part of an advertisement.

(*The words in square brackets were added by the Cable and Broadcasting Act 1984.*)

40. Provisions as to Northern Ireland

(1) This Act shall apply to Northern Ireland subject to the following modifications, that is to say—

(*a*) section 19(2) shall apply as if for the references to [section 127(1) of

the Magistrates' Courts Act 1980] and the trial and laying of an information there were substituted respectively references to section 34 of the Magistrates' Courts Act (Northern Ireland) 1964 and the hearing and determination and making of a complaint;
- (*b*) section 26 and subsections (2) to (4) of section 30 shall not apply but it shall be the duty of the Ministry of Commerce for Northern Ireland to enforce the provisions of this Act and of any order made under it (other than the provisions of section 42 of this Act);
- (*c*) sections 27 to 29 and 33 shall apply as if for references to a local weights and measures authority and any officer of such an authority there were substituted respectively references to the said Ministry and any of its officers.

(2)–(4) (*Subsections (2) to (4) were repealed by the Northern Ireland Constitution Act 1973.*)

(*The words in square brackets were substituted by the Magistrates' Courts Act 1980.*)

(5) (*This subsection was repealed by the Northern Ireland (Modifications of Enactments No. 1) Order 1973.*)

(6) Nothing in this Act shall authorise any department of the Government of Northern Ireland to incur any expenses attributable to the provisions of this Act until provision has been made by the Parliament of Northern Ireland for those expenses to be defrayed out of moneys provided by that Parliament.

(7) (*This subsection was repealed by the Northern Ireland Constitution Act 1973.*)

41. Consequential amendments and repeals

(1) The enactments mentioned in Schedule 1 to this Act shall have effect subject to the amendments specified in that Schedule.

(2) (*Subsection (2) was repealed by the Statute Law (Repeals) Act 1975.*)

42. Continuation, for three years, of Orders in Council requiring indication of origin

(*This subsection was repealed by the Statute Law (Repeals) Act 1975.*)

43. Short title and commencement

(1) This Act may be cited as the Trade Descriptions Act 1968.

(2) This Act shall come into force on the expiration of the period of six months beginning with the day on which it is passed.

SCHEDULES

Schedule 1

CONSEQUENTIAL AMENDMENTS

Schedule 2

REPEALS

Auctions (Bidding Agreements) Act 1969
Chapter 56

An Act to amend the law with respect to proceedings for offences under the Auctions (Bidding Agreements) Act 1927; to make fresh provision as to the rights of a seller of goods by auction where an agreement subsists that a person or persons shall abstain from bidding for the goods; and for connected purposes.
[22nd October 1969]

1. Offences under Auctions (Bidding Agreements) Act 1927 to be indictable as well as triable summarily, and extension of time for bringing summary proceedings

(1) Offences under section 1 of the Auctions (Bidding Agreements) Act 1927 (which, as amended by the Criminal Justice Act 1967, renders a dealer who agrees to give, or gives, or offers a gift or consideration to another as an inducement or reward for abstaining, or for having abstained, from bidding at a sale by auction punishable on summary conviction with a fine not exceeding £400 or imprisonment for a term not exceeding six months, or both, and renders similarly punishable a person who agrees to accept, or accepts, or attempts to obtain from a dealer any such gift or consideration as aforesaid) shall be triable on indictment as well as summarily; and the penalty that may be imposed on a person on conviction on indictment of an offence under that section shall be imprisonment for a term not exceeding two years or a fine or both.

(2) (*This subsection was repealed by the Criminal Law Act 1977.*)

(3) Summary proceedings in Scotland for an offence under the said section 1 shall not be commenced after the expiration of five years from the commission of the offence, but, subject to the foregoing limitation and notwithstanding anything in section 23 of the Summary Jurisdiction (Scotland) Act 1954, such proceedings may be commenced at any time within three months after the date on which evidence sufficient in the opinion of the Lord Advocate to justify the proceedings comes to his knowledge, and subsection (2) of the said section 23 shall apply for the purposes of this subsection as it applies for the purposes of that section.

(4) (*This subsection was repealed by the Criminal Law Act 1977.*)

(5) This section applies only to offences committed after the commencement of this Act.

2. Persons convicted not to attend or participate in auctions

(1) On any such summary conviction or conviction on indictment as is mentioned in section 1 above, the court may order that the person so convicted or that person and any representative of him shall not (without leave of the court) for a period from the date of such conviction—

(*a*) in the case of a summary conviction, of not more than one year, or

(*b*) in the case of a conviction on indictment, of not more than three years,

enter upon any premises where goods intended for sale by auction are on display or to attend or participate in any way in any sale by auction.

(2) In the event of a contravention of an order under this section, the person who contravenes it (and, if he is the representative of another, that other also) shall be guilty of an offence and liable—

(a) on summary conviction, to a fine not exceeding £400;
(b) on conviction on indictment, to imprisonment for a term not exceeding two years or to a fine or to both.

(3) In any proceedings against a person in respect of a contravention of an order under this section consisting in the entry upon premises where goods intended for sale by auction were on display, it shall be a defence for him to prove that he did not know, and had no reason to suspect, that goods so intended were on display on the premises, and in any proceedings against a person in respect of a contravention of such an order consisting in his having done something as the representative of another, it shall be a defence for him to prove that he did not know, and had no reason to suspect, that that other was the subject of such an order.

(4) A person shall not be guilty of an offence under this section by reason only of his selling property by auction or causing it to be so sold.

3. Rights of seller of goods by auction where agreement subsists that some person shall abstain from bidding for the goods

(1) Where goods are purchased at an auction by a person who has entered into an agreement with another or others that the other or the others (or some of them) shall abstain from bidding for the goods (not being an agreement to purchase the goods bona fide on a joint account) and he or the other party, or one of the other parties, to the agreement is a dealer, the seller may avoid the contract under which the goods are purchased.

(2) Where a contract is avoided by virtue of the foregoing subsection, then, if the purchaser has obtained possession of the goods and restitution thereof is not made, the persons who were parties to the agreement that one or some of them should abstain from bidding for the goods the subject of the contract shall be jointly and severally liable to make good to the seller the loss (if any) he sustained by reason of the operation of the agreement.

(3) Subsection (1) above applies to a contract made after the commencement of this Act whether the agreement as to the abstention of a person or persons from bidding for the goods the subject of the contract was made before or after that commencement.

(4) Section 2 of the Auctions (Bidding Agreements) Act 1927 (right of vendors to treat certain sales as fraudulent) shall not apply to a sale the contract for which is made after the commencement of this Act.

(5) In this section, 'dealer' has the meaning assigned to it by section 1(2) of the Auctions (Bidding Agreements) Act 1927.

4. Copy of Act to be exhibited at sale

Section 3 of the Auctions (Bidding Agreements) Act 1927 (copy of Act to be exhibited at sale) shall have effect as if the reference to that Act included a reference to this Act.

Auctions (Bidding Agreements) Act 1969

5. Short title, commencement and extent

(1) This Act may be cited as the Auctions (Bidding Agreements) Act 1969.

(2) This Act shall come into force at the expiration of one month beginning with the day on which it is passed.

(3) This Act shall not extend to Northern Ireland.

Administration of Justice Act 1970
Chapter 31

An Act to make further provision about the courts (including assizes), their business, jurisdiction and procedure; to enable a High Court judge to accept appointment as arbitrator or umpire under an arbitration agreement; to amend the law respecting the enforcement of debt and other liabilities; to amend section 106 of the Rent Act 1968; and for miscellaneous purposes connected with the administration of justice. [29th May 1970]

PART V

MISCELLANEOUS PROVISIONS

40. Punishment for unlawful harassment of debtors

(1) A person commits an offence if, with the object of coercing another person to pay money claimed from the other as a debt due under a contract, he—

   (*a*) harasses the other with demands for payment which, in respect of their frequency or the manner or occasion of making any such demand, or of any threat or publicity by which any demand is accompanied, are calculated to subject him or members of his family or household to alarm, distress or humiliation;
   (*b*) falsely represents, in relation to the money claimed, that criminal proceedings lie for failure to pay it;
   (*c*) falsely represents himself to be authorised in some official capacity to claim or enforce payment; or
   (*d*) utters a document falsely represented by him to have some official character or purporting to have some official character which he knows it has not.

(2) A person may be guilty of an offence by virtue of subsection 1(*a*) above if he concerts with others in the taking of such action as is described in that paragraph, notwithstanding that his own course of conduct does not by itself amount to harassment.

(3) Subsection (1)(*a*) above does not apply to anything done by a person which is reasonable (and otherwise permissible in law) for the purpose—

   (*a*) of securing the discharge of an obligation due, or believed by him to be due, to himself or to persons for whom he acts, or protecting himself or them from future loss; or
   (*b*) of the enforcement of any liability by legal process.

(4) A person guilty of an offence under this section shall be liable on summary conviction to a fine [not exceeding level 5 on the standard scale].

[*The words in square brackets were substituted by the Criminal Justice Act 1982, sections 35, 37, 38 and 46, as further amended by the Criminal Penalties etc (Increase) Order 1984 (S.I. 1984 No. 447).*]

Unsolicited Goods and Services Act 1971
Chapter 30

An Act to make provision for the greater protection of persons receiving unsolicited goods, and to amend the law with respect to charges for entries in directories. [12th May 1971]

1. Rights of recipient of unsolicited goods

(1) In the circumstances specified in the following subsection, a person who after the commencement of this Act receives unsolicited goods, may as between himself and the sender, use, deal with or dispose of them as if they were an unconditional gift to him, and any right of the sender to the goods shall be extinguished.

(2) The circumstances referred to in the preceding subsection are that the goods were sent to the recipient with a view to his acquiring them, that the recipient has no reasonable cause to believe that they were sent with a view to their being acquired for the purposes of a trade or business and has neither agreed to acquire nor agreed to return them, and either—

   (*a*) that during the period of six months beginning with the day on which the recipient received the goods the sender did not take possession of them and the recipient did not unreasonably refuse to permit the sender to do so; or
   (*b*) that not less than thirty days before the expiration of the period aforesaid the recipient gave notice to the sender in accordance with the following subsection, and that during the period of thirty days beginning with the day on which the notice was given the sender did not take possession of the goods and the recipient did not unreasonably refuse to permit the sender to do so.

(3) A notice in pursuance of the preceding subsection shall be in writing and shall—

   (*a*) state the recipient's name and address and, if possession of the goods in question may not be taken by the sender at that address, the address at which it may be so taken;
   (*b*) contain a statement, however expressed, that the goods are unsolicited,

and may be sent by post.

(4) In this section 'sender', in relation to any goods, includes any person on whose behalf or with whose consent the goods are sent, and any other person claiming through or under the sender or any such person.

2. Demands and threats regarding payment

(1) A person who, not having reasonable cause to believe there is a right to payment, in the course of any trade or business makes a demand for payment, or asserts a present or prospective right to payment, for what he knows are unsolicited goods sent (after the commencement of this Act) to another person

Unsolicited Goods and Services Act 1971

with a view to his acquiring them, shall be guilty of an offence and on summary conviction shall be liable to a fine not exceeding £200.

(2) A person who, not having reasonable cause to believe there is a right to payment, in the course of any trade or business and with a view to obtaining any payment for what he knows are unsolicited goods sent as aforesaid—

(*a*) threatens to bring any legal proceedings; or
(*b*) places or causes to be placed the name of any person on a list of defaulters or debtors or threatens to do so; or
(*c*) invokes or causes to be invoked any other collection procedure or threatens to do so,

shall be guilty of an offence and shall be liable on summary conviction to a fine not exceeding £400.

3. Directory entries

(1) A person shall not be liable to make any payment, and shall be entitled to recover any payment made by him, by way of charge for including or arranging for the inclusion in a directory of an entry relating to that person or his trade or business, unless there has been signed by him or on his behalf an order complying with this section or a note complying with this section of his agreement to the charge and, in the case of a note of agreement to the charge, before the note was signed, a copy of it was supplied, for retention by him, to him or to a person acting on his behalf.

(2) A person shall be guilty of an offence punishable on summary conviction with a fine not exceeding £400 if, in a case where a payment in respect of a charge would, in the absence of an order or note of agreement to the charge complying with this section, be recoverable from him in accordance with the terms of subsection (1) above, he demands payment, or asserts a present or prospective right to payment, of the charge or any part of it, without knowing or having reasonable cause to believe that the entry to which the charge relates was ordered in accordance with this section or a proper note of agreement has been duly signed.

(3) For the purposes of subsection (1) above, an order for an entry in a directory must be made by means of an order form or other stationery belonging to the person to whom, or to whose trade or business, the entry is to relate and bearing, in print, the name and address (or one or more of the addresses) of that person; and the note required by this section of a person's agreement to a charge [shall comply with the requirements of regulations under section 3A of this Act.]

(*The words in square brackets were substituted by the Unsolicited Goods and Services (Amendment) Act 1975.*)

(4) Nothing in this section shall apply to a payment due under a contract entered into before the commencement of this Act, or entered into by the acceptance of an offer made before that commencement.

[3A. Contents and form of notes of agreement, invoices and similar documents

(1) For the purposes of this Act, the Secretary of State may make regulations as to the contents and form of notes of agreement, invoices and similar documents;

and, without prejudice to the generality of the foregoing, any such regulations may—

(a) require specified information to be included,
(b) prescribe the manner in which specified information is to be included,
(c) prescribe such other requirements (whether as to presentation, type, size, colour or disposition of lettering, quality or colour of paper or otherwise) as the Secretary of State may consider appropriate for securing that specified information is clearly brought to the attention of the recipient of any note of agreement, invoice or similar document,
(d) make different provision for different classes or descriptions of notes of agreement, invoices and similar documents or for the same class or description in different circumstances,
(e) contain such supplementary and incidental provisions as the Secretary of State may consider appropriate.

(2) Any reference in this section to a note of agreement includes any such copy as is mentioned in section 3(1) of this Act.

(3) Regulations under this section shall be made by statutory instrument and shall be subject to annulment in pursuance of a resolution of either House of Parliament.]

(*Section 3A was added by the Unsolicited Goods and Services (Amendment) Act 1975.*)

4. Unsolicited publications

(1) A person shall be guilty of an offence if he sends or causes to be sent to another person any book, magazine or leaflet (or advertising material for any such publication) which he knows or ought reasonably to know is unsolicited and which describes or illustrates human sexual techniques.

(2) A person found guilty of an offence under this section shall be liable on summary conviction to a fine not exceeding £100 for a first offence and to a fine not exceeding £400 for any subsequent offence.

(3) A prosecution for an offence under this section shall not in England and Wales be instituted except by, or with the consent of, the Director of Public Prosecutions.

5. Offences by corporations

(1) Where an offence under this Act which has been committed by a body corporate is proved to have been committed with the consent or connivance of, or to be attributable to any neglect on the part of, any director, manager, secretary, or other similar officer of the body corporate, or of any person who was purporting to act in any such capacity, he as well as the body corporate shall be guilty of that offence and shall be liable to be proceeded against and punished accordingly.

(2) Where the affairs of a body corporate are managed by its members, this section shall apply in relation to the acts or defaults of a member in connection with his functions of management as if he were a director of the body corporate.

6. Interpretation

(1) In this Act, unless the context or subject matter otherwise requires—

'acquire' includes hire;
'send' includes deliver, and 'sender' shall be construed accordingly;
'unsolicited' means, in relation to goods sent to any person, that they are sent without any prior request made by him or on his behalf.

[(2) For the purpose of this Act any invoice or similar document stating the amount of any payment and not complying with the requirements of regulations under section 3A of this Act applicable thereto shall be regarded as asserting a right to the payment]

(Subsection (2) was substituted by the Unsolicited Goods and Services (Amendment) Act 1975.)

7. Citation, commencement and extent

(1) This Act may be cited as the Unsolicited Goods and Services Act 1971.

(2) This Act shall come into force at the expiration of three months beginning with the day on which it is passed.

(3) This Act does not extend to Northern Ireland.

Unsolicited Goods and Services (Amendment) Act 1975
Chapter 13

1–2. (*Sections 1 and 2 amend the Unsolicited Goods and Services Act 1971. The amendments are incorporated in the 1971 Act above.*)

3. Provision for offence under section 3(2) of the Act of 1971 to be prosecuted on indictment

(1) An offence under section 3(2) of the Act of 1971 may be prosecuted on indictment; and a person convicted on indictment of an offence under that section shall be liable to a fine.

(2) This section applies only to offences committed after the coming into operation of this section.

4. Short title, citation, commencement, transitional provisions and extent

(1) This Act may be cited as the Unsolicited Goods and Services (Amendment) Act 1975 and the Unsolicited Goods and Services Act 1971 and this Act may be cited together as the Unsolicited Goods and Services Acts 1971 and 1975.

(2) Sections 1 and 3 of this Act and this section shall come into operation on the passing of this Act but any regulations made by virtue of the said section 1 shall not come into operation before the date appointed by order under subsection (3) below for the coming into operation of section 2 of this Act.

(3) Section 2 of this Act shall come into operation on such date as the Secretary of State may by order made by statutory instrument appoint; and different dates may be appointed by order under this subsection for different provisions of that section.

(4) The amendments made to sections 3(3) and 6(2) of the Act of 1971 by section 2 of this Act and any regulations made by virtue of section 1 of this Act shall not apply to any note of agreement signed, or invoice or similar document sent before the date appointed by order under subsection (3) above for the coming into operation of the said section 2.

(5) This Act shall not extend to Northern Ireland.

Supply of Goods (Implied Terms) Act 1973

Supply of Goods (Implied Terms) Act 1973
Chapter 13

ARRANGEMENT OF SECTIONS

Hire-purchase agreements

Section
 8. Implied terms as to title
 9. Letting by description
 10. Implied undertakings as to quality or fitness
 11. Samples
 12. Exclusion of implied terms and conditions
 13. Conflict of laws
 14. Special provisions as to conditional sale agreements
 15. Supplementary
 [. . .]

Miscellaneous

17. Northern Ireland
18. Short title, citation, interpretation, commencement, repeal and saving

An Act to amend the law with respect to the terms to be implied in contracts of sale of goods and hire-purchase agreements and on the exchange of goods for trading stamps, and with respect to the terms of conditional sale agreements; and for connected purposes.

[18th April 1973]

[*Sections 1 to 7 were repealed by the Sale of Goods Act 1979, section* 63(2) *and Schedule* 3.]

Hire-purchase agreements

[8. Implied terms as to title

(1) In every hire-purchase agreement, other than one to which subsection (2) below applies, there is—

 (*a*) an implied condition on the part of the creditor that he will have a right to sell the goods at the time when the property is to pass; and
 (*b*) an implied warranty that—
  (i) the goods are free, and will remain free until the time when the property is to pass, from any charge or encumbrance not disclosed or known to the person to whom the goods are bailed or (in Scotland) hired before the agreement is made, and
  (ii) that person will enjoy quiet possession of the goods except so far as it may be disturbed by any person entitled to the benefit of any charge or encumbrance so disclosed or known.

(2) In a hire-purchase agreement, in the case of which there appears from the agreement or is to be inferred from the circumstances of the agreement

Supply of Goods (Implied Terms) Act 1973

an intention that the creditor should transfer only such title as he or a third person may have, there is—

(*a*) an implied warranty that all charges or encumbrances known to the creditor and not known to the person to whom the goods are bailed or hired have been disclosed to that person before the agreement is made; and

(*b*) an implied warranty that neither—
  (i) the creditor; nor
  (ii) in a case where the parties to the agreement intend that any title which may be transferred shall be only such title as a third person may have, that person; nor
  (iii) anyone claiming through or under the creditor or that third person otherwise than under a charge or encumbrance disclosed or known to the person to whom the goods are bailed or hired, before the agreement is made;

will disturb the quiet possession of the person to whom the goods are bailed or hired.

[*See note at foot of section 12.*]

9. Bailing or hiring by description

(1) Where under a hire-purchase agreement goods are bailed or (in Scotland) hired by description, there is an implied condition that the goods will correspond with the description, and if under the agreement the goods are bailed or hired by reference to a sample as well as a description, it is not sufficient that the bulk of the goods corresponds with the sample if the goods do not also correspond with the description.

(2) Goods shall not be prevented from being bailed or hired by description by reason only that, being exposed for sale, bailment or hire, they are selected by the person to whom they are bailed or hired.

[*See note at foot of section 12.*]

10. Implied undertaking as to quality or fitness

(1) Except as provided by this section and section 11 below and subject to the provisions of any other enactment, including any enactment of the Parliament of Northern Ireland or the Northern Ireland Assembly, there is no implied condition or warranty as to the quality of fitness for any particular purpose of goods bailed or (in Scotland) hired under a hire-purchase agreement.

(2) Where the creditor bails or hires goods under a hire-purchase agreement in the course of a business, there is an implied condition that the goods [supplied under the agreement] are of merchantable quality, except that there is no such condition—

(*a*) as regards defects specifically drawn to the attention of the person to whom the goods are bailed or hired before the agreement is made; or
(*b*) if that person examines the goods before the agreement is made, as regards defects which that examination ought to reveal.

(3) Where the creditor bails or hires goods under a hire-purchase agreement in the course of a business and the person to whom the goods are bailed or hired, expressly or by implication makes known—

Supply of Goods (Implied Terms) Act 1973

(*a*) to the creditor in the course of negotiations conducted by the creditor in relation to the making of the hire-purchase agreement, or

(*b*) to a credit-broker in the course of negotiations conducted by that broker in relation to goods sold by him to the creditor before forming the subject matter of the hire-purchase agreement.

any particular purpose for which the goods are being bailed or hired, there is an implied condition that the goods supplied under the agreement are reasonably fit for that purpose, whether or not that is a purpose for which such goods are commonly supplied, except where the circumstances show that the person to whom the goods are bailed or hired does not rely, or that it is unreasonable for him to rely, on the skill or judgment of the creditor or credit-broker.

(4) An implied condition or warranty as to quality or fitness for a particular purpose may be annexed to a hire-purchase agreement by usage.

(5) The preceding provisions of this section apply to a hire-purchase agreement made by a person who in the course of a business is acting as agent for the creditor as they apply to an agreement made by the creditor in the course of a business, except where the creditor is not bailing or hiring in the course of a business and either the person to whom the goods are bailed or hired knows that fact or reasonable steps are taken to bring it to the notice of that person before the agreement is made.

(6) In subsection (3) above and this subsection—

(*a*) 'credit-broker' means a person acting in the course of a business of credit brokerage;

(*b*) 'credit brokerage' means the effecting of introduction of individuals desiring to obtain credit—

(i) to persons carrying on any business so far as it relates to the provision of credit,

or

(ii) to other persons engaged in credit brokerage.

[*See note at foot of section 12.*]

[*The words in square brackets in subsection (2) were introduced by the Supply of Goods and Services Act 1982, section 17(1).*]

11. Samples

Where under a hire-purchase agreement goods are bailed or (in Scotland) hired by reference to a sample, there is an implied condition—

(*a*) that the bulk will correspond with the sample in quality; and

(*b*) that the person to whom the goods are bailed or hired will have a reasonable opportunity of comparing the bulk with the sample; and

(*c*) that the goods will be free from any defect, rendering them unmerchantable, which would not be apparent on reasonable examination of the sample.

[*See note at foot of section 12.*]

12. Exclusion of implied terms and conditions

(1) An express condition or warranty does not negative a condition or warranty implied by this Act unless inconsistent with it.]

Supply of Goods (Implied Terms) Act 1973

[*Sections 8 to 12 were substituted, by the Consumer Credit Act 1974, section 192(3)(a) and Schedule 4, Part I, paragraph 35. The amendments are to accommodate changes in terminology only.*]

[*Section 13 was repealed by the Unfair Contract Terms Act 1977, section 31(4) and Schedule 4.*]

14. Special provisions as to conditional sale agreements

(1) *Section 11(4) of the Sale of Goods Act 1979* (whereby in certain circumstances a breach of condition in a contract of sale is treated only as a breach of warranty) shall not apply to [a conditional sale agreement where the buyer deals as consumer within Part I of the Unfair Contract Terms Act 1977 . . .]

[*In the above subsection, the words in italics were substituted by the Sale of Goods Act 1979, section 63(2) and Schedule 2, paragraph 16, the words within square brackets were substituted by the Unfair Contract Terms Act 1977, section 31(3) and Schedule 3, and the words omitted were repealed by the Statute Law (Repeals) Act 1981.*]

(2) In England and Wales and Northern Ireland a breach of a condition (whether express or implied) to be fulfilled by the seller under any such agreement shall be treated as a breach of warranty, and not as grounds for rejecting the goods and treating the agreement as repudiated, if (but only if) it would have fallen to be so treated had the condition been contained or implied in corresponding hire-purchase agreement as a condition to be fulfilled by the creditor.

[*See note at foot of section 15.*]

15. Supplementary

(1) In sections 8 to 14 above and this section—

'business' includes a profession and the activities of any Government department (including a Northern Ireland department), [or local or public authority];

[*The words within square brackets in the above definition were substituted by the Unfair Contract Terms Act 1977, section 31(3) and Schedule 3.*]

'buyer' and 'seller' includes a person to whom rights and duties under a conditional sale agreement have passed by assignment or operation of law;

'condition' and 'warranty', in relation to Scotland, mean stipulation, and any stipulation referred to in sections 8(1)(a), 9, 10 and 11 above shall be deemed to be material to the agreement;

'conditional sale agreement' means an agreement for the sale of goods under which the purchase price or part of it is payable by instalments, and the property in the goods is to remain in the seller (notwithstanding that the buyer is to be in possession of the goods) until such conditions as to the payment of instalments or otherwise as may be specified in the agreement are fulfilled;

['consumer sale' has the same meaning as in section 55 of the Sale of Goods Act 1979 (as set out in paragraph 11 of Schedule 1 to that Act)]

[The above definition was inserted by the Sale of Goods Act 1979, Schedule 2, para. 17.]

'creditor' means the person by whom the goods are bailed or (in Scotland) hired under a hire-purchase agreement or the person to whom his rights and duties under the agreement have passed by assignment or operation of law; and

'hire-purchase agreement' means an agreement, other than conditional sale agreement, under which—

(*a*) goods are bailed or (in Scotland) hired in return for periodical payments by the person to whom they are bailed or hired, and

(*b*) the property in the goods will pass to that person if the terms of the agreement are complied with and one or more of the following occurs—

(i) the exercise of an option to purchase by that person,
(ii) the doing of any other specified act by any party to the agreement,
(iii) the happening of any other specified event.

(2) Goods of any kind are of merchantable quality within the meaning of section 10(2) above if they are as fit for the purpose or purposes for which goods of that kind are commonly bought as it is reasonable to expect having regard to any description applied to them, the price (if relevant) and all the other relevant circumstances; and in section 11 above 'unmerchantable' shall be construed accordingly.

(3) In section 14(2) above 'corresponding hire-purchase agreement' means, in relation to a conditional sale agreement, a hire-purchase agreement relating to the same goods as the conditional sale agreement and made between the same parties and at the same time and in the same circumstances and, as nearly as may be, in the same terms as the conditional sale agreement.

(4) Nothing in sections 8 to 13 above shall prejudice the operation of any other enactment including any enactment of the Parliament of Northern Ireland or the Northern Ireland Assembly or any rule of law whereby any condition or warranty, other than one relating to quality or fitness, is to be implied in any hire-purchase agreement.]

[Sections 14 and 15 were substituted by the Consumer Credit Act 1974, section 192(3)(a) and Schedule 4, Part I, paragraph 36. The amendments are to accommodate changes in terminology only.]

Trading stamps

16. Terms to be implied on redemption of trading stamps for goods

(This section amends the Trading Stamps Act 1964 and the amendments are incorporated therein.)

Miscellaneous

17. Northern Ireland

(1) It is hereby declared that this Act extends to Northern Ireland.

[Subsection (2) was repealed by the Northern Ireland Constitution Act 1973, section 4(1) and Schedule 6, Part I.]

18. Short title, citation, interpretation, commencement, repeal and saving

(1) This Act may be cited as the Supply of Goods (Implied Terms) Act 1973.

[*Subsection (2) was repealed by the Sale of Goods Act 1979, section 63(2) and Schedule 3.*]

(3) This Act shall come into operation at the expiration of a period of one month beginning with the date on which it is passed.

(4) Sections 17 to 20 and 29(3)(*c*) of each of the following Acts, that is to say, the Hire-Purchase Act 1965, the Hire-Purchase (Scotland) Act 1965 and the Hire-Purchase Act (Northern Ireland) 1966 (provisions as to conditions, warranties and stipulations in hire-purchase agreements) shall cease to have effect.

(5) This Act does not apply to contracts of sale or hire-purchase agreements made before its commencement.

Fair Trading Act 1973
Chapter 41

ARRANGEMENT OF SECTIONS

PART I

INTRODUCTORY

Section
1. Director General of Fair Trading
2. General functions of Director
3. Consumer Protection Advisory Committee

* * *

12. Powers of Secretary of State in relation to functions of Director

PART II

REFERENCES OF CONSUMER PROTECTION ADVISORY COMMITTEE

General provisions

13. Meaning of 'consumer trade practice'
14. General provisions as to references to Advisory Committee
15. Exclusion from s. 14 in respect of certain services
16. Restriction on references under s. 14 in respect of certain goods and services
17. References to Advisory Committee proposing recommendation to Secretary of State to make an order
18. No such recommendation to be made except in pursuance of reference to which s. 17 applies
19. Scope of recommendation proposed in reference to which s. 17 applies
20. Time-limit and quorum for report on reference to which s. 17 applies
21. Report of Advisory Committee on reference to which s. 17 applies

Order in pursuance of report of Advisory Committee

22. Order of Secretary of State in pursuance of report of Advisory Committee
23. Penalties for contravention of order under s. 22
24. Offences due to default of other person
25. Defences in proceedings under s. 23
26. Limitation of effect of orders under s. 22

Enforcement of orders

27. Enforcing authorities
28. Power to make test purchases
29. Power to enter premises and inspect and seize goods and documents
30. Offences in connection with exercise of powers under s. 29
31. Notice of test
32. Compensation for loss in respect of goods seized under s. 29

Section
33. Application of Part II to Northern Ireland

PART III

ADDITIONAL FUNCTIONS OF DIRECTOR FOR PROTECTION OF CONSUMERS

34. Action by Director with respect to course of conduct detrimental to interests of consumers
35. Proceedings before Restrictive Practices Court
36. Evidence in proceedings under s. 35
37. Order of, or undertaking given to, Court in proceedings under s. 35
38. Provisions as to persons consenting to or conniving at courses of conduct detrimental to interests of consumers
39. Order of, or undertaking given to, Court in proceedings under s. 38
40. Provisions as to interconnected bodies corporate
41. Concurrent jurisdiction of other courts in certain cases
42. Appeals from decisions or orders of courts under Part III

* * *

PART VII

PROVISIONS RELATING TO REFERENCES TO ADVISORY COMMITTEE OR TO COMMISSION

81. Procedure in carrying out investigations
82. General provisions as to reports
83. Laying before Parliament and publication of reports

* * *

PART XII

MISCELLANEOUS AND SUPPLEMENTARY PROVISIONS

* * *

125. Annual and other reports of Director

* * *

129. Time-limit for prosecutions

* * *

131. Notification of convictions and judgments to Director

* * *

138. Supplementary interpretation provisions

* * *

140. Short title, citation, commencement and extent.

SCHEDULES:

Schedule 1—Director General of Fair Trading

Schedule 2—Consumer Protection Advisory Committee

* * *

Schedule 6—Matters falling within scope of proposals under section 17

* * *

An Act to provide for the appointment of a Director General of Fair Trading and of a Consumer Protection Advisory Committee, and to confer on the Director General and the Committee so appointed, on the Secretary of State, on the Restrictive Practices Court and on certain other courts new functions for the protection of consumers; to make provision, in substitution for the Monopolies and Restrictive Practices (Inquiry and Control) Act 1948 and the Monopolies and Mergers Act 1965, for the matters dealt with in those Acts and related matters, including restrictive labour practices; to amend the Restrictive Trade Practices Act 1956 and the Restrictive Trade Practices Act 1968, to make provision for extending the said Act of 1956 to agreements relating to services, and to transfer to the Director General of Fair Trading the functions of the Registrar of Restrictive Trading Agreements; to make provision with respect to pyramid selling and similar trading schemes; to make new provision in place of section 30(2) to (4) of the Trade Descriptions Act 1968; and for purposes connected with those matters.

[25th July 1973]

PART I

INTRODUCTORY

1. Director General of Fair Trading

(1) The Secretary of State shall appoint an officer to be known as the Director General of Fair Trading (in this Act referred to as 'the Director') for the purpose of performing the functions assigned or transferred to the Director by or under this Act.

(2) An appointment of a person to hold office as the Director shall not be for a term exceeding five years; but previous appointment to that office shall not affect eligibility for re-appointment.

(3) The Director may at any time resign his office as the Director by notice in writing addressed to the Secretary of State; and the Secretary of State may remove any person from that office on the ground of incapacity or misbehaviour.

(4) Subject to subsections (2) and (3) of this section, the Director shall hold and vacate office as such in accordance with the terms of his appointment.

(5) The Director may appoint such staff as he may think fit, subject to the approval of the Minister for the Civil Service as to numbers and as to terms and conditions of service.

(6) The provisions of Schedule 1 to this Act shall have effect with respect to the Director.

2. General functions of Director

(1) Without prejudice to any other functions assigned or transferred to him by or under this Act, it shall be the duty of the Director, so far as appears to him to be practicable from time to time,—

(*a*) to keep under review the carrying on of commercial activities in the United Kingdom which relate to goods supplied to consumers in the United Kingdom or produced with a view to their being so supplied, or which relate to services supplied for consumers in the United Kingdom, and to collect information with respect to such activities, and the persons by whom they are carried on, with a view to his becoming aware of, and ascertaining the circumstances relating to, practices which may adversely affect the economic interests of consumers in the United Kingdom, and

(*b*) to receive and collate evidence becoming available to him with respect to such activities as are mentioned in the preceding paragraph and which appears to him to be evidence of practices which may adversely affect the interests (whether they are economic interests or interests with respect to health, safety or other matters) of consumers in the United Kingdom.

(2) It shall also be the duty of the Director, so far as appears to him to be practicable from time to time, to keep under review the carrying on of commercial activities in the United Kingdom, and to collect information with respect to those activities, and the persons by whom they are carried on, with a view to his becoming aware of, and ascertaining the circumstances relating to, monopoly situations or uncompetitive practices.

(3) It shall be the duty of the Director, where either he considers it expedient or he is requested by the Secretary of State to do so,—

(*a*) to give information and assistance to the Secretary of State with respect to any of the matters in respect of which the Director has any duties under subsections (1) and (2) of this section, or

(*b*) subject to the provisions of Part II of this Act in relation to recommendations under that Part of this Act, to make recommendations to the Secretary of State as to any action which in the opinion of the Director it would be expedient for the Secretary of State or any other Minister to take in relation to any of the matters in respect of which the Director has any such duties.

(4) It shall also be the duty of the Director to have regard to evidence becoming available to him with respect to any course of conduct on the part of a person carrying on a business which appears to be conduct detrimental to the interests of consumers in the United Kingdom and (in accordance with the provisions of Part III of this Act) to be regarded as unfair to them, with a view to considering what action (if any) he should take under Part III of this Act.

(5) It shall be the duty of the Director to have regard to the need of regional development and to the desirability of dispersing administrative offices from London in making decisions on the location of offices for his staff.

3. Consumer Protection Advisory Committee

(1) There shall be established an advisory committee to be called the Consumer Protection Advisory Committee (in this Act referred to as 'the Advisory

Fair Trading Act 1973

Committee') for the purpose of performing the functions assigned to that Committee by Part II of this Act.

(2) Subject to subsection (6) of this section, the Advisory Committee shall consist of not less than ten and not more than fifteen members, who shall be appointed by the Secretary of State.

(3) The Secretary of State may appoint persons to the Advisory Committee either as full-time members or as part-time members.

(4) Of the members of the Advisory Committee, the Secretary of State shall appoint one to be chairman and one to be deputy chairman of the Advisory Committee.

(5) In appointing persons to be members of the Advisory Committee, the Secretary of State shall have regard to the need for securing that the Advisory Committee will include—

(*a*) one or more persons appearing to him to be qualified to advise on practices relating to goods supplied to consumers in the United Kingdom or produced with a view to their being so supplied, or relating to services supplied for consumers in the United Kingdom, by virtue of their knowledge of or experience in the supply (whether to consumers or not) of such goods or by virtue of their knowledge of or experience in the supply of such services;

(*b*) one or more persons appearing to him to be qualified to advise on such practices as are mentioned in the preceding paragraph by virtue of their knowledge of or experience in the enforcement of the [Weights and Measures Act 1985] or the Trade Descriptions Act 1968 or other similar enactments; and

(*c*) one or more persons appearing to him to be qualified to advise on such practices by virtue of their knowledge of or experience in organisations established, or activities carried on, for the protection of consumers.

(6) The Secretary of State may by order made by statutory instrument increase the maximum number of members of the Advisory Committee to such number as he may think fit.

(7) The provisions of Schedule 2 to this Act shall have effect with respect to the Advisory Committee.

[*The words in square brackets were substituted by the Weights and Measures Act 1985, section 97, Schedule 12, paragraph 6.*]

* * *

12. Powers of Secretary of State in relation to functions of Director

(1) The Secretary of State may give general directions indicating considerations to which the Director should have particular regard in determining the order of priority in which—

(*a*) matters are to be brought under review in the performance of his duty under section 2(1) of this Act, or

(*b*) classes of goods or services are to be brought under review by him for the purpose of considering whether a monopoly situation exists or may exist in relation to them.

(2) The Secretary of State may also give general directions indicating—

(*a*) considerations to which, in cases where it appears to the Director that a practice may adversely affect the interests of consumers in the United Kingdom, he should have particular regard in determining whether to make a recommendation to the Secretary of State under section 2(3)(*b*) of this Act, or

(*b*) considerations to which, in cases where it appears to the Director that a consumer trade practice may adversely affect the economic interest of consumers in the United Kingdom, he should have particular regard in determining whether to make a reference to the Advisory Committee under Part II of this Act, or

(*c*) considerations to which, in cases where it appears to the Director that a monopoly situation exists or may exist, he should have particular regard in determining whether to make a monopoly reference to the Commission under Part IV of this Act.

(3) The Secretary of State, on giving any directions under this section, shall arrange for those directions to be published in such manner as the Secretary of State thinks most suitable in the circumstances.

PART II
REFERENCES TO CONSUMER PROTECTION ADVISORY COMMITTEE

General provisions

13. Meaning of 'consumer trade practice'

In this Act 'consumer trade practice' means any practice which is for the time being carried on in connection with the supply of goods (whether by way of sale or otherwise) to consumers or in connection with the supply of services for consumers and which relates—

(*a*) to the terms or conditions (whether as to price or otherwise) on or subject to which goods or services are or are sought to be supplied, or

(*b*) to the manner in which those terms or conditions are communicated to persons to whom goods are or are sought to be supplied or for whom services are or are sought to be supplied, or

(*c*) to promotion (by advertising, labelling or marking of goods, canvassing or otherwise) of the supply of goods or of the supply of services, or

(*d*) to methods of salesmanship employed in dealing with consumers, or

(*e*) to the way in which goods are packed or otherwise got up for the purpose of being supplied, or

(*f*) to methods of demanding or securing payment for goods or services supplied.

14. General provisions as to references to Advisory Committee

(1) Subject to sections 15 and 16 of this Act, the Secretary of State or any other Minister or the Director may refer to the Advisory Committee the question whether a consumer trade practice specified in the reference adversely affects the economic interests of consumers in the United Kingdom.

(2) The Secretary of State or any other Minister by whom a reference is made under this section shall transmit a copy of the reference to the Director.

(3) On any reference made to the Advisory Committee under this section the Advisory Committee shall consider the question so referred to them and shall prepare a report on that question and (except as otherwise provided by section 21(3) of this Act) submit that report to the person by whom the reference was made.

(4) Subject to the provisions of section 133 of this Act, it shall be the duty of the Director, where he is requested by the Advisory Committee to do so for the purpose of assisting the Committee in carrying out an investigation on a reference made to them under this section, to give to the Committee—

   (*a*) any information which is in his possession and which relates to matters falling within the scope of the investigation, and
   (*b*) any other assistance which the Committee may require, and which it is within his power to give, in relation to any such matters.

(5) The Advisory Committee shall transmit to the Secretary of State a copy of every report which is made by them under this section to a person other than the Secretary of State, and shall transmit to the Director a copy of every report which is made by them under this section to a person other than the Director.

15. Exclusion from section 14 in respect of certain services

No reference under section 14 of this Act shall be made to the Advisory Committee by the Secretary of State or by any other Minister or by the Director if it appears to him—

   (*a*) that the consumer trade practice in question is carried on in connection only with the supply of services of a description specified in Schedule 4 to this Act, and
   (*b*) that a monopoly situation exists or may exist in relation to the supply of services of that description.

16. Restriction on references under section 14 in respect of certain goods and services

(1) No reference under section 14 of this Act shall be made to the Advisory Committee by the Director except with the consent of the appropriate Minister, if it appears to the Director that the consumer trade practice in question—

   (*a*) is carried on in connection only with the supply, by a body corporate to which this section applies, of goods or services of a description specified in Part I of Schedule 5 to this Act,
   [. . .]

(2) This section applies to any body corporate which fulfils the following conditions, that is to say—

   (*a*) that the affairs of the body corporate are managed by its members, and
   (*b*) that by virtue of an enactment those members are appointed by a Minister;

and in this section 'Minister' includes a Minister of the Government of Northern Ireland, and 'the appropriate Minister', in relation to a body corporate, means the Minister by whom members of that body corporate are appointed.

(3) The Secretary of State may by order made by statutory instrument vary any of the provisions of Schedule 5 to this Act, either by adding one or more

further entries or by altering or deleting any entry for the time being contained in it; and any reference in this Act to that Schedule shall be construed as a reference to that Schedule as for the time being in force.

[*Section 16(1)(b) was repealed by the Telecommunications Act 1984, Schedule 7, Part I.*]

17. Reference to Advisory Committee proposing recommendation to Secretary of State to make an order

(1) This section applies to any reference made to the Advisory Committee by the Director under section 14 of this Act which includes proposals in accordance with the following provisions of this section.

(2) Where it appears to the Director that a consumer trade practice has the effect, or is likely to have the effect,—

- (*a*) of misleading consumers as to, or withholding from them adequate information as to, or an adequate record of, their rights and obligations under relevant consumer transactions, or
- (*b*) of otherwise misleading or confusing consumers with respect to any matter in connection with relevant consumer transactions, or
- (*c*) of subjecting consumers to undue pressure to enter into relevant consumer transactions, or
- (*d*) of causing the terms or conditions, on or subject to which consumers enter into relevant consumer transactions, to be so adverse to them as to be inequitable,

any reference made by the Director under section 14 of this Act with respect to that consumer trade practice may, if the Director thinks fit, include proposals for recommending to the Secretary of State that he should exercise his powers under the following provisions of this Part of this Act with respect to that consumer trade practice.

(3) A reference to which this section applies shall state which of the effects specified in subsection (2) of this section it appears to the Director that the consumer trade practice in question has or is likely to have.

(4) Where the Director makes a reference to which this section applies, he shall arrange for it to be published in full in the London, Edinburgh and Belfast Gazettes.

(5) In this Part of this Act 'relevant consumer transaction', in relation to a consumer trade practice, means any transaction to which a person is, or may be invited to become, a party in his capacity as a consumer in relation to that practice.

18. No such recommendation to be made except in pursuance of reference to which section 17 applies

The Director shall not make any recommendation to the Secretary of State to exercise his powers under the following provisions of this Part of this Act except by way of making a reference to the Advisory Committee to which section 17 of this Act applies.

19. Scope of recommendation proposed in reference to which section 17 applies

(1) In formulating any proposals which, in accordance with the provisions of section 17 of this Act, are included in a reference to which that section applies, the Director shall have regard—

- (*a*) to the particular respects in which it appears to him that the consumer trade practice specified in the reference may adversely affect the economic interests of consumers in the United Kingdom, and
- (*b*) to the class of relevant consumer transactions, or the classes (whether being some or all classes) of such transactions, in relation to which it appears to him that the practice may so affect those consumers;

and the proposed recommendation shall be for an order making, in relation to relevant consumer transactions of that class or of those classes, as the case may be, such provision specified in the proposals as the Director may consider requisite for the purpose of preventing the continuance of that practice, or causing it to be modified, in so far as it may so affect those consumers in those respects.

(2) Without prejudice to the generality of the preceding subsection, for the purpose mentioned in that subsection any such proposals may in particular recommend the imposition by such an order of prohibitions or requirements of any description specified in Schedule 6 to this Act.

(3) In that Schedule, in its application to any such proposals, 'the specified consumer trade practice' means the consumer trade practice specified in the reference in which the proposals are made, 'specified consumer transactions' means transactions which are relevant consumer transactions in relation to that consumer trade practice and are of a description specified in the proposals, and 'specified' (elsewhere than in those expressions) means specified in the proposals.

20. Time-limit and quorum for report on reference to which s 17 applies

(1) A report of the Advisory Committee on a reference to which section 17 of this Act applies shall not have effect, and no action shall be taken in relation to it under the following provisions of this Part of this Act, unless the report is made before the end of the period of three months beginning with the date of the reference or of such further period or periods (if any) as may be allowed by the Secretary of State.

(2) The Secretary of State shall not allow any further period for such a report except after consulting the Advisory Committee and considering any representations made by them with respect to the proposal to allow a further period.

(3) No such further period shall be longer than three months; but (subject to subsection (2) of this section) two or more further periods may be allowed in respect of the same reference.

(4) The quorum necessary for a meeting of the Advisory Committee held for the final settling of a report of the Committee on a reference to which section 17 of this Act applies shall be not less than two-thirds of the members of the Committee.

21. Report of the Advisory Committee on reference to which s 17 applies

(1) A report of the Advisory Committee on a reference to which section 17 of this Act applies shall state the conclusions of the Committee on the questions—

  (*a*) whether the consumer trade practice specified in the reference adversely affects the economic interests of consumers in the United Kingdom, and
  (*b*) if so, whether it does so by reason, or partly by reason, that it has or is likely to have such one or more of the effects specified in section 17(2) of this Act as are specified in the report.

(2) If, in their conclusions set out in such a report, the Advisory Committee find that the consumer trade practice specified in the reference does adversely affect the economic interests of consumers in the United Kingdom, and does so wholly or partly for the reason mentioned in subsection (1)(*b*) of this section, the report shall state whether the Committee—

  (*a*) agree with the proposals set out in the reference, or
  (*b*) would agree with those proposals if they were modified in a manner specified in the report, or
  (*c*) disagree with the proposals and do not desire to suggest any such modifications.

(3) Every report of the Advisory Committee on a reference to which section 17 of this Act applies shall be made to the Secretary of State, and shall set out in full the reference on which it is made.

Order in pursuance of report of Advisory Committee

22. Order of Secretary of State in pursuance of report on reference to which s 17 applies

(1) The provisions of this section shall have effect where a report of the Advisory Committee on a reference to which section 17 of this Act applies has been laid before Parliament in accordance with the provisions of Part VII of this Act, and the report states that the Committee—

  (*a*) agree with the proposals set out in the reference, or
  (*b*) would agree with those proposals if they were modified in a manner specified in the report.

(2) In the circumstances mentioned in the preceding subsection, the Secretary of State may, if he thinks fit, by an order made by statutory instrument make such provision as—

  (*a*) in a case falling within paragraph (*a*) of the preceding subsection, is in his opinion appropriate for giving effect to the proposals set out in the reference, or
  (*b*) in a case falling within paragraph (*b*) of that subsection, is in his opinion appropriate for giving effect either to the proposals as set out in the reference or to those proposals as modified in the manner specified in the report, as the Secretary of State may in his discretion determine.

(3) Any such order may contain such supplementary or incidental provisions as the Secretary of State may consider appropriate in the circumstances; and (without prejudice to the generality of this subsection) any such order may restrict the prosecution of offences under the next following section in respect of

Fair Trading Act 1973

contraventions of the order where those contraventions also constitute offences under another enactment.

(4) No such order, and no order varying or revoking any such order, shall be made under this section unless a draft of the order has been laid before Parliament and approved by a resolution of each House of Parliament.

23. Penalties for contravention of order under s 22

Subject to the following provisions of this Part of this Act, any person who contravenes a prohibition imposed by an order under section 22 of this Act, or who does not comply with a requirement imposed by such an order which applies to him, shall be guilty of an offence and shall be liable—

  (*a*) on summary conviction, to a fine not exceeding [the prescribed sum];
  (*b*) on conviction on indictment, to a fine or to imprisonment for a term not exceeding two years or both.

[*The words in square brackets were substituted by the Magistrates' Courts Act 1980, section 32(9) and the Criminal Penalties etc (Increase) Order 1984 (S.I. 1984 No. 447).*]

24. Offences due to default of other person

Where the commission by any person of an offence under section 23 of this Act is due to the act or default of some other person, that other person shall be guilty of the offence, and a person may be charged with and convicted of the offence by virtue of this section whether or not proceedings are taken against the first-mentioned person.

25. Defences in proceedings under s 23

(1) In any proceedings for an offence under section 23 of this Act it shall, subject to subsection (2) of this section, be a defence for the person charged to prove—

  (*a*) that the commission of the offence was due to a mistake, or to reliance on information supplied to him, or to the act or default of another person, an accident or some other cause beyond his control, and
  (*b*) that he took all reasonable precautions and exercised all due diligence to avoid the commission of such an offence by himself or any person under his control.

(2) If in any case the defence provided by the preceding subsection involves the allegation that the commission of the offence was due to the act or default of another person or to reliance on information supplied by another person, the person charged shall not, without leave of the court, be entitled to rely on that defence unless, within a period ending seven clear days before the hearing, he has served on the prosecutor a notice in writing, giving such information identifying or assisting in the identification of that other person as was then in his possession.

(3) In proceedings for an offence under section 23 of this Act committed by the publication of an advertisement, it shall be a defence for the person charged to prove that he is a person whose business it is to publish or arrange for the publication of advertisements, and that he received the advertisement for publication in the ordinary course of business and did not know and had

no reason to suspect that its publication would amount to an offence under section 23 of this Act.

26. Limitation of effect of orders under section 22

A contract for the supply of goods or services shall not be void or unenforceable by reason only of a contravention of an order made under section 22 of this Act; and, subject to the provisions of section 33 of the Interpretation Act 1889 (which relates to offences under two or more laws), the provisions of this Part of this Act shall not be construed as—

- (*a*) conferring a right of action in any civil proceedings (other than proceedings for the recovery of a fine) in respect of any contravention of such an order, or
- (*b*) affecting any restriction imposed by or under any other enactment, whether public, local or private, or
- (*c*) derogating from any right of action or other remedy (whether civil or criminal) in proceedings instituted otherwise than under this Part of this Act.

Enforcement of orders

27. Enforcing authorities

(1) It shall be the duty of every local weights and measures authority to enforce within their area the provisions of any order made under section 22 of this Act [. . .]

(2) Nothing in subsection (1) shall be taken as authorising a local weights and measures authority in Scotland to institute proceedings for an offence.

[*The words in square brackets were omitted by the Weights and Measures Act 1985, section 98, Schedule 13, Part I.*]

28. Power to make test purchases

A local weights and measures authority may make, or may authorise any of their officers to make on their behalf, such purchases of goods, and may authorise any of their officers to obtain such services, as may be expedient for the purpose of determining whether or not the provisions of any order made under section 22 of this Act are being complied with.

29. Power to enter premises and inspect and seize goods and documents

(1) A duly authorised officer of a local weights and measures authority, or a person duly authorised in writing by the Secretary of State, may at all reasonable hours, and on production, if required, of his credentials, exercise the following powers, that is to say—

- (*a*) he may, for the purpose of ascertaining whether any offence under section 23 of this Act has been committed, inspect any goods and enter any premises other than premises used only as a dwelling;
- (*b*) if he has reasonable cause to suspect that an offence under that section has been committed, he may, for the purpose of ascertaining whether it has been committed, require any person carrying on a business or employed in connection with a business to produce any books or

documents relating to the business and may take copies of, or of any entry in, any such book or document;

(c) if he has reasonable cause to believe that such an offence has been committed, he may seize and detain any goods for the purpose of ascertaining, by testing or otherwise, whether the offence has been committed;

(d) he may seize and detain any goods or documents which he has reason to believe may be required as evidence in proceedings for such an offence;

(e) he may, for the purpose of exercising his powers under this subsection to seize goods, but only if and to the extent that it is reasonably necessary in order to secure that the provisions of an order made under section 22 of this Act are duly observed, require any person having authority to do so to break open any container or open any vending machine and, if that person does not comply with the requirement, he may do so himself.

(2) A person seizing any goods or documents in the exercise of his powers under this section shall inform the person from whom they are seized and, in the case of goods seized from a vending machine, the person whose name and address are stated on the machine as being the proprietor's or, if no name and address are so stated, the occupier of the premises on which the machine stands or to which it is affixed.

(3) If a justice of the peace, on sworn information in writing,—

(a) is satisfied that there is reasonable ground to believe either—

(i) that any goods, books or documents which a person has power under this section to inspect are on any premises and that their inspection is likely to disclose evidence of the commission of an offence under section 23 of this Act, or

(ii) that any offence under section 23 has been, is being or is about to be committed on any premises, and

(b) is also satisfied either—

(i) that admission to the premises has been or is likely to be refused and that notice of intention to apply for a warrant under this subsection has been given to the occupier, or

(ii) that an application for admission, or the giving of such a notice, would defeat the object of the entry or that the premises are unoccupied or that the occupier is temporarily absent, and it might defeat the object of the entry to await his return,

the justice may by warrant under his hand, which shall continue in force for a period of one month, authorise any such officer or other person as is mentioned in subsection (1) of this section to enter the premises, if need be by force.

In the application of this subsection to Scotland, 'justice of the peace' shall be construed as including a sheriff and a magistrate.

(4) A person entering any premises by virtue of this section may take with him such other persons and such equipment as may appear to him necessary; and on leaving any premises which he has entered by virtue of a warrant under subsection (3) of this section he shall, if the premises are unoccupied or the occupier is temporarily absent, leave them as effectively secured against trespassers as he found them.

(5) Nothing in this section shall be taken to compel the production by a barrister,

advocate or solicitor of a document containing a privileged communication made by or to him in that capacity or to authorise the taking of possession of any such document which is in his possession.

30. Offences in connection with exercise of powers under s 29

(1) Subject to subsection (6) of this section, any person who—

   (*a*) wilfully obstructs any such officer or person as is mentioned in subsection (1) of section 29 of this Act acting in the exercise of any powers conferred on him by or under that section, or
   (*b*) wilfully fails to comply with any requirement properly made to him by such an officer or person under that section, or
   (*c*) without reasonable cause fails to give to such an officer or person so acting any other assistance or information which he may reasonably require of him for the purpose of the performance of his functions under this Part of this Act,

shall be guilty of an offence.

(2) If any person, in giving any such information as is mentioned in subsection (1)(*c*) of this section, makes any statement which he knows to be false, he shall be guilty of an offence.

(3) If any person discloses to any other person—

   (*a*) any information with respect to any manufacturing process or trade secret obtained by him in premises which he has entered by virtue of section 29 of this Act, or
   (*b*) any information obtained by him under that section or by virtue of subsection (1) of this section,

he shall, unless the disclosure was made in the performance of his duty, be guilty of an offence.

(4) If any person who is neither a duly authorised officer of a weights and measures authority nor a person duly authorised in that behalf by the Secretary of State purports to act as such under section 29 of this act or under this section, he shall be guilty of an offence.

(5) Any person guilty of an offence under subsection (1) of this section shall be liable on summary conviction to a fine not exceeding [level 3 on the standard scale]; and any person guilty of an offence under subsection (2), subsection (3) or subsection (4) of this section shall be liable—

   (*a*) on summary conviction, to a fine not exceeding [the prescribed sum];
   (*b*) on conviction on indictment, to a fine or to imprisonment for a term not exceeding two years or to both.

(6) Nothing in this section shall be construed as requiring a person to answer any question or give any information if to do so might incriminate that person or (where that person is married) the husband or wife of that person.

[*The words in square brackets were substituted by the Magistrates' Courts Act 1980, section 32(9); the Criminal Justice Act 1982, sections 37, 38 and 46; and the Criminal Penalties etc (Increase) Order 1984 (S.I. 1984 No. 447).*]

31. Notice of test

Where any goods seized or purchased by a person in pursuance of this Part of this Act are submitted to a test, then—

(a) if the goods were seized, he shall inform any such person as is mentioned in section 29(2) of this act of the result of the test;

(b) if the goods were purchased and the test leads to the institution of proceedings for an offence under section 23 of this Act, he shall inform the person from whom the goods were purchased, or, in the case of goods sold through a vending machine, the person mentioned in relation to such goods in section 29(2) of this Act, of the result of the test;

and where, as a result of the test, proceedings for an offence under section 23 of this Act are instituted against any person, he shall allow that person to have the goods tested on his behalf if it is reasonably practicable to do so.

32. Compensation for loss in respect of goods seized under s 29

(1) Where in the exercise of his powers under section 29 of this Act a person seizes and detains any goods, and their owner suffers loss by reason of their being seized or by reason that the goods, during the detention, are lost or damaged or deteriorate, unless the owner is convicted of an offence under section 23 of this Act committed in relation to the goods, the appropriate authority shall be liable to compensate him for the loss so suffered.

(2) Any disputed question as to the right to or the amount of any compensation payable under this section shall be determined by arbitration and, in Scotland, by a single arbiter appointed, failing agreement between the parties, by the sheriff.

(3) In this section 'the appropriate authority'—

(a) in relation to goods seized by an officer of a local weights and measures authority, means that authority, and

(b) in any other case, means the Secretary of State.

33. Application of Part II to Northern Ireland

(1) It shall be the duty of the Ministry of Commerce for Northern Ireland to enforce in Northern Ireland the provisions of any order under section 22 of this Act.

(2) In the application of this Part of this Act to Northern Ireland—

(a) section 27 shall not apply;

(b) in sections 28 and 29, any reference to a local weights and measures authority shall be construed as a reference to the Ministry of Commerce for Northern Ireland, and the provisions of sections 30 to 32 shall be construed accordingly;

(c) in section 29(3), any reference to a justice of the peace shall be construed as a reference to a resident magistrate; and

(d) the provisions of the Arbitration Act (Northern Ireland) 1937, except the provisions set out in Schedule 3 thereto, shall apply to an arbitration under section 32 of this Act as if the arbitration were pursuant to an arbitration agreement (as defined in section 30(1) of that Act).

Fair Trading Act 1973

PART III

Additional Functions of Director for Protection of Consumers

34. Action by Director with respect to course of conduct detrimental to interests of consumers

(1) Where it appears to the Director that the person carrying on a business has in the course of that business persisted in a course of conduct which—

- (*a*) is detrimental to the interests of consumers in the United Kingdom, whether those interests are economic interests or interests in respect of health, safety or other matters, and
- (*b*) in accordance with the following provisions of this section is to be regarded as unfair to consumers,

the Director shall use his best endeavours, by communication with that person or otherwise, to obtain from him a satisfactory written assurance that he will refrain from continuing that course of conduct and from carrying on any similar course of conduct in the course of that business.

(2) For the purposes of subsection (1)(*b*) of this section a course of conduct shall be regarded as unfair to consumers if it consists of contraventions of one or more enactments which impose duties, prohibitions or restrictions enforceable by criminal proceedings, whether any such duty, prohibition or restriction is imposed in relation to consumers as such or not and whether the person carrying on the business has or has not been convicted of any offence in respect of any such contravention.

(3) A course of conduct on the part of the person carrying on a business shall also be regarded for those purposes as unfair to consumers if it consists of things done, or omitted to be done, in the course of that business in breach of contract or in breach of a duty (other than a contractual duty) owed to any person by virtue of any enactment or rule of law and enforceable by civil proceedings, whether (in any such case) civil proceedings in respect of the breach of contract or breach of duty have been brought or not.

(4) For the purpose of determining whether it appears to him that a person has persisted in such a course of conduct as is mentioned in subsection (1) of this section, the Director shall have regard to either or both of the following, that is to say—

- (*a*) complaints received by him, whether from consumers or from other persons;
- (*b*) any other information collected by or furnished to him, whether by virtue of this Act or otherwise.

35. Proceedings before Restrictive Practices Court

If, in the circumstances specified in subsection (1) of section 34 of this Act,—

- (*a*) the Director is unable to obtain from the person in question such an assurance as is mentioned in that subsection, or
- (*b*) that person has given such an assurance and it appears to the Director that he has failed to observe it,

the Director may bring proceedings against him before the Restrictive Practices Court.

Fair Trading Act 1973

36. Evidence in proceedings under s 35

(1) For the purposes of section 11 of the Civil Evidence Act 1968, section 10 of the Law Reform (Miscellaneous Provisions) (Scotland) Act 1968 or section 7 of the Civil Evidence Act (Northern Ireland) 1971 (each of which relates to convictions as evidence in civil proceedings), proceedings under section 35 of this Act shall (without prejudice to the generality of the relevant definition) be taken to be civil proceedings within the meaning of the Act in question.

(2) Where in any proceedings under section 35 of this Act the Director alleges such a breach of contract or breach of duty as is mentioned in section 34(3) of this Act, a judgment of any court given in civil proceedings, which includes a finding that the breach of contract or breach of duty in question was committed,—

- (*a*) shall be admissible in evidence for the purpose of proving the breach of contract or breach of duty, and
- (*b*) shall, unless the contrary is proved, be taken to be sufficient evidence that the breach of contract or breach of duty was committed.

(3) For the purposes of subsection (2) of this section no account shall be taken of a judgment given in any civil proceedings if it has subsequently been reversed on appeal, or has been varied on appeal so as to negative the finding referred to in that subsection.

(4) In subsection (1) of this section 'the relevant definition' means section 18(1) of the Civil Evidence Act 1968, section 17(1) of the Law Reform (Miscellaneous Provisions) (Scotland) Act 1968 or section 14(1) of the Civil Evidence Act (Northern Ireland) 1971, as the case may be.

37. Order of, or undertaking given to, Court in proceedings under s 35

(1) Where in any proceedings before the Restrictive Practices Court under section 35 of this Act—

- (*a*) the Court finds that the person against whom the proceedings are brought (in this section referred to as 'the respondent') has in the course of a business carried on by him persisted in such a course of conduct as it mentioned in section 34(1) of this Act, and
- (*b*) the respondent does not give an undertaking to the Court under subsection (3) of this section which is accepted by the Court, and
- (*c*) it appears to the Court that, unless an order is made against the respondent under this section, he is likely to continue that course of conduct or to carry on a similar course of conduct.

the Court may make an order against the respondent under this section.

(2) An order of the Court under this section shall (with such degree of particularity as appears to the Court to be sufficient for the purposes of the order) indicate the nature of the course of conduct to which the finding of the Court under subsection (1)(*a*) of this section relates, and shall direct the respondent—

- (*a*) to refrain from continuing that course of conduct, and
- (*b*) to refrain from carrying on any similar course of conduct in the course of his business.

(3) Where in any proceedings under section 35 of this Act the Court makes

such a finding as is mentioned in subsection (1)(*a*) of this section, and the respondent offers to give to the Court an undertaking either—

> (*a*) to refrain as mentioned in paragraphs (*a*) and (*b*) of subsection (2) of this section, or
>
> (*b*) to take particular steps which, in the opinion of the Court, would suffice to prevent a continuance of the course of conduct to which the complaint relates and to prevent the carrying on by the respondent of any similar course of conduct in the course of his business,

the Court may, if it thinks fit, accept that undertaking instead of making an order under this section.

38. Provisions as to persons consenting to or conniving at courses of conduct detrimental to interests of consumers

(1) The provisions of this section shall have effect where it appears to the Director—

> (*a*) that a body corporate has in the course of a business carried on by that body persisted in such a course of conduct as is mentioned in section 34(1) of this Act, and
>
> (*b*) that the course of conduct in question has been so persisted in with the consent or connivance of a person (in this and the next following section referred to as 'the accessory') who at a material time fulfilled the relevant conditions in relation to that body.

(2) For the purposes of this section a person shall be taken to fulfil the relevant conditions in relation to a body corporate at any time if that person either—

> (*a*) is at that time a director, manager, secretary or other similar officer of the body corporate or a person purporting to act in any such capacity, or
>
> (*b*) whether being an individual or a body of persons, corporate or unincorporate, has at that time a controlling interest in that body corporate.

(3) If, in the circumstances specified in subsection (1) of this section,—

> (*a*) the Director has used his best endeavours to obtain from the accessory such an assurance as is mentioned in the next following subsection and has been unable to obtain such an assurance from him, or
>
> (*b*) the accessory has given such an assurance to the Director and it appears to the Director that he has failed to observe it,

the Director may bring proceedings against the accessory before the Restrictive Practices Court.

(4) The assurance referred to in subsection (3) of this section is a satisfactory written assurance given by the accessory that he will refrain—

> (*a*) from continuing to consent to or connive at the course of conduct in question;
>
> (*b*) from carrying on any similar course of conduct in the course of any business which may at any time be carried on by him; and
>
> (*c*) from consenting to or conniving at the carrying on of any such course of conduct by any other body corporate in relation to which, at any

Fair Trading Act 1973

time when that course of conduct is carried on, he fulfils the relevant conditions.

(5) Proceedings may be brought against the accessory under this section whether or not any proceedings are brought under section 35 of this Act against the body corporate referred to in subsection (1) of this section.

(6) Section 36 of this Act shall have effect in relation to proceedings under this section as it has effect in relation to proceedings under section 35 of this Act.

(7) For the purposes of this section a person (whether being an individual or a body of persons, corporate or unincorporate) has a controlling interest in a body corporate if (but only if) that person can, directly or indirectly, determine the manner in which one-half of the votes which could be cast at a general meeting of the body corporate are to be cast on matters, and in circumstances, not of such a description as to bring into play any special voting rights or restrictions on voting rights.

39. Order of, or undertaking given to, Court in proceedings under s 38

(1) Where in any proceedings brought against the accessory before the Restrictive Practices Court under section 38 of this Act—

- (*a*) the Court finds that the conditions specified in paragraphs (*a*) and (*b*) of subsection (1) of that section are fulfilled in the case of the accessory, and
- (*b*) the accessory does not given an undertaking to the Court under subsection (3) of this section which is accepted by the Court, and
- (*c*) it appears to the Court that, unless an order is made against the accessory under this section, it is likely that he will not refrain from acting in one or more of the ways mentioned in paragraphs (*a*) to (*c*) of subsection (4) of that section,

the Court may make an order against the accessory under this section.

(2) An order of the Court under this section shall (with such degree of particularity as appears to the Court to be sufficient for the purposes of the order) indicate the nature of the course of conduct to which the finding of the Court under subsection (1)(*a*) of this section relates, and shall direct the accessory, in relation to the course of conduct so indicated, to refrain from acting in any of the ways mentioned in paragraphs (*a*) to (*c*) of subsection (4) of section 38 of this Act.

(3) Where in any proceedings under section 38 of this Act the Court makes such a finding as is mentioned in subsection (1)(*a*) of this section, and the accessory offers to the Court an undertaking either—

- (*a*) to refrain from acting in any of the ways mentioned in paragraphs (*a*) to (*c*) of subsection (4) of that section, or
- (*b*) to take particular steps which, in the opinion of the Court, would suffice to prevent him from acting in any of those ways,

the Court may, if it thinks fit, accept that undertaking instead of making an order under this section.

40. Provisions as to interconnected bodies corporate

(1) This section applies to any order made under section 37 or section 39 of this Act.

(2) Where an order to which this section aplies is made against a body corporate which is a member of a group of interconnected bodies corporate, the Restrictive Practices Court, on making the order, may direct that it shall be binding upon all members of the group as if each of them were the body corporate against which the order is made.

(3) Where an order to which this section applies has been made against a body corporate, and at a time when that order is in force—

  (*a*) the body corporate becomes a member of a group of interconnected bodies corporate, or
  (*b*) a group of interconnected bodies corporate of which it is a member is increased by the addition of one or more further members,

the Restrictive Practices Court, on the application of the Director, may direct that the order shall thereafter be binding upon each member of the group as if it were the body corporate against which the order was made.

(4) The power conferred by subsection (3) of this section shall be exercisable—

  (*a*) whether, at the time when the original order was made, the body corporate against which it was made was a member of a group of interconnected bodies corporate or not, and
  (*b*) if it was such a member, whether a direction under subsection (2) of this section was given or not.

41. Concurrent jurisdiction of other courts in certain cases

(1) In any case where—

  (*a*) the Director could bring proceedings against a person before the Restrictive Practices Court under section 35 or section 38 of this Act, and
  (*b*) it appears to the Director that the conditions specified in the next following subsection are fulfilled,

the Director may, if he thinks fit, bring those proceedings in an appropriate alternative court instead of bringing them before the Restrictive Practices Court; and, in relation to any proceedings brought by virtue of this section, the appropriate alternative court in which they are brought shall have the like jurisdiction as the Restrictive Practices Court would have had if they had been brought in that Court.

(2) The conditions referred to in the proceeding subsection are—

  (*a*) that neither the person against whom the proceedings are to be brought nor the person against whom any associated proceedings have been or are intended to be brought is a body corporate having a share capital, paid up or credited as paid up, of an amount exceeding £10,000, and
  (*b*) that neither those proceedings nor any associated proceedings involve or are likely to involve the determination of a question (whether of law of or fact) of such general application as to justify its being reserved for determination by the Restrictive Practices Court.

(3) For the purposes of this section, the following shall be appropriate alternative courts in relation to proceedings in respect of a course of conduct maintained in the course of a business, that is to say, the county court for any district (or, in Northern Ireland, any division) in which, or, in Scotland, any sheriff court within whose jurisdiction, that business is carried on.

(4) In relation to any proceedings brought in an appropriate alternative court by virtue of this section, or to any order made in any such proceedings, any reference in section 37, in section 39 or section 40 of this Act to the Restrictive Practices Court shall be construed as a reference to the appropriate alternative court in which the proceedings are brought.

(5) In this section 'associated proceedings'—

- (*a*) in relation to proceedings under section 35 of this Act, means proceedings under section 38 of this Act against a person as being a person consenting to or conniving at the course of conduct in question, and
- (*b*) in relation to proceedings under section 38 of this Act, means proceedings under section 35 of this Act against a person as being the person by whom the course of conduct in question has been maintained.

42. Appeals from decisions or orders of courts under Part III

(1) Notwithstanding anything in any other enactment, an appeal, whether on a question of fact or on a question of law, shall lie from any decision or order of any court in proceedings under Part III of this Act.

(2) Any such appeal shall lie—

- (*a*) in the case of proceedings in England and Wales, to the Court of Appeal;
- (*b*) in the case of proceedings in Scotland, to the Court of Session;
- (*c*) in the case of proceedings in Northern Ireland, to the Court of Appeal in Northern Ireland

* * *

PART VII

PROVISIONS RELATING TO REFERENCES TO ADVISORY COMMITTEE OR TO COMMISSION

81. Procedure in carrying out investigations

(1) The Advisory Committee, in carrying out an investigation on a reference to which section 17 of this Act applies, and the Commission, in carrying out an investigation on a reference made to them under this Act (whether it is a monopoly reference or a merger reference or a reference under Part VI of this Act),—

- (*a*) shall take into consideration any representations made to them by persons appearing to them to have a substantial interest in the subject-matter of the reference, or by bodies appearing to them to represent substantial numbers of persons who have such an interest, and
- (*b*) unless in all the circumstances they consider it not reasonably necessary or not reasonably practicable to do so, shall permit any such person or body to be heard orally by the Advisory Committee or the Commission, as the case may be, or by a member of the Committee or of the Commission nominated by them for that purpose.

(2) Subject to subsection (1) of this section, the Advisory Committee or the Commission may determine their own procedure for carrying out any investigation on a reference under this Act, and in particular may determine—

  (*a*) the extent, if any, to which persons interested or claiming to be interested in the subject-matter of the reference are allowed to be present or to be heard, either by themselves or by their representatives, or to cross-examine witnesses or otherwise take part in the investigation, and
  (*b*) the extent, if any, to which the sittings of the Advisory Committee or of the Commission are to be held in public.

(3) In determining their procedure under subsection (2) of this section, and, in the case of the Commission, in exercising any powers conferred on them by section 85 of this Act, the Advisory Committee or the Commission, as the case may be, shall act in accordance with any general directions which may from time to time be given to them by the Secretary of State.

(4) The Secretary of State shall lay before each House of Parliament a copy of any directions given by him under subsection (3) of this section.

82. General provisions as to reports

(1) In making any report under this Act the Advisory Committee or the Commission shall have regard to the need for excluding, so far as that is practicable,—

  (*a*) any matter which relates to the private affairs of an individual, where the publication of that matter would or might, in their opinion, seriously and prejudicially affect the interests of that individual, and
  (*b*) any matter which relates specifically to the affairs of a particular body of persons, whether corporate or uncorporate, where publication of that matter would or might, in the opinion of the Advisory Committee or the Commission, as the case may be, seriously and prejudicially affect the interests of that body, unless in their opinion the inclusion of that matter relating specifically to that body is necessary for the purposes of the report.

(2) For the purposes of the law relating to defamation, absolute privilege shall attach to any report of the Advisory Committee or of the Commission under this Act.

(3) Subject to the next following subsection, if—

  (*a*) on a reference to the Advisory Committee under this Act, or
  (*b*) on a reference to the Commission, other than a monopoly reference limited to the facts,

a member of the Advisory Committee or of the Commission, as the case may be, dissents from any conclusions contained in the report on the reference as being conclusions of the committee or of the Commission, the report shall, if that member so desires, include a statement of his dissent and of his reasons for dissenting.

(4) In relation to a report made by a group of members of the Commission in pursuance of paragraph 10 or paragraph 11 of Schedule 3 to this Act, subsection (3) of this section shall have effect subject to paragraph 14(1) of that Schedule.

Fair Trading Act 1973

83. Laying before Parliament and publication of reports

(1) [Subject to subsection (1A) below] the Minister or Ministers to whom any report of the Advisory Committee on a reference to which section 17 of this Act applies, or any report of the Commission under this Act, is made shall lay a copy of the report before each House of Parliament, and shall arrange for the report to be published in such manner as appears to the Minister or Ministers to be appropriate.

[(1A) the Minister or Ministers to whom a report of the Commission or a monopoly reference is made shall not lay a copy of the report before either House of Parliament unless at least twenty-four hours before doing so he transmits or they transmit to every person named in the report as a person in whose favour a monopoly situation exists a copy of the report in the form in which it is laid (or by virtue of subsection (2) below is treated as being laid) before each House of Parliament.]

(2) If such a report is presented by command of Her Majesty to either House of Parliament otherwise than at or during the time of a sitting of that House, the presentation of the report shall for the purposes of this section be treated as the laying of a copy of it before that House by the Minister or Ministers to whom the report was made.

(3) If it appears to the Minister or Ministers to whom any report of the Advisory Committee or of the Commission under this Act is made that the publication of any matter in the report would be against the public interest, the Minister or Ministers shall exclude that matter from the copies of the report as laid before Parliament and from the report as published under this section.

(4) Any reference in this Act to a report to the Advisory Committee or of the Commission as laid before Parliament shall be construed as a reference to the report in the form in which copies of it are laid (or by virtue of subsection (2) of this section are treated as having been laid) before each House of Parliament under this section.

[*The words within square brackets in subsection (1) were substituted, and subsection (1A) was added by the Competition Act 1980, section 22 and the Competition Act 1980 (Commencement No. 1) Order 1980 (S.I. 1980 No. 497) r. 3(b) and Sched, Pt II.*]

* * *

118. Trading schemes to which Part XI applies

(1) This Part of this Act applies to any trading scheme which includes the following elements, that is to say—

- (*a*) goods or services, or both, are to be provided by the person promoting the scheme (in this Part of this Act referred to as 'the promoter') or, in the case of a scheme promoted by two or more persons acting in concert (in this Part of this Act referred to as 'the promoters'), are to be provided by one or more of those persons;
- (*b*) the goods or services so provided are to be supplied to or for other persons under transactions effected by persons (other than the promoter or any of the promoters) who participate in the scheme (each of whom is in this Part of this Act referred to as a 'participant');
- (*c*) those transactions, or most of them, are to be effected elsewhere than

Fair Trading Act 1973

at premises at which the promoter or any of the promoters or the participant effecting the transaction carries on business; and

(*d*) the prospect is held out to participants of receiving payments or other benefits in respect of any one or more of the matters specified in the next following subsection.

(2) The matters referred to in paragraph (*d*) of subsection (1) of this section are—

(*a*) the introduction of other persons who become participants;
(*b*) the promotion, transfer or other change of status of participants within the trading scheme;
(*c*) the supply of goods to other participants;
(*d*) the supply of training facilities or other services for other participants;
(*e*) transactions effected by other participants under which goods are to be supplied to, or services are to be supplied for, other persons.

(3) For the purposes of this Part of this Act a trading scheme shall be taken to include the element referred to in paragraph (*b*) of subsection (1) of this section whether the transactions referred to in that paragraph are to be effected by participants in the capacity of servants or agents of the promoter or of one of the promoters or in any other capacity.

(4) In determining, for the purposes of paragraph (*c*) of subsection (1) of this section, whether any premises are premises at which a participant in a trading scheme carries on business, no account shall be taken of transactions effected or to be effected by him under that trading scheme.

(5) For the purposes of this Part of this Act such a prospect as is mentioned in paragraph (*d*) of subsection (1) of this section shall be taken to be held out to a participant—

(*a*) whether it is held out so as to confer on him a legally enforceable right or not, and
(*b*) in so far as it relates to the introduction of new participants, whether it is limited to the introduction of new participants by him or extends to the introduction of new participants by other persons.

(6) In this Part of this Act 'trading scheme' includes any arrangements made in connection with the carrying on of a business, whether those arrangements are made or recorded wholly or partly in writing or not.

(7) In this section any reference to the provision of goods or services by a person shall be construed as including a reference to the provision of goods or services under arrangements to which that person is a party.

119. Regulations relating to such trading schemes

(1) Regulations made by the Secretary of State by statutory instrument may make provision with respect to the issue, circulation or distribution of documents, whether being advertisements, prospectuses, circulars or notices, which—

(*a*) contain any invitation to persons to become participants in a trading scheme to which this Part of this Act applies, or
(*b*) contain any information calculated to lead directly or indirectly to persons becoming participants in such a trading scheme,

and may prohibit any such document from being issued, circulated or distributed

Fair Trading Act 1973

unless it complies with such requirements as to the matters to be included or not included in it as may be prescribed by the regulations.

(2) Regulations made by the Secretary of State by statutory instrument may prohibit the promoter or any of the promoters of, or any participant in, a trading scheme to which this Part of this Act applies from—

    (*a*) supplying any goods to a participant in the trading scheme, or

    (*b*) supplying any training facilities or other services for such a participant, or

    (*c*) providing any goods or services under a transaction effected by such a participant, or

    (*d*) being a party to any arrangements under which goods or services are supplied or provided as mentioned in any of the preceding paragraphs, or

    (*e*) accepting from any such participant any payment, or any undertaking to make a payment, in respect of any goods or services supplied or provided as mentioned in any of paragraphs (*a*) to (*d*) of this subsection or in respect of any goods or services to be so supplied or provided.

unless (in any such case) such requirements as prescribed by the regulations are complied with.

(3) Any requirements prescribed by regulations under subsection (2) of this section shall be such as the Secretary of State considers necessary or expedient for the purpose of preventing participants in trading schemes to which this Part of this Act applies from being unfairly treated; and, without prejudice to the generality of this subsection, any such requirements may include provisions—

    (*a*) requiring the rights and obligations of every participant under such a trading scheme to be set out in full in an agreement in writing made between the participant and the promoter or (if more than one) each of the promoters;

    (*b*) specifying rights required to be conferred on every such participant, and obligations required to be assumed by the promoter or promoters, under any such trading scheme; or

    (*c*) imposing restrictions on the liabilities to be incurred by such a participant in respect of any of the matters mentioned in paragraphs (*a*) to (*e*) of subsection (2) of this section.

(4) Regulations made under subsection (2) of this section—

    (*a*) may include provision for enabling a person who has made a payment as a participant in a trading scheme to which this Part of this Act applies, in circumstances where any of the requirements prescribed by the regulations were not complied with, to recover the whole or part of that payment from any person to whom or for whose benefit it was paid, and

    (*b*) subject to any provision made in accordance with the preceding paragraph, may prescribe the degree to which anything done in contravention of the regulations is to be treated as valid or invalid for the purposes of any civil proceedings.

(5) The power to make regulations under this section may be exercised so as to make different provision—

in relation to different descriptions of trading schemes to which this Part of this Act applies, or

(*b*) in relation (*a*) trading schemes which are or were in operation on a date specified in the regulations and trading schemes which are or were not in operation on that date,

or in relation to different descriptions of participants in such trading schemes.

120. Offences under Part XI

(1) Subject to the next following section, any person who issues, circulates or distributes, or causes another person to issue, circulate or distribute, a document in contravention of any regulations made under subsection (1) of section 119 of this Act shall be guilty of an offence.

(2) Any person who contravenes any regulations made under subsection (2) of that section shall be guilty of an offence.

(3) If any person who is a participant in a trading scheme to which this Part of this Act applies, or has applied or been invited to become a participant in such a trading scheme,—

(*a*) makes any payment to or for the benefit of the promoter of (if there is more than one) any of the promoters, or to or for the benefit of a participant in the trading scheme, and

(*b*) is induced to make that payment by reason that the prospect is held out to him of receiving payments of other benefits in respect of the introduction of other persons who become participants in the trading scheme.

any person to whom or for whose benefit that payment is made shall be guilty of an offence.

(4) If the promoter or any of the promoters of a trading scheme to which this part of this Act applies, or any other person acting in accordance with such a trading scheme, by holding out to any person such a prospect as is mentioned in subsection (3)(*b*) of this section, attempts to induce him—

(*a*) if he is already a participant in the trading scheme, to make any payment to or for the benefit of the promoter or any of the promoters or to or for the benefit of a participant in the trading scheme, or

(*b*) if he is not already a participant in the trading scheme, to become such a participant and to make any such payment as is mentioned in the preceding paragraph,

the person attempting to induce him to make that payment shall be guilty of an offence.

(5) In determining, for the purposes of subsection (3) or subsection (4) of this section, whether an inducement or attempt to induce is made by holding out such a prospect as is therein mentioned, it shall be sufficient if such a prospect constitutes or would constitute a substantial part of the inducement.

(6) Where the person by whom an offence is committed under subsection (3) or subsection (4) of this section is not the sole promoter of the trading scheme in question, any other person who is the promoter or (as the case may be) one of the promoters of the trading scheme shall, subject to the next following section, also be guilty of that offence.

(7) Nothing is subsections (3) to (6) of this section shall be construed as limiting the circumstances in which the commission of any act may constitute an offence under subsection (1) or subsection (2) of this section.

(8) In this section any reference to the making of a payment to or for the benefit of a person shall be construed as including the making of a payment partly to or for the benefit of that person and partly to or for the benefit of one or more other persons.

121. Defences in certain proceedings under Part XI

(1) Where a person is charged with an offence under subsection (1) of section 120 of this Act in respect of an advertisement, it shall be a defence for him to prove that he is a person whose business it is to publish or arrange for the publication of advertisements, and that he received the advertisement for publication in the ordinary course of business and did not know, and had no reason to suspect, that its publication would amount to an offence under that subsection.

(2) Where a person is charged with an offence by virtue of subsection (6) of section 120 of this Act, it shall be a defence for him to prove—

- (*a*) that the trading scheme to which the charge relates was in operation before the commencement of this Act, and
- (*b*) that the act constituting the offence was committed without his consent or connivance.

122. Penalties for offences under Part XI

A person guilty of an offence under this Part of this Act shall be liable—

- (*a*) on summary conviction, to a fine not exceeding £400 or to imprisonment for a term not exceeding three months or to both;
- (*b*) on conviction on indictment, to a fine or to imprisonment for a term not exceeding two years or to both.

123. Enforcement provisions

(1) The provisions of sections 29 to 32 of this Act shall have effect for the purposes of this Part of this Act as if in those provisions—

- (*a*) references to a weights and measures authority or a duly authorised officer of such an authority were omitted, and
- (*b*) any reference to an offence under section 23 of this Act were a reference to an offence under this Part of this Act.

(2) For the purposes of the application to Northern Ireland of those provisions as applied by the preceding subsection—

- (*a*) any reference to the Secretary of State shall be construed as a reference to the Ministry of Commerce for Northern Ireland, and
- (*b*) paragraphs (*c*) and (*d*) of section 33(2) of this Act shall have effect as they have effect for the purposes of the application of Part II of this Act to Northern Ireland.

* * *

Fair Trading Act 1973

PART XII

MISCELLANEOUS AND SUPPLEMENTARY PROVISIONS

* * *

125. Annual and other reports of Director

(1) The Director shall, as soon as practicable after the end of the year 1974 and of each subsequent calendar year, make to the Secretary of State a report on his activities, and the activities of the Advisory Committee and of the Commission during that year.

(2) Every such report shall include a general survey of developments, during the year to which it relates, in respect of matters falling within the scope of the Director's duties under any enactment (including any enactment contained in this Act, other than this section) [and shall set out any directions given to the Director under section 2(2) of the Consumer Credit Act 1974 during that year.]

(3) The Secretary of State shall lay a copy of every report made by the Director under subsection (1) of this section before each House of Parliament, and shall arrange for every such report to be published in such manner as he may consider appropriate.

(4) The Director may also prepare such other reports as appear to him to be expedient with respect to such matters as are mentioned in subsection (2) of this section, and may arrange for any such report to be published in such manner as he may consider appropriate.

(5) In making any report under this Act the Director shall have regard to the need for excluding, so far as that is practicable, any such matter as is specified in paragraph (*a*) or paragraph (*b*) of section 124(2) of this Act.

(6) For the purposes of this section any period between the commencement of this Act and the end of the year 1973 shall be treated as included in the year 1974.

[*The words in square brackets were inserted by the Consumer Credit Act 1974, section 5.*]

* * *

129. Time-limit for prosecutions

(1) No prosecution for an offence under this Act shall be commenced after the expiration of three years from the commission of the offence or one year from its discovery by the prosecutor, whichever is the earlier.

(2) Notwithstanding anything in [section 127(1) of the Magistrates' Courts Act 1980], a magistrates' court may try an information for an offence under this Act if the information was laid within twelve months from the commission of the offence.

(3) Notwithstanding anything in section 23 of the Summary Jurisdiction (Scotland) Act 1954, summary proceedings in Scotland for an offence under this Act may be commenced within twelve months from the commission of the offence, and subsection (2) of the said section 23 shall apply for the purposes of this subsection as it applies for the purposes of that section.

(4) In the application of this section to Northern Ireland, for the references in subsection (2) to [section 127(1) of the Magistrates' Courts Act 1980] and to the trial and laying of an information there shall be substituted respectively references to [Article 19(1) of the Magistrates' Courts (Northern Ireland) Order 1981] and to the hearing and determination and making of a complaint [and as if in that subsection for the words 'an offence under this Act' there were substituted the words 'an offence under sections 30(1) or 46(2) of this Act.'].

[*The words in square brackets were substituted by the Magistrates' Courts Act 1980, section 154(1) and Schedule 7, the Criminal Justice (Northern Ireland) Order 1980 (S.I. 1980 No. 704), and the Magistrates' Courts (Northern Ireland) Order 1981 (S.I. 1981 No. 1675).*]

* * *

131. Notification of convictions and judgments to Director

(1) Where in any criminal proceedings a person is convicted of an offence by or before a court in the United Kingdom, or a judgment is given against a person in civil proceedings in any such court, and it appears to the court—

(a) having regard to the functions of the Director under Part III of this Act [or under the Estate Agents Act 1979], that it would be expedient for the conviction or judgment to be brought to his attention, and

(b) that it may not be brought to his attention unless arrangements for the purpose are made by the court,

the court may make arrangements for that purpose notwithstanding that the proceedings have been finally disposed of by the court.

(2) In this section 'judgment' includes any order or decree, and any reference to the giving of a judgment shall be construed accordingly.

[*The words in square brackets were inserted by the Estate Agents Act 1979, section 9(5).*]

132. Offences by bodies corporate

(1) Where an offence under section 23, section 46, section 85(6) or Part XI of this Act, which has been committed by a body corporate, is proved to have been committed with the consent or connivance of, or to be attributable to any neglect on the part of, any director, manager, secretary or other similar officer of the body corporate, or any person who was purporting to act in any such capacity, he as well as the body corporate shall be guilty of that offence and be liable to be proceeded against and punished accordingly.

(2) Where the affairs of a body corporate are managed by its members, subsection (1) of this section shall apply in relation to the acts and defaults of a member in connection with his functions of management as if he were a director of the body corporate.

* * *

137. General interpretation provisions

(1) In this Act—

'the Act of 1948' means the Monopolies and Restrictive Practices (Inquiry and Control) Act 1948;

Fair Trading Act 1973

'[the Act of 1976' means the Restrictive Trade Practices Act 1976];
[. . .]

'the Act of 1965' means the Monopolies and Mergers Act 1965;
[. . .]

'assignment,' in relation to Scotland, means assignation;

'contract of employment' means a contract of service or of apprenticeship, whether it is express or implied, and (if it is express) whether it is oral or in writing;

'scale' (where the reference is to the scale on which any services are, or are to be, made available, supplied or obtained) means scale measured in terms of money or money's worth or in any other manner.

(2) Except in so far as the context otherwise requires, in this Act, [. . .], the following expressions have the meanings hereby assigned to them respectively, that is to say—

'the Advisory Committee' means the Consumer Protection Advisory Committee;

'agreement' means any agreement or arrangement, in whatever way and in whatever form it is made, and whether it is, or is intended to be, legally enforceable or not;

'business' includes a professional practice and includes any other undertaking which is carried on for gain or reward or which is an undertaking in the course of which goods or services are supplied otherwise than free of charge;

'commercial activities in the United Kingdom' means any of the following, that is to say, the production and supply of goods in the United Kingdom, the supply of services in the United Kingdom and the export of goods from the United Kingdom;

'the Commission' means the Monopolies and Mergers Commission;

'complex monopoly situation' has the meaning assigned to it by section 11 of this Act;

'consumer' (subject to subsection (6) of this section) means any person who is either—

(*a*) a person to whom goods are or are sought to be supplied (whether by way of sale or otherwise) in the course of a business carried on by the person supplying or seeking to supply them, or

(*b*) a person for whom services are or are sought to be supplied in the course of a business carried on by the person supplying or seeking to supply them,

and who does not receive or seek to receive the goods or services in the course of a business carried on by him;

'the Director' means the Director General of Fair Trading;

'enactment' includes an enactment of the Parliament of Northern Ireland;

'goods' includes buildings and other structures, and also includes ships, aircraft and hovercraft, but does not include electricity;

'group' (where the reference is to a group of persons fulfilling specified conditions, other than the condition of being interconnected bodies corporate) means any two or more persons fulfilling those conditions, whether apart from fulfilling them they would be regarded as constituting a group or not;

'merger reference' has the meaning assigned to it by section 5(3) of this Act;

'merger situation qualifying for investigation' has the meaning assigned to it by section 64(8) of this Act;

'Minister' includes a Government department but shall not by virtue of this provision be taken to include the establishment consisting of the Director and his staff, and, except where the contrary is expressly provided, does not include any Minister or department of the Government of Northern Ireland;

'monopoly reference' and 'monopoly situation' have the meanings assigned to them by section 5(3) of this Act;

'newspaper merger reference' has the meaning assigned to it by section 59(3) of this Act;

'practice' means any practice, whether adopted in pursuance of an agreement or otherwise;

'price' includes any charge or fee, by whatever name called;

'produce,' in relation to the production of minerals or other substances, includes getting them, and, in relation to the production of animals or fish, includes taking them;

'supply,' in relation to the supply of goods, includes supply by way of sale, lease, hire or hire-purchase, and, in relation to buildings or other structures, includes the construction of them by a person for another person;

'uncompetitive practices' means practices having the effect of preventing, restricting or distorting competition in connection with any commercial activities in the United Kingdom;

'worker' (subject to subsection (7) of this section) has the meaning assigned to it by section 167 of the Industrial Relations Act 1971.

(3) In the provisions of this Act [. . .] 'the supply of services' does not include the rendering of any services under a contract of employment but, [. . .]—

- (a) includes the undertaking and performance for gain or reward of engagements (whether professional or other) for any matter other than the supply of goods, and
- (b) includes both the rendering of services to order and the provision of services by making them available to potential users; [and
- (c) includes the making of arrangements for a person to put or keep on land a caravan (within the meaning of Part I of the Caravan Sites and Control of Development Act 1960) other than arrangements by virtue of which the person may occupy the caravan as his only or main residence]; [and
- (d) includes arrangements for the use by public-service vehicles (within the meaning of the Public Passenger Vehicles Act 1981) of a parking place which is used as a point at which passengers on services provided by means of such vehicles may be taken up or set down.]

Fair Trading Act 1973

and any reference in those provisions to services supplied or to be supplied, or to services provided or to be provided, shall be construed accordingly.

(Subsection 3(c) was inserted by the Competition Act 1980 and subsection 3(d) was inserted by the Transport Act 1985.)

(4) For the purposes of this Act, [. . .], 'services' includes electricity.

(5) For the purposes of the provisions of this Act [. . .], any two bodies corporate are to be treated as interconnected if one of them is a body corporate of which the other is a subsidiary (within the meaning of [section 736 of the Companies Act 1985]) or if both of them are subsidiaries (within the meaning of that section) of one and the same body corporate; and in those provisions 'interconnected bodies corporate' shall be construed accordingly, and 'group of interconnected bodies corporate' means a group consisting of two or more bodies corporate all of whom are interconnected with each other.

(6) For the purposes of the application of any provision of this Act in relation to goods or services of a particular description or to which a particular practice applies, 'consumers' means persons who are consumers (as defined by subsection (2) of this section) in relation to goods or services of that description or in relation to goods or services to which that practice applies.

(7) For the purposes of the application of this Act to Northern Ireland, the definition of 'worker' in subsection (2) of this section shall apply as if the Industrial Relations Act 1971 extended to Northern Ireland but, in section 167(2)(*a*) of that Act, references to general medical services, pharmaceutical services, general dental services or general ophthalmic services provided under the enactments mentioned in that subsection were references to the corresponding services provided in Northern Ireland under the corresponding enactments there in force.

(8) Except in so far as the context otherwise requires, any reference in this Act to an enactment shall be construed as a reference to that enactment as amended or extended by or under any other enactment, including this Act.

(Throughout section 137, the words omitted were repealed by the Restrictive Trade Practices Act 1976.)

* * *

138. Supplementary interpretation provisions

(1) This section applies to the following provisions of this Act, that is to say, section 2(4), Parts II and III, section 137(7), and the definition of 'consumer' contained in section 137(2).

(2) For the purposes of any provisions to which this section applies it is immaterial whether any person supplying goods or services has a place of business in the United Kingdom or not.

(3) For the purposes of any provisions to which this section applies any goods or services supplied wholly or partly outside the United Kingdom, if they are supplied in accordance with arrangements made in the United Kingdom, whether made orally or by one or more documents delivered in the United Kingdom or by correspondence posted from and to addresses in the United Kingdom, shall be treated as goods supplied to, or services supplied for, persons in the United Kingdom.

(4) In relation to the supply of goods under a hire-purchase agreement, a

credit-sale agreement or a conditional sale agreement, the person conducting any antecedent negotiations, as well as the owner or seller, shall for the purposes of any provisions to which this section applies be treated as a person supplying or seeking to supply the goods.

[(5) In subsection (4) of this section, the following expressions have the meanings given by, or referred to in, section 189 of the Consumer Credit Act 1974—
>'antecedent negotiations',
>'conditional sale agreement',
>'credit-sale agreement',
>'hire-purchase agreement'.]

(6) In any provisions to which this section applies.
- (a) any reference to a person to or for whom goods or services are supplied shall be construed as including a reference to any guarantor of such a person, and
- (b) any reference to the terms or conditions on or subject to which goods or services are supplied shall be construed as including a reference to the terms or conditions on or subject to which any person undertakes to act as such a guarantor;

and in this subsection 'guarantor', in relation to a person to or for whom goods or services are supplied, includes a person who undertakes to indemnify the supplier of the goods or services against any loss which he may incur in respect of the supply of the goods or services to or for that person.

(7) For the purposes of any provisions to which this section applies goods or services supplied by a person carrying on a business shall be taken to be supplied in the course of that business if payment for the supply of goods or services is made or (whether under a contract or by virtue of an enactment or otherwise) is required to be made.

[*Subsection (5) was substituted by the Consumer Credit Act 1974, section 192(3)(a) and (4), and Schedule 4, Part I, paragraph 37.*]

* * *

140. Short title, citation, commencement and extent

This Act may be cited as the Fair Trading Act 1973.

Powers of Criminal Courts Act 1973
Chapter 62
Sections 35 to 38 only

* * *

35. Compensation orders against convicted persons

(1) Subject to the provisions of this Part of this Act [and to section 40 of the Magistrates' Courts Act 1980 (which imposes a monetary limit on the powers of a magistrates' court under this section)], a court by or before which a person is convicted of an offence, instead of or in addition to dealing with him in any other way, may, on application or otherwise, make an order (in this Act referred to as 'a compensation order') requiring him to pay compensation for any personal injury, loss or damage resulting from that offence or any other offence which is taken into consideration by the court in determining sentence [or to make payments for funeral expenses or bereavement in respect of a death resulting from any such offence, other than a death due to an accident arising out of the presence of a motor vehicle on a road; and a court shall give reasons, on passing sentence, if it does not make such an order in a case where this section empowers it to do so.]

(Subsection 1 was substituted by the Criminal Justice Act 1982, section 67 and the words in square brackets were added by the Criminal Justice Act 1988, section 104.)

[(1A) Compensation under subsection (1) above shall be of such amount as the court considers appropriate, having regard to any evidence and to any representations that are made by or on behalf of the accused or the prosecutor.]

(Subsection (1A) was inserted by the Criminal Justice Act 1982, section 67.)

(2) In the case of an offence under the Theft Act 1968, where the property in question is recovered, any damage to the property occurring while it was out of the owner's possession shall be treated for the purposes of subsection (1) above as having resulted from the offence, however and by whomsoever the damage was caused.

[(3) A compensation order may only be made in respect of injury loss or damage (other than loss suffered by a person's dependants in consequence of his death) which was due to an accident arising out of the presence of a motor vehicle on a road, if—

    (*a*) it is in respect of damage which is treated by subsection (2) above as resulting from an offence under the Theft Act 1968; or
    (*b*) it is in respect of injury, loss or damage as respects which—
        (i) the offender is uninsured in relation to the use of the vehicle; and
        (ii) compensation is not payable under any arrangements to which the Secretary of State is a party;

and, where a compensation order is made in respect of injury, loss or damage

Powers of Criminal Courts Act 1973

due to such an accident, the amount to be paid may include an amount representing the whole or part of any loss of or reduction in preferential rates of insurance attributable to the accident.

(3A) A vehicle the use of which is exempted from insurance by section 144 of the Road Traffic Act 1972 is not uninsured for the purposes of subsection (3) above.

(3B) A compensation order in respect of funeral expenses may be made for the benefit of anyone who incurred the expenses.

(3C) A compensation order in respect of bereavement may only be made for the benefit of a person for whose benefit a claim for damages for bereavement could be made under section 1A of the Fatal Accidents Act 1976.

(3D) The amounts of compensation in respect of bereavement shall not exceed the amount for the time being specified in section 1A(3) of the Fatal Accidents Act 1976.]

(Subsections (3) to (3D) were substituted by the Criminal Justice Act 1988, section 104.)

(4) In determining whether to make a compensation order against any person, and in determining the amount to be paid by any person under such an order, the court shall have regard to his means so far as they appear or are known to the court.

[(4A) Where the court considers—

  (*a*) that it would be appropriate both to impose a fine and to make a compensation order; but
  (*b*) that the offender has insufficient means to pay both an appropriate fine and appropriate compensation, the court shall give preference to compensation (though it may impose a fine as well).]

(Subsection (4A) was inserted by the Criminal Justice Act 1982, section 67.)

(5) *(Subsection (5) was repealed by the Magistrates' Courts Act 1980.)*

[36. Enforcement and appeals

(1) A person in whose favour a compensation order is made shall not be entitled to receive the amount due to him until (disregarding any power of a court to grant leave to appeal out of time) there is no further possibility of an appeal on which the order could be varied or set aside.

(2) Rules under section 144 of the Magistrates' Courts Act 1980 may make provision regarding the way in which the magistrates' court for the time being having functions (by virtue of section 41(1) of the Administration of Justice Act 1970) in relation to the enforcement of a compensation order is to deal with money paid in satisfaction of the order where the entitlement of the person in whose favour it was made is suspended.

(3) The Court of Appeal may by order annul or vary any compensation order made by the court of trial, although the conviction is not quashed; and the order, if annulled, shall not take effect and, if varied, shall take effect as varied.

(4) Where the House of Lords restores a conviction, it may make any compensation order which the court of trial could have made.

(5) Where a compensation order has been made against any person in respect of an offence taken into consideration in determining his sentence—

(*a*) the order shall cease to have effect if he successfully appeals against his conviction of the offence or, if more than one, all the offences, of which he was convicted in the proceedings in which the order was made;

(*b*) he may appeal against the order as if it were part of the sentence imposed in respect of the offence or, if more than one, any of the offences, of which he was so convicted.]

(Section 36 was substituted by the Criminal Justice Act 1988, section 105.)

[37. **Review of compensation orders**

At any time before the person against whom a compensation order has been made has paid into court the whole of the compensation which the order requires him to pay, but at a time when (disregarding any power of a court to grant leave to appeal out of time) there is no further possibility of an appeal on which the order could be varied or set aside, the magistrates' court for the time being having functions in relation to the enforcement of the order may, on the application of the person against whom it was made, discharge the order, or reduce the amount which remains to be paid, if it appears to the court—

(*a*) that the injury, loss or damage in respect of which the order was made has been held in civil proceedings to be less than it was taken to be for the purposes of the order; or

(*b*) in the case of an order in respect of the loss of any property, that the property has been recovered by the person in whose favour the order was made; or

(*c*) that the means of the person against whom the order was made are insufficient to satisfy in full both the order and a confiscation order under Part VI of the Criminal Justice Act 1988 made against him in the same proceedings; or

(*d*) that the person against whom the order was made has suffered a substantial reduction in his means which was unexpected at the time when the compensation order was made, and that his means seem unlikely to increase for a considerable period;

but where the order was made by the Crown Court, a magistrates' court shall not exercise any power conferred by this section in a case where it is satisfied as mentioned in paragraph (c) or (d) above unless it has first obtained the consent of the Crown Court.]

(Section 37 was substituted by the Criminal Justice Act 1988, section 105.)

[38. **Effect of compensation order on subsequent award of damages in civil proceedings**

(1) This section shall have effect where a compensation order has been made in favour of any person in respect of any injury, loss or damage and a claim by him in civil proceedings for damages in respect of the injury, loss or damage subsequently falls to be determined.

(2) The damages in the civil proceedings shall be assessed without regard to the order; but the plaintiff may only recover an amount equal to the aggregate of the following—

Powers of Criminal Courts Act 1973

(*a*) any amount by which they exceed the compensation; and
(*b*) a sum equal to any portion of the compensation which he fails to recover,

and may not enforce the judgment, so far as it relates to a sum such as is mentioned in paragraph (*b*) above, without the leave of the court.]

(Section 38 was substituted by the Criminal Justice Act 1988, section 105.)

Consumer Credit Act 1974
Chapter 39

ARRANGEMENT OF SECTIONS

PART I

DIRECTOR GENERAL OF FAIR TRADING

Section
1. General functions of Director
2. Powers of Secretary of State
3. Supervision by Council on Tribunals
4. Dissemination of information and advice
5. Annual and other Reports
6. Form etc. of applications
7. Penalty for false information

PART II

CREDIT AGREEMENTS, HIRE AGREEMENTS AND LINKED TRANSACTIONS

8. Consumer credit agreements
9. Meaning of credit
10. Running-account credit and fixed-sum credit
11. Restricted-use credit and unrestricted-use credit
12. Debtor-credit-supplier agreements
13. Debtor-creditor agreements
14. Credit-token agreements
15. Consumer hire agreements
16. Exempt agreements
17. Small agreements
18. Multiple agreements
19. Linked transactions
20. Total charge for credit

PART III

LICENSING OF CREDIT AND HIRE BUSINESS

Licensing principles

21. Business needing a licence
22. Standard and group licences
23. Authorisation of specific activities
24. Control of name of business
25. Licensee to be a fit person
26. Conduct of business

Issue of licences

Section
27. Determination of applications
28. Exclusion from group licence

Renewal, variation, suspension and revocation of licences

29. Renewal
30. Variation by request
31. Compulsory variation
32. Suspension and revocation
33. Application to end suspension

Miscellaneous

34. Representations to Director
35. The register
36. Duty to notify changes
37. Death, bankruptcy etc. of licensee
38. Application of s. 37 to Scotland and Northern Ireland
39. Offences against Part III
40. Enforcement of agreements made by unlicensed trader
41. Appeals to Secretary of State under Part III
42. Further appeal on point of law

PART IV

SEEKING BUSINESS

Advertising

43. Advertisements to which Part IV applies
44. Form and content of advertisements
45. Prohibition of advertisement where goods etc. not sold for cash
46. False or misleading advertisements
47. Advertising infringements

Canvassing etc.

48. Definition of canvassing off trade premises (regulated agreements.)
49. Prohibition of canvassing debtor-creditor agreements off trade premises
50. Circulars to minors
51. Prohibition of unsolicited credit-tokens.

Miscellaneous

52. Quotations
53. Duty to display information
54. Conduct of business regulations

Consumer Credit Act 1974

PART V

ENTRY INTO CREDIT OR HIRE AGREEMENTS

Preliminary matters

Section
55. Disclosure of information
56. Antecedent negotiations
57. Withdrawal from prospective agreement
58. Opportunity for withdrawal from prospective land mortgage
59. Agreement to enter future agreement void

Making the agreement

60. Form and content of agreements
61. Signing of agreement
62. Duty to supply copy of unexecuted agreement
63. Duty to supply copy of executed agreement
64. Duty to give notice of cancellation rights
65. Consequences of improper execution
66. Acceptance of credit-tokens

Cancellation of certain agreements within cooling-off period

67. Cancellable agreements
68. Cooling-off period
69. Notice of cancellation
70. Cancellation: recovery of money paid by debtor or hirer
71. Cancellation: repayment of credit
72. Cancellation: return of goods
73. Cancellation: goods given in part-exchange

Exclusion of certain agreements from Part V

74. Exclusion of certain agreements from Part V

PART VI

MATTERS ARISING DURING CURRENCY OF CREDIT OR HIRE AGREEMENTS

75. Liability of creditor for breaches by supplier
76. Duty to give notice before taking certain action
77. Duty to give information to debtor under fixed-sum credit agreement
78. Duty to give information to debtor under running-account credit agreement
79. Duty to give hirer information
80. Debtor or hirer to give information about goods
81. Appropriation of payments
82. Variation of agreements
83. Liability for misuse of credit facilities
84. Misuse of credit-tokens
85. Duty on issue of new credit-tokens
86. Death of debtor or hirer

Consumer Credit Act 1974

PART VII

DEFAULT AND TERMINATION

Default notices

Section
87 Need for default notice
88. Contents and effect of default notice
89. Compliance with default notice

Further restriction of remedies for default

90. Retaking of protected hire-purchase etc. goods
91. Consequences of breach of s. 90
92. Recovery of possession of goods or land
93. Interest not to be increased on default

Early payment by debtor

94. Right to complete payments ahead of time
95. Rebate on early settlement
96. Effect on linked transactions
97. Duty to give information

Termination of agreements

98. Duty to give notice of termination (non-default cases)
99. Right to terminate hire-purchase etc. agreements
100. Liability of debtor on termination of hire-purchase etc. agreement
101. Right to terminate hire agreement
102. Agency for receiving notice of rescission
103. Termination statements
104. Goods not to be treated as subject to landlord's hypothec in Scotland

PART VIII

SECURITY

General

105. Form and content of securities
106. Ineffective securities
107. Duty to give information to surety under fixed-sum credit agreement
108. Duty to give information to surety under running-account credit agreement
109. Duty to give information to surety under consumer hire agreement
110. Duty to give information to debtor or hirer
111. Duty to give surety copy of default etc. notice
112. Realisation of securities
113. Act not to be evaded by use of security

Pledges

114. Pawn-receipts
115. Penalty for failure to supply copies of pledge agreement etc.
116. Redemption period
117. Redemption procedure

Section
118. Loss etc. of pawn-receipt
119. Unreasonable refusal to deliver pawn
120. Consequence of failure to redeem
121. Realisation of pawn
122. Order in Scotland to deliver pawn

Negotiable instruments

123. Restrictions on taking and negotiating instruments
124. Consequences of breach of s. 123
125. Holders in due course

Land mortgages

126. Enforcement of land mortgages

PART IX

JUDICIAL CONTROL

Enforcement of certain regulated agreements and securities

127. Enforcement orders in cases of infringement
128. Enforcement orders on death of debtor or hirer

Extension of time

129. Time orders
130. Supplemental provisions about time orders

Protection of property pending proceedings

131. Protection orders

Hire and hire-purchase etc. agreements

132. Financial relief for hirer
133. Hire-purchase etc. agreements: special powers of court
134. Evidence of adverse detention in hire-purchase etc. cases

Supplemental provisions as to orders

135. Power to impose conditions, or suspend operation of order
136. Power to vary agreements and securities

Extortionate credit bargains

137. Extortionate credit bargains
138. When bargains are extortionate
139. Reopening of extortionate agreements
140. Interpretation of sections 137 to 139

Miscellaneous

141. Jurisdiction and parties
142. Power to declare rights of parties

Northern Ireland

Section
143. Jurisdiction of county court in Northern Ireland
144. Appeal from county court in Northern Ireland

PART X

ANCILLARY CREDIT BUSINESS

Definitions

145. Types of ancillary credit business
146. Exceptions from section 145

Licensing

147. Application of Part III
148. Agreement for services of unlicensed trader
149. Regulated agreements made on introductions by unlicensed credit-broker
150. Appeals to Secretary of State against licensing decisions

Seeking business

151. Advertisements
152. Application of sections 52 to 54 to credit brokerage etc.
153. Definition of canvassing off trade premises (agreements for ancillary credit services)
154. Prohibition of canvassing certain ancillary credit services off trade premises.
155. Right to recover brokerage fees.

Entry into agreements

156. Entry into agreements

Credit reference agencies

157. Duty to disclose name etc. of agency
158. Duty of agency to disclose filed information
159. Correction of wrong information
160. Alternative procedure for business consumers

PART XI

ENFORCEMENT OF ACT

161. Enforcement authorities
162. Powers of entry and inspection
163. Compensation for loss
164. Power to make test purchases etc.
165. Obstruction of authorised officers
166. Notification of convictions and judgments to Director
167. Penalties
168. Defences
169. Offences by bodies corporate
170. No further sanctions for breach of Act
171. Onus of proof in various proceedings

Section
172. Statements by creditor or owner to be binding
173. Contracting-out forbidden

PART XII

SUPPLEMENTAL

General

174. Restrictions on disclosure of information
175. Duty of persons deemed to be agents
176. Service of documents
177. Saving for registered charges
178. Local Acts

Regulations, orders etc.

179. Power to prescribe form etc. of secondary documents
180. Power to prescribe form etc. of copies
181. Power to alter monetary limits etc.
182. Regulations and orders
183. Determinations etc. by Director

Interpretation

184. Associates
185. Agreement with more than one debtor or hirer
186. Agreement with more than one creditor or owner
187. Arrangements between creditor and supplier
188. Examples of use of new terminology
189. Definitions

Miscellaneous

190. Financial provisions
191. Special provisions as to Northern Ireland
192. Transitional and commencement provisions, amendments and repeals
193. Short title and extent.

SCHEDULES:

Schedule 1—Prosecution and punishment of offences
Schedule 2—Examples of use of new terminology
Schedule 3—Transitional and commencement provisions
Schedule 4—Minor and consequential amendments
Schedule 5—Repeals

Consumer Credit Act 1974
Chapter 39

An Act to establish for the protection of consumers a new system, administered by the Director General of Fair Trading, of licensing and other control of traders concerned with the provision of credit, or the supply of goods on hire or hire-purchase, and their transactions, in place of the present enactments regulating moneylenders, pawnbrokers and hire-purchase traders and their transactions; and for related matters. [31st July 1974]

PART I

DIRECTOR GENERAL OF FAIR TRADING

1. General functions of Director

(1) It is the duty of the Director General of Fair Trading ('the Director')—

(*a*) to administer the licensing system set up by this Act,
(*b*) to exercise the adjudicating functions conferred on him by this Act in relation to the issue, renewal, variation, suspension and revocation of licences, and other matters,
(*c*) generally to superintend the working and enforcement of this Act, and regulations made under it, and
(*d*) where necessary or expedient, himself to take steps to enforce this Act, and regulations so made.

(2) It is the duty of the Director, so far as appears to him to be practicable and having regard both to the national interest and the interests of persons carrying on businesses to which this Act applies and their customers, to keep under review and from time to time advise the Secretary of State about—

(*a*) social and commercial developments in the United Kingdom and elsewhere relating to the provision of credit or bailment or (in Scotland) hiring of goods to individuals, and related activities; and
(*b*) the working and enforcement of this Act and orders and regulations made under it.

2. Powers of Secretary of State

(1) The Secretary of State may by order—

(*a*) confer on the Director additional functions concerning the provision of credit or bailment or (in Scotland) hiring of goods to individuals, and related activities, and
(*b*) regulate the carrying out by the Director of his functions under this Act.

(2) The Secretary of State may give general directions indicating considerations to which the Director should have particular regard in carrying out his functions under this Act, and may give specific directions on any matter connected with the carrying out by the Director of those functions.

(3) The Secretary of State, on giving any directions under subsection (2), shall

arrange for them to be published in such manner as he thinks most suitable for drawing them to the attention of interested persons.

(4) With the approval of the Secretary of State and the Treasury, the Director may charge, for any service or facility provided by him under this Act, a fee of an amount specified by general notice (the 'specified fee').

(5) Provision may be made under subsection (4) for reduced fees, or no fees at all, to be paid for certain services or facilities by persons of a specified description, and references in this Act to the specified fee shall, in such cases, be construed accordingly.

(6) An order under subsection (1)(*a*) shall be made by statutory instrument and shall be of no effect unless a draft of the order has been laid before and approved by each House of Parliament.

(7) References in subsection (2) to the functions of the Director under this Act do not include the making of a determination to which section 41 or 150 (appeals from Director to Secretary of State) applies.

3. Supervision by Council on Tribunals

The Tribunals and Inquiries Act 1971 is amended as follows (the amendments bringing the adjudicating functions of the Director under this Act under the supervision of the Council on Tribunals)—

(*a*) in section 8(2), insert '5A' after 'paragraph';
(*b*) in section 19(4), insert 'or the Director General of Fair Trading referred to in paragraph 5A' after 'or 46';
(*c*) in Schedule 1, after paragraph 5, insert—

'Consumer credit   5A. The Director General of Fair Trading, in respect of his functions under the Consumer Credit Act 1974 (c. 39), and any member of the Director's staff authorised to exercise those functions under paragraph 7 of Schedule 1 to the Fair Trading Act 1973.'

4. Dissemination of information and advice

The Director shall arrange for the dissemination, in such form and manner as he considers appropriate, of such information and advice as it may appear to him expedient to give to the public in the United Kingdom about the operation of this Act, the credit facilities available to them, and other matters within the scope of his functions under this Act.

5. Annual and other reports

At the end of subsection (2) of section 125 (annual and other reports of Director) of the Fair Trading Act 1973 insert 'and shall set out any directions given to the Director under section 2(2) of the Consumer Credit Act 1974 during that year'.

6. Form etc. of applications

(1) An application to the Director under this Act is of no effect unless the requirements of this section are satisfied.

(2) The application must be in writing, and in such form, and accompanied

by such particulars, as the Director may specify by general notice, and must be accompanied by the specified fee.

(3) After giving preliminary consideration to an application, the Director may by notice require the applicant to furnish him with such further information relevant to the application as may be described in the notice, and may require any information furnished by the applicant (whether at the time of the application or subsequently) to be verified in such manner as the Director may stipulate.

(4) The Director may by notice require the applicant to publish details of his application at a time or times and in a manner specified in the notice.

7. Penalty for false information

A person who, in connection with any application or request to the Director under this Act, or in response to any invitation or requirement of the Director under this Act, knowingly or recklessly gives information to the Director which, in a material particular, is false or misleading, commits an offence.

PART II

CREDIT AGREEMENTS, HIRE AGREEMENTS AND LINKED TRANSACTIONS

8. Consumer credit agreements

(1) A personal credit agreement is an agreement between an individual ('the debtor') and any other person ('the creditor') by which the creditor provides the debtor with credit of any amount.

(2) A consumer credit agreement is a personal credit agreement by which the creditor provides the debtor with credit not exceeding [£15,000.]

[*The figure in square brackets was substituted by the Consumer Credit (Increase of Monetary Limits) Order 1983, Article 4, Schedule, Part II (S.I. 1983 No. 1878).*]

(3) A consumer credit agreement is a regulated agreement within the meaning of this Act if it is not an agreement (an 'exempt agreement') specified in or under section 16.

9. Meaning of credit

(1) In this Act 'credit' includes a cash loan, and any other form of financial accommodation.

(2) Where credit is provided otherwise than in sterling it shall be treated for the purposes of this Act as provided in sterling of an equivalent amount.

(3) Without prejudice to the generality of subsection (1), the person by whom goods are bailed or (in Scotland) hired to an individual under a hire-purchase agreement shall be taken to provide him with fixed-sum credit to finance the transaction of an amount equal to the total price of the goods less the aggregate of the deposit (if any) and the total charge for credit.

(4) For the purposes of this Act, an item entering into the total charge for credit shall not be treated as credit even though time is allowed for its payment.

10. Running-account credit and fixed-sum credit

(1) For the purposes of this Act—

(a) running-account credit is a facility under a personal credit agreement whereby the debtor is enabled to receive from time to time (whether in his own person, or by another person) from the creditor or a third party cash, goods and services (or any of them) to an amount or value such that, taking into account payments made by or to the credit of the debtor, the credit limit (if any) is not at any time exceeded; and

(b) fixed-sum credit is any other facility under a personal credit agreement whereby the debtor is enabled to receive credit (whether in one amount or by instalments).

(2) In relation to running-account credit, 'credit limit' means, as respects any period, the maximum debit balance which, under the credit agreement, is allowed to stand on the account during that period, disregarding any term of the agreement allowing that maximum to be exceeded merely temporarily.

(3) For the purposes of section 8(2), running-account credit shall be taken not to exceed the amount specified in that subsection ('the specified amount') if—

(a) the credit limit does not exceed the specified amount; or
(b) whether or not there is a credit limit, and if there is, notwithstanding that it exceeds the specified amount,—

(i) the debtor is not enabled to draw at any one time an amount which, so far as (having regard to section 9(4)) it represents credit, exceeds the specified amount, or

(ii) the agreement provides that, if the debit balance rises above a given amount (not exceeding the specified amount), the rate of the total charge for credit increases or any other condition favouring the creditor or his associate comes into operation, or

(iii) at the time the agreement is made it is probable, having regard to the terms of the agreement and any other relevant considerations, that the debit balance will not at any time rise above the specified amount.

11. Restricted-use credit and unrestricted-use credit

(1) A restricted-use credit agreement is a regulated consumer credit agreement—

(a) to finance a transaction between the debtor and the creditor, whether forming part of that agreement or not, or
(b) to finance a transaction between the debtor and a person (the 'supplier') other than the creditor, or
(c) to refinance any existing indebtedness of the debtor, whether to the creditor or another person,

and 'restricted-use credit' shall be construed accordingly.

(2) An unrestricted-use credit agreement is a regulated consumer credit agreement not falling within subsection (1), and 'unrestricted-use credit' shall be construed accordingly.

(3) An agreement does not fall within subsecton (1) if the credit is in fact provided in such a way as to leave the debtor free to use it as he chooses, even though certain uses would contravene that or any other agreement.

(4) An agreement may fall within subsection (1)(*b*) although the identity of the supplier is unknown at the time the agreement is made.

12. Debtor-creditor-supplier agreements

A debtor-creditor-supplier agreement is a regulated consumer credit agreement being—

- (*a*) a restricted-use credit agreement which falls within section 11(1)(*a*), or
- (*b*) a restricted-use credit agreement which falls within section 11(1)(*b*) and is made by the creditor under pre-existing arrangements, or in contemplation of future arrangements, between himself and the supplier, or
- (*c*) an unrestricted-use credit agreement which is made by the creditor under pre-existing arrangements between himself and a person (the 'supplier') other than the debtor in the knowledge that the credit is to be used to finance a transaction between the debtor and the supplier.

13. Debtor-creditor agreements

A debtor-creditor agreement is a regulated consumer credit agreement being—

- (*a*) a restricted-use credit agreement which falls within section 11(1)(*b*) but is not made by the creditor under pre-existing arrangements, or in contemplation of future arrangements, between himself and the supplier, or
- (*b*) a restricted-use credit agreement which falls within section 11(1)(*c*), or
- (*c*) an unrestricted-use credit agreement which is not made by the creditor under pre-existing arrangements between himself and a person (the 'supplier') other than the debtor in the knowledge that the credit is to be used to finance a transaction between the debtor and the supplier.

14. Credit-token agreements

(1) A credit-token is a card, check, voucher, coupon, stamp, form, booklet or other document or thing given to an individual by a person carrying on a consumer credit business, who undertakes—

- (*a*) that on the production of it (whether or not some other action is also required) he will supply cash, goods and services (or any of them) on credit, or
- (*b*) that where, on the production of it to a third party (whether or not any other action is also required), the third party supplies cash, goods and services (or any of them), he will pay the third party for them (whether or not deducting any discount or commission), in return for payment to him by the individual.

(2) A credit-token agreement is a regulated agreement for the provision of credit in connection with the use of a credit-token.

(3) Without prejudice to the generality of section 9(1), the person who gives to an individual an undertaking falling within subsection (1)(*b*) shall be taken to provide him with credit drawn on whenever a third party supplies him with cash, goods or services.

(4) For the purposes of subsection (1), use of an object to operate a machine

provided by the person giving the object or a third party shall be treated as the production of the object to him.

15. Consumer hire agreements

(1) A consumer hire agreement is an agreement made by a person with an individual (the 'hirer') for the bailment or (in Scotland) the hiring of goods to the hirer, being an agreement which—

    (*a*) is not a hire-purchase agreement, and
    (*b*) is capable of subsisting for more than three months, and
    (*c*) does not require the hirer to make payments exceeding [£15,000.]

[*The figure in square brackets was increased by the Consumer Credit (Increase of Monetary Limits) Order 1983, Article 4, Schedule, Part II (S.I. 1983 No. 1878).*]

(2) A consumer hire agreement is a regulated agreement if it is not an exempt agreement.

16. Exempt agreements

(1) This Act does not regulate a consumer credit agreement where the creditor is a local authority [. . .], or a body specified, or of a description specified, in an order made by the Secretary of State, being—

    (*a*) an insurance company,
    (*b*) a friendly society,
    (*c*) an organisation of employers or organisation of workers,
    (*d*) a charity,
    (*e*) a land improvement company, [. . .]
    (*f*) a body corporate named or specifically referred to in any public general Act.
[(ff) a body corporate named or specifically referred to in an order made under—
        section 156(4), 444(1) or 447(2)(*a*) or the Housing Act 1985,
        section 2 of the Home Purchase Assistance and Housing Corporation Guarantee Act 1978 of section 31 of the Tenants' Rights, etc. (Scotland) Act 1980,
        or
        Article 154(1)(*a*) or 156AA of the Housing (Northern Ireland) Order 1981 or Article 10(6A) of the Housing (Northern Ireland) Order 1983; or]

[(*g*) a building society] [or

    (*h*) an authorised institution or wholly owned subsidiary (within the meaning of the Companies Act 1985) of such an institution]

[*Square brackets containing dots indicate words repealed by the Building Societies Act 1986, section 120 and Schedule 19, Part I*]

[*Paragraph (ff) was added by the Housing and Planning Act 1986, section 22. Paragraph (g) was added by the Building Societies Act 1986, section 120 and Schedule 18, paragraph 10. Paragraph (h) was added by the Banking Act 1987, section 88, with effect from 1st October 1987 (see S.I. 1987 No. 1664).*]

(2) Subsection (1) applies only where the agreement is—

    (*a*) a debtor-creditor-supplier agreement financing—

(i) the purchase of land, or
(ii) the provision of dwellings on any land, and secured by a land mortgage on that land; or
(b) a debtor-creditor agreement secured by any land mortgage; or
(c) a debtor-creditor-supplier agreement financing a transaction which is a linked transaction in relation to—
(i) an agreement falling within paragraph (a), or
(ii) an agreement falling within paragraph (b) financing—
(aa) the purchase of any land, or
(bb) the provision of dwellings on any land,
and secured by a land mortgage on the land referred to in paragraph (a) or, as the case may be, the land referred to in sub-paragraph (ii).

(3) The Secretary of State shall not make, vary or revoke an order—

(a) under subsection (1)(a) without consulting the Minister of the Crown responsible for insurance companies,
(b) under subsection (1)(b) [or (c)] without consulting the Chief Registrar of Friendly Societies,
(c) under subsection (1)(d) without consulting the Charity Commissioners, [...]
(d) under subsection (1)(e) [(f) or (ff)] without consulting any Minister of the Crown with responsibilities concerning the body in question[, or
(e) under subsection (1)(g) without consulting the Building Societies Commission and the Treasury] [or
(f) under subsection (1)(h) without consulting the Treasury and the Bank of England.]

[*The words in square brackets in subsection 3(b) were repealed, as respects England and Wales, by the Employment Protection Act 1975, section 125(3) and Schedule 18.*

The words in square brackets in subsection 3(c) were repealed by the Building Societies Act 1986, section 120 and Schedule 19, Part I.

The words in square brackets in subsection (3)(d) were substituted by the Housing and Planning Act 1986, section 22.

Subsection (3)(e) was added by the Building Societies Act 1986, section 120 and Schedule 18, paragraph 10(3).

Subsection 3(f) was added by the Banking Act 1987, section 88, at the same time as paragraph (h) was added to subsection (1) above)]

(4) An order under subsection (1) relating to a body may be limited so as to apply only to agreements by that body of a description specified in the order.

(5) The Secretary of State may by order provide that this Act shall not regulate other consumer credit agreements where—

(a) the number of payments to be made by the debtor does not exceed the number specified for that purpose in the order, or
(b) the rate of the total charge for credit does not exceed the rate so specified, or
(c) an agreement has a connection with a country outside the United Kingdom.

Consumer Credit Act 1974

(6) The Secretary of State may by order provide that this Act shall not regulate consumer hire agreements of a description specified in the order where—

(a) the owner is a body corporate authorised by or under any enactment to supply electricity, gas or water, and

(b) the subject of the agreement is a meter or metering equipment,

[or where the owner is a public telecommunications operator specified in the order].

[(6A) This Act does not regulate a consumer credit agreement where the creditor is a housing authority and the agreement is secured by a land mortgage of a dwelling.

(6B) In subsection (6A) 'housing authority' means—

(a) as regards England and Wales, an authority or body within section 80(1) of the Housing Act 1985 (the landlord condition for secure tenancies), other than a housing association or a housing trust which is a charity;

(b) as regards Scotland, a development corporation established under an order made, or having effect as if made under the New Towns (Scotland) Act 1968, the Scottish Special Housing Association or the Housing Corporation;

(c) as regards Northern Ireland, the Northern Ireland Housing Executive.]

[*The words in square brackets at the end of subsection (6) were amended by the Telecommunications Act 1984, s 109, Sch 4, para 60.*]

[*Subsections (6A) and (6B) were added by the Housing and Planning Act 1986, section 22.*]

(7) Nothing in this section affects the application of sections 137 to 140 (extortionate credit bargains).

(8) In the application of this section to Scotland subsection (3)(c) shall not have effect.

(9) In the application of this section to Northern Ireland subsection (3) shall have effect as if any reference to a Minister of the Crown were a reference to a Northern Ireland department, any reference to the Chief Registrar of Friendly Societies were a reference to the Registrar of Friendly Societies for Northern Ireland, and any reference to the Charity Commissioners were a reference to the Department of Finance for Northern Ireland.

17.

(1) A small agreement is—

(a) a regulated consumer credit agreement for credit not exceeding [£50], other than a hire-purchase or conditional sale agreement; or

(b) a regulated consumer hire agreement which does not require the hirer to make payments exceeding [£50].

being an agreement which is either unsecured or secured by a guarantee or indemnity only (whether or not the guarantee or indemnity is itself secured).

[*The figures in square brackets were amended by Consumer Credit (Increase of Monetary Limits) Order 1983, Article 3, Schedule, Part I (S.I. 1983 No. 1878).*]

Consumer Credit Act 1974

(2) Section 10(3)(*a*) applies for the purposes of subsection (1) as it applies for the purposes of section 8(2).

(3) Where—
- (*a*) two or more small agreements are made at or about the same time between the same parties, and
- (*b*) it appears probable that they would instead have been made as a single agreement but for the desire to avoid the operation of provisions of this Act which would have applied to that single agreement but, apart from this subsection, are not applicable to the small agreements,

this Act applies to the small agreements as if they were regulated agreements other than small agreements.

(4) If, apart from this subsection, subsection (3) does not apply to any agreements but would apply if, for any party or parties to any of the agreements, there were substituted an associate of that party, or associates of each of those parties, as the case may be, then subsection (3) shall apply to the agreements.

18. Multiple agreements

(1) This section applies to an agreement (a 'multiple agreement') if its terms are such as—
- (*a*) to place a part of it within one category of agreement mentioned in this Act, and another part of it within a different category of agreement so mentioned, or within a category of agreement not so mentioned, or
- (*b*) to place it, or a part of it, within two or more categories of agreement so mentioned.

(2) Where a part of an agreement falls within subsection (1), that part shall be treated for the purposes of this Act as a separate agreement.

(3) Where an agreement falls within subsection (1)(*b*), it shall be treated as an agreement in each of the categories in question, and this Act shall apply to it accordingly.

(4) Where under subsection (2) a part of a multiple agreement is to be treated as a separate agreement, the multiple agreement shall (with any necessary modifications) be construed accordingly; and any sum payable under the multiple agreement, if not apportioned by the parties, shall for the purposes of proceedings in any court relating to the multiple agreement be apportioned by the court as may be requisite.

(5) In the case of an agreement for running-account credit, a term of the agreement allowing the credit limit to be exceeded merely temporarily shall not be treated as a separate agreement or as providing fixed-sum credit in respect of the excess.

(6) This Act does not apply to a multiple agreement so far as the agreement relates to goods if under the agreement payments are to be made in respect of the goods in the form of rent (other than a rentcharge) issuing out of land.

19. Linked transactions

(1) A transaction entered into by the debtor or hirer, or a relative of his, with any other person ('the other party'), except one for the provision of security,

is a linked transaction in relation to an actual or prospective regulated agreement (the 'principal agreement') of which it does not form part if—
- (*a*) the transaction is entered into in compliance with a term of the principal agreement; or
- (*b*) the principal agreement is a debtor-creditor-supplier agreement and the transaction is financed, or to be financed, by the principal agreement; or
- (*c*) the other party is a person mentioned in subsection (2), and a person so mentioned initiated the transaction by suggesting it to the debtor or hirer, or his relative, who enters into it—
   - (i) to induce the creditor or owner to enter into the principal agreement, or
   - (ii) for another purpose related to the principal agreement, or
   - (iii) where the principal agreement is a restricted-use credit agreement, for a purpose related to a transaction financed, or to be financed, by the principal agreement.

(2) The persons referred to in subsection (1)(*c*) are—
- (*a*) the creditor or owner, or his associate;
- (*b*) a person who, in the negotiation of the transaction, is represented by a credit-broker who is also a negotiator in antecedent negotiations for the principal agreement;
- (*c*) a person who, at the time the transaction is initiated, knows that the principal agreement has been made or contemplates that it might be made.

(3) A linked transaction entered into before the making of the principal agreement has no effect until such time (if any) as that agreement is made.

(4) Regulations may exclude linked transactions of the prescribed description from the operation of subsection (3).

20. Total charge for credit

(1) The Secretary of State shall make regulations containing such provisions as appear to him appropriate for determining the true cost to the debtor of the credit provided or to be provided under an actual or prospective consumer credit agreement (the 'total charge for credit'), and regulations so made shall prescribe—
- (*a*) what items are to be treated as entering into the total charge for credit, and how their amount is to be ascertained;
- (*b*) the method of calculating the rate of the total charge for credit.

(2) Regulations under subsection (1) may provide for the whole or part of the amount payable by the debtor or his relative under any linked transaction to be included in the total charge for credit, whether or not the creditor is a party to the transaction or derives benefit from it.

PART III

LICENSING OF CREDIT AND HIRE BUSINESSES

Licensing principles

21. Businesses needing a licence

(1) Subject to this section, a licence is required to carry on a consumer credit business or consumer hire business.

(2) A local authority does not need a licence to carry on a business.

(3) A body corporate empowered by a public general Act naming it to carry on a business does not need a licence to do so.

22. Standard and group licences

(1) A licence may be—
  (*a*) a standard licence, that is a licence, issued by the Director to a person named in the licence on an application made by him, which, during the prescribed period, covers such activities as are described in the licence, or
  (*b*) a group licence, that is a licence, issued by the Director (whether on the application of any person or of his own motion), which, during such period as the Director thinks fit or, if he thinks fit, indefinitely, covers such persons and activities as are described in the licence.

(2) A licence is not assignable or, subject to section 37, transmissible on death or in any other way.

(3) Except in the case of a partnership or an unincorporated body of persons, a standard licence shall not be issued to more than one person.

(4) A standard licence issued to a partnership or an unincorporated body of persons shall be issued in the name of the partnership or body.

(5) The Director may issue a group licence only if it appears to him that the public interest is better served by doing so than by obliging the persons concerned to apply separately for standard licences.

(6) The persons covered by a group licence may be described by general words, whether or not coupled with the exclusion of named persons, or in any other way the Director thinks fit.

(7) The fact that a person is covered by a group licence in respect of certain activities does not prevent a standard licence being issued to him in respect of those activities or any of them.

(8) A group licence issued on the application of any person shall be issued to that person, and general notice shall be given of the issue of any group licence (whether on application or not).

23. Authorisation of specific activities

(1) Subject to this section, a licence to carry on a business covers all lawful activities done in the course of that business, whether by the licensee or other persons on his behalf.

(2) A licence may limit the activities it covers, whether by authorising the licensee to enter into certain types of agreement only, or in any other way.

(3) A licence covers the canvassing off trade premises of debtor-creditor-supplier agreements or regulated consumer hire agreements only if, and to the extent that, the licence specifically so provides; and such provision shall not be included in a group licence.

(4) Regulations may be made specifying other activities which, if engaged in by or on behalf of the person carrying on a business, require to be covered by an express term in his licence.

24. Control of name of business

A standard licence authorises the licensee to carry on a business under the name or names specified in the licence, but not under any other name.

25. Licensee to be a fit person

(1) A standard licence shall be granted on the application of any person if he satisfies the Director that—

> (a) he is a fit person to engage in activities covered by the licence, and
> (b) the name or names under which he applies to be licensed is or are not misleading or otherwise undesirable.

(2) In determining whether an applicant for a standard licence is a fit person to engage in any activities, the Director shall have regard to any circumstances appearing to him to be relevant, and in particular any evidence tending to show that the applicant, or any of the applicant's employees, agents or associates (whether past or present) or, where the applicant is a body corporate, any person appearing to the Director to be a controller of the body corporate or an associate of any such person, has—

> (a) committed any offence involving fraud or other dishonesty, or violence,
> (b) contravened any provision made by or under this Act, or by or under any other enactment regulating the provision of credit to individuals or other transactions with individuals,
> (c) practised discrimination on grounds of sex, colour, race or ethnic or national origins in, or in connection with, the carrying on of any business, or
> (d) engaged in business practices appearing to the Director to be deceitful or oppressive, or otherwise unfair or improper (whether unlawful of not).

(3) In subsection (2), 'associate', in addition to the persons specified in section 184, includes a business associate.

26. Conduct of business

Regulations may be made as to the conduct by a licensee of his business, and may in particular specify—

> (a) the books and other records to be kept by him, and
> (b) the information to be furnished by him to persons with whom he does business or seeks to do business, and the way it is to be furnished.

Issue of licences

27. Determination of applications

(1) Unless the Director determines to issue a licence in accordance with an application he shall, before determining the application, by notice—

- (*a*) inform the applicant, giving his reasons, that, as the case may be, he is minded to refuse the application, or to grant it in terms different from those applied for, describing them, and
- (*b*) invite the applicant to submit to the Director representations in support of his application in accordance with section 34.

(2) If the Director grants the application in terms different from those applied for then, whether or not the applicant appeals, the Director shall issue the licence in the terms approved by him unless the applicant by notice informs him that he does not desire a licence in those terms.

28. Exclusion from group licence

Where the Director is minded to issue a group licence (whether on the application of any person or not), and in doing so to exclude any person from the group by name, he shall, before determining the matter,—

- (*a*) give notice of that fact to the person proposed to be excluded, giving his reasons, and
- (*b*) invite that person to submit to the Director representations against his exclusion in accordance with section 34.

Renewal, variation, suspension and revocation of licences

29. Renewal

(1) If the licensee under a standard licence, or the original applicant for, or any licensee under, a group licence of limited duration, wishes the Director to renew the licence, whether on the same terms (except as to expiry) or on varied terms, he must, during the period specified by the Director by general notice or such longer period as the Director may allow, make an application to the Director for its renewal.

(2) The Director may of his own motion renew any group licence.

(3) The preceding provisions of this Part apply to the renewal of a licence as they apply to the issue of a licence, except that section 28 does not apply to a person who was already excluded in the licence up for renewal.

(4) Until the determination of an application under subsection (1) and, where an appeal lies from the determination, until the end of the appeal period, the licence shall continue in force, notwithstanding that apart from this subsection it would expire earlier.

(5) On the refusal of an application under this section, the Director may give directions authorising a licensee to carry into effect agreements made by him before the expiry of the licence.

(6) General notice shall be given of the renewal of a group licence.

30. Variation by request

(1) On an application made by the licensee, the Director may if he thinks fit by notice to the licensee vary a standard licence in accordance with the application.

(2) In the case of a group licence issued on the application of any person, the Director, on an application made by that person, may if he thinks fit by notice to that person vary the terms of the licence in accordance with the application; but the Director shall not vary a group licence under this subsection by excluding a named person, other than the person making the request, unless that named person consents in writing to his exclusion.

(3) In the case of a group licence from which (whether by name or description) a person is excluded, the Director, on an application made by that person, may if he thinks fit, by notice to that person, vary the terms of the licence so as to remove the exclusion.

(4) Unless the Director determines to vary a licence in accordance with an application he shall, before determining the application, by notice—

(*a*) inform the applicant, giving his reasons, that he is minded to refuse the application, and

(*b*) invite the applicant to submit to the Director representations in support of his application in accordance with section 34.

(5) General notice shall be given that a variation of a group licence has been made under this section.

31. Compulsory variation

(1) Where at a time during the currency of a licence the Director is of the opinion that, if the licence had expired at that time, he would, on an application for its renewal or further renewal on the same terms (except as to expiry), have been minded to grant the application but on different terms, and that therefore the licence should be varied, he shall proceed as follows.

(2) In the case of a standard licence the Director shall, by notice—

(*a*) inform the licensee of the variations the Director is minded to make in the terms of the licence, stating his reasons, and

(*b*) invite him to submit to the Director representations as to the proposed variations in accordance with section 34.

(3) In the case of a group licence the Director shall—

(*a*) give general notice of the variations he is minded to make in the terms of the licence, stating his reasons, and

(*b*) in the notice invite any licensee to submit to him representations as to the proposed variations in accordance with section 34.

(4) In the case of a group licence issued on application the Director shall also—

(*a*) inform the original applicant of the variations the Director is minded to make in the terms of the licence, stating his reasons, and

(*b*) invite him to submit to the Director representations as to the proposed variations in accordance with section 34.

(5) If the Director is minded to vary a group licence by excluding any person (other than the original applicant) from the group by name the Director shall, in addition, take the like steps under section 28 as are required in the case mentioned in that section.

(6) General notice shall be given that a variation of any group licence has been made under this section.

(7) A variation under this section shall not take effect before the end of the appeal period.

32. Suspension and revocation

(1) Where at a time during the currency of a licence the Director is of the opinion that if the licence had expired at that time he would have been minded not to renew it, and that therefore it should be revoked or suspended, he shall proceed as follows.

(2) In the case of a standard licence the Director shall, by notice—

  (*a*) inform the licensee that, as the case may be, the Director is minded to revoke the licence, or suspend it until a specified date or indefinitely, stating his reasons, and
  (*b*) invite him to submit representations as to the proposed revocation or suspension in accordance with section 34.

(3) In the case of a group licence the Director shall—

  (*a*) give general notice that, as the case may be, he is minded to revoke the licence, or suspend it until a specified date or indefinitely, stating his reasons, and
  (*b*) in the notice invite any licensee to submit to him representations as to the proposed revocation or suspension in accordance with section 34.

(4) In the case of a group licence issued on application the Director shall also—

  (*a*) inform the original applicant that, as the case may be, the Director is minded to revoke the licence, or suspend it until a specified date or indefinitely, stating his reasons, and
  (*b*) invite him to submit representations as to the proposed revocation or suspension in accordance with section 34.

(5) If he revokes or suspends the licence, the Director may give directions authorising a licensee to carry into effect agreements made by him before the revocation or suspension.

(6) General notice shall be given of the revocation or suspension of a group licence.

(7) A revocation or suspension under this section shall not take effect before the end of the appeal period.

(8) Except for the purposes of section 29, a licensee under a suspended licence shall be treated, in respect of the period of suspension, as if the licence had not been issued; and where the suspension is not expressed to end on a specified date it may, if the Director thinks fit, be ended by notice given by him to the licensee or, in the case of a group licence, by general notice.

33. Application to end suspension

(1) On an application made by a licensee the Director may, if he thinks fit, by notice to the licensee end the suspension of a licence, whether the suspension was for a fixed or indefinite period.

(2) Unless the Director determines to end the suspension in accordance with the application he shall, before determining the application, by notice—

(*a*) inform the applicant, giving his reasons, that he is minded to refuse the application, and
(*b*) invite the applicant to submit to the Director representations in support of his application in accordance with section 34.

(3) General notice shall be given that a suspension of a group licence has been ended under this section.

(4) In the case of a group licence issued on application—

(*a*) the references in subsection (1) to a licensee include the original applicant;
(*b*) the Director shall inform the original applicant that a suspension of a group licence has been ended under this section.

Miscellaneous

34. Representations to Director

(1) Where this section applies to an invitation by the Director to any person to submit representations, the Director shall invite that person, within 21 days after the notice containing the invitation is given to him or published, or such longer period as the Director may allow,—

(*a*) to submit his representations in writing to the Director, and
(*b*) to give notice to the Director, if he thinks fit, that he wishes to make representations orally,

and where notice is given under paragraph (*b*) the Director shall arrange for the oral representations to be heard.

(2) In reaching his determination the Director shall take into account any representations submitted or made under this section.

(3) The Director shall give notice of his determination to the persons who were required to be invited to submit representations about it or, where the invitation to submit representations was required to be given by general notice, shall give general notice of the determination.

35. The register

(1) The Director shall establish and maintain a register, in which he shall cause to be kept particulars of—

(*a*) applications not yet determined for the issue, variation or renewal of licences, or for ending the suspension of a licence;
(*b*) licences which are in force, or have at any time been suspended or revoked, with details of any variation of the terms of a licence;
(*c*) decisions given by him under this Act, and any appeal from those decisions; and
(*d*) such other matters (if any) as he thinks fit.

(2) The Director shall give general notice of the various matters required to be entered in the register, and of any change in them made under subsection (1)(*d*).

(3) Any person shall be entitled on payment of the specified fee—

   (*a*) to inspect the register during ordinary office hours and take copies of any entry, or
   (*b*) to obtain from the Director a copy, certified by the Director to be correct, of any entry in the register.

(4) The Director may, if he thinks fit, determine that the right conferred by subsection (3)(*a*) shall be exercisable in relation to a copy of the register instead of, or in addition to, the original.

(5) The Director shall give general notice of the place or places where, and times when, the register or a copy of it may be inspected.

36. Duty to notify changes

(1) Within 21 working days after a change takes place in any particulars entered in the register in respect of a standard licence or the licensee under section 35(1)(*d*) (not being a change resulting from action taken by the Director), the licensee shall give the Director notice of the change; and the Director shall cause any necessary amendment to be made in the register.

(2) Within 21 working days after—

   (*a*) any change takes place in the officers of—
      (i) a body corporate, or an unincorporated body of persons, which is the licensee under a standard licence, or
      (ii) a body corporate which is a controller of a body corporate which is such a licensee, or
   (*b*) a body corporate which is such a licensee becomes aware that a person has become or ceased to be a controller of the body corporate, or
   (*c*) any change takes place in the members of a partnership which is such a licensee (including a change on the amalgamation of the partnership with another firm, or a change whereby the number of partners is reduced to one),

the licensee shall give the Director notice of the change.

(3) Within 14 working days after any change takes place in the officers of a body corporate which is a controller of another body corporate which is a licensee under a standard licence, the controller shall give the licensee notice of the change.

(4) Within 14 working days after a person becomes or ceases to be a controller of a body corporate which is a licensee under a standard licence, that person shall give the licensee notice of the fact.

(5) Where a change in a partnership has the result that the business ceases to be carried on under the name, or any of the names, specified in a standard licence the licence shall cease to have effect.

(6) Where the Director is given notice under subsection (1) or (2) of any change, and subsection (5) does not apply, the Director may by notice require the licensee to furnish him with such information, verified in such manner, as the Director may stipulate.

37. Death, bankruptcy etc. of licensee

(1) A licence held by one individual terminates if he—

(*a*) dies, or
(*b*) is adjudged bankrupt, or
(*c*) becomes a patient within the meaning of Part VIII of the Mental Health Act 1959.

(2) In relation to a licence held by one individual, or a partnership or other unincorporated body of persons, or a body corporate, regulations may specify other events relating to the licensee on the occurrence of which the licence is to terminate.

(3) Regulations may—

(*a*) provide for the termination of a licence by subsection (1), or under subsection (2), to be deferred for a period not exceeding 12 months, and
(*b*) authorise the business of the licensee to be carried on under the licence by some other person during the period of deferment, subject to such conditions as may be prescribed.

(4) This section does not apply to group licences.

38. Application of s. 37 to Scotland and Northern Ireland

(1) In the application of section 37 to Scotland the following shall be substituted for paragraphs (*b*) and (*c*) of subsection (1)—

'(*b*) has his estate sequestrated, or
(*c*) becomes incapable of managing his own affairs.'

(2) In the application of section 37 to Northern Ireland the following shall be substituted for subsection (1)—

'(1) A licence held by one individual terminates if—

(*a*) he dies, or
(*b*) he is adjudged bankrupt or his estate and effects vest in the official assignee under section 349 of the Irish Bankrupt and Insolvent Act 1857, or
(*c*) a delcaration is made under section 15 of the Lunacy Regulation (Ireland) Act 1871 that he is of unsound mind and incapable of managing his person or property, or an order is made under section 68 of that Act in consequence of its being found that he is of unsound mind and incapable of managing his affairs.'

39. Offences against Part III

(1) A person who engages in any activities for which a licence is required when he is not a licensee under a licence covering those activities commits an offence.

(2) A licensee under a standard licence who carries on business under a name not specified in the licence commits an offence.

(3) A person who fails to give the Director or a licensee notice under section 36 within the period required commits an offence.

40. Enforcement of agreements made by unlicensed trader

(1) A regulated agreement, other than a non-commercial agreement, if made when the creditor or owner was unlicensed, is enforceable against the debtor or hirer only where the Director has made an order under this section which applies to the agreement.

(2) Where during any period an unlicensed person (the 'trader') was carrying on a consumer credit business or consumer hire business, he or his successor in title may apply to the Director for an order that regulated agreements made by the trader during that period are to be treated as if he had been licensed.

(3) Unless the Director determines to make an order under subsection (2) in accordance with the application, he shall, before determining the application, by notice—

- (a) inform the applicant, giving his reasons, that, as the case may be, he is minded to refuse the application, or to grant it in terms different from those applied for, describing them, and
- (b) invite the applicant to submit to the Director representations in support of his application in accordance with section 34.

(4) In determining whether or not to make an order under subsection (2) in respect of any period the Director shall consider, in addition to any other relevant factors—

- (a) how far, if at all, debtors or hirers under regulated agreements made by the trader during that period were prejudiced by the trader's conduct.
- (b) whether or not the Director would have been likely to grant a licence covering that period on an application by the trader, and
- (c) the degree of culpability for the failure to obtain a licence.

(5) If the Director thinks fit, he may in an order under subsection (2)—

- (a) limit the order to specified agreements, or agreements of a specified description or made at a specified time;
- (b) make the order conditional on the doing of specified acts by the applicant.

41. Appeals to Secretary of State under Part III

(1) If, in the case of a determination by the Director such as is mentioned in column 1 of the table set out at the end of this section, a person mentioned in relation to that determination in column 2 of the table is aggrieved by the determination he may, within the prescribed period, and in the prescribed manner, appeal to the Secretary of State.

(2) Regulations may make provision as to the persons by whom (on behalf of the Secretary of State) appeals under this section are to be heard, the manner in which they are to be conducted, and any other matter connected with such appeals.

(3) On an appeal under this section, the Secretary of State may give such directions for disposing of the appeal as he thinks just, including a direction for the payment of costs by any party to the appeal.

(4) A direction under subsection (3) for payment of costs may be made a rule of the High Court on the application of the party in whose favour it is given.

(5) In Scotland a direction under subsection (3) for payment of expenses may be enforced in like manner as a recorded decree arbitral.

TABLE

Determination	Appellant
Refusal to issue, renew or vary licence in accordance with terms of application.	The applicant.
Exclusion of person from group licence.	The person excluded.
Refusal to give directions in respect of a licensee under section 29(5) or 32(5).	The licensee.
Compulsory variation, or suspension or revocation, of standard licence.	The licensee.
Compulsory variation, or suspension or revocation, of group licence.	The original applicant or any licensee.
Refusal to end suspension of licence in accordance with terms of application.	The applicant.
Refusal to make order under section 40(2) in accordance with terms of application.	The applicant.

42. Further appeal on point of law

(1) In section 13 of the Tribunals and Inquiries Act 1971 (subsection (1) of which provides that on a point of law an appeal shall lie to the High Court from a decision of any tribunal mentioned in that subsection or the tribunal may be required to state a case for the opinion of the High Court), insert the following new subsection after subsection (5)—

'(5A) Subsection (1) of this section shall apply to a decision of the Secretary of State on an appeal under section 41 of the Consumer Credit Act 1974 from a determination of the Director General of Fair Trading as it applies to a decision of any of the tribunals mentioned in that subsection, but with the substitution for the reference to a party to proceedings of a reference to any person who had a right to appeal to the Secretary of State (whether or not he has exercised that right); and accordingly references in subsections (1) and (3) of this section to a tribunal shall be construed, in relation to such an appeal, as references to the Secretary of State.'

(2) In subsection (6)(*a*) of the said section 13 (application to Scotland), after the word 'commissioners' there shall be inserted the words 'or on an appeal under section 41 of the Consumer Credit Act 1974 by a company registered in Scotland or by any other person whose principal or prospective principal place of business in the United Kingdom is in Scotland'.

(3) In subsection (7) of the said section 13 (application to Northern Ireland) after 'subsection (1) of this section' insert 'and in relation to a decision of the Secretary of State on an appeal under section 41 of the Consumer Credit Act 1974 by a company registered in Northern Ireland or by any other person whose

principal or prospective principal place of business in the United Kingdom is in Northern Ireland.'

PART IV

Seeking Business

Advertising

43. Advertisements to which Part IV applies

(1) This Part applies to any advertisement, published for the purposes of a business carried on by the advertiser, indicating that he is willing—

- (*a*) to provide credit, or
- (*b*) to enter into an agreement for the bailment or (in Scotland) the hiring of goods by him.

(2) An advertisement does not fall within subsection (1) if the advertiser does not carry on—

- (*a*) a consumer credit business or consumer hire business, or
- (*b*) a business in the course of which he provides credit to individuals secured on land, or
- (*c*) a business which comprises or relates to unregulated agreements where—
    - (i) the proper law of the agreement is the law of a country outside the United Kingdom, and
    - (ii) if the proper law of the agreement were the law of a part of the United Kingdom it would be a regulated agreement.

(3) An advertisement does not fall within subsection (1)(*a*) if it indicates—

- (*a*) that the credit must exceed [£15,000,] and that no security is required, or the security is to consist of property other than land, or
- (*b*) that the credit is available only to a body corporate.

[*The figure in square brackets was substituted by the Consumer Credit (Increase of Monetary Limits) Order 1983, Article 4, Schedule, Part II (S.I. 1983 No. 1878).*]

(4) An advertisement does not fall within subsection (1)(*b*) if it indicates that the advertiser is not willing to enter into a consumer hire agreement.

(5) The Secretary of State may by order provide that this Part shall not apply to other advertisements of a description specified in the order.

44. Form and content of advertisements

(1) The Secretary of State shall make regulations as to the form and content of advertisements to which this Part applies, and the regulations shall contain such provisions as appear to him appropriate with a view to ensuring that, having regard to its subject-matter and the amount of detail included in it, an advertisement conveys a fair and reasonably comprehensive indication of the nature of the credit or hire facilities offered by the advertiser and of their true cost to persons using them.

(2) Regulations under subsection (1) may in particular—

- (*a*) require specified information to be included in the prescribed manner in advertisements, and other specified material to be excluded;
- (*b*) contain requirements to ensure that specified information is clearly

brought to the attention of persons to whom advertisements are directed, and that one part of an advertisement is not given insufficient or excessive prominence compared with another.

45. Prohibition of advertisement where goods etc. not sold for cash

If an advertisement to which this Part applies indicates that the advertiser is willing to provide credit under a restricted-use credit agreement relating to goods or services to be supplied by any person, but at the time when the advertisement is published that person is not holding himself out as prepared to sell the goods or provide the services (as the case may be) for cash, the advertiser commits an offence.

46. False or misleading advertisements

(1) If an advertisement to which this Part applies conveys information which in a material respect is false or misleading the advertiser commits an offence.

(2) Information stating or implying an intention on the advertiser's part which he has not got is false.

47. Advertising infringements

(1) Where an advertiser commits an offence against regulations made under section 44 or against section 45 or 46 or would be taken to commit such an offence but for the defence provided by section 168, a like offence is committed by—

    (*a*) the publisher of the advertisement, and
    (*b*) any person who, in the course of a business carried on by him, devised the advertisement, or a part of it relevant to the first-mentioned offence, and
    (*c*) where the advertiser did not procure the publication of the advertisement, the person who did procure it.

(2) In proceedings for an offence under subsection (1)(*a*) it is a defence for the person charged to prove that—

    (*a*) the advertisement was published in the course of a business carried on by him, and
    (*b*) he received the advertisement in the course of that business, and did not know and had no reason to suspect that its publication would be an offence under this Part.

Canvassing etc.

48. Definition of canvassing off trade premises (regulated agreements)

(1) An individual (the 'canvasser') canvasses a regulated agreement off trade premises if he solicits the entry (as debtor or hirer) of another individual (the 'consumer') into the agreement by making oral representations to the consumer, or any other individual, during a visit by the canvasser to any place (not excluded by subsection (2)) where the consumer, or that other individual, as the case may be, is, being a visit—

    (*a*) carried out for the purpose of making such oral representations to individuals who are at that place, but
    (*b*) not carried out in response to a request made on a previous occasion.

(2) A place is excluded from subsection (1) if it is a place where a business is carried on (whether on a permanent or temporary basis) by—

   (*a*) the creditor or owner, or
   (*b*) a supplier, or
   (*c*) the canvasser, or the person whose employee or agent the canvasser is, or
   (*d*) the consumer.

49. Prohibition of canvassing debtor-creditor agreements off trade premises

(1) It is an offence to canvass debtor-creditor agreements off trade premises.

(2) It is also an offence to solicit the entry of an individual (as debtor) into a debtor-creditor agreement during a visit carried out in response to a request made on a previous occasion, where—

   (*a*) the request was not in writing signed by or on behalf of the person making it, and
   (*b*) if no request for the visit had been made, the soliciting would have constituted the canvassing of a debtor-creditor agreement off trade premises.

(3) Subsections (1) and (2) do not apply to any soliciting for an agreement enabling the debtor to overdraw on a current account of any description kept with the creditor, where—

   (*a*) the Director has determined that current accounts of that description kept with the creditor are excluded from subsections (1) and (2), and
   (*b*) the debtor already keeps an account with the creditor (whether a current account or not).

(4) A determination under subsection (3)(*a*)—

   (*a*) may be made subject to such conditions as the Director thinks fit, and
   (*b*) shall be made only where the Director is of opinion that it is not against the interests of debtors.

(5) If soliciting is done in breach of a condition imposed under subsection (4)(*a*), the determination under subsection (3)(*a*) does not apply to it.

50. Circulars to minors

(1) A person commits an offence who, with a view to financial gain, sends to a minor any document inviting him to—

   (*a*) borrow money, or
   (*b*) obtain goods on credit or hire, or
   (*c*) obtain services on credit, or
   (*d*) apply for information or advice on borrowing money or otherwise obtaining credit, or hiring goods.

(2) In proceedings under subsection (1) in respect of the sending of a document to a minor, it is a defence for the person charged to prove that he did not know, and had no reasonable cause to suspect, that he was a minor.

(3) Where a document is received by a minor at any school or other educational establishment for minors, a person sending it to him at that establishment knowing

or suspecting it to be such an establishment shall be taken to have reasonable cause to suspect that he is a minor.

51. Prohibition of unsolicited credit-tokens

(1) It is an offence to give a person a credit-token if he has not asked for it.

(2) To comply with subsection (1) a request must be contained in a document signed by the person making the request, unless the credit-token agreement is a small debtor-creditor-supplier agreement.

(3) Subsection (1) does not apply to the giving of a credit-token to a person—

  (*a*) for use under a credit-token agreement already made, or
  (*b*) in renewal or replacement of a credit-token previously accepted by him under a credit-token agreement which continues in force, whether or not varied.

Miscellaneous

52. Quotations

(1) Regulations may be made—

  (*a*) as to the form and content of any document (a 'quotation') by which a person who carried on a consumer credit business or consumer hire business, or a business in the course of which he provides credit to individuals secured on land, gives prospective customers information about the terms on which he is prepared to do business;
  (*b*) requiring a person carrying on such a business to provide quotations to such persons and in such circumstances as are prescribed.

(2) Regulations under subsection (1)(*a*) may in particular contain provisions relating to quotations such as are set out in relation to advertisements in section 44.

53. Duty to display information

Regulations may require a person who carries on a consumer credit business or consumer hire business, or a business in the course of which he provides credit to individuals secured on land, to display in the prescribed manner, at any premises where the business is carried on to which the public have access, prescribed information about the business.

54. Conduct of business regulations

Without prejudice to the generality of section 26, regulations under that section may include provisions further regulating the seeking of business by a licensee who carries on a consumer credit business or a consumer hire business.

PART V

Entry into Credit or Hire Agreements

Preliminary matters

55. Disclosure of information

(1) Regulations may require specified information to be disclosed in the prescribed manner to the debtor or hirer before a regulated agreement is made.

(2) A regulated agreement is not properly executed unless regulations under subsection (1) were complied with before the making of the agreement.

56. Antecedent negotiations

(1) In this Act 'antecedent negotiations' means any negotiations with the debtor or hirer—

- (*a*) conducted by the creditor or owner in relation to the making of any regulated agreement, or
- (*b*) conducted by a credit-broker in relation to goods sold or proposed to be sold by the credit-broker to the creditor before forming the subject-matter of a debtor-creditor-supplier agreement within section 12(*a*), or
- (*c*) conducted by the supplier in relation to a transaction financed or proposed to be financed by a debtor-creditor-supplier agreement within section 12(*b*) or (*c*),

and 'negotiator' means the person by whom negotiations are so conducted with the debtor or hirer.

(2) Negotiations with the debtor in a case falling within subsection (1)(*b*) or (*c*) shall be deemed to be conducted by the negotiator in the capacity of agent of the creditor as well as in his actual capacity.

(3) An agreement is void if, and to the extent that, it purports in relation to an actual or prospective regulated agreement—

- (*a*) to provide that a person acting as, or on behalf of, a negotiator is to be treated as the agent of the debtor or hirer, or
- (*b*) to relieve a person from liability for acts or omissions of any person acting as, or on behalf of, a negotiator.

(4) For the purposes of this Act, antecedent negotiations shall be taken to begin when the negotiator and the debtor or hirer first enter into communication (including communication by advertisement), and to include any representations made by the negotiator to the debtor or hirer and any other dealings between them.

57. Withdrawal from prospective agreement

(1) The withdrawal of a party from a prospective regulated agreement shall operate to apply this Part to the agreement, any linked transaction and any other thing done in anticipation of the making of the agreement as it would apply if the agreement were made and then cancelled under section 69.

(2) The giving to a party of a written or oral notice which, however expressed, indicates the intention of the other party to withdraw from a prospective regulated agreement operates as a withdrawal from it.

(3) Each of the following shall be deemed to be the agent of the creditor or owner for the purpose of receiving a notice under subsection (2)—

- (*a*) a credit-broker or supplier who is the negotiator in antecedent negotiations, and

(b) any person who, in the course of a business carried on by him, acts on behalf of the debtor or hirer in any negotiations for the agreement.

(4) Where the agreement, if made, would not be a cancellable agreement, subsection (1) shall nevertheless apply as if the contrary were the case.

58. Opportunity for withdrawal from prospective land mortgage

(1) Before sending to the debtor or hirer, for his signature, an unexecuted agreement in a case where the prospective regulated agreement is to be secured on land (the 'mortgaged land'), the creditor or owner shall give the debtor or hirer a copy of the unexecuted agreement which contains a notice in the prescribed form indicating the right of the debtor or hirer to withdraw from the prospective agreement, and how and when the right is exercisable, together with a copy of any other document referred to in the unexecuted agreement.

(2) Subsection (1) does not apply to—

(a) a restricted-use credit agreement to finance the purchase of the mortgaged land, or
(b) an agreement for a bridging loan in connection with the purchase of the mortgaged land or other land.

59. Agreement to enter future agreement void

(1) An agreement is void if, and to the extent that, it purports to bind a person to enter as debtor or hirer into a prospective regulated agreement.

(2) Regulations may exclude from the operation of subsection (1) agreements such as are described in the regulations.

Making the agreement

60. Form and content of agreements

(1) The Secretary of State shall make regulations as to the form and content of documents embodying regulated agreements, and the regulations shall contain such provisions as appear to him appropriate with a view to ensuring that the debtor or hirer is made aware of—

(a) the rights and duties conferred or imposed on him by the agreement,
(b) the amount and rate of the total charge for credit (in the case of a consumer credit agreement),
(c) the protection and remedies available to him under this Act, and
(d) any other matters which, in the opinion of the Secretary of State, it is desirable for him to know about in connection with the agreement.

(2) Regulations under subsection (1) may in particular—

(a) require specified information to be included in the prescribed manner in documents, and other specified material to be excluded;
(b) contain requirements to ensure that specified information is clearly brought to the attention of the debtor or hirer, and that one part of a document is not given insufficient or excessive prominence compared with another.

(3) If, on an application made to the Director by a person carrying on a consumer credit business or a consumer hire business, it appears to the Director impracticable for the applicant to comply with any requirement of regulations

under subsection (1) in a particular case, he may, by notice to the applicant direct that the requirement be waived or varied in relation to such agreements, and subject to such conditions (if any), as he may specify, and this Act and the regulations shall have effect accordingly.

(4) The Director shall give a notice under subsection (3) only if he is satisfied that to do so would not prejudice the interests of debtor or hirers.

61. Signing of agreement

(1) A regulated agreement is not properly executed unless—

  (*a*) a document in the prescribed form itself containing all the prescribed terms and conforming to regulations under section 60(1) is signed in the prescribed manner both by the debtor or hirer and by or on behalf of the creditor or owner, and
  (*b*) the document embodies all the terms of the agreement, other than implied terms, and
  (*c*) the document is, when presented or sent to the debtor or hirer for signature, in such a state that all its terms are readily legible.

(2) In addition, where the agreement is one to which section 58(1) applies, it is not properly executed unless—

  (*a*) the requirements of section 58(1) were complied with, and
  (*b*) the unexecuted agreement was sent, for his signature, to the debtor or hirer by post not less than seven days after a copy of it was given to him under section 58(1), and
  (*c*) during the consideration period, the creditor or owner refrained from approaching the debtor or hirer (whether in person, by telephone or letter, or in any other way) except in response or letter, or in any other way) except in response to a specific request made by the debtor or hirer after the beginning of the consideration period, and
  (*d*) no notice of withdrawal by the debtor or hirer was received by the creditor or owner before the sending of the unexecuted agreement.

(3) In subsection (2)(*c*), 'the consideration period' means the period beginning with the giving of the copy under section 58(1) and ending—

  (*a*) at the expiry of seven days after the day on which the unexecuted agreement is sent, for his signature, to the debtor or hirer, or
  (*b*) on its return by the debtor or hirer after signature by him,

whichever first occurs.

(4) Where the debtor or hirer is a partnership or an unincorporated body of persons, subsection (1)(*a*) shall apply with the substitution for 'by the debtor or hirer' of 'by or on behalf of the debtor or hirer'.

62. Duty to supply copy of unexecuted agreement

(1) If the unexecuted agreement is presented personally to the debtor or hirer for his signature, but on the occasion when he signs it the document does not become an executed agreement, a copy of it, and of any other document referred to in it, must be there and then delivered to him.

(2) If the unexecuted agreement is sent to the debtor or hirer for his signature,

a copy of it, and of any other document referred to in it, must be sent to him at the same time.

(3) A regulated agreement is not properly executed if the requirements of this section are not observed.

63. Duty to supply copy of executed agreement

(1) If the unexecuted agreement is presented personally to the debtor or hirer for his signature, and on the occasion when he signs it the document becomes an executed agreement, a copy of the executed agreement, and of any other document referred to in it, must be there and then delivered to him.

(2) A copy of the executed agreement, and of any other document referred to in it, must be given to the debtor or hirer within the seven days following the making of the agreement unless—

   (*a*) subsection (1) applies, or
   (*b*) the unexecuted agreement was sent to the debtor or hirer for his signautre and, on the occasion of his signing it, the document became an executed agreement.

(3) In the case of a cancellable agreement, a copy under subsection (2) must be sent by post.

(4) In the case of a credit-token agreement, a copy under subsection (2) need not be given within the seven days following the making of the agreement if it is given before or at the time when the credit-token is given to the debtor.

(5) A regulated agreement is not properly executed if the requirements of this section are not observed.

64. Duty to give notice of cancellation rights

(1) In the case of a cancellable agreement, a notice in the prescribed form indicating the right of the debtor or hirer to cancel the agreement, how and when that right is exercisable, and the name and address of a person to whom notice of cancellation may be given,—

   (*a*) must be included in every copy given to the debtor or hirer under section 62 or 63, and
   (*b*) except where section 63(2) applied, must also be sent by post to the debtor or hirer within the seven days following the making of the agreement.

(2) In the case of a credit-token agreement, a notice under subsection (1)(*b*) need not be sent by post within the seven days following the making of the agreement if either—

   (*a*) it is sent by post to the debtor or hirer before the credit-token is given to him, or
   (*b*) it is sent by post to him together with the credit-token.

(3) Regulations may provide that except where section 63(2) applied a notice sent under subsection (1)(*b*) shall be accompanied by a further copy of the executed agreement, and of any other document referred to in it.

(4) Regulations may provide that subsection (1)(*b*) is not to apply in the case

of agreements such as are described in the regulations, being agreements made by a particular person, if—

- (*a*) on an application by that person to the Director, the Director has determined that, having regard to—
  - (i) the manner in which antecedent negotiations for agreements with the applicant of that description are conducted, and
  - (ii) the information provided to debtors or hirers before such agreements are made,

  the requirement imposed by subsection (1)(*b*) can be dispensed with without prejudicing the interests of debtor or hirers; and
- (*b*) any conditions imposed by the Director in making the determination are complied with.

(5) A cancellable agreement is not properly executed if the requirements of this section are not observed.

65. Consequences of improper execution

(1) An improperly executed regulated agreement is enforceable against the debtor or hirer on an order of the court only.

(2) A retaking of goods or land to which a regulated agreement relates is an enforcement of the agreement.

66. Acceptance of credit-tokens

(1) The debtor shall not be liable under a credit-token agreement for use made of the credit-token by any person unless the debtor had previously accepted the credit-token, or the use constituted an acceptance of it by him.

(2) The debtor accepts a credit-token when—

- (*a*) it is signed, or
- (*b*) a receipt for it is signed, or
- (*c*) it is first used,

either by the debtor himself or by a person who, pursuant to the agreement, is authorised by him to use it.

Cancellation of certain agreements within cooling-off period

67. Cancellable agreements

A regulated agreement may be cancelled by the debtor or hirer in accordance with this Part if the antecedent negotiations included oral representations made when in the presence of the debtor or hirer by an individual acting as, or on behalf of, the negotiator, unless—

- (*a*) the agreement is secured on land, or is a restricted-use credit agreement to finance the purchase of land or is an agreement for a bridging loan in connection with the purchase of land, or
- (*b*) the unexecuted agreement is signed by the debtor or hirer at premises at which any of the following is carrying on any business (whether on a permanent or temporary basis)—
  - (i) the creditor or owner;
  - (ii) any party to a linked transaction (other than the debtor or hirer or a relative of his);

(iii) the negotiator in any antecedent negotiations.

68. Cooling-off period

The debtor or hirer may serve notice of cancellation of a cancellable agreement between his signing of the executed agreement and—

(*a*) the end of the fifth day following the day on which he received a copy under section 63(2) or a notice under section 64(1)(*b*), or

(*b*) if (by virtue of regulations made under section 64(4)) section 64(1)(*b*) does not apply, the end of the fourteenth day following the day on which he signed the unexecuted agreement.

69. Notice of cancellation

(1) If within the period specified in section 68 the debtor or hirer under a cancellable agreement serves on—

(*a*) the creditor or owner, or
(*b*) the person specified in the notice under section 64(1), or
(*c*) a person who (whether by virtue of subsection (6) or otherwise) is the agent of the creditor or owner,

a notice (a 'notice of cancellation') which, however expressed and whether or not conforming to the notice given under section 64(1), indicates the intention of the debtor or hirer to withdraw from the agreement, the notice shall operate—

(i) to cancel the agreement, and any linked transaction, and
(ii) to withdraw any offer by the debtor or hirer, or his relative, to enter into a linked transaction.

(2) In the case of a debtor-creditor-supplier agreement for restricted-use credit financing—

(*a*) the doing of work or supply of goods to meet an emergency, or
(*b*) the supply of goods which, before service of the notice of cancellation, had by the act of the debtor or his relative become incorporated in any land or thing not comprised in the agreement or any linked transaction,

subsection (1) shall apply with the substitution of the following for paragraph (i)—

'(i) to cancel only such provisions of the agreement and any linked transaction as—
(*aa*) relate to the provision of credit, or
(*bb*) require the debtor to pay an item in the total charge for credit, or
(*cc*) subject the debtor to any obligation other than to pay for the doing of the said work, or the supply of the said goods'.

(3) Except so far as is otherwise provided, references in this Act to the cancellation of an agreement or transaction do not include a case within subsection (2).

(4) Except as otherwise provided by or under this Act, an agreement or transaction cancelled under subsection (1) shall be treated as if it had never been entered into.

(5) Regulations may exclude linked transactions of the prescribed description from subsection (1)(i) or (ii).

(6) Each of the following shall be deemed to be the agent of the creditor or owner for the purpose of receiving a notice of cancellation—

  (*a*) a credit-broker or supplier who is the negotiator in antecedent negotiations, and
  (*b*) any person who, in the course of a business carried on by him, acts on behalf of the debtor or hirer in any negotiations for the agreement.

(7) Whether or not it is actually received by him, a notice of cancellation sent by post to a person shall be deemed to be served on him at the time of posting.

70. Cancellation: recovery of money paid by debtor or hirer

(1) On the cancellation of a regulated agreement, and of any linked transaction,—

  (*a*) any sum paid by the debtor or hirer, or his relative, under or in contemplation of the agreement or transaction, including any item in the total charge for credit, shall become repayable, and
  (*b*) any sum, including any item in the total charge for credit, which but for the cancellation is, or would or might become, payable by the debtor or hirer, or his relative, under the agreement or transaction shall cease to be, or shall not become, so payable, and
  (*c*) in the case of a debtor-creditor-supplier agreement falling within section 12(*b*), any sum paid on the debtor's behalf by the creditor to the supplier shall become repayable to the creditor.

(2) If, under the terms of a cancelled agreement or transaction, the debtor or hirer, or his relative, is in possession of any goods, he shall have a lien on them for any sum repayable to him under subsection (1) in respect of that agreement or transaction, or any other linked transaction

(3) A sum repayable under subsection (1) is repayable by the person to whom it was originally paid, but in the case of a debtor-creditor-supplier agreement falling within section 12(*b*) the creditor and the supplier shall be under a joint and several liability to repay sums paid by the debtor, or his relative, under the agreement or under a linked transaction falling within section 19(1)(*b*) and accordingly, in such a case, the creditor shall be entitled, in accordance with rules of court, to have the supplier made a party to any proceedings brought against the creditor to recover any such sums.

(4) Subject to any agreement between them, the creditor shall be entitled to be indemnified by the supplier for loss suffered by the creditor in satisfying his liability under subsection (3), including costs reasonably incurred by him in defending proceedings instituted by the debtor.

(5) Subsection (1) does not apply to any sum which, if not paid by a debtor, would be payable by virtue of section 71, and applies to a sum paid or payable by a debtor for the issue of a credit-token only where the credit-token has been returned to the creditor or surrendered to a supplier.

(6) If the total charge for credit includes an item in respect of a fee or commission charged by a credit-broker, the amount repayable under subsection (1) in respect of that item shall be the excess over [£3] of the fee or commission.

[*The figure in square brackets was substituted by the Consumer Credit (Increase of Monetary Amounts) Order 1983, Article 4, Schedule, Part II (S.I. 1983 No. 1571).*]

(7) If the total charge for credit includes any sum payable or paid by the debtor to a credit-broker otherwise than in respect of a fee or commission charged by him, that sum shall for the purposes of subsection (6) be treated as if it were such a fee or commission.

(8) So far only as is necessary to give effect to section 69(2), this section applies to an agreement or transaction within that subsection as it applies to a cancelled agreement or transaction.

71. Cancellation: repayment of credit

(1) Notwithstanding the cancellation of a regulated consumer credit agreement, other than a debtor-creditor-supplier agreement for restricted-use credit, the agreement shall continue in force so far as it relates to repayment of credit and payment of interest.

(2) If, following the cancellation of a regulated consumer credit agreement, the debtor repays the whole or a portion of the credit—

(*a*) before the expiry of one month following service of the notice of cancellation, or
(*b*) in the case of a credit repayable by instalments, before the date on which the first instalment is due,

no interest shall be payable on the amount repaid.

(3) If the whole of a credit repayable by instalments is not repaid on or before the date specified in subsection (2)(*b*), the debtor shall not be liable to repay any of the credit except on receipt of a request in writing in the prescribed form, signed by or on behalf of the creditor, stating the amounts of the remaining instalments (recalculated by the creditor as nearly as may be in accordance with the agreement and without extending the repayment period), but excluding any sum other than principal and interest.

(4) Repayment of a credit, or payment of interest, under a cancelled agreement shall be treated as duly made if it is made to any person on whom, under section 69, a notice of cancellation could have been served, other than a person referred to in section 69(6)(*b*).

72. Cancellation: cancellation return of goods

(1) This section applies where any agreement or transaction relating to goods, being—

(*a*) a restricted-use debtor-creditor-supplier agreement, a consumer hire agreement, or a linked transaction to which the debtor or hirer under any regulated agreement is a party, or
(*b*) a linked transaction to which a relative of the debtor or hirer under any regulated agreement is a party,

is cancelled after the debtor or hirer (in a case within paragraph (*a*)) or the relative (in a case within paragraph (*b*)) has acquired possession of the goods by virtue of the agreement or transaction.

(2) In this section—

(a) 'the possessor' means the person who has acquired possession of the goods as mentioned in subsection (1),
   (b) 'the other party' means the person from whom the possessor acquired possession, and
   (c) 'the pre-cancellation period' means the period beginning when the possessor acquired possession and ending with the cancellation.

(3) The possessor shall be treated as having been under a duty throughout the pre-cancellation period—
   (a) to retain possession of the goods, and
   (b) to take reasonable care of them.

(4) On the cancellation, the possessor shall be under a duty, subject to any lien, to restore the goods to the other party in accordance with this section, and meanwhile to retain possession of the goods and take reasonable care of them.

(5) The possessor shall not be under any duty to deliver the goods except at his own premises and in pursuance of a request in writing signed by or on behalf of the other party and served on the possessor either before, or at the time when, the goods are collected from those premises.

(6) If the possessor—
   (a) delivers the goods (whether at his own premises or elsewhere) to any person on whom, under section 69, a notice of cancellation could have been served (other than a person referred to in section 69(6)(b)), or
   (b) sends the goods at his own expense to such a person,

he shall be discharged from any duty to retain the goods or deliver them to any person.

(7) Where the possessor delivers the goods as mentioned in subsection (6)(a), his obligation to take care of the goods shall cease; and if he sends the goods as mentioned in subsection (6)(b), he shall be under a duty to take reasonable care to see that they are received by the other party and not damaged in transit, but in other respects his duty to take care of the goods shall cease.

(8) Where, at any time during the period of 21 days following the cancellation, the possessor receives such a request as is mentioned in subsection (5), and unreasonably refuses or unreasonably fails to comply with it, his duty to take reasonable care of the goods shall continue until he delivers or sends the goods as mentioned in subsection (6), but if within that period he does not receive such a request his duty to take reasonable care of the goods shall cease at the end of that period.

(9) The preceding provisions of this section do not apply to—
   (a) perishable goods, or
   (b) goods which by their nature are consumed by use and which, before the cancellation, were so consumed, or
   (c) goods supplied to meet an emergency, or
   (d) goods which, before the cancellation, had become incorporated in any land or thing not comprised in the cancelled agreement or a linked transaction.

(10) Where the address of the possessor is specified in the executed agreement, references in this section to his own premises are to that address and no other.

(11) Breach of a duty imposed by this section is actionable as a breach of statutory duty.

73. Cancellation: goods given in part-exchange

(1) This section applies on the cancellation of a regulated agreement where, in antecedent negotiations, the negotiator agreed to take goods in part-exchange (the 'part-exchange goods') and those goods have been delivered to him.

(2) Unless, before the end of the period of ten days beginning with the date of cancellation, the part-exchange goods are returned to the debtor or hirer in a condition substantially as good as when they were delivered to the negotiator, the debtor or hirer shall be entitled to recover from the negotiator a sum equal to the part-exchange allowance (as defined in subsection (7)(*b*)).

(3) In the case of a debtor-creditor-supplier agreement within section 12(*b*), the negotiator and the creditor shall be under a joint and several liability to pay to the debtor a sum recoverable under subsection (2).

(4) Subject to any agreement between them, the creditor shall be entitled to be indemnified by the negotiator for loss suffered by the creditor in satisfying his liability under subsection (3), including costs reasonably incurred by him in defending proceedings instituted by the debtor.

(5) During the period of ten days beginning with the date of cancellation, the debtor or hirer, if he is in possession of goods to which the cancelled agreement relates, shall have a lien on them for—

(*a*) delivery of the part-exchange goods, in a condition substantially as good as when they were delivered to the negotiator, or
(*b*) a sum equal to the part-exchange allowance;

and if the lien continues to the end of that period it shall thereafter subsist only as a lien for a sum equal to the part-exchange allowance.

(6) Where the debtor or hirer recovers from the negotiator or creditor, or both of them jointly, a sum equal to the part-exchange allowance, then, if the title of the debtor or hirer to the part-exchange goods has not vested in the negotiator, it shall so vest on the recovery of that sum.

(7) For the purposes of this section—

(*a*) the negotiator shall be treated as having agreed to take goods in part-exchange if, in pursuance of the antecedent negotiations, he either purchased or agreed to purchase those goods or accepted or agreed to accept them as part of the consideration for the cancelled agreement, and
(*b*) the part-exchange allowance shall be the sum agreed as such in the antecedent negotiations or, if no such agreement was arrived at, such sum as it would have been reasonable to allow in respect of the part-exchange goods if no notice of cancellation had been served.

(8) In an action brought against the creditor for a sum recoverable under subsection (2), he shall be entitled, in accordance with rules of court, to have the negotiator made a party to the proceedings.

Exclusion of certain agreements from Part V

74. Exclusion of certain agreements from Part V

(1) This Part (except section 56) does not apply to—

(*a*) a non-commercial agreement, or

(*b*) a debtor-creditor agreement enabling the debtor to overdraw on a current account, or

(*c*) a debtor-creditor agreement to finance the making of such payments arising on, or connected with, the death of a person as may be prescribed.

(2) This Part (except sections 55 and 56) does not apply to a small debtor-creditor-supplier agreement for restricted-use credit.

[(2A) In the case of an agreement to which the Consumer Protection (Cancellation of Contracts Concluded away from Business Premises) Regulations 1987 apply the reference in subsection (2) to a small agreement shall be construed as if in section 17(1)(*a*) and (*b*) '£35' were substituted for '£50'.]

(3) Subsection (1)(*b*) or (*c*) applies only where the Director so determines, and such a determination—

(*a*) may be made subject to such conditions as the Director thinks fit, and

(*b*) shall be made only if the Director is of opinion that it is not against the interests of debtors.

[(3A) Notwithstanding anything in subsection (3)(*b*) above, in relation to a debtor-creditor agreement under which the creditor is the Bank of England or a bank within the meaning of the Bankers' Books Evidence Act 1879, the Director shall make a determination that subsection (1)(*b*) above applies unless he considers that it would be against the public interest to do so.]

(4) If any term of an agreement falling within subsection (1) . . . (*c*) or (2) is expressed in writing, regulations under section 60(1) shall apply to that term (subject to section 60(3)) as if the agreement were a regulated agreement not falling within subsection (1) . . .(*c*) or (2).

[*Subsection (2A) was added, with effect from 1 July 1988, by the Consumer Protection (Cancellation of Contracts Concluded away from Business Premises) Regulations 1987, (S.I. 1987 No. 2117).*]

[*Subsection (3A) was added, and the words in subsection (4) deleted, by the Banking Act 1979, s 38(1), which was brought into force on 1 October 1979 by the Banking Act 1979 (Commencement No. 1) Order 1979 (S.I. 1979 No. 938).*]

PART VI

MATTERS ARISING DURING CURRENCY OF CREDIT OR HIRE AGREEMENTS

75. Liability of creditor for breaches by supplier

(1) If the debtor under a debtor-creditor-supplier agreement falling within section 12(*b*) or (*c*) has, in relation to a transaction financed by the agreement, any claim against the supplier in respect of a misrepresentation or breach of contract, he shall have a like claim against the creditor, who, with the supplier, shall accordingly be jointly and severally liable to the debtor.

(2) Subject to any agreement between them, the creditor shall be entitled to be indemnified by the supplier for loss suffered by the creditor in satisfying

his liability under subsection (1), including costs reasonably incurred by him in defending proceedings instituted by the debtor.

(3) Subsection (1) does not apply to a claim—

(*a*) under a non-commercial agreement, or
(*b*) so far as the claim relates to any single item to which the supplier has attached a cash price not exceeding [£100] or more than [£30,000].

[*The figures in square brackets were amended by Consumer Credit (Increase of Monetary Limits) Order 1983, Articles 3 and 4, Schedule, Parts I and II (S.I. 1983 No. 1878).*]

(4) This section applies notwithstanding that the debtor, in entering into the transaction, exceeded the credit limit or otherwise contravened any term of the agreement.

(5) In an action brought against the creditor under subsection (1) he shall be entitled, in accordance with rules of court, to have the supplier made a party to the proceedings.

76. Duty to give notice before taking certain action

(1) The creditor or owner is not entitled to enforce a term of a regulated agreement by—

(*a*) demanding earlier payment of any sum, or
(*b*) recovering possession of any goods or land, or
(*c*) treating any right conferred on the debtor or hirer by the agreement as terminated, restricted or deferred,

except by or after giving the debtor or hirer not less than seven days' notice of his intention to do so.

(2) Subsection (1) applies only where—

(*a*) a period for the duration of the agreement is specified in the agreement, and
(*b*) that period has not ended when the creditor or owner does an act mentioned in subsection (1),

but so applies notwithstanding that, under the agreement, any party is entitled to terminate it before the end of the period so specified.

(3) A notice under subsection (1) is ineffective if not in the prescribed form.

(4) Subsection (1) does not prevent a creditor from treating the right to draw on any credit as restricted or deferred and taking such steps as may be necessary to make the restriction or deferment effective.

(5) Regulations may provide that subsection (1) is not to apply to agreements described by the regulations.

(6) Subsection (1) does not apply to a right of enforcement arising by reason of any breach by the debtor or hirer of the regulated agreement.

77. Duty to given information to debtor under fixed-sum credit agreement

(1) The creditor under a regulated agreement for fixed-sum credit, within the prescribed period after receiving a request in writing that effect from the debtor and payment of a fee of [50] new pence, shall give the debtor a copy of the

Consumer Credit Act 1974

executed agreement (if any) and of any other document referred to in it, together with a statement signed by or on behalf of the creditor showing, according to the information to which it is practicable for him to refer,—

(a) the total sum paid under the agreement by the debtor;

(b) the total sum which has become payable under the agreement by the debtor but remains unpaid, and the various amount comprised in that total sum, with the date when each became due; and

(c) the total sum which is to become payable under the agreement by the debtor, and the various amounts comprised in that total sum, with the date, or mode of determining the date, when each becomes due.

[*The figure in square brackets was substituted by the Consumer Credit (Increase of Monetary Amounts) Order 1983, Article 4, Schedule, Part II (S.I. 1983 No. 1571).*]

(2) If the creditor possesses insufficient information to enable him to ascertain the amounts and dates mentioned in subsection (1)(c), he shall be taken to comply with that paragraph if his statement under subsection (1) gives the basis on which, under the regulated agreement, they would fall to be ascertained.

(3) Subsection (1) does not apply to—

(a) an agreement under which no sum is, or will or may become, payable by the debtor, or

(b) a request made less than one month after a previous request under that subsection relating to the same agreement was complied with.

(4) If the creditor under an agreement fails to comply with subsection (1)—

(a) he is not entitled, while the default continues, to enforce the agreement; and

(b) if the default continues for one month he commits an offence.

(5) This section does not apply to a non-commercial agreement.

78. Duty to give information to debtor under running-account credit agreement

(1) The creditor under a regulated agreement for running-account credit, within the prescribed period after receiving a request in writing to that effect from the debtor and payment of a fee of [50] new pence, shall give the debtor a copy of the executed agreement (if any) and of any other document referred to in it, together with a statement signed by or on behalf of the creditor showing, according to the information to which it is practicable for him to refer,—

(a) the state of the account, and

(b) the amount, if any, currently payable under the agreement by the debtor to the creditor, and

(c) the amounts and due dates of any payments which, if the debtor does not draw further on the account, will later become payable under the agreement by the debtor to the creditor.

[*The figure in square brackets was substituted by the Consumer Credit (Increase of Monetary Amounts) Order 1983, Article 4, Schedule, Part II (S.I. 1983 No. 1571).*]

(2) If the creditor possesses insufficient information to enable him to ascertain the amounts and dates mentioned in subsection (1)(c), he shall be taken to comply

with that paragraph if his statement under subsection (1) gives the basis on which, under the regulated agreement, they would fall to be ascertained.

(3) Subsection (1) does not apply to—

(*a*) an agreement under which no sum is, or will or may become, payable by the debtor, or
(*b*) a request made less than one month after a previous request under that subsection relating to the same agreement was complied with.

(4) Where running-account credit is provided under a regulated agreement, the creditor shall give the debtor statements in the prescribed form, and with the prescribed contents—

(*a*) showing according to the information to which it is practicable for him to refer, the state of the account at regular intervals of not more than twelve months, and
(*b*) where the agreement provides, in relation to specified periods, for the making of payments by the debtor, or the charging against him of interest or any other sum, showing according to the information to which it is practicable for him to refer the state of the account at the end of each of those periods during which there is any movement in the account.

(5) A statement under subsection (4) shall be given within the prescribed period after the end of the period to which the statement relates.

(6) If the creditor under an agreement fails to comply with subsection (1)—

(*a*) he is not entitled, while the default continues, to enforce the agreement; and
(*b*) if the default continues for one month he commits an offence.

(7) This section does not apply to a non-commercial agreement, and subsections (4) and (5) do not apply to a small agreement.

79. Duty to give hirer information

(1) The owner under a regulated consumer hire agreement, within the prescribed period after receiving a request in writing to that effect from the hirer and payment of a fee of [50] new pence, shall give to the hirer a copy of the executed agreement and of any other document referred to in it, together with a statement signed by or on behalf of the owner showing, according to the information to which it is practicable for him to refer, the total sum which has become payable under the agreement by the hirer but remains unpaid and the various amounts comprised in that total sum, with the date when each became due.

[*The figure in square brackets was substituted by the Consumer Credit (Increase of Monetary Amounts) Order 1983, Article 4, Schedule, Part II (S.I. 1983 No. 1571).*]

(2) Subsection (1) does not apply to—

(*a*) an agreement under which no sum is, or will or may become, payable by the hirer, or
(*b*) a request made less than one month after a previous request under that subsection relating to the same agreement was complied with.

(3) If the owner under an agreement fails to comply with subsection (1)—

Consumer Credit Act 1974

(*a*) he is not entitled, while the default continues, to enforce the agreement; and

(*b*) if the default continues for one month he commits an offence.

(4) This section does not apply to a non-commercial agreement.

80. Debtor or hirer to give information about goods

(1) Where a regulated agreement, other than a non-commercial agreement, requires the debtor or hirer to keep goods to which the agreement relates in his possession or control, he shall, within seven working days after he has received a request in writing to that effect from the creditor or owner, tell the creditor or owner where the goods are.

(2) If the debtor or hirer fails to comply with subsection (1), and the default continues for 14 days, he commits an offence.

81. Appropriation of payments

(1) Where a debtor or hirer is liable to make to the same person payments in respect of two or more regulated agreements, he shall be entitled, on making any payment in respect of the agreements which is not sufficient to discharge the total amount then due under all the agreements, to appropriate the sum so paid by him—

(*a*) in or towards the satisfaction of the sum due under any one of the agreements, or

(*b*) in or towards the satisfaction of the sums due under any two or more of the agreements in such proportions as he thinks fit.

(2) If the debtor or hirer fails to make any such appropriation where one or more of the agreements is—

(*a*) a hire-purchase agreement or conditional sale agreement, or

(*b*) a consumer hire agreement, or

(*c*) an agreement in relation to which any security is provided,

the payment shall be appropriated towards the satisfaction of the sums due under the several agreements respectively in the proportions which those sums bear to one another.

82. Variation of agreements

(1) Where, under a power contained in a regulated agreement, the creditor or owner varies the agreement, the variation shall not take effect before notice of it is given to the debtor or hirer in the prescribed manner.

(2) Where an agreement (a 'modifying agreement') varies or supplements an earlier agreement, the modifying agreement shall for the purposes of this Act be treated as—

(*a*) revoking the earlier agreement, and

(*b*) containing provisions reproducing the combined effect of the two agreements,

and obligations outstanding in relation to the earlier agreement shall accordingly be treated as outstanding instead in relation to the modifying agreement.

(3) If the earlier agreement is a regulated agreement but (apart from this

Consumer Credit Act 1974

subsection) the modifying agreement is not then, unless the modifying agreement is for running-account credit, it shall be treated as a regulated agreement.

(4) If the earlier agreement is a regulated agreement for running-account credit, and by the modifying agreement the creditor allows the credit limit to be exceeded but intends the excess to be merely temporary, Part V (except section 56) shall not apply to the modifying agreement.

(5) If—
- (*a*) the earlier agreement is a cancellable agreement, and
- (*b*) the modifying agreement is made within the period applicable under section 68 to the earlier agreement,

then, whether or not the modifying agreement would, apart from this subsection, be a cancellable agreement, it shall be treated as a cancellable agreement in respect of which a notice may be served under section 68 not later than the end of the period applicable under that section to the earlier agreement.

(6) Except under subsection (5), a modifying agreement shall not be treated as a cancellable agreement.

(7) This section does not apply to a non-commercial agreement.

83. Liability for misuse of credit facilities

(1) The debtor under a regulated consumer credit agreement shall not be liable to the creditor for any loss arising from use of the credit facility by another person not acting, or to be treated as acting, as the debtor's agent.

(2) This section does not apply to a non-commercial agreement, or to any loss in so far as it arises from misuse of an instrument to which section 4 of the Cheques Act 1957 applies.

84. Misuse of credit-tokens

(1) Section 83 does not prevent the debtor under a credit-token agreement from being made liable to the extent of [£50] (or the credit limit if lower) for loss to the creditor arising from use of the credit-token by other persons during a period beginning when the credit-token ceases to be in the possession of any authorised person and ending when the credit-token is once more in the possession of an authorised person.

[*The figure in square brackets was substituted by the Consumer Credit (Increase of Monetary Amounts) Order 1983, Article 4, Schedule, Part II (S.I. 1983 No. 1571).*]

(2) Section 83 does not prevent the debtor under a credit-token agreement from being made liable to any extent for loss to the creditor from use of the credit-token by a person who acquired possession of it with the debtor's consent.

(3) Subsections (1) and (2) shall not apply to any use of the credit-token after the creditor has been given oral or written notice that it is lost or stolen, or is for any other reason liable to misuse.

(4) Subsections (1) and (2) shall not apply unless there are contained in the credit-token agreement in the prescribed manner particulars of the name, address and telephone number of a person stated to be the person to whom notice is to be given under subsection (3).

(5) Notice under subsection (3) takes effect when received, but where it is given orally, and the agreement so requires, it shall be treated as not taking effect if not confirmed in writing within seven days.

(6) Any sum paid by the debtor for the issue of the credit-token, to the extent (if any) that it is not been previously offset by use made of the credit-token, shall be treated as paid towards satisfaction of any liability under subsection (1) or (2).

(7) The debtor, the creditor, and any person authorised by the debtor to use the credit-token, shall be authorised persons for the purposes of subsection (1).

(8) Where two or more credit-tokens are given under one credit-token agreement, the preceding provisions of this section apply to each credit-token separately.

85. Duty on issue of new credit-tokens

(1) Whenever, in connection with a credit-token agreement, a credit-token (other than the first) is given by the creditor to the debtor, the creditor shall give the debtor a copy of the executed agreement (if any) and of any other document referred to in it.

(2) If the creditor fails to comply with this section—

    (*a*) he is not entitled, while the default continues, to enforce the agreement; and

    (*b*) if the default continues for one month he commits an offence.

(3) This section does not apply to a small agreement.

86. Death of debtor or hirer

(1) The creditor or owner under a regulated agreement is not entitled, by reason of the death of the debtor or hirer, to do an act specified in paragraphs (*a*) to (*e*) of section 87(1) if at the death the agreement is fully secured.

(2) If at the death of the debtor or hirer a regulated agreement is only partly secured or is unsecured, the creditor or owner is entitled, by reason of the death of the debtor or hirer, to do an act specified in paragraphs (*a*) to (*e*) of section 87(1) on an order of the court only.

(3) This section applies in relation to the termination of an agreement only where—

    (*a*) a period for its duration is specified in the agreement, and

    (*b*) that period has not ended when the creditor or owner purports to terminate the agreement,

but so applies notwithstanding that, under the agreement, any party is entitled to terminate it before the end of the period so specified.

(4) This section does not prevent the creditor from treating the right to draw on any credit as restricted or deferred, and taking such steps as may be necessary to make the restriction or deferment effective.

(5) This section does not affect the operation of any agreement providing for payment of sums—

    (*a*) due under the regulated agreement, or

(b) becoming due under it on the death of the debtor or hirer,

out of the proceeds of a policy of assurance on his life.

(6) For the purposes of this section an act is done by reason of the death of the debtor or hirer if it is done under a power conferred by the agreement which is—

(a) exercisable on his death, or
(b) exercisable at will and exercised at any time after his death.

PART VII

DEFAULT AND TERMINATION

Default notices

87. Need for default notice

(1) Service of a notice on the debtor or hirer in accordance with section 88 (a 'default notice') is necessary before the creditor or owner can become entitled, by reason of any breach by the debtor or hirer of a regulated agreement,—

(a) to terminate the agreement, or
(b) to demand earlier payment of any sum, or
(c) to recover possession of any goods or land, or
(d) to treat any right conferred on the debtor or hirer by the agreement as terminated, restricted or deferred, or
(e) to enforce any security

(2) Subsection (1) does not prevent the creditor from treating the right to draw upon any credit as restricted or deferred, and taking such steps as may be necessary to make the restriction or deferment effective.

(3) The doing of an act by which a floating charge becomes fixed is not enforcement of a security.

(4) Regulations may provide that subsection (1) is not to apply to agreements described by the regulations.

88. Contents and effect of default notice

(1) The default notice must be in the prescribed form and specify—

(a) the nature of the alleged breach;
(b) if the breach is capable of remedy, what action is required to remedy it and the date before which that action is to be taken;
(c) if the breach is not capable of remedy, the sum (if any) required to be paid as compensation for the breach, and the date before which it is to be paid.

(2) A date specified under subsection (1) must not be less than seven days after the date of service of the default notice, and the creditor or owner shall not take action such as is mentioned in section 87(1) before the date so specified or (if no requirement is made under subsection (1)) before those seven days have elapsed.

(3) The default notice must not treat as a breach failure to comply with a provision of the agreement which becomes operative only on breach of some other provision, but if the breach of that other provision is not duly remedied

or compensation demanded under subsection (1) is not duly paid, or (where no requirement is made under subsection (1)) if the seven days mentioned in subsection (2) have elapsed, the creditor or owner may treat the failure as a breach and section 87(1) shall not apply to it.

(4) The default notice must contain information in the prescribed terms about the consequences of failure to comply with it.

(5) A default notice making a requirement under subsection (1) may include a provision for the taking of action such as is mentioned in section 87(1) at any time after the restriction imposed by subsection (2) will cease, together with a statement that the provision will be ineffective if the breach is duly remedied or the compensation duly paid.

89. Compliance with default notice

If before the date specified for that purpose in the default notice the debtor or hirer takes the action specified under section 88(1)(*b*) or (*c*) the breach shall be treated as not having occurred.

Further restriction of remedies for default

90. Retaking of protected hire-purchase etc. goods

(1) At any time when—

   (*a*) the debtor is in breach of a regulated hire-purchase or a regulated conditional sale agreement relating to goods, and
   (*b*) the debtor has paid to the creditor one-third or more of the total price of the goods, and
   (*c*) the property in the goods remains in the creditor,

the creditor is not entitled to recover possession of the goods from the debtor except on an order of the court.

(2) Where under a hire-purchase or conditional sale agreement the creditor is required to carry out any installation and the agreement specifies, as part of the total price, the amount to be paid in respect of the installation (the 'installation charge') the reference in subsection (1)(*b*) to one-third of the total price shall be construed as a reference to the aggregate of the installation charge and one-third of the remainder of the total price.

(3) In a case where—

   (*a*) subsection (1)(*a*) is satisfied, but not subsection (1)(*b*), and
   (*b*) subsection (1)(*a*) was satisfied on a previous occasion in relation to an earlier agreement, being a regulated hire-purchase or regulated conditional sale agreement, between the same parties, and relating to any of the goods comprised in the later agreement (whether or not other goods were also included),

subsection (1) shall apply to the later agreement with the omission of paragraph (*b*).

(4) If the later agreement is a modifying agreement, subsection (3) shall apply with the substitution, for the second reference to the later agreement, of a reference to the modifying agreement.

(5) Subsection (1) shall not apply, or shall cease to apply, to an agreement if the debtor has terminated, or terminates, the agreement.

(6) Where subsection (1) applies to an agreement at the death of the debtor, it shall continue to apply (in relation to the possessor of the goods) until the grant of probate or administration, or (in Scotland) confirmation (on which the personal representative would fall to be treated as the debtor).

(7) Goods falling within this section are in this Act referred to as 'protected goods'.

91. Consequences of breach of s 90

If goods are recovered by the creditor in contravention of section 90—

- (*a*) the regulated agreement, if not previously terminated, shall terminate, and
- (*b*) the debtor shall be released from all liability under the agreement, and shall be entitled to recover from the creditor all sums paid by the debtor under the agreement.

92. Recovery of possession of goods or land

(1) Except under an order of the court, the creditor or owner shall not be entitled to enter any premises to take possession of goods subject to a regulated hire-purchase agreement, regulated conditional sale agreement or regulated consumer hire agreement.

(2) At any time when the debtor is in breach of a regulated conditional sale agreement relating to land, the creditor is entitled to recover possession of the land from the debtor, or any person claiming under him, on an order of the court only.

(3) An entry in contravention of subsection (1) or (2) is actionable as a breach of statutory duty.

93. Interest not to be increased on default

The debtor under a regulated consumer credit agreeement shall not be obliged to pay interest on sums which, in breach of the agreement, are unpaid by him at a rate—

- (*a*) where the total charge for credit includes an item in respect of interest, exceeding the rate of that interest, or
- (*b*) in any other case, exceeding what would be the rate of the total charge for credit if any items included in the total charge for credit by virtue of section 20(2) were disregarded.

(3A) Summary diligence shall not be competent in Scotland to enforce payment of a debt due under a regulated agreement or under any security thereto.

[*Subsection (3A) was added by the Debtors (Scotland) Act 1987.*]

Early payment by debtor

94. Right to complete payments ahead of time

(1) The debtor under a regulated consumer credit agreement is entitled at any time, by notice to the creditor and the payment to the creditor of all amounts

payable by the debtor to him under the agreement (less any rebate allowable under section 95), to discharge the debtor's indebtedness under the agreement.

(2) A notice under subsection (1) may embody the exercise by the debtor of any option to purchase goods conferred on him by the agreement, and deal with any other matter arising on, or in relation to, the termination of the agreement.

95. Rebate on early settlement

(1) Regulations may provide for the allowance of a rebate of charges for credit to the debtor under a regulated consumer credit agreement where, under section 94, on refinancing, on breach of the agreement, or for any other reason, his indebtedness is discharged or becomes payable before the time fixed by the agreement, or any sum becomes payable by him before the time so fixed.

(2) Regulations under subsection (1) may provide for calculation of the rebate by reference to any sums paid or payable by the debtor or his relative under or in connection with the agreement (whether to the creditor or some other person), including sums under linked transactions and other items in the total charge for credit.

96. Effect of linked transactions

(1) Where for any reason the indebtedness of the debtor under a regulated consumer credit agreement is discharged before the time fixed by the agreement, he, and any relative of his, shall at the same time be discharged from any liability under a linked transaction, other than a debt which has already become payable.

(2) Subsection (1) does not apply to a linked transaction which is itself an agreement providing the debtor or his relative with credit.

(3) Regulations may exclude linked transactions of the prescribed description from the operation of subsection (1).

97. Duty to give information

(1) The creditor under a regulated consumer credit agreement, within the prescribed period after he has received a request in writing to that effect from the debtor, shall give the debtor a statement in the prescribed form indicating, according to the information to which it is practicable for him to refer, the amount of the payment required to discharge the debtor's indebtedness under the agreement, together with the prescribed particulars showing how the amount is arrived at.

(2) Subsection (1) does not apply to a request made less than one month after a previous request under that subsection relating to the same agreement was complied with.

(3) If the creditor fails to comply with subsection (1)—

    (a) he is not entitled, while the default continues, to enforce the agreement; and

    (b) if the default continues for one month he commits an offence.

Consumer Credit Act 1974

Termination of agreements

98. Duty to give notice of termination (non-default cases)

(1) The creditor or owner is not entitled to terminate a regulated agreement except by or after giving the debtor or hirer not less than seven days' notice of the termination.

(2) Subsection (1) applies only where—

(*a*) a period for the duration of the agreement is specified in the agreement, and

(*b*) that period has not ended when the creditor or owner does an act mentioned in subsection (1),

but so applies notwithstanding that, under the agreement, any party is entitled to terminate it before the end of the period so specified.

(3) A notice under subsection (1) is ineffective if not in the prescribed form.

(4) Subsection (1) does not prevent a creditor from treating the right to draw on any credit as restricted or deferred and taking such steps as may be necessary to make the restriction of deferment effective.

(5) Regulations may provide that subsection (1) is not to apply to agreements described by the regulations.

(6) Subsection (1) does not apply to the termination of a regulated agreement by reason of any breach by the debtor or hirer of the agreement.

99. Right to terminate hire-purchase etc. agreements

(1) At any time before the final payment by the debtor under a regulated hire-purchase or regulated conditional sale agreement falls due, the debtor shall be entitled to terminate the agreement by giving notice to any person entitled or authorised to receive the sums payable under the agreement.

(2) Termination of an agreement under subsection (1) does not affect any liability under the agreement which has accrued before the termination.

(3) Subsection (1) does not apply to a conditional sale agreement relating to land after the title to the land has passed to the debtor.

(4) In the case of a conditional sale agreement relating to goods, where the property in the goods, having become vested in the debtor, is transferred to a person who does not become the debtor under the agreement, the debtor shall not thereafter be entitled to terminate the agreement under subsection (1).

(5) Subject to subsection (4), where a debtor under a conditional sale agreement relating to goods terminates the agreement under this section after the property in the goods has become vested in him, the property in the goods shall thereupon vest in the person (the 'previous owner') in whom it was vested immediately before it became vested in the debtor:

Provided that if the previous owner has died, or any other event has occurred whereby that property, if vested in him immediately before that event, would thereupon have vested in some other person, the property shall be treated as having devolved as if it had been vested in the previous owner immediately before his death or immediately before that event, as the case may be.

100. Liability of debtor on termination of hire-purchase etc. agreement

(1) Where a regulated hire-purchase or regulated conditional sale agreement is terminated under section 99 the debtor shall be liable, unless the agreement provides for a smaller payment, or does not provide for any payment, to pay to the creditor the amount (if any) by which one-half of the total price exceeds the aggregate of the sums paid and the sums due in respect of the total price immediately before the termination.

(2) Where under a hire-purchase or conditional sale agreement the creditor is required to carry out any installation and the agreement specifies, as part of the total price, the amount to be paid in respect of the installation (the 'installation charge') the reference in subsection (1) to one-half of the total price shall be construed as a reference to the aggregate of the installation charge and one-half of the remainder of the total price.

(3) If in any action the court is satisfied that a sum less than the amount specified in subsection (1) would be equal to the loss sustained by the creditor in consequence of the termination of the agreement by the debtor, the court may make an order for the payment of that sum in lieu of the amount specified in subsection (1).

(4) If the debtor has contravened an obligation to take reasonable care of the goods or land, the amount arrived at under subsection (1) shall be increased by the sum required to recompense the creditor for that contravention, and subsection (2) shall have effect accordingly.

(5) Where the debtor, on the termination of the agreement, wrongfully retains possession of goods to which the agreement relates, then, in any action brought by the creditor to recover possession of the goods from the debtor, the court, unless it is satisfied that having regard to the circumstances it would not be just to do so, shall order the goods to be delivered to the creditor without giving the debtor an option to pay the value of the goods.

101. Right to terminate hire agreement

(1) The hirer under a regulated consumer hire agreement is entitled to terminate the agreement by giving notice to any person entitled or authorised to receive the sums payable under the agreement.

(2) Termination of an agreement under subsection (1) does not affect any liability under the agreement which has accrued before the termination.

(3) A notice under subsection (1) shall not expire earlier than eighteen months after the making of the agreement, but apart from that the minimum period of notice to be given under subsection (1), unless the agreement provides for a shorter period, is as follows.

(4) If the agreement provides for the making of payments by the hirer to the owner at equal intervals, the minimum period of notice is the length of one interval or three months, whichever is less.

(5) If the agreement provides for the making of such payments at differing intervals, the minimum period of notice is the length of the shortest interval or three months, whichever is less.

(6) In any other case, the minimum period of notice is three months.

(7) This section does not apply to—

(a) any agreement which provides for the making by the hirer of payments which in total (and without breach of the agreement) exceed [£900] in any year, or

(b) any agreement where—

(i) goods are bailed or (in Scotland) hired to the hirer for the purposes of a business carried on by him, or the hirer holds himself out as requiring the goods for those purposes, and

(ii) the goods are selected by the hirer, and acquired by the owner for the purposes of the agreement at the request of the hirer from any person other than the owner's associate, or

(c) any agreement where the hirer requires, or holds himself out as requiring, the goods for the purpose of bailing or hiring them to other persons in the course of a business carried on by him.

[*The figure in square brackets was substituted by the Consumer Credit (Increase of Monetary Amounts) Order 1983, Article 4, Schedule, Part II (S.I. 1983 No. 1571).*]

(8) If, on an application made to the Director by a person carrying on a consumer hire business, it appears to the Director that it would be in the interest of hirers to do so, he may by notice to the applicant direct that this section shall not apply to consumer hire agreements made by the applicant, and subject to such conditions (if any) as the Director may specify, this Act shall have effect accordingly.

(9) In the case of a modifying agreement, subsection (3) shall apply with the substitution, for 'the making of the agreement' of 'the making of the original agreement'.

102. Agency for receiving notice of rescission

(1) Where the debtor or hirer under a regulated agreement claims to have a right to rescind the agreement, each of the following shall be deemed to be the agent of the creditor or owner for the purpose of receiving any notice rescinding the agreement which is served by the debtor or hirer—

(a) a credit-broker or supplier who was the negotiator in antecedent negotiations, and

(b) any person who, in the course of a business carried on by him, acted on behalf of the debtor or hirer in any negotiations for the agreement.

(2) In subsection (1) 'rescind' does not include—

(a) service of a notice of cancellation, or

(b) termination of an agreement under section 99 or 101 or by the exercise of a right or power in that behalf expressly conferred by the agreement.

103. Termination statements

(1) If an individual (the 'customer') serves on any person (the 'trader') a notice—

(a) stating that—

(i) the customer was the debtor or hirer under a regulated agreement described in the notice, and the trader was the creditor or owner under the agreement, and

(ii) the customer has discharged his indebtedness to the trader under the agreement, and

(iii) the agreement has ceased to have any operation; and
(b) requiring the trader to give the customer a notice, signed by or on behalf of the trader, confirming that those statements are correct,

the trader shall, within the prescribed period after receiving the notice, either comply with it or serve on the customer a counter-notice stating that, as the case may be, he disputes the correctness of the notice or asserts that the customer is not indebted to him under the agreement.

(2) Where the trader disputes the correctness of the notice he shall give particulars of the way in which he alleges it to be wrong.

(3) Subsection (1) does not apply in relation to any agreement if the trader has previously complied with that subsection on the service of a notice under it with respect to that agreement.

(4) Subsection (1) does not apply to a non-commercial agreement.

(5) If the trader fails to comply with subsection (1), and the default continues for one month, he commits an offence.

104. Goods not to be treated as subject to landlord's hypothec in Scotland

Goods comprised in a hire-purchase agreement or goods comprised in a conditional sale agreement which have not become vested in the debtor shall not be treated in Scotland as subject to the landlord's hypothec—

(a) during the period between the service of a default notice in respect of the goods and the date on which the notice expires or is earlier complied with; or
(b) if the agreement is enforceable on an order of the court only, during the period between the commencement and termination of an action by the creditor to enforce the agreement.

PART VIII
SECURITY

General

105. Form and content of securities

(1) Any security provided in relation to a regulated agreement shall be expressed in writing.

(2) Regulations may prescribe the form and content of documents ('security instruments') to be made in compliance with subsection (1).

(3) Regulations under subsection (2) may in particular—

(a) require specified information to be included in the prescribed manner in documents, and other specified material to be excluded;
(b) contain requirements to ensure that specified information is clearly brought to the attention of the surety, and that one part of a document is not given insufficient or excessive prominence compared with another.

(4) A security instrument is not properly executed unless—

(a) a document in the prescribed form, itself containing all the prescribed terms and conforming to regulations under subsection (2), is signed in the prescribed manner by or on behalf of the surety, and

(*b*) the document embodies all the terms of the security, other than implied terms, and

(*c*) the document, when presented or sent for the purpose of being signed by or on behalf of the surety, is in such state that its terms are readily legible, and

(*d*) when the document is presented or sent for the purpose of being signed by or on behalf of the surety there is also presented or sent a copy of the document.

(5) A security instrument is not properly executed unless—

(*a*) where the security is provided after, or at the time when, the regulated agreement is made, a copy of the executed agreement, together with a copy of any other document referred to in it, is given to the surety at the time the security is provided, or

(*b*) where the security is provided before the regulated agreement is made, a copy of the executed agreement, together with a copy of any other document referred to in it, is given to the surety within seven days after the regulated agreement is made.

(6) Subsection (1) does not apply to a security provided by the debtor or hirer.

(7) If—

(*a*) in contravention of subsection (1) a security is not expressed in writing, or

(*b*) a security instrument is improperly executed,

the security, so far as provided in relation to a regulated agreement, is enforceable against the surety on an order of the court only.

(8) If an application for an order under subsection (7) is dismissed (except on technical grounds only) section 106 (ineffective securities) shall apply to the security.

(9) Regulations under section 60(1) shall include provision requiring documents embodying regulated agreements also to embody any security provided in relation to a regulated agreement by the debtor or hirer.

106. Ineffective securities

Where, under any provision of this Act, this section is applied to any security provided in relation to a regulated agreement, then, subject to section 177 (saving for registered charges,—

(*a*) the security, so far as it is so provided, shall be treated as never having effect;

(*b*) any property lodged with the creditor or owner solely for the purposes of the security as so provided shall be returned by him forthwith;

(*c*) the creditor or owner shall take any necessary action to remove or cancel an entry in any register, so far as the entry relates to the security as so provided; and

(*d*) any amount received by the creditor or owner on realisation of the security shall, so far as it is referable to the agreement, be repaid to the surety.

107. Duty to give information to surety under fixed-sum credit agreement

(1) The creditor under a regulated agreement for fixed-sum credit in relation to which security is provided, within the prescribed period after receiving a request in writing to that effect from the surety and payment of a fee of [50] new pence, shall give to the surety (if a different person from the debtor)—

- (*a*) a copy of the executed agreement (if any) and of any other document referred to in it;
- (*b*) a copy of the security instrument (if any); and
- (*c*) a statement signed by or on behalf of the creditor showing, according to the information to which it is practicable for him to refer,—
    - (i) the total sum paid under the agreement by the debtor,
    - (ii) the total sum which has become payable under the agreement by the debtor but remains unpaid, and the various amounts comprised in that total sum, with the date when each became due, and
    - (iii) the total sum which is to become payable under the agreement by the debtor, and the various amounts comprised in that total sum, with the date, or mode of determining the date, when each becomes due.

[*The figure in square brackets was substituted by the Consumer Credit (Increase of Monetary Amounts) Order 1983, Article 4, Schedule, Part II (S.I. 1983 No. 1571).*]

(2) If the creditor possesses insufficient information to enable him to ascertain the amounts and dates mentioned in subsection (1)(*c*)(iii), he shall be taken to comply with that sub-paragraph if his statement under subsection (1)(*c*) gives the basis on which, under the regulated agreement, they would fall to be ascertained.

(3) Subsection (1) does not apply to—

- (*a*) an agreement under which no sum is, or will or may become, payable by the debtor, or
- (*b*) a request made less than one month after a previous request under that subsection relating to the same agreement was complied with.

(4) If the creditor under an agreement fails to comply with subsection (1)—

- (*a*) he is not entitled, while the default continues, to enforce the security, so far as provided in relation to the agreement; and
- (*b*) if the default continues for one month he commits an offence.

(5) This section does not apply to a non-commercial agreement.

108. Duty to give information to surety under running-account credit agreement

(1) The creditor under a regulated agreement for running-account credit in relation to which security is provided, within the prescribed period after receiving a request in writing to that effect from the surety and payment of a fee of [50] new pence, shall give to the surety (if a different person from the debtor)—

- (*a*) a copy of the executed agreement (if any) and of any other document referred to in it;
- (*b*) a copy of the security instrument (if any); and
- (*c*) a statement signed by or on behalf of the creditor showing, according to the information to which it is practicable for him to refer,—
    - (i) the state of the account, and

(ii) the amount, if any, currently payable under the agreement by the debtor to the creditor, and

(iii) the amounts and due dates of any payments which, if the debtor does not draw further on the account, will later become payable under the agreement by the debtor to the creditor.

[*The figure in square brackets was substituted by the Consumer Credit (Increase of Monetary Amounts) Order 1983, Article 4, Schedule, Part II (S.I. 1983 No. 1571).*]

(2) If the creditor possesses insufficient information to enable him to ascertain the amounts and dates mentioned in subsection (1)(*c*)(iii), he shall be taken to comply with that sub-paragraph if his statement under subsection (1)(*c*) gives the basis on which, under the regulated agreement, they would fall to be ascertained.

(3) Subsection (1) does not apply to—

(*a*) an agreement under which no sum is, or will or may become, payable by the debtor, or

(*b*) a request made less than one month after a previous request under that subsection relating to the same agreement was complied with.

(4) If the creditor under an agreement fails to comply with subsection (1)—

(*a*) he is not entitled, while the default continues, to enforce the security, so far as provided in relation to the agreement; and

(*b*) if the default continues for one month he commits an offence.

(5) This section does not apply to a non-commercial agreement.

109. Duty to give information to surety under consumer hire agreement

(1) The owner under a regulated consumer hire agreement in relation to which security is provided, within the prescribed period after receiving a request in writing to that effect from the surety and payment of a fee of [50] new pence, shall give to the surety (if a different person from the hirer)—

(*a*) a copy of the executed agreement and of any other document referred to in it;

(*b*) a copy of the security instrument (if any); and

(*c*) a statement signed by or on behalf of the owner showing, according to the information to which it is practicable for him to refer, the total sum which has become payable under the agreement by the hirer but remains unpaid and the various amounts comprised in that total sum, with the date when each became due.

[*The figure in square brackets was substituted by the Consumer Credit (Increase of Monetary Amounts) Order 1983, Article 4, Schedule, Part II (S.I. 1983 No. 1571).*]

(2) Subsection (1) does not apply to—

(*a*) an agreement under which no sum is, or will or may become, payable by the hirer, or

(*b*) a request made less than one month after a previous request under that subsection relating to the same agreement was complied with.

(3) If the owner under an agreement fails to comply with subsection (1)—

(*a*) he is not entitled, while the default continues, to enforce the security, so far as provided in relation to the agreement; and

(*b*) if the default continues for one month he commits an offence.

(4) This section does not apply to a non-commercial agreement.

110. Duty to give information to debtor or hirer

(1) The creditor or owner under a regulated agreement, within the prescribed period after receiving a request in writing to that effect from the debtor or hirer and payment of a fee of [50] new pence, shall give the debtor or hirer a copy of any security instrument executed in relation to the agreement after the making of the agreement.

[*The figure in square brackets was substituted by the Consumer Credit (Increase of Monetary Amounts) Order 1983, Article 4, Schedule, Part II (S.I. 1983 No. 1571).*]

(2) Subsection (1) does not apply to—

(*a*) a non-commercial agreement, or

(*b*) an agreement under which no sum is, or will or may become, payable by the debtor or hirer, or

(*c*) a request made less than one month after a previous request under subsection (1) relating to the same agreement was complied with.

(3) If the creditor or owner under an agreement fails to comply with subsection (1)—

(*a*) he is not entitled, while the default continues, to enforce the security (so far as provided in relation to the agreement); and

(*b*) if the default continues for one month he commits an offence.

111. Duty to give surety copy of default etc. notice

(1) When a default notice or a notice under section 76(1) or 98(1) is served on a debtor or hirer, a copy of the notice shall be served by the creditor or owner on any surety (if a different person from the debtor or hirer).

(2) If the creditor or owner fails to comply with subsection (1) in the case of any surety, the security is enforceable against the surety (in respect of the breach or other matter to which the notice relates) on an order of the court only.

112. Realisation of securities

Subject to section 121, regulations may provide for any matters relating to the sale or other realisation, by the creditor or owner, of property over which any right has been provided by way of security in relation to an actual or prospective regulated agreement, other than a non-commercial agreement.

113. Act not to be evaded by use of security

(1) Where a security is provided in relation to an actual or prospective regulated agreement, the security shall not be enforced so as to benefit the creditor or owner, directly or indirectly, to an extent greater (whether as respects the amount of any payment or the time or manner of its being made) than would be the case if the security were not provided and any obligations of the debtor or

Consumer Credit Act 1974

hirer, or his relative, under or in relation to the agreement were carried out to the extent (if any) to which they would be enforced under this Act.

(2) In accordance with subsection (1), where a regulated agreement is enforceable on an order of the court or the Director only, any security provided in relation to the agreement is enforceable (so far as provided in relation to the agreement) where such an order has been made in relation to the agreement, but not otherwise.

(3) Where—

- (*a*) a regulated agreement is cancelled under section 69(1) or becomes subject to section 69(2), or
- (*b*) a regulated agreement is terminated under section 91, or
- (*c*) in relation to any agreement an application for an order under section 40(2), 65(1), 124(1) or 149(2) is dismissed (except on technical grounds only), or
- (*d*) a declaration is made by the court under section 142(1) (refusal of enforcement order) as respects any regulated agreement,

section 106 shall apply to any security provided in relation to the agreement.

(4) Where subsection (3)(*d*) applies and the declaration relates to a part only of the regulated agreement, section 106 shall apply to the security only so far as it concerns that part.

(5) In the case of a cancelled agreement, the duty imposed on the debtor or hirer by section 71 or 72 shall not be enforceable before the creditor or owner has discharged any duty imposed on him by section 106 (as applied by subsection (3)(*a*)).

(6) If the security is provided in relation to a prospective agreement or transaction, the security shall be enforceable in relation to the agreement or transaction only after the time (if any) when the agreement is made; and until that time the person providing the security shall be entitled, by notice to the creditor or owner, to require that section 106 shall thereupon apply to the security.

(7) Where an indemnity [or guarantee] is given in a case where the debtor or hirer is a minor, or [an indemnity is given in a case where he] is otherwise not of full capacity, the reference in subsection (1) to the extent to which his obligations would be enforced shall be read in relation to the indemnity [or guarantee] as a reference to the extent to which [those obligations] would be enforced if he were of full capacity.

(8) Subsections (1) to (3) also apply where a security is provided in relation to an actual or prospective linked transaction, and in that case—

- (*a*) references to the agreement shall be read as references to the linked transaction, and
- (*b*) references to the creditor or owner shall be read as references to any person (other than the debtor or hirer, or his relative) who is a party, or prospective party, to the linked transaction.

[*The words in square brackets in subsection (7) were inserted by the Minors' Contracts Act 1987, section 4(1).*]

Pledges

114. Pawn-receipts

(1) At the time he receives the article, a person who takes any article in pawn under a regulated agreement shall give to the person from whom he receives it a receipt in the prescribed form (a 'pawn-receipt').

(2) A person who takes any article in pawn from an individual whom he knows to be, or who appears to be and is, a minor commits an offence.

(3) This section and sections 115 to 122 do not apply to—

(*a*) a pledge of documents of title [or of bearer bonds], or

(*b*) a non-commercial agreement.

[*The words in square brackets were added by the Banking Act 1979, s 38(2), which was brought into force on 1 October 1979 by the Banking Act 1979 (Commencement No. 1) Order 1979 (S.I. 1979 No. 938).*]

115. Penalty for failure to supply copies of pledge agreement, etc.

If the creditor under a regulated agreement to take any article in pawn fails to observe the requirements of sections 62 to 64 or 114(1) in relation to the agreement he commits an offence.

116. Redemption period

(1) A pawn is redeemable at any time within six months after it was taken.

(2) Subject to subsection (1), the period within which a pawn is redeemable shall be the same as the period fixed by the parties for the duration of the credit secured by the pledge, or such longer period as they may agree.

(3) If the pawn is not redeemed by the end of the period laid down by subsections (1) and (2) (the 'redemption period'), it nevertheless remains redeemable until it is realised by the pawnee under section 121 except where under section 120(1)(*a*) the property in it passes to the pawnee.

(4) No special charge shall be made for redemption of a pawn after the end of the redemption period, and charges in respect of the safe keeping of the pawn shall not be at a higher rate after the end of the redemption period than before.

117. Redemption procedure

(1) On surrender of the pawn-receipt, and payment of the amount owing, at any time when the pawn is redeemable, the pawnee shall deliver the pawn to the bearer of the pawn-receipt.

(2) Subsection (1) does not apply if the pawnee knows or has reasonable cause to suspect that the bearer of the pawn-receipt is neither the owner of the pawn nor authorised by the owner to redeem it.

(3) The pawnee is not liable to any person in tort or delict for delivering the pawn where subsection (1) applies, or refusing to deliver it where the person demanding delivery does not comply with subsection (1) or, by reason of subsection (2), subsection (1) does not apply.

118. Loss etc. of pawn-receipt

(1) A person (the 'claimant') who is not in possession of the pawn-receipt but claims to be the owner of the pawn, or to be otherwise entitled or authorised to redeem it, may do so at any time when it is redeemable by tendering to the pawnee in place of the pawn-receipt—

  (a) a statutory declaration made by the claimant in the prescribed form, and with the prescribed contents, or
  (b) where the pawn in security for fixed-sum credit not exceeding [£25] or running-account credit on which the credit limit does not exceed [£25], and the pawnee agrees, a statement in writing in the prescribed form, and with the prescribed contents, signed by the claimant.

[*The figures in square brackets were substituted by the Consumer Credit (Increase of Monetary Amounts) Order 1983, Article 4, Schedule, Part II (S.I. 1983 No. 1571).*]

(2) On compliance by the claimant with subsection (1), section 117 shall apply as if the declaration or statement were the pawn-receipt, and the pawn-receipt itself shall become inoperative for the purposes of section 117.

119. Unreasonable refusal to deliver pawn

(1) If a person who has taken a pawn under a regulated agreement refuses without reasonable cause to allow the pawn to be redeemed, he commits an offence.

(2) On the conviction in England or Wales of a pawnee under subsection (1) where the offence does not amount to theft, section 28 (orders for restitution) of the Theft Act 1968, and any provision of the Theft Act 1968 relating to that section, shall apply as if the pawnee had been convicted of stealing the pawn.

(3) On the conviction in Northern Ireland of a pawnee under subsection (1) where the offence does not amount to theft, section 27 (orders for restitution) of the Theft Act (Northern Ireland) 1969, and any provision of the Theft Act (Northern Ireland) 1969 relating to that section, shall apply as if the pawnee had been convicted of stealing the pawn.

120. Consequence of failure to redeem

(1) If at the end of the redemption period the pawn has not been redeemed—

  (a) notwithstanding anything in section 113, the property in the pawn passes to the pawnee where the redemption period is six months and the pawn is security for fixed-sum credit not exceeding £15 or running-account credit on which the credit limit does not exceed [£25]; or
  (b) in any other case the pawn becomes realisable by the pawnee.

[*The figure in square brackets was substituted by the Consumer Credit (Increase of Monetary Amounts) Order 1983, Article 4, Schedule, Part II (S.I. 1983 No. 1571).*]

(2) Where the debtor or hirer is entitled to apply to the court for a time order under section 129, subsection (1) shall apply with the substitution, for 'at the end of the redemption period' of 'after the expiry of five days following the end of the redemption period'.

121. Realisation of pawn

(1) When a pawn has become realisable by him, the pawnee may sell it, after giving to the pawnor (except in such cases as may be prescribed) not less than the prescribed period of notice of the intention to sell, indicating in the notice the asking price and such other particulars as may be prescribed.

(2) Within the prescribed period after the sale takes place, the pawnee shall give the pawnor the prescribed information in writing as to the sale, its proceeds and expenses.

(3) Where the net proceeds of sale are not less than the sum which, if the pawn had been redeemed on the date of the sale, would have been payable for its redemption, the debt secured by the pawn is discharged and any surplus shall be paid by the pawnee to the pawnor.

(4) Where subsection (3) does not apply, the debt shall be treated as from the date of sale as equal to the amount by which the net proceeds of sale fall short of the sum which would have been payable for the redemption of the pawn on that date.

(5) In this section the 'net proceeds of sale' is the amount realised (the 'gross amount') less the expenses (if any) of the sale.

(6) If the pawnor alleges that the gross amount is less than the true market value of the pawn on the date of sale, it is for the pawnee to prove that he and any agents employed by him in the sale used reasonable care to ensure that the true market value was obtained, and if he fails to do so subsections (3) and (4) shall have effect as if the reference in subsection (5) to the gross amount were a reference to the true market value.

(7) If the pawner alleges that the expenses of the sale were unreasonably high, it is for the pawnee to prove that they were reasonable, and if he fails to do so subsections (3) and (4) shall have effect as if the reference in subsection (5) to expenses were a reference to reasonable expenses.

122. Order in Scotland to deliver pawn

(1) As respects Scotland where—

  (*a*) a pawn is either—
    (i) an article which has been stolen, or
    (ii) an article which has been obtained by fraud, and a person is convicted of any offence in relation to the theft or, as the case may be, the fraud; or
  (*b*) a person is convicted of an offence under section 119(1),

the court by which that person is so convicted may order delivery of the pawn to the owner or the person otherwise entitled thereto.

(2) A court making an order under subsection (1)(*a*) for delivery of a pawn may make the order subject to such conditions as to payment of the debt secured by the pawn as it thinks fit.

Consumer Credit Act 1974

Negotiable instruments

123. Restrictions on taking and negotiating instruments

(1) A creditor or owner shall not take a negotiable instrument, other than a bank note or cheque, in discharge of any sum payable—

(*a*) by the debtor or hirer under a regulated agreement, or

(*b*) by any person as surety in relation to the agreement.

(2) The creditor or owner shall not negotiate a cheque taken by him in discharge of a sum payable as mentioned in subsection (1) except to a banker (within the meaning of the Bills of Exchange Act 1882).

(3) The creditor or owner shall not take a negotiable instrument as security for the discharge of any sum payable as mentioned in subsection (1).

(4) A person takes a negotiable instrument as security for the discharge of a sum if the sum is intended to be paid in some other way, and the negotiable instrument is to be presented for payment only if the sum is not paid in that way.

(5) This section does not apply where the regulated agreement is a non-commercial agreement.

(6) The Secretary of State may by order provide that this section shall not apply where the regulated agreement has a connection with a country outside the United Kingdom.

124. Consequences of breach of s. 123

(1) After any contravention of section 123 has occurred in relation to a sum payable as mentioned in section 123(1)(*a*), the agreement under which the sum is payable is enforceable against the debtor or hirer on an order of the court only.

(2) After any contravention of section 123 has occurred in relation to a sum payable by any surety, the security is enforceable on an order of the court only.

(3) Where an application for an order under subsection (2) is dismissed (except on technical grounds only) section 106 shall apply to the security.

125. Holders in due course

(1) A person who takes a negotiable instrument in contravention of section 123(1) or (3) is not a holder in due course, and is not entitled to enforce the instrument.

(2) Where a person negotiates a cheque in contravention of section 123(2), his doing so constitutes a defect in his title within the meaning of the Bills of Exchange Act 1882.

(3) If a person mentioned in section 123(1)(*a*) or (*b*) ('the protected person') becomes liable to a holder in due course of an instrument taken from the protected person in contravention of section 123(1) or (3), or taken from the protected person and negotiated in contravention of section 123(2), the creditor or owner shall indemnify the protected person in respect of that liability.

(4) Nothing in this Act affects the rights of the holder in due course of any negotiable instrument.

Consumer Credit Act 1974

Land mortgages

126. Enforcement of land mortgages

A land mortgage securing a regulated agreement is enforceable (so far as provided in relation to the agreement) on an order of the court only.

PART IX
JUDICIAL CONTROL

Enforcement of certain regulated agreements and securities

127. Enforcement orders in cases of infringement

(1) In the case of an application for an enforcement order under—

(*a*) section 65(1) (improperly executed agreements), or

(*b*) section 105(7)(*a*) or (*b*) (improperly executed security instruments), or

(*c*) section 111(2) (failure to serve copy of notice on surety), or

(*d*) section 124(1) or (2) (taking of negotiable instrument in contravention of section 123),

the court shall dismiss the application if, but (subject to subsections (3) and (4)) only if, it considers it just to do so having regard to—
  (i) prejudice caused to any person by the contravention in question, and the degree of culpability for it; and
  (ii) the powers conferred on the court by subsection (2) and sections 135 and 136.

(2) If it appears to the court just to do so, it may in an enforcement order reduce or discharge any sum payable by the debtor or hirer, or any surety, so as to compensate him for prejudice suffered as a result of the contravention in question.

(3) The court shall not make an enforcement order under section 65(1) if section 61(1)(*a*) (signing of agreements) was not complied with unless a document (whether or not in the prescribed form and complying with regulations under section 60(1)) itself containing all the prescribed terms of the agreement was signed by the debtor or hirer (whether or not in the prescribed manner).

(4) The court shall not make an enforcement order under section 65(1) in the case of a cancellable agreement if—

(*a*) a provision of section 62 or 63 was not complied with, and the creditor or owner did not give a copy of the executed agreement, and of any other document referred to in it, to the debtor or hirer before the commencement of the proceedings in which the order is sought, or

(*b*) section 64(1) was not complied with.

(5) Where an enforcement order is made in a case to which subsection (3) applies, the order may direct that the regulated agreement is to have effect as if it did not include a term omitted from the document signed by the debtor or hirer.

128. Enforcement orders on death of debtor or hirer

The court shall make an order under section 86(2) if, but only if, the creditor or owner proves that he has been unable to satisfy himself that the present and future obligations of the debtor or hirer under the agreement are likely to be discharged.

Extension of time

129. Time orders

(1) [Subject to subsection (3) below, if] it appears to the court just to do so—

    (*a*) on an application for an enforcement order; or

    (*b*) on an application made by a debtor or hirer under this paragraph after service on him of—
        (i) a default notice, or
        (ii) a notice under section 76(1) or 98(1); or

    (*c*) in an action brought by a creditor or owner to enforce a regulated agreement or any security, or recover possession of any goods or land to which a regulated agreement relates,

the court may make an order under this section (a 'time order').

(2) A time order shall provide for one or both of the following, as the court considers just—

    (*a*) the payment by the debtor or hirer or any surety of any sum owed under a regulated agreement or a security by such instalments, payable at such times, as the court, having regard to the means of the debtor or hirer and any surety, considers reasonable;

    (*b*) the remedying by the debtor or hirer of any breach of a regulated agreement (other than non-payment of money) within such period as the court may specify.

[(3) Where in Scotland a time to pay direction or a time to pay order has been made in relation to a debt, it shall not thereafter be competent to make a time order in relation to the same debt.]

[*Subsection (3) and the words in square brackets in subsection (1) was added by the Debtors (Scotland) 1987, section 108(1) and Schedule 6, paragraph 16.*]

130. Supplemental provisions about time orders

(1) Where in accordance with rules of court an offer to pay any sum by instalments is made by the debtor or hirer and accepted by the creditor or owner, the court may in accordance with rules of court make a time order under section 129(2)(*a*) giving effect to the offer without hearing evidence of means.

(2) In the case of a hire-purchase or conditional sale agreement only, a time order under section 129(2)(*a*) may deal with sums which, although not payable by the debtor at the time the order is made, would if the agreement continued in force become payable under it subsequently.

(3) A time order under section 129(2)(*a*) shall not be made where the regulated agreement is secured by a pledge if, by virtue of regulations made under section

76(5), 87(4) or 98(5), service of a notice is not necessary for enforcement of the pledge.

(4) Where, following the making of a time order in relation to a regulated hire-purchase or conditional sale agreement or a regulated consumer hire agreement, the debtor or hirer is in possession of the goods, he shall be treated (except in the case of a debtor to whom the creditor's title has passed) as a bailee or (in Scotland) a custodier of the goods under the terms of the agreement, notwithstanding that the agreement has been terminated.

(5) Without prejudice to anything done by the creditor or owner before the commencement of the period specified in a time order made under section 129(2)(*b*) ('the relevant period'),—

> (*a*) he shall not while the relevant period subsists take in relation to the agreement any action such as is mentioned in section 87(1);
> (*b*) where—
>> (i) a provision of the agreement ('the secondary provision') becomes operative only on breach of another provision of the agreement ('the primary provision'), and
>> (ii) the time order provides for the remedying of such a breach of the primary provision within the relevant period,
>
> he shall not treat the secondary provision as operative before the end of that period;
> (*c*) if while the relevant period subsists the breach to which the order relates is remedied it shall be treated as not having occurred.

(6) On the application of any person affected by a time order, the court may vary or revoke the order.

Protection of property pending proceedings

131. Protection orders

The court, on the application of the creditor or owner under a regulated agreement, may make such orders as it thinks just for protecting any property of the creditor or owner, or property subject to any security, from damage or depreciation pending the determination of any proceedings under this Act, including orders restricting or prohibiting use of the property or giving directions as to its custody.

Hire and hire-purchase etc. agreements

132. Financial relief for hirer

(1) Where the owner under a regulated consumer hire agreement recovers possession of goods to which the agreement relates otherwise than by action, the hirer may apply to the court for an order that—

> (*a*) the whole or part of any sum paid by the hirer to the owner in respect of the goods shall be repaid, and
> (*b*) the obligation to pay the whole or part of any sum owed by the hirer to the owner in respect of the goods shall cease,

and if it appears to the court just to do so, having regard to the extent of the enjoyment of the goods by the hirer, the court shall grant the application in full or in part.

(2) Where in proceedings relating to a regulated consumer hire agreement the court makes an order for the delivery to the owner of goods to which the agreement relates the court may include in the order the like provision as may be made in an order under subsection (1).

133. Hire-purchase etc. agreements: special powers of court

(1) If, in relation to a regulated hire-purchase or conditional sale agreement, it appears to the court just to do so—

    (*a*) on an application for an enforcement order or time order; or
    (*b*) in an action brought by the creditor to recover possession of goods to which the agreement relates.

the court may—

    (i) make an order (a 'return order') for the return to the creditor of goods to which the agreement relates;
    (ii) make an order (a 'transfer order') for the transfer to the debtor of the creditor's title to certain goods to which the agreement relates ('the transferred goods'), and the return to the creditor of the remainder of the goods.

(2) In determining for the purposes of this section how much of the total price has been paid ('the paid-up sum'), the court may—

    (*a*) treat any sum paid by the debtor, or owed by the creditor, in relation to the goods as part of the paid-up sum;
    (*b*) deduct any sum owed by the debtor in relation to the goods (otherwise than as part of the total price) from the paid-up sum,

and make corresponding reductions in amounts so owed.

(3) Where a transfer order is made, the transferred goods shall be such of the goods to which the agreement relates as the court thinks just; but a transfer order shall be made only where the paid-up sum exceeds the part of the total price referable to the transferred goods by an amount equal to at least one-third of the unpaid balance of the total price.

(4) Notwithstanding the making of a return order or transfer order, the debtor may at any time before the goods enter the possession of the creditor, on payment of the balance of the total price and the fulfilment of any other necessary conditions, claim the goods ordered to be returned to the creditor.

(5) When, in pursuance of a time order or under this section, the total price of goods under a regulated hire-purchase agreement or regulated conditional sale agreement is paid and any other necessary conditions are fulfilled, the creditor's title to the goods vests in the debtor.

(6) If, in contravention of a return order or transfer order, any goods to which the order relates are not returned to the creditor, the court, on the application of the creditor, may—

    (*a*) revoke so much of the order as relates to those goods, and
    (*b*) order the debtor to pay the creditor the unpaid portion of so much of the total price as is referable to those goods.

(7) For the purposes of this section, the part of the total price referable to

any goods is the part assigned to those goods by the agreement or (if no such assignment is made) the part determined by the court to be reasonable.

134. Evidence of adverse detention in hire-purchase etc. cases

(1) Where goods are comprised in a regulated hire-purchase agreement, regulated conditional sale agreement or regulated consumer hire agreement, and the creditor or owner—

> (*a*) brings an action or makes an application to enforce a right to recover possession of the goods from the debtor or hirer, and
> (*b*) proves that a demand for the delivery of the goods was included in the default notice under section 88(5), or that, after the right to recover possession of the goods accured but before the action was begun or the application was made, he made a request in writing to the debtor or hirer to surrender the goods,

then, for the purposes of the claim of the creditor or owner to recover possession of the goods, the possession of them by the debtor or hirer shall be deemed to be adverse to the creditor or owner.

(2) In subsection (1) 'the debtor or hirer' includes a person in possession of the goods at any time between the debtor's or hirer's death and the grant of probate or administration, or (in Scotland) confirmation.

(3) Nothing in this section affects a claim for damages for conversion or (in Scotland) for delict.

Supplemental provisions as to orders

135. Power to impose conditions, or suspend operation of order

(1) If it considers it just to do so, the court may in an order made by it in relation to a regulated agreement include provisions—

> (*a*) making the operation of any term of the order conditional on the doing of specified acts by any party to the proceedings;
> (*b*) suspending the operation of any term of the order either—
>> (i) until such time as the court subsequently directs, or
>> (ii) until the occurrence of a specified act or omission.

(2) The court shall not suspend the operation of a term requiring the delivery up of goods by any person unless satisfied that the goods are in his possession or control.

(3) In the case of a consumer hire agreement, the court shall not so use its powers under subsection (1)(*b*) as to extend the period for which, under the terms of the agreement, the hirer is entitled to possession of the goods to which the agreement relates.

(4) On the application of any person affected by a provision included under subsection (1), the court may vary the provision.

136. Power to vary agreements and securities

The court may in an order made by it under this Act include such provision as it considers just for amending any agreement or security in consequence of a term of the order.

Extortionate credit bargains

137. Extortionate credit bargains

(1) If the court finds a credit bargain extortionate it may reopen the credit agreement so as to do justice between the parties.

(2) In this section and sections 138 to 140,—

(a) 'credit agreement' means any agreement between an individual (the 'debtor') and any other person (the 'creditor') by which the creditor provides the debtor with credit of any amount, and
(b) 'credit bargain'—
   (i) where no transaction other than the credit agreement is to be taken into account in computing the total charge for credit, means the credit agreement, or
   (ii) where one or more other transactions are to be so taken into account, means the credit agreement and those other transactions, taken together.

138. When bargains are extortionate

(1) A credit bargain is extortionate if it—

(a) requires the debtor or a relative of his to make payments (whether unconditionally, or on certain contingencies) which are grossly exorbitant, or
(b) otherwise grossly contravenes ordinary principles of fair dealing.

(2) In determining whether a credit bargain is extortionate, regard shall be had to such evidence as is adduced concerning—

(a) interest rates prevailing at the time it was made,
(b) the factors mentioned in subsections (3) to (5), and
(c) any other relevant considerations.

(3) Factors applicable under subsection (2) in relation to the debtor include—

(a) his age, experience, business capacity and state of health; and
(b) the degree to which, at the time of making the credit bargain, he was under financial pressure, and the nature of that pressure.

(4) Factors applicable under subsection (2) in relation to the creditor include—

(a) the degree of risk accepted by him, having regard to the value of any security provided;
(b) his relationship to the debtor; and
(c) whether or not a colourable cash price was quoted for any goods or services included in the credit bargain.

(5) Factors applicable under subsection (2) in relation to a linked transaction included the question how far the transaction was reasonably required for the protection of debtor or creditor, or was in the interest of the debtor.

139. Reopening of extortionate agreements

(1) A credit agreement may, if the court thinks just, be reopened on the ground that the credit bargain is extortionate—

(a) on an application for the purpose made by the debtor or any surety

to the High Court, county court or sheriff court; or
- (b) at the instance of the debtor or a surety in any proceedings to which the debtor and creditor are parties, being proceedings to enforce the credit agreement, any security relating to it, or any linked transaction; or
- (c) at the instance of the debtor or a surety in other proceedings in any court where the amount paid or payable under the credit agreement is relevant.

(2) In reopening the agreement, the court may, for the purpose of relieving the debtor or a surety from payment of any sum in excess of that fairly due and reasonable, by order—

- (a) direct accounts to be taken, or (in Scotland) an accounting to be made, between any persons,
- (b) set aside the whole or part of any obligation imposed on the debtor or a surety by the credit bargain or any related agreement,
- (c) require the creditor to repay the whole or part of any sum paid under the credit bargain or any related agreement by the debtor or a surety, whether paid to the creditor or any other person,
- (d) direct the return to the surety of any property provided for the purposes of the security, or
- (e) alter the terms of the credit agreement or any security instrument.

(3) An order may be made under subsection (2) notwithstanding that its effect is to place a burden on the creditor in respect of an advantage unfairly enjoyed by another person who is a party to a linked transaction.

(4) An order under subsection (2) shall not alter the effect of any judgment.

(5) In England and Wales an application under subsection (1)(a) shall be brought only in the county court in the case of—

- (a) a regulated agreement, or
- (b) an agreement (not being a regulated agreement) under which the creditor provides the debtor with fixed-sum credit not exceeding [the county court limit] or running-account credit on which the credit limit does not exceed [the county court limit].

[*The words in square brackets were substituted by the Administration of Justice Act 1982, s 37, Sch 3, Pt II, paras 2-3.*]

[(5A) In the preceding subsection 'the county court limit' means the county court limit for the time being specified by an Order in Council under section 145 of the County Courts Act 1984 as the county court limit for the purposes of that subsection.]

[*The words in square brackets were inserted by the Administration of Justice Act 1982, s 37, Sch 3, Pt II, para 4, as amended by s 148(1), Sch 2, Pt V, para 47.*]

(6) In Scotland an application under subsection (1)(a) may be brought in the sheriff court for the district in which the debtor or surety resides or carries on business.

(7) In Northern Ireland an application under subsection (1)(a) may be brought in the county court in the case of—

- (a) a regulated agreement, or

(*b*) an agreement (not being a regulated agreement) under which the creditor provides the debtor with fixed-sum credit not exceeding [£5,000] or running-account credit on which the credit limit does not exceed [£5,000].

[*The figures in square brackets were substituted by the County Courts (Amendment) Rules (Northern Ireland) 1982 (S.I. 1982 No. 120).*]

140. Interpretation of sections 137 to 139

Where the credit agreement is not a regulated agreement, expressions used in sections 137 to 139 which, apart from this section, apply only to regulated agreements, shall be construed as nearly as may be as if the credit agreement were a regulated agreement.

Miscellaneous

141. Jurisdiction and parties

(1) In England and Wales the county court shall have jurisdiction to hear and determine—

(*a*) any action by the creditor or owner to enforce a regulated agreement or any security relating to it;

(*b*) any action to enforce any linked transaction against the debtor or hirer or his relative,

and such an action shall not be brought in any other court.

(2) Where an action or application is brought in the High Court which, by virtue of this Act, ought to have been brought in the county court it shall not be treated as improperly brought, but shall be transferred to the county court.

[(3) In Scotland the sheriff court shall have jurisdiction to hear and determine any action referred to in subsection (1) and such an action shall not be brought in any other court.

(3A) Subject to subsection (3B) an action which is brought in the sheriff court by virtue of subsection (3) shall be brought only in one of the following courts, namely—

(*a*) the court for the place where the debtor or hirer is domiciled (within the meaning of section 41 or 42 of the Civil Jurisdiction and Judgments Act 1982);

(*b*) the court for the place where the debtor or hirer carries on business; and

(*c*) where the purpose of the action is to assert, declare or determine proprietary or possessory rights, or rights of security, in or over moveable property, or to obtain authority to dispose of moveable property, the court for the place where the property is situated.

(3B) Subsection (3A) shall not apply—

(*a*) where Rule 3 of Schedule 8 to the said Act of 1982 applies; or

(*b*) where the jurisdiction of another court has been prorogated by an agreement entered into after the dispute has arisen.]

[*Subsections (3) (3A) and (3B) were substituted for subsection (3) by the Civil Jurisdiction and Judgments Act 1982 with effect from 1st January 1987 (S.I. 1986 No. 2044).*]

(4) In Northern Ireland the county court shall have jurisdiction to hear and determine any action or application falling within subsection (1).

(5) Except as may be provided by rules of court, all the parties to a regulated agreement, and any surety, shall be made parties to any proceedings relating to the agreement.

142. Power to declare rights of parties

(1) Where under any provision of this Act a thing can be done by a creditor or owner on an enforcement order only, and either—

- (a) the court dismisses (except on technical grounds only) an application for an enforcement order, or
- (b) where no such application has been made or such an application has been dismissed on technical grounds only, an interested party applies to the court for a declaration under this subsection,

the court may if it thinks just make a declaration that the creditor or owner is not entitled to do that thing, and thereafter no application for an enforcement order in respect of it shall be entertained.

(2) Where—

- (a) a regulated agreement or linked transaction is cancelled under section 69(1), or becomes subject to section 69(2), or
- (b) a regulated agreement is terminated under section 91,

and an interested party applies to the court for a declaration under this subsection, the court may make a declaration to that effect.

Northern Ireland

143. Jurisdiction of county court in Northern Ireland

Without prejudice to any provision which may be made by rules of court made in relation to county courts in Northern Ireland such rules may provide—

- (a) that any action or application such as is mentioned in section 141(4) which is brought against the debtor or hirer in the county court may be brought in the county court for the division in which the debtor or hirer resided or carried on business at the date on which he last made a payment under the regulated agreement;
- (b) that an application by a debtor or hirer or any surety under section 129(1)(b), 132(1), 139(1)(a) or 142(1)(b) which is brought in the county court may be brought in the county court for the division in which the debtor, or, as the case may be, the hirer or surety resides or carries on business;
- (c) for service of process on persons outside Northern Ireland.

144. Appeal from county court in Northern Ireland

Any person dissatisfied—

- (a) with an order, whether adverse to him or in his favour, made by a county court in Northern Ireland in the exercise of any jurisdiction conferred by this Act, or
- (b) with the dismissal or refusal by such a county court of any action or application instituted by him under the provisions of this Act,

shall be entitled to appeal from the order or from the dismissal or refusal as if the order, dismissal or refusal had been made in exercise of the jurisdiction conferred by Part III of the County Courts [(Northern Ireland) Order 1980 and the appeal brought under Part VI of that Order and Articles 61 and 62 of that Order shall apply accordingly].

[*The words in square brackets were substituted by the County Courts (Northern Ireland) Order 1980 (S.I. 1980 No. 397).*]

PART X

ANCILLARY CREDIT BUSINESSES

Definitions

145. Types of ancillary credit business

(1) An ancillary credit business is any business so far as it comprises or relates to—

    (*a*) credit brokerage,
    (*b*) debt-adjusting,
    (*c*) debt-counselling,
    (*d*) debt-collecting, or
    (*e*) the operation of a credit reference agency.

(2) Subject to section 146(5), credit brokerage is the effecting of introductions—

    (*a*) of individuals desiring to obtain credit—
        (i) to persons carrying on business to which this sub-paragraph applies, or
        (ii) in the case of an individual desiring to obtain credit to finance the acquisition or provision of a dwelling occupied or to be occupied by himself or his relative, to any person carrying on a business in the course of which he provides credit secured on land, or
    (*b*) of individuals desiring to obtain goods on hire to persons carrying on business to which this paragraph applies, or
    (*c*) of individuals desiring to obtain credit, or to obtain goods on hire, to other credit-brokers

(3) Subsection (2)(*a*)(*i*) applies to—

    (*a*) a consumer credit business;
    (*b*) a business which comprises or relates to consumer credit agreements being, otherwise than by virtue of section 16(5)(*a*), exempt agreement;
    (*c*) a business which comprises or relates to unregulated agreements where—
        (i) the proper law of the agreement is the law of a country outside the United Kingdom, and
        (ii) if the proper law of the agreement were the law of a part of the United Kingdom it would be a regulated consumer credit agreement.

(4) Subsection (2)(*b*) applies to—

    (*a*) a consumer hire business;
    (*b*) a business which comprises or relates to unregulated agreements where—
        (i) the proper law of the agreement is the law of a country outside the United Kingdom, and

(ii) if the proper law of the agreement were the law of a part of the United Kingdom it would be a regulated consumer hire agreement.

(5) Subject to section 146(6), debt-adjusting is, in relation to debts due under consumer credit agreements or consumer hire agreements,—

- (*a*) negotiating with the creditor or owner, on behalf of the debtor or hirer, terms for the discharge of a debt, or
- (*b*) taking over, in return for payments by the debtor or hirer, his obligation to discharge a debt, or
- (*c*) any similar activity concerned with the liquidation of a debt.

(6) Subject to section 146(6), debt-counselling is the giving of advice to debtors or hirers about the liquidation of debts due under consumer credit agreements or consumer hire agreements.

(7) Subject to section 146(6), debt-collecting is the taking of steps to procure payment of debts due under consumer credit agreements or consumer hire agreements.

(8) A credit reference agency is a person carrying on a business comprising the furnishing of persons with information relevant to the financial standing of individuals, being information collected by the agency for that purpose.

146. Exceptions from section 145

(1) A barrister or advocate acting in that capacity is not to be treated as doing so in the course of any ancillary credit business.

(2) A solicitor engaging in contentious business (as defined in section 86(1) of the Solicitors Act 1957) is not to be treated as doing so in the course of any ancillary credit business.

(3) A solicitor within the meaning of the Solicitors (Scotland) Act 1933 engaging in business done in or for the purposes of proceedings before a court or before an arbiter is not to be treated as doing so in the course of any ancillary credit business.

(4) A solicitor in Northern Ireland engaging in business done, whether as solicitor or advocate, in or for the purposes of proceedings begun before a court (including the Lands Tribunal for Northern Ireland) or before an aribtrator appointed under the Arbitration Act (Northern Ireland) 1937, not being business [which falls within the definition of non-contentious probate business contained in Article 2(2) of the Administration of Estates (Northern Ireland) Order 1979] is not to be treated as doing so in the course of any ancillary credit business.

(5) For the purposes of section 145(2), introductions effected by an individual by canvassing off trade premises either debtor-creditor-supplier agreements falling within section 12(*a*) or regulated consumer hire agreements shall be disregarded if—

- (*a*) the introductions are not effected by him in the capacity of an employee, and
- (*b*) he does not by any other method effect introductions falling within section 145(2).

(6) It is not debt-adjusting, debt-counselling or debt-collecting for a person to do anything in relation to a debt arising under an agreement if—

(a) he is the creditor or owner under the agreement, otherwise than by virtue of an assignment, or
(b) he is the creditor or owner under the agreement by virtue of an assignment made in connection with the transfer to the assignee of any business other than a debt-collecting business, or
(c) he is the supplier in relation to the agreement, or
(d) he is a credit-broker who has acquired the business of the person who was the supplier in relation to the agreement, or
(e) he is a person prevented by subsection (5) from being treated as a credit-broker, and the agreement was made in consequence of an introduction (whether made by him or another person) which, under subsection (5), is to be disregarded.

[*The words in square brackets in subsection (4) were substituted by the Tax, Consumer Credit and Judicature (Northern Ireland Consequential Amendments) Order 1979 (S.I. 1979 No. 1576), article 4.*]

Licensing

147. Application of Part III

(1) The provisions of Part III (except section 40) apply to an ancillary credit business as they apply to a consumer credit business.

(2) Without prejudice to the generality of section 26, regulations under that section (as applied by subsection (1) may include provisions regulating the collection and dissemination of information by credit reference agencies.

148. Agreement for services of unlicensed trader

(1) An agreement for the services of a person carrying on an ancillary credit business (the 'trader'), if made when the trader was unlicensed, in enforceable against the other party (the 'customer') only where the Director has made an order under subsection (2) which applies to the agreement.

(2) The trader or his successor in title may apply to the Director for an order that agreements within subsection (1) are to be treated as if made when the trader was licensed.

(3) Unless the Director determines to make an order under subsection (2) in accordance with the application, he shall, before determining the application, by notice—

(a) inform the trader, giving his reasons, that, as the case may be, he is minded to refuse the application, or to grant it in terms different from those applied for, describing them, and
(b) invite the trader to submit to the Director representations in support of his application in accordance with section 34.

(4) In determining whether or not to make an order under subsection (2) in respect of any period the Director shall consider, in addition to any other relevant factors,—

(a) how far, if at all, customers under agreements made by the trader during that period were prejudiced by the trader's conduct.
(b) whether or not the Director would have been likely to grant a licence covering that period on application by the trader, and
(c) the degree of culpability for the failure to obtain a licence.

Consumer Credit Act 1974

(5) If the Director thinks fit, he may in an order under subsection (2)—

  (*a*) limit the order to specified agreements, or agreements of a specified description or made at a specified time;
  (*b*) make the order conditional on the doing of specified acts by the trader.

149. Regulated agreements made on introductions by unlicensed credit-broker

(1) A regulated agreement made by a debtor or hirer who, for the purpose of making that agreement, was introduced to the creditor or owner by an unlicensed credit-broker is enforceable against the debtor or hirer only where—

  (*a*) on the application of the credit-broker, the Director has made an order under section 148(2) in respect of a period including the time when the introduction was made, and the order does not (whether in general terms or specifically) exclude the application of this paragraph to the regulated agreement, or
  (*b*) the Director has made an order under subsection (2) which applies to the agreement.

(2) Where during any period individuals were introduced to a person carrying on a consumer credit business or consumer hire business by an unlicensed credit-broker for the purpose of making regulated agreements with the person carrying on that business, that person or his successor in title may apply to the Director for an order that regulated agreements so made are to be treated as if the credit-broker had been licensed at the time of the introduction.

(3) Unless the Director determines to make an order under subsection (2) in accordance with the application, he shall, before determining the application, by notice—

  (*a*) inform the applicant, giving his reasons, that, as the case may be, he is minded to refuse the application, or to grant it in terms different from those applied for, describing them, and
  (*b*) invite the applicant to submit to the Director representations in support of his application in accordance with section 34.

(4) In determining whether or not to make an order under subsection (2) the Director shall consider, in additon to any other relevant factors—

  (*a*) how far, if at all, debtors or hirers under regulated agreements to which the application relates were prejudiced by the credit-broker's conduct, and
  (*b*) the degree of culpability of the applicant in facilitating the carrying on by the credit-broker of his business when unlicensed.

(5) If the Director thinks fit, he may in an order under subsection (2)—

  (*a*) limit the order to specified agreements, or agreements of a specified description or made at a specified time;
  (*b*) make the order conditional on the doing of specified acts by the applicant.

150. Appeals to Secretary of State against licensing decisions

Section 41 (as applied by section 147(1)) shall have effect as if the following entry were included in the table set out at the end—

Determination	Appellant
Refusal to make order under section 148(2) or 149(2) in accordance with terms of application.	The applicant.

Seeking business

151. Advertisements

(1) Sections 44 to 47 apply to an advertisement published for the purposes of a business of credit brokerage carried on by any person, whether it advertises the services of that person or the services of persons to whom he effects introductions, as they apply to an advertisement to which Part IV applies.

(2) Sections 44, 46 and 47 apply to an advertisement, published for the purposes of a business carried on by the advertiser, indicating that he is willing to advise on debts, or engage in transactions concerned with the liquidation of debts, as they apply to an advertisement to which Part IV applies.

(3) The Secretary of State may by order provide that an advertisement published for the purposes of a business of credit brokerage, debt-adjusting or debt-counselling shall not fall within subsection (1) or (2) if it is of a description specified in the order.

(4) An advertisement does not fall within subsection (2) if it indicates that the advertiser is not willing to act in relation to consumer credit agreements and consumer hire agreements.

(5) In subsections (1) and (3) 'credit brokerage' includes the effecting of introductions of individuals desiring to obtain credit to any person carrying on a business in the course of which he provides credit secured on land.

152. Applications of sections 52 to 54 to credit brokerage etc.

(1) Sections 52 to 54 apply to a business of credit brokerage, debt-adjusting or debt-counselling as they apply to a consumer credit business.

(2) In their application to a business of credit brokerage, sections 52 and 53 shall apply to the giving of quotations and information about the business of any person to whom the credit-broker effects introductions as well as to the giving of quotations and information about his own business.

153. Definition of canvassing off trade premises (agreements for ancillary credit services)

(1) An individual (the 'canvasser') canvasses off trade premises the services of a person carrying on an ancillary credit business if he solicits the entry of another individual (the 'consumer') into an agreement for the provision to the consumer of those services by making oral representations to the consumer, or any other individual, during a visit by the canvasser to any place (not excluded by subsection (2)) where the consumer, or that other individual as the case may be, is, being a visit—

(*a*) carried out for the purpose of making such oral representations to individuals who are at that place, but
(*b*) not carried out in response to a request made on a previous occasion.

(2) A place is excluded from subsection (1) if it is a place where (whether on a permanent or temporary basis)—

(*a*) the ancillary credit business is carried on, or
(*b*) any business is carried on by the canvasser or the person whose employee or agent the canvasser is, or by the consumer.

154. Prohibition of canvassing certain ancillary credit services off trade premises

It is an offence to canvass off trade premises the services of a person carrying on a business of credit brokerage, debt-adjusting or debt-counselling.

155. Right to recover brokerage fees

(1) The excess over [£3] of a fee or commission for his services charged by a credit-broker to an individual to whom this subsection applies shall cease to be payable or, as the case may be, shall be recoverable by the individual if the introduction does not result in his entering into a relevant agreement within the six months following the introduction (disregarding any agreement which is cancelled under section 69(1) or becomes subject to section 69(2)).

[*The figure in square brackets was substituted by The Consumer Credit (Increase of Monetary Amounts) Order 1983 (S.I. 1983 No. 1571).*]

(2) Subsection (1) applies to an individual who sought an introduction for a purpose which would have been fulfilled by his entry into—

(*a*) a regulated agreement, or
(*b*) in the case of an individual such as is referred to in section 145(2)(*a*)(ii), an agreement for credit secured on land, or
(*c*) an agreement such as is referred to in section 145(3)(*b*) or (*c*) or (4)(*b*).

(3) An agreement is a relevant agreement for the purposes of subsection (1) in relation to an individual if it is an agreement such as is referred to in subsection (2) in relation to that individual.

(4) In the case of an individual desiring to obtain credit under a consumer credit agreement, any sum payable or paid by him to a credit-broker otherwise than as a fee or commission for the credit-broker's services shall for the purposes of subsection (1) be treated as such a fee or commission if it enters or would enter, into the total charge for credit.

Entry into agreements

156. Entry into agreements

Regulations may make provision, in relation to agreements entered into in the course of a business of credit brokerage, debt-adjusting or debt-counselling, corresponding, with such modifications as the Secretary of State thinks fit, to the provision which is or may be made by or under sections 55, 60, 61, 62, 63, 65, 127, 179 or 180 in relation to agreements to which those sections apply.

Credit reference agencies

157. Duty to disclose name etc. of agency

(1) A creditor, owner or negotiator, within the prescribed period after receiving a request in writing to that effect from the debtor or hirer, shall give him notice of the name and address of any credit reference agency from which the creditor,

owner or negotiator has, during the antecedent negotiations, applied for information about his financial standing.

(2) Subsection (1) does not apply to a request received more than 28 days after the termination of the antecedent negotiations, whether on the making of the regulated agreement or otherwise.

(3) If the creditor, owner or negotiator fails to comply with subsection (1) he commits an offence.

158. Duty of agency to disclose filed information

(1) A credit reference agency, within the prescribed period after receiving,—

(*a*) a request in writing to that effect from any individual (the 'consumer'), and
(*b*) such particulars as the agency may reasonably require to enable them to identify the file, and
(*c*) a fee of [£1],

shall give the consumer a copy of the file relating to him kept by the agency.

[*The figure in square brackets was substituted by The Consumer Credit (Increase of Monetary Amounts) Order 1983 (S.I. 1983 No. 1571).*]

(2) When giving a copy of the file under subsection (1), the agency shall also give the consumer a statement in the prescribed form of his rights under section 159.

(3) If the agency does not keep a file relating to the consumer it shall give him notice of that fact, but need not return any money paid.

(4) If the agency contravenes any provision of this section it commits an offence.

(5) In this Act 'file', in relation to an individual, means all the information about him kept by a credit reference agency, regardless of how the information is stored, and 'copy of the file', as respects information not in plain English, means a transcript reduced into plain English.

159. Correction of wrong information

(1) A consumer given information under section 158 who considers that an entry in his file is incorrect, and that if it is not corrected he is likely to be prejudiced, may give notice to the agency requiring it either to remove the entry from the file or amend it.

(2) Within 28 days after receiving a notice under subsection (1), the agency shall by notice inform the consumer that it has—

(*a*) removed the entry from the file, or
(*b*) amended the entry, or
(*c*) taken no action,

and if the notice states that the agency has amended the entry it shall include a copy of the file so far as it comprises the amended entry.

(3) Within 28 days after receiving a notice under subsection (2), or where no such notice was given, within 28 days after the expiry of the period mentioned in subsection (2), the consumer may, unless he has been informed by the agency that it has removed the entry from his file, serve a further notice on the agency

requiring it to add to the file an accompanying notice of correction (not exceeding 200 words) drawn up by the consumer, and include a copy of it when furnishing information included in or based on that entry.

(4) Within 28 days after receiving a notice under subsection (3), the agency, unless it intends to apply to the Director under subsection (5), shall by notice inform the consumer that it has received the notice under subsection (3) and intends to comply with it.

(5) If—

(a) the consumer has not received a notice under subsection (4) within the time required, or
(b) it appears to the agency that it would be improper for it to publish a notice of correction because it is incorrect, or unjustly defames any person, or is frivolous or scandalous, or is for any other reason unsuitable,

the consumer or, as the case may be, the agency may, in the prescribed manner and on payment of the specified fee, apply to the Director, who may make such order on the application as he thinks fit.

(6) If a person to whom an order under this section is directed fails to comply with it within the period specified in the order he commits an offence.

160. Alternative procedure for business consumers

(1) The Director, on an application made by a credit reference agency, may direct that this section shall apply to the agency if he is satisfied—

(a) that compliance with section 158 in the case of consumers who carry on a business would adversely affect the service provided to its customers by the agency, and
(b) that, having regard to the methods employed by the agency and to any other relevant factors, it is probable that consumers carrying on a business would not be prejudiced by the making of the direction.

(2) Where an agency to which this section applies receives a request, particulars and a fee under section 158(1) from a consumer who carries on a business, and section 158(3) does not apply, the agency, instead of complying with section 158, may elect to deal with the matter under the following subsections.

(3) Instead of giving the consumer a copy of the file, the agency shall within the prescribed period give notice to the consumer that it is proceeding under this section, and by notice give the consumer such information included in or based on entries in the file as the Director may direct, together with a statement in the prescribed form of the consumer's rights under subsections (4) and (5).

(4) If within 28 days after receiving the information given him under subsection (3), or such longer period as the Director may allow, the consumer—

(a) gives notice to the Director that he is dissatisfied with the information, and
(b) satisfies the Director that he has taken such steps in relation to the agency as may be reasonable with a view to removing the cause of his dissatisfaction, and
(c) pays the Director the specified fee,

the Director may direct the agency to give the Director a copy of the file, and the Director may disclose to the consumer such of the information on the file as the Director thinks fit.

(5) Section 159 applies with any necessary modifications to information given to the consumer under this section as it applies to information given under section 158.

(6) If an agency making an election under subsection (2) fails to comply with subsection (3) or (4) it commits an offence.

PART XI
ENFORCEMENT OF ACT

161. Enforcement authorities

(1) The following authorities ('enforcement authorities') have a duty to enforce this Act and regulations made under it—

    (*a*) the Director,
    (*b*) in Great Britain, the local weights and measures authority,
    (*c*) in Northern Ireland, the Department of Commerce for Northern Ireland.

(2) Where a local weights and measures authority in England or Wales propose to institute proceedings for an offence under this Act (other than an offence under section 162(6), 165(1) or (2) or 174(5)) it shall, as between the authority and the Director, be the duty of the authority to give the Director notice of the intended proceedings, together with a summary of the facts on which the charges are to be founded, and postpone institution of the proceedings until either—

    (*a*) 28 days have expired since that notice was given, or
    (*b*) the Director has notified them of receipt of the notice and summary.

(3) Every local weights and measures authority shall, whenever the Director requires, report to him in such form and with such particulars as he requires on the exercise of their functions under this Act.

[*Subsections (4)(5) and (6) were repealed as from 13 November 1980 by the Local Government, Planning and Land Act 1980, section 1(4) and Schedule 4, paragraph 10 and section 194 and Schedule 34, Part IV.*]

162. Powers of entry and inspection

(1) A duly authorised officer of an enforcement authority, at all reasonable hours and on production, if required, of his credentials, may—

    (*a*) in order to ascertain whether a breach of any provision of or under this Act has been committed, inspect any goods and enter any premises (other than premises used only as a dwelling);
    (*b*) if he has reasonable cause to suspect that a breach of any provision of or under this Act has been committed, in order to ascertain whether it has been committed, require any person—
        (i) carrying on, or employed in connection with, a business to produce any books or documents relating to it; or
        (ii) having control of any information relating to a business recorded otherwise than in a legible form to provide a document containing a legible reproduction of the whole or part of the information,

and take copies of, or of any entry in, the books or documents;
- (c) if he has reasonable cause to believe that a breach of any provision of or under this Act has been committed, seize and detain any goods in order to ascertain (by testing or otherwise) whether such a breach has been committed;
- (d) seize and detain any goods, books or documents which he has reason to believe may be required as evidence in proceedings for an offence under this Act;
- (e) for the purpose of exercising his powers under this subsection to seize goods, books or documents, but only if and to the extent that it is reasonably necessary for securing that the provisions of this Act and of any regulations made under it are duly observed, require any person having authority to do so to break open any container and, if that person does not comply, break it open himself.

(2) An officer seizing goods, books or documents in exercise of his powers under this section shall not do so without informing the person he seizes them from.

(3) If a justice of the peace, on sworn information in writing, or, in Scotland, a sheriff or a magistrate or justice of the peace, on evidence on oath,—
- (a) is satisfied that there is reasonable ground to believe either—
    - (i) that any goods, books or documents which a duly authorised officer has power to inspect under this section are on any premises and their inspection is likely to disclose evidence of a breach of any provision of or under this Act; or
    - (ii) that a breach of any provision of or under this Act has been, is being or is about to be committed on any premises; and
- (b) is also satisfied either—
    - (i) that admission to the premises has been or is likely to be refused and that notice of intention to apply for a warrant under this subsection has been given to the occupier; or
    - (ii) that an application for admission, or the giving of such a notice, would defeat the object of the entry or that the premises are unoccupied or that the occupier is temporarily absent and it might defeat the object of the entry to wait for his return,

the justice or, as the case may be, the sheriff or magistrate may by warrant under his hand, which shall continue in force for a period of one month, authorise an officer of an enforcement authority to enter the premises (by force if need be).

(4) An officer entering premises by virtue of this section may take such other persons and equipment with him as he thinks necessary; and on leaving premises entered by virtue of a warrant under subsection (3) shall, if they are unoccupied or the occupier is temporarily absent, leave them as effectively secured against trespassers as he found them.

(5) Regulations may provide that, in cases described by the regulations, an officer of a local weights and measures authority is not to be taken to be duly authorised for the purposes of this section unless he is authorised by the Director.

(6) A person who is not a duly authorised officer of an enforcement authority, but purports to act as such under this section, commits an offence.

(7) Nothing in this section compels a barrister, advocate or solicitor to produce

a document containing a privileged communication made by or to him in that capacity or authorises the seizing of any such document in his possession.

163. Compensation for loss

(1) Where, in exercising his powers under section 162, an officer of an enforcement authority seizes and detains goods and their owner suffers loss by reason of—

   (*a*) that seizure, or
   (*b*) the loss, damage or deterioration of the goods during detention,

then, unless the owner is convicted of an offence under this Act committed in relation to the goods, the authority shall compensate him for the loss so suffered.

(2) Any dispute as to the right to or amount of any compensation under subsection (1) shall be determined by arbitration.

164. Power to make test purchases etc.

(1) An enforcement authority may—

   (*a*) make, or authorise any of their officers to make on their behalf, such purchases of goods; and
   (*b*) authorise any of their officers to procure the provision of such services or facilities or to enter into such agreements or other transactions,

as may appear to them expedient for determining whether any provisions made by or under this Act are being complied with.

(2) Any act done by an officer authorised to do it under subsection (1) shall be treated for the purposes of this Act as done by him as an individual on his own behalf.

(3) Any goods seized by an officer under this Act may be tested, and in the event of such a test he shall inform the person mentioned in section 162(2) of the test results.

(4) Where any test leads to proceedings under this Act, the enforcement authority shall—

   (*a*) if the goods were purchased, inform the person they were purchased from of the test results, and
   (*b*) allow any person against whom the proceedings are taken to have the goods tested on his behalf if it is reasonably practicable to do so.

165. Obstruction of authorised officers

(1) Any person who—

   (*a*) wilfully obstructs an officer of an enforcement authority acting in pursuance of this Act; or
   (*b*) wilfully fails to comply with any requirement properly made to him by such an officer under section 162; or
   (*c*) without reasonable cause fails to give such an officer (so acting) other assistance or information he may reasonably require in performing his functions under this Act,

commits an offence.

Consumer Credit Act 1974

(2) If any person, in giving such information as is mentioned in subsection (1)(*c*), makes any statement which he knows to be false, he commits an offence.

(3) Nothing in this section requires a person to answer any question or give any information if to do so might incriminate that person or (where that person is married) the husband or wife of that person.

166. Notification of convictions and judgments to Director

Where a person is convicted of an offence or has a judgment given against him by or before any court in the United Kingdom and it appears to the court—

(*a*) having regard to the functions of the Director under this Act, that the conviction or judgment should be brought to the Director's attention, and

(*b*) that it may not be brought to his attention unless arrangements for that purpose are made by the court,

the court may make such arrangements notwithstanding that the proceedings have been finally disposed of.

167. Penalties

(1) An offence under a provision of this Act specified in column 1 of Schedule 1 is triable in the mode or modes indicated in column 3, and on conviction is punishable as indicated in column 4 (where a period of time indicates the maximum term of imprisonment, and a monetary amount indicates the maximum fine, for the offence in question).

(2) A person who contravenes any regulations made under section 44, 52, 53, or 112, or made under section 26 by virtue of section 54, commits an offence.

168. Defences

(1) In any proceedings for an offence under this Act it is a defence for the person charged to prove—

(*a*) that his act or omission was due to a mistake, or to reliance on information supplied to him, or to an act or omission by another person, or to an accident or some other cause beyond his control, and

(*b*) that he took all reasonable precautions and exercised all due diligence to avoid such an act or omission by himself or any person under his control.

(2) If in any case the defence provided by subsection (1) involves the allegation that the act or omission was due to an act or omission by another person or to reliance on information supplied by another person, the person charged shall not, without leave of the court, be entitled to rely on that defence unless, within a period ending seven clear days before the hearing, he has served on the prosecutor a notice giving such information identifying or assisting in the identification of that other person as was then in his possession.

169. Offences by bodies corporate

Where at any time a body corporate commits an offence under this Act with the consent or connivance of, or because of neglect by, any individual, the individual commits the like offence if at that time—

(*a*) he is a director, manager, secretary or similar officer of the body corporate, or
(*b*) he is purporting to act as such an officer, or
(*c*) the body corporate is managed by its members of whom he is one.

170. No further sanctions for breach of Act

(1) A breach of any requirement made (otherwise than by any court) by or under this Act shall incur no civil or criminal sanction as being such a breach, except to the extent (if any) expressly provided by or under this Act.

(2) In exercising his functions under this Act the Director may take account of any matter appearing to him to constitute a breach of a requirement made by or under this Act, whether or not any sanction for that breach is provided by or under this Act and, if it is so provided, whether or not proceedings have been brought in respect of the breach.

(3) Subsection (1) does not prevent the grant of an injunction, or the making of an order of certiorari, mandamus or prohibition or as respects Scotland the grant of an interdict or of an order under section 91 of the Court of Session Act 1868 (order for specific performance of statutory duty).

171. Onus of proof in various proceedings

(1) If an agreement contains a term signifying that in the opinion of the parties section 10(3)(*b*)(iii) does not apply to the agreement, it shall be taken not to apply unless the contrary is proved.

(2) It shall be assumed in any proceedings, unless the contrary is proved, that when a person initiated a transaction as mentioned in section 19(1)(*c*) he knew the principal agreement had been made, or contemplated that it might be made.

(3) Regulations under section 44 or 52 may make provision as to the onus of proof in any proceedings to enforce the regulations.

(4) In proceedings brought by the creditor under a credit-token agreement—

(*a*) it is for the creditor to prove that the credit-token was lawfully supplied to the debtor, and was accepted by him, and
(*b*) if the debtor alleges that any use made of the credit-token was not authorised by him, it is for the creditor to prove either—
(i) that the use was so authorised, or
(ii) that the use occurred before the creditor had been given notice under section 84(3).

(5) In proceedings under section 50(1) in respect of a document received by a minor at any school or other educational establishment for minors, it is for the person sending it to him at that establishment to prove that he did not know or suspect it to be such an establishment.

(6) In proceedings under section 119(1) it is for the pawnee to prove that he had reasonable cause to refuse to allow the pawn to be redeemed.

(7) If, in proceedings referred to in section 139(1), the debtor or any surety alleges that the credit bargain is extortionate it is for the creditor to prove the contrary.

172. Statements by creditor or owner to be binding

(1) A statement by a creditor or owner is binding on him if given under—

> section 77(1),
> section 78(1),
> section 79(1),
> section 97(1),
> section 107(1)(c),
> section 108(1)(c), or
> section 109(1)(c).

(2) Where a trader—

(a) gives a customer a notice in compliance with section 103(1)(b), or
(b) gives a customer a notice under section 103(1) asserting that the customer is not indebted to him under an agreement,

the notice is binding on the trader.

(3) Where in proceedings before any court—

(a) it is sought to reply on a statement or notice given as mentioned in subsection (1) or (2), and
(b) the statement or notice is shown to be incorrect,

the court may direct such relief (if any) to be given to the creditor or owner from the operation of subsection (1) or (2) as appears to the court to be just.

173. Contracting-out forbidden

(1) A term contained in a regulated agreement or linked transaction, or in any other agreement relating to an actual or prospective regulated agreement or linked transaction, is void if, and to the extent that, it is inconsistent with a provision for the protection of the debtor or hirer or his relative or any surety contained in this Act or in any regulation made under this Act.

(2) Where a provision specifies the duty or liability of the debtor or hirer or his relative or any surety in certain circumstances, a term is inconsistent with that provision if it purports to impose, directly or indirectly, an additional duty or liability on him in those circumstances.

(3) Notwithstanding subsection (1), a provision of this Act under which a thing may be done in relation to any person on an order of the court or the Director only shall not be taken to prevent its being done at any time with that person's consent given at that time, but the refusal of such consent shall not give rise to any liability.

PART XII

SUPPLEMENTAL

174. Restrictions on disclosure of information

(1) No information obtained under or by virtue of this Act about any individual shall be disclosed without his consent.

(2) No information obtained under or by virtue of this Act about any business shall be disclosed except, so long as the business continues to be carried on, with the consent of the person for the time being carrying it on.

(3) Subsections (1) and (2) do not apply to any disclosure of information made—

(*a*) for the purpose of facilitating the performance of any functions, under this Act, the Trade Descriptions Act 1968 or Part II or III or section 125 (annual and other reports of Director) of the Fair Trading Act 1973, [or the Estate Agents Act 1979, or the Competition Act 1980, or the Telecommunications Act 1984 or the Gas Act 1986 or the Airports Act 1986 or the Consumer Protection Act 1987 or the Control of Misleading Advertisements Regulations 1988] of the Secretary of State, any other Minister, [the Director General of Telecommunications, the Director General of Gas Supply, the Civil Aviation Authority] any enforcement authority or any Northern Ireland department, or

(*b*) in connection with the investigation of any criminal offence or for the purposes of any criminal proceedings, or

(*c*) for the purposes of any civil proceedings brought under or by virtue of this Act or under Part III of the Fair Trading Act 1973 [or under the Control of Misleading Advertisements Regulations].

[*The words in square brackets were inserted by the Estate Agents Act 1979, s 10(4)(b), by the Competition Act 1980, s 19(4)(d), by the Telecommunications Act 1984, s 109, Sch 4, para 60, by the Gas Act 1986, s 67(1), Sch 7, para 19, by the Airports Act 1986, s 83(1), Sch 4, para 4, by the Consumer Protection Act 1987, s 48, Sch 4, para 4 and by the Control of Misleading Advertisements Regulations 1988, regulation 7(6)(b).*]

(4) Nothing in subsections (1) and (2) shall be construed—

(*a*) as limiting the particulars which may be entered in the register; or

(*b*) as applying to any information which has been made public as part of the register.

(5) Any person who discloses information in contravention of this section commits an offence.

175. Duty of persons deemed to be agents

Where under this Act a person is deemed to receive a notice or payment as agent of the creditor or owner under a regulated agreement, he shall be deemed to be under a contractual duty to the creditor or owner to transmit the notice, or remit the payment, to him forthwith.

176. Service of documents

(1) A document to be served under this Act by one person ('the server') on another person ('the subject') is to be treated as properly served on the subject if dealt with as mentioned in the following subsections.

(2) The document may be delivered or sent by post to the subject, or addressed to him by name and left at his proper address.

(3) For the purposes of this Act, a document sent by post to, or left at, the address last known to the server as the address of a person shall be treated as sent by post to, or left at, his proper address.

(4) Where the document is to be served on the subject as being the person having any interest in land, and it is not practicable after reasonable inquiry to ascertain the subject's name or address, the document may be served by—

(a) addressing it to the subject by the description of the person having that interest in the land (naming it), and

(b) delivering the document to some responsible person on the land or affixing it, or a copy of it, in a conspicuous position on the land.

(5) Where a document to be served on the subject as being a debtor, hirer or surety, or as having any other capacity relevant for the purposes of this Act, is served at any time on another person who—

(a) is the person last known to the server as having that capacity, but

(b) before that time had ceased to have it,

the document shall be treated as having been served at that time on the subject.

(6) Anything done to a document in relation to a person who (whether to the knowledge of the server or not) has died shall be treated for the purposes of subsection (5) as service of the document on that person if it would have been so treated had he not died.

(7) Neither of the following enactments (which provide for the vesting of the estate of an intestate in the Probate Judge) shall be construed as authorising service on the Probate Judge of any document which is to be served under this Act—

section 9 of the Administration of Estates Act 1925;
section 3 of the Administration of Estates Act (Northern Ireland) 1955.

(8) References in the preceding subsections to the serving of a document on a person include the giving of the document to that person.

177. Saving for registered charges

(1) Nothing in this Act affects the rights of a proprietor of a registered charge (within the meaning of the Land Registration Act (1925), who—

(a) became the proprietor under a transfer for valuable consideration without notice of any defect in the title arising (apart from this section) by virtue of this Act, or

(b) derives title from such a proprietor.

(2) Nothing in this Act affects the operation of section 104 of the Law of Property Act 1925 (protection of purchaser where mortgagee exercises power of sale).

(3) Subsection (1) does not apply to a proprietor carrying on a business of debt-collecting.

(4) Where, by virtue of subsection (1), a land mortgage is enforced which apart from this section would be treated as never having effect, the original creditor or owner shall be liable to indemnify the debtor or hirer against any loss thereby suffered by him.

(5) In the application of this section to Scotland for subsections (1) to (3) there shall be substituted the following subsections—

'(1) Nothing in this Act affects the rights of a creditor in a heritable security who—

(a) became the creditor under a transfer for value without notice of any defect in the title arising (apart from this section) by virtue of this Act; or

(b) derives title from such a creditor.

(2) Nothing in this Act affects the operation of section 41 of the Conveyancing (Scotland) Act 1924 (protection of purchasers), or of that section as applied to standard securities by section 32 of the Conveyancing and Feudal Reform (Scotland) Act 1970.

(3) Subsection (1) does not apply to a creditor carrying on a business of debt-collecting.'.

(6) In the application of this section to Northern Ireland—

(a) any reference to the proprietor of a registered charge (within the meaning of the Land Registration Act 1925) shall be construed as a reference to the registered owner of a charge under the Local Registration of Title (Ireland) Act 1891 or Part VI of the Land Registration Act (Northern Ireland) 1970, and

(b) for the reference to section 104 of the Law of Property Act 1925 there shall be substituted a reference to section 21 of the Conveyancing and Law of Property Act 1881 and section 5 of the Conveyancing Act 1911.

178. Local Acts

The Secretary of State or the Department of Commerce for Northern Ireland may by order make such amendments or repeals of any provision of any local Act as appears to the Secretary of State or, as the case may be, the Department, necessary or expedient in consequence of the replacement by this Act of the enactments relating to pawnbrokers and moneylenders.

Regulations, orders, etc.

179. Power to prescribe form etc. of secondary documents

(1) Regulations may be made as to the form and content of credit-cards, trading-checks, receipts, vouchers and other documents or things issued by creditors, owners or suppliers under or in connection with regulated agreements or by other persons in connection with linked transactions, and may in particular—

(a) require specified information to be included in the prescribed manner in documents, and other specified material to be excluded;

(b) contain requirements to ensure that specified information is clearly brought to the attention of the debtor or hirer, or his relative, and that one part of a document is not given insufficient or excessive prominence compared with another.

(2) If a person issues any document or thing in contravention of regulations under subsection (1) then, as from the time of the contravention but without prejudice to anything done before it, this Act shall apply as if the regulated agreement had been improperly executed by reason of a contravention of regulations under section 60(1).

180. Power to prescribe form etc. of copies

(1) Regulations may be made as to the form and content of documents to be issued as copies of any executed agreement, security instrument or other document referred to in this Act, and may in particular—

(a) require specified information to be included in the prescribed manner in any copy, and contain requirements to ensure that such information is clearly brought to the attention of a reader of the copy;

(b) authorise the omission from a copy of certain material contained in the original, or the inclusion of such material in condensed form.

(2) A duty imposed by any provision of this Act (except section 35) to supply a copy of any document—

(a) is not satisfied unless the copy supplied is in the prescribed form and conforms to the prescribed requirements;

(b) is not infringed by the omission of any material, or its inclusion in condensed form, if that is authorised by regulations;

and reference in this Act to copies shall be construed accordingly.

(3) Regulations may provide that a duty imposed by this Act to supply a copy of a document referred to in an unexecuted agreement or an executed agreement shall not apply to documents of a kind specified in the regulations.

181. Power to alter monetary limits etc.

(1) The Secretary of State may by order by statutory instrument amend, or further amend, any of the following provisions of this Act so as to reduce or increase a sum mentioned in that provision, namely, sections 8(2), 15(1)(c), 17(1), 43(3)(a), 70(6), 75(3)(b), 77(1), 78(1), 79(1), 84(1), 101(7)(a), 107(1), 108(1), 109(1), 110(1), 118(1)(b), 120(1)(a), 139(5) and (7), 155(1) and 158(1).

(2) An order under subsection (1) amending section 8(2), 15(1)(c), 17(1), 43(3)(a), 75(3)(b) or 139(5) or (7) shall be of no effect unless a draft of the order has been laid before and approved by each House of Parliament.

182. Regulations and orders

(1) Any power of the Secretary of State to make regulations or orders under this Act, except the power conferred by sections 2(1)(a), 181 and 192 shall be exercisable by statutory instrument subject to annulment in pursuance of a resolution of either House of Parliament.

(2) Where a power to make regulations or orders is exercisable by the Secretary of State by virtue of this Act, regulations or orders made in the exercise of that power may—

(a) make different provision in relation to different cases or classes of case, and

(b) exclude certain cases or classes of case, and

(c) contain such transitional provisions as the Secretary of State thinks fit.

(3) Regulations may provide that specified expressions, when used as described by the regulations, are to be given the prescribed meaning, notwithstanding that another meaning is intended by the person using them.

(4) Any power conferred on the Secretary of State by this Act to make orders includes power to vary or revoke an order so made.

183. Determinations etc. by Director

The Director may vary or revoke any determination or direction made or given by him under this Act (other than Part III, or Part III as applied by section 147).

Interpretation

184. Associates

(1) A person is an associate of an individual if that person is the individual's husband or wife, or is a relative, or the husband or wife of a relative, of the individual or of the individual's husband or wife.

(2) A person is an associate of any person with whom he is in partnership, and of the husband or wife or a relative of any individual with whom he is in partnership.

(3) A body corporate is an associate of another body corporate—

(*a*) if the same person is a controller of both, or a person is a controller of one and persons who are his associates, or he and persons who are his associates, are controllers of the other: or

(*b*) if a group of two or more persons is a controller of each company, and the groups either consist of the same persons or could be regarded as consisting of the same persons by treating (in one or more cases) a member of either group as replaced by a person of whom he is an associate.

(4) A body corporate is an associate of another person if that person is a controller of it or if that person and persons who are his associates together are controllers of it.

(5) In this section 'relative' means brother, sister, uncle, aunt, nephew, niece, lineal ancestor or lineal descendant, and references to a husband or wife include a former husband or wife and a reputed husband or wife; and for the purposes of his subsection a relationship shall be established as if any illegitimate child, step-child or adopted child of a person had been a child born to him in wedlock.

185. Agreement with more than one debtor or hirer

(1) Where an actual or prospective regulated agreement has two or more debtors or hirers (not being a partnership or an unincorporated body of persons)—

(*a*) anything required by or under this Act to be done to or in relation to the debtor or hirer shall be done to or in relation to each of them; and

(*b*) anything done under this Act by or on behalf of one of them shall have effect as if done by or on behalf of all of them.

(2) Notwithstanding subsection (1)(*a*), where running-account credit is provided to two or more debtors jointly, any of them may by a notice signed by him (a 'dispensing notice') authorise the creditor not to comply in his case with section 78(4) (giving of periodical statement of account); and the dispensing notice shall have effect accordingly until revoked by a further notice given by the debtor to the creditor:

Provided that:

(*a*) a dispensing notice shall not take effect if previous dispensing notices are operative in the case of the other debtor, or each of the other debtors, as the case may be;

(b) any dispensing notices operative in relation to an agreement shall cease to have effect if any of the debtors dies;

[(c) a dispensing notice which is operative in relation to an agreement shall be operative also in relation to any subsequent agreement which, in relation to the earlier agreement, is a modifying agreement].

(3) Subsection (1)(b) does not apply for the purposes of section 61(1)(a) or 127(3).

(4) Where a regulated agreement has two or more debtors or hirers (not being a partnership or an unincorporated body of persons), section 86 applies to the death of any of them.

(5) An agreement for the provision of credit, or the bailment or (in Scotland) the hiring of goods, to two or more persons jointly where—

(a) one or more of those persons is an individual, and
(b) one or more of them is a body corporate,

is a consumer credit agreement or consumer hire agreement if it would have been one had they all been individuals; and the body corporate or bodies corporate shall accordingly be included among the debtors or hirers under the agreement.

(6) Where subsection (5) applies, references in this Act to the signing of any document by the debtor or hirer shall be construed in relation to a body corporate as referring to a signing on behalf of the body corporate.

[Paragraph (c) in subsection (2) was added by the Banking Act 1979, s 38(3), which was brought into force on 1 October 1979 by the Banking Act 1979 (Commencement No. 1) Order 1979 (S.I. 1979 No. 938).]

186. Agreement with more than one creditor or owner

Where an actual or prospective regulated agreement has two or more creditors or owners, anything required by or under this Act to be done to, or in relation to, or by, the creditor or owners shall be effective if done to, or in relation to, or by, any one of them.

187. Arrangements between creditor and supplier

(1) A consumer credit agreement shall be treated as entered into under pre-existing arrangements between a creditor and a supplier if it is entered into in accordance with, or in furtherance of, arrangements previously made between persons mentioned in subsection (4)(a), (b) or (c).

(2) A consumer credit agreement shall be treated as entered into in contemplation of further arrangements between a creditor and a supplier if it is entered into in the expectation that arrangements will subsequently be made between persons mentioned in subsection (4)(a), (b) or (c) for the supply of cash, goods and services (or any of them) to be financed by the consumer credit agreement.

(3) Arrangements shall be disregarded for the purposes of subsection (1) or (2) if—

(a) they are arrangements for the making, in specified circumstances, of payments to the supplier by the creditor, and
(b) the creditor holds himself out as willing to make, in such circumstances, payments of the kind to suppliers generally.

[(3A) Arrangements shall also be disregarded for the purposes of subsections (1) and (2), if they are arrangements for the electronic transfer of funds from a current account at a bank within the meaning of the Bankers' Books Evidence Act 1879.]

[*Subsection (3A) was added by the Banking Act 1987, section 89 with effect from 1st October 1987 (see S.I. 1987 No 1664).*]

(4) The persons referred to in subsections (1) and (2) are—

    (*a*) the creditor and the supplier;

    (*b*) one of them and an associate of the other;

    (*c*) an associate of one and an associate of the other.

(5) Where the creditor is an associate of the supplier, the consumer credit agreement shall be treated, unless the contrary is proved, as entered into under pre-existing arrangements between the creditor and the supplier.

188. Examples of use of new terminology

(1) Schedule 2 shall have effect for illustrating the use of terminology employed in this Act.

(1) The examples given in Schedule 2 are not exhaustive.

(3) In the case of conflict between Schedule 2 and any other provision of this Act, that other provision shall prevail.

(4) The Secretary of State may by order amend Schedule 2 by adding further examples or in any other way.

189. Definitions

(1) In this Act, unless the context otherwise requires—

    'advertisement' includes every form of advertising, whether in a publication, by television or radio, by display of notices, signs, labels, showcards or goods, by distribution of samples, circulars, catalogues, price lists or other material, by exhibition of pictures, models or films, or in any other way, and references to the publishing of advertisements shall be construed accordingly;

    'advertiser' in relation to an advertisement, means any person indicated by the advertisement as willing to enter into transactions to which the advertisement relates;

    'ancillary credit business' has the meaning given by section 145(1);

    'antecedent negotiations' has the meaning given by section 56;

    'appeal period' means the period beginning on the first day on which an appeal to the Secretary of State may be brought and ending on the last day on which it may be brought or, if it is brought, ending on its final determination, or abandonment;

    'assignment', in relation to Scotland, means assignation;

    'associate' shall be construed in accordance with section 184;

    ['authorised institution' means an institution authorised under the Banking Act 1987;]

[*The definition of 'authorised institution' was added by the Banking Act 1987, section 88.*]

'bill of sale' has the meaning given by section 4 of the Bills of Sale Act 1878 or, for Northern Ireland, by section 4 of the Bills of Sale (Ireland) Act 1879;

'building society' [means a building society within the meaning of the Building Societies Act 1986;]

[*The definition, given in square brackets, of 'building society' was substituted by the Building Societies Act 1986, section 120 and Schedule 18, paragraph 10(4).*]

'business' includes profession or trade, and references to a business apply subject to subsection (2);

'cancellable agreement' means a regulated agreement which, by virtue of section 67, may be cancelled by the debtor or hirer;

'canvass' shall be construed in accordance with sections 48 and 153;

'cash' includes money in any form;

'charity' means as respects England and Wales a charity registered under the Charities Act 1960 or an exempt charity (within the meaning of that Act), and as respects Scotland and Northern Ireland an institution or other organisation established for charitable purposes only ('organisation' including any persons administering a trust and 'charitable' being construed in the same way as if it were contained in the Income Tax Acts);

'conditional sale agreement' means an agreement for the sale of goods or land under which the purchase price or part of it is payable by instalments, and the property in the goods or land is to remain in the seller (notwithstanding that the buyer is to be in possession of the goods or land) until such conditions as to the payment of instalments or otherwise as may be specified in the agreement are fulfilled;

'consumer credit agreement' has the meaning given by section 8, and includes a consumer credit agreement which is cancelled under section 69(1), or becomes subject to section 69(2), so far as the agreement remains in force;

'consumer credit business' means any business so far as it comprises or relates to the provision of credit under regulated consumer credit agreements;

'consumer hire agreement' has the meaning given by section 15;

'consumer hire business' means any business so far as it comprises or relates to the bailment or (in Scotland) the hiring of goods under regulated consumer hire agreements;

'controller', in relation to a body corporate, means a person— (*a*) in accordance with whose directions or instructions the directors of the body corporate or of another body corporate which is its controller (or any of them) are accustomed to act, or (*b*) who, either alone or with any associate or associates, is entitled to exercise, or control the

Consumer Credit Act 1974

exercise of, one-third or more of the voting power at any general meeting of the body corporate or of another body corporate which is its controller;

'copy' shall be construed in accordance with section 180;

'costs', in relation to Scotland, means expenses;

'court' means in relation to England and Wales the county court, in relation to Scotland the sheriff court and in relation to Northern Ireland the High Court or the county court;

'credit' shall be construed in accordance with section 9;

'credit-broker' means a person carrying on a business of credit brokerage;

'credit brokerage' has the meaning given by section 145(2);

'credit limit' has the meaning given by section 10(2);

'creditor' means the person providing credit under a consumer credit agreement or the person to whom his rights and duties under the agreement have passed by assignment or operation of law, and in relation to a prospective consumer credit agreement, includes the prospective creditor;

'credit reference agency' has the meaning given by section 145(8);

'credit-sale agreement' means an agreement for the sale of goods, under which the purchase price or part of it is payable by instalments, but which is not a conditional sale agreement;

'credit-token' has the meaning given by section 14(1);

'credit-token agreement' means a regulated agreement for the provision of credit in connection with the use of a credit-token;

'debt-adjusting' has the meaning given by section 145(5);

'debt-collecting' has the meaning given by section 145(7);

'debt-counselling' has the meaning given by section 145(6);

'debtor' means the individual receiving credit under a consumer credit agreement or the person to whom his rights and duties under the agreement have passed by assignment or operation of law, and in relation to a prospective consumer credit agreement includes the prospective debtor;

'debtor-creditor agreement' has the meaning given by section 13;

'debtor-creditor-supplier agreement' has the meaning given by section 12;

'default notice' has the meaning given by section 87(1);

'deposit' means any sum payable by a debtor or hirer by way of deposit or down-payment, or credited or to be credited to him on account of any deposit or down-payment, whether the sum is to be or has been paid to the creditor or owner or any other person, or is to be or has been discharged by a payment of money or a transfer or delivery of goods or by any other means;

'Director' means the Director General of Fair Trading;

'electric line' has the meaning given by the Electric Lighting Act 1882 or,

Consumer Credit Act 1974

for Northern Ireland, the Electricity Supply (Northern Ireland) Order 1972;

'embodies' and related words shall be construed in accordance with subsection (4);

'enforcement authority' has the meaning given by section 161(1);

'enforcement order' means an order under section 65(1), 105(7)(*a*) or (*b*), 111(2) or 124(1) or (2);

'executed agreement' means a document, signed by or on behalf of the parties, embodying the terms of a regulated agreement, or such of them as have been reduced to writing;

'exempt agreement' means an agreement specified in or under section 16;

'finance' means to finance wholly or partly, and 'financed' and 'refinanced' shall be construed accordingly;

'file' and 'copy of the file' have the meanings given by section 185(5);

'fixed-sum credit' has the meaning given by section 10(1)(*b*);

'friendly society' means a society registered under the Friendly Societies Acts 1896 to 1971 or a society within the meaning of the Friendly Societies Act (Northern Ireland) 1970;

'future arrangements' shall be construed in accordance with section 187;

'general notice' means a notice published by the Director at a time and in a manner appearing to him suitable for securing that the notice is seen within a reasonable time by persons likely to be affected by it;

'give' means deliver or send by post to;

'goods' has the meaning given by [section 61(1) of the Sale of Goods Act 1979];

[*The words in square brackets were substituted by the Sale of Goods Act 1979, section 63(2) and Schedule 2, paragraph 18.*]

'group licence' has the meaning given in section 22(1)(*b*);

'High Court' means Her Majesty's High Court of Justice, or the Court of Session in Scotland or the High Court of Justice in Northern Ireland;

'hire-purchase agreement' means an agreement, other than a conditional sale agreement, under which—

    (*a*) goods are bailed or (in Scotland) hired in return for periodical payments by the person to whom they are bailed or hired, and
    (*b*) the property in the goods will pass to that person if the terms of the agreement are complied with and one or more of the following occurs—
        (i) the exercise of an option to purchase by that person,
        (ii) the doing of any other specified act by any party to the agreement,
        (iii) the happening of any other specified event;

'hirer' means the individual to whom goods are bailed or (in Scotland) hired under a consumer hire agreement, or the person to whom his rights and duties under the agreement have passed by assignment or operation of law, and in relation to a prospective consumer hire agreement includes the prospective hirer;

'individual' includes a partnership or other unincorporated body of persons not consisting entirely of bodies corporate;

'installation' means—

(a) the installing of any electric line or any gas or water pipe,
(b) the fixing of goods to the premises where they are to be used, and the alteration of premises to enable goods to be used on them,
(c) where it is reasonably necessary that goods should be constructed or erected on the premises where they are to be used, any work carried out for the purpose of constructing or erecting them on those premises;

'insurance company' has the meaning given by [section 96(1) of the Insurance Companies Act 1982], but does not include a friendly society or an organisation of workers or organisation of employers;

[*The words in square brackets were substituted by the Insurance Companies Act 1982, s 99(2), Sch 5, para 14.*]

'judgment' includes an order or decree made by any court;

'land' includes an interest in land, and in relation to Scotland includes heritable subjects of whatever description;

'land improvement company' means an improvement company as defined by section 7 of the Improvement of Land Act 1899;

'land mortgage' includes any security charged on land;

'licence' means a licence under Part III (including that Part as applied to ancillary credit businesses by section 147);

'licensed', in relation to any act, means authorised by a licence to do the act or cause or permit another person to do it;

'licensee', in the case of a group licence, includes any person covered by the licence;

'linked transaction' has the meaning given by section 19(1);

'local authority', in relation to England and Wales, means [. . .], a county council, a London borough council, a district council, the Common Council of the City of London, or the Council of the Isles of Scilly, and in relation to Scotland, means a regional, islands or district council, and, in relation to Northern Ireland, means a district council;

[*The words omitted above were repealed by Schedule 17 of the Local Government Act 1985.*]

'minor', in relation to Scotland, includes pupil;

'modifying agreement' has the meaning given by section 82(2);

'mortgage', in relation to Scotland, includes any heritable security;

'multiple agreement' has the meaning given by section 18(1);

'negotiator' has the meaning given by section 56(1);

'non-commercial agreement' means a consumer credit agreement or a consumer hire agreement not made by the creditor or owner in the course of a business carried on by him;

'notice' means notice in writing;

'notice of cancellation' has the meaning given by section 69(1);

'owner' means a person who bails or (in Scotland) hires out goods under a consumer hire agreement or the person to whom his rights and duties under the agreement have passed by assignment or operation of law, and in relation to a prospective consumer hire agreement, includes the prospective bailor or person from whom the goods are to be hired;

'pawn' means any article subject to a pledge;

'pawn-receipt' has the meaning given by section 114;

'pawnee' and 'pawnor' include any person to whom the rights and duties of the original pawnee or the original pawnor, as the case may be, have passed by assignment or operation of law;

'payment' includes tender;

'personal credit agreement' has the meaning given by section 8(1);

'pledge' means the pawnee's rights over an article taken in pawn;

'prescribed' means prescribed by regulations made by the Secretary of State;

'pre-existing arrangements' shall be construed in accordance with section 187;

'principal agreement' has the meaning given by section 19(1);

'protected goods' has the meaning given by section 90(7);

'quotation' has the meaning given by section 52(1)(*a*);

'redemption period' has the meaning given by section 116(3);

'register' means the register kept by the Director under section 35;

'regulated agreement' means a consumer credit agreement, or consumer hire agreement, other than an exempt agreement, and 'regulated' and 'unregulated' shall be construed accordingly;

'regulations' means regulations made by the Secretary of State;

'relative', except in section 184, means a person who is an associate by virtue of section 184(1);

'representation' includes any condition or warranty, and any other statement or undertaking, whether oral or in writing;

'restricted-use credit agreement' and 'restricted-use credit' have the meanings given by section 11(1);

'rules of court', in relation to Northern Ireland means, in relation to the High Court, rules made under section 7 of the Northern Ireland Act 1962, and, in relation to any other court, rules made by the authority

Consumer Credit Act 1974

having for the time being power to make rules regulating the practice and procedure in that court;

'running-account credit' shall be construed in accordance with section 10;

'security', in relation to an actual or prospective consumer credit agreement or consumer hire agreement, or any linked transaction, means a mortgage, charge, pledge, bond, debenture, indemnity, guarantee, bill, note or other right provided by the debtor or hirer, or at his request (express or implied), to secure the carrying out of the obligations of the debtor or hirer under the agreement;

'security instrument' has the meaning given by section 105(2);

'serve on' means delivery or send by post to;

'signed' shall be construed in accordance with subsection (3);

'small agreement' has the meaning given by section 17(1), and 'small' in relation to an agreement within any category shall be construed accordingly;

'specified fee' shall be construed in accordance with section 2(4) and (5);

'standard licence' has the meaning given by section 22(1)(*a*);

'supplier' has the meaning given by section 11(1)(*b*) or 12(*c*) or 13(*c*) or, in relation to an agreement falling within section 11(1)(*a*), means the creditor, and includes a person to whom the rights and duties of a supplier (as so defined) have passed by assignment or operation of law;

'technical grounds' shall be construed in accordance with subsection (5);

'time order' has the meaning given by section 129(1);

'total charge for credit' means a sum calculated in accordance with regulations under section 20(1);

'total price' means the total sum payable by the debtor under a hire-purchase agreement or a conditional sale agreement, including any sum payable on the exercise of an option to purchase, but excluding any sum payable as a penalty or as compensation or damages for a breach of the agreement.

'unexecuted agreement' means a document embodying the terms of a prospective regulated agreement, or such of them as it is intended to reduce to writing;

'unlicensed' means without a licence, but applies only in relation to acts for which a licence is required;

'unrestricted-use credit agreement' and 'unrestricted-use credit' have the meanings given by section 11(2);

'working day' means any day other than—

    (*a*) Saturday or Sunday,
    (*b*) Christmas Day or Good Friday,
    (*c*) a bank holiday within the meaning given by section 1 of the Banking and Financial Dealings Act 1971.

(2) A person is not to be treated as carrying on a particular type of business

merely because occasionally he enters into transactions belonging to a business of that type.

(3) Any provision of this Act requiring a document to be signed is complied with by a body corporate if the document is sealed by that body.
This subsection does not apply to Scotland.

(4) A document embodies a provision if the provision is set out either in the document itself or in another document referred to in it.

(5) An application dismissed by the court or the Director shall, if the court or the Director (as the case may be) so certifies, be taken to be dismissed on technical grounds only.

(6) Except in so far as the context otherwise requires, any reference to this Act to an enactment shall be construed as a reference to that enactment as amended by or under any other enactment, including this Act.

(7) In this Act, except where otherwise indicated—

    (*a*) a reference to a number Part, section or Schedule is a reference to the Part or section of, of the Schedule to, this Act so numbered, and

    (*b*) a reference in a section to a numbered subsection is a reference to the subsection of that section so numbered, and

    (*c*) a reference in a section, subsection or Schedule to a numbered paragraph is a reference to the paragraph of that section, subsection or Schedule so numbered.

190. Financial provisions

(1) There shall be defrayed out of money provided by Parliament—

    (*a*) all expenses incurred by the Secretary of State in consequence of the provisions of this Act;

    (*b*) any expenses incurred in consequence of those provisions by any other Minister of the Crown or Government department;

    (*c*) any increase attributable to this Act in the sums payable out of money so provided under the Superannuation Act 1972 or the Fair Trading Act 1973.

(2) Any fees received by the Director under this Act shall be paid into the Consolidated Fund.

191. Special provisions as to Northern Ireland

(1) The Director may make arrangements with the Department of Commerce for Northern Ireland for the Department, on his behalf,—

    (*a*) to receive applications, notices and fees;

    (*b*) to maintain, and make available for inspection and copying, copies of entries in the register; and

    (*c*) to provide certified copies of entries in the register,

to the extent that seems to him desirable for the convenience of persons in Northern Ireland.

(2) The Director shall give general notice of any arrangements made under subsection (1).

(3) Nothing in this Act shall authorise any Northern Ireland department to

incur any expenses attributable to the provisions of this Act until provision has been made for those expenses to be defrayed out of money appropriated for the purpose.

(4) The power of the Department of Commerce for Northern Ireland to make an order under section 178 shall be exercisable by statutory rule for the purposes of the [Statutory Rules (Northern Ireland) Order 1979], and any such order shall be subject to negative resolution within the meaning of the Interpretation Act (Northern Ireland) 1954 as if it were a statutory instrument within the meaning of that Act.

[*The words in square brackets were substituted by the Statutory Rules (Northern Ireland) Order 1979 (S.I. 1979 No. 1573).*]

(5) In this Act 'enactment' includes an enactment of the Parliament of Northern Ireland or the Northern Ireland Assembly, and 'Act' shall be construed in a corresponding manner; and (without prejudice to section 189(6)) any reference in this Act to such an enactment shall include a reference to any enactment re-enacting it with or without modifications.

(6) Section 38 of the Interpretation Act 1889 (effect of repeals) shall have the same operation in relation to any repeal by this Act of an enactment of the Parliament of Northern Ireland as it has in relation to the repeal of an Act of the Parliament of the United Kingdom, references in that section of the Act of 1889 to Acts and enactments being construed accordingly.

192. Transitional and commencement provisions, amendments and repeals

(1) The provisions of Schedule 3 shall have effect for the purposes of this Act.

(2) The appointment of a day for the purposes of any provision of Schedule 3 shall be effected by an order of the Secretary of State made by statutory instrument; and any such order shall include a provision amending Schedule 3 so as to insert an express reference to the day appointed.

(3) Subject to subsection (4)—

  (*a*) the enactments specified in Schedule 4 shall have effect subject to the amendments specified in that Schedule (being minor amendments or amendments consequential on the preceding provisions of this Act), and
  (*b*) the enactments specified in Schedule 5 are hereby repealed to the extent shown in column 3 of that Schedule.

(4) The Secretary of State shall by order made by statutory instrument provide for the coming into operation of the amendments contained in Schedule 4 and the repeals contained in Schedule 5, and those amendments and repeals shall have effect only as provided by an order so made.

193. Short title and extent

(1) This Act may be cited as the Consumer Credit Act 1974.

(2) This Act extends to Northern Ireland.

Consumer Credit Act 1974

SCHEDULES

SCHEDULE 1

Prosecution and Punishment of Offences

Section 167.

1 Section	2 Offence	3 Mode of prosecution	4 Imprisonment or fine
7	Knowingly or recklessly giving false information to Director.	(a) Summarily. (b) On indictment.	[The prescribed sum] 2 years or a fine or both.
39(1)	Engaging in activities requiring a licence when not a licensee.	(a) Summarily. (b) On indictment.	[The prescribed sum] 2 years or a fine or both.
39(2)	Carrying on a business under a name not specified in licence.	(a) Summarily. (b) On indictment.	[The prescribed sum] 2 years or a fine or both.
39(3)	Failure to notify changes in register particulars.	(a) Summarily. (b) On indictment.	[The prescribed sum] 2 years or a fine or both.
45	Advertising credit where goods etc. not available for cash.	(a) Summarily. (b) On indictment.	[The prescribed sum] 2 years or a fine or both.
46(1)	False or misleading advertisements.	(a) Summarily. (b) On indictment.	[The prescribed sum] 2 years or a fine or both.
47(1)	Advertising infringements.	(a) Summarily. (b) On indictment.	[The prescribed sum] 2 years or a fine or both.
49(1)	Canvassing debtor-creditor agreements off trade premises.	(a) Summarily. (b) On indictment.	[The prescribed sum] 1 year or a fine or both.
49(2)	Soliciting debtor-creditor agreements during visits made in response to previous oral requests.	(a) Summarily. (b) On indictment.	[The prescribed sum] 1 year or a fine or both.
50(1)	Sending circulars to minors.	(a) Summarily. (b) On indictment.	[The prescribed sum] 1 year or a fine or both.
51(1)	Supplying unsolicited credit-tokens.	(a) Summarily. (b) On indictment.	[The prescribed sum] 2 years or a fine or both.
77(4)	Failure of creditor under fixed-sum agreement to supply copies of documents etc.	Summarily.	[Level 4]

255

Consumer Credit Act 1974

1 Section	2 Offence	3 Mode of prosecution	4 Imprisonment or fine
78(6)	Failure of creditor under running-account credit agreement to supply copies of documents etc.	Summarily.	[Level 4]
79(3)	Failure of owner under consumer hire agreement to supply copies of documents etc.	Summarily.	[Level 4]
80(2)	Failure to tell creditor or owner whereabouts of goods.	Summarily.	[Level 3]
85(2)	Failure of creditor to supply copy of credit-token agreement.	Summarily.	[Level 4]
97(3)	Failure to supply debtor with statement of amount required to discharge agreement.	Summarily.	[Level 3]
103(5)	Failure to deliver notice relating to discharge of agreements.	Summarily.	[Level 3]
107(4)	Failure of creditor to give information to surety under fixed-sum credit agreement.	Summarily.	[Level 4]
108(4)	Failure of creditor to give information to surety under running-account credit agreement.	Summarily.	[Level 4]
109(3)	Failure of owner to give information to surety under consumer hire agreement.	Summarily.	[Level 4]
110(3)	Failure of creditor or owner to supply a copy of any security instrument to debtor or hirer.	Summarily.	[Level 4]
114(2)	Taking pledges from minors.	(a) Summarily. (b) On indictment.	[The prescribed sum] 1 year or a fine or both.
115	Failure to supply copies of a pledge agreement or pawn-receipt.	Summarily.	[Level 4]
119(1)	Unreasonable refusal to allow pawn to be redeemed.	Summarily.	[Level 4]
154	Canvassing ancillary credit services off trade premises.	(a) Summarily. (b) On indictment.	[The prescribed sum] 1 year or a fine or both.
157(3)	Refusal to give name etc. of credit reference agency.	Summarily.	[Level 4]
158(4)	Failure of credit reference agency to disclose filed information.	Summarily.	[Level 4]
159(6)	Failure of credit reference agency to correct information.	Summarily.	[Level 4]
160(6)	Failure of credit reference agency to comply with section 160(3) or (4).	Summarily.	[Level 4]

Consumer Credit Act 1974

1 Section	2 Offence	3 Mode of prosecution	4 Imprisonment or fine
162(6) ...	Impersonation of enforcement authority officers.	(a) Summarily. (b) On indictment.	[The prescribed sum] 2 years or a fine or both.
165(1) ...	Obstruction of enforcement authority officers.	Summarily.	[Level 4]
165(2) ...	Giving false information to enforcement authority officers.	(a) Summarily. (b) On indictment.	[The prescribed sum] 2 years or a fine or both.
167(2) ...	Contravention of regulations under section 44, 52, 53, 54, or 112.	(a) Summarily. (b) On indictment.	[The prescribed sum] 2 years or a fine or both.
174(5) ...	Wrongful disclosure of information.	(a) Summarily. (b) On indictment.	[The prescribed sum] 2 years or a fine or both.

The Standard Scale of Fines

Level on the Scale	Amount of fine
1	£50
2	£100
3	£400
4	£1,000
5	£2,000

[*The Standard Scale of Fines was introduced by the Criminal Justice Act 1982 sections 35–50 and Schedules 2–5 and was amended by the Criminal Penalties etc. (Increase) Order 1984 (S.I. 1984 No. 447). The 'prescribed sum' was increased to £2,000 by the Criminal Penalties etc. (Increase) Order 1984 (S.I. 1984 No. 447).*]

Consumer Credit Act 1974

SCHEDULE 2

Examples of Use of New terminology

PART I

List of Terms

Term	Defined in section	Illustrated by example(s)
Advertisement	189(1)	2
Advertiser	189(1)	2
Antecedent negotiations	56	1, 2, 3, 4
Cancellable agreement	67	4
Consumer credit agreement	8	5, 6, 7, 15, 21
Consumer hire agreement	15	20, 24
Credit	9	16, 19, 21
Credit-broker	189(1)	2
Credit limit	10(2)	6, 7, 19, 22, 23
Creditor	189(1)	1, 2, 3, 4
Credit-sale agreement	189(1)	5
Credit-token	14	3, 14, 16
Credit-token agreement	14	3, 14, 16, 22
Debtor-creditor agreement	13	8, 16, 17, 18
Debtor-creditor-supplier agreement	12	8, 16
Fixed-sum credit	10	9, 10, 17, 23
Hire-purchase agreement	189(1)	10
Individual	189(1)	19, 24
Linked transaction	19	11
Modifying agreement	82(2)	24
Multiple agreement	18	16, 18
Negotiator	56(1)	1, 2, 3, 4
Personal credit agreement	8(1)	19
Pre-existing arrangements	187	8, 21
Restricted-use credit	11	10, 12, 13, 14, 16
Running-account credit	10	15, 16, 18, 23
Small agreement	17	16, 17, 22
Supplier	189(1)	3, 14
Total charge for credit	20	5, 10
Total price	189(1)	10
Unrestricted-use credit	11	8, 12, 16, 17, 18

Part II

EXAMPLES

Example 1

Facts. Correspondence passes between an employee of a moneylending company (writing on behalf of the company) and an individual about the terms on which the company would grant him a loan under a regulated agreement.

Analysis. The correspondence constitutes antecedent negotiations falling within section 56(1)(*a*), the moneylending company being both creditor and negotiator.

EXAMPLE 2

Facts. Representations are made about goods in a poster displayed by a shopkeeper near the goods, the goods being selected by a customer who has read the poster and then sold by the shopkeeper to a finance company introduced by him (with whom he has a business relationship). The goods are disposed of by the finance company to the customer under a regulated hire-purchase agreement.

Analysis. The representations in the poster constitute antecedent negotiations falling within section 56(1)(*b*), the shopkeeper being the credit-broker and negotiator and the finance company being the creditor. The poster is an advertisement and the shopkeeper is the advertiser.

EXAMPLE 3

Facts. Discussions take place between a shopkeeper and a customer about goods the customer wishes to buy using a credit-card issued by the D Bank under a regulated agreement.

Analysis. The discussions constitute antecedent negotiations falling within section 56(1)(*c*), the shopkeeper being the supplier and negotiator and the D Bank the creditor. The credit-card is a credit-token as defined in section 14(1), and the regulated agreement under which it was issued is a credit-token agreement as defined in section 14(2).

EXAMPLE 4

Facts. Discussions take place and correspondence passes between a second-hand car dealer and a customer about a car, which is then sold by the dealer to the customer under a regulated conditional sale agreement. Subsequently, on a revocation of that agreement by consent, the car is resold by the dealer to a finance company introduced by him (with whom he has a business relationship), who in turn dispose of it to the same customer under a regulated hire-purchase agreement.

Analysis. The discussions and correspondence constitute antecedent negotiations in relation both to the conditional sale agreement and the hire-purchase agreement. They fall under section 56(1)(*a*) in relation to the conditional sale agreement, the dealer being the creditor and the negotiator. In relation to the hire-purchase agreement they fall within section 56(1)(*b*), the dealer continuing to be treated as the negotiator but the finance company now being the creditor. Both agreements are cancellable if the discussions took place when the individual conducting the negotiations (whether the 'negotiator' or his employee or agent) was in the presence of the debtor, unless the unexecuted agreement was signed by the debtor at trade premises (as defined in section 67(*b*)). If the discussions all took place by telephone however, or the unexecuted agreement was signed by the debtor on trade premises (as so defined) the agreements are not cancellable.

EXAMPLE 5

Facts. E agrees to sell to F (an individual) an item of furniture in return for 24 monthly instalments of £10 payable in arrear. The property in the goods passes to F immediately.

Analysis. This is a credit-sale agreement (see definition of 'credit-sale agreement' in section 189(1)). The credit provided amounts to £240 less the amount which, according to regulations made under section 20(1), constitutes the total charge for credit. (This amount is required to be deducted by section 9(4)). Accordingly the agreement falls within section 8(2) and is a consumer credit agreement.

EXAMPLE 6

Facts. The G Bank grants H (an individual) an unlimited overdraft, with an increased rate of interest on so much of any debit balance as exceeds £2,000.

Analysis. Although the overdraft purports to be unlimited, the stipulation for increased interest above £2,000 brings the agreement within section 10(3)(*b*)(ii) and it is a consumer credit agreement.

EXAMPLE 7

Facts. J is an individual who owns a small shop which usually carries a stock worth about £1,000. K makes a stocking agreement under which he undertakes to provide on short-term credit the stock needed from time to time by J without any specified limit.

Analysis. Although the agreement appears to provide unlimited credit, it is probable, having regard to the stock usually carried by J, that his indebtedness to K will not at any time rise above £5,000. Accordingly the agreement falls within section 10(3)(*b*)(iii) and is a consumer credit agreement.

EXAMPLE 8

Facts. U, a moneylender, lends £500 to V (an individual) knowing he intends to use it to buy office equipment from W. W introduced V to U, it being his practice to introduce customers needing finance to him. Sometimes U gives W a commission for this and sometimes not. U pays the £500 direct to V.

Analysis. Although this appears to fall under section 11(1)(*b*), it is excluded by section 11(3) and is therefore (by section 11(2)) an unrestricted-use credit agreement. Whether it is a debtor-creditor agreement (by section 13(*c*)) or a debtor-creditor-supplier agreement (by section 12(*c*)) depends on whether the previous dealings between U and W amount to 'pre-existing arrangements', that is whether the agreement can be taken to have been entered into 'in accordance with, or in furtherance of' arrangements previously made between U and W, as laid down in section 187(1).

EXAMPLE 9

Facts. A agrees to lend B (an individual) £4,500 in nine monthly instalments of £500.

Analysis. This is a cash loan and is a form of credit (see section 9 and definition of 'cash' in section 189(1)). Accordingly it falls within section 10(1)(*b*) and is fixed-sum credit amounting to £4,500.

Consumer Credit Act 1974

Example 10

Facts. C (in England) agrees to bail goods to D (an individual) in return for periodical payments. The agreement provides for the property in the goods to pass to D on payment of a total of £7,500 and the exercise by D of an option to purchase. The sum of £7,500 includes a down-payment of £1,000. It also includes an amount which, according to regulations made under section 20(1), constitutes a total charge for credit of £1,500.

Analysis. This is a hire-purchase agreement with a deposit of £1,000 and a total price of £7,500 (see definitions of 'hire-purchase agreement', 'deposit' and 'total price' in section 189(1)). By section 9(3), it is taken to provide credit amounting to £7,500 — (£1,500 + £1,000), which equals £5,000. Under section 8(2), the agreement is therefore a consumer credit agreement, and under sections 9(3) and 11(1) it is a restricted-use credit agreement for fixed-sum credit. A similar result would follow if the agreement by C had been a hiring agreement in Scotland.

Example 11

Facts. X (an individual) borrows £500 from Y (Finance). As a condition of the granting of the loan X is required—

(*a*) to execute a second mortgage on his house in favour of Y (Finance), and
(*b*) to take out a policy of insurance on his life with Y (Insurances).

In accordance with the loan agreement, the policy is charged to Y (Finance) as collateral security for the loan. The two companies are associates within the meaning of section 184(3).

Analysis. The second mortgage is a transaction for the provision of security and accordingly does not fall within section 19(1), but the taking out of the insurance policy is a linked transaction falling within section 19(1)(*a*). The charging of the policy is a separate transaction (made between different parties) for the provision of security and again is excluded from section 19(1). The only linked transaction is therefore the taking out of the insurance policy. If X had not been required by the loan agreement to take out the policy, but it had been done at the suggestion of Y (Finance) to induce them to enter into the loan agreement, it would have been a linked transaction under section 19(1)(*c*)(i) by virtue of section 19(2)(*a*).

Example 12

Facts. The N Bank agrees to lend O (an individual) £2,000 to buy a car from P. To make sure the loan is used as intended, the N Bank stipulates that the money must be paid by it direct to P.

Analysis. The agreement is a consumer credit agreement by virtue of section 8(2). Since it falls within section 11(1)(*b*), it is a restricted-use credit agreement, P being the supplier. If the N Bank had not stipulated for direct payment to the supplier, section 11(3) would have operated and made the agreement into one for unrestricted-use credit.

Example 13

Facts. Q, a debt-adjuster, agrees to pay off debts owed by R (an individual) to various moneylenders. For this purpose the agreement provides for the making of a loan by Q to R in return for R agreeing to repay the loan by instalments with interest. The loan money is not paid over to R but retained by Q and used to pay off the moneylenders.

Analysis. This is an agreement to refinance existing indebtedness of the debtor, and if the loan by Q does not exceed £5,000 is a restricted-use credit agreement falling within section 11(1)(*c*).

EXAMPLE 14

Facts. On payment of £1, S issues to T (an individual) a trading check under which T can spend up to £20 at any shop which has agreed, or in future agrees, to accept S's trading checks.

Analysis. The trading check is a credit-token falling within section 14(1)(*b*). The credit-token agreement is a restricted-use credit agreement within section 11(1)(*b*), any shop in which the credit-token is used being the 'supplier'. The fact that further shops may be added after the issue of the credit-token is irrelevant in view of section 11(4).

EXAMPLE 15

Facts. A retailer L agrees with M (an individual) to open an account in M's name and, in return for M's promise to pay a specified minimum sum into the account each month and to pay a monthly charge for credit, agrees to allow to be debited to the account, in respect of purchases made by M from L, such sums as will not increase the debit balance at any time beyond the credit limit, defined in the agreement as a given multiple of the specified minimum sum.

Analysis. This agreement provides credit falling within the definition of running-account credit in section 10(1)(*a*). Provided the credit limit is not over £5,000, the agreement falls within section 8(2) and is a consumer credit agreement for running-account credit.

EXAMPLE 16

Facts. Under an unsecured agreement, A (Credit), an associate of the A Bank, issues to B (an individual) a credit-card for use in obtaining cash on credit from A (Credit), to be paid by branches of the A Bank (acting as agent of A (Credit)), or goods or cash from suppliers or banks who have agreed to honour credit-cards issued by A (Credit). The credit limit is £30.

Analysis. This is a credit-token agreement falling within section 14(1)(*a*) and (*b*). It is a regulated consumer credit agreement for running-account credit. Since the credit limit does not exceed £30, the agreement is a small agreement. So far as the agreement relates to goods it is a debtor-creditor-supplier agreement within section 12(*b*), since it provides restricted-use credit under section 11(1)(*b*). So far as it relates to cash it is a debtor-creditor agreement within section 13(*c*) and the credit it provides is unrestricted-use credit. This is therefore a multiple agreement. In that the whole agreement falls within several of the categories of agreement mentioned in this Act, it is, by section 18(3), to be treated as an agreement in each of those categories. So far as it is a debtor-creditor-supplier agreement providing restricted-use credit it is, by section 18(2), to be treated as a separate agreement; and similarly so far as it is a debtor-creditor agreement providing unrestricted-use credit. (See also Example 22.)

Consumer Credit Act 1974

Example 17

Facts. The manager of the C Bank agrees orally with D (an individual) to open a current account in D's name. Nothing is said about overdraft facilities. After maintaining the account in credit for some weeks, D draws a cheque in favour of E for an amount exceeding D's credit balance by £20. E presents the cheque and the Bank pay it.

Analysis. In drawing the cheque D, by implication, requests the Bank to grant him an overdraft of £20 on its usual terms as to interest and other charges. In deciding to honour the cheque, the Bank by implication accepts the offer. This constitutes a regulated small consumer credit agreement for unrestricted-use, fixed-sum credit. It is a debtor-creditor agreement, and falls within section 74(1)(*b*) if covered by a determination under section 74(3). (Compare Example 18.)

Example 18

Facts. F (an individual) has had a current account with the G Bank for many years. Although usually in credit, the account has been allowed by the Bank to become overdrawn from time to time. The maximum such overdraft has been is about £1,000. No explicit agreement has ever been made about overdraft facilities. Now, with a credit balance of £500, F draws a cheque for £1,300.

Analysis. It might well be held that the agreement with F (express or implied) under which the Bank operate his account includes an implied term giving him the right to overdraft facilities up to say £1,000. If so, the agreement is a regulated consumer credit agreement for unrestricted-use, running-account credit. It is a debtor-credit agreement, and falls within section 74(1)(*b*) if covered by a direction under section 74(3). It is also a multiple agreement, part of which (i.e. the part not dealing with the overdraft), as referred to in section 18(1)(*a*), falls within a category of agreement not mentioned in this Act. (Compare Example 17.)

Example 19

Facts. H (a finance house) agrees with J (a partnership of individuals) to open an unsecured loan account in J's name on which the debit balance is not to exceed £7,000 (having regard to payments into the account made from time to time by J). Interest is to be payable in advance on this sum, with provision for yearly adjustments. H is entitled to debit the account with interest, a 'setting-up' charge, and other charges. Before J has an opportunity to draw on the account it is initially debited with £2,250 for advance interest and other charges.

Analysis. This is a personal running-account credit agreement (see section 8(1) and 10(1)(*a*), and definition of 'individual' in section 189(1)). By section 10(2) the credit limit is £7,000. By section 9(4) however the initial debit of £2,250, and any other charges later debited to the account by H, are not to be treated as credit even though time is allowed for their payment. Effect is given to this by section 10(3). Although the credit limit of £7,000 exceeds the amount (£5,000) specified in section 8(2) as the maximum for a consumer credit agreement, so that the agreement is not within section 10(3)(*a*), it is caught by section 10(3)(*b*)(i). At the beginning J can effectively draw (as credit) no more than £4,750, so the agreement is a consumer credit agreement.

Example 20

Facts. K (in England) agrees with L (an individual) to bail goods to L for a period of three years certain at £2,000 a year, payable quarterly. The agreement contains no provision for the passing of the property in the goods to L.

Analysis. This is not a hire-purchase agreement (see paragraph (*b*) of the definition of that term in section 189(1), and is capable of subsisting for more than three months. Paragraphs (*a*) and (*b*) of section 15(1) are therefore satisfied, but paragraph (*c*) is not. The payments by L must exceed £5,000 if he conforms to the agreement. It is true that under section 101 L has a right to terminate the agreement on giving K three months' notice expiring not earlier than eighteen months after the making of the agreement, but that section applies only where the agreement is a regulated consumer hire agreement apart from the section (see subsection (1)). So the agreement is not a consumer hire agreement, though it would be if the hire charge were say £1,500 a year, or there were a 'break' clause in it operable by either party before the hire charges exceeded £5,000. A similar result would follow if the agreement by K had been a hiring agreement in Scotland.

Example 21

Facts. The P Bank decides to issue cheque cards to its customers under a scheme whereby the bank undertakes to honour cheques of up to £30 in every case where the payee has taken the cheque in reliance on the cheque card, whether the customer has funds in his account or not. The P Bank writes to the major retailers advising them of this scheme and also publicises it by advertising. The Bank issues a cheque card to Q (an individual), who uses it to pay by cheque for goods costing £20 bought by Q from R, a major retailer. At the time, Q has £500 in his account at the P Bank.

Analysis. The agreement under which the cheque card is used to Q is a consumer credit agreement even though at all relevant times Q has more than £30 in his account. This is because Q is free to draw out his whole balance and then use the cheque card, in which case the Bank has bound itself to honour the cheque. In other words the cheque card agreement provides Q with credit, whether he avails himself of it or not. Since the amount of the credit is not subject to any express limit, the cheque card can be used any number of times. It may be presumed however that section 10(3)(*b*)(iii) will apply. The agreement is an unrestricted-use debtor-creditor agreement (by section 13(*c*)). Although the P Bank wrote to R informing R of the P Bank's willingness to honour any cheque taken by R in reliance on a cheque card, this does not constitute pre-existing arrangements as mentioned in section 13(*c*) because section 187(3) operates to prevent it. The agreement is not a credit-token agreement within section 14(1)(*b*) because payment by the P Bank to R, would be a payment of the cheque and not a payment for the goods.

Example 22

Facts. The facts are as in Example 16. On one occasion B uses the credit-card in a way which increases his debit balance with A (Credit) to £40. A (Credit) writes to B agreeing to allow the excess on that occason only, but stating that it must be paid off within one month.

Analysis. In exceeding his credit limit B, by implication, requests A (Credit) to allow him a temporary excess (compare Example 17). A (Credit) is thus faced by B's action with the choice of treating it as a breach of contract or granting his implied request. He does the latter. If he had done the former, B would be treated as taking credit to which he was not entitled (see section 14(3)) and, subject to the terms of his contract with A (Credit), would be liable to damages for breach of contract. As it is, the agreement to allow the excess varies the original credit-token agreement by adding a new term. Under section 10(2), the new term is to be disregarded in arriving at the credit limit, so that the credit-token agreement at no time ceases to be a small agreement. By section 82(2) the later agreement is deemed to revoke the original agreement and contain provisions reproducing the combined effect of the two agreements. By section 82(4), this later agreement is exempted from Part V (except section 56).

Example 23

Facts. Under an oral agreement made on 10th January, X (an individual) has an overdraft on his current account at the Y bank with a credit limit of £100. On 15th February, when his overdraft stands at £90, X draws a cheque for £25. It is the first time that X has exceeded his credit limit, and on 16th February the bank honours the cheque.

Analysis. The agreement of 10th January is a consumer credit agreement for running-account credit. The agreement of 15th-16th February varies the earlier agreement by adding a term allowing the credit limit to be exceeded merely temporarily. By section 82(2) the later agreement is deemed to revoke the earlier agreement and reproduce the combined effect of the two agreements. By section 82(4), Part V of this Act (except section 56) does not apply to the later agreement. By section 18(5), a term allowing a merely temporary excess over the credit limit is not to be treated as a separate agreement, or as providing fixed-sum credit. The whole of the £115 owed to the bank by X on 16th February is therefore running-account credit.

Example 24

Facts. On 1st March 1975 Z (in England) enters into an agreement with A (an unincorporated body of persons) to bail to A equipment consisting of two components (component P and component Q). The agreement is not a hire-purchase agreement and is for a fixed term of 3 years, so paragraphs (*a*) and (*b*) of section 15(1) are both satisfied. The rental is payable monthly at a rate of £2,400 a year, but the agreement provides that this is to be reduced to £1,200 a year for the remainder of the agreement if at any time during its currency A returns component Q to the owner Z. On 5th May 1976 A is incorporated as A Ltd., taking over A's assets and liabilities. On 1st March 1977, A Ltd. returns component Q. On 1st January 1978, Z and A Ltd. agree to extend the earlier agreement by one year, increasing the rental for the final year by £250 to £1,450.

Analysis. When entered into on 1st March 1975, the agreement is a consumer hire agreement. A falls within the definition of 'individual' in section 189(1) and if A returns component Q before 1st May 1976 the total rental will not exceed £5,000 (see section 15(1)(*c*)). When this date is passed without component Q having been returned it is obvious that the total rental must now exceed £5,000. Does this mean that the agreement then ceases to be a consumer hire agreement? The answer is no, because there has been no change in the terms of the agreement, and without such a change the agreement cannot move from one category to the other. Similarly, the fact that A's rights and duties under the agreement pass to a body corporate on 5th May 1976 does not cause the agreement to cease to be a consumer hire agreement (see the definition of 'hirer' in section 189(1)).

The effect of the modifying agreement of 1st January 1978 is governed by section 82(2), which requires it to be treated as containing provisions reproducing the combined effect of the two actual agreements, that is to say as providing that—

(a) obligations outstanding on 1st January 1978 are to be treated as outstanding under the modifying agreement;
(b) the modifying agreement applies at the old rate of hire for the months of January and February 1978, and
(c) for the year beginning 1st March 1978 A Ltd. will be the bailee of component P at a rental of £1,450.

The total rental under the modifying agreement is £1,850. Accordingly the modifying agreement is a regulated agreement. Even if the total rental under the modifying agreement exceeded £5,000 it would still be regulated because of the provisions of section 82(3).

SCHEDULE 3

Transitional and Commencement Provisions

Note. Except as otherwise mentioned in this Schedule, the provisions of this Act came into operation on its passing, that is on 31st July, 1974.

Part II of Act

Credit Agreements, Hire Agreements and Linked Transactions

Regulated agreements

1.—(1) An agreement made before [1st April 1977] is not a regulated agreement within the meaning of this Act.

(2) In this Act 'prospective regulated agreement' does not include a prospective agreement which, if made as expected, would be made before the day appointed for the purposes of this paragraph.

[*The date in square brackets was substituted by the Consumer Credit Act 1974 (Commencement No. 2) Order 1977 (S.I. 1977 No. 325).*]

Linked transactions

2. A transaction may be a linked transaction in relation to a regulated agreement or prospective regulated agreement even though the transaction was entered into before the day appointed for the purposes of paragraph 1.

3. Section 19(3) applies only to transactions entered into on or after [19th May 1985.]

[*The date in square brackets was substituted by the Consumer Credit Act 1974 (Commencement No. 8) Order 1983 (S.I. 1983 No. 1551).*]

Total charge for credit

4. Section 20 applies to consumer credit agreements whenever made.

Consumer Credit Act 1974

Part III of Act

Licensing of Credit and Hire Businesses

Businesses needing a licence

5.—(1) Section 21 does not apply to the carrying on of any description of consumer credit business or consumer hire business—

[(a) before 1st October 1977 in the case of a consumer credit business, not being a consumer credit business which is carried on by an individual and in the course of which only the following regulated consumer credit agreements (excluding agreements made before that date) are made, namely—
  (i) agreements for fixed-sum credit not exceeding £30, and
  (ii) agreements for running-account credit where the credit limit does not exceed that amount,]
(b) before the day appointed for the purposes of this paragraph [in the case of any other description of consumer credit business and
(c) before 1st October 1977 in the case of any consumer hire business.]

(2) Where the person carrying on any description of consumer credit business or consumer hire business applies for a licence before the day [specified or referred to in sub-paragraph (1) above] in relation to a business of that description, he shall be deemed to have been granted on that day a licence covering that business and continuing in force until the licence applied for is granted or, if the application is refused, until the end of the appeal period.

[*The dates and words in square brackets were substituted by the Consumer Credit Act 1974 (Commencement No. 2) Order 1977 (S.I. 1977 No. 325).*]

The register

6. Sections 35 and 36 come into operation on the [2nd February 1976].

[*The date in square brackets was substituted by the Consumer Credit Act 1974 (Commencement No. 1) Order 1975 (S.I. 1975 No. 2123).*]

Enforcement of agreements made by unlicensed trader

7. Section 40 does not apply to a regulated agreement made in the course of any business before the day [specified or referred to in paragraph 5(1) in relation to the description of business in question.]

[*The words in square brackets were substituted by the Consumer Credit Act 1974 (Commencement No. 2) Order 1977 (S.I. 1977 No. 325).*]

Part IV of Act

Seeking Business

Advertisements

8. Part IV does not apply to any advertisement published before [6th October 1980].

[*The date in square brackets was substituted by the Consumer Credit Act 1974 (Commencement No. 6) Order 1980 (S.I. 1980 No. 50).*]

Consumer Credit Act 1974

Canvassing

9. Section 49 comes into operation on [1st October 1977].

Circulars to minors

10. Section 50 comes into operation on [1st July 1977].

Unsolicited credit-tokens

11.—(1) Section 51(1) does not apply to the giving of a credit-token before [1st July 1977].

(2) In section 51(3), 'agreement' means an agreement whenever made.

[*In paragraphs 9, 10 and 11, the dates in square brackets were substituted by the Consumer Credit Act 1974 (Commencement No. 3) Order 1977 (S.I. 1977 No. 802).*]

PART V OF ACT

ENTRY INTO CREDIT OR HIRE AGREEMENTS

Antecedent negotiations

12.—(1) Section 56 applies to negotiations in relation to an actual or prospective regulated agreement where the negotiations begin after [16th May 1977].

(2) In section 56(3), 'agreement' where it first occurs, means an agreement whenever made.

[*The date in square brackets was substituted by the Consumer Credit Act 1977 (Commencement No. 2) Order 1977 (S.I. 1977 No. 325).*]

General

13. Sections 57 to 59, 61 to 65 and 67 to 73 come into operation on [19th May 1985].

14. Section 66 comes into operation on [19th May 1985].

[*The date in square brackets was substituted by the Consumer Credit Act 1974 (Commencement No. 8) Order 1983 (S.I. 1983 No. 1551).*]

PART VI OF ACT

MATTERS ARISING DURING CURRENCY OF CREDIT OR HIRE AGREEMENTS

Liability of creditor for breaches by supplier

15. Section 75 comes into operation on [1st July 1977 but only in relation to regulated agreements made on or after that day].

[*The words in square brackets were substituted by the Consumer Credit Act 1974 (Commencement No. 3) Order 1977 (S.I. 1977 No. 802).*]

Duty to give notice

16.—(1) Section 76 comes into operation on [19th May 1985].

(2) Section 76 applies to an agreement made before [19th May 1985] where the agreement would have been a regulated agreement if made on that day.

Consumer Credit Act 1974

[*The date in square brackets was substituted by the Consumer Credit Act 1974 (Commencement No. 8) Order 1983 (S.I. 1983 No. 1551).*]

Duty to give information

17.—(1) Sections 77 to 80 come into operation on [19th May 1985].

(2) Sections 77 to 79 apply to an agreement made before [19th May 1985] where the agreement would have been a regulated agreement if made on that day.

[*The date in square brackets was substituted by the Consumer Credit Act 1974 (Commencement No. 8) Order 1983 (S.I. 1983 No. 1551).*]

Appropriation of payments

18. Section 81 comes into operation on [19th May 1985].

[*The date in square brackets was substituted by the Consumer Credit Act 1974 (Commencement No. 8) Order 1983 (S.I. 1983 No. 1551).*]

Variation of agreements

19. Section 82 comes into operation on [1st April 1977].

[*The date in square brackets was substituted by the Consumer Credit Act 1974 (Commencement No. 2) Order 1977 (S.I. 1977 No. 325).*]

Misuse of credit facilities

20.—(1) Sections 83 and 84 come into operation on [19th May 1985].

(2) Subject to sub-paragraph (4), section 83 applies to an agreement made before [19th May 1985] where the agreement would have been a regulated consumer credit agreement if made on that day.

(3) Subject to sub-paragraph (4), section 84 applies to an agreement made before [19th May 1985] where the agreement would have been a credit-token agreement if made on that day.

(4) Sections 83 and 84 do not apply to losses arising before [19th May 1985].

(5) Section 84(4) shall be taken to be satisfied in relation to an agreement made before [19th May 1985] if, within 28 days after that day, the creditor gives notice to the debtor of the name, address and telephone number of a person stated in that notice to be the person to whom notice is to be given under section 84(3).

[*The date in square brackets was substituted by the Consumer Credit Act 1974 (Commencement No. 8) Order 1983 (S.I. 1983 No. 1551).*]

Duty on issue of new credit-tokens

21.—(1) Section 85 comes into operation on [19th May 1985].

(2) Section 85 applies to an agreement made before [19th May 1985] where the agreement would have been a regulated agreement if made on that day.

[*The date in square brackets was substituted by the Consumer Credit Act 1974 (Commencement No. 8) Order 1983 (S.I. 1983 No. 1551).*]

Consumer Credit Act 1974

Death of debtor or hirer

22.—(1) Section 86 comes into operation on [19th May 1985].

(2) Section 86 applies to an agreement made before [19th May 1985] where the agreement would have been a regulated agreement if made on that day.

[*The date in square brackets was substituted by the Consumer Credit Act 1974 (Commencement No. 8) Order 1983 (S.I. 1983 No. 1551).*]

Part VII of Act

Default and Termination

Default notices

23. Sections 87 to 89 come into operation on [19th May 1985].

[*The date in square brackets was substituted by the Consumer Credit Act 1974 (Commencement No. 8) Order 1983 (S.I. 1983 No. 1551).*]

Retaking of goods and land

24. Sections 90 and 91 come into operation on [19th May 1985].

25. Section 92 comes into operation on [19th May 1985].

[*The dates in square brackets were substituted by the Consumer Credit Act 1974 (Commencement No. 8) Order 1983 (S.I. 1983 No. 1551).*]

Interest on default

26. Section 93 comes into operation on [19th May 1985].

[*The date in square brackets was substituted by the Consumer Credit Act 1974 (Commencement No. 8) Order 1983 (S.I. 1983 No. 1551).*]

Early payment by debtor

27. Sections 94 to 97 come into operation on [19th May 1985].

[*The date in square brackets was substituted by the Consumer Credit Act 1974 (Commencement No. 8) Order 1983 (S.I. No. 1551).*]

Termination of agremeents

28. Section 98 comes into operation on [19th May 1985].
29. Section 99 comes into operation on [19th May 1985].
30. Section 100 comes into operation on [19th May 1985].
31. Section 101 comes into operation on [19th May 1985].
32. Section 102 comes into operation on [19th May 1985].
33. Section 103 comes into operation on [19th May 1985].
34. Section 104 comes into operation on [19th May 1985].

[*The date in square brackets was substituted by the Consumer Credit Act 1974 (Commencement No. 8) Order 1983 (S.I. 1983 No. 1551).*]

Old agreements

35. Part VII (except sections 90, 91, 93 and 99 to 102 and 104) applies to

an agreement made before [19th May 1985] where the agreement would have been a regulated agreement if made on that day.

[*The date in square brackets was substituted by the Consumer Credit Act 1974 (Commencement No. 8) Order 1983 (S.I. 1983 No. 1551).*]

PART VII OF ACT
DEFAULT AND TERMINATION
General

36. Section 105 comes into operation on [19th May 1985].

37.—(1) Sections 107 to 110 come into operation on [19th May 1985].

(2) Sections 107 to 110 apply to an agreement made before [19th May 1985] where the agreement would have been a regulated agreement if made on that day.

38—(1) Section 111 comes into operation on [19th May 1985].

(2) Section 111 applies to an agreement made before [19th May 1985] where the agreement would have been a regulated agreement if made on that day.

[*The date in square brackets was substituted by the Consumer Credit Act 1974 (Commencement No. 8) Order 1983 (S.I. 1983 No. 1551).*]

Pledges

39. Sections 114 to 122 come into operation on [19th May 1985 but only in respect of articles taken in pawn under a regulated consumer credit agreement].

[*The date and words in square brackets were substituted by the Consumer Credit Act 1974 (Commencement No. 8) Order 1983 (S.I. 1983 No. 1551).*]

Negotiable instruments

40. Sections 123 to 125 come into operation on [19th May 1985].

[*The date in square brackets was substituted by the Consumer Credit Act 1974 (Commencement No. 9) Order 1984 (S.I. 1984 No. 436).*]

Land mortgages

41. Section 126 comes into operation on [19th May 1985].

[*The date in square brackets was substituted by the Consumer Credit Act 1974 (Commencement No. 8) Order 1983 (S.I. 1983 No. 1551).*]

PART IX OF ACT

JUDICIAL CONTROL

42. Sections 137 to 140 (extortionate credit bargains) come into operation on [16th May 1977] and apply to agreements and transactions whenever made.

[*The date in square brackets was substituted by the Consumer Credit Act 1974 (Commencement No. 2) Order 1977 (S.I. 1977 No. 325).*]

43. Subject to paragraph 42, Part IX comes into operation on [19th May 1985].

Consumer Credit Act 1974

[*The date in square brackets was substituted by the Consumer Credit Act 1974 (Commencement No. 8) Order 1983 (S.I. 1983 No. 1551).*]

PART X OF ACT

ANCILLARY CREDIT BUSINESSES

Licensing

44.—(1) Section 21(1) does not apply (by virtue of section 147(1)) to the carrying on of any ancillary credit business before [3rd August 1976 in the case of any business so far as it comprises or relates to—

(a) debt-adjusting,
(b) debt-counselling,
(c) debt-collecting, or
(d) the operation of a credit reference agency.]

[or the day appointed for the purposes of this paragraph in the case of any ancillary credit business so far as it comprises or relates to credit brokerage.]

[(1A) Section 21(1) does not apply (by virtue of section 147(1)) to the carrying on of any ancillary credit business before 1st July 1978 so far as it comprises or relates to credit brokerage, not being a business which is carried on by an individual and in the course of which introductions are effected only of individuals desiring to obtain credit—

(a) under debtor-creditor-supplier agreements which fall within section 12(a) and where, in the case of any such agreement—
(i) the person carrying on the business would be willing to sell the goods which are the subject of the agreement to the debtor under a transaction not financed by credit, and
(ii) the amount of credit does not exceed £30; and
(b) under debtor-creditor-supplier agreements which fall within section 12(b) or (c) and where, in the case of any such agreement—
(i) the person carrying on the business is the supplier,
(ii) the creditor is a person referred to in section 145(2)(a)(i), and
(iii) the amount of credit or, in the case of an agreement for running-account credit, the credit limit does not exceed £30.

(1B) Section 21(1) does not apply (by virtue of section 147(1)) to the carrying on of any ancillary credit business before the day appointed for the purpose of this paragraph in the case of any description of ancillary credit business in relation to which no day is appointed under the foregoing provisions of this paragraph.]

(2) Where the person carrying on an ancillary credit business applies for a licence before—

(a) 3rd August 1976 [in the case of an ancillary credit business of a description to which sub-paragraph (1) above applies;
(b) 1st July 1978 in the case of an ancillary credit business of a description to which sub-paragraph (1A) above applies; or
(c) the day appointed for the purposes of this paragraph in the case of an ancillary credit business to which sub-paragraph (1B) Above applies,]

he shall be deemed to have been granted on 3rd August 1976, [1st July 1978 or the day so appointed, as the case may be,] a licence covering the description of ancillary credit business in question and continuing in force until the licence applied for is granted or, if the application is refused, until the end of the appeal period.

[*In sub-paragraph (1) the first set of words in square brackets was substituted by the Consumer Credit Act 1974 (Commencement No. 1) Order 1975 (S.I. 1975 No. 2123). The remaining words in square brackets were substituted by the Consumer Credit Act 1974 (Commencement No. 2) Order 1977 (S.I. 1977 No. 325). Sub-paragraphs (1A) and (1B) were added, and in sub-paragraph (2), the words in square brackets were substituted, by the Consumer Credit Act 1974 (Commencement No. 4) Order 1977 (S.I. 1977 No. 2163).*].

Enforcement of agreements made by unlicensed trader

45. Section 148(1) does not apply to an agreement made in the course of any business before [3rd August 1976 in the case of any business so far as it comprises or relates to—

(*a*) debt-adjusting,
(*b*) debt-counselling,
(*c*) debt-collecting, or
(*d*) the operation of a credit agency.]

[or before 1st July 1989 in the case of an ancillary credit business of a description to which sub-paragraph (1A) of paragraph 44 applies or before the day appointed for the purposes of that paragraph in the case of an ancillary credit business to which sub-paragraph (1B) of that paragraph applies.]

[*The first set of words in square brackets was substituted by the Consumer Credit Act 1974 (Commencement No. 1) Order 1975 (S.I. 1975 No. 2123). The second set of words in square brackets was substituted by the Consumer Credit Act 1974 (Commencement No. 4) Order 1977 (S.I. 1977 No. 2163).*]

Introductions by unlicensed credit-broker

46. Section 149 does not apply to a regulated agreement made on an introduction effected in the course of any business if the introduction was effected before [1st July 1978 in the case of an ancillary credit business to which sub-paragraph (1A) of paragraph 44 applies or before the day appointed for the purposes of that paragraph in the case of an ancillary credit business to which sub-paragraph (1B) of that paragraph applies.]

[*The words in square brackets were substituted by the Consumer Credit Act 1974 (Commencement No. 4) Order 1977 (S.I. 1977 No. 2163).*]

Advertisements

47. Subsections (1) and (2) of section 151 do not apply to any advertisement published before [6th October 1980].

[*The date in square brackets was substituted by the Consumer Credit Act 1974 (Commencement No. 6) Order 1980 (S.I. 1980 No. 50).*]

Credit reference agencies

48. Sections 157 and 158 do not apply to a request received before [16th May 1977].

[The date in square brackets was substituted by the Consumer Credit Act 1974 (Commencement No. 2) Order 1977 (S.I. 1977 No. 325).]

PART XII OF ACT

SUPPLEMENTAL

Interpretation

49.—(1) In the case of an agreement—
   (*a*) which was made before [19th May 1985], and
   (*b*) to which (by virtue of paragraph 17(2)) section 78(4) applies, section 185(2) shall have effect as respects a notice given before that day in relation to the agreement (whether given before or after the passing of this Act) as it would have effect if section 78(4) had been in operation when the notice was given.

(2) Paragraph (1) applies to an agreement made on or after [19th May 1985] to provide credit on a current account opened before that day as it applied to an agreement made before that day.

[The date in square brackets was substituted by the Consumer Credit Act 1974 (Commencement No. 8) Order 1983 (S.I. 1983 No. 1551).]

50. In section 189, the definition of 'local authority' shall have effect in relation to matters arising before 16th May 1975 as if for the words 'regional, islands or district council' there were substituted 'a county council or town council'.

SCHEDULE 4
MINOR AND CONSEQUENTIAL AMENDMENTS

SCHEDULE 5
REPEALS

Torts (Interference with Goods) Act 1977
Chapter 32

An Act to amend the law concerning conversion and other torts affecting goods. [22nd July 1977]

Preliminary

1. Definition of 'wrongful interference with goods'

In this Act 'wrongful interference', or 'wrongful interference with goods', means—

- (*a*) conversion of goods (also called trover),
- (*b*) trespass to goods,
- (*c*) negligence so far as it results in damage to goods or to an interest in goods,
- (*d*) subject to section 2, any other tort so far as it results in damage to goods or to an interest in goods,

[and references in this Act (however worded) to proceedings for wrongful interference or to a claim or right to claim for wrongful interference shall include references to proceedings by virtue of Part I of the Consumer Protection Act 1987 (product liability) in respect of any damage to goods or to an interest in goods or, as the case may be, to a claim or right to claim by virtue of that Part in respect of any such damage.]

(The words in square brackets were added by the Consumer Protection Act 1987, section 48 and Schedule 4.)

Detention of goods

2. Abolition of detinue

(1) Detinue is abolished.

(2) An action lies in conversion for loss or destructon of goods which a bailee has allowed to happen in breach of his duty to his bailor (that is to say it lies in a case which is not otherwise conversion, but would have been detinue before detinue was abolished).

3. Form of judgment where goods are detained

(1) In proceedings for wrongful interference against a person who is in possession or in control of the goods relief may be given in accordance with this section, so far as appropriate.

(2) The relief is—

- (*a*) an order for delivery of the goods, and for payment of any consequential damages, or
- (*b*) an order for delivery of the goods, but giving the defendant the alternative of paying damages by reference to the value of the goods, together in either alternative with payment of any consequential damages, or

(c) damages.

(3) Subject to rules of court—

(a) relief shall be given under only one of paragraphs (a), (b) and (c) of subsection (2),

(b) relief under paragraph (a) of subsection (2) is at the discretion of the court, and the claimant may choose between the others.

(4) If it is shown to the satisfaction of the court that an order under subsection (2)(a) has not been complied with, the court may—

(a) revoke the order, or the relevant part of it, and
(b) make an order for payment of damages by reference to the value of the goods.

(5) Where an order is made under subsection (2)(b) the defendant may satisfy the order by returning the goods at any time before execution of judgment, but without prejudice to liability to pay any consequential damages.

(6) An order for delivery of the goods under subsection (2)(a) or (b) may impose such conditions as may be determined by the court, or pursuant to rules of court, and in particular, where damages by reference to the value of the goods would not be the whole of the value of the goods, may require an allowance to be made by the claimant to reflect the difference.

For example, a bailor's action against the bailee may be one in which the measure of damages is not the full value of the goods, and then the court may order delivery of the goods, but require the bailor to pay the bailee a sum reflecting the difference.

(7) Where under subsection (1) or subsection (2) of section 6 an allowance is to be made in respect of an improvement of the goods, and an order is made under subsection (2)(a) or (b), the court may assess the allowance to be made in respect of the improvement, and by the order require, as a condition for delivery of the goods, that allowance to be made by the claimant.

(8) This section is without prejudice—

(a) to the remedies afforded by section 133 of the Consumer Credit Act 1974, or
(b) to the remedies afforded by sections 35, 42 and 44 of the Hire-Purchase Act 1965, or to those sections of the Hire-Purchase Act (Northern Ireland) 1966 (so long as those sections respectively remain in force), or
(c) to any jurisdiction to afford ancillary or incidental relief.

4. Interlocutory relief where goods are detained

(1) In this section 'proceedings' means proceedings for wrongful interference.

(2) On the application of any person in accordance with rules of court, the High Court shall, in such circumstances as may be specified in the rules, have power to make an order providing for the delivery up of any goods which are or may become the subject matter of subsequent proceedings in the court, or as to which any question may arise in proceedings.

(3) Delivery shall be, as the order may provide, to the claimant or to a person appointed by the court for the purpose, and shall be on such terms and conditions as may be specified in the order.

(4) The power to make rules of court under section [84 of the Supreme Court Act 1981] or under section 7 of the Northern Ireland Act 1962 shall include power to make rules of court as to the manner in which an application for such an order can be made, and as to the circumstances in which such an order can be made; and any such rules may include such incidental, supplementary and consequential provisions as the authority making the rules may consider necessary or expedient.

(The substitution in square brackets was made by the Supreme Court Act 1981.)

(5) The preceding provisions of this section shall have effect in relation to county courts as they have effect in relation to the High Court, and as if in those provisions references to rules of court and to section [84] of the said Act of [1981] or section 7 of the Northern Ireland Act 1962 included references to county court rules and to [section 75 of the County Courts Act 1984] or section 146 of the County Courts Act (Northern Ireland) 1959.

(The substitutions in square brackets were made by the Acts mentioned therein.)

Damages

5. Extinction of title on satisfaction of claim for damages

(1) Where damages for wrongful interference are, or would fall to be, assessed on the footing that the claimant is being compensated—

(a) for the whole of his interest in the goods, or
(b) for the whole of his interest in the goods subject to a reduction for contributory negligence,

payment of the assessed damages (under all heads), or as the case may be settlement of a claim for damages for the wrong (under all heads), extinguishes the claimant's title to that interest.

(2) In subsection (1) the reference to the settlement of the claim includes—

(a) where the claim is made in court proceedings, and the defendant has paid a sum into court to meet the whole claim, the taking of that sum by the claimant, and
(b) where the claim is made in court proceedings, and the proceedings are settled or compromised, the payment of what is due in accordance with the settlement or compromise, and
(c) where the claim is made out of court and is settled or compromised, the payment of what is due in accordance with the settlement or compromise.

(3) It is hereby declared that subsection (1) does not apply where damages are assessed on the footing that the claimant is being compensated for the whole of his interest in the goods, but the damages paid are limited to some lesser amount by virtue of any enactment or rule of law.

(4) Where under section 7(3) the claimant accounts over to another person (the 'third party') so as to compensate (under all heads) the third party for the whole of his interest in the goods, the third party's title to that interest is extinguished.

(5) This section has effect subject to any agreement varying the respective rights of the parties to the agreement, and where the claim is made in court proceedings has effect subject to any order of the court.

6. Allowance for improvement of the goods

(1) If in proceedings for wrongful interference against a person (the 'improver') who has improved the goods, it is shown that the improver acted in the mistaken but honest belief that he had a good title to them, an allowance shall be made for the extent to which, at the time as at which the goods fall to be valued in assessing damages, the value of the goods is attributable to the improvement.

(2) If, in proceedings for wrongful interference against a person ('the purchaser') who has purported to purchase the goods—

(*a*) from the improver, or

(*b*) where after such a purported sale the goods passed by a further purported sale on one or more occasions, on any such occasion.

it is shown that the purchaser acted in good faith, an allowance shall be made on the principle set out in subsection (1).

For example, where a person in good faith buys a stolen car from the improver and is sued in conversion by the true owner the damages may be reduced to reflect the improvement, but if the person who bought the stolen car from the improver sues the improver for failure of consideration, and the improver acted in good faith, subsection (3) below will ordinarily make a comparable reduction in the damages he recovers from the improver.

(3) If in a case within subsection (2) the person purporting to sell the goods acted in good faith, then in proceedings by the purchaser for recovery of the purchase price because of failure of consideration, or in any other proceedings founded on that failure of consideration, an allowance shall, where appropriate, be made on the principle set out in subsection (1).

(4) This section applies, with the necessary modifications, to a purported bailment or other disposition of goods as it applies to a purported sale of goods.

Liability to two or more claimants

7. Double liability

(1) In this section 'double liability' means the double liability of the wrongdoer which can arise—

(*a*) where one of two or more rights of action for wrongful interference is founded on a possessory title, or

(*b*) where the measure of damages in an action for wrongful interference founded on a proprietary title is or includes the entire value of the goods, although the interest is one of two or more interests in the goods.

(2) In proceedings to which any two or more claimants are parties, the relief shall be such as to avoid double liability of the wrongdoer as between those claimants.

(3) On satisfaction, in whole or in part, of any claim for an amount exceeding that recoverable if subsection (2) applied, the claimant is liable to account over to the other person having a right to claim to such extent as will avoid double liability.

(4) Where, as the result of enforcement of a double liability, any claimant is unjustly enriched to any extent, he shall be liable to reimburse the wrongdoer to that extent.

Torts (Interference with Goods) Act 1977

For example, if a converter of goods pays damages first to a finder of the goods, and then to the true owner, the finder is unjustly enriched unless he accounts over to the true owner under subsection (3); and then the true owner is unjustly enriched and becomes liable to reimburse the converter of the goods.

8. Competing rights to the goods

(1) The defendant in an action for wrongful interference shall be entitled to show, in accordance with rules of court, that a third party has a better right than the plaintiff as respects all or any part of the interest claimed by the plaintiff, or in right of which he sues, and any rule of law (sometimes called jus tertii) to the contrary is abolished.

(2) Rules of court relating to proceedings for wrongful interference may—

   (a) require the plaintiff to give particulars of his title,
   (b) require the plaintiff to identify any person who, to his knowledge, has or claims any interest in the goods,
   (c) authorise the defendant to apply for directions as to whether any person should be joined with a view to establishing whether he has a better right than the plaintiff, or has a claim as a result of which the defendant might be doubly liable,
   (d) where a party fails to appear on an application within paragraph (c), or to comply with any direction given by the court on such an application, authorise the court to deprive him of any right of action against the defendant for the wrong either unconditionally, or subject to such terms or conditions as may be specified.

(3) Subsection (2) is without prejudice to any other power of making rules of court.

9. Concurrent actions

(1) This section applies where goods are the subject of two or more claims for wrongful interference (whether or not the claims are founded on the same wrongful act, and whether or not any of the claims relates also to other goods).

(2) Where goods are the subject of two or more claims under section 6 this section shall apply as if any claim under section 6(3) were a claim for wrongful interference.

(3) If proceedings have been brought in a county court on one of those claims, county court rules may waive, or allow a court to waive, any limit (financial or territorial) on the jurisdiction of county courts in [the County Courts Act 1984] or the County Courts Act (Northern Ireland) 1959 so as to allow another of those claims to be brought in the same county court.

(The words in square brackets were substituted by the County Courts Act 1984.)

(4) If proceedings are brought on one of the claims in the High Court, and proceedings on any other are brought in a county court, whether prior to the High Court proceedings or not, the High Court may, on the application of the defendant, after notice has been given to the claimant in the county court proceedings—

   (a) order that the county court proceedings be transferred to the High Court, and

(b) order security for costs or impose such other terms as the court thinks fit.

Conversion and trespass to goods

10. Co-owners

(1) Co-ownership is no defence to an action founded on conversion or trespass to goods where the defendant without the authority of the other co-owner—

(a) destroys the goods, or disposes of the goods in a way giving a good title to the entire property in the goods, or otherwise does anything equivalent to the destruction of the other's interest in the goods, or

(b) purports to dispose of the goods in a way which would give a good title to the entire property in the goods if he was acting with the authority of all co-owners of the goods.

(2) Subsection (1) shall not affect the law concerning execution or enforcement of judgments, or concerning any form of distress.

(3) Subsection (1)(a) is by way of restatement of existing law so far as it relates to conversion.

11. Minor amendments

(1) Contributory negligence is no defence in proceedings founded on conversion, or on intentional trespass to goods.

(2) Receipt of goods by way of pledge is conversion if the delivery of the goods is conversion.

(3) Denial of title is not of itself conversion.

Uncollected goods

12. Bailee's power of sale

(1) This section applies to goods in the possession or under the control of a bailee where—

(a) the bailor is in breach of an obligation to take delivery of the goods or, if the terms of the bailment so provide, to give directions as to their delivery, or

(b) the bailee could impose such an obligation by giving notice to the bailor, but is unable to trace or communicate with the bailor, or

(c) the bailee can reasonably expect to be relieved of any duty to safeguard the goods on giving notice to the bailor, but is unable to trace or communicate with the bailor.

(2) In the cases in Part I of Schedule 1 to this Act a bailee may, for the purposes of subsection (1), impose an obligation on the bailor to take delivery of the goods, or as the case may be to give directions as to their delivery, and in those cases the said Part I sets out the method of notification.

(3) If the bailee—

(a) has in accordance with Part II of Schedule 1 to this Act given notice to the bailor of his intention to sell the goods under this subsection, or

(b) has failed to trace or communicate with the bailor with a view to giving him such a notice, after having taken reasonable steps for the purpose,

and is reasonably satisfied that the bailor owns the goods, he shall be entitled, as against the bailor, to sell the goods.

(4) Where subsection (3) applies but the bailor did not in fact own the goods, a sale under this section, or under section 13, shall not give a good title as against the owner, or as against a person claiming under the owner.

(5) A bailee exercising his powers under subsection (3) shall be liable to account to the bailor for the proceeds of sale, less any costs of sale, and—

(a) the account shall be taken on the footing that the bailee should have adopted the best method of sale reasonably available in the circumstances, and
(b) where subsection (3)(a) applies, any sum payable in respect of the goods by the bailor to the bailee which accrued due before the bailee gave notice of intention to sell the goods shall be deductible from the proceeds of sale.

(6) A sale duly made under this section gives a good title to the purchaser as against the bailor.

(7) In this section, section 13, and Schedule 1 to this Act,

(a) 'bailor' and 'bailee' include their respective successors in title, and
(b) references to what is payable, paid or due to the bailee in respect of the goods include references to what would be payable by the bailor to the bailee as a condition of delivery of the goods at the relevant time.

(8) This section, and Schedule 1 to this Act, have effect subject to the terms of the bailment.

(9) This section shall not apply where the goods were bailed before the commencement of this Act.

13. Sale authorised by the court

(1) If a bailee of the goods to which section 12 applies satisfies the court that he is entitled to sell the goods under section 12, or that he would be so entitled if he had given any notice required in accordance with Schedule 1 to this Act, the court—

(a) may authorise the sale of the goods subject to such terms and conditions, if any, as may be specified in the order, and
(b) may authorise the bailee to deduct from the proceeds of sale any costs of sale and any amount due from the bailor to the bailee in respect of the goods, and
(c) may direct the payment into court of the net proceeds of sale, less any amount deducted under paragraph (b), to be held to the credit of the bailor.

(2) A decision of the court authorising a sale under this section shall, subject to any right of appeal, be conclusive, as against the bailor, of the bailee's entitlement to sell the goods, and gives a good title to the purchaser as against the bailor.

(3) In this section 'the court' means the High Court or a county court, and a county court shall have jurisdiction in the proceedings if the value of the goods does not exceed the county court limit.

Supplemental

14. Interpretation

(1) In this Act, unless the context otherwise requires—

'county court limit' means the [amount which for the time being is the county court limit for the purposes of section 15 of the County Courts Act 1984], or in Northern Ireland the current amount mentioned in section 10(1) of the County Courts Act (Northern Ireland) 1959,

(The words in square brackets were substituted by the County Courts Act 1984.)

'enactment' includes an enactment contained in an Act of the Parliament of Northern Ireland or an Order in Council made under the Northern Ireland (Temporary Provisions) Act 1972, or in a Measure of the Northern Ireland Assembly,

'goods' includes all chattels personal other than things in action and money,

'High Court' includes the High Court of Justice in Northern Ireland.

(2) References in this Act to any enactment include references to that enactment as amended, extended or applied by or under that or any other enactment.

15. Repeal

(1) The Disposal of Uncollected Goods Act 1952 is hereby repealed.

(2) In England and Wales that repeal shall not affect goods bailed before the commencement of this Act.

(3) In Scotland that repeal shall not affect the rights of the person with whom the goods are deposited where the notice of intention to sell the goods under section 1(3)(*c*) of the said Act of 1952 was delivered before the commencement of this Act.

16. Extent and application to the Crown

(1) Section 15 shall extend to Scotland, but otherwise this Act shall not extend to Scotland.

(2) This Act, except section 15, extends to Northern Ireland.

(3) This Act shall bind the Crown, but as regards the Crown's liability in tort shall not bind the Crown further than the Crown is made liable in tort by the Crown Proceedings Act 1947.

17. Short title, etc.

(1) This Act may be cited as the Torts (Interference with Goods) Act 1977.

(2) This Act shall come into force on such day as the Lord Chancellor may by order contained in a statutory instrument appoint, and such an order may appoint different dates for different provisions or for different purposes.

(3) Schedule 2 to this Act contains transitional provisions.

Torts (Interference with Goods) Act 1977

SCHEDULES
SCHEDULE 1

Uncollected Goods

Part I

Power to Impose Obligation to Collect Goods

1. Power to impose obligations to collect goods

(1) For the purposes of section 12(1) a bailee may, in the circumstances specified in this Part of this Schedule, by notice given to the bailor impose on him an obligation to take delivery of the goods.

(2) The notice shall be in writing, and may be given either—

- (*a*) by delivering it to the bailor, or
- (*b*) by leaving it at his proper address, or
- (*c*) by post.

(3) The notice shall—

- (*a*) specify the name and address of the bailee, and give sufficient particulars of the goods and the address or place where they are held, and
- (*b*) state that the goods are ready for delivery to the bailor, or where combined with a notice terminating the contract of bailment, will be ready for delivery when the contract is terminated, and
- (*c*) specify the amount, if any, which is payable by the bailor to the bailee in respect of the goods and which became due before the giving of the notice.

(4) Where the notice is sent by post it may be combined with a notice under Part II of this Schedule if the notice is sent by post in a way complying with paragraph 6(4).

(5) References in this Part of this Schedule to taking delivery of the goods include, where the terms of the bailment admit, references to giving directions as to their delivery.

(6) This Part of this Schedule is without prejudice to the provisions of any contract requiring the bailor to take delivery of the goods.

2. Goods accepted for repair or other treatment

If a bailee has accepted goods for repair or other treatment on the terms (expressed or implied) that they will be redelivered to the bailor when the repair or other treatment has been carried out, the notice may be given at any time after the repair or other treatment has been carried out.

3. Goods accepted for valuation or appraisal

If a bailee has accepted goods in order to value or appraise them, the notice may be given at any time after the bailee has carried out the valuation or appraisal.

4. Storage, warehousing, etc.

(1) If a bailee is in possession of goods which he has held as custodian, and his obligation as custodian has come to an end, the notice may be given at any time after the ending of the obligation, or may be combined with any notice terminating his obligation as custodian.

(2) This paragraph shall not apply to goods held by a person as mercantile agent, that is to say by a person having in the customary course of his business as a mercantile agent authority either to sell goods or to consign goods for the purpose of sale, or to buy goods, or to raise money on the security of goods.

5. Supplemental

Paragraphs 2, 3 and 4 apply whether or not the bailor has paid any amount due to the bailee in respect of the goods, and whether or not the bailment is for reward, or in the course of business, or gratuitous.

Part II

Notice of Intention to Sell Goods

6.

(1) A notice under section 12(3) shall—

(a) specify the name and address of the bailee, and give sufficient particulars of the goods and the address or place where they are held, and
(b) specify the date on or after which the bailee proposes to sell the goods, and
(c) specify the amount, if any, which is payable by the bailor to the bailee in respect of the goods, and which became due before the giving of the notice.

(2) The period between giving of the notice and the date specified in the notice as that on or after which the bailee proposes to exercise the power of sale shall be such as will afford the bailor a reasonable opportunity of taking delivery of the goods.

(3) If any amount is payable in respect of the goods by the bailor to the bailee, and became due before giving of the notice, the said period shall be not less than three months.

(4) The notice shall be in writing and shall be sent by post in a registered letter, or by the recorded delivery service.

7.

(1) The bailee shall not give a notice under section 12(3), or exercise his right to sell the goods pursuant to such a notice, at a time when he has notice that, because of a dispute concerning the goods, the bailor is questioning or refusing to pay all or any part of what the bailee claims to be due to him in respect of the goods.

(2) This paragraph shall be left out of account in determining under section

3(1) whether a bailee of goods is entitled to sell the goods under section 12, or would be so entitled if he had given any notice required in accordance with this Schedule.

8. Supplemental

For the purposes of this Schedule, and of section 26 of the Interpretation Act 1889 in its application to this Schedule, the proper address of the person to whom a notice is to be given shall be—

- (*a*) in this case of a body corporate, a registered or principal office of the body corporate, and
- (*b*) in any other case, the last known address of the person.

SCHEDULE 2

Transitional

1.

This Act shall not affect any action or arbitration brought before the commencement of this Act or any proceedings brought to enforce a decision in the action or arbitration.

2.

Subject to paragraph 1, this Act applies to acts or omissions before it comes into force as well as to later ones, and for the purposes of the Limitation Act 1939, the Statute of Limitations (Northern Ireland) 1958, or any other limitation enactment, the cause of action shall be treated as having accrued at the time of the act or omission even if proceedings could not have been brought before the commencement of this Act.

3.

For the purposes of this Schedule, any claim by way of set-off or counterclaim shall be deemed to be a separate action, and to have been brought on the same date as the action in which the set-off or counterclaim is pleaded.

Unfair Contract Terms Act 1977
Chapter 50

ARRANGEMENT OF SECTIONS

PART I

AMENDMENT OF LAW FOR ENGLAND AND WALES AND NORTHERN IRELAND

Introductory

Section
1. Scope of Part I

Avoidance of liability for negligence, breach of contract, etc.

2. Negligence liability
3. Liability arising in contract
4. Unreasonable indemnity clauses

Liability arising from sale or supply of goods

5. 'Guarantee' of consumer goods
6. Sale and hire-purchase
7. Miscellaneous contracts under which goods pass

Other provisions about contracts

8. Misrepresentation
9. Effect of breach
10. Evasion by means of secondary contract

Explanatory provisions

11. The 'unreasonableness' test
12. 'Dealing as consumer'
13. Varieties of exemption clause
14. Interpretation of Part I

PART II

AMENDMENT OF LAW FOR SCOTLAND

15. Scope of Part II
16. Liability for breach of duty
17. Control of unreasonable exemptions in consumer or standard form contracts
18. Unreasonable indemnity clauses in consumer contract
19. 'Guarantee' of consumer goods
20. Obligations implied by law in sale and hire-purchase contracts
21. Obligations implied by law in other contracts for the supply of goods
22. Consequences of breach

Section
23. Evasion by means of secondary contract
24. The 'reasonableness' test
25. Interpretation of Part II

PART III

PROVISIONS APPLYING TO WHOLE OF UNITED KINGDOM

Miscellaneous

26. International supply contracts
27. Choice of law clauses
28. Temporary provision for sea carriage of passengers
29. Saving for other relevant legislation
30. Obligations under Consumer Protection Acts

General

31. Commencement; amendments; repeals
32. Citation and extent

SCHEDULES:

Schedule 1—Scope of ss 2 to 4 and 7
Schedule 2—'Guidelines' for application of reasonableness test
Schedule 3—Amendment of enactments
Schedule 4—Repeals

An Act to impose further limits on the extent to which under the law of England and Wales and Northern Ireland civil liability for breach of contract, or for negligence or other breach of duty, can be avoided by means of contract terms and otherwise, and under the law of Scotland civil liability can be avoided by means of contract terms. [26th October 1977]

PART I

AMENDMENT OF LAW FOR ENGLAND AND WALES AND NORTHERN IRELAND

Introductory

1. Scope of Part I

(1) For the purposes of this Part of this Act, 'negligence' means the breach—

  (*a*) of any obligation, arising from the express or implied terms of a contract, to take reasonable care or exercise reasonable skill in the performance of the contract;
  (*b*) of any common law duty to take reasonable care or exercise reasonable skill (but not any stricter duty);
  (*c*) of the common duty of care imposed by the Occupiers' Liability Act 1957 or the Occupiers' Liability Act (Northern Ireland) 1957.

(2) This Part of this Act is subject to Part III; and in relation to contracts, the operation of sections 2 to 4 and 7 is subject to the exceptions made by Schedule 1.

(3) In the case of both contract and tort, sections 2 to 7 apply (except where

the contrary is stated in section 6(4)) only to business liability, that is liability for breach of obligations or duties arising—

(*a*) from things done or to be done by a person in the course of a business (whether his own business or another's); or

(*b*) from the occupation of premises used for business purposes of the occupier;

and references to liability are to be read accordingly, [but liability of an occupier of premises for breach of an obligation or duty towards a person obtaining access to the premises for recreational or educational purposes, being liability for loss or damage suffered by reason of the dangerous state of the premises, is not a business liability of the occupier unless granting that person such access for the purposes concerned falls within the business purposes of the occupier].

[*The words in square brackets were inserted by the Occupiers' Liability Act 1984, section 2.*]

(4) In relation to any breach of duty or obligation, it is immaterial for any purpose of this Part of this Act whether the breach was inadvertent or intentional, or whether liability for it arises directly or vicariously.

Avoidance of liability for negligence, breach of contracts, etc.

2. Negligence liability

(1) A person cannot by reference to any contract term or to a notice given to persons generally or to particular persons exclude or restrict his liability for death or personal injury resulting from negligence.

(2) In the case of other loss or damage, a person cannot so exclude or restrict his liability for negligence except in so far as the term or notice satisfies the requirement of reasonableness.

(3) Where a contract term or notice purports to exclude or restrict liability for negligence a person's agreement to or awareness of it is not of itself to be taken as indicating his voluntary acceptance of any risk.

3. Liability arising in contract

(1) This section applies as between contracting parties where one of them deals as consumer or on the other's written standard terms of business.

(2) As against that party, the other cannot by reference to any contract term—

(*a*) when himself in breach of contract, exclude or restrict any liability of his in respect of the breach; or

(*b*) claim to be entitled—

(i) to render a contractual performance substantially different from that which was reasonably expected of him, or

(ii) in respect of the whole or any part of his contractual obligation, to render no performance at all,

except in so far as (in any of the cases mentioned above in this subsection) the contract term satisfies the requirement of reasonableness.

4. Unreasonable indemnity clauses

(1) A person dealing as consumer cannot by reference to any contract term

Unfair Contract Terms Act 1977

be made to indemnify another person (whether a party to the contract or not) in respect of liability that may be incurred by the other for negligence or breach of contract, except in so far as the contract term satisfies the requirement of reasonableness.

(2) This section applies whether the liability in question—

(*a*) is directly that of the person to be indemnified or is incurred by him vicariously:
(*b*) is to the person dealing as consumer or to someone else.

Liability arising from sale or supply of goods

5. 'Guarantee' of consumer goods

(1) In the case of goods of a type ordinarily supplied for private use or consumption, where loss or damage—

(*a*) arises from the goods proving defective while in consumer use; and
(*b*) results from the negligence of a person concerned in the manufacture or distribution of the goods,

liability for the loss or damage cannot be excluded or restricted by reference to any contract term or notice contained in or operating by reference to a guarantee of the goods.

(2) For these purposes—

(*a*) goods are to be regarded as 'in consumer use' when a person is using them, or has them in his possession for use, otherwise than exclusively for the purposes of a business; and
(*b*) anything in writing is a guarantee if it contains or purports to contain some promise or assurance (however worded or presented) that defects will be made good by complete or partial replacement, or by repair, monetary compensation or otherwise.

(3) This section does not apply as between the parties to a contract under or in pursuance of which possession or ownership of the goods passed.

6. Sale and hire-purchase

(1) Liability for breach of the obligations arising from—

(*a*) [section 12 of the Sale of Goods Act 1979] (seller's implied undertakings as to title, etc.);
(*b*) section 8 of the Supply of Goods (Implied Terms) Act 1973 (the corresponding thing in relation to hire-purchase),

cannot be excluded or restricted by reference to any contract term.

(2) As against a person dealing as consumer, liability for breach of the obligations arising from—

(*a*) [section 13, 14 or 15 of the 1979 Act] (seller's implied undertakings as to conformity of goods with description or sample, or as to their quality or fitness for a particular purpose);
(*b*) section 9, 10 or 11 of the 1973 Act (the corresponding things in relation to hire-purchase),

cannot be excluded or restricted by reference to any contract term.

(3) As against a person dealing otherwise than as consumer, the liability specified in subsection (2) above can be excluded or restricted by reference to a contract term, but only in so far as the term satisfies the requirement of reasonableness.

(4) The liabilities referred to in this section are not only the business liabilities defined by section 1(3), but include those arising under any contract of sale of goods or hire-purchase agreement.

[*The words in square brackets in subsection (1)(a) and (2)(a) were substituted by the Sale of Goods Act 1979, section 63(2) and Schedule 2, paragraph 19(a) and (b) respectively.*]

7. Miscellaneous contracts under which goods pass

(1) Where the possession or ownership of goods passes under or in pursuance of a contract not governed by the law of sale of goods or hire-purchase, subsection (2) to (4) below apply as regards the effect (if any) to be given to contract terms excluding or restricting liability for breach of obligation arising by implication of law from the nature of the contract.

(2) As against a person dealing as consumer, liability in respect of the goods correspondence with description or sample, or their quality or fitness for any particular purpose, cannot be excluded or restricted by reference to any such term.

(3) As against a person dealing otherwise than as consumer, that liability can be excluded or restricted by reference to such a term, but only in so far as the term satisfies the requirement of reasonableness.

[(3A) Liability for breach of the obligations arising under section 2 of the Supply of Goods and Services Act 1982 (implied terms about title etc. in certain contracts for the transfer of the property in goods) cannot be excluded or restricted by references to any such term.]

(4) Liability in respect of—

(a) the right to transfer ownership of the goods, or give possession; or
(b) the assurance of quiet possession to a person taking goods in pursuance of the contract,

cannot [(in a case to which subsection (3A) above does not apply)] be excluded or restricted by reference to any such term except in so far as the term satisfies the requirement of reasonableness.

(5) This section does not apply in the case of goods passing on a redemption of trading stamps within the Trading Stamps Act 1964 or the Trading Stamps Act (Northern Ireland) 1965.

[*Subsection (3A) and the words in square brackets in subsection (4) were introduced by the Supply of Goods and Services Act 1982, section 17(2), 3.*]

Other provisions about contracts

8. Misrepresentation

(1) In the Misrepresentation Act 1967, the following is substituted for section 3—

3. If a contract contains a term which would exclude or restrict—

(*a*) any liability to which a party to a contract may be subject by reason of any misrepresentation made by him before the contract was made; or

(*b*) any remedy available to another party to the contract by reason of such a misrepresentation,

the term shall be of no effect except in so far as it satisfies the requirement of reasonableness as stated in section 11(1) of the Unfair Contract Terms Act 1977; and it is for those claiming that the term satisfies that requirement to show that it does.'

(2) The same section is substituted for section 3 of the Misrepresentation Act (Northern Ireland) 1967.

9. Effect of breach

(1) Where for reliance upon it a contract term has to satisfy the requirement of reasonableness, it may be found to do so and be given effect accordingly notwithstanding that the contract has been terminated either by breach or by a party electing to treat it as repudiated.

(2) Where on a breach the contract is nevertheless affirmed by a party entitled to treat it as repudiated, this does not of itself exclude the requirement of reasonableness in relation to any contract term.

10. Evasion by means of secondary contract

A person is not bound by any contract term prejudicing or taking away rights of his which arise under, or in connection with the performance of, another contract, so far as those rights extend to the enforcement of another's liability which this Part of this Act prevents that other from excluding or restricting.

Explanatory provisions

11. The 'reasonableness' test

(1) In relation to a contract term, the requirement of reasonableness for the purposes of this Part of this Act, section 3 of the Misrepresentation Act 1967 and section 3 of the Misrepresentation Act (Northern Ireland) 1967 is that the term shall have been a fair and reasonable one to be included having regard to the circumstances which were, or ought reasonably to have been, known to or in the contemplation of the parties when the contract was made.

(2) In determining for the purposes of section 6 or 7 above whether a contract term satisfies the requirement of reasonableness, regard shall be had in particular to the matters specified in Schedule 2 to this Act; but this subsection does not prevent the court or arbitrator from holding, in accordance with any rule of law, that a term which purports to exclude or restrict any relevant liability is not a term of the contract.

(3) In relation to a notice (not being a notice having contractual effect), the requirement of reasonableness under this Act is that it should be fair and reasonable to allow reliance on it, having regard to all the circumstances obtaining when the liability arose or (but for the notice) would have arisen.

(4) Whereby reference to a contract term or notice a person seeks to restrict liability to a specified sum of money, and the question arises (under this or any other Act) whether the term or notice satisfies the requirement of

reasonableness, regard shall be had in particular (but without prejudice to subsection (2) above in the case of contract terms) to—

(a) the resources which he could expect to be available to him for the purpose of meeting the liability should it arise; and
(b) how far it was open to him to cover himself by insurance.

(5) It is for those claiming that a contract term or notice satisfies the requirement of reasonableness to show that it does.

12. 'Dealing as consumer'

(1) A party to a contract 'deals as consumer' in relation to another party if—

(a) he neither makes the contract in the course of a business nor holds himself out as doing so; and
(b) the other party does make the contract in the course of a business; and
(c) in the case of a contract governed by the law of sale of goods or hire-purchase, or by section 7 of this Act, the goods passing under or in pursuance of the contract are of a type ordinarily supplied for private use or consumption.

(2) But on a sale by auction or by competitive tender the buyer is not in any circumstances to be regarded as dealing as consumer.

(3) Subject to this, it is for those claiming that a party does not deal as consumer to show that he does not.

13. Varieties of exemption clause

(1) To the extent that this Part of this Act prevents the exclusion or restriction of any liability it also prevents—

(a) making the liability or its enforcement subject to restrictive or onerous conditions;
(b) excluding or restricting any right or remedy in respect of the liability, or subjecting a person to any prejudice in consequence of his pursuing any such right or remedy;
(c) excluding or restricting rules of evidence or procedure;

and (to that extent) sections 2 and 5 to 7 also prevent excluding or restricting liability by reference to terms and notices which exclude or restrict the relevant obligation or duty.

(2) But an agreement in writing to submit present or future differences to arbitration is not to be treated under this Part of this Act as excluding or restricting any liability.

14. Interpretation of Part I

In this Part of this Act—

'business' includes a profession and the activities of any Government department or local or public authority;

'goods' has the same meaning as in the [Sale of Goods Act 1979];

'hire-purchase agreement' has the same meaning as in the Consumer Credit Act 1974;

'negligence' has the meaning given by section 1(1);

'notice' includes an announcement, whether or not in writing, and any other communication or pretended communication; and

'personal injury' includes any disease and any impairment of physical or mental condition.

[*The words in square brackets were substituted by the Sale of Goods Act 1979, section 63(2) and Schedule 2, paragraph 20.*]

PART II

AMENDMENT OF LAW FOR SCOTLAND

15. Scope of Part II

(1) This Part of this Act applies only to contracts, is subject to Part III of this Act and does not affect the validity of any discharge or indemnity given by a person in consideration of the receipt by him of compensation in settlement of any claim which he has.

(2) Subject to subsection (3) below, sections 16 to 18 of this Act apply to any contract only to the extent that the contract—

(*a*) relates to the transfer of the ownership or possession of goods from one person to another (with or without work having been done on them);
(*b*) constitutes a contract of service or apprenticeship;
(*c*) relates to services of whatever kind, including (without prejudice to the foregoing generality) carriage, deposit and pledge, care and custody, mandate, agency, loan and services relating to the use of land;
(*d*) relates to the liability of an occupier of land to persons entering upon or using that land;
(*e*) relates to a grant of any right or permission to enter upon or use land not amounting to an estate or interest in the land.

(3) Notwithstanding anything in subsection (2) above, sections 16 to 18—

(*a*) do not apply to any contract to the extent that the contract—
   (i) is a contract of insurance (including a contract to pay an annuity on human life);
   (ii) relates to the formation, constitution or dissolution of any body corporate or unincorporated association or partnership;

(*b*) apply to—
   a contract of marine salvage or towage;
   a charter party of a ship or hovercraft;
   a contract for the carriage of goods by ship or hovercraft; or,
   a contract to which subsection (4) below relates.
   only to the extent that—
   (i) both parties deal or hold themselves out as dealing in the course of a business (and then only in so far as the contract purports to exclude or restrict liability for breach of duty in respect of death or personal injury); or

(ii) the contract is a consumer contract (and then only in favour of the consumer).

(4) This subsection relates to a contract in pursuance of which goods are carried by ship or hovercraft and which either—

(*a*) specifies ship or hovercraft as the means of carriage over part of the journey to be covered; or

(*b*) makes no provision as to the means of carriage and does not exclude ship or hovercraft as that means,

in so far as the contract operates for and in relation to the carriage of the goods by that means.

16. Liability for breach of duty

(1) Where a term of contract purports to exclude or restrict liability for breach of duty arising in the course of any business or from the occupation of any premises used for business purposes of the occupier, that term—

(*a*) shall be void in any case where such exclusion or restriction is in respect of death or personal injury;

(*b*) shall, in any other case, have no effect if it was not fair and reasonable to incorporate the term in the contract.

(2) Subsection (1)(*a*) above does not affect the validity of any discharge and indemnity given by a person, on or in connection with an award to him of compensation for pneumoconiosis attributable to employment in the coal industry, in respect of any further claim arising from his contracting that disease.

(3) Where under subsection (1) above a term of a contract is void or has no effect, the fact that a person agreed to, or was aware of, the term shall not of itself be sufficient evidence that he knowingly and voluntarily assumed any risk.

17. Control of unreasonable exemptions in consumer or standard form contracts

(1) Any term of a contract which is a consumer contract or a standard form contract shall have no effect for the purpose of enabling a party to the contract—

(*a*) who is in breach of a contractual obligation, to exclude or restrict any liability of his to the consumer or customer in respect of the breach;

(*b*) in respect of a contractual obligation, to render no performance, or to render a performance substantially different from that which the consumer or customer reasonably expected from the contract;

if it was not fair and reasonable to incorporate the term in the contract.

(2) In this section 'customer' means a party to a standard form contract who deals on the basis of written standard terms of business of the other party to the contract who himself deals in the course of a business.

18. Unreasonable indemnity clauses in consumer contracts

(1) Any term of a contract which is a consumer contract shall have no effect for the purpose of making the consumer indemnify another person (whether a party to the contract or not) in respect of liability which that other person may incur as a result of breach of duty or breach of contract, if it was not fair and reasonable to incorporate the term in the contract.

(2) In this section 'liability' means liability arising in the course of any business or from the occupation of any premises used for business purposes of the occupier.

19. 'Guarantee' of consumer goods

(1) This section applies to a guarantee—

    (*a*) in relation to goods which are of a type ordinarily supplied for private use or consumption; and

    (*b*) which is not a guarantee given by one party to the other party to a contract under or in pursuance of which the ownership or possession of the goods to which the guarantee relates is transferred.

(2) A term of a guarantee to which this section applies shall be void in so far as it purports to exclude or restrict liability for loss or damage (including death or personal injury)—

    (*a*) arising from the goods proving defective while—
        (i) in use otherwise than exclusively for the purposes of a business; or
        (ii) in the possession of a person for such use; and

    (*b*) resulting from the breach of duty of a person concerned in the manufacture or distribution of the goods.

(3) For the purposes of this section, any document is a guarantee if it contains or purports to contain some promise or assurance (however worded or presented) that defects will be made good by complete or partial replacement, or by repair, monetary compensation or otherwise.

20. Obligations implied by law in sale and hire-purchase contracts

(1) Any term of a contract which purports to exclude or restrict liability for breach of the obligations arising from—

    (*a*) section 12 of the Sale of Goods Act [1979] (seller's implied undertakings as to title etc.);

    (*b*) section 8 of the Supply of Goods (Implied Terms) Act 1973 (implied terms as to title in hire-purchase agreements),

shall be void.

(2) Any term of a contract which purports to exclude or restrict liability for breach of the obligations arising from—

    (*a*) section 13, 14 or 15 of the said Act of [1979] (seller's implied undertakings as to conformity of goods with description or sample, or as to their quality or fitness for a particular purpose);

    (*b*) section 9, 10 or 11 of the said Act of 1973 (the corresponding provisions in relation to hire-purchase),

shall—
    (i) in the case of a consumer contract, be void against the consumer;
    (ii) in any other case, have no effect if it was not fair and reasonable to incorporate the term in the contract.

[*The dates within square brackets in subsections (1)(a) and (2)(a) were substituted by the Sale of Goods Act 1979, section 63(2) and Schedule 2, paragraph 21.*]

21. Obligations implied by law in other contracts for the supply of goods

(1) Any term of a contract to which this section applies purporting to exclude or restrict liability for breach of an obligation—

(*a*) such as is referred to in subsection (3)(*a*) below—
  (i) in the case of a consumer contract, shall be void against the consumer, and
  (ii) in any other case, shall have no effect if it was not fair and reasonable to incorporate the term in the contract;

(*b*) such as is referred to in subsection (3)(*b*) below, shall have no effect if it was not fair and reasonable to incorporate the term in the contract.

(2) This section applies to any contract to the extent that it relates to any such matter as is referred to in section 15(2)(*a*) of this Act, but does not apply to—

(*a*) a contract of sale of goods or a hire-purchase agreement; or
(*b*) a charter party of a ship or hovercraft unless it is a consumer contract (and then only in favour of the consumer).

(3) An obligation referred to in this subsection is an obligation incurred under a contract in the course of a business and arising by implication of law from the nature of the contract which relates—

(*a*) to the correspondence of goods with description or sample, or to the quality or fitness of the goods for any particular purpose; or
(*b*) to any right to transfer ownership or possession of goods, or to the enjoyment of quiet possession of goods.

(4) Nothing in this section applies to the supply of goods on a redemption of trading stamps within the Trading Stamps Act 1964.

22. Consequence of breach

For the avoidance of doubt, where any provision of this Part of this Act requires that the incorporation of a term in a contract must be fair and reasonable for that term to have effect—

(*a*) if that requirement is satisfied, the term may be given effect to notwithstanding that the contract has been terminated in consequence of breach of that contract;
(*b*) for the term to be given effect to, that requirement must be satisfied even where a party who is entitled to rescind the contract elects not to rescind it.

23. Evasion by means of secondary contract

Any term of any contract shall be void which purports to exclude or restrict, or has the effect of excluding or restricting—

(*a*) the exercise, by a party to any other contract, of any right or remedy which arises in respect of that other contract in consequence of breach of duty, or of obligation, liability for which could not by virtue of the provisions of this Part of this Act be excluded or restricted by a term of that other contract;
(*b*) the application of the provisions of this Part of this Act in respect of that or any other contract.

24. The 'reasonableness' test

(1) In determining for the purposes of this Part of this Act whether it was fair and reasonable to incorporate a term in a contract, regard shall be had only to the circumstances which were, or ought reasonably to have been, known to or in the contemplation of the parties to the contract at the time the contract was made.

(2) In determining for the purposes of section 20 or 21 of this Act whether it was fair and reasonable to incorporate a term in a contract, regard shall be had in particular to the matters specified in Schedule 2 to this Act; but this subsection shall not prevent a court or arbiter from holding, in accordance with any rule of law, that a term which purports to exclude or restrict any relevant liability is not a term of the contract.

(3) Where a term in a contract purports to restrict liability to a specified sum of money, and the question arises for the purpose of this Part of this Act whether it was fair and reasonable to incorporate the term in the contract, then, without prejudice to subsection (2) above, regard shall be had in particular to—

 (*a*) the resources which the party seeking to rely on that term could expect to be available to him for the purpose of meeting the liability should it arise;
 (*b*) how far it was open to that party to cover himself by insurance.

(4) The onus of proving that it was fair and reasonable to incorporate a term in a contract shall lie on the party so contending.

25. Interpretation of Part II

(1) In this Part of this Act—
'breach of duty' means the breach—

 (*a*) of any obligation, arising from the express or implied terms of a contract, to take reasonable care or exercise reasonable skill in the performance of the contract;
 (*b*) of any common law duty to take reasonable care or exercise reasonable skill;
 (*c*) of the duty of reasonable care imposed by section 2(1) of the Occupiers' Liability (Scotland) Act 1960;

 'business' includes a profession and the activities of any Government department or local or public authority;

 'consumer' has the meaning assigned to that expression in the definition in this section of 'consumer contract';

 'consumer contract' means a contract (not being a contract of sale by auction or competitive tender) in which—

 (*a*) one party to the contract deals, and the other party to the contract ('the consumer') does not deal or hold himself out as dealing, in the course of a business, and
 (*b*) in the case of a contract such as is mentioned in section 15(2)(*a*) of this Act, the goods are of a type ordinarily supplied for private use or consumption;

and for the purposes of this Part of this Act the onus of proving that a contract is not to be regarded as a consumer contract shall lie on the party so contending;

Unfair Contract Terms Act 1977

'goods' has the same meaning as in the [Sale of Goods Act 1979];

[*The words within square brackets were substituted by the Sale of Goods Act 1979, section 63(2) and Schedule 2, paragraph 22.*]

'hire-purchase agreement' has the same meaning as in section 189(1) of the Consumer Credit Act 1974;

'personal injury' includes any disease and any impairment of physical or mental condition.

(2) In relation to any breach of duty or obligation, it is immaterial for any purpose of this Part of this Act whether the act or omission giving rise to that breach was inadvertent or intentional, or whether liability for it arises directly or vicariously.

(3) In this Part of this Act, any reference to excluding or restricting any liability includes—

(*a*) making the liability or its enforcement subject to any restrictive or onerous conditions;
(*b*) excluding or restricting any right or remedy in respect of the liability, or subjecting a person to any prejudice in consequence of his pursuing any such right or remedy;
(*c*) excluding or restricting any rule of evidence or procedure;
(*d*) excluding or restricting any liability by reference to a notice having contractual effect,

but does not include an agreement to submit any question to arbitration.

(4) In subsection (3)(*d*) above 'notice' includes an announcement, whether or not in writing, and any other communication or pretended communication.

(5) In sections 15 and 16 and 19 to 21 of this Act, any reference to excluding or restricting liability for breach of an obligation or duty shall include a reference to excluding or restricting the obligation or duty itself.

PART III

PROVISIONS APPLYING TO WHOLE OF UNITED KINGDOM

Miscellaneous

26. International supply contracts

(1) The limits imposed by this Act on the extent to which a person may exclude or restrict liability by reference to a contract term do not apply to liability arising under such a contract as is described in subsection (3) below.

(2) The terms of such a contract are not subject to any requirement of reasonableness under section 3 or 4; and nothing in Part II of this Act shall require the incorporation of the terms of such a contract to be fair and reasonable for them to have effect.

(3) Subject to subsection (4), that description of contract is one whose characteristics are the following—

(*a*) either it is a contract of sale of goods or it is one under or in pursuance of which the possession or ownership of goods passes; and
(*b*) it is made by parties whose places of business (or, if they have none,

Unfair Contract Terms Act 1977

habitual residences) are in the territories of different States (the Channel Islands and the Isle of Man being treated for this purpose as different States from the United Kingdom).

(4) A contract falls within subsection (3) above only if either—

   (a) the goods in question are, at the time of the conclusion of the contract, in the course of carriage, or will be carried, from the territory of one State to the territory of another; or

   (b) the acts constituting the offer and acceptance have been done in the territories of different States; or

   (c) the contract provides for the goods to be delivered to the territory of a State other than that within whose territory those acts were done.

27. Choice of law clauses

(1) Where the proper law of a contract is the law of any part of the United Kingdom only by choice of the parties (and apart from that choice would be the law of some country outside the United Kingdom) sections 2 to 7 and 16 to 21 of this Act do not operate as part of the proper law.

(2) This Act has effect notwithstanding any contract term which applies or purports to apply the law of some country outside the United Kingdom, where (either or both)—

   (a) the term appears to the court, or arbitrator or arbiter to have been imposed wholly or mainly for the purpose of enabling the party imposing it to evade the operation of this Act; or

   (b) in the making of the contract one of the parties dealt as consumer, and he was then habitually resident in the United Kingdom, and the essential steps necessary for the making of the contract were taken there, whether by him or by others on his behalf.

(3) In the application of subsection (2) above to Scotland, for paragraph (b) there shall be substituted—

   '(b) the contract is a consumer contract as defined in Part II of this Act, and the consumer at the date when the contract was made was habitually resident in the United Kingdom, and the essential steps necessary for the making of the contract were taken there, whether by him or by others on his behalf.'.

28. Temporary provision for sea carriage of passengers

(1) This section applies to a contract for carriage by sea of a passenger or of a passenger and his luggage where the provisions of the Athens Convention (with or without modification) do not have, in relation to the contract, the force of law in the United Kingdom.

(2) In a case where—

   (a) the contract is not made in the United Kingdom, and
   (b) neither the place of departure nor the place of destination under it is in the United Kingdom,

a person is not precluded by this Act from excluding or restricting liability for loss or damage, being loss or damage for which the provisions of the Convention would, if they had the force of law in relation to the contract, impose liability on him.

(3) In any other case, a person is not precluded by this Act from excluding or restricting liability for that loss or damage—

(*a*) in so far as the exclusion or restriction would have been effective in that case had the provisions of the Convention had the force of law in relation to the contract; or

(*b*) in such circumstances and to such extent as may be prescribed, by reference to a prescribed term of the contract.

(4) For the purposes of subsection (3)(*a*), the values which shall be taken to be the official values in the United Kingdom of the amounts (expressed in gold francs) by reference to which liability under the provisions of the Convention is limited shall be such amounts in sterling as the Secretary of State may from time to time by order made by statutory instrument specify.

(5) In this section,—

(*a*) the references to excluding or restricting liability include doing any of those things in relation to the liability which are mentioned in section 13 or section 25(3) and (5); and

(*b*) 'the Athens Convention' means the Athens Convention relating to the Carriage of Passengers and their Luggage by Sea, 1974; and

(*c*) 'prescribed' means prescribed by the Secretary of State by regulations made by statutory instrument;

and a statutory instrument containing the regulation shall be subject to annulment in pursuance of a resolution of either House of Parliament.

29. Saving for other relevant legislation

(1) Nothing in this Act removes or restricts the effect of, or prevents reliance upon, any contractual provision which—

(*a*) is authorised or required by the express terms or necessary implication of an enactment; or

(*b*) being made with a view to compliance with an international agreement to which the United Kingdom is a party, does not operate more restrictively than is contemplated by the agreement.

(2) A contract term is to be taken—

(*a*) for the purposes of Part I of this Act, as satisfying the requirement of reasonableness; and

(*b*) for those of Part II, to have been fair and reasonable to incorporate,

if it is incorporated or approved by, or incorporated pursuant to a decision or ruling of, a competent authority acting in the exercise of any statutory jurisdiction or function and is not a term in a contract to which the competent authority is itself a party.

(3) In this section—

'competent authority' means any court, arbitrator or arbiter, Government department or public authority;

'enactment' means any legislation (including subordinate legislation) of the United Kingdom or Northern Ireland and any instrument having effect by virtue of such legislation; and 'statutory' means conferred by an enactment.

30. Obligations under Consumer Protection Acts

[*Amends section 3, Consumer Protection Act 1961.*]

General

31. Commencement; amendments; repeals

(1) This Act comes into force on 1st February 1978.

(2) Nothing in this Act applies to contracts made before the date on which it comes into force; but subject to this, it applies to liability for any loss or damage which is suffered on or after that date.

(3) The enactments specified in Schedule 3 to this Act are amended as there shown.

(4) The enactments specified in Schedule 4 to this Act are repealed to the extent specified in column 3 of that Schedule.

32. Citation and extent

(1) This Act may be cited as the Unfair Contract Terms Act 1977.

(2) Part I of this Act extends to England and Wales and to Northern Ireland; but it does not extend to Scotland.

(3) Part II of this Act extends to Scotland only.

(4) This Part of this Act extends to the whole of the United Kingdom.

SCHEDULES

SCHEDULE 1

Scope of sections 2 to 4 and 7

1. Sections 2 to 4 of this Act do not extend to—
    (*a*) any contract of insurance (including a contract to pay an annuity on human life);
    (*b*) any contract so far as it relates to the creation or transfer of an interest in land, or to the termination of such in interest, whether by extinction, merger, surrender, forfeiture or otehwise;
    (*c*) any contract so far as it relates to the creation or transfer of a right or interest in any patent, trade mark, copyright, registered design, technical or commercial information or other intellectual property, or relates to the termination of any such right or interest;
    (*d*) any contract so far as it relates—
        (i) to the formation or dissolution of a company (which means any body corporate or unincorporated association and includes a partnership), or
        (ii) to its constitution or the rights or obligations of its corporators or members;
    (*e*) any contract so far as it relates to the creation or transfer of securities or of any right or interest in securities.

[*The reference in paragraph 1(c) to a trade mark includes a reference to a service mark, Patents, Designs and Marks Act 1986, section 2 and Schedule 2.*]

2. Section 2(1) extends to—
   (*a*) any contract of marine salvage or towage;
   (*b*) any charter party of a ship or hovercraft; and
   (*c*) any contract for the carriage of goods by ship or hovercraft;

but subject to this sections 2 to 4 and 7 do not extend to any such contract except in favour of a person dealing as consumer.

3. Where goods are carried by ship or hovercraft in pursuance of a contract which either—

   (*a*) specifies that as the means of carriage over part of the journey to be covered, or
   (*b*) make no provision as to the means of carriage and does not exclude that means,

then sections 2(2), 3 and 4 do not, except in favour of a person dealing as a consumer, extend to the contract as it operates for and in relation to the carriage of the goods by that means.

4. Section 2(1) and (2) do not extend to a contract of employment, except in favour of the employee.

5. Section 2(1) does not affect the validity of any discharge and indemnity given by a person, on or in connection with an award to him of compensation for pneumoconiosis attributable to employment in the coal industry, in respect of any further claim arising from his contracting that disease.

SCHEDULE 2

'Guidelines' for Application of Reasonableness Test

The matters to which regard is to be had in particular for the purposes of sections 6(3), 7(3) and (4), 20 and 21 are any of the following which appear to be relevant—

   (*a*) the strength of the bargaining positions of the parties relative to each other, taking into account (among other things) alternative means by which the customer's requirements could have been met;
   (*b*) whether the customer received an inducement to agree to the term, or in accepting it had an opportunity of entering into a similar contract with other persons, but without having to accept a similar term;
   (*c*) whether the customer knew or ought reasonably to have known of the existence and extent of the term (having regard, among other things, to any custom of the trade and any previous course of dealing between the parties);
   (*d*) where the term excludes or restricts any relevant liability if some condition is not complied with, whether it was reasonable at the time of the contract to expect that compliance with that condition would be practicable;
   (*e*) whether the goods were manufactured, processed or adapted to the special order of the customer.

Unfair Contract Terms Act 1977

SCHEDULE 3
AMENDMENTS OF ENACTMENTS

SCHEDULE 4
Repeals

Estate Agents Act 1979
Chapter 38

ARRANGEMENT OF SECTIONS

Application of Act

Section
1. Estate agency work.
2. Interests in land.

Orders by Director General of Fair Trading

3. Orders prohibiting unfit persons from doing estate agency work.
4. Warning orders.
5. Supplementary provisions as to orders under sections 3 and 4.
6. Revocation and variation of orders under sections 3 and 4.
7. Appeals.
8. Register of orders etc.

Information, entry and inspection

9. Information for the Director.
10. Restriction on disclosure of information.
11. Powers of entry and inspection.

Clients' money and accounts

12. Meaning of 'clients' money' etc.
13. Clients' money held on trust or as agent.
14. Keeping of client accounts.
15. Interest on clients' money.
16. Insurance cover for clients' money.
17. Exemptions from section 16.

Regulation of other aspects of estate agency work

18. Information to client of prospective liabilities.
19. Regulation of pre-contract deposits outside Scotland.

Supervision, enforcement, publicity etc.

20. Prohibition of pre-contract deposits in Scotland.
21. Transactions in which an estate agent has a personal interest.
22. Standards of competence.
23. Bankrupts not to engage in estate agency work.
24. Supervision by Council on Tribunals.
25. General duties of Director.
26. Enforcement authorities.
27. Obstruction and personation of authorised officers.

Estate Agents Act 1979

Supplementary

Section
28. General provisions as to offences.
29. Service of notices etc.
30. Orders and regulations.
31. Meaning of 'business associate' and 'controller'.
32. Meaning of 'associate'.
33. General interpretation provisions.
34. Financial provisions.
35. Scotland.
36. Short title, commencement and extent.

SCHEDULES:
Schedule 1—Provisions supplementary to section 3(1).
Schedule 2—Procedure etc.

An Act to make provision with respect to the carrying on of and to persons who carry on, certain activities in connection with the disposal and acquisition of interests in land; and for purposes connected therewith.

[4th April 1979]

1. Application of Act

(1) This Act applies, subject to subsections (2) to (4) below to things done by any person in the course of a business (including a business in which he is employed) pursuant to instructions received from another person (in this section referred to as 'the client') who wishes to dispose of or acquire an interest in land—

(*a*) for the purpose of, or with a view to, effecting the introduction to the client of a third person who wishes to acquire or, as the case may be, dispose of such an interest; and

(*b*) after such an introduction has been effected in the course of that business, for the purpose of securing the disposal or, as the case may be, the acquisition of that interest;

and in this Act the expression 'estate agency work' refers to things done as mentioned above to which this Act applies.

(2) This Act does not apply to things done—

(*a*) in the course of his profession by a practising solicitor or a person employed by him [or by an incorporated practice (within the meaning of the Solicitors (Scotland) Act 1980) or a person employed by it]; or

(*b*) in the course of credit brokerage, within the meaning of the Consumer Credit Act 1974; or

(*c*) in the course of insurance brokerage by a person who is for the time being registered under section 2, or enrolled under section 4, of the Insurance Brokers (Registration) Act 1977; or

(*d*) in the course of carrying out any survey or valuation pursuant to a contract which is distinct from that under which other things falling within subsection (1) above are done; or

(*e*) in connection with applications and other matters arising under the Town and Country Planning Act 1971 or the Town and Country Planning (Scotland) Act 1972 or the Planning (Northern Ireland) Order 1972.

(The words in brackets in subsection (2)(a) were added by the Law Reform (Miscellaneous Provisions) (Scotland) Act 1985.)

(3) This Act does not apply to things done by any person—

  (*a*) pursuant to instructions received by him in the course of his employment in relation to an interest in land if his employer is the person who, on his own behalf, wishes to dispose of or acquire that interest; or
  (*b*) in relation to any interest in any property if the property is subject to a mortgage and he is the receiver of the income of it; or
  (*c*) in relation to a present, prospective or former employee of his or of any person by whom he also is employed if the things are done by reason of the employment (whether past, present or future).

(4) This Act does not apply to the publication of advertisements or the dissemination of information by a person who does no other acts which fall within subsection (1) above.

(5) In this section—

  (*a*) 'practising solicitor' means, except in Scotland, a solicitor who is qualified to act as such under section 1 of the Solicitors Act 1974 or Article 4 of the Solicitors (Northern Ireland) Order 1976, and in Scotland includes a firm of practising solicitors;
  (*b*) 'mortgage' includes a debenture and any other charge on property for securing money or money's worth; and
  (*c*) any reference to employment is a reference to employment under a contract of employment.

2. Interests in land

(1) Subject to subsection (3) below, any reference in this Act to disposing of an interest in land is a reference to—

  (*a*) transferring a legal estate in fee simple absolute in possession; or
  (*b*) transferring or creating, elsewhere than in Scotland, a lease which, by reason of the level of the rent, the length of the term or both, has a capital value which may be lawfully realised on the open market; or
  (*c*) transferring or creating in Scotland any estate or interest in land which is capable of being owned or held as a separate interest and to which a title may be recorded in the Register of Sasines;

and any reference to acquiring an interest in land shall be construed accordingly.

(2) In subsection (1)(*b*) above the expression 'lease' includes the rights and obligations arising under an agreement to grant a lease.

(3) Notwithstanding anything in subsections (1) and (2) above, references in this Act to disposing of an interest in land do not extend to disposing of—

  (*a*) the interest of a creditor whose debt is secured by way of a mortgage or charge of any kind over land or an agreement for any such mortgage or charge; or
  (*b*) in Scotland, the interest of a creditor in a heritable security as defined

in section 9(8) of the Conveyancing and Feudal Reform (Scotland) Act 1970.

Orders by Director General of Fair Trading

3. Orders prohibiting unfit persons from doing estate agency work

(1) The power of the Director General of Fair Trading (in this Act referred to as 'the Director') to make an order under this section with respect to any person shall not be exercisable unless the Director is satisfied that that person—

  (*a*) has been convicted of—
    (i) an offence involving fraud or other dishonesty or violence, or
    (ii) an offence under any provision of this Act, other than section 10(6), section 22(3) or section 23(4), or
    (iii) any other offence which, at the time it was committed, was specified for the purposes of this section by an order made by the Secretary of State; or
  (*b*) has committed discrimination in the course of estate agency work; or
  (*c*) has failed to comply with any obligation imposed on him under any of sections 15 and 18 to 21 below; or
  (*d*) has engaged in a practice which, in relation to estate agency work, has been declared undesirable by an order made by the Secretary of State;

and the provisions of Schedule 1 to the Act shall have effect for supplementing paragraphs (*a*) and (*b*) above.

(2) Subject to subsection (1) above, if the Director is satisfied that any person is unfit to carry on estate agency work generally or of a particular description he may make an order prohibiting that person—

  (*a*) from doing any estate agency work at all; or
  (*b*) from doing estate agency work of a description specified in the order;

and in determining whether a person is so unfit the Director may, in addition to taking account of any matters falling within subsection (1) above, also take account of whether, in the course of estate agency work or any other business activity, that person has engaged in any practice which involves breaches of a duty owed by virtue of any enactment, contract or rule of law and which is material to his fitness to carry on estate agency work.

(3) For the purposes of paragraphs (*c*) and (*d*) of subsection (1) above,—

  (*a*) anything done by a person in the course of his employment shall be treated as done by his employer as well as by him, whether or not it was done with the employer's knowledge or approval, unless the employer shows that he took such steps as were reasonably practicable to prevent the employee from doing that act, or from doing in the course of his employment acts of that description; and
  (*b*) anything done by a person as agent for another person with the authority (whether express or implied, and whether precedent or subsequent) of that person shall be treated as done by that other person as well as by him; and
  (*c*) anything done by a business associate of a person shall be treated as done by that person as well, unless he can show that the act was done without his connivance or consent.

(4) In an order under this section the Director shall specify as the grounds

for the order those matters falling within paragraphs (*a*) to (*d*) of subsection (1) above as to which he is satisfied and on which, accordingly, he relies to give him power to make the order.

(5) If the Director considers it appropriate, he may in an order under this section limit the scope of the prohibition imposed by the order to a particular part of or area within the United Kingdom.

(6) An order under paragraph (*a*)(iii) or paragraph (*d*) of subsection (1) above—

 (*a*) shall be made by statutory instrument;
 (*b*) shall be laid before Parliament after being made; and
 (*c*) shall cease to have effect (without prejudice to anything previously done in reliance on the order) after the expiry of the period of twenty-eight days beginning with the date on which it was made unless within that period it has been approved by a resolution of each House of Parliament.

(7) In reckoning for the purposes of subsection (6)(*c*) above any period of twenty-eight days, no account shall be taken of any period during which Parliament is dissolved or prorogued or during which both Houses are adjourned for more than four days.

(8) A person who fails without reasonable excuse to comply with an order of the Director under this section shall be liable on conviction on indictment or on summary conviction to a fine which on summary conviction shall not exceed the statutory maximum.

4. Warning orders

(1) If the Director is satisfied that—

 (*a*) in the course of estate agency work any person has failed to comply with any such obligation as is referred to in section 3(1)(*c*) above (in this section referred to as a 'relevant statutory obligation') or has engaged in such a practice as is referred to in section 3(1)(*d*) above, and
 (*b*) if that person were again to fail to comply with a relevant statutory obligation or, as the case may be, were to continue to engage in that practice, the Director would consider him unfit as mentioned in subsection (2) of section 3 above and would proceed to make an order under that section,

the Director may by order notify that person that he is so satisfied.

(2) An order under this section shall state whether, in the opinion of the Director, a further failure to comply with a relevant statutory obligation or, as the case may be, continuation of the practice specified in the order would render the person to whom the order is addressed unfit to carry on estate agency work generally or estate agency work of a description specified in the order.

(3) If, after an order has been made under this section, the person to whom it is addressed fails to comply with a relevant statutory obligation or, as the case may be, engages in the practice specified in the order then, for the purposes of this Act, that fact shall be treated as conclusive evidence that he is unfit to carry on estate agency work as stated in the order in accordance with subsection (2) above; and the Director may proceed to make an order under section 3 above accordingly.

5. Supplementary provisions as to orders under sections 3 and 4

(1) The provisions of Part I of Schedule 2 to this Act shall have effect—

   (a) with respect to the procedure to be followed before an order is made by the Director under section 3 or section 4 above; and

   (b) in connection with the making and coming into operation of any such order.

(2) Where an order is made by the Director under section 3 or section 4 above against a partnership, it may, if the Director thinks it appropriate, have effect also as an order against some or all of the partners individually, and in such a case the order shall so provide and shall specify the names of the partners affected by the order.

(3) Nothing in section 62 of the Sex Discrimination Act 1975, section 53 of the Race Relations Act 1976 or Article 62 of the Sex Discrimination (Northern Ireland) Order 1976 (restriction of sanctions for breaches of those Acts and that Order) shall be construed as applying to the making of an order by the Director under section 3 above.

(4) In any case where—

   (a) an order of the Director under section 3 above specifies a conviction as a ground for the order, and

   (b) the conviction becomes spent for the purposes of the Rehabilitation of Offenders Act 1974 or any corresponding enactment for the time being in force in Northern Ireland.

then, unless the order also specified other grounds which remain valid, the order shall cease to have effect on the day on which the conviction becomes so spent.

(5) In any case where—

   (a) an order of the Director under section 3 above specifies as grounds for the order the fact that the person concerned committed discrimination by reason of the existence of any such finding or notice as is referred to in paragraph 2 of Schedule 1 to this Act, and

   (b) the period expires at the end of which, by virtue of paragraph 3 of that Schedule, the person concerned would no longer be treated for the purposes of section 3(1)(b) above as having committed discrimination by reason only of that finding or notice,

then, unless the order also specifies other grounds which remain valid, the order shall cease to have effect at the end of that period.

6. Revocation and variation of orders under sections 3 and 4

(1) On an application made to him by the person in respect of whom the Director has made an order under section 3 or section 4 above, the Director may revoke or vary the order.

(2) An application under subsection (1) above—

   (a) shall state the reasons why the applicant considers that the order should be revoked or varied;

   (b) in the case of an application for a variation, shall indicate the variation which the applicant seeks; and

   (c) shall be accompanied by the prescribed fee.

(3) If the Director decides to accede to an application under subsection (1) above, he shall give notice in writing of his decision to the applicant and, upon the giving of that notice, the revocation or, as the case may be, the variation specified in the application shall take effect.

(4) The Director may decide to refuse an application under subsection (1) above—

>   (a) where it relates to an order under section 3 above, if he considers that the applicant remains unfit to carry on any estate agency work at all or, as the case may be, estate agency work of the description which is prohibited by the order; and
>   (b) where it relates to an order under section 4 above, if he considers that the applicant may again fail to comply with a relevant statutory obligation or, as the case may be, again engage in the practice specified in the order.

(5) If, on an application under subsection (1) above, the Director decides that—

>   (a) he cannot accede to the application because he considers that the applicant remains unfit to carry on any estate agency work at all in a particular part of or area within the United Kingdom or remains unfit to carry on estate agency work of a particular description (either throughout the United Kingdom or in a particular part of or area within it) of, as the case may be, remains likely to fail to comply with a relevant statutory obligation or to engage in a particular practice, but
>   (b) the order to which the application relates could, without detriment to the public, be varied in favour of the applicant,

the Director may make such a variation accordingly.

(6) The provisions of Part II of Schedule 2 to this Act shall have effect in relation to any application to the Director under subsection (1) above and the provisions of Part I of that Schedule shall have effect—

>   (a) with respect to the procedure to be followed before the Director comes to a decision under subsection (4) or subsection (5) above; and
>   (b) in connection with the making and coming into operation of such a decision.

(7) In this section 'relevant statutory obligation' has the meaning assigned to it by section 4(1)(a) above.

7. Appeals

(1) A person who receives notice under paragraph 9 of Schedule 2 to this Act of—

>   (a) a decision of the Director to make an order in respect of him under section 3 or section 4 above, or
>   (b) a decision of the Director under subsection (4) or subsection (5) of section 6 above on an application made by him,

may appeal against the decision to the Secretary of State.

(2) On an appeal under subsection (1) above the Secretary of State may give such directions for disposing of the appeal as he thinks just, including a direction for the payment of costs or expenses by any party to the appeal.

(3) The Secretary of State shall make provision by regulations with respect to appeals under subsection (1) above—

(a) as to the period within which and the manner in which such appeals are to be brought;
(b) as to the persons by whom such appeals are to be heard on behalf of the Secretary of State;
(c) as to the manner in which such appeals are to be conducted;
(d) for taxing or otherwise settling any costs or expenses directed to be paid under subsection (2) above and for the enforcement of any such direction; and
(e) as to any other matter connected with such appeals;

and such regulations shall be made by statutory instrument which shall be subject to annulment in pursuance of a resolution of either House of Parliament.

(4) If the appellant is dissatisfied in point of law with a decision of the Secretary of State under this section he may appeal against that decision to the High Court, the Court of Session or a judge of the High Court in Northern Ireland.

(5) No appeal to the Court of Appeal or to the Court of Appeal in Northern Ireland shall be brought from a decision under subsection (4) above except with the leave of that Court or of the court or judge from whose decision the appeal is brought.

(6) An appeal shall lie, with the leave of the Court of Session or the House of Lords, from any decision of the Court of Session under this section, and such leave may be given on such terms as to costs or otherwise as the Court of Session or the House of Lords may determine.

8. Register of orders etc.

(1) The Director shall establish and maintain a register on which there shall be entered particulars of every order made by him under section 3 or section 4 above and of his decision on any application for revocation or variation of such an order.

(2) The particulars referred to in subsection (1) above shall include—

(a) the terms of the order and of any variation of it; and
(b) the date on which the order or variation came into operation or is expected to come into operation or if an appeal against the decision is pending and the order or variation has in consequence not come into operation, a statement to that effect.

(3) The Director may, of his own motion or on the application of any person aggrieved, rectify the register by the addition, variation or removal of any particulars; and the provisions of Part II of Schedule 2 to this Act shall have effect in relation to an application under this subsection.

(4) If it comes to the attention of the Director that any order of which particulars appear in the register is no longer in operation, he shall remove those particulars from the register.

(5) Any person shall be entitled on payment of the prescribed fee—

(a) to inspect the register during such office hours as may be specified by a general notice made by the Director and to take copies of any entry, or (*b*) to obtain from the Director a copy, certified by him to be correct, of any entry in the register.

(6) A certificate given by the Director under subsection (5)(*b*) above shall be conclusive evidence of the fact that, on the date on which the certificate was given, the particulars contained in the copy to which the certificate relates were entered on the register; and particulars of any matters required to be entered on the register which are so entered shall be evidence and, in Scotland, sufficient evidence of those matters and shall be presumed, unless the contrary is proved, to be correct.

Information, entry and inspection

9. Information for the Director

(1) The Director may, for the purpose of assisting him—

(*a*) to determine whether to make an order under section 3 or section 4 above, and

(*b*) in the exercise of any of his functions under section 5, 6 and 8 above and 13 and 17 below,

by notice require any person to furnish to him such information as may be specified or described in the notice or to produce to him any documents so specified or described.

(2) A notice under this section—

(*a*) may specify the way in which and the time within which it is to be complied with and, in the case of a notice requiring the production of documents, the facilities to be afforded for making extracts, or taking copies of, the documents; and

(*b*) may be varied or revoked by a subsequent notice.

(3) Nothing in this section shall be taken to require a person who has acted as counsel or solicitor for any person to disclose any privileged communication made by or to him in that capacity.

(4) A person who—

(*a*) refuses or wilfully neglects to comply with a notice under this section, or

(*b*) in furnishing any information in compliance with such a notice, makes any statement which he knows to be false in a material particular or recklessly makes any statement which is false in a material particular, or

(*c*) with intent to deceive, produces in compliance with such a notice a document which is false in a material particular,

shall be liable on conviction on indictment or on summary conviction to a fine which, on summary conviction, shall not exceed the statutory maximum.

(5) In section 131 of the Fair Trading Act 1973 (which provides for the Director to be notified by courts of convictions and judgments which may be relevant to his functions under Part III of that Act) after the words 'this Act' there shall be inserted the words 'or under the Estate Agents Act 1979'.

(6) It shall be the duty of—

(*a*) the Equal Opportunities Commission,

(b) the Equal Opportunities Commission for Northern Ireland, and
(c) the Commission for Racial Equality,

to furnish to the Director such information relating to any finding, notice, injunction or order falling within paragraph 2 of Schedule 1 to this Act as is in their possession and appears to them to be relevant to the functions of the Director under this Act.

10. Restriction on disclosure of information

(1) Subject to subsections (3) to (5) below, no information obtained under or by virtue of this Act about any individual shall be disclosed without his consent.

(2) Subject to subsections (3) to (5) below, no information obtained under or by virtue of this Act about any business shall be disclosed except, so long as the business continues to be carried on, with the consent of the person for the time being carrying it on.

(3) Subsections (1) and (2) above do not apply to any disclosure of information made—

(a) for the purpose of facilitating the performance of any functions under this Act, the Trade Descriptions Act 1968, the Fair Trading Act 1973, the Consumer Credit Act 1974 or the Restrictive Trade Practices Act 1976 [or the Competition Act 1980 or the Telecommunications Act 1984 or the Gas Act 1986 or the Airports Act 1986 or the Consumer Protection Act 1987 or the Control of Misleading Advertisements Regulations 1988] of any Minister of the Crown, any Northern Ireland department, [the Director General of Telecommunications, the Director General of Gas Supply, the Civil Aviation Authority,] the Director or a local weights and measures authority in Great Britain, or

(The words in square brackets were inserted by the statutes and regulations appearing within the square brackets.)

(b) in connection with the investigation of any criminal offence or for the purposes of any criminal proceedings, or
(c) for the purposes of any civil proceedings brought under or by virtue of this Act or any of the other enactments [or subordinate legislation] specified in paragraph (a) above.

(The words in square brackets were added by the Control of Misleading Advertisements Regulations 1988.)

(4) For the purpose of enabling the Director to use, in connection with his functions under this Act, information obtained by him in the exercise of functions under certain other enactments, the following amendments shall be made in provisions restricting disclosure of information, namely,—

(a) at the end of paragraph (a) of subsection (2) of section 133 of the Fair Trading Act 1973 there shall be added the words 'the Estate Agents Act 1979, or';
(b) in paragraph (a) of subsection (3) of section 174 of the Consumer Credit Act 1974 after the words 'Fair Trading Act 1973' there shall be added the words 'or the Estate Agents Act 1979'; and
(c) at the end of paragraph (a) of subsection (1) of section 41 of the Restrictive

Estate Agents Act 1979

Trade Practices Act 1976 there shall be added the words 'or the Estate Agents Act 1979'.

(5) Nothing in subsections (1) and (2) above shall be construed—

(*a*) as limiting the particulars which may be entered in the register; or

(*b*) as applying to any information which has been made public as part of the register.

(6) Any person who discloses information in contravention of this section shall be liable on summary conviction to a fine not exceeding the statutory maximum and, on conviction on indictment, to imprisonment for a term not exceeding two years or to a fine or both.

11. Powers of entry and inspection

(1) A duly authorised officer of an enforcement authority, at all reasonable hours and on production, if required, of his credentials may—

(*a*) if he has reasonable cause to suspect that an offence has been committed under this Act, in order to ascertain whether it has been committed, enter any premises (other than premises used only as a dwelling);

(*b*) if he has reasonable cause to suspect that an offence has been committed under this Act, in order to ascertain whether it has been committed, require any person—
  (i) carrying on, or employed in connection with, a business to produce any books or documents relating to it, or
  (ii) having control of any information relating to a business recorded otherwise than in a legible form, to provide a document containing a legible reproduction of the whole or any part of the information;
and take copies of, or of any entry in, the books or documents;

(*c*) seize and detain any books or documents which he has reason to believe may be required as evidence in proceedings for an offence under this Act;

(*d*) for the purpose of exercising his powers under this subsection to seize books and documents, but only if and to the extent that it is reasonably necessary for securing that the provisions of this Act are duly observed, require any person having authority to do so to break open any container and, if that person does not comply, break it open himself.

(2) An officer seizing books or documents in exercise of his powers under this section shall not do so without informing the person from whom he seizes them.

(3) If and so long as any books or documents which have been seized under this section are not required as evidence in connection with proceedings which have been begun for an offence under this Act, the enforcement authority by whose officer they were seized shall afford to the person authorised by him in writing reasonable facilities to inspect them and to take copies of or make extracts from them.

(4) If a justice of the peace, on sworn information in writing, or, in Scotland, a sheriff or a justice of the peace, on evidence on oath,—

(*a*) is satisfied that there is reasonable ground to believe either—
  (i) that any books or documents which a duly authorised officer has power to inspect under this section are on any premises and their

inspection is likely to disclose evidence of the commission of an offence under this Act, or
   (ii) that an offence under this Act has been, or is being or is about to be, committed on any premises; and
 (b) is also satisfied either—
   (i) that admission to the premises has been or is likely to be refused and that notice of intention to apply for a warrant under this subsection has been given to the occupier, or
   (ii) that an application for admission, or the giving of such a notice, would defeat the object of the entry or that the premises are unoccupied or that the occupier is temporarily absent and it might defeat the object of the entry to wait for his return,

the justice or, as the case may be, the sheriff may by warrant under his hand, which shall continue in force for a period of one month, authorise an officer of an enforcement authority to enter the premises, by force if need be.

(5) An officer entering premises by virtue of this section may take such other persons and equipment with him as he thinks necessary, and on leaving premises entered by virtue of a warrant under subsection (4) above shall, if the premises are unoccupied or the occupier is temporarily absent, leave them as effectively secured against trespassers as he found them.

(6) The Secretary of State may by regulations provide that, in cases specified in the regulations, an officer of a local weights and measures authority is not to be taken to be duly authorised for the purposes of this section unless he is authorised by the Director.

(7) The power to make regulations under section (6) above shall be exercisable by statutory instrument which shall be subject to annulment in pursuance of a resolution of either House of Parliament.

(8) Nothing in this section shall be taken to require a person who has acted as counsel or solicitor for any person to produce a document containing a privileged communication made by or to him in that capacity or authorises the seizing of any such document in his possession.

Clients' money and accounts

12. Meaning of 'clients' money' etc.

(1) In this Act 'clients' money', in relation to a person engaged in estate agency work, means any money received by him in the course of that work which is a contract or pre-contract deposit—

 (a) in respect of the acquisition of an interest in land in the United Kingdom, or
 (b) in respect of a connected contract,

whether that money is held or received by him as agent, bailee, stakeholder or in any other capacity.

(2) In this Act 'contract deposit' means any sum paid by a purchaser—

 (a) which in whole or in part is, or is intended to form part of, the consideration for acquiring such an interest as is referred to in subsection (1)(a) above or for a connected contract; and

(b) which is paid by him at or after the time at which he acquires the interest or enters into an enforceable contract to acquire it.

(3) In this Act 'pre-contract deposit' means any sum paid by any person—

(a) in whole or in part as an earnest of his intention to acquire such an interest as is referred to in subsection (1)(a) above, or
(b) in whole or in part towards meeting any liability of his in respect of the consideration for the acquisition of such an interest which will arise if he acquires or enters into an enforceable contract to acquire the interest, or
(c) in respect of a connected contract,

and which is paid by him at a time before he either acquires the interest or enters into an enforceable contract to acquire it.

(4) In this Act 'connected contract', in relation to the acquisition of an interest in land, means a contract which is conditional upon such an acquisition or upon entering into an enforceable contract for such an acquisition (whether or not it is also conditional on other matters).

13. Clients' money held on trust or as agent

(1) It is hereby declared that clients' money received by any person in the course of estate agency work in England, Wales or Northern Ireland—

(a) is held by him on trust for the person who is entitled to call for it to be paid over to him or to be paid on his direction or to have it otherwise credited to him, or
(b) if it is received by him as stakeholder, is held by him on trust for the person who may become so entitled on the occurrence of the event against which the money is held.

(2) It is hereby declared that clients' money received by any person in the course of estate agency work in Scotland is held by him as agent for the person who is entitled to call for it to be paid over to him or to be paid on his direction or to have it otherwise credited to him.

(3) The provisions of sections 14 and 15 below as to the investment of clients' money, the keeping of accounts and records and accounting for interest shall have effect in place of the corresponding duties which would be owed by a person holding clients' money as trustee, or in Scotland as agent, under the general law.

(4) Where an order of the Director under section 3 above has the effect of prohibiting a person from holding clients' money the order may contain provision—

(a) appointing another person as trustee, or in Scotland as agent, in place of the person to whom the order relates to hold and deal with clients' money held by that person when the order comes into effect; and
(b) requiring the expenses and such reasonable remuneration of the new trustee or agent as may be specified in the order to be paid by the person to whom the order relates or, if the order so provides, out of the clients' money;

but nothing in this subsection shall affect the power conferred by section 41 of the Trustee Act 1925 or section 40 of the Trustee Act (Northern Ireland) 1958 to appoint a new trustee to hold clients' money.

(5) For the avoidance of doubt it is hereby declared that the fact that any person has or may have a lien on clients' money held by him does not affect the operation of this section and also that nothing in this section shall prevent such a lien from being given effect.

14. Keeping of client accounts

(1) Subject to such provision as may be made by accounts regulations, every person who receives clients' money in the course of estate agency work shall, without delay, pay the money into a client account maintained by him or by a person in whose employment he is.

(2) In this Act a 'client account' means a current or deposit account which—

   (*a*) is with an institution authorised for the purposes of this section, and
   (*b*) is in the name of a person who is or has been engaged in estate agency work; and
   (*c*) contains in its title the word 'client'.

(3) The Secretary of State may make provision by regulations (in this section referred to as 'accounts regulations') as to the opening and keeping of client accounts, the keeping of accounts and records relating to clients' money and the auditing of those accounts; and such regulations shall be made by statutory instrument which shall be subject to annulment in pursuance of a resolution of either House of Parliament.

(4) As to the opening and keeping of client accounts, accounts regulations may in particular specify—

   (*a*) the institutions which are authorised for the purposes of this section;
   (*b*) any persons or classes of persons to whom, or any circumstances in which, the obligation imposed by subsection (1) above does not apply;
   (*c*) any circumstances in which money other than clients' money may be paid into a client account; and
   (*d*) the occasions on which, and the persons to whom, money held in a client account may be paid out.

(5) As to the auditing of accounts relating to clients' money, accounts regulations may in particular make provision—

   (*a*) requiring such accounts to be drawn up in respect of specified accounting periods and to be audited by a qualified auditor within a specified time after the end of each such period;
   (*b*) requiring the auditor to report whether in his opinion the requirements of this Act and of the accounts regulations have been complied with or have been substantially complied with;
   (*c*) as to the matters to which such a report is to relate and the circumstances in which a report of substantial compliance may be given; and
   (*d*) requiring a person who maintains a client account to produce on demand to a duly authorised officer of an enforcement authority the latest auditor's report.

(6) Subject to subsection (7) below, 'qualified auditor' in subsection (5)(*a*) above means—

(a) a person who is a member of one or more bodies of accountants established in the United Kingdom and for the time being recognised by the Secretary of State for the purposes of [section 389(1)(a) of the Companies Act 1985] or, in Northern Ireland, recognised by the Department of Commerce for Northern Ireland for the purposes of section 155(1)(a) of the Companies Act (Northern Ireland) 1960; or

(b) a person who is for the time being authorised by the Secretary of State under [section 389(1)(b) of the Companies Act 1985] or, in Northern Ireland, by the Department of Commerce for Northern Ireland under section 155(1)(b) of the Companies Act (Northern Ireland) 1960; or

(c) in the case of a client account maintained by a company, a person who is qualified to audit the accounts of the company by virtue of [section 389(2) of the Companies Act 1985] (unqualified auditors of former exempt private companies); or

(d) a Scottish firm of which all the members are qualified auditors within paragraphs (a) to (c) above.

(The words in square brackets were substituted by the Companies Consolidation (Consequential Provisions) Act 1985.)

(7) A person is not a qualified auditor for the purposes of subsection (5)(a) above if, in the case of a client account maintained by a company, he is disqualified from auditing the accounts of the company [either by subsection (6), subsection (7) or subsection (8) of section 389 of the Companies Act 1985 or by subsection (2), subsection (3) or subsection (4) of section 155 of the Companies Act (Northern Ireland) 1960.

(The words in square brackets were substituted and inserted by the Companies Consolidation (Consequential Provisions) Act 1985.)

(8) A person who—

(a) contravenes any provision of this Act or of accounts regulations as to the manner in which clients' money is to be dealt with or accounts and records relating to such money are to be kept, or

(b) fails to produce an auditor's report when required to do so by accounts regulations,

shall be liable on summary conviction to a fine not exceeding £500.

15. Interest on clients' money

(1) Accounts regulations may make provision for requiring a person who has received any clients' money to account, in such cases as may be prescribed by the regulations, to the person who is or becomes entitled to the money for the interest which was, or could have been, earned by putting the money in a separate deposit account at an institution authorised for the purposes of section 14 above.

(2) The cases in which a person may be required by accounts regulations to account for interest as mentioned in subsection (1) above may be defined, amongst other things, by reference to the amount of the sum held or received by him or the period for which it is likely to be retained, or both.

(3) Except as provided by accounts regulations and subject to subsection (4) below, a person who maintains a client account in which he keeps clients' money

generally shall not be liable to account to any person for interest received by him on money in that account.

(4) Nothing in this section or in accounts regulations shall affect any arrangement in writing, whenever made, between a person engaged in estate agency work and any other person as to the application of, or of any interest on, money in which that other person has or may have an interest.

(5) Failure of any person to comply with any provision of accounts regulations made by virtue of this section may be taken into account by the Director in accordance with section 3(1)(c) above and may form the basis of a civil claim for interest which was or should have been earned on clients' money but shall not render that person liable to any criminal penalty.

(6) In this section 'accounts regulations' have the same meaning as in section 14 above.

16. Insurance cover for clients' money

(1) Subject to the provisions of this section, a person may not accept clients' money in the course of estate agency work unless there are in force authorised arrangements under which, in the event of his failing to account for such money to the person entitled to it, his liability will be made good by another.

(2) The Secretary of State may by regulations made by statutory instrument, which shall be subject to annulment in pursuance of a resolution of either House of Parliament,—

(a) specify any persons or classes of persons to whom subsection (1) above does not apply;
(b) specify arrangements which are authorised for the purposes of this section including arrangements to which an enforcement authority nominated for the purpose by the Secretary of State or any other person so nominated is a party;
(c) specify the terms and condition upon which any payment is to be made under such arrangements and any circumstances in which the right to any such payment may be excluded or modified;
(d) provide that any limit on the amount of any such payment is to be not less than a specified amount;
(e) require a person providing authorised arrangements covering any person carrying on estate agency work to issue a certificate in a form specified in the regulations certifying that arrangements complying with the regulations have been made with respect to that person; and
(f) prescribe any matter required to be precribed for the purposes of subsection (4) below.

(3) Every guarantee entered into by a person (in this subsection referred to as 'the insurer') who provides authorised arrangements covering another person (in this subsection referred to as 'the agent') carrying on estate agency work shall enure for the benefit of every person from whom the agent has received clients' money as if—

(a) the guarantee were contained in a contract made by the insurer with every such person; and
(b) except in Scotland, that contract were under seal; and
(c) where the guarantee is given by two or more insurers, they had bound themselves jointly and severally.

Estate Agents Act 1979

(4) No person who carries on estate agency work may describe himself as an 'estate agent' or so use any name or in any way hold himself out as to indicate or reasonably be understood to indicate that he is carrying on a business in the course of which he is prepared to act as a broker in the acquisition or disposal of interests in land unless, in such manner as may be prescribed,—

(*a*) there is displayed at his place of business, and
(*b*) there is included in any relevant document issued or displayed in connection with his business,

any prescribed information relating to arrangements authorised for the purposes of this section.

(5) For the purposes of subsection (4) above,—

(*a*) any business premises at which a person carries on estate agency work and to which the public has access is a place of business of his; and
(*b*) 'relevant document' means any advertisement, notice or other written material which might reasonably induce any person to use the services of another in connection with the acquisition or disposal of an interest in land.

(6) A person who fails to comply with any provision of subsection (1) or subsection (4) above or of regulations under subsection (2) above which is binding on him shall be liable on conviction on indictment or on summary conviction to a fine which, on summary conviction, shall not exceed the statutory maximum.

17. Exemptions from section 16

(1) If, on an application made to him in that behalf, the Director considers that a person engaged in estate agency work may, without loss of adequate protection to consumers, be exempted from all or any of the provisions of subsection (1) of section 16 above or of regulations under subsection (2) of that section, he may issue to that person a certificate of exemption under this section.

(2) An application under subsection (1) above—

(*a*) shall state the reasons why the applicant considers that he should be granted a certificate of exemption; and
(*b*) shall be accompanied by the prescribed fee.

(3) A certificate of exemption under this section—

(*a*) may impose conditions of exemption on the person to whom it is issued;
(*b*) may be issued to have effect for a period specified in the certificate or without limit of time.

(4) If and so long as—

(*a*) a certificate of exemption has effect, and
(*b*) the person to whom it is issued complies with any conditions of exemption specified in the certificate,

that person shall be exempt, to the extent so specified, from the provisions of subsection (1) of section 16 above and of any regulations made under subsection (2) of that section.

(5) If the Director decides to refuse an application under subsection (1) above

Estate Agents Act 1979

he shall give the applicant notice of his decision and of the reasons for it, including any facts which in his opinion justify the decision.

(6) If a person who made an application under subsection (1) above is aggrieved by a decision of the Director—

(*a*) to refuse his application, or
(*b*) to grant him a certificate of exemption subject to conditions,

he may appeal against the decision to the Secretary of State; and subsections (2) to (6) of section 7 above shall apply to such an appeal as they apply to an appeal under that section.

(7) A person who fails to comply with any condition of exemption specified in a current certificate of exemption issued to him shall be liable on conviction on indictment or on summary conviction to a fine which, on summary conviction, shall not exceed the statutory maximum.

Regulation of other aspects of estate agency work

18. Information to clients of prospective liabilities

(1) Subject to subsection (2) below, before any person (in this section referred to as 'the client') enters into a contract with another (in this section referred to as 'the agent') under which the agent will engage in estate agency work on behalf of the client, the agent shall give the client—

(*a*) the information specified in subsection (2) below; and
(*b*) any additional information which may be prescribed under subsection (4) below.

(2) The following is the information to be given under subsection (1)(*a*) above—

(*a*) particulars of the circumstances in which the client will become liable to pay remuneration to the agent for carrying out estate agency work;
(*b*) particulars of the amount of the agent's remuneration for carrying out estate agency work or, if that amount is not ascertainable at the time the information is given, particulars of the manner in which the remuneration will be calculated;
(*c*) particulars of any payments which do not form part of the agent's remuneration for carrying out estate agency work or a contract or pre-contract deposit but which, under the contract referred to in subsection (1) above, will or may in certain circumstances be payable by the client to the agent or any other person and particulars of the circumstances in which any such payments will become payable; and
(*d*) particulars of the amount of any payment falling within paragraph (*c*) above or, if that amount is not ascertainable at the time the information is given, an estimate of that amount together with particulars of the manner in which it will be calculated.

(3) If, at any time after the client and the agent have entered into such a contract as is referred to in subsection (1) above, the parties are agreed that the terms of the contract should be varied so far as they relate to the carrying out of estate agency work or any payment falling within subsecton (2)(*c*) above, the agent shall give the client details of any changes which, at the time the statement is given, fall to be made in the information which was given to the client under subsection (1) above before the contract was entered into.

(4) The Secretary of State may by regulations—

(*a*) prescribe for the purposes of subsection (1)(*b*) above additional information relating to any estate agency work to be performed under the contract; and
(*b*) make provision with respect to the time and the manner in which the obligation of the agent under subsection (1) or subsection (3) above is to be performed;

and the power to make regulations under this subsection shall be exercisable by statutory instrument which shall be subject to annulment in pursuance of a resolution of either House of Parliament.

(5) If any person—

(*a*) fails to comply with the obligation under subsection (1) above with respect to a contract or with any provision of regulations under subsection (4) above relating to that obligation, or
(*b*) fails to comply with the obligation under subsection (3) above with respect to any variation of a contract or with any provision of regulations under subsection (4) above relating to that obligation,

the contract or, as the case may be, the variation of it shall not be enforceable by him except pursuant to an order of the court under subsection (6) below.

(6) If, in a case where subsection (5) above applies in relation to a contract or a variation of a contract, the agent concerned makes an application to the court for the enforcement of the contract or, as the case may be, of a contract as varied by the variation,—

(*a*) the court shall dismiss the application if, but only if, it considers it just to do so having regard to prejudice caused to the client by the agent's failure to comply with his obligation and the degree of culpability for the failure; and
(*b*) where the court does not dismiss the application, it may nevertheless order that any sum payable by the client under the contract or, as the case may be, under the contract as varied shall be reduced or discharged so as to compensate the client for prejudice suffered as a result of the agent's failure to comply with his obligation.

(7) In this section—

(*a*) references to the enforcement of a contract or variation include the withholding of money in pursuance of a lien for money alleged to be due under the contract or as a result of the variation; and
(*b*) 'the court' means any court having jurisdiction to hear and determine matters arising out of the contract.

19. Regulation of pre-contract deposits outside Scotland

(1) No person may, in the course of estate agency work in England, Wales or Northern Ireland, seek from any other person (in this section referred to as a 'prospective purchaser') who wishes to acquire an interest in land in the United Kingdom, a payment which, if made, would constitute a pre-contract deposit in excess of the prescribed limit.

(2) If, in the course of estate agency work, any person receives from a prospective purchaser a pre-contract deposit which exceeds the prescribed limit,

so much of that deposit as exceeds the prescribed limit shall forthwith be either repaid to the prospective purchaser or paid to such other person as the prospective purchaser may direct.

(3) In relation to a prospective purchaser, references in subsections (1) and (2) above to a pre-contract deposit shall be treated as references to the aggregate of all the payments which constitute pre-contract deposits in relation to his proposed acquisition of a particular interest in land in the United Kingdom.

(4) In this section 'the prescribed limit' means such limit as the Secretary of State may by regulations prescribe; and such a limit may be so prescribed either as a specific amount or as a percentage or fraction of a price or other amount determined in any particular case in accordance with the regulations.

(5) The power to make regulations under this section shall be exercisable by statutory instrument which shall be subject to annulment in pursuance of a resolution of either House of Parliament.

(6) Failure by any person to comply with subsection (1) or subsection (2) above may be taken into account by the Director in accordance with section 3(1)(c) above but shall not render that person liable to any criminal penalty nor constitute a ground for any civil claim, other than a claim for the recovery of such an excess as is referred to in subsection (2) above.

(7) This section does not form part of the law of Scotland.

20. Prohibition of pre-contract deposit in Scotland

(1) No person may, in the course of estate agency work in Scotland, seek or accept from any person (in this section referred to as a 'prospective purchaser') who wishes to acquire an interest in land in the United Kingdom a payment which, if made, would constitute a pre-contract deposit or, as the case may be, which constitutes such a deposit.

(2) If, in the course of estate agency work in Scotland, any person receives from a prospective purchaser a payment which constitutes a pre-contract deposit, it shall forthwith be either repaid to the prospective purchaser or paid to such person as the prospective purchaser shall direct.

(3) Failure by any person to comply with subsection (1) or subsection (2) above may be taken into account by the Director in accordance with section 3(1)(c) above but shall not render that person liable to any criminal penalty nor constitute a ground for any civil claim, other than a claim under subsection (2) above for the recovery of the pre-contract deposit.

(4) This section forms part of the law of Scotland only.

21. Transactions in which an estate agent has a personal interest

(1) A person who is engaged in estate agency work (in this section referred to as an 'estate agent') and has a personal interest in any land shall not enter into negotiations with any person with respect to the acquisition or disposal by that person of any interest in that land until the estate agent has disclosed to that person the nature and extent of his personal interest in it.

(2) In any case where the result of a proposed disposal of an interest in land or of such a proposed disposal and other transactions would be that an estate agent would have a personal interest in that land, the estate agent shall not

Estate Agents Act 1979

enter into negotiations with any person with respect to the proposed disposal until he has disclosed to that person the nature and extent of that personal interest.

(3) Subsections (1) and (2) above apply where an estate agent is negotiating on his own behalf as well as where he is negotiating in the course of estate agency work.

(4) An estate agent may not seek or receive a contract or pre-contract deposit in respect of the acquisition or proposed acquisition of—

    (*a*) a personal interest of his in land in the United Kingdom; or

    (*b*) any other interest in any such land in which he has a personal interest.

(5) For the purposes of this section, an estate agent has a personal interest in land if—

    (*a*) he has a beneficial interest in the land or in the proceeds of sale of an interest in it; or

    (*b*) he knows or might reasonably be expected to know that any of the following persons has such a beneficial interest, namely,—
        (i) his employer or principal, or
        (ii) any employee or agent of his, or
        (iii) any associate of his or of any person mentioned in sub-paragraphs (i) and (ii) above.

(6) Failure by an estate agent to comply with any of the preceding provisions of this section may be taken into account by the Director in accordance with section 3(1)(*c*) above but shall not render the estate agent liable to any criminal penalty nor constitute a ground for any civil claim.

22. Standards of competence

(1) The Secretary of State may by regulations made by statutory instrument make provision for ensuring that persons engaged in estate agency work satisfy minimum standards of competence.

(2) If the Secretary of State exercises his power to make regulations under subsection (1) above, he shall in the regulations prescribe a degree of practical experience which is to be taken as evidence of competence and, without prejudice to the generality of subsection (1) above, the regulations may, in addition,—

    (*a*) prescribe professional or academic qualifications which shall also be taken to be evidence of competence;

    (*b*) designate any body of persons as a body which may itself specify professional qualifications the holding of which is to be taken as evidence of competence;

    (*c*) make provision for and in connection with the establishment of a body having power to examine and inquire into the competence of persons engaged or professing to engage in estate agency work; and

    (*d*) delegate to a body established as mentioned in paragraph (*c*) above powers of the Secretary of State with respect to the matters referred to in paragraph (*a*) above;

and any reference in the following provisions of this section to a person who has attained the required standard of competence is a reference to a person who has that degree of practical experience which, in accordance with the regulations, is to be taken as evidence of competence or, where the regulations so provide, holds such qualifications or otherwise fulfils such conditions as, in accordance with the regulations, are to be taken to be evidence of competence.

(3) After the day appointed for the coming into force of this subsection,—

(a) no individual may engage in estate agency work on his own account unless he has attained the required standard of competence;

(b) no member of a partnership may engage in estate agency work on the partnership's behalf unless such number of the partners as may be prescribed have attained the required standard of competence; and

(c) no body corporate or unincorporated association may engage in estate agency work unless such numbers and descriptions of the officers, members or employees as may be prescribed have attained the required standard of competence;

and any person who contravenes this subsection shall be liable on conviction on indictment or on summary conviction to a fine which, on summary conviction, shall not exceed the statutory maximum.

(4) In subsection (3) above 'prescribed' means prescribed by the Secretary of State by order made by statutory instrument, which shall be subject to annulment in pursuance of a resolution of either House of Parliament.

(5) No regulations shall be made under this section unless a draft of them has been laid before Parliament and approved by a resolution of each House.

23. Bankrupts not to engage in estate agency work

(1) An individual who is adjudged bankrupt after the day appointed for the coming into force of this section or, in Scotland, whose estate is sequestrated after that day shall not engage in estate agency work of any description except as an employee of another person.

(2) The prohibition imposed on an individual by subsection (1) above shall cease to have effect if and when—

(a) the adjudication of bankruptcy against him is annulled, or, in Scotland, the sequestration of his estate is recalled [or reduced]; or

[(b) he is discharged from bankruptcy.]

(The words in square brackets in paragraph (a) were added by the Bankruptcy Scotland Act 1985. Paragraph (b) was substituted by the Insolvency Act 1985.)

(3) The reference in subsection (1) above to employment of an individual by another person does not include employment of him by a body corporate of which he is a director or controller

(4) If a person engages in estate agency work in contravention of subsection (1) above he shall be liable on conviction on indictment or on summary conviction to a fine which on summary conviction shall not exceed the statutory maximum.

Supervision, enforcement, publicity etc.

24. Supervision by Council on Tribunals

(1) The Tribunals and Inquiries Act 1971 shall be amended as follows (the amendments bringing the adjudicating functions of the Director under this Act under the supervision of the Council on Tribunals)—

(*a*) in section 8(2) and section 19(4), for '5A' there shall be substituted '6A'; and

(*b*) in Schedule 1, paragraph 5A is hereby repealed and after paragraph 6 there shall be inserted—

'**Fair Trading** 6A. The Director General of Fair Trading in respect of his functions under the Consumer Credit Act 1974 (c. 39) and the Estate Agents Act 1979 (c. 38), and any member of the Director's staff authorised to exercise those functions under paragraph 7 of Schedule 1 to the Fair Trading Act 1973 (c. 41).'

(2) Any member of the Council on Tribunals or of the Scottish Committee of the Council, in his capacity as such, may attend any hearing of representations conducted in accordance with Part I of Schedule 2 to this Act.

25. General duties of Director

(1) Subject to section 26(3) below, it is the duty of the Director—

(*a*) generally to superintend the working and enforcement of this Act, and

(*b*) where necessary or expedient, himself to take steps to enforce this Act.

(2) It is the duty of the Director, so far as appears to him to be practicable and having regard both to the national interest and the interests of persons engaged in estate agency work and of consumers, to keep under review and from time to time advise the Secretary of State about—

(*a*) social and commercial developments in the United Kingdom and elsewhere relating to the carrying on of estate agency work and related activities; and

(*b*) the working and enforcement of this Act.

(3) The Director shall arrange for the dissemination, in such form and manner as he considers appropriate, of such information and advice as it may appear to him expedient to give the public in the United Kingdom about the operation of this Act.

26. Enforcement authorities

(1) Without prejudice to section 25(1) above, the following authorities (in this Act referred to as 'enforcement authorities') have a duty to enforce this Act—

(*a*) the Director,

(*b*) in Great Britain, a local weights and measures authority, and

(*c*) in Northern Ireland, the Department of Commerce for Northern Ireland.

(2) Where a local weights and measures authority in England and Wales propose to institute proceedings for an offence under this Act it shall, as between the authority and the Director, be the duty of the authority to give the Director notice of the intended proceedings, together with a summary of the facts on which the charges are to be founded, and postpone the institution of the proceedings until either—

(*a*) twenty-eight days have expired since that notice was given, or

(*b*) the Director has notified them of receipt of the notice and summary.

(3) Nothing in this section or in section 25 above authorises an enforcement authority to institute proceedings in Scotland for an offence.

(4) Every local weights and measures authority shall, whenever the Director requires, report to him in such form and with such particulars as he requires on the exercise of their functions under this Act.

(5)–(8) (*Subsections (5) to (8) were repealed by the Local Government, Planning and Land Act 1980.*)

27. Obstruction and personation of authorised officers

(1) Any person who—

- (*a*) wilfully obstructs an authorised officer, or
- (*b*) wilfully fails to comply with any requirement properly made to him under section 11 above by an authorised officer, or
- (*c*) without reasonable cause fails to give an authorised officer other assistance or information he may reasonably require in performing his functions under this Act, or
- (*d*) in giving information to an authorised officer, makes any statement which he knows to be false,

shall be liable on summary conviction to a fine not exceeding £500.

(2) A person who is not an authorised officer but purports to act as such shall be liable on summary conviction to a fine not exceeding £1,000.

(3) In this section 'authorised officer' means a duly authorised officer of an enforcement authority who is acting in pursuance of this Act.

(4) Nothing in subsection (1) above requires a person to answer any question or given any information if to do so might incriminate that person or that person's husband or wife.

Supplementary

28. General provisions as to offences

(1) In any proceedings for an offence under this Act it shall be a defence for the person charged to prove that he took all reasonable precautions and exercised all due diligence to avoid the commission of an offence by himself or any person under his control.

(2) Where an offence under this Act committed by a body corporate is proved to have been committed with the consent or connivance of, or to be attributable to any neglect on the part of, any director, manager, secretary or other similar officer of the body corporate, or any person who was purporting to act in any such capacity, he as well as the body corporate shall be guilty of that offence and shall be liable to be proceeded against and punished accordingly.

29. Service of notices etc.

(1) Any notice which under this Act is to be given to any person by the Director shall be so given—

- (*a*) by delivering it to him, or
- (*b*) by leaving it at his proper address, or
- (*c*) by sending it by post to him at that address.

(2) Any such notice may,—

Estate Agents Act 1979

(*a*) in the case of a body corporate or unincorporated association, be given to the secretary or clerk of that body or association; and

(*b*) in the case of a partnership, be given to a partner or a person having the control or management of the partnership business.

(3) Any application or other document which under this Act may be made or given to the Director may be so made or given by sending it by post to the Director at such address as may be specified for the purposes of this Act by a general notice.

(4) For the purposes of subsections (1) and (2) above and section 7 of the Interpretation Act 1978 (service of documents by post) in its application to those subsections, the proper address of any person to whom a notice is to be given shall be his last known address, except that—

(*a*) in the case of a body corporate or their secretary or clerk, it shall be the address of the registered or principal office of that body;

(*b*) in the case of an unincorporated association or their secretary or clerk, it shall be that of the principal office of that association;

(*c*) in the case of a partnership or a person having the control or management of the partnership business, it shall be that of the principal office of the partnership;

and for the purposes of this subsection the principal office of a company registered outside the United Kingdom or of an unincorporated association or partnership carrying on business outside the United Kingdom shall be their principal office within the United Kingdom.

(5) If the person to be given any notice mentioned in subsection (1) above has specified an address within the United Kingdom other than his proper address, within the meaning of subsection (4) above, as the one at which he or someone on his behalf will accept notices under this Act, that address shall also be treated for the purposes mentioned in subsection (4) above as his proper address.

30. Orders and regulations

(1) Before making any order or regulations under any provision of this Act to which this subsection applies, the Secretary of State shall consult the Director, such bodies representative of persons carrying on estate agency work, such bodies representative of consumers and such other persons as he thinks fit.

(2) Subsection (1) above applies to paragraphs (*a*)(iii) and (*d*) of section 3(1) above and to sections 14, 15, 16, 18, 19 and 22 above.

(3) Any power of the Secretary of State to make orders or regulations under this Act—

(*a*) may be so exercised as to make different provision in relation to different cases or classes of cases and to exclude certain cases or classes of case; and

(*b*) includes power to make such supplemental, incidental and transitional provisions as he thinks fit.

31. Meaning of 'business associate' and 'controller'

(1) The provisions of this section shall have effect for determining the meaning of 'business associate' and 'controller' for the purposes of this Act.

Estate Agents Act 1979

(2) As respects acts done in the course of a business carried on by a body corporate, every director and controller of that body is a business associate of it.

(3) As respects acts done in the course of a business carried on by a partnership, each partner is a business associate of every other member of the partnership and also of the partnership itself and, in the case of a partner which is a body corporate, every person who, by virtue of subsection (2) above, is a business associate of that body is also a business associate of every other member of the partnership.

(4) As respects acts done in the course of a business carried on by an unincorporated association, every officer of the association and any other person who has the management or control of its activities is a business associate of that association.

(5) In relation to a body corporate 'controller' means a person—

   (*a*) in accordance with whose directions or instructions the directors of the body corporate or of any other body corporate which is its controller (or any of them) are accustomed to act; or
   (*b*) who, either alone or with any associate or associates, is entitled to exercise, or control the exercise of, one-third or more of the voting power at any general meeting of the body corporate or of another body corporate which is its controller.

32. Meaning of 'associate'

(1) In this Act 'associate' includes a business associate and otherwise has the meaning given by the following provisions of this section.

(2) A person is an associate of another if he is the spouse or a relative of that other or of a business associate of that other

(3) In subsection (2) above 'relative' means brother, sister, uncle, aunt, nephew, niece, lineal ancester or linear descendant, and references to a spouse include a former spouse and a reputed spouse; and for the purposes of this subsection a relationship shall be established as if an illegitimate child or step-child of a person had been a child born to him in wedlock.

(4) A body corporate is an associate of another body corporate—

   (*a*) if the same person is a controller of both, or a person is a controller of one and persons who are his associates, or he and persons who are his associates, are controllers of the other; or
   (*b*) if a group of two or more persons is a controller of each company, and the groups either consist of the same persons or could be regarded as consisting of the same persons by treating (in one or more cases) a member of either group as replaced by a person of whom he is an associate.

(5) An incorporated association is an associate of another unincorporated association if any person—

   (*a*) is an officer of both associations;
   (*b*) has the management or control of the activities of both associations; or

(c) is an officer of one association and has the management or control of the activities of the other association.

(6) A partnership is an associate of another partnership if—

(a) any person is a member of both partnerships; or
(b) a person who is a member of one partnership is an associate of a member of the other partnership; or
(c) a member of one partnership has an associate who is also an associate of a member of the other partnership.

33. General interpretation provisions

(1) In this Act, unless the context otherwise requires,—

'associate' has the meaning assigned to it by section 32 above and 'business associate' has the meaning assigned to it by section 31 above;

'client account' has the meaning assigned to it by section 14(2) above;

'clients' money' has the meaning assigned to it by section 12(1) above;

'connected contract', in relation to the acquisition of an interest in land, has the meaning assigned to it by section 12(4) above;

'contract deposit' has the meaning assigned to it by section 12(2) above;

'controller', in relation to a body corporate, has the meaning assigned to it by section 31(5) above;

'Director' means the Director General of Fair Trading;

'enforcement authority' has the meaning assigned to it by section 26(1) above;

'estate agency work' has the meaning assigned to it by section 1(1) above;

'general notice' means a notice published by the Director at a time and in a manner appearing to him suitable for securing that the notice is seen within a reasonable time by persons likely to be affected by it.

'pre-contract deposit' has the meaning assigned to it by section 12(3) above;

'prescribed fee' means such fee as may be prescribed by regulations made by the Secretary of State;

'the statutory maximum', in relation to a fine on summary conviction, means—

(a) in England and Wales and Northern Ireland, the prescribed sum within the meaning of section 28 of the Criminal Law Act 1977 (£2000); and
(b) in Scotland, the prescribed sum within the meaning of section 289B of the Criminal Procedure (Scotland) Act 1975 (£2000);

and for the purposes of the application of this definition in Northern Ireland the provisions of the Criminal Law Act 1977 which relate to the sum mentioned in paragraph (a) above shall extend to Northern Ireland; and

'unincorporated association' does not include a partnership.

(2) The power to make regulations under subsection (1) above prescribing

fees shall be exercisable by statutory instrument which shall be subject to annulment in pursuance of a resolution of either House of Parliament.

34. Financial provisions

35. [*This section was repealed by the Statute Law (Repeals) Act 1981.*]

36. Short title, commencement and extent

(1) This Act may be cited as the Estate Agents Act 1979.

(2) This Act shall come into force on such day as the Secretary of State may by order made by statutory instrument appoint and different days may be so appointed for different provisions and for different purposes.

(3) This Act extends to Northern Ireland.

Estate Agents Act 1979

SCHEDULES
SCHEDULE 1

PROVISIONS SUPPLEMENTARY TO SECTION 3(1)

Spent convictions

1. A conviction which is to be treated as spent for the purposes of the Rehabilitation of Offenders Act 1974 or any corresponding enactment for the time being in force in Northern Ireland shall be disregarded for the purposes of section 3(1)(*a*) of this Act.

Discrimination

2. A person shall be deemed to have committed discrimination for the purposes of section 3(1)(*b*) of this Act in the following cases only, namely,—

(*a*) where a finding of discrimination has been made against him in proceedings under section 66 of the Sex Discrimination Act 1975 (in this Schedule referred to as 'the 1975 Act') and the finding has become final;

(*b*) where a non-discrimination notice has been served on him under the 1975 Act and the notice has become final;

(*c*) if he is for the time being subject to the restraints of an injunction or order granted against him in proceedings under section 71 (persistent discrimination) or section 72(4) (enforcement of sections 38 to 40) of the 1975 Act;

(*d*) if, on an application under section 72(2)(*a*) of the 1975 Act, there has been a finding against him that a contravention of section 38, section 39 or section 40 of that Act has occurred and that finding has become final;

(*e*) where a finding of discrimination has been made against him in proceedings under section 57 of the Race Relations Act 1976 (in this Schedule referred to as 'the 1976 Act') and the finding has become final;

(*f*) where a non-discrimination notice has been served on him under the 1976 Act and the notice has become final;

(*g*) if he is for the time being subject to the restraints of an injunction or order granted against him in proceedings under section 62 (persistent discrimination) or section 63(4) (enforcement of sections 29 to 31) of the 1976 Act; or

(*h*) if, on an application under section 63(2)(*a*) of the 1976 Act, there has been a finding against him that a contravention of section 29, section 30 or section 31 of that Act has occurred and that finding has become final;

and the finding, notice, injunction or order related or relates to discrimination falling within Part III of the 1975 Act or the 1976 Act (discrimination in fields other than employment).

3. After the expiry of the period of five years beginning on the day on which any such finding or notice as is referred to in paragraph 2 above became final, no person shall be treated for the purposes of section 3(1)(*b*) of this Act as having committed discrimination by reason only of that finding or notice.

Estate Agents Act 1979

4. (1) So far as paragraphs 2 and 3 above relate to findings and notices under the 1975 Act, subsections (1) and (4) of section 82 of that Act (general interpretation provisions) shall have effect as if those paragraphs were contained in that Act.

(2) So far as paragraphs 2 and 3 above relate to findings and notices under the 1976 Act, subsections (1) and (4) of section 78 of that Act (general interpretation provisions) shall have effect as if those paragraphs were contained in that Act.

5. In the application of paragraphs 2 to 4 above to Northern Ireland references to the 1975 Act shall be construed as references to the Sex Discrimination (Northern Ireland) Order 1976, and in particular—

- (*a*) the references to sections 38, 39 and 40 of the 1975 Act shall be construed as references to Articles 39, 40 and 41 of that Order;
- (*b*) the reference to subsections (1) and (4) of section 82 of the 1975 Act shall be construed as a reference to paragraphs (1), (2) and (5) of Article 2 of that Order; and
- (*c*) other references to numbered sections of the 1975 Act shall be construed as references to the Articles of that Order bearing the same number;

and there shall be omitted sub-paragraphs (*e*) to (*h*) of paragraph 2, sub-paragraph (2) of paragraph 4 and so much of paragraph 3 as relates to findings or notices under the 1976 Act.

SCHEDULE 2

Procedure Etc.

Part I

Orders and Decisions Under Sections 3, 4 and 6

Introductory

1. In this Schedule—

- (*a*) subject to sub-paragraph (2) below, references to 'the person affected' are to the person in respect of whom the Director proposes to make, or has made, an order under section 3 or section 4 of this Act, or who has made an application under section 6 of this Act for the variation or revocation of such an order; and
- (*b*) references to the Director's 'proposal' are to any proposal of his to make such an order or to make a decision under subsection (4) or subsection (5) of section 6 of this Act on such an application.

(2) In the case of a proposal of the Director to make an order under section 3 or section 4 of this Act against a partnership where, by virtue of section 5(2) of this Act, he intends that the order shall have effect as an order against some or all of the partners individually, references in the following provisions of this Schedule to the person affected shall be construed, except where the

Estate Agents Act 1979

contrary is provided, as references to each of the partners affected by the order, as well as to the partnership itself.

Notice of proposal

2. (1) The Director shall give to the person affected a notice informing him of the proposal and of the Director's reason for it; but paragraph 1(2) above shall not apply for the purposes of this sub-paragraph.

(2) In the case of a proposal to make an order, the notice under sub-paragraph (1) above shall inform the person affected of the substance of the proposed order and, in the case of a proposal to make an order under section 3 of this Act, shall—

- (*a*) set out those matters falling within subsection (1) of that section which the Director intends should be specified as the grounds for the order, and
- (*b*) specify any other matters of which the Director has taken account under subsection (2) of that section, and
- (*c*) if the Director proposes to rely on section 4(3) of this Act to establish the unfitness of the person affected, state that fact.

(3) The notice given under sub-paragraph (1) above shall invite the person affected, within such period of not less than twenty-one days as may be specified in the notice,—

- (*a*) to submit to the Director his representations in writing as to why the order should not be made or, as the case may be, should be varied or revoked in accordance with the application, and
- (*b*) to give notice to the Director, if he thinks fit, that he wishes to make such representations orally,

and where notice is given under paragraph (*b*) above the Director shall arrange for the oral representations to be heard.

Hearing of representations

3. Where the Director receives notice under paragraph 2(3)(*b*) above he shall give the person affected not less than twenty-one days notice, or such shorter notice as the person affected may consent to accept, of the date, time and place at which his representations are to be heard.

4. (1) In the course of the hearing of oral representations the Director shall, at the request of the person affected, permit any other person (in addition to the person affected) to make representations on his behalf or to give evidence or to introduce documents for him.

(2) The Director shall not refuse to admit evidence solely on the grounds that it would not be admissible in a court of law.

5. If the Director adjourns the hearing he shall give the person affected reasonable notice of the date, time and place at which the hearing is to be resumed.

Estate Agents Act 1979

Decision

6. (1) The Director shall take into account in deciding whether to proceed with his proposal any written or oral representations made in accordance with the preceding provisions of this Schedule.

(2) If the Director considers that he should proceed with his proposal but for a reason which differs, or on grounds which differ, from those set out in the notice of the proposal under paragraph 2 above, he shall give a further notice under that paragraph.

(3) In any case where—

  (*a*) a notice under paragraph 2 above gives more than one reason for the proposal or (in the case of a proposal to make an order under section 3 of this Act) sets out more than one matter which the Director intends should be specified as the grounds for the order, and
  (*b*) it appears to the Director that one or more of those reasons should be abandoned or, as the case may be, that one or more of those matters should not be so specified,

the Director may nevertheless decide to proceed with his proposal on the basis of any other reason given in the notice or, as the case may be, on any other grounds set out in the notice.

7. If the Director decides not to proceed with his proposal he shall give notice of that decision to the person affected and, in the case of a notice of a decision on an application under section 6 of this Act, such a notice shall be combined with a notice under subsection (3) of that section.

8. If the Director decides to proceed with his proposal he may, if he thinks fit having regard to any representations made to him—

  (*a*) where the proposal is for the making of an order, make the order in a form which varies from that of the proposed order mentioned in the notice under paragraph 2 above, or
  (*b*) where the proposal is to vary an order, make a variation other than that mentioned in the notice under paragraph 2 above, or
  (*c*) where the proposal is to refuse to revoke an order, vary the order.

Notification of decision

9. (1) Notice of the decision to make the order, and of the terms of the order or, as the case may be, notice of the decision on the application for variation or revocation of the order, shall be given to the person affected, together with the Director's reasons for his decision, including the facts which in his opinion justify the decision.

(2) The notice referred to in sub-paragraph (1) above shall also inform the person affected of his right to appeal against the decision and of the period within which an appeal may be brought and of how notice of appeal may be given.

10. (1) Subject to sub-paragraph (2) below, the order to which the decision relates or, as the case may be, any variation of an order for which the decision provides shall not come into operation until any appeal under section 7(1) of this Act and any further appeal has been finally determined or the period within which such an appeal may be brought has expired.

(2) Where the Director states in the notice referred to in paragraph 9(1) above that he is satisfied that there are special circumstances which require it, an order shall come into operation immediately upon the giving of notice of the decision to make it.

Part II

Applications Under Sections 6(1) and 8(3)

11. Any reference in this Part of this Schedule to an application is a reference to an application to the Director under section 6(1) or section 8(3) of this Act, and any reference to the applicant shall be construed accordingly.

12. An application shall be in writing and be in such form and accompanied by such particulars as the Director may specify by general notice.

13. The Director may by notice require the applicant to publish details of his application at a time or times and in a manner specified in the notice.

14. If an application does not comply with paragraph 12 above or if an applicant fails to comply with a notice under section 9 of this Act requiring the furnishing of information or the production of documents in connection with the application, the Director may decline to proceed with the application.

Sale of Goods Act 1979
Chapter 54

ARRANGEMENT OF SECTIONS

PART I

CONTRACTS TO WHICH ACT APPLIES

Section
1. Contracts to which Act applies

PART II

FORMATION OF THE CONTRACT

Contract of sale

2. Contract of sale
3. Capacity of buy and sell

Formalities of contract

4. How contract of sale is made

Subject matter of contract

5. Existing or future goods
6. Goods which have perished
7. Goods perishing before sale but after agreement to sell

The price

8. Ascertainment of price
9. Agreement to sell at valuation

Conditions and warranties

10. Stipulations about time
11. When condition to be treated as warranty
12. Implied terms about title, etc.
13. Sale by description
14. Implied terms about quality or fitness

Sale by sample

15. Sale by sample

Sale of Goods Act 1979

PART III

Effects of the Contract

Transfer of property as between seller and buyer

Section
16. Goods must be ascertained
17. Property passes when intended to pass
18. Rules for ascertaining intention
19. Reservation of right of disposal
20. Risk prima facie passes with property

Transfer of title

21. Sale by persons not the owner
22. Market overt
23. Sale under voidable title
24. Seller in possession after sale
25. Buyer in possession after sale
26. Supplementary to sections 24 and 25

PART IV

Performance of the Contract

27. Duties of seller and buyer
28. Payment and delivery are concurrent conditions
29. Rules about delivery
30. Delivery of wrong quantity
31. Instalment deliveries
32. Delivery to carrier
33. Risk where goods are delivered at distant places
34. Buyer's right of examining the goods
35. Acceptance
36. Buyer not bound to return rejected goods
37. Buyer's liability for not taking delivery of goods

PART V

Rights of Unpaid Seller against the Goods

Preliminary

38. Unpaid seller defined
39. Unpaid seller's rights
40. Attachment by seller in Scotland

Unpaid seller's lien

41. Seller's lien
42. Part delivery
43. Termination of lien

Sale of Goods Act 1979

Stoppage in transit

Section
44. Right of stoppage in transit
45. Duration of transit
46. How stoppage in transit is effected

Re-sale etc. by buyer

47. Effect of sub-sale etc. by buyer

Rescission: and re-sale by seller

48. Rescission: and re-sale by seller

PART VI

ACTIONS FOR BREACH OF THE CONTRACT

Seller's remedies

49. Action for price
50. Damages for non-acceptance

Buyer's remedies

51. Damages for non-delivery
52. Specific performance
53. Remedy for breach of warranty

Interest, etc.

54. Interest, etc.

PART VII

SUPPLEMENTARY

55. Exclusion of implied terms
56. Conflict of laws
57. Auction sales
58. Payment into court in Scotland
59. Reasonable time a question of fact
60. Rights etc. enforceable by action
61. Interpretation
62. Savings: rules of law etc.
63. Consequential amendments, repeals and savings
64. Short title and commencement

SCHEDULES:
Schedule 1—Modification of Act for certain contracts
Schedule 2—Consequential amendments
Schedule 3—Repeals
Schedule 4—Savings

An Act to consolidate the law relating to the sale of goods

[6th December 1979]

Sale of Goods Act 1979

PART I

CONTRACTS TO WHICH ACT APPLIES

1. Contracts to which Act applies

(1) This Act applies to contracts of sale of goods made on or after (but not to those made before) 1 January 1894.

(2) In relation to contracts made on certain dates, this Act applies subject to the modification of certain of its sections as mentioned in Schedule 1 below.

(3) Any such modification is indicated in the section concerned by a reference to Schedule 1 below.

(4) Accordingly, where a section does not contain such a reference, this Act applies in relation to the contract concerned without such modification of the section.

PART II

FORMATION OF THE CONTRACT

Contract of sale

2. Contract of sale

(1) A contract of sale of goods is a contract by which the seller transfers or agrees to transfer the property in goods to the buyer for a money consideration, called the price.

(2) There may be a contract of sale between one part-owner and another.

(3) A contract of sale may be absolute or conditional.

(4) Where under a contract of sale the property in the goods is transferred from the seller to the buyer the contract is called a sale.

(5) Where under a contract of sale the transfer of the property in the goods is to take place at a future time or subject to some condition later to be fulfilled the contract is called an agreement to sell.

(6) An agreement to sell becomes a sale when the time elapses or the conditions are fulfilled subject to which the property in the goods is to be transferred.

3. Capacity to buy and sell

(1) Capacity to buy and sell is regulated by the general law concerning capacity to contract and to transfer and acquire property.

(2) Where necessaries are sold and delivered to a minor or to a person who by reason of mental incapacity or drunkenness is incompetent to contract, he must pay a reasonable price for them.

(3) In subsection (2) above 'necessaries' means goods suitable to the condition in life of the minor or other person concerned and to his actual requirements at the time of the sale and delivery.

Formalities of contract

4. How contract of sale is made

(1) Subject to this and any other Act, a contract of sale may be made in

writing (either with or without seal), or by word of mouth, or partly in writing and partly by word of mouth, or may be implied from the conduct of the parties.

(2) Nothing in this section affects the law relating to corporations.

Subject matter of contract

5. Existing or future goods

(1) The goods which form the subject of a contract of sale may be either existing goods, owned or possessed by the seller, or goods to be manufactured or acquired by him after the making of the contract of sale, in this Act called future goods.

(2) There may be a contract for the sale of goods the acquisition of which by the seller depends on a contingency which may or may not happen.

(3) Where by a contract of sale the seller purports to effect a present sale of future goods, the contract operates as an agreement to sell the goods.

6. Goods which have perished

Where there is a contract for the time of specific goods, and the goods without the knowledge of the seller have perished at the time when the contract is made, the contract is void.

7. Goods perishing before sale but after agreement to sell

Where there is an agreement to sell specific goods and subsequently the goods, without any fault on the part of the seller or buyer, perish before the risk passes to the buyer, the agreement is avoided.

The price

8. Ascertainment of price

(1) The price in a contract of sale may be fixed by the contract, or may be left to be fixed in a manner agreed by the contract, or may be determined by the course of dealing between the parties.

(2) Where the price is not determined as mentioned in subsection (1) above the buyer must pay a reasonable price.

(3) What is a reasonable price is a question of fact dependent on the circumstances of each particular case.

9. Agreements to sell at valuation

(1) Where there is an agreement to sell goods on the terms that the price is to be fixed by the valuation of a third party, and he cannot or does not make the valuation, the agreement is avoided; but if the goods or any part of then have been delivered to and appropriated by the buyer he must pay a reasonable price for them.

(2) Where the third party is prevented from making the valuation by the fault of the seller or buyer, the party not at fault may maintain an action for damages against the party at fault.

Sale of Goods Act 1979

Conditions and warranties

10. Stipulations about time

(1) Unless a different intention appears from the terms of the contract, stipulations as to time of payment are not of the essence of a contract of sale.

(2) Whether any other stipulation as to time is or is not of the essence of the contract depends on the terms of the contract.

(3) In a contract of sale 'month' prima facie means calendar month.

11. When condition to be treated as warranty

(1) Subsections (2) to (4) and (7) below do not apply to Scotland and subsection (5) below applies only to Scotland.

(2) Where a contract of sale is subject to a condition to be fulfilled by the seller, the buyer may waive the condition, or may elect to treat the breach of the condition as a breach of warranty and not as a ground for treating the contract as repudiated.

(3) Whether a stipulation in a contract of sale is a condition, the breach of which may give rise to a right to treat the contract as repudiated, or a warranty, the breach of which may give rise to a claim for damages but not to a right to reject the goods and treat the contract as repudiated, depends in each case on the construction of the contract; and a stipulation may be a condition, though called a warranty in the contract.

(4) Where a contract of sale is not severable and the buyer has accepted the goods or part of them, the breach of a condition to be fulfilled by the seller can only be treated as a breach of warranty, and not as a ground for rejecting the goods and treating the contract as repudiated, unless there is an express or implied term of the contract to that effect.

(5) In Scotland, failure by the seller to perform any material part of a contract of sale is a breach of contract, which entitles the buyer either within a reasonable time after delivery to reject the goods and treat the contract as repudiated, or to retain the goods and treat the failure to perform such material part as a breach which may give rise to a claim for compensation or damages.

(6) Nothing in this section affects a condition or warranty whose fulfilment is excused by law by reason of impossibility or otherwise.

(7) Paragraph 2 of Schedule 1 below applies in relation to a contract made before 22 April 1967 or (in the application of this Act to Northern Ireland) 28 July 1967.

12. Implied terms about title, etc.

(1) In a contract of sale, other than one to which subsection (3) below applies, there is an implied condition on the part of the seller that in the case of a sale he has a right to sell the goods, and in the case of an agreement to sell he will have such a right at the time when the property is to pass.

(2) In a contract of sale, other than one to which subsection (3) below applies, there is also an implied warranty that—

    (*a*) the goods are free, and will remain free until the time when the property is to pass, from any charge or encumbrance not disclosed or known to the buyer before the contract is made, and

    (*b*) the buyer will enjoy quiet possession of the goods except so far as it may be disturbed by the owner or other person entitled to the benefit of any charge or encumbrance so disclosed or known.

(3) This subsection applies to a contract of sale in the case of which there appears from the contract or is to be inferred from its circumstances an intention that the seller should transfer only such title as he or a third person may have.

(4) In a contract to which subsection (3) above applies there is an implied warranty that all charges or encumbrances known to the seller and not known to the buyer have been disclosed to the buyer before the contract is made.

(5) In a contract to which subsection (3) above applies there is also an implied warranty that none of the following will disturb the buyer's quiet possession of the goods, namely—

(a) the seller;

(b) in a case where the parties to the contract intend that the seller should transfer only such title as a third person may have, that person;

(c) anyone claiming through or under the seller or that third person otherwise than under a charge or encumbrance disclosed or known to the buyer before the contract is made.

(6) Paragraph 3 of Schedule 1 below applies in relation to a contract made before 18 May 1973.

13. Sale by description

(1) Where there is a contract for the sale of goods by description, there is an implied condition that the goods will correspond with the description.

(2) If the sale is by sample as well as by description it is not sufficient that the bulk of the goods corresponds with the sample if the goods do not also correspond with the description.

(3) A sale of goods is not prevented from being a sale by description by reason only that, being exposed for sale or hire, they are selected by the buyer.

(4) Paragraph 4 of Schedule 1 below applies in relation to a contract made before 18 May 1973.

14. Implied terms about quality or fitness

(1) Except as provided by this section and section 15 below and subject to any other enactment, there is no implied condition or warranty about the quality or fitness for any particular purpose of goods supplied under a contract of sale.

(2) Where the seller sells goods in the course of a business, there is an implied condition that the goods supplied under the contract are of merchantable quality, except that there is no such condition—

(a) as regards defects specifically drawn to the buyer's attention before the contract is made; or

(b) if the buyer examines the goods before the contract is made, as regards defects which that examination ought to reveal.

(3) Where the seller sells goods in the course of a business and the buyer, expressly or by implication, makes known—

(a) to the seller, or

(b) where the purchase price or part of it is payable by instalments and the goods were previously sold by a credit-broker to the seller, to that credit-broker, any particular purpose for which the goods are being bought, there is an implied condition that the goods supplied under the contract are reasonably fit for that purpose, whether or not that is a purpose for which such goods are commonly supplied, except where the circumstances show that the buyer does not rely, or that it is unreasonable for him to rely, on the skill or judgment of the seller or credit-broker.

(4) An implied condition or warranty about quality or fitness for a particular purpose may be annexed to a contract of sale by usage.

(5) The preceding provisions of this section apply to a sale by a person who in the course of a business is acting as agent for another as they apply to a sale by a principal in the course of a business, except where that other is not selling in the course of a business and either the buyer knows that fact or reasonable steps are taken to bring it to the notice of the buyer before the contract is made.

(6) Goods of any kind are of merchantable quality within the meaning of subsection (2) above if they are as fit for the purpose or purposes for which goods of that kind are commonly bought as it is reasonable to expect having regard to any description applied to them, the price (if relevant) and all the other relevant circumstances.

(7) Paragraph 5 of Schedule 1 below applies in relation to a contract made on or after 18 May 1973 and before the appointed day, and paragraph 6 in relation to one made before 18 May 1973.

(8) In subsection (7) above and paragraph 5 of Schedule 1 below references to the appointed day are to the day appointed for the purposes of those provisions by an order of the Secretary of State made by statutory instrument.

Sale of sample

15. Sale of sample

(1) A contract of sale is a contract for sale by sample where there is an express or implied term to the effect in the contract.

(2) In the case of a contract for sale by sample there is an implied condition—

(*a*) that the bulk will correspond with the sample in quality;
(*b*) that the buyer will have a reasonable opportunity of comparing the bulk with the sample;
(*c*) that the goods will be free from any defect, rendering them unmerchantable, which would not be apparent on reasonable examination of the sample.

(3) In subsection (2)(*c*) above 'unmerchantable' is to be construed in accordance with section 14(6) above.

(4) Paragraph 7 of Schedule 1 below applies in relation to a contract made before 18 May 1973.

Sale of Goods Act 1979

PART III

EFFECTS OF THE CONTRACT

Transfer of property as between seller and buyer

16. Goods must be ascertained

Where there is a contract for the sale of unascertained goods no property in the goods is transferred to the buyer unless and until the goods are ascertained.

17. Property passes when intended to pass

(1) Where there is a contract for the sale of specific or ascertained goods the property in them is transferred to the buyer at such time as the parties to the contract intend it to be transferred.

(2) For the purpose of ascertaining the intention of the parties regard shall be had to the terms of the contract, the conduct of the parties and the circumstances of the case.

18. Rules for ascertaining intention

Unless a different intention appears, the following are rules for ascertaining the intention of the parties as to the time at which the property in the goods is to pass to the buyer.

Rule 1—Where there is an unconditional contract for the sale of specific goods in a deliverable state the property in the goods passes to the buyer when the contract is made, and it is immaterial whether the time of payment or the time of delivery, or both, be postponed.

Rule 2—Where there is a contract for the sale of specific goods and the seller is bound to do something to the goods for the purpose of putting them into a deliverable state, the property does not pass until the thing is done and the buyer has notice that it has been done.

Rule 3—Where there is a contract for the sale of specific goods in a deliverable state but the seller is bound to weigh, measure, test, or do some other act or thing with reference to the goods for the purpose of ascertaining the price, the property does not pass until the act or thing is done and the buyer has notice that it has been done.

Rule 4—When goods are delivered to the buyer on approval or on sale or return or other similar terms the property in the goods passes to the buyer:—

  (a) when he signifies his approval or acceptance to the seller or does any other act adopting the transaction.
  (b) if he does not signify his approval or acceptance to the seller but retains the goods without giving notice of rejection, then, if a time has been fixed for the return of the goods, on the expiration of that time, and, if no time has been fixed, on the expiration of a reasonable time.

Rule 5—(1) Where there is a contract for the sale of unascertained or future goods by description, and goods of that description and in a deliverable state are unconditionally appropriated to the contract, either by the seller with the assent of the buyer or by the buyer with the assent of the seller, the property in the goods then passes to the buyer, and the assent may be express or implied, and may be given either before or after the appropriation is made.

(2) Where, in pursuance of the contract, the seller delivers the goods to the buyer or to a carrier or other bailee or custodier (whether named by the buyer or not) for the purpose of transmission to the buyer, and does not reserve the right of disposal, he is to be taken to have unconditionally appropriated the goods to the contract.

19. Reservation of right of disposal

(1) Where there is a contract for the sale of specific goods or where goods are subsequently appropriated to the contract, the seller may, by the terms of the contract or appropriation, reserve the right of disposal of the goods until certain conditions are fulfilled; and in such a case, notwithstanding the delivery of the goods to the buyer, or to a carrier or other bailee or custodier for the purpose of transmission to the buyer, the property in the goods does not pass to the buyer until the conditions imposed by the seller are fulfilled.

(2) Where goods are shipped, and by the bill of lading the goods are deliverable to the order of the seller or his agent, the seller is prima facie to be taken to reserve the right of disposal.

(3) Where the seller of goods draws on the buyer for the price, and transmits the bill of exchange and bill of lading to the buyer together to secure acceptance or payment of the bill of exchange, the buyer is bound to return the bill of lading if he does not honour the bill of exchange, and if he wrongfully retains the bill of lading the property in the goods does not pass to him.

20. Risk prima facie passes with property

(1) Unless otherwise agreed, the goods remain at the seller's risk until the property in them is transferred to the buyer, but when the property in them is transferred to the buyer the goods are at the buyer's risk whether delivery has been made or not.

(2) But where delivery has been delayed through the fault of either buyer or seller the goods are at the risk of the party at fault as regards any loss which might not have occurred but for such fault.

(3) Nothing in this section affects the duties or liabilities of either seller or buyer as a bailee or custodier of the goods of the other party.

Transfer of title

21. Sale by person not the owner

(1) Subject to this Act, where goods are sold by a person who is not their owner, and who does not sell them under the authority or with the consent of the owner, the buyer acquires no better title to the goods than the seller had, unless the owner of the goods is by his conduct precluded from denying the seller's authority to sell.

(2) Nothing in this Act affects—

    (*a*) the provisions of the Factors Acts or any enactment enabling the apparent owner of goods to dispose of them as if he were their true owner;

    (*b*) the validity of any contract of sale under any special common law or statutory power of sale or under the order of a court of competent jurisdiction.

22. Market overt

(1) Where goods are sold in market overt, according to the usage of the market, the buyer acquires a good title to the goods, provided he buys them in good faith and without notice of any defect or want of title on the part of the seller.

(2) This section does not apply to Scotland.

(3) Paragraph 8 of Schedule 1 below applies in relation to a contract under which goods were sold before 1 January 1968 or (in the application of this Act to Northern Ireland) 29 August 1967.

23. Sale under voidable title

Where the seller of goods has a voidable title to them, but his title has not been avoided at the time of the sale, the buyer acquires a good title to the goods, provided he buys them in good faith and without notice of the seller's defect of title.

24. Seller in possession after sale

Where a person having sold goods continues or is in possession of the goods, or of the documents of title to the goods, the delivery or transfer by that person, or by a mercantile agent acting for him, of the goods or documents of title under any sale, pledge, or other disposition thereof, to any person receiving the same in good faith and without notice of the previous sale, has the same effect as if the person making the delivery or transfer were expressly authorised by the owner of the goods to make the same.

25. Buyer in possession after sale

(1) Where a person having bought or agreed to buy goods obtains, with the consent of the seller, possession of the goods or the documents of title to the goods, the delivery or transfer by that person, or by a mercantile agent acting for him, of the goods or documents of title, under any sale, pledge, or other disposition thereof, to any person receiving the same in good faith and without notice of any lien or other right of the original seller in respect of the goods, has the same effect as if the person making the delivery or transfer were a mercantile agent in possession of the goods or documents of title with the consent of the owner.

(2) For the purposes of subsection (1) above—

(*a*) the buyer under a conditional sale agreement is to be taken not to be a person who has bought or agreed to buy goods, and
(*b*) 'conditional sale agreement' means an agreement for the sale of goods which is a consumer credit agreement within the meaning of the Consumer Credit Act 1974 under which the purchase price or part of it is payable by instalments, and the property in the goods is to remain in the seller (notwithstanding that the buyer is to be in possession of the goods) until such conditions as to the payment of instalments or otherwise as may be specified in the agreement are fulfilled.

(3) Paragraph 9 of Schedule 1 below applies in relation to a contract under which a person buys or agrees to buy goods and which is made before the appointed day.

(4) In subsection (3) above and paragraph 9 of Schedule 1 below references

26. Supplementary to sections 24 and 25

In sections 24 and 25 above 'mercantile agent' means a mercantile agent having in the customary course of his business as such agent authority either—

(*a*) to sell goods, or
(*b*) to consign goods for the purpose of sale, or
(*c*) to buy goods, or
(*d*) to raise money on the security of goods

PART IV

Performance of the Contract

27. Duties of seller and buyer

It is the duty of the seller to deliver the goods, and of the buyer to accept and pay for them, in accordance with the terms of the contract of sale.

28. Payment and delivery are concurrent conditions

Unless otherwise agreed, delivery of the goods and payment of the price are concurrent conditions, that is to say, the seller must be ready and willing to give possession of the goods to the buyer in exchange for the price and the buyer must be ready and willing to pay the price in exchange for possession of the goods.

29. Rules about delivery

(1) Whether it is for the buyer to take possession of the goods or for the seller to send them to the buyer is a question depending in each case on the contract, express or implied, between the parties.

(2) Apart from any such contract, express or implied, the place of delivery is the seller's place of business if he has one, and if not, his residence; except that, if the contract is for sale of specific goods, which to the knowledge of the parties when the contract is made are in some other place, then that place is the place of delivery.

(3) Where under the contract of sale the seller is bound to send the goods to the buyer, but no time for sending them is fixed, the seller is bound to send them within a reasonable time.

(4) Where the goods at the time of sale are in the possession of a third person, there is no delivery by seller to buyer unless and until the third person acknowledges to the buyer that he holds the goods on his behalf; but nothing in this section affects the operation of the issue or transfer of any document of title to goods.

(5) Demand or tender of delivery may be treated as ineffectual unless made at a reasonable hour; and what is a reasonable hour is a question of fact.

(6) Unless otherwise agreed, the expenses of and incidental to putting the goods into a deliverable state must be borne by the seller.

30. Delivery of wrong quantity

(1) Where the seller delivers to the buyer a quantity of goods less than he contracted to sell, the buyer may reject them, but if the buyer accepts the goods so delivered he must pay for them at the contract rate.

(2) Where the seller delivers to the buyer a quantity of goods larger than he contracted to sell, the buyer may accept the goods included in the contract and reject the rest, or he may reject the whole.

(3) Where the seller delivers to the buyer a quantity of goods larger than he contracted to sell and the buyer accepts the whole of the goods so delivered he must pay for them at the contract rate.

(4) Where the seller delivers to the buyer the goods he contracted to sell mixed with goods of a different description not included in the contract, the buyer may accept the goods which are in accordance with the contract and reject the rest, or he may reject the whole.

(5) This section is subject to any usage of trade, special agreement, or course of dealing between the parties.

31. Instalment deliveries

(1) Unless otherwise agreed, the buyer of goods is not bound to accept delivery of them by instalments.

(2) Where there is a contract for the sale of goods to be delivered by stated instalments, which are to be separately paid for, and the seller makes defective deliveries in respect of one or more instalments, or the buyer neglects or refuses to take delivery of or pay for one or more instalments, it is a question in each case depending on the terms of the contract and the circumstances of the case whether the breach of contract is a repudiation of the whole contract or whether it is a severable breach giving rise to a claim for compensation but not to a right to treat the whole contract as repudiated.

32. Delivery to carrier

(1) Where, in pursuance of a contract of sale is authorised or required to send the goods to the buyer, delivery of the goods to a carrier (whether named by the buyer or not) for the purpose of transmission to the buyer is prima facie deemed to be delivery of the goods to the buyer.

(2) Unless otherwise authorised by the buyer, the seller must make such contract with the carrier on behalf of the buyer as may be reasonable having regard to the nature of the goods and the other circumstances of the case; and if the seller omits to do so, and the goods are lost or damaged in course of transit, the buyer may decline to treat the delivery to the carrier as a delivery to himself or may hold the seller responsible in damages.

(3) Unless otherwise agreed, where goods are sent by the seller to the buyer by a route involving sea transit, under circumstances in which it is usual to insure, the seller must give such notice to the buyer as may enable him to insure them during their sea transit; and if the seller fails to do so, the goods are at his risk during such sea transit.

33. Risk where goods are delivered at distant place

Where the seller of goods agrees to deliver them at his own risk at a place other than that where they are when sold, the buyer must nevertheless (unless otherwise agreed) take any risk of deterioration in the goods necessarily incident to the course of transit.

34. Buyer's right of examining goods

(1) Where goods are delivered to the buyer, and he has not previously examined them, he is not deemed to have accepted them until he has had a reasonable opportunity of examining them for the purpose of ascertaining whether they are in conformity with the contract.

(2) Unless otherwise agreed when the seller tenders delivery of the goods to the buyer, he is bound on request to afford the buyer a reasonable opportunity of examining the goods for the purpose of ascertaining whether they are in conformity with the contract.

35. Acceptance

(1) The buyer is deemed to have accepted the goods when he intimates to the seller that he has accepted them, or (except where section 34 above otherwise provides) when the goods have been delivered to him and he does any act in relation to them which is inconsistent with the ownership of the seller, or when after the lapse of a reasonable time he retains the goods without intimating to the seller that he has rejected them.

(2) Paragraph 10 of Schedule 1 below applies in relation to a contract made before 22 April 1967 or (in the application of this Act to Northern Ireland) 28 July 1967.

36. Buyer not bound to return rejected goods

Unless otherwise agreed, where goods are delivered to the buyer, and he refuses to accept them, having the right to do so, he is not bound to return them to the seller, but it is sufficient if he intimates to the seller that he refuses to accept them.

37. Buyer's liability for not taking delivery of goods

(1) When the seller is ready and willing to deliver the goods, and requests the buyer to take delivery, and the buyer does not within a reasonable time after such request take delivery of the goods, he is liable to the seller for any loss occasioned by his neglect or refusal to take delivery, and also for a reasonable charge for the care and custody of the goods.

(2) Nothing in this section affects the rights of the seller where the neglect or refusal of the buyer to take delivery amounts to a repudiation of the contract.

PART V

RIGHTS OF UNPAID SELLER AGAINST THE GOODS

Preliminary

38. Unpaid seller defined

(1) The seller of goods is an unpaid seller within the meaning of this Act—

    (*a*) when the whole of the price has not been paid or tendered;
    (*b*) when a bill of exchange or other negotiable instrument has been received

Sale of Goods Act 1979

as conditional payment, and the condition on which it was received has not been fulfilled by reason of the dishonour of the instrument or otherwise.

(2) In this Part of this Act 'seller' includes any person who is in the position of a seller, as, for instance, an agent of the seller to whom the bill of lading has been indorsed, or a consignor or agent who has himself paid (or is directly responsible for) the price.

39. Unpaid seller's rights

(1) Subject to this and any other Act, notwithstanding that the property in the goods may have passed to the buyer, the unpaid seller of goods, as such, has by implication of law—

   (*a*) a lien on the goods or right to retain them for the price while he is in possession of them;
   (*b*) in case of the insolvency of the buyer, a right of stopping the goods in transit after he has parted with the possession of them;
   (*c*) a right of re-sale as limited by this Act.

(2) Where the property in goods has not passed to the buyer, the unpaid seller has (in addition to his other remedies) a right of withholding delivery similar to and co-extensive with his rights of lien or retention and stoppage in transit where the property has passed to the buyer.

[40 . . .]

[*Section 40 was repealed by the Debtors (Scotland) Act 1987, section 108(3) and Schedule 8.*]

Unpaid seller's lien

41. Seller's lien

(1) Subject to this Act, the unpaid seller of goods who is in possession of them is entitled to retain possession of them until payment or tender of the price in the following cases:—

   (*a*) where the goods have been sold without any stipulation as to credit;
   (*b*) where the goods have been sold on credit but the term of credit has expired;
   (*c*) where the buyer becomes insolvent.

(2) The seller may exercise his lien or right of retention notwithstanding that he is in possession of the goods as agent or bailee or custodier for the buyer.

42. Part delivery

Where an unpaid seller has made part delivery of the goods, he may exercise his lien or right of retention on the remainder, unless such part delivery has been made under such circumstances as to show an agreement to waive the lien or right of retention.

43. Termination of lien

(1) The unpaid seller of goods loses his lien or right of retention in respect of them—

(*a*) when he delivers the goods to a carrier or other bailee or custodier for the purpose of transmission to the buyer without reserving the right of disposal of the goods;
(*b*) when the buyer or his agent lawfully obtains possession of the goods;
(*c*) by waiver of the lien or right of retention.

(2) An unpaid seller of goods who has a lien or right of retention in respect of them does not lose his lien or right of retention by reason only that he has obtained judgment or decree for the price of the goods.

Stoppage in transit

44. Right of stoppage in transit

Subject to this Act, when the buyer of goods becomes insolvent the unpaid seller who has parted with the possession of the goods has the right of stopping them in transit, that is to say, he may resume possession of the goods as long as they are in course of transit, and may retain them until payment or tender of the price.

45. Duration of transit

(1) Goods are deemed to be in course of transit from the time when they are delivered to a carrier or other bailee or custodier for the purpose of transmission to the buyer, until the buyer or his agent in that behalf takes delivery of them from the carrier or other bailee or custodier.

(2) If the buyer or his agent in that behalf obtains delivery of the goods before their arrival at the appointed destination, the transit is at an end.

(3) If, after the arrival of the goods at the appointed destination, the carrier or other bailee or custodier acknowledges to the buyer or his agent that he holds the goods on his behalf and continues in possession of them as bailee or custodier for the buyer or his agent, the transit is at an end, and it is immaterial that a further destination for the goods may have been indicated by the buyer.

(4) If the goods are rejected by the buyer, and the carrier or other bailee or custodier continues in possession of them, the transit is not deemed to be at an end, even if the seller has refused to receive them back.

(5) When goods are delivered to a ship chartered by the buyer it is a question depending on the circumstances of the particular case whether they are in the possession of the master as a carrier or as agent to the buyer.

(6) Where the carrier or other bailee or custodier wrongfully refuses to deliver the goods to the buyer or his agent in that behalf, the transit is deemed to be at an end.

(7) Where part delivery of the goods has been made to the buyer or his agent in that behalf, the remainder of the goods may be stopped in transit, unless such part delivery has been made under such circumstances as to show an agreement to give up possession of the whole of the goods.

46. How stoppage in transit is effected

(1) The unpaid seller may exercise his right of stoppage in transit either by taking actual possession of the goods or by giving notice of his claim to the carrier or other bailee or custodier in whose possession the goods are.

Sale of Goods Act 1979

(2) The notice may be given either to the person in actual possession of the goods or to his principal.

(3) If given to the principal, the notice is ineffective unless given at such time and under such circumstances that the principal, by the exercise of reasonable diligence, may communicate it to his servant or agent in time to prevent a delivery to the buyer.

(4) When notice of stoppage in transit is given by the seller to the carrier or other bailee or custodier in possession of the goods, he must redeliver the goods to, or according to the directions of, the seller; and the expenses of the redelivery must be borne by the seller.

Re-sale etc. by buyer

47. Effect of sub-sale etc. by buyer

(1) Subject to this Act, the unpaid seller's right of lien or retention or stoppage in transit is not affected by any sale or other disposition of the goods which the buyer may have made, unless the seller has assented to it.

(2) Where a document of title to goods has been lawfully transferred to any person as buyer or owner of the goods, and that person transfers the document to a person who takes it in good faith and for valuable consideration, then—

(*a*) if the last-mentioned transfer was by way of sale the unpaid seller's right of lien or retention or stoppage in transit is defeated; and
(*b*) if the last-mentioned transfer was made by way of pledge or other disposition for value, the unpaid seller's right of lien or retention or stoppage in transit can only be exercised subject to the rights of the transferee.

Rescission: and re-sale by seller

48. Rescission: and re-sale by seller

(1) Subject to this section, a contract of sale is not rescinded by the mere exercise by an unpaid seller of his right of lien or retention or stoppage in transit.

(2) Where an unpaid seller who has exercised his right of lien or retention or stoppage in transit resells the goods, the buyer acquires a good title to them as against the original buyer.

(3) Where the goods are of a perishable nature, or where the unpaid seller gives notice to the buyer of his intention to resell, and the buyer does not within a reasonable time pay or tender the price, the unpaid seller may re-sell the goods and recover from the original buyer damages for any loss occasioned by his breach of contact.

(4) Where the seller expressly reserves the right of re-sale in case the buyer should make default, and on the buyer making default resells the goods, the original contract of sale is rescinded but without prejudice to any claim the seller may have for damages.

Sale of Goods Act 1979

PART VI

ACTIONS FOR BREACH OF THE CONTRACT

Seller's remedies

49. Action for price

(1) Where, under a contract of sale, the property in the goods has passed to the buyer and he wrongfully neglects or refuses to pay for the goods according to the terms of the contract, the seller may maintain an action against him for the price of the goods.

(2) Where, under a contract of sale, the price is payable on a day certain irrespective of delivery and the buyer wrongfully neglects or refuses to pay such price, the seller may maintain an action for the price, although the property in the goods has not passed and the goods have not been appropriated to the contract.

(3) Nothing in this section prejudices the right of the seller in Scotland to recover interest on the price from the date of tender of the goods, or from the date on which the price was payable, as the case may be.

50. Damages for non-acceptance

(1) Where the buyer wrongfully neglects or refuses to accept and pay for the goods, the seller may maintain an action against him for damages for non-acceptance.

(2) The measure of damages is the estimated loss directly and naturally resulting, in the ordinary course of events, from the buyer's breach of contract.

(3) Where there is an available market for the goods in question the measure of damages is prima facie to be ascertained by the difference between the contract price and the market or current price at the time or times when the goods ought to have been accepted or (if no time was fixed for acceptance) at the time of the refusal to accept.

Buyer's remedies

51. Damages for non-delivery

(1) Where the seller wrongfully neglects or refuses to deliver the goods to the buyer, the buyer may maintain an action against the seller for damages for non-delivery.

(2) The measure of damages is the estimated loss directly and naturally resulting, in the ordinary course of events, from the seller's breach of contract.

(3) Where there is an available market for the goods in question the measure of damages is prima facie to be ascertained by the difference between the contract price and the market or current price of the goods at the time or times when they ought to have been delivered or (if no time was fixed) at the time of the refusal to deliver.

52. Specific performance

(1) In any action for breach of contract to deliver specific or ascertained goods the court may, if it thinks fit, on the plaintiff's application, by its judgment

or decree direct that the contract shall be performed specifically, without giving the defendant the option of retaining the goods on payment of damages.

(2) The plaintiff's application may be made at any time before judgment or decree.

(3) The judgment or decree may be unconditional, or on such terms and conditions as to damages, payment of the price and otherwise as seem just to the court.

(4) The provisions of this section shall be deemed to be supplementary to, and not in derogation of, the right of specific implement in Scotland.

53. Remedy for breach of warranty

(1) Where there is a breach of warranty by the seller or where the buyer elects (or is compelled) to treat any breach of a condition on the part of the seller as a breach of warranty, the buyer is not by reason only of such breach of warranty entitled to reject the goods; but he may—

  (*a*) set up against the seller the breach of warranty in diminution or extinction of the price, or
  (*b*) maintain an action against the seller for damages for the breach of warranty.

(2) The measure of damages for breach of warranty is the estimated loss directly and naturally resulting, in the ordinary course of events, from the breach of warranty.

(3) In the case of breach of warranty of quality such loss is prima facie the difference between the value of the goods at the time of delivery to the buyer and the value they would have had if they had fulfilled the warranty.

(4) The fact that the buyer has set up the breach of warranty in diminution or extinction of the price does not prevent him from maintaining an action for the same breach of warranty if he has suffered further damage.

(5) Nothing in this section prejudices or affects the buyer's right of rejection in Scotland as declared by this Act.

Interest, etc.

54. Interest, etc.

Nothing in this Act affects the right of the buyer or the seller to recover interest or special damages in any case where by law interest or special damages may be recoverable, or to recover money paid where the consideration for the payment of it has failed.

PART VII

Supplementary

55. Exclusion of implied terms

(1) Where a right, duty or liability would arise under a contract of sale of goods by implication of law, it may (subject to the Unfair Contract Terms Act 1977) be negatived or varied by express agreement, or by the course of dealing between the parties, or by such usage as binds both parties to the contract.

(2) An express condition or warranty does not negative a condition or warranty implied by this Act unless inconsistent with it.

(3) Paragraph 11 of Schedule 1 below applies in relation to a contract made on or after 18 May 1973 and before 1 February 1978, and paragraph 12 in relation to one made before 18 May 1973.

56. Conflict of laws

Paragraph 13 of Schedule 1 below applies in relation to a contract made on or after 18 May 1973 and before 1 February 1978, so as to make provision about conflict of laws in relation to such a contact.

57. Auction sales

(1) Where goods are put up for sale by auction in lots, each lot is prima facie deemed to be the subject of a separate contract of sale.

(2) A sale by auction is complete when the auctioneer announces its completion by the fall of the hammer, or in other customary manner; and until the announcement is made any bidder may retract his bid.

(3) A sale by auction may be notified to be subject to a reserve or upset price, and a right to bid may also be reserved expressly by or on behalf of the seller.

(4) Where a sale by auction is not notified to be subject to a right to bid by or on behalf of the seller, it is not lawful for the seller to bid himself or to employ any person to bid at the sale, or for the auctioneer knowingly to take any bid from the seller or any such person.

(5) A sale contravening subsection (4) above may be treated as fraudulent by the buyer.

(6) Where, in respect of a sale by auction, a right to bid is expressly reserved (but not otherwise) the seller or any one person on his behalf may bid at the auction.

58. Payment into court in Scotland

In Scotland where a buyer has elected to accept goods which he might have rejected, and to treat a breach of contract as only giving rise to a claim for damages, he may, in an action by the seller for the price, be required, in the discretion of the court before which the action depends, to consign or pay into court the price of the goods, or part of the price, or to give other reasonable security for its due payment.

59. Reasonable time a question of fact

Where a reference is made in this Act to a reasonable time the question what is a reasonable time is a question of fact.

60. Rights etc. enforceable by action

Where a right, duty or liability is declared by this Act, it may (unless otherwise provided by this Act) be enforced by action.

61. Interpretation

(1) In this Act, unless the context or subject matter otherwise requires,—

'action' includes counterclaim and set-off, and in Scotland condescendence and claim and compensation;

'business' includes a profession and the activities of any Government department (including a Northern Ireland deparment) or local or public authority;

'buyer' means a person who buys or agrees to buy goods;

'contract of sale' includes an agreement to sell as well as a sale;

'credit-broker' means a person acting in the course of a business of credit brokerage carried on by him, that is a business of effecting introductions of individuals desiring to obtain credit—

(*a*) to persons carrying on any business so far as it relates to the provision of credit, or

(*b*) to other persons engaged in credit brokerage;

'defendant' includes in Scotland defender, respondent, and claimant in a multiplepoinding;

'delivery' means voluntary transfer of possession from one person to another;

'document of title to goods' has the same meaning as it has in the Factors Acts;

'Factors Acts' means the Factors Act 1889, the Factors (Scotland) Act 1890, and any enactment amending or substituted for the same;

'fault' means wrongful act or default;

'future goods' means goods to be manufactured or acquired by the seller after the making of the contract of sale;

'goods' includes all personal chattels other than things in action and money, and in Scotland all corporeal moveables except money; and in particular 'goods' includes emblements, industrial growing crops, and things attached to or forming part of the land which are agreed to be severed before sale or under the contract of sale;

'plaintiff' includes pursuer, complainer, claimant in a multiplepoinding and defendant or defender counterclaiming;

'property' means the general property in goods, and not merely a special property;

'quality', in relation to goods, includes their state or condition;

'sale' includes a bargain and sale as well as a sale and delivery

'seller' means a person who sells or agrees to sell goods;

'specific goods' means goods identified and agreed on at the time a contract of sale is made;

'warranty' (as regards England and Wales and Northern Ireland) means an agreement with reference to goods which are the subject of a contract of sale, but collateral to the main purpose of such contract, the breach of which gives rise to a claim for damages, but not to a right to reject the goods and treat the contract as repudiated.

(2) As regards Scotland a breach of warranty shall be deemed to be a failure to perform a material part of the contract.

(3) A thing is deemed to be done in good faith within the meaning of this Act when it is in fact done honestly, whether it is done negligently or not.

(4) A person is deemed to be insolvent within the meaning of this Act if he has either ceased to pay his debts in the ordinary course of business or he cannot pay his debts as they become due. [. . .].

Sale of Goods Act 1979

[*The words omitted were repealed by Schedule 8 of the Bankruptcy (Scotland) Act 1985 and Schedule 10 of the Insolvency Act 1985.*]

(5) Goods are in a deliverable state within the meaning of this Act when they are in such a state that the buyer would under the contract be bound to take delivery of them.

(6) As regards the definition of 'business' in subsection (1) above, paragraph 14 of Schedule 1 below applies in relation to a contract made on or after 18 May 1973 and before 1 February 1978, and paragraph 15 in relation to one made before 18 May 1973.

62. Savings: rules of law etc.

(1) The rules in bankruptcy relating to contracts of sale apply to those contracts, notwithstanding anything in this Act.

(2) The rules of common law, including the law merchant, except in so far as they are inconsistent with the provisions of this Act, and in particular the rules relating to the law of principal and agent and the effect of fraud, misrepresentation, duress or coercion, mistake, or other invalidating cause, apply to contract for the sale of goods.

(3) Nothing in this Act or the Sale of Goods Act 1893 affects the enactments relating to bills of sale, or any enactment relating to the sale of goods which is not expressly repealed or amended by this Act or that.

(4) The provisions of this Act about contracts of sale do not apply to a transaction in the form of a contract of sale which is intended to operate by way of mortgage, pledge, charge, or other security.

(5) Nothing in this Act prejudices or affects the landlord's right of hypothec or sequestration for rent in Scotland.

63. Consequential amendment, repeals and savings

(1) Without prejudice to section 17 of the Interpretation Act 1978 (repeal and re-enactment), the enactments mentioned in Schedule 2 below have effect subject to the amendments there specified (being amendments consequential on this Act).

(2) The enactments mentioned in Schedule 3 below are repealed to the extent specified in column 3, but subject to the savings in Schedule 4 below.

(3) The savings in Schedule 4 below have effect.

64. Short title and commencement

(1) This Act may be cited as the Sale of Goods Act 1979.

(2) This Act comes into force on 1 January 1980.

Sale of Goods Act 1979

SCHEDULES

SCHEDULE 1

Modification of Act for Certain Contracts

Preliminary

1.—(1) This Schedule modifies this Act as it applies to contracts of sale of goods made on certain dates.

(2) In this Schedule references to sections are to those of this Act and references to contracts are to contracts of sale of goods.

Nothing in this Schedule affects a contract made before 1 January 1894.

Section 11: condition treated as warranty

2. In relation to contract made before 22 April 1967 or (in the application of this Act to Northern Ireland) 28 July 1967, in section 11(4) after 'or part of them,' insert 'or where the contract is for specific goods, the property in which has passed to the buyer,'.

Section 12: implied terms about title etc.

3. In relation to a contract made before 18 May 1973 substitute the following for section 12:—

Implied terms about title, etc.

12. In a contract of sale, unless the circumstances of the contract are such as to show a different intention, there is—

(*a*) an implied condition on the part of the seller that in the case of a sale he has a right to sell the goods, and in the case of an agreement to sell he will have such a right at the time when the property is to pass;

(*b*) an implied warranty that the buyer will have and enjoy quiet possession of the goods;

(*c*) an implied warranty that the goods will be free from any charge or encumbrance in favour of any third party, not declared or known to the buyer before or at the time when the contract is made.

Section 13: sale by description

4. In relation to a contract made before 18 May 1973, omit section 13(3).

Section 14: quality or fitness (i)

5. In relation to a contract made on or after 18 May 1973 and before the appointed day, substitute the following for section 14:—

Implied terms about quality or fitness

14.—(1) Except as provided by this section and section 15 below and subject to any other enactment, there is no implied condition or warranty about the quality or fitness for any particular purpose of goods supplied under a contract of sale.

(2) Where the seller sells goods in the course of a business, there is an

Sale of Goods Act 1979

implied condition that the goods supplied under the contract are of merchantable quality, except that there is no such condition—

(*a*) as regards defects specifically drawn to the buyer's attention before the contract is made; or

(*b*) if the buyer examines the goods before the contract is made, as regards defects which that examination ought to reveal.

(3) Where the seller sells goods in the course of a business and the buyer, expressly or by implication, makes known to the seller any particular purpose for which the goods are being bought, there is an implied condition that the goods supplied under the contract are reasonably fit for that purpose, whether or not that is a purpose for which such goods are commonly supplied, except where the circumstances show that the buyer does not rely, or that it is unreasonable for him to rely, on the seller's skill or judgment.

(4) An implied condition or warranty about quality or fitness for a particular purpose may be annexed to a contract of sale by usage.

(5) The preceding provisions of this section apply to a sale by a person who in the course of a business is acting as agent for another as they apply to a sale by a principal in the course of a business, except where that other is not selling in the course of a business and either the buyer knows that fact or reasonable steps are taken to bring it to the notice of the buyer before the contract is made.

(6) Goods of any kind are of merchantable quality within the meaning of subsection (2) above if they are as fit for the purpose or purposes for which goods of that kind are commonly bought as it is reasonable to expect having regard to any description applied to them, the price (if relevant) and all the other relevant circumstances.

(7) In the application of subsection (3) above to an agreement for the sale of goods under which the purchase price or part of it is payable by instalments any reference to the seller includes a reference to the person by whom any antecedent negotiations are conducted; and section 58(3) and (5) of the Hire-Purchase Act 1965, section 54(3) and (5) of the Hire-Purchase (Scotland) Act 1965 and section 65(3) and (5) of the Hire-Purchase Act (Northern Ireland) 1966 (meaning of antecedent negotiations and related expressions) apply in relation to this subsection as in relation to each of those Acts, but as if a reference to any such agreement were included in the references in subsection (3) of each of those sections to the agreements there mentioned.

Section 14: quality or fitness (ii)

6. In relation to a contract made before 18 May 1973 substitute the following for section 14:—

Implied terms about quality or fitness

14.—(1) Subject to this and any other Act, there is no implied condition or warranty about the quality or fitness for any particular purpose of goods supplied under a contract of sale.

(2) Where the buyer, expressly or by implication, makes known to the seller the particular purpose for which the goods are required, so as to show

Sale of Goods Act 1979

that the buyer relies on the seller's skill or judgment, and the goods are of a description which it is in the course of the seller's business to supply (whether he is the manufacturer or not), there is an implied condition that the goods will be reasonably fit for such purpose, except that in the case of a contract for the sale of a specified article under its patent or other trade name there is no implied condition as to its fitness for any particular purpose.

(3) Where goods are bought by description from a seller who deals in goods of that description (whether he is the manufacturer or not), there is an implied condition that the goods will be of merchantable quality; but if the buyer has examined the goods, there is no implied condition as regards defects which such examination ought to have revealed.

(4) An implied condition or warranty about quality or fitness for a particular purpose may be annexed by the usage of trade.

(5) An express condition or warranty does not negative a condition or warranty implied by this Act unless inconsistent with it.

Section 15: sale by sample

7. In relation to a contract made before 18 May 1973, omit section 15(3).

Section 22: market overt

8. In relation to a contract under which goods were sold before 1 January 1968 or (in the application of this Act to Northern Ireland) 29 August 1967, add the following paragraph at the end of section 22(1):—

'Nothing in this subsection affects the law relating to the sale of horses.'

Section 25: buyer in possession

9. In relation to a contract under which a person buys or agrees to buy goods and which is made before the appointed day, omit section 25(2).

Section 35: acceptance

10. In relation to a contract made before 22 April 1967 or (in the application of this Act to Northern Irleand) 28 July 1967, in section 35(1) omit '(except where section 34 above otherwise provides)'.

Section 55: exclusion of implied terms (i)

11. In relation to a contract made on or after 18 May 1973 and before 1 February 1978 substitute the following for section 55:—

Exclusion of implied terms

55.—(1) Where a right, duty or liability would arise under a contract of sale of goods by implication of law, it may be negatived or varied by express agreement, or by the course of dealing between the parties, or by such usage as binds both parties to the contract, but the preceding provision has effect subject to the following provisions of this section.

(2) An express condition or warranty does not negative a condition or warranty implied by this Act unless inconsistent with it.

(3) In the case of a contract of sale of goods, any term of that or any other

contract exempting from all or any of the provisions of section 12 above is void.

(4) In the case of a contract of sale of goods, any term of that or any other contract exempting from all or any of the provisions of section 13, 14 or 15 above is void in the case of a consumer sale and is, in any other case, not enforceable to the extent that it is shown that it would not be fair or reasonable to allow reliance on the term.

(5) In determining for the purposes of subsection (4) above whether or not reliance on any such term would be fair or reasonable regard shall be had to all the circumstances of the case and in particular to the following matters—

  (*a*) the strength of the bargaining positions of the seller and buyer relative to each other, taking into account, among other things, the availability of suitable alternative products and sources of supply;
  (*b*) whether the buyer received an inducement to agree to the term or in accepting it had an opportunity of buying the goods or suitable alternatives without it from any source of supply;
  (*c*) whether the buyer knew or ought reasonably to have known of the existence and extent of the term (having regard, among other things, to any custom of the trade and any previous course of dealing between the parties);
  (*d*) where the term exempts from all or any of the provisions of section 13, 14 or 15 above if some condition is not complied with, whether it was reasonable at the time of the contract to expect that compliance with that condition would be practicable;
  (*e*) whether the goods were manufactured, processed, or adapted to the special order of the buyer.

(6) Subsection (5) above does not prevent the court from holding, in accordance with any rule of law, that a term which purports to exclude or restrict any of the provisions of section 13, 14 or 15 above is not a term of the contract.

(7) In this section 'consumer sale' means a sale of goods (other than a sale by auction or by competitive tender) by a seller in the course of a business where the goods—

  (*a*) are of a type ordinarily bought for private use or consumption; and
  (*b*) are sold to a person who does not buy or hold himself out as buying them in the course of a business.

(8) The onus of proving that a sale falls to be treated for the purposes of this section as not being a consumer sale lies on the party so contending.

(9) Any reference in this section to a term exempting from all or any of the provisions of any section of this Act is a reference to a term which purports to exclude or restrict, or has the effect of excluding or restricting, the operation of all or any of the provisions of that section, or the exercise of a right conferred by any provision of that section, or any liability of the seller for breach of a condition or warranty implied by any provision of that section.

(10) It is hereby declared that any reference in this section to a term of a contract includes a reference to a term which although not contained in a contract is incorporated in the contract by another term of the contract.

(11) Nothing in this section prevents the parties to a contract for the international sale of goods from negativing or varying any right, duty or liability which would otherwise arise by implication of law under sections 12 to 15 above.

(12) In subsection (11) above 'contract for the international sale of goods' means a contract of sale of goods made by parties whose places of business (or, if they have none, habitual residences) are in the territories of different States (the Channel Islands and the Isle of Man being treated for this purpose as different States from the United Kingdom) and in the case of which one of the following conditions is satisfied:—

> (*a*) the contract involves the sale of goods which are at the time of the conclusion of the contract in the course of carriage or will be carried from the territory of one State to the territory of another; or
> (*b*) the acts constituting the offer and acceptance have been effected in the territories of different States; or
> (*c*) delivery of the goods is to be made in the territory of a State other than that within whose territory the acts constituting the offer and the acceptance have been effected.

Section 55: exclusion of implied terms (ii)

12. In relation to a contract made before 18 May 1973 substitute the following, for section 55:—

Exclusion of implied terms

55. Where a right, duty or liability would arise under a contract of sale by implication of law, it may be negatived or varied by express agreement, or by the course of dealing between the parties, or by such usage as binds both parties to the contract.

Section 56: conflict of laws

13.—(1) In relation to a contract made on or after 18 May 1973 and before 1 February 1978 substitute for section 56 the section set out in sub-paragraph (3) below.

(2) In relation to a contract made otherwise than as mentioned in sub-paragraph (1) above, ignore section 56 and this paragraph.

(3) The section mentioned in sub-paragraph (1) above is as follows:—

Conflict of laws

56.—(1) Where the proper law of a contract for the sale of goods would, apart from a term that it should be the law of some other country or a term to the like effect, be the law of any part of the United Kingdom, or where any such contract contains a term which purports to substitute, or has the effect of substituting, provisions of the law of some other country for all or any of the provisions of sections 12 to 15 and 55 above, those sections shall, notwithstanding that term but subject to subsection (2) below, apply to the contract.

(2) Nothing in subsection (1) above prevents the parties to a contract for the international sale of goods from negativing or varying any right, duty or liability which would otherwise arise by implication of law under sections 12 to 15 above.

(3) In subsection (2) above 'contract for the international sale of goods' means a contract of sale of goods made by parties whose places of business (or, if they have none, habitual residences) are in the territories of different States

(the Channel Islands and the Isle of Man being treated for this purpose as different States from the United Kingdom) and in the case of which one of the following conditions is satisfied:—

 (a) the contract involves the sale of goods which are at the time of the conclusion of the contract in the course of carriage or will be carried from the territory of one State to the territory of another; or
 (b) the acts constituting the offer and acceptance have been effected in the territories of different States; or
 (c) delivery of the goods is to be made in the territory of a State other than that within whose territory the acts constituting the offer and the acceptance have been effected.

Section 61(1): definition of 'business' (i)

14. In relation to a contract made on or after 18 May 1973 and before 1 February 1978, in the defintion of 'business' in section 61(1) for 'or local or public authority' substitute ', local authority or statutory undertaker'.

Section 61(1): definition of 'business' (ii)

15. In relation to a contract made before 18 May 1973 omit the definition of 'business' in section 61(1).

SCHEDULE 2

CONSEQUENTIAL AMENDMENTS

SCHEDULE 3

REPEALS

SCHEDULE 4

SAVINGS

Magistrates' Courts Act 1980
Chapter 43

40.

(1) The compensation to be paid under a compensation order by a magistrates' court in respect of any offence of which the court has convicted the offender shall not exceed £2,000, and the compensation or total compensation to be paid under a compensation order or compensation orders made by a magistrates' court in respect of any offence or offences taken into consideration in determining the sentence shall not exceed the difference (if any) between the amount or total amount which under the preceding provisions of this subsection is the maximum for the offence or offences of which the offender has been convicted and the amount or total amounts (if any) which are in fact ordered to be paid in respect of that offence or those offences.

Supreme Court Act 1981
Chapter 54

138. Effect of writs of execution against goods

(1) Subject to subsection (2), a writ of fieri facias or other writ of execution against goods issued from the High Court shall bind the property in the goods of the execution debtor as from the time when the writ is delivered to the sheriff to be executed.

(2) Such a writ shall not prejudice the title to any goods of the execution debtor acquired by a person in good faith and for valuable consideration unless he had, at the time when he acquired his title—

- (*a*) notice that that writ or any such writ by virtue of which the goods of the execution debtor might be seized or attached had been delivered to and remained unexecuted in the hands of the sheriff; or
- (*b*) notice that an application for the issue of a warrant of execution against the goods of the execution debtor had been made to the registrar of a county court and that the warrant issued on the application either—
  - (i) remained unexecuted in the hands of the registrar of the court from which it was issued; or
  - (ii) had been sent for execution to, and received by, the registrar of another county court, and remained unexecuted in the hands of the registrar of that court.

(3) For the better manifestation of the time mentioned in subsection (1), it shall be the duty of the sheriff (without fee) on receipt of any such writ as is there mentioned to endorse on its back the hour, day, month and year when he received it.

(4) For the purpose of this section—

- (*a*) 'property' means the general property in goods, and not merely a special property;
- (*b*) 'sheriff' includes any officer charged with the enforcement of a writ of execution;
- (*c*) any reference to the goods of the execution debtor includes a reference to anything else that may lawfully be seized in execution; and
- (*d*) a thing shall be treated as done in good faith if it is in fact done honestly, whether it is done negligently or not.

Supply of Goods and Services Act 1982

Supply of Goods and Services Act 1982
Chapter 29

ARRANGEMENT OF SECTIONS

PART I

SUPPLY OF GOODS

Contracts for the transfer of property in goods

Section
1. The contracts concerned.
2. Implied terms about title, etc.
3. Implied terms where transfer is by description.
4. Implied terms about quality or fitness.
5. Implied terms where transfer is by sample.

Contracts for the hire of goods

6. The contracts concerned.
7. Implied terms about right to transfer possession, etc.
8. Implied terms where hire is by description.
9. Implied terms about quality or fitness.
10. Implied terms where hire is by sample.

Exclusion of implied terms, etc.

11. Exclusion of implied terms, etc.

PART II

SUPPLY OF SERVICES

12. The contracts concerned.
13. Implied term about care and skill.
14. Implied term about time for performance.
15. Implied term about consideration.
16. Exclusion of implied terms, etc.

PART III

SUPPLEMENTARY

17. Minor and consequential amendments.
18. Interpretation: general.
19. Interpretation: references to Acts.
20. Citation, transitional provisions, commencement and extent.

SCHEDULE—Transitional provisions.

Supply of Goods and Services Act 1982

An Act to amend the law with respect to the terms to be implied in certain contracts for the transfer of the property in goods, in certain contracts for the hire of goods and in certain contracts for the supply of a service; and for connected purposes.

[13th July 1982]

PART I

Supply of Goods

Contracts for the transfer of property in goods

1. The contracts concerned

(1) In this Act a 'contract for the transfer of goods' means a contract under which one person transfers or agrees to transfer to another the property in goods, other than an excepted contract.

(2) For the purposes of this section an excepted contract means any of the following:—
- (*a*) a contract of sale of goods;
- (*b*) a hire-purchase agreement;
- (*c*) a contract under which the property in goods is (or is to be) transferred in exchange for trading stamps on their redemption;
- (*d*) a transfer or agreement to transfer which is made by deed and for which there is no consideration other than the presumed consideration imported by the deed;
- (*e*) a contract intended to operate by way of mortgage, pledge, charge or other security.

(3) For the purposes of this Act a contract is a contract for the transfer of goods whether or not services are also provided or to be provided under the contract, and (subject to subsection (2) above) whatever is the nature of the consideration for the transfer or agreement to transfer.

2. Implied terms about title, etc.

(1) In a contract for the transfer of goods, other than one to which subsection (3) below applies, there is an implied condition on the part of the transferor that in the case of a transfer of the property in the goods he has a right to transfer the property and in the case of an agreement to transfer the property in the goods he will have such a right at the time when the property is to be transferred.

(2) In a contract for the transfer of goods, other than one to which subsection (3) below applies, there is also an implied warranty that—
- (*a*) the goods are free, and will remain free until the time when the property is to be transferred, from any charge or encumbrance not disclosed or known to the transferee before the contract is made, and
- (*b*) the transferee will enjoy quiet possession of the goods except so far as it may be disturbed by the owner or other person entitled to the benefit of any charge or encumbrance so disclosed or known.

(3) This subsection applies to a contract for the transfer of goods in the case of which there appears from the contract or is to be inferred from its circumstances

Supply of Goods and Services Act 1982

an intention that the transferor should transfer only such title as he or a third person may have.

(4) In a contract to which subsection (3) above applies there is an implied warranty that all charges or encumbrances known to the transferor and not known to the transferee have been disclosed to the transferee before the contract is made.

(5) In a contract to which subsection (3) above applies there is also an implied warranty that none of the following will disturb the transferee's quiet possession of the goods, namely—

- (*a*) the transferor;
- (*b*) in a case where the parties to the contract intend that the transferor should transfer only such title as a third person may have, that person;
- (*c*) anyone claiming through or under the transferor or that third person otherwise than under a charge or encumbrance disclosed or known to the transferee before the contract is made.

3. Implied terms where transfer is by description

(1) This section applies where, under a contract for the transfer of goods, the transferor transfers or agrees to transfer the property in the goods by description.

(2) In such a case there is an implied condition that the goods will correspond with the description.

(3) If the transferor transfers or agrees to transfer the property in the goods by sample as well as by description it is not sufficient that the bulk of the goods corresponds with the sample if the goods do not also correspond with the description.

(4) A contract is not prevented from falling within subsection (1) above by reason only that, being exposed for supply, the goods are selected by the transferee.

4. Implied terms about quality or fitness

(1) Except as provided by this section and section 5 below and subject to the provisions of any other enactment, there is no implied condition or warranty about the quality or fitness for any particular purpose of goods supplied under a contract for the transfer of goods.

(2) Where, under such a contract, the transferor transfers the property in goods in the course of a business, there is (subject to subsection (3) below) an implied condition that the goods supplied under the contract are of merchantable quality.

(3) There is no such condition as is mentioned in subsection (2) above—

- (*a*) as regards defects specifically drawn to the transferee's attention before the contract is made; or
- (*b*) if the transferee examines the goods before the contract is made, as regards defects which that examination ought to reveal.

(4) Subsection (5) below applies where, under a contract for the transfer of goods, the transferor transfers the property in goods in the course of a business and the transferee, expressly or by implication, makes known—

(*a*) to the transferor, or

(*b*) where the consideration or part of the consideration for the transfer is a sum payable by instalments and the goods were previously sold by a credit-broker to the transferor, to that credit-broker,

any particular purpose for which the goods are being acquired.

(5) In that case there is (subject to subsection (6) below) an implied condition that the goods supplied under the contract are reasonably fit for that purpose, whether or not that is a purpose for which such goods are commonly supplied.

(6) Subsection (5) above does not apply where the circumstances show that the transferee does not rely, or that it is unreasonable for him to rely, on the skill or judgment of the transferor or credit-broker.

(7) An implied condition or warranty about quality or fitness for a particular purpose may be annexed by usage to a contract for the transfer of goods.

(8) The preceding provisions of this section apply to a transfer by a person who in the course of a business is acting as agent for another as they apply to a transfer by a principal in the course of a business, except where that other is not transferring in the course of a business and either the transferee knows that fact or reasonable steps are taken to bring it to the transferee's notice before the contract concerned is made.

(9) Goods of any kind are of merchantable quality within the meaning of subsection (2) above if they are as fit for the purpose or purposes for which goods of that kind are commonly supplied as it is reasonable to expect having regard to any description applied to them, the price (if relevant) and all the other relevant circumstances.

5. Implied terms where transfer is by sample

(1) This section applies where, under a contract for the transfer of goods, the transferor transfers or agrees to transfer the property in the goods by reference to a sample.

(2) In such a case there is an implied condition—

(*a*) that the bulk will correspond with the sample in quality; and

(*b*) that the transferee will have a reasonable opportunity of comparing the bulk with the sample; and

(*c*) that the goods will be free from any defect, rendering them unmerchantable, which would not be apparent on reasonable examination of the sample.

(3) In subsection (2)(*c*) above 'unmerchantable' is to be construed in accordance with section 4(9) above.

(4) For the purposes of this section a transferor transfers or agrees to transfer the property in goods by reference to a sample where there is an express or implied term to that effect in the contract concerned.

Supply of Goods and Services Act 1982

Contracts for the hire of goods

6. The contracts concerned

(1) In this Act a 'contract for the hire of goods' means a contract under which one person bails or agrees to bail goods to another by way of hire, other than an excepted contract.

(2) For the purposes of this section an excepted contract means any of the following:—

- (*a*) a hire-purchase agreement;
- (*b*) a contract under which goods are (or are to be) bailed in exchange for trading stamps on their redemption.

(3) For the purposes of this Act a contract is a contract for the hire of goods whether or not services are also provided or to be provided under the contract, and (subject to subsection (2) above) whatever is the nature of the consideration for the bailment or agreement to bail by way of hire.

7. Implied terms about right to transfer possession, etc.

(1) In a contract for the hire of goods there is an implied condition on the part of the bailor that in the case of a bailment he has a right to transfer possession of the goods by way of hire for the period of the bailment and in the case of an agreement to bail he will have such a right at the time of the bailment.

(2) In a contract for the hire of goods there is also an implied warranty that the bailee will enjoy quiet possession of the goods for the period of the bailment except so far as the possession may be disturbed by the owner or other person entitled to the benefit of any charge or encumbrance disclosed or known to the bailee before the contract is made.

(3) The preceding provisions of this section do not affect the right of the bailor to repossess the goods under an express or implied term of the contract.

8. Implied terms where hire is by description

(1) This section applies where, under a contract for the hire of goods, the bailor bails or agrees to bail the goods by description.

(2) In such a case there is an implied condition that the goods will correspond with the description.

(3) If under the contract the bailor bails or agrees to bail the goods by reference to a sample as well as a description it is not sufficient that the bulk of the goods corresponds with the sample if the goods do not also correspond with the description.

(4) A contract is not prevented from falling within subsection (1) above by reason only that, being exposed for supply, the goods are selected by the bailee.

9. Implied terms about quality or fitness

(1) Except as provided by this section and section 10 below and subject to the provisions of any other enactment, there is no implied condition or warranty

about the quality or fitness for any particular purpose of goods bailed under a contract for the hire of goods.

(2) Where, under such a contract, the bailor bails goods in the course of a business, there is (subject to subsection (3) below) an implied condition that the goods supplied under the contract are of merchantable quality.

(3) There is no such condition as is mentioned in subsection (2) above—

   (*a*) as regards defects specifically drawn to the bailee's attention before the contract is made; or
   (*b*) if the bailee examines the goods before the contract is made, as regards defects which that examination ought to reveal.

(4) Subsection (5) below applies where, under a contract for the hire of goods, the bailor bails goods in the course of a business and the bailee, expressly or by implication, makes known—

   (*a*) to the bailor in the course of negotiations conducted by him in relation to the making of the contract, or
   (*b*) to a credit-broker in the course of negotiations conducted by that broker in relation to goods sold by him to the bailor before forming the subject matter of the contract,

any particular purpose for which the goods are being bailed.

(5) In that case there is (subject to subsection (6) below) an implied condition that the goods supplied under the contract are reasonably fit for that purpose, whether or not that is a purpose for which such goods are commonly supplied.

(6) Subsection (5) above does not apply where the circumstances show that the bailee does not rely, or that it is unreasonable for him to rely, on the skill or judgment of the bailor or credit-broker.

(7) An implied condition or warranty about quality or fitness for a particular purpose may be annexed by usage to a contract for the hire of goods.

(8) The preceding provisions of this section apply to a bailment by a person who in the course of a business is acting as agent for another as they apply to a bailment by a principal in the course of a business, except where that other is not bailing in the course of a business and either the bailee knows that fact or reasonable steps are taken to bring it to the bailee's notice before the contract concerned is made.

(9) Goods of any kind are of merchantable quality within the meaning of subsection (2) above if they are as fit for the purpose or purposes for which goods of that kind are commonly supplied as it is reasonable to expect having regard to any description applied to them, the consideration for the bailment (if relevant) and all the other relevant circumstances.

10. Implied terms where hire is by sample

(1) This section applies where, under a contract for the hire of goods, the bailor bails or agrees to bail the goods by reference to a sample.

(2) In such a case there is an implied condition—

   (*a*) that the bulk will correspond with the sample in quality; and
   (*b*) that the bailee will have a reasonable opportunity of comparing the bulk with the sample; and

(*c*) that the goods will be free from any defect, rendering them unmerchantable, which would not be apparent on reasonable examination of the sample.

(3) In subsection (2)(*c*) above 'unmerchantable' is to be construed in accordance with section 9(9) above.

(4) For the purposes of this section a bailor bails or agrees to bail goods by reference to a sample where there is an express or implied term to that effect in the contract concerned.

Exclusion of implied terms, etc.

11. Exclusion of implied terms, etc.

(1) Where a right, duty or liability would arise under a contract for the transfer of goods or a contract for the hire of goods by implication of law, it may (subject to subsection (2) below and the 1977 Act) be negatived or varied by express agreement, or by the course of dealing between the parties, or by such usage as binds both parties to the contract.

(2) An express condition or warranty does not negative a condition or warranty implied by the preceding provisions of this Act unless inconsistent with it.

(3) Nothing in the preceding provisions of this Act prejudices the operation of any other enactment or any rule of law whereby any condition or warranty (other than one relating to quality or fitness) is to be implied in a contract for the transfer of goods or a contract for the hire of goods.

PART II

SUPPLY OF SERVICES

12. The contracts concerned

(1) In this Act a 'contract for the supply of a service' means, subject to subsection (2) below, a contract under which a person ('the supplier') agrees to carry out a service.

(2) For the purposes of this Act, a contract of service or apprenticeship is not a contract for the supply of a service.

(3) Subject to subsection (2) above, a contract is a contract for the supply of a service for the purposes of this Act whether or not goods are also—

(*a*) transferred or to be transferred, or
(*b*) bailed or to be bailed by way of hire.

under the contract, and whatever is the nature of the consideration for which the service is to be carried out.

(4) The Secretary of State may by order provide that one or more of sections 13 to 15 below shall not apply to services of a description specified in the order, and such an order may make different provision for different circumstances.

(5) The power to make an order under subsection (4) above shall be exercisable by statutory instrument subject to annulment in pursuance of a resolution of either House of Parliament.

13. Implied term about care and skill

In a contract for the supply of a service where the supplier is acting in the course of a business, there is an implied term that the supplier will carry out the service with reasonable care and skill.

14. Implied term about time for performance

(1) Where, under a contract for the supply of a service by a supplier acting in the course of a business, the time for the service to be carried out is not fixed by the contract, left to be fixed in a manner agreed by the contract or determined by the course of dealing between the parties, there is an implied term that the supplier will carry out the service within a reasonable time.

(2) What is a reasonable time in a question of fact.

15. Implied term about consideration

(1) Where, under a contract for the supply of a service, the consideration for the service is not determined by the contract, left to be determined in a manner agreed by the contract or determined by the course of dealing between the parties, there is an implied term that the party contracting with the supplier will pay a reasonable charge.

(2) What is a reasonable charge is a question of fact.

16. Exclusion of implied terms, etc.

(1) Where a right, duty or liability would arise under a contract for the supply of a service by virtue of this Part of this Act, it may (subject to subsection (2) below and the 1977 Act) be negatived or varied by express agreement, or by the course of dealing between the parties, or by such usage as binds both parties to the contract.

(2) An express term does not negative a term implied by this Part of this Act unless inconsistent with it.

(3) Nothing in this Part of this Act prejudices—

   (*a*) any rule of law which imposes on the supplier a duty stricter than that imposed by section 13 or 14 above; or
   (*b*) subject to paragraph (*a*) above, any rule of law whereby any term not inconsistent with this Part of this Act is to be implied in a contract for the supply of a service.

(4) This Part of this Act has effect subject to any other enactment which defines or restricts the rights, duties or liabilities arising in connection with a service of any description.

PART III

SUPPLEMENTARY

17. Minor and consequential amendments

(1) In section 10(2) of the 1973 Act, as originally enacted and as prospectively substituted by paragraph 35 of Schedule 4 to the 1974 Act (implied condition

in hire-purchase agreement that goods are of merchantable quality), after 'implied condition that the goods' there shall be inserted 'supplied under the agreement'.

(2) The following subsection shall be inserted after section 7(3) of the 1977 Act:—

'(3A) Liability for breach of the obligations arising under section 2 of the Supply of Goods and Services Act 1982 (implied terms about title etc. in certain contracts for the transfer of the property in goods) cannot be excluded or restricted by reference to any such term.'

(3) In consequence of subsection (2) above, in section 7(4) of the 1977 Act, after 'cannot' there shall be inserted '(in a case to which subsection (3A) above does not apply)'.

18. Interpretation: general

(1) In the preceding provisions of this Act and this section—

'bailee', in relation to a contract for the hire of goods means (depending on the context) a person to whom the goods are bailed under the contract, or a person to whom they are to be so bailed, or a person to whom the rights under the contract of either of those persons have passed;

'bailor', in relation to a contract for the hire of goods, means (depending on the context) a person who bails the goods under the contract, or a person who agrees to do so, or a person to whom the duties under the contract of either of those persons have passed;

'business' includes a profession and the activities of any government department or local or public authority;

'credit-broker' means a person acting in the course of a business of credit brokerage carried on by him;

'credit brokerage' means the effecting of introductions—
   (*a*) of individuals desiring to obtain credit to persons carrying on any business so far as it relates to the provision of credit; or
   (*b*) of individuals desiring to obtain goods on hire to persons carrying on a business which comprises or relates to the bailment of goods under a contract for the hire of goods; or
   (*c*) of individuals desiring to obtain credit, or to obtain goods on hire, to other credit-brokers;

'enactment' means any legislation (including subordinate legislation) of the United Kingdom or Northern Ireland;

'goods' include all personal chattels (including emblements, industrial growing crops, and things attached to or forming part of the land which are agreed to be severed before the transfer or bailment concerned or under the contract concerned), other than things in action and money;

'hire-purchase agreement' has the same meaning as in the 1974 Act;

'property', in relation to goods, means the general property in them and not merely a special property;

'quality', in relation to goods, includes their state or condition;

'redemption', in relation to trading stamps, has the same meaning as in the Trading Stamps Act 1964 or, as respects Northern Ireland, the Trading Stamps Act (Northern Ireland) 1965;

'trading stamps' has the same meaning as in the said Act of 1964 or, as respects Northern Ireland, the said Act of 1965;

'transferee', in relation to a contract for the transfer of goods, means (depending on the context) a person to whom the property in the goods is transferred under the contract, or a person to whom the property is to be transferred, or a person to whom the rights under the contract of either of those persons have passed;

'transferor', in relation to a contract for the transfer of goods, means (depending on the context) a person who transfers the property in the goods under the contract, or a person who agrees to do so, or a person to whom the duties under the contract of either of those persons have passed.

(2) In subsection (1) above, in the definitions of bailee, bailor, transferee and transferor, a reference to rights or duties passing is to their passing by assignment, operation of law or otherwise.

19. Interpretation: references to Acts

In this Act—

'the 1973 Act' means the Supply of Goods (Implied Terms) Act 1973;

'the 1974 Act' means the Consumer Credit Act 1974;

'the 1977 Act' means the Unfair Contract Terms Act 1977; and

'the 1979 Act' means the Sale of Goods Act 1979.

20. Citation, transitional provisions, commencement and extent

(1) This Act may be cited as the Supply of Goods and Services Act 1982.

(2) The transitional provisions in the Schedule to this Act shall have effect.

(3) Part I of this Act together with section 17 and so much of sections 18 and 19 above as relates to that Part shall not come into operation until 4th January 1983; and Part II of this Act together with so much of sections 18 and 19 above as relates to that Part shall not come into operation until such day as may be appointed by an order made by the Secretary of State.

(4) The power to make an order under subsection (3) above shall be exercisable by statutory instrument.

(5) No provision of this Act applies to a contract made before the provision comes into operation.

(6) This Act extends to Northern Ireland but not to Scotland.

SCHEDULE

Transitional Provisions

1.

(1) If section 4 of this Act comes into operation before the day appointed for the purposes of section 14(7) of and paragraph 5 of Schedule 1 to the 1979

Act, then until that day, section 4 of this Act shall have effect with the modifications set out in sub-paragraphs (2) to (4) below.

(2) For subsection (4) substitute:

'(4) Subsection (5) below applies where, under a contract for the transfer of goods, the transferor transfers the property in goods in the course of a business and the transferee, expressly or by implication, makes known to the transferor any particular purpose for which the goods are being acquired.'

(3) In subsection (6) omit 'or credit-broker'.

(4) After subsection (9) insert:—

'(10) In the application of subsections (4) to (6) above to a contract for the transfer of goods under which the consideration or part of the consideration for the transfer is a sum payable by instalments any reference to the transferor includes a reference to the person by whom any antecedent negotiations are conducted.

(11) Section 58(3) and (5) of the Hire-Purchase Act 1965 (meaning of antecedent negotiations and related expressions) apply, with the appropriate modifications, in relation to subsection (10) above as in relation to that Act.'

2.

(1) If section 9 of this Act comes into operation before paragraph 35 of Schedule 4 to the 1974 Act (which, among other things, amends section 10(3) of the 1973 Act so as to make it refer to credit-brokers), then, until the paragraph comes into operation, section 9 of this Act shall have effect with the modifications set out in sub-paragraphs (2) to (4) below.

(2) For subsection (4) substitute:—

'(4) Subsection (5) below applies where, under a contract for the hire of goods, the bailor bails goods in the course of a business and the bailee, expressly or by implication, makes known to the bailor or the person by whom any antecedent negotiations are conducted any particular purpose for which the goods are being bailed.'

(3) In subsection (6), for 'credit-broker' substitute 'person by whom the antecedent negotiations are conducted'.

(4) After subsection (9) insert:—

'(10) Section 58(3) and (5) of the Hire-Purchase Act 1965 (meaning of antecedent negotiations and related expressions) apply, with the appropriate modifications, in relation to subsections (4) to (6) above as in relation to that Act.'

County Courts Act 1984
Chapter 28

(Sections 99 and 103 only)

Claims in respect of goods seized

99. Effects of warrants of execution

(1) Subject

(*a*) to subsection (2); and

(*b*) to section 103(2),

a warrant of execution against goods issued from a county court shall bind the property in the goods of the execution debtor as from the time at which application for the warrant was made to the registrar of the county court.

(2) Such a warrant shall not prejudice the title to any goods of the execution debtor acquired by a person in good faith and for valuable consideration unless he had at the time when he acquired his title—

(*a*) notice that an application for the issue of a warrant of execution against the goods of the execution debtor had been made to the registrar of a county court and that the warrant issued on the application either—

(i) remained unexecuted in the hands of the registrar of the court from which it was issued; or

(ii) had been sent for execution to, and received by, the registrar of another county court, and remained unexecuted in the hands of the registrar of that court; or

(*b*) notice that a writ of fieri facias or other writ of execution by virtue of which the goods of the execution debtor might be seized or attached had been delivered to and remained unexecuted in the hands of the sheriff.

(3) It shall be the duty of the registrar (without fee) on application for a warrant of execution being made to him to endorse on its back the hour, day, month and year when he received the application.

(4) For the purposes of this section—

(*a*) 'property' means the general property in goods, and not merely a special property;

(*b*) 'sheriff' includes any officer charged with the enforcement of a writ of execution; and

(*c*) a thing shall be treated as done in good faith if it is in fact done honestly whether it is done negligently or not.

Execution out of jurisdiction of court

103. Execution out of jurisdiction of court

(1) Where a warrant of execution has been issued from a county court (hereafter in this section referred to as a 'home court') against the goods of any person

and the goods are out of the jurisdiction of that court, the registrar of that court may send the warrant of execution to the registrar of any other county court within the jurisdiction of which the goods are or are believed to be, with a warrant endorsed on it or annexed to it requiring execution of the original warrant.

(2) The original warrant shall bind the property in goods of the execution debtor which are within the jurisdiction of the court to which it is sent as from the time when it is received by the registrar of that court.

(3) It shall be the duty of the registrar of the court to which the warrant is sent (without fee) on receipt of the warrant to endorse on its back the hour, day, month and year when he received it.

(4) On the receipt of the warrant, the registrar of the other county court shall act in all respects as if the original warrant of execution had been issued by the court of which he is registrar and shall within the prescribed time—

  (*a*) report to the registrar of the home court what he has done in the execution of the warrant; and
  (*b*) pay over all moneys received in pursuance of the warrant.

(5) Where a warrant of execution is sent by the registrar of a home court to the registrar of another court for execution under this section, that other court shall have the same power as the home court of staying the execution under section 88 as respects any goods within the jurisdiction of that other court.

Data Protection Act 1984
Chapter 35

An Act to regulate the use of automatically processed information relating to individuals and the provision of services in respect of such information.

[12th July 1984]

Part I
Preliminary

1. Definition of 'data' and related expressions

(1) The following provisions shall have effect for the interpretation of this Act.

(2) 'Data' means information recorded in a form in which it can be processed by equipment operating automatically in response to instructions given for that purpose.

(3) 'Personal data' means data consisting of information which relates to a living individual who can be identified from that information (or from that and other information in the possession of the data user), including any expression of opinion about the individual but not any indication of the intentions of the data user in respect of that individual.

(4) 'Data subject' means an individual who is the subject of personal data.

(5) 'Data user' means a person who holds data, and a person 'holds' data if—
   (a) the data form part of a collection of data processed or intended to be processed by or on behalf of that person as mentioned in subsection (2) above; and
   (b) that person (either alone or jointly or in common with other persons) controls the contents and use of the data comprised in the collection; and
   (c) the data are in the form in which they have been or are intended to be processed as mentioned in paragraph (a) above or (though not for the time being in that form) in a form into which they have been converted after being so processed and with a view to being further so processed on a subsequent occasion.

* * *

Part III
Rights of Data Subjects

21. Rights of access to personal data

(1) Subject to the provisions of this section, an individual shall be entitled—
   (a) to be informed by any data user whether the data held by him include personal data of which that individual is the data subject; and

(*b*) to be supplied by any data user with a copy of the information constituting any such personal data held by him;

and where any of the information referred to in paragraph (*b*) above is expressed in terms which are not intelligible without explanation the information shall be accompanied by an explanation of those terms.

(2) A data user shall not be obliged to supply any information under subsection (1) above except in response to a request in writing and on payment of such fee (not exceeding the prescribed maximum) as he may require; but a request for information under both paragraphs of that subsection shall be treated as a single request and a request for information under paragraph (*a*) shall, in the absence of any indication to the contrary, be treated as extending also to information under paragraph (*b*).

(3) In the case of a data user having separate entries in the register in respect of data held for different purposes a separate request must be made and a separate fee paid under this section in respect of the data to which each entry relates.

(4) A data user shall not be obliged to comply with a request under this section—

(*a*) unless he is supplied with such information as he may reasonably require in order to satisfy himself as to the identity of the person making the request and to locate the information which he seeks; and
(*b*) if he cannot comply with the request without disclosing information relating to another individual who can be identified from that information, unless he is satisfied that the other individual has consented to the disclosure of the information to the person making the request.

(5) In paragraph (*b*) of subsection (4) above the reference to information relating to another individual includes a reference to information identifying that individual as the source of the information sought by the request; and that paragraph shall not be construed as excusing a data user from supplying so much of the information sought by the request as can be supplied without disclosing the identity of the other individual concerned, whether by the omission of names or other identifying particulars or otherwise.

(6) A data user shall comply with a request under this section within forty days of receiving the request or, if later, receiving the information referred to in paragraph (*a*) of subsection (4) above and, in a case where it is required, the consent referred to in paragraph (*b*) of that subsection.

(7) The information to be supplied pursuant to a request under this section shall be supplied by reference to the data in question at the time when the request is received except that it may take account of any amendment or deletion made between that time and the time when the information is supplied, being an amendment or deletion that would have been made regardless of the receipt of the request.

(8) If a court is satisfied on the application of any person who has made a request under the foregoing provisions of this section that the data user in question has failed to comply with the request in contravention of those provisions, the court may order him to comply with the request; but a court shall not make an order under this subsection if it considers that it would in all the circumstances be unreasonable to do so, whether because of the frequency with

which the applicant has made requests to the data user under those provisions or for any other reason.

(9) The Secretary of State may by order provide for enabling a request under this section to be made on behalf of any individual who is incapable by reason of mental disorder of managing his own affairs.

* * *

Part IV

Exemptions

* * *

34. Other Exemptions

(3) Where all the personal data relating to a data subject held by a data user (or all such data in respect of which a data user has a separate entry in the register) consist of information in respect of which the data subject is entitled to make a request to the data user under section 158 of the Consumer Credit Act 1974 (files of credit reference agencies)—

    (*a*) the data are exempt from the subject access provisions; and

    (*b*) any request in respect of the data under section 21 above shall be treated for all purposes as if it were a request under the said section 158.

42. Commencement and transitional provisions

(1) No application for registration shall be made until such day as the Secretary of State may by order appoint, and sections 5 and 15 above shall not apply until the end of the period of six months beginning with that day.

(2) Until the end of the period of two years beginning with the day appointed under subsection (1) above the Registrar shall not have power—

    (*a*) to refuse an application made in accordance with section 6 above except on the ground mentioned in section 7(2)(*a*) above; or

    (*b*) to serve an enforcement notice imposing requirements to be complied with, a de-registration notice expiring, or a transfer prohibition notice imposing a prohibition taking effect, before the end of that period.

(3) Where the Registrar proposes to serve any person with an enforcement notice before the end of the period mentioned in subsection (2) above he shall, in determining the time by which the requirements of the notice are to be complied with, have regard to the probable cost to that person of complying with those requirements.

(4) Section 21 above and paragraph 1(*b*) of Schedule 4 to this Act shall not apply until the end of the period mentioned in subsection (2) above.

* * *

[*By the Data Protection Act 1984 (Appointed Day) Order 1985 (S.I. 1985 No. 1055), the appointed day for the purposes of section 42(1) was 11 November 1985).*]

Law Reform (Miscellaneous Provisions) (Scotland) Act 1985
Chapter 73

(Section 10 only)

10. Negligent misrepresentation

(1) A party to a contract who has been induced to enter into it by negligent misrepresentation made by or on behalf of another party to the contract shall not be disentitled, by reason only that the misrepresentation is not fraudulent, from recovering damages from the other party in respect of any loss or damage he has suffered as a result of the misrepresentation; and any rule of law that such damages cannot be recovered unless fraud is proved shall cease to have effect.

(2) Subsection (1) applies to any proceedings commenced on or after the date on which it comes into force, whether or not the negligent misrepresentation was made before or after that date, but does not apply to any proceedings commenced before that date.

Minors' Contracts Act 1987
Chapter 13

An Act to amend the law relating to minors' contracts. [9th April 1987]

1. Disapplication of Infants Relief Act 1874 etc.

The following enactments shall not apply to any contract made by a minor after the commencement of this Act—

(a) the Infants Relief Act 1874 (which invalidates certain contracts made by minors and prohibits actions to enforce contracts ratified after majority); and

(b) section 5 of the Betting and Loans (Infants) Act 1892 (which invalidates contracts to repay loans advanced during minority).

2. Guarantees

Where—

(a) a guarantee is given in respect of an obligation of a party to a contract made after the commencement of this Act, and

(b) the obligation is unenforceable against him (or he repudiates the contract) because he was a minor when the contract was made,

the guarantee shall not for that reason alone be unenforceable against the guarantor.

3. Restitution

(1) Where—

(a) a person ('the plaintiff') has after the commencement of this Act entered into a contract with another ('the defendant'), and

(b) the contract is unenforceable against the defendant (or he repudiates it) because he was a minor when the contract was made,

the court may, if it is just and equitable to do so, require the defendant to transfer to the plaintiff any property acquired by the defendant under the contract, or any property representing it.

(2) Nothing in this section shall be taken to prejudice any other remedy available to the plaintiff.

4. Consequential amendment and repeals

(1) In section 113 of the Consumer Credit Act 1974 (that Act not to be evaded by use of security) in subsection (7)—

(a) after the word 'indemnity', in both places where it occurs, there shall be inserted 'or guarantee';

Minors' Contracts Act 1987

(b) after the words 'minor, or' there shall be inserted 'an indemnity is given in a case where he'; and

(c) for the word 'they' there shall be substituted 'those obligations'.

(2) The Infants Relief Act 1874 and the Betting and Loans (Infants) Act 1892 are hereby repealed (in accordance with section 1 of this Act).

5. Short title, commencement and extent

(1) This Act may be cited as the Minors' Contracts Act 1987.

(2) This Act shall come into force at the end of the period of two months beginning with the date on which it is passed.

(3) This Act extends to England and Wales only.

Consumer Protection Act 1987
Chapter 43

ARRANGEMENT OF SECTIONS

Part I
Product Liability

Section
1. Purpose and construction of Part I.
2. Liability for defective products.
3. Meaning of 'defect'.
4. Defences.
5. Damage giving rise to liability.
6. Application of certain enactments etc.
7. Prohibition on exclusions from liability.
8. Power to modify Part I.
9. Application of Part I to Crown.

Part II
Consumer Safety

10. The general safety requirement.
11. Safety regulations.
12. Offences against the safety regulations.
13. Prohibition notices and notices to warn.
14. Suspension notices.
15. Appeals against suspension notices.
16. Forfeiture: England and Wales and Northern Ireland.
17. Forfeiture: Scotland.
18. Power to obtain information.
19. Interpretation of Part II.

Part III
Misleading Price Indications

20. Offence of giving misleading indication.
21. Meaning of 'misleading'.
22. Application to provision of services and facilities.
23. Application to provision of accommodation etc.
24. Defences.
25. Code of practice.
26. Power to make regulations.

Part IV
Enforcement of Parts II and III

27. Enforcement.
28. Test purchases.

Section
29. Powers of search etc.
30. Provisions supplemental to s.29.
31. Power of customs officer to detain goods.
32. Obstruction of authorised officer.
33. Appeals against detention of goods.
34. Compensation for seizure and detention.
35. Recovery of expenses of enforcement.

PART V

MISCELLANEOUS AND SUPPLEMENTAL

36. Amendments of Part I of the Health and Safety at Work etc. Act 1974.
37. Power of Commissioners of Customs and Excise to disclose information.
38. Restrictions on disclosure of information.
39. Defence of due diligence.
40. Liability of persons other than principal offender.
41. Civil proceedings.
42. Reports etc.
43. Financial provisions.
44. Service of documents etc.
45. Interpretation.
46. Meaning of 'supply'.
47. Savings for certain privileges.
48. Minor and consequential amendments and repeals.
49. Northern Ireland.
50. Short title, commencement and transitional provision.

Schedule 1—Limitation of actions under Part I.
    Part   I—England and Wales.
    Part II—Scotland.

Schedule 2—Prohibition notices and notices to warn.
    Part   I—Prohibition notices.
    Part II—Notices to warn.
    Part III—General.

Schedule 3—Amendments of Part I of the Health and Safety at Work etc. Act 1974.
Schedule 4—Minor and consequential amendments.
Schedule 5—Repeals.

An Act to make provision with respect to the liability of persons for damage caused by defective products; to consolidate with amendments the Consumer Safety Act 1978 and the Consumer Safety (Amendment) Act 1986; to make provision with respect to the giving of price indications; to amend Part I of the Health and Safety at Work etc. Act 1974 and sections 31 and 80 of the Explosives Act 1875; to repeal the Trade Descriptions Act 1972 and the Fabrics (Misdescription) Act 1913; and for connected purposes.

[15th May 1987]

Part I

Product Liability

1. Purpose and construction of Part I

(1) This Part shall have effect for the purpose of making such provision as is necessary in order to comply with the product liability Directive and shall be construed accordingly.

(2) In this Part, except in so far as the context otherwise requires—

'agricultural produce' means any produce of the soil, of stock-farming or of fisheries;

'dependant' and 'relative' have the same meaning as they have in, respectively, the Fatal Accidents Act 1976 and the Damages (Scotland) Act 1976;

'producer', in relation to a product, means—

(a) the person who manufactured it;
(b) in the case of a substance which has not been manufactured but has been won or abstracted, the person who won or abstracted it;
(c) in the case of a product which has not been manufactured, won or abstracted but essential characteristics of which are attributable to an industrial or other process having been carried out (for example, in relation to agricultural produce), the person who carried out that process;

'product' means any goods or electricity and (subject to subsection (3) below) includes a product which is comprised in another product, whether by virtue of being a component part or raw material or otherwise; and

'the product liability Directive' means the Directive of the Council of the European Communities, dated 25th July 1985, (No. 85/374/EEC) on the approximation of the laws, regulations and administrative provisions of the member States concerning liability for defective products.

(3) For the purposes of this Part a person who supplies any product in which products are comprised, whether by virtue of being component parts or raw materials or otherwise, shall not be treated by reason only of his supply of that product as supplying any of the products so comprised.

2. Liability for defective products

(1) Subject to the following provisions of this Part, where any damage is caused wholly or partly by a defect in a product, every person to whom subsection (2) below applies shall be liable for the damage.

(2) This subsection applies to—

(a) the producer of the product;
(b) any person who, by putting his name on the product or using a trade mark or other distinguishing mark in relation to the product, has held himself out to be the producer of the product;
(c) any person who has imported the product into a Member State from a place outside the Member States in order, in the course of any business of his, to supply it to another.

(3) Subject as aforesaid, where any damage is caused wholly or partly by a defect in a product, any person who supplied the product (whether to the

Consumer Protection Act 1987

person who suffered the damage, to the producer of any product in which the product in question is comprised or to any other person) shall be liable for the damage if—

(a) the person who suffered the damage requests the supplier to identify one or more of the persons (whether still in existence or not) to whom subsection (2) above applies in relation to the product;
(b) that request is made within a reasonable period after the damage occurs and at a time when it is not reasonably practicable for the person making the request to identify all those persons; and
(c) the supplier fails, within a reasonable period after receiving the request, either to comply with the request or to identify the person who supplied the product to him.

(4) Neither subsection (2) nor subsection (3) above shall apply to a person in respect of any defect in any game or agricultural produce if the only supply of the game or produce by that person to another was at a time when it had not undergone an industrial process.

(5) Where two or more persons are liable by virtue of this Part for the same damage, their liability shall be joint and several.

(6) This section shall be without prejudice to any liability arising otherwise than by virtue of this Part.

3. Meaning of 'defect'

(1) Subject to the following provisions of this section, there is a defect in a product for the purposes of this Part if the safety of the product is not such as persons generally are entitled to expect; and for those purposes 'safety', in relation to a product, shall include safety with respect to products comprised in that product and safety in the context of risks of damage to property, as well as in the context of risks of death or personal injury.

(2) In determining for the purposes of subsection (1) above what persons generally are entitled to expect in relation to a product all the circumstances shall be taken into account, including—

(a) the manner in which, and purposes for which, the product has been marketed, its get-up, the use of any mark in relation to the product and any instructions for, or warnings with respect to, doing or refraining from doing anything with or in relation to the product;
(b) what might reasonably be expected to be done with or in relation to the product; and
(c) the time when the product was supplied by its producer to another;

and nothing in this section shall require a defect to be inferred from the fact alone that the safety of a product which is supplied after that time is greater than the safety of the product in question.

4. Defences

(1) In any civil proceedings by virtue of this Part against any person ('the person proceeded against') in respect of a defect in a product it shall be a defence for him to show—

(a) that the defect is attributable to compliance with any requirement

imposed by or under any enactment or with any Community obligation; or
(b) that the person proceeded against did not at any time supply the product to another; or
(c) that the following conditions are satisfied, that is to say—
  (i) that the only supply of the product to another by the person proceeded against was otherwise than in the course of a business of that person; and
  (ii) that section 2(2) above does not apply to that person or applies to him by virtue only of things done otherwise than with a view to profit; or
(d) that the defect did not exist in the product at the relevant time; or
(e) that the state of scientific and technical knowledge at the relevant time was not such that a producer of products of the same description as the product in question might be expected to have discovered the defect if it had existed in his products while they were under his control; or
(f) that the defect—
  (i) constituted a defect in a product ('the subsequent product') in which the product in question had been comprised; and
  (ii) was wholly attributable to the design of the subsequent product or to compliance by the producer of the product in question with instructions given by the producer of the subsequent product.

(2) In this section 'the relevant time', in relation to electricity, means the time at which it was generated, being a time before it was transmitted or distributed, and in relation to any other product, means—

(a) if the person proceeded against is a person to whom subsection (2) of section 2 above applies in relation to the product, the time when he supplied the product to another;
(b) if that subsection does not apply to that person in relation to the product, the time when the product was last supplied by a person to whom that subsection does apply in relation to the product.

5. Damage giving rise to liability

(1) Subject to the following provisions of this section, in this Part 'damage' means death or personal injury or any loss of or damage to any property (including land).

(2) A person shall not be liable under section 2 above in respect of any defect in a product for the loss of or any damage to the product itself or for the loss of or any damage to the whole or any part of any product which has been supplied with the product in question comprised in it.

(3) A person shall not be liable under section 2 above for any loss of or damage to any property which, at the time it is lost or damaged, is not—

(a) of a description of property ordinarily intended for private use, occupation or consumption; and
(b) intended by the person suffering the loss or damage mainly for his own private use, occupation or consumption.

(4) No damages shall be awarded to any person by virtue of this Part in respect of any loss of or damage to any property if the amount which would

fall to be so awarded to that person, apart from this subsection and any liability for interest, does not exceed £275.

(5) In determining for the purposes of this Part who has suffered any loss of or damage to property and when any such loss or damage occurred, the loss or damage shall be regarded as having occurred at the earliest time at which a person with an interest in the property had knowledge of the material facts about the loss or damage.

(6) For the purposes of subsection (5) above the material facts about any loss of or damage to any property are such facts about the loss or damage as would lead a reasonable person with an interest in the property to consider the loss or damage sufficiently serious to justify his instituting proceedings for damages against a defendant who did not dispute liability and was able to satisfy a judgment.

(7) For the purposes of subsection (5) above a person's knowledge includes knowledge which he might reasonably have been expected to acquire—

(*a*) from facts observable or ascertainable by him; or
(*b*) from facts ascertainable by him with the help of appropriate expert advice which it is reasonable for him to seek;

but a person shall not be taken by virtue of this subsection to have knowledge of a fact ascertainable by him only with the help of expert advice unless he has failed to take all reasonable steps to obtain (and, where appropriate, to act on) that advice.

(8) Subsections (5) to (7) above shall not extend to Scotland.

6. Application of certain enactments etc.

(1) Any damage for which a person is liable under section 2 above shall be deemed to have been caused—

(*a*) for the purposes of the Fatal Accidents Act 1976, by that person's wrongful act, neglect or default;
(*b*) for the purposes of section 3 of the Law Reform (Miscellaneous Provisions) (Scotland) Act 1940 (contribution among joint wrongdoers), by that person's wrongful act or negligent act or omission;
(*c*) for the purposes of section 1 of the Damages (Scotland) Act 1976 (rights of relatives of a deceased), by that person's act or omission; and
(*d*) for the purposes of Part II of the Administration of Justice Act 1982 (damages for personal injuries, etc.—Scotland), by an act or omission giving rise to liability in that person to pay damages.

(2) Where—

(*a*) a person's death is caused wholly or partly by a defect in a product, or a person dies after suffering damage which has been so caused;
(*b*) a request such as mentioned in paragraph (a) of subsection (3) of section 2 above is made to a supplier of the product by that person's personal representatives or, in the case of a person whose death is caused wholly or partly by the defect, by any dependant or relative of that person; and
(*c*) the conditions specified in paragraphs (b) and (c) of that subsection are satisfied in relation to that request,

this Part shall have effect for the purposes of the Law Reform (Miscellaneous Provisions) Act 1934, the Fatal Accidents Act 1976 and the Damages (Scotland) Act 1976 as if liability of the supplier to that person under that subsection did not depend on that person having requested the supplier to identify certain persons or on the said conditions having been satisfied in relation to a request made by that person.

(3) Section 1 of the Congenital Disabilities (Civil Liability) Act 1976 shall have effect for the purposes of this Part as if—

  (*a*) a person were answerable to a child in respect of an occurrence caused wholly or partly by a defect in a product if he is or has been liable under section 2 above in respect of any effect of the occurrence on a parent of the child, or would be so liable if the occurrence caused a parent of the child to suffer damage;
  (*b*) the provisions of this Part relating to liability under section 2 above applied in relation to liability by virtue of paragraph (a) above under the said section 1; and
  (*c*) subsection (6) of the said section 1 (exclusion of liability) were omitted.

(4) Where any damage is caused partly by a defect in a product and partly by the fault of the person suffering the damage, the Law Reform (Contributory Negligence) Act 1945 and section 5 of the Fatal Accidents Act 1976 (contributory negligence) shall have effect as if the defect were the fault of every person liable by virtue of this Part for the damage caused by the defect.

(5) In subsection (4) above 'fault' has the same meaning as in the said Act of 1945.

(6) Schedule 1 to this Act shall have effect for the purpose of amending the Limitation Act 1980 and the Prescription and Limitation (Scotland) Act 1973 in their application in relation to the bringing of actions by virtue of this Part.

(7) It is hereby declared that liability by virtue of this Part is to be treated as liability in tort for the purposes of any enactment conferring jurisdiction on any court with respect to any matter.

(8) Nothing in this Part shall prejudice the operation of section 12 of the Nuclear Installations Act 1965 (rights to compensation for certain breaches of duties confined to rights under that Act).

7. Prohibition on exclusions from liability

The liability of a person by virtue of this Part to a person who has suffered damage caused wholly or partly by a defect in a product, or to a dependant or relative of such a person, shall not be limited or excluded by any contract term, by any notice or by any other provision.

8. Power to modify Part I

(1) Her Majesty may by Order in Council make such modifications of this Part and of any other enactment (including an enactment contained in the following Parts of this Act, or in an Act passed after this Act) as appear to Her Majesty in Council to be necessary or expedient in consequence of any modification of the product liability Directive which is made at any time after the passing of this Act.

(2) An Order in Council under subsection (1) above shall not be submitted

9. Application of Part I to Crown

(1) Subject to subsection (2) below, this Part shall bind the Crown.

(2) The Crown shall not, as regards the Crown's liability by virtue of this Part, be bound by this Part further than the Crown is made liable in tort or in reparation under the Crown Proceedings Act 1947, as that Act has effect from time to time.

Part II

Consumer Safety

10. The general safety requirement

(1) A person shall be guilty of an offence if he—

   (a) supplies any consumer goods which fail to comply with the general safety requirement;
   (b) offers or agrees to supply any such goods; or
   (c) exposes or possesses any such goods for supply.

(2) For the purposes of this section consumer goods fail to comply with the general safety requirement if they are not reasonably safe having regard to all the circumstances, including—

   (a) the manner in which, and purposes for which, the goods are being or would be marketed, the get-up of the goods, the use of any mark in relation to the goods and any instructions or warnings which are given or would be given with respect to the keeping, use or consumption of the goods;
   (b) any standards of safety published by any person either for goods of a description which applies to the goods in question or for matters relating to goods of that description; and
   (c) the existence of any means by which it would have been reasonable (taking into account the cost, likelihood and extent of any improvement) for the goods to have been made safer.

(3) For the purposes of this section consumer goods shall not be regarded as failing to comply with the general safety requirement in respect of—

   (a) anything which is shown to be attributable to compliance with any requirement imposed by or under any enactment or with any Community obligation;
   (b) any failure to do more in relation to any matter than is required by—
       (i) any safety regulations imposing requirements with respect to that matter;
       (ii) any standards of safety approved for the purposes of this subsection by or under any such regulations and imposing requirements with respect to that matter;
       (iii) any provision of any enactment or subordinate legislation imposing such requirements with respect to that matter as are designated for the purposes of this subsection by any such regulations.

(4) In any proceedings against any person for an offence under this section in respect of any goods it shall be a defence for that person to show—

(a) that he reasonably believed that the goods would not be used or consumed in the United Kingdom; or
(b) that the following conditions are satisfied, that is to say—
(i) that he supplied the goods, offered or agreed to supply them or, as the case may be, exposed or possessed them for supply in the course of carrying on a retail business; and
(ii) that, at the time he supplied the goods or offered or agreed to supply them or exposed or possessed them for supply, he neither knew nor had reasonable grounds for believing that the goods failed to comply with the general safety requirement; or
(c) that the terms on which he supplied the goods or agreed or offered to supply them or, in the case of goods which he exposed or possessed for supply, the terms on which he intended to supply them—
(i) indicated that the goods were not supplied or to be supplied as new goods; and
(ii) provided for, or contemplated, the acquisition of an interest in the goods by the persons supplied or to be supplied.

(5) For the purposes of subsection (4)(b) above goods are supplied in the course of carrying on a retail business if—

(a) whether or not they are themselves acquired for a person's private use or consumption, they are supplied in the course of carrying on a business of making a supply of consumer goods available to persons who generally acquire them for private use or consumption; and
(b) the descriptions of goods the supply of which is made available in the course of that business do not, to a significant extent, include manufactured or imported goods which have not previously been supplied in the United Kingdom.

(6) A person guilty of an offence under this section shall be liable on summary conviction to imprisonment for a term not exceeding six months or to a fine not exceeding level 5 on the standard scale or to both.

(7) In this section 'consumer goods' means any goods which are ordinarily intended for private use or consumption, not being—

(a) growing crops or things comprised in land by virtue of being attached to it;
(b) water, food, feeding stuff or fertiliser;
(c) gas which is, is to be or has been supplied by a person authorised to supply it by or under section 6, 7 or 8 of the Gas Act 1986 (authorisation of supply of gas through pipes);
(d) aircraft (other than hang-gliders) or motor vehicles;
(e) controlled drugs or licensed medicinal products;
(f) tobacco.

11. Safety regulations

(1) The Secretary of State may by regulations under this section ('safety regulations') make such provision as he considers appropriate for the purposes of section 10(3) above and for the purpose of securing—

(a) that goods to which this section applies are safe;

(b) that goods to which this section applies which are unsafe, or would be unsafe in the hands of persons of a particular description, are not made available to persons generally or, as the case may be, to persons of that description; and

(c) that appropriate information is, and inappropriate information is not, provided in relation to goods to which this section applies.

(2) Without prejudice to the generality of subsection (1) above, safety regulations may contain provision—

(a) with respect to the composition or contents, design, construction, finish or packing of goods to which this section applies, with respect to standards for such goods and with respect to other matters relating to such goods;

(b) with respect to the giving, refusal, alteration or cancellation of approvals of such goods, of descriptions of such goods or of standards for such goods;

(c) with respect to the conditions that may be attached to any approval given under the regulations;

(d) for requiring such fees as may be determined by or under the regulations to be paid on the giving or alteration of any approval under the regulations and on the making of an application for such an approval or alteration;

(e) with respect to appeals against refusals, alterations and cancellations of approvals given under the regulations and against the conditions contained in such approvals;

(f) for requiring goods to which this section applies to be approved under the regulations or to conform to the requirements of the regulations or to descriptions or standards specified in or approved by or under the regulations;

(g) with respect to the testing or inspection of goods to which this section applies (including provision for determining the standards to be applied in carrying out any test or inspection);

(h) with respect to the ways of dealing with goods of which some or all do not satisfy a test required by or under the regulations or a standard connected with a procedure so required;

(i) for requiring a mark, warning or instruction or any other information relating to goods to be put on or to accompany the goods or to be used or provided in some other manner in relation to the goods, and for securing that inappropriate information is not given in relation to goods either by means of misleading marks or otherwise;

(j) for prohibiting persons from supplying, or from offering to supply, agreeing to supply, exposing for supply or possessing for supply, goods to which this section applies and component parts and raw materials for such goods;

(k) for requiring information to be given to any such person as may be determined by or under the regulations for the purpose of enabling that person to exercise any function conferred on him by the regulations.

(3) Without prejudice as aforesaid, safety regulations may contain provision—

(a) for requiring persons on whom functions are conferred by or under section 27 below to have regard, in exercising their functions so far as relating to any provision of safety regulations, to matters specified in a direction issued by the Secretary of State with respect to that provision;

(b) for securing that a person shall not be guilty of an offence under section

12 below unless it is shown that the goods in question do not conform to a particular standard;

(c) for securing that proceedings for such an offence are not brought in England and Wales except by or with the consent of the Secretary of State or the Director of Public Prosecutions;

(d) for securing that proceedings for such an offence are not brought in Northern Ireland except by or with the consent of the Secretary of State or the Director of Public Prosecutions for Northern Ireland;

(e) for enabling a magistrates' court in England and Wales or Northern Ireland to try an information or, in Northern Ireland, a complaint in respect of such an offence if the information was laid or the complaint made within twelve months from the time when the offence was committed;

(f) for enabling summary proceedings for such an offence to be brought in Scotland at any time within twelve months from the time when the offence was committed; and

(g) for determining the persons by whom, and the manner in which, anything required to be done by or under the regulations is to be done.

(4) Safety regulations shall not provide for any contravention of the regulations to be an offence.

(5) Where the Secretary of State proposes to make safety regulations it shall be his duty before he makes them—

(a) to consult such organisations as appear to him to be representative of interests substantially affected by the proposal;

(b) to consult such other persons as he considers appropriate; and

(c) in the case of proposed regulations relating to goods suitable for use at work, to consult the Health and Safety Commission in relation to the application of the proposed regulations to Great Britain;

but the preceding provisions of this subsection shall not apply in the case of regulations which provide for the regulations to cease to have effect at the end of a period of not more than twelve months beginning with the day on which they come into force and which contain a statement that it appears to the Secretary of State that the need to protect the public requires that the regulations should be made without delay.

(6) The power to make safety regulations shall be exercisable by statutory instrument subject to annulment in pursuance of a resolution of either House of Parliament and shall include power—

(a) to make different provision for different cases; and

(b) to make such supplemental, consequential and transitional provision as the Secretary of State considers appropriate.

(7) This section applies to any goods other than—

(a) growing crops and things comprised in land by virtue of being attached to it;

(b) water, food, feeding stuff and fertiliser;

(c) gas which is, is to be or has been supplied by a person authorised to supply it by or under section 6, 7 or 8 of the Gas Act 1986 (authorisation of supply of gas through pipes);

(d) controlled drugs and licensed medicinal products.

12. Offences against the safety regulations

(1) Where safety regulations prohibit a person from supplying or offering or agreeing to supply any goods or from exposing or possessing any goods for supply, that person shall be guilty of an offence if he contravenes the prohibition.

(2) Where safety regulations require a person who makes or processes any goods in the course of carrying on a business—

   (a) to carry out a particular test or use a particular procedure in connection with the making or processing of the goods with a view to ascertaining whether the goods satisfy any requirements of such regulations; or
   (b) to deal or not to deal in a particular way with a quantity of the goods of which the whole or part does not satisfy such a test or does not satisfy standards connected with such a procedure,

that person shall be guilty of an offence if he does not comply with the requirement.

(3) If a person contravenes a provision of safety regulations which prohibits or requires the provision, by means of a mark or otherwise, of information of a particular kind in relation to goods, he shall be guilty of an offence.

(4) Where safety regulations require any person to give information to another for the purpose of enabling that other to exercise any function, that person shall be guilty of an offence if—

   (a) he fails without reasonable cause to comply with the requirement; or
   (b) in giving the information which is required of him—
      (i) he makes any statement which he knows is false in a material particular; or
      (ii) he recklessly makes any statement which is false in a material particular.

(5) A person guilty of an offence under this section shall be liable on summary conviction to imprisonment for a term not exceeding six months or to a fine not exceeding level 5 on the standard scale or to both.

13. Prohibition notices and notices to warn

(1) The Secretary of State may—

   (a) serve on any person a notice ('a prohibition notice') prohibiting that person, except with the consent of the Secretary of State, from supplying, or from offering to supply, agreeing to supply, exposing for supply or possessing for supply, any relevant goods which the Secretary of State considers are unsafe and which are described in the notice;
   (b) serve on any person a notice ('a notice to warn') requiring that person at his own expense to publish, in a form and manner and on occasions specified in the notice, a warning about any relevant goods which the Secretary of State considers are unsafe, which that person supplies or has supplied and which are described in the notice.

(2) Schedule 2 to this Act shall have effect with respect to prohibition notices and notices to warn; and the Secretary of State may by regulations make provision specifying the manner in which information is to be given to any person under that Schedule.

(3) A consent given by the Secretary of State for the purposes of a prohibition

notice may impose such conditions on the doing of anything for which the consent is required as the Secretary of State considers appropriate.

(4) A person who contravenes a prohibition notice or a notice to warn shall be guilty of an offence and liable on summary conviction to imprisonment for a term not exceeding six months or to a fine not exceeding level 5 on the standard scale or to both.

(5) The power to make regulations under subsection (2) above shall be exercisable by statutory instrument subject to annulment in pursuance of a resolution of either House of Parliament and shall include power—

(a) to make different provision for different cases; and
(b) to make such supplemental, consequential and transitional provision as the Secretary of State considers appropriate.

(6) In this section 'relevant goods' means—

(a) in relation to a prohibition notice, any goods to which section 11 above applies; and
(b) in relation to a notice to warn, any goods to which that section applies or any growing crops or things comprised in land by virtue of being attached to it.

14. Suspension notices

(1) Where an enforcement authority has reasonable grounds for suspecting that any safety provision has been contravened in relation to any goods, the authority may serve a notice ('a suspension notice') prohibiting the person on whom it is served, for such period ending not more than six months after the date of the notice as is specified therein, from doing any of the following things without the consent of the authority, that is to say, supplying the goods, offering to supply them, agreeing to supply them or exposing them for supply.

(2) A suspension notice served by an enforcement authority in respect of any goods shall—

(a) describe the goods in a manner sufficient to identify them;
(b) set out the grounds on which the authority suspects that a safety provision has been contravened in relation to the goods; and
(c) state that, and the manner in which, the person on whom the notice is served may appeal against the notice under section 15 below.

(3) A suspension notice served by an enforcement authority for the purpose of prohibiting a person for any period from doing the things mentioned in subsection (1) above in relation to any goods may also require that person to keep the authority informed of the whereabouts throughout that period of any of those goods in which he has an interest.

(4) Where a suspension notice has been served on any person in respect of any goods, no further such notice shall be served on that person in respect of the same goods unless—

(a) proceedings against that person for an offence in respect of a contravention in relation to the goods of a safety provision (not being an offence under this section); or
(b) proceedings for the forfeiture of the goods under section 16 or 17 below,

are pending at the end of the period specified in the first-mentioned notice.

(5) A consent given by an enforcement authority for the purposes of subsection (1) above may impose such conditions on the doing of anything for which the consent is required as the authority considers appropriate.

(6) Any person who contravenes a suspension notice shall be guilty of an offence and liable on summary conviction to imprisonment for a term not exceeding six months or to a fine not exceeding level 5 on the standard scale or to both.

(7) Where an enforcement authority serves a suspension notice in respect of any goods, the authority shall be liable to pay compensation to any person having an interest in the goods in respect of any loss or damage caused by reason of the service of the notice if—

(a) there has been no contravention in relation to the goods of any safety provision; and
(b) the exercise of the power is not attributable to any neglect or default by that person.

(8) Any disputed question as to the right to or the amount of any compensation payable under this section shall be determined by arbitration or, in Scotland, by a single arbiter appointed, failing agreement between the parties, by the sheriff.

15. Appeals against suspension notices

(1) Any person having an interest in any goods in respect of which a suspension notice is for the time being in force may apply for an order setting aside the notice.

(2) An application under this section may be made—

(a) to any magistrates' court in which proceedings have been brought in England and Wales or Northern Ireland—
  (i) for an offence in respect of a contravention in relation to the goods of any safety provision; or
  (ii) for the forfeiture of the goods under section 16 below;
(b) where no such proceedings have been so brought, by way of complaint to a magistrates' court; or
(c) in Scotland, by summary application to the sheriff.

(3) On an application under this section to a magistrates' court in England and Wales or Northern Ireland the court shall make an order setting aside the suspension notice only if the court is satisfied that there has been no contravention in relation to the goods of any safety provision.

(4) On an application under this section to the sheriff he shall make an order setting aside the suspension notice only if he is satisfied that at the date of making the order—

(a) proceedings for an offence in respect of a contravention in relation to the goods of any safety provision; or
(b) proceedings for the forfeiture of the goods under section 17 below,

have not been brought or, having been brought, have been concluded.

(5) Any person aggrieved by an order made under this section by a magistrates' court in England and Wales or Northern Ireland, or by a decision of such a court not to make such an order, may appeal against that order or decision—

(a) in England and Wales, to the Crown Court;
(b) in Northern Ireland, to the county court;

and an order so made may contain such provision as appears to the court to be appropriate for delaying the coming into force of the order pending the making and determination of any appeal (including any application under section 111 of the Magistrates' Courts Act 1980 or Article 146 of the Magistrates' Courts (Northern Ireland) Order 1981 (statement of case)).

16. Forfeiture: England and Wales and Northern Ireland

(1) An enforcement authority in England and Wales or Northern Ireland may apply under this section for an order for the forfeiture of any goods on the grounds that there has been a contravention in relation to the goods of a safety provision.

(2) An application under this section may be made—

(a) where proceedings have been brought in a magistrates' court for an offence in respect of a contravention in relation to some or all of the goods of any safety provision, to that court;
(b) where an application with respect to some or all of the goods has been made to a magistrates' court under section 15 above or section 33 below, to that court; and
(c) where no application for the forfeiture of the goods has been made under paragraph (a) or (b) above, by way of complaint to a magistrates' court.

(3) On an application under this section the court shall make an order for the forfeiture of any goods only if it is satisfied that there has been a contravention in relation to the goods of a safety provision.

(4) For the avoidance of doubt it is declared that a court may infer for the purposes of this section that there has been a contravention in relation to any goods of a safety provision if it is satisfied that any such provision has been contravened in relation to goods which are representative of those goods (whether by reason of being of the same design or part of the same consignment or batch or otherwise).

(5) Any person aggrieved by an order made under this section by a magistrates' court, or by a decision of such a court not to make such an order, may appeal against that order or decision—

(a) in England and Wales, to the Crown Court;
(b) in Northern Ireland, to the county court;

and an order so made may contain such provision as appears to the court to be appropriate for delaying the coming into force of the order pending the making and determination of any appeal (including any application under section 111 of the Magistrates' Courts Act 1980 or Article 146 of the Magistrates' Courts (Northern Ireland) Order 1981 (statement of case)).

(6) Subject to subsection (7) below, where any goods are forfeited under this section they shall be destroyed in accordance with such directions as the court may give.

(7) On making an order under this section a magistrates' court may, if it considers it appropriate to do so, direct that the goods to which the order relates

shall (instead of being destroyed) be released, to such person as the court may specify, on condition that that person—

 (a) does not supply those goods to any person otherwise than as mentioned in section 46(7)(a) or (b) below; and
 (b) complies with any order to pay costs or expenses (including any order under section 35 below) which has been made against that person in the proceedings for the order for forfeiture.

17. Forfeiture: Scotland

(1) In Scotland a sheriff may make an order for forfeiture of any goods in relation to which there has been a contravention of a safety provision—

 (a) on an application by the procurator-fiscal made in the manner specified in section 310 of the Criminal Procedure (Scotland) Act 1975; or
 (b) where a person is convicted of any offence in respect of any such contravention, in addition to any other penalty which the sheriff may impose.

(2) The procurator-fiscal making an application under subsection (1)(a) above shall serve on any person appearing to him to be the owner of, or otherwise to have an interest in, the goods to which the application relates a copy of the application, together with a notice giving him the opportunity to appear at the hearing of the application to show cause why the goods should not be forfeited.

(3) Service under subsection (2) above shall be carried out, and such service may be proved, in the manner specified for citation of an accused in summary proceedings under the Criminal Procedure (Scotland) Act 1975.

(4) Any person upon whom notice is served under subsection (2) above and any other person claiming to be the owner of, or otherwise to have an interest in, goods to which an application under this section relates shall be entitled to appear at the hearing of the application to show cause why the goods should not be forfeited.

(5) The sheriff shall not make an order following an application under subsection (1)(a) above—

 (a) if any person on whom notice is served under subsection (2) above does not appear, unless service of the notice on that person is proved; or
 (b) if no notice under subsection (2) above has been served, unless the court is satisfied that in the circumstances it was reasonable not to serve notice on any person.

(6) The sheriff shall make an order under this section only if he is satisfied that there has been a contravention in relation to those goods of a safety provision.

(7) For the avoidance of doubt it is declared that the sheriff may infer for the purposes of this section that there has been a contravention in relation to any goods of a safety provision if he is satisfied that any such provision has been contravened in relation to any goods which are representative of those goods (whether by reason of being of the same design or part of the same consignment or batch or otherwise).

(8) Where an order for the forfeiture of any goods is made following an

application by the procurator-fiscal under subsection (1)(a) above, any person who appeared, or was entitled to appear, to show cause why goods should not be forfeited may, within twenty-one days of the making of the order, appeal to the High Court by Bill of Suspension on the ground of an alleged miscarriage of justice; and section 452(4)(a) to (e) of the Criminal Procedure (Scotland) Act 1975 shall apply to an appeal under this subsection as it applies to a stated case under Part II of that Act.

(9) An order following an application under subsection (1)(a) above shall not take effect—

(a) until the end of the period of twenty-one days beginning with the day after the day on which the order is made; or

(b) if an appeal is made under subsection (8) above within that period, until the appeal is determined or abandoned.

(10) An order under subsection (1)(b) above shall not take effect—

(a) until the end of the period within which an appeal against the order could be brought under the Criminal Procedure (Scotland) Act 1975; or

(b) if an appeal is made within that period, until the appeal is determined or abandoned.

(11) Subject to subsection (12) below, goods forfeited under this section shall be destroyed in accordance with such directions as the sheriff may give.

(12) If he thinks fit, the sheriff may direct that the goods be released, to such person as he may specify, on condition that that person does not supply those goods to any other person otherwise than as mentioned in section 46(7)(a) or (b) below.

18. Power to obtain information

(1) If the Secretary of State considers that, for the purpose of deciding whether—

(a) to make, vary or revoke any safety regulations; or

(b) to serve, vary or revoke a prohibition notice; or

(c) to serve or revoke a notice to warn,

he requires information which another person is likely to be able to furnish, the Secretary of State may serve on the other person a notice under this section.

(2) A notice served on any person under this section may require that person—

(a) to furnish to the Secretary of State, within a period specified in the notice, such information as is so specified;

(b) to produce such records as are specified in the notice at a time and place so specified and to permit a person appointed by the Secretary of State for the purpose to take copies of the records at that time and place.

(3) A person shall be guilty of an offence if he—

(a) fails, without reasonable cause, to comply with a notice served on him under this section; or

(b) in purporting to comply with a requirement which by virtue of paragraph (a) of subsection (2) above is contained in such a notice—

(i) furnishes information which he knows is false in a material particular; or

(ii) recklessly furnishes information which is false in a material particular.

(4) A person guilty of an offence under subsection (3) above shall—

(a) in the case of an offence under paragraph (a) of that subsection, be liable on summary conviction to a fine not exceeding level 5 on the standard scale; and

(b) in the case of an offence under paragraph (b) of that subsection be liable—

(i) on conviction on indictment, to a fine;

(ii) on summary conviction, to a fine not exceeding the statutory maximum.

19. Interpretation of Part II

(1) In this Part—

'controlled drug' means a controlled drug within the meaning of the Misuse of Drugs Act 1971;

'feeding stuff' and 'fertiliser' have the same meanings as in Part IV of the Agriculture Act 1970;

'food' does not include anything containing tobacco but, subject to that, has the same meaning as in the Food Act 1984 or, in relation to Northern Ireland, the same meaning as in the Food and Drugs Act (Northern Ireland) 1958;

'licensed medicinal product' means—

(a) any medicinal product within the meaning of the Medicines Act 1968 in respect of which a product licence within the meaning of that Act is for the time being in force; or

(b) any other article or substance in respect of which any such licence is for the time being in force in pursuance of an order under section 104 or 105 of that Act (application of Act to other articles and substances);

'safe', in relation to any goods, means such that there is no risk, or no risk apart from one reduced to a minimum, that any of the following will (whether immediately or after a definite or indefinite period) cause the death of, or any personal injury to, any person whatsoever, that is to say—

(a) the goods;
(b) the keeping, use or consumption of the goods;
(c) the assembly of any of the goods which are, or are to be, supplied unassembled;
(d) any emission or leakage from the goods or, as a result of the keeping, use or consumption of the goods, from anything else; or
(e) reliance on the accuracy of any measurement, calculation or other reading made by or by means of the goods,

and 'safer' and 'unsafe' shall be construed accordingly;

'tobacco' includes any tobacco product within the meaning of the Tobacco Products Duty Act 1979 and any article or substance containing tobacco and intended for oral or nasal use.

(2) In the definition of 'safe' in subsection (1) above, references to the keeping, use or consumption of any goods are references to—

(*a*) the keeping, use or consumption of the goods by the persons by whom, and in all or any of the ways or circumstances in which, they might reasonably be expected to be kept, used or consumed; and

(*b*) the keeping, use or consumption of the goods either alone or in conjunction with other goods in conjunction with which they might reasonably be expected to be kept, used or consumed.

Part III

Misleading Price Indications

20. Offence of giving misleading indication

(1) Subject to the following provisions of this Part, a person shall be guilty of an offence if, in the course of any business of his, he gives (by any means whatever) to any consumers an indication which is misleading as to the price at which any goods, services, accommodation or facilities are available (whether generally or from particular persons).

(2) Subject as aforesaid, a person shall be guilty of an offence if—

(*a*) in the course of any business of his, he has given an indication to any consumers which, after it was given, has become misleading as mentioned in subsection (1) above; and

(*b*) some or all of those consumers might reasonably be expected to rely on the indication at a time after it has become misleading; and

(*c*) he fails to take all such steps as are reasonable to prevent those consumers from relying on the indication.

(3) For the purposes of this section it shall be immaterial—

(*a*) whether the person who gives or gave the indication is or was acting on his own behalf or on behalf of another;

(*b*) whether or not that person is the person, or included among the persons, from whom the goods, services, accommodation or facilities are available; and

(*c*) whether the indication is or has become misleading in relation to all the consumers to whom it is or was given or only in relation to some of them.

(4) A person guilty of an offence under subsection (1) or (2) above shall be liable—

(*a*) on conviction on indictment, to a fine;

(*b*) on summary conviction, to a fine not exceeding the statutory maximum.

(5) No prosecution for an offence under subsection (1) or (2) above shall be brought after whichever is the earlier of the following, that is to say—

(*a*) the end of the period of three years beginning with the day on which the offence was committed; and

(*b*) the end of the period of one year beginning with the day on which

Consumer Protection Act 1987

the person bringing the prosecution discovered that the offence had been committed.

(6) In this Part—

'consumer'—

(*a*) in relation to any goods, means any person who might wish to be supplied with the goods for his own private use or consumption;

(*b*) in relation to any services or facilities, means any person who might wish to be provided with the services or facilities otherwise than for the purposes of any business of his; and

(*c*) in relation to any accommodation, means any person who might wish to occupy the accommodation otherwise than for the purposes of any business of his;

'price', in relation to any goods, services, accommodation or facilities, means—

(*a*) the aggregate of the sums required to be paid by a consumer for or otherwise in respect of the supply of the goods or the provision of the services, accommodation or facilities; or

(*b*) except in section 21 below, any method which will be or has been applied for the purpose of determining that aggregate.

21. Meaning of 'misleading'

(1) For the purposes of section 20 above an indication given to any consumers is misleading as to a price if what is conveyed by the indication, or what those consumers might reasonably be expected to infer from the indication or any omission from it, includes any of the following, that is to say—

(*a*) that the price is less than in fact it is;

(*b*) that the applicability of the price does not depend on facts or circumstances on which its applicability does in fact depend;

(*c*) that the price covers matters in respect of which an additional charge is in fact made;

(*d*) that a person who in fact has no such expectation—

(i) expects the price to be increased or reduced (whether or not at a particular time or by a particular amount); or

(ii) expects the price, or the price as increased or reduced, to be maintained (whether or not for a particular period); or

(*e*) that the facts or circumstances by reference to which the consumers might reasonably be expected to judge the validity of any relevant comparison made or implied by the indication are not what in fact they are.

(2) For the purposes of section 20 above, an indication given to any consumers is misleading as to a method of determining a price if what is conveyed by the indication, or what those consumers might reasonably be expected to infer from the indication or any omission from it, includes any of the following, that is to say—

(*a*) that the method is not what in fact it is;

(*b*) that the applicability of the method does not depend on facts or circumstances on which its applicability does in fact depend;

(c) that the method takes into account matters in respect of which an additional charge will in fact be made;
(d) that a person who in fact has no such expectation—
   (i) expects the method to be altered (whether or not at a particular time or in a particular respect); or
   (ii) expects the method, or that method as altered, to remain unaltered (whether or not for a particular period); or
(e) that the facts or circumstances by reference to which the consumers might reasonably be expected to judge the validity of any relevant comparison made or implied by the indication are not what in fact they are.

(3) For the purposes of subsections (1)(e) and (2)(e) above a comparison is a relevant comparison in relation to a price or method of determining a price if it is made between that price or that method, or any price which has been or may be determined by that method, and—

(a) any price or value which is stated or implied to be, to have been or to be likely to be attributed or attributable to the goods, services, accommodation or facilities in question or to any other goods, services, accommodation or facilities; or
(b) any method, or other method, which is stated or implied to be, to have been or to be likely to be applied or applicable for the determination of the price or value of the goods, services, accommodation or facilities in question or of the price or value of any other goods, services, accommodation or facilities.

22. Application to provision of services and facilities

(1) Subject to the following provisions of this section, references in this Part to services or facilities are references to any services or facilities whatever including, in particular—

(a) the provision of credit or of banking or insurance services and the provision of facilities incidental to the provision of such services;
(b) the purchase or sale of foreign currency;
(c) the supply of electricity;
(d) the provision of a place, other than on a highway, for the parking of a motor vehicle;
(e) the making of arrangements for a person to put or keep a caravan on any land other than arrangements by virtue of which that person may occupy the caravan as his only or main residence.

(2) References in this Part to services shall not include references to services provided to an employer under a contract of employment.

(3) References in this Part to services or facilities shall not include references to services or facilities which are provided by an authorised person or appointed representative in the course of the carrying on of an investment business.

(4) In relation to a service consisting in the purchase or sale of foreign currency, references in this Part to the method by which the price of the service is determined shall include references to the rate of exchange.

(5) In this section—

Consumer Protection Act 1987

'appointed representative', 'authorised person' and 'investment business' have the same meanings as in the Financial Services Act 1986;

'caravan' has the same meaning as in the Caravan Sites and Control of Development Act 1960;

'contract of employment' and 'employer' have the same meanings as in the Employment Protection (Consolidation) Act 1978;

'credit' has the same meaning as in the Consumer Credit Act 1974.

23. Application to provision of accommodation etc.

(1) Subject to subsection (2) below, references in this Part to accommodation or facilities being available shall not include references to accommodation or facilities being available to be provided by means of the creation or disposal of an interest in land except where—

- (*a*) the person who is to create or dispose of the interest will do so in the course of any business of his; and
- (*b*) the interest to be created or disposed of is a relevant interest in a new dwelling and is to be created or disposed of for the purpose of enabling that dwelling to be occupied as a residence, or one of the residences, of the person acquiring the interest.

(2) Subsection (1) above shall not prevent the application of any provision of this Part in relation to—

- (*a*) the supply of any goods as part of the same transaction as any creation or disposal of an interest in land; or
- (*b*) the provision of any services or facilities for the purposes of, or in connection with, any transaction for the creation or disposal of such an interest.

(3) In this section—

'new dwelling' means any building or part of a building in Great Britain which—

- (*a*) has been constructed or adapted to be occupied as a residence; and
- (*b*) has not previously been so occupied or has been so occupied only with other premises or as more than one residence, and includes any yard, garden, out-houses or appurtenances which belong to that building or part or are to be enjoyed with it;

'relevant interest'—

- (*a*) in relation to a new dwelling in England and Wales, means the freehold estate in the dwelling or a leasehold interest in the dwelling for a term of years absolute of more than twenty-one years, not being a term of which twenty-one years or less remains unexpired;
- (*b*) in relation to a new dwelling in Scotland, means the dominium utile of the land comprising the dwelling, or a leasehold interest in the dwelling where twenty-one years or more remains unexpired.

24. Defences

(1) In any proceedings against a person for an offence under subsection (1)

or (2) of section 20 above in respect of any indication it shall be a defence for that person to show that his acts or omissions were authorised for the purposes of this subsection by regulations made under section 26 below.

(2) In proceedings against a person for an offence under subsection (1) or (2) of section 20 above in respect of an indication published in a book, newspaper, magazine, film or radio or television broadcast or in a programme included in a cable programme service, it shall be a defence for that person to show that the indication was not contained in an advertisement.

(3) In proceedings against a person for an offence under subsection (1) or (2) of section 20 above in respect of an indication published in an advertisement it shall be a defence for that person to show that—

(a) he is a person who carries on a business of publishing or arranging for the publication of advertisements;
(b) he received the advertisement for publication in the ordinary course of that business; and
(c) at the time of publication he did not know and had no grounds for suspecting that the publication would involve the commission of the offence.

(4) In any proceedings against a person for an offence under subsection (1) of section 20 above in respect of any indication, it shall be a defence for that person to show that—

(a) the indication did not relate to the availability from him of any goods, services, accommodation or facilities;
(b) a price had been recommended to every person from whom the goods, services, accommodation or facilities were indicated as being available;
(c) the indication related to that price and was misleading as to that price only by reason of a failure by any person to follow the recommendation; and
(d) it was reasonable for the person who gave the indication to assume that the recommendation was for the most part being followed.

(5) The provisions of this section are without prejudice to the provisions of section 39 below.

(6) In this section—

'advertisement' includes a catalogue, a circular and a price list;

'cable programme service' has the same meaning as in the Cable and Broadcasting Act 1984.

25. Code of practice

(1) The Secretary of State may, after consulting the Director General of Fair Trading and such other persons as the Secretary of State considers it appropriate to consult, by order approve any code of practice issued (whether by the Secretary of State or another person) for the purpose of—

(a) giving practical guidance with respect to any of the requirements of section 20 above; and
(b) promoting what appear to the Secretary of State to be desirable practices as to the circumstances and manner in which any person gives an indication as to the price at which any goods, services, accommodation

or facilities are available or indicates any other matter in respect of which any such indication may be misleading.

(2) A contravention of a code of practice approved under this section shall not of itself give rise to any criminal or civil liability, but in any proceedings against any person for an offence under section 20(1) or (2) above—

(*a*) any contravention by that person of such a code may be relied on in relation to any matter for the purpose of establishing that that person committed the offence or of negativing any defence; and

(*b*) compliance by that person with such a code may be relied on in relation to any matter for the purpose of showing that the commission of the offence by that person has not been established or that that person has a defence.

(3) Where the Secretary of State approves a code of practice under this section he may, after such consultation as is mentioned in subsection (1) above, at any time by order—

(*a*) approve any modification of the code; or
(*b*) withdraw his approval;

and references in subsection (2) above to a code of practice approved under this section shall be construed accordingly.

(4) The power to make an order under this section shall be exercisable by statutory instrument subject to annulment in pursuance of a resolution of either House of Parliament.

26. Power to make regulations

(1) The Secretary of State may, after consulting the Director General of Fair Trading and such other persons as the Secretary of State considers it appropriate to consult, by regulations make provision—

(*a*) for the purpose of regulating the circumstances and manner in which any person—
  (i) gives any indication as to the price at which any goods, services, accommodation or facilities will be or are available or have been supplied or provided; or
  (ii) indicates any other matter in respect of which any such indication may be misleading;
(*b*) for the purpose of facilitating the enforcement of the provisions of section 20 above or of any regulations made under this section.

(2) The Secretary of State shall not make regulations by virtue of subsection (1)(*a*) above except in relation to—

(*a*) indications given by persons in the course of business; and
(*b*) such indications given otherwise than in the course of business as—
  (i) are given by or on behalf of persons by whom accommodation is provided to others by means of leases or licences; and
  (ii) relate to goods, services or facilities supplied or provided to those others in connection with the provision of the accommodation.

(3) Without prejudice to the generality of subsection (1) above, regulations under this section may—

(*a*) prohibit an indication as to a price from referring to such matters as may be prescribed by the regulations;
(*b*) require an indication as to a price or other matter to be accompanied or supplemented by such explanation or such additional information as may be prescribed by the regulations;
(*c*) require information or explanations with respect to a price or other matter to be given to an officer of an enforcement authority and to authorise such an officer to require such information or explanations to be given;
(*d*) require any information or explanation provided for the purposes of any regulations made by virtue of paragraph (b) or (c) above to be accurate;
(*e*) prohibit the inclusion in indications as to a price or other matter of statements that the indications are not to be relied upon;
(*f*) provide that expressions used in any indication as to a price or other matter shall be construed in a particular way for the purposes of this Part;
(*g*) provide that a contravention of any provision of the regulations shall constitute a criminal offence punishable—
   (i) on conviction on indictment, by a fine;
   (ii) on summary conviction, by a fine not exceeding the statutory maximum;
(*h*) apply any provision of this Act which relates to a criminal offence to an offence created by virtue of paragraph (*g*) above.

(4) The power to make regulations under this section shall be exercisable by statutory instrument subject to annulment in pursuance of a resolution of either House of Parliament and shall include power—

(*a*) to make different provision for different cases; and
(*b*) to make such supplemental, consequential and transitional provision as the Secretary of State considers appropriate.

(5) In this section 'lease' includes a sub-lease and an agreement for a lease and a statutory tenancy (within the meaning of the Landlord and Tenant Act 1985 or the Rent (Scotland) Act 1984).

Part IV

Enforcement of Parts II and III

27. Enforcement

(1) Subject to the following provisions of this section—

(*a*) it shall be the duty of every weights and measures authority in Great Britain to enforce within their area the safety provisions and the provisions made by or under Part III of this Act; and
(*b*) it shall be the duty of every district council in Northern Ireland to enforce within their area the safety provisions.

(2) The Secretary of State may by regulations—

(*a*) wholly or partly transfer any duty imposed by subsection (1) above on a weights and measures authority or a district council in Northern Ireland to such other person who has agreed to the transfer as is specified in the regulations;

(b) relieve such an authority or council of any such duty so far as it is exercisable in relation to such goods as may be described in the regulations.

(3) The power to make regulations under subsection (2) above shall be exercisable by statutory instrument subject to annulment in pursuance of a resolution of either House of Parliament and shall include power—

(a) to make different provision for different cases; and
(b) to make such supplemental, consequential and transitional provision as the Secretary of State considers appropriate.

(4) Nothing in this section shall authorise any weights and measures authority, or any person on whom functions are conferred by regulations under subsection (2) above, to bring proceedings in Scotland for an offence.

28. Test purchases

(1) An enforcement authority shall have power, for the purpose of ascertaining whether any safety provision or any provision made by or under Part III of this Act has been contravened in relation to any goods, services, accommodation or facilities—

(a) to make, or to authorise an officer of the authority to make, any purchase of any goods; or
(b) to secure, or to authorise an officer of the authority to secure, the provision of any services, accommodation or facilities.

(2) Where—

(a) any goods purchased under this section by or on behalf of an enforcement authority are submitted to a test; and
(b) the test leads to—
    (i) the bringing of proceedings for an offence in respect of a contravention in relation to the goods of any safety provision or of any provision made by or under Part III of this Act or for the forfeiture of the goods under section 16 or 17 above; or
    (ii) the serving of a suspension notice in respect of any goods; and
(c) the authority is requested to do so and it is practicable for the authority to comply with the request,

the authority shall allow the person from whom the goods were purchased or any person who is a party to the proceedings or has an interest in any goods to which the notice relates to have the goods tested.

(3) The Secretary of State may by regulations provide that any test of goods purchased under this section by or on behalf of an enforcement authority shall—

(a) be carried out at the expense of the authority in a manner and by a person prescribed by or determined under the regulations; or
(b) be carried out either as mentioned in paragraph (a) above or by the authority in a manner prescribed by the regulations.

(4) The power to make regulations under subsection (3) above shall be exercisable by statutory instrument subject to annulment in pursuance of a resolution of either House of Parliament and shall include power—

(a) to make different provision for different cases; and

(*b*) to make such supplemental, consequential and transitional provision as the Secretary of State considers appropriate.

(5) Nothing in this section shall authorise the acquisition by or on behalf of an enforcement authority of any interest in land.

29. Powers of search etc.

(1) Subject to the following provisions of this Part, a duly authorised officer of an enforcement authority may at any reasonable hour and on production, if required, of his credentials exercise any of the powers conferred by the following provisions of this section.

(2) The officer may, for the purpose of ascertaining whether there has been any contravention of any safety provision or of any provision made by or under Part III of this Act, inspect any goods and enter any premises other than premises occupied only as a person's residence.

(3) The officer may, for the purpose of ascertaining whether there has been any contravention of any safety provision, examine any procedure (including any arrangements for carrying out a test) connected with the production of any goods.

(4) If the officer has reasonable grounds for suspecting that any goods are manufactured or imported goods which have not been supplied in the United Kingdom since they were manufactured or imported he may—

(*a*) for the purpose of ascertaining whether there has been any contravention of any safety provision in relation to the goods, require any person carrying on a business, or employed in connection with a business, to produce any records relating to the business;
(*b*) for the purpose of ascertaining (by testing or otherwise) whether there has been any such contravention, seize and detain the goods;
(*c*) take copies of, or of any entry in, any records produced by virtue of paragraph (*a*) above.

(5) If the officer has reasonable grounds for suspecting that there has been a contravention in relation to any goods of any safety provision or of any provision made by or under Part III of this Act, he may—

(*a*) for the purpose of ascertaining whether there has been any such contravention, require any person carrying on a business, or employed in connection with a business, to produce any records relating to the business;
(*b*) for the purpose of ascertaining (by testing or otherwise) whether there has been any such contravention, seize and detain the goods;
(*c*) take copies of, or of any entry in, any records produced by virtue of paragraph (*a*) above.

(6) The officer may seize and detain—

(*a*) any goods or records which he has reasonable grounds for believing may be required as evidence in proceedings for an offence in respect of a contravention of any safety provision or of any provision made by or under Part III of this Act;
(*b*) any goods which he has reasonable grounds for suspecting may be liable to be forfeited under section 16 or 17 above.

(7) If and to the extent that it is reasonably necessary to do so to prevent a contravention of any safety provision or of any provision made by or under Part III of this Act, the officer may, for the purpose of exercising his power under subsection (4), (5) or (6) above to seize any goods or records—

(a) require any person having authority to do so to open any container or to open any vending machine; and
(b) himself open or break open any such container or machine where a requirement made under paragraph (a) above in relation to the container or machine has not been complied with.

30. Provisions supplemental to s 29

(1) An officer seizing any goods or records under section 29 above shall inform the following persons that the goods or records have been so seized, that is to say—

(a) the person from whom they are seized; and
(b) in the case of imported goods seized on any premises under the control of the Commissioners of Customs and Excise, the importer of those goods (within the meaning of the Customs and Excise Management Act 1979).

(2) If a justice of the peace—

(a) is satisfied by any written information on oath that there are reasonable grounds for believing either—

(i) that any goods or records which any officer has power to inspect under section 29 above are on any premises and that their inspection is likely to disclose evidence that there has been a contravention of any safety provision or of any provision made by or under Part III of this Act; or
(ii) that such a contravention has taken place, is taking place or is about to take place on any premises; and

(b) is also satisfied by any such information either

(i) that admission to the premises has been or is likely to be refused and that notice of intention to apply for a warrant under this subsection has been given to the occupier; or
(ii) that an application for admission, or the giving of such a notice, would defeat the object of the entry or that the premises are unoccupied or that the occupier is temporarily absent and it might defeat the object of the entry to await his return,

the justice may by warrant under his hand, which shall continue in force for a period of one month, authorise any officer of an enforcement authority to enter the premises, if need be by force.

(3) An officer entering any premises by virtue of section 29 above or a warrant under subsection (2) above may take with him such other persons and such equipment as may appear to him necessary.

(4) On leaving any premises which a person is authorised to enter by a warrant under subsection (2) above, that person shall, if the premises are unoccupied or the occupier is temporarily absent, leave the premises as effectively secured against trespassers as he found them.

(5) If any person who is not an officer of an enforcement authority purports

to act as such under section 29 above or this section he shall be guilty of an offence and liable on summary conviction to a fine not exceeding level 5 on the standard scale.

(6) Where any goods seized by an officer under section 29 above are submitted to a test, the officer shall inform the persons mentioned in subsection (1) above of the result of the test and, if—

    (a) proceedings are brought for an offence in respect of a contravention in relation to the goods of any safety provision or of any provision made by or under Part III of this Act or for the forfeiture of the goods under section 16 or 17 above, or a suspension notice is served in respect of any goods; and

    (b) the officer is requested to do so and it is practicable to comply with the request,

the officer shall allow any person who is a party to the proceedings or, as the case may be, has an interest in the goods to which the notice relates to have the goods tested.

(7) The Secretary of State may by regulations provide that any test of goods seized under section 29 above by an officer of an enforcement authority shall—

    (a) be carried out at the expense of the authority in a manner and by a person prescribed by or determined under the regulations; or

    (b) be carried out either as mentioned in paragraph (a) above or by the authority in a manner prescribed by the regulations.

(8) The power to make regulations under subsection (7) above shall be exercisable by statutory instrument subject to annulment in pursuance of a resolution of either House of Parliament and shall include power—

    (a) to make different provision for different cases; and

    (b) to make such supplemental, consequential and transitional provision as the Secretary of State considers appropriate.

(9) In the application of this section to Scotland, the reference in subsection (2) above to a justice of the peace shall include a reference to a sheriff and the references to written information on oath shall be construed as references to evidence on oath.

(10) In the application of this section to Northern Ireland, the references in subsection (2) above to any information on oath shall be construed as references to any complaint on oath.

31. Power of customs officer to detain goods

(1) A customs officer may, for the purpose of facilitating the exercise by an enforcement authority or officer of such an authority of any functions conferred on the authority or officer by or under Part II of this Act, or by or under this Part in its application for the purposes of the safety provisions, seize any imported goods and detain them for not more than two working days.

(2) Anything seized and detained under this section shall be dealt with during the period of its detention in such manner as the Commissioners of Customs and Excise may direct.

(3) In subsection (1) above the reference to two working days is a reference to a period of forty-eight hours calculated from the time when the goods in

question are seized but disregarding so much of any period as falls on a Saturday or Sunday or on Christmas Day, Good Friday or a day which is a bank holiday under the Banking and Financial Dealings Act 1971 in the part of the United Kingdom where the goods are seized.

(4) In this section and section 32 below 'customs officer' means any officer within the meaning of the Customs and Excise Management Act 1979.

32. Obstruction of authorised officer

(1) Any person who—

  (*a*) intentionally obstructs any officer of an enforcement authority who is acting in pursuance of any provision of this Part or any customs officer who is so acting; or
  (*b*) intentionally fails to comply with any requirement made of him by any officer of an enforcement authority under any provision of this Part; or
  (*c*) without reasonable cause fails to give any officer of an enforcement authority who is so acting any other assistance or information which the officer may reasonably require of him for the purposes of the exercise of the officer's functions under any provision of this Part,

shall be guilty of an offence and liable on summary conviction to a fine not exceeding level 5 on the standard scale.

(2) A person shall be guilty of an offence if, in giving any information which is required of him by virtue of subsection (1)(*c*) above—

  (*a*) he makes any statement which he knows is false in a material particular; or
  (*b*) he recklessly makes a statement which is false in a material particular.

(3) A person guilty of an offence under subsection (2) above shall be liable—

  (*a*) on conviction on indictment, to a fine;
  (*b*) on summary conviction, to a fine not exceeding the statutory maximum.

33. Appeals against detention of goods

(1) Any person having an interest in any goods which are for the time being detained under any provision of this Part by an enforcement authority or by an officer of such an authority may apply for an order requiring the goods to be released to him or to another person.

(2) An application under this section may be made—

  (*a*) to any magistrates' court in which proceedings have been brought in England and Wales or Northern Ireland—
    (i) for an offence in respect of a contravention in relation to the goods of any safety provision or of any provision made by or under Part III of this Act; or
    (ii) for the forfeiture of the goods under section 16 above;
  (*b*) where no such proceedings have been so brought, by way of complaint to a magistrates' court; or
  (*c*) in Scotland, by summary application to the sheriff.

(3) On an application under this section to a magistrates' court or to the

Consumer Protection Act 1987

sheriff, an order requiring goods to be released shall be made only if the court or sheriff is satisfied—

(*a*) that proceedings—
(i) for an offence in respect of a contravention in relation to the goods of any safety provision or of any provision made by or under Part III of this Act; or
(ii) for the forfeiture of the goods under section 16 or 17 above,

have not been brought or, having been brought, have been concluded without the goods being forfeited; and
(*b*) where no such proceedings have been brought, that more than six months have elapsed since the goods were seized.

(4) Any person aggrieved by an order made under this section by a magistrates' court in England and Wales or Northern Ireland, or by a decision of such a court not to make such an order, may appeal against that order or decision—

(*a*) in England and Wales, to the Crown Court;
(*b*) in Northern Ireland, to the county court;

and an order so made may contain such provision as appears to the court to be appropriate for delaying the coming into force of the order pending the making and determination of any appeal (including any application under section 111 of the Magistrates' Courts Act 1980 or Article 146 of the Magistrates' Courts (Northern Ireland) Order 1981 (statement of case)).

34. Compensation for seizure and detention

(1) Where an officer of an enforcement authority exercises any power under section 29 above to seize and detain goods, the enforcement authority shall be liable to pay compensation to any person having an interest in the goods in respect of any loss or damage caused by reason of the exercise of the power if—

(*a*) there has been no contravention in relation to the goods of any safety provision or of any provision made by or under Part III of this Act; and
(*b*) the exercise of the power is not attributable to any neglect or default by that person.

(2) Any disputed question as to the right to or the amount of any compensation payable under this section shall be determined by arbitration or, in Scotland, by a single arbiter appointed, failing agreement between the parties, by the sheriff.

35. Recovery of expenses of enforcement

(1) This section shall apply where a court—
(*a*) convicts a person of an offence in respect of a contravention in relation to any goods of any safety provision or of any provision made by or under Part III of this Act; or
(*b*) makes an order under section 16 or 17 above for the forfeiture of any goods.

(2) The court may (in addition to any other order it may make as to costs or expenses) order the person convicted or, as the case may be, any person having an interest in the goods to reimburse an enforcement authority for any expenditure which has been or may be incurred by that authority—

(a) in connection with any seizure or detention of the goods by or on behalf of the authority; or

(b) in connection with any compliance by the authority with directions given by the court for the purposes of any order for the forfeiture of the goods.

Part V

Miscellaneous and Supplemental

36. Amendments of Part I of the Health and Safety at Work etc. Act 1974

Part I of the Health and Safety at Work etc. Act 1974 (which includes provision with respect to the safety of certain articles and substances) shall have effect with the amendments specified in Schedule 3 to this Act; and, accordingly, the general purposes of that Part of that Act shall include the purpose of protecting persons from the risks protection from which would not be afforded by virtue of that Part but for those amendments.

37. Power of Commissioners of Customs and Excise to disclose information

(1) If they think it appropriate to do so for the purpose of facilitating the exercise by any person to whom subsection (2) below applies of any functions conferred on that person by or under Part II of this Act, or by or under Part IV of this Act in its application for the purposes of the safety provisions, the Commissioners of Customs and Excise may authorise the disclosure to that person of any information obtained for the purposes of the exercise by the Commissioners of their functions in relation to imported goods.

(2) This subsection applies to an enforcement authority and to any officer of an enforcement authority.

(3) A disclosure of information made to any person under subsection (1) above shall be made in such manner as may be directed by the Commissioners of Customs and Excise and may be made through such persons acting on behalf of that person as may be so directed.

(4) Information may be disclosed to a person under subsection (1) above whether or not the disclosure of the information has been requested by or on behalf of that person.

38. Restrictions on disclosure of information

(1) Subject to the following provisions of this section, a person shall be guilty of an offence if he discloses any information—

(a) which was obtained by him in consequence of its being given to any person in compliance with any requirement imposed by safety regulations or regulations under section 26 above;

(b) which consists in a secret manufacturing process or a trade secret and was obtained by him in consequence of the inclusion of the information—

(i) in written or oral representations made for the purposes of Part I or II of Schedule 2 to this Act; or

(ii) in a statement of a witness in connection with any such oral representations;

(c) which was obtained by him in consequence of the exercise by the Secretary of State of the power conferred by section 18 above;

(d) which was obtained by him in consequence of the exercise by any person of any power conferred by Part IV of this Act; or

(e) which was disclosed to or through him under section 37 above.

(2) Subsection (1) above shall not apply to a disclosure of information if the information is publicised information or the disclosure is made—

(a) for the purpose of facilitating the exercise of a relevant person's functions under this Act or any enactment or subordinate legislation mentioned in subsection (3) below;

(b) for the purposes of compliance with a Community obligation; or

(c) in connection with the investigation of any criminal offence or for the purposes of any civil or criminal proceedings.

(3) The enactments and subordinate legislation referred to in subsection (2)(a) above are—

(a) the Trade Descriptions Act 1968;

(b) Parts II and III and section 125 of the Fair Trading Act 1973;

(c) the relevant statutory provisions within the meaning of Part I of the Health and Safety at Work etc. Act 1974 or within the meaning of the Health and Safety at Work (Northern Ireland) Order 1978;

(d) the Consumer Credit Act 1974;

(e) the Restrictive Trade Practices Act 1976;

(f) the Resale Prices Act 1976;

(g) the Estate Agents Act 1979;

(h) the Competition Act 1980;

(i) the Telecommunications Act 1984;

(j) the Airports Act 1986;

(k) the Gas Act 1986;

(l) any subordinate legislation made (whether before or after the passing of this Act) for the purpose of securing compliance with the Directive of the Council of the European Communities, dated 10th September 1984 (No. 84/450/EEC) on the approximation of the laws, regulations and administrative provisions of the member States concerning misleading advertising.

(4) In subsection (2)(a) above the reference to a person's functions shall include a reference to any function of making, amending or revoking any regulations or order.

(5) A person guilty of an offence under this section shall be liable—

(a) on summary conviction, to a fine not exceeding the statutory maximum;

(b) on conviction on indictment, to imprisonment for a term not exceeding two years or to a fine or to both.

(6) In this section—

'publicised information' means any information which has been disclosed in any civil or criminal proceedings or is or has been required to be contained in a warning published in pursuance of a notice to warn; and

'relevant person' means any of the following, that is to say—

(a) a Minister of the Crown, Government department or Northern Ireland department;

(b) the Monopolies and Mergers Commission, the Director General of Fair Trading, the Director General of Telecommunications or the Director General of Gas Supply;
(c) the Civil Aviation Authority;
(d) any weights and measures authority, any district council in Northern Ireland or any person on whom functions are conferred by regulations under section 27(2) above;
(e) any person who is an enforcing authority for the purposes of Part I of the Health and Safety at Work etc. Act 1974 or for the purposes of Part II of the Health and Safety at Work (Northern Ireland) Order 1978.

39. Defence of due diligence

(1) Subject to the following provisions of this section, in proceedings against any person for an offence to which this section applies it shall be a defence for that person to show that he took all reasonable steps and exercised all due diligence to avoid committing the offence.

(2) Where in any proceedings against any person for such an offence the defence provided by subsection (1) above involves an allegation that the commission of the offence was due—

(a) to the act or default of another; or
(b) to reliance on information given by another,

that person shall not, without the leave of the court, be entitled to rely on the defence unless, not less than seven clear days before the hearing of the proceedings, he has served a notice under subsection (3) below on the person bringing the proceedings.

(3) A notice under this subsection shall give such information identifying or assisting in the identification of the person who committed the act or default or gave the information as is in the possession of the person serving the notice at the time he serves it.

(4) It is hereby declared that a person shall not be entitled to rely on the defence provided by subsection (1) above by reason of his reliance on information supplied by another, unless he shows that it was reasonable in all the circumstances for him to have relied on the information, having regard in particular—

(a) to the steps which he took, and those which might reasonably have been taken, for the purpose of verifying the information; and
(b) to whether he had any reason to disbelieve the information.

(5) This section shall apply to an offence under section 10, 12(1), (2) or (3), 13(4), 14(6) or 20(1) above.

40. Liability of persons other than principal offender

(1) Where the commission by any person of an offence to which section 39 above applies is due to an act or default committed by some other person in the course of any business of his, the other person shall be guilty of the offence and may be proceeded against and punished by virtue of this subsection whether or not proceedings are taken against the first-mentioned person.

(2) Where a body corporate is guilty of an offence under this Act (including where it is so guilty by virtue of subsection (1) above) in respect of any act

or default which is shown to have been committed with the consent or connivance of, or to be attributable to any neglect on the part of, any director, manager, secretary or other similar officer of the body corporate or any person who was purporting to act in any such capacity he, as well as the body corporate, shall be guilty of that offence and shall be liable to be proceeded against and punished accordingly.

(3) Where the affairs of a body corporate are managed by its members, subsection (2) above shall apply in relation to the acts and defaults of a member in connection with his functions of management as if he were a director of the body corporate.

41. Civil proceedings

(1) An obligation imposed by safety regulations shall be a duty owed to any person who may be affected by a contravention of the obligation and, subject to any provision to the contrary in the regulations and to the defences and other incidents applying to actions for breach of statutory duty, a contravention of any such obligation shall be actionable accordingly.

(2) This Act shall not be construed as conferring any other right of action in civil proceedings, apart from the right conferred by virtue of Part I of this Act, in respect of any loss or damage suffered in consequence of a contravention of a safety provision or of a provision made by or under Part III of this Act.

(3) Subject to any provision to the contrary in the agreement itself, an agreement shall not be void or unenforceable by reason only of a contravention of a safety provision or of a provision made by or under Part III of this Act.

(4) Liability by virtue of subsection (1) above shall not be limited or excluded by any contract term, by any notice or (subject to the power contained in subsection (1) above to limit or exclude it in safety regulations) by any other provision.

(5) Nothing in subsection (1) above shall prejudice the operation of section 12 of the Nuclear Installations Act 1965 (rights to compensation for certain breaches of duties confined to rights under that Act).

(6) In this section 'damage' includes personal injury and death.

42. Reports etc.

(1) It shall be the duty of the Secretary of State at least once in every five years to lay before each House of Parliament a report on the exercise during the period to which the report relates of the functions which under Part II of this Act, or under Part IV of this Act in its application for the purposes of the safety provisions, are exercisable by the Secretary of State, weights and measures authorities, district councils in Northern Ireland and persons on whom functions are conferred by regulations made under section 27(2) above.

(2) The Secretary of State may from time to time prepare and lay before each House of Parliament such other reports on the exercise of those functions as he considers appropriate.

(3) Every weights and measures authority, every district council in Northern Ireland and every person on whom functions are conferred by regulations under subsection (2) of section 27 above shall, whenever the Secretary of State so directs, make a report to the Secretary of State on the exercise of the functions

exercisable by that authority or council under that section or by that person by virtue of any such regulations.

(4) A report under subsection (3) above shall be in such form and shall contain such particulars as are specified in the direction of the Secretary of State.

(5) The first report under subsection (1) above shall be laid before each House of Parliament not more than five years after the laying of the last report under section 8(2) of the Consumer Safety Act 1978.

43. Financial provisions

(1) There shall be paid out of money provided by Parliament—

(*a*) any expenses incurred or compensation payable by a Minister of the Crown or Government department in consequence of any provision of this Act; and

(*b*) any increase attributable to this Act in the sums payable out of money so provided under any other Act.

(2) Any sums received by a Minister of the Crown or Government department by virtue of this Act shall be paid into the Consolidated Fund.

44. Service of documents etc.

(1) Any document required or authorised by virtue of this Act to be served on a person may be so served—

(*a*) by delivering it to him or by leaving it at his proper address or by sending it by post to him at that address; or

(*b*) if the person is a body corporate, by serving it in accordance with paragraph (*a*) above on the secretary or clerk of that body; or

(*c*) if the person is a partnership, by serving it in accordance with that paragraph on a partner or on a person having control or management of the partnership business.

(2) For the purposes of subsection (1) above, and for the purposes of section 7 of the Interpretation Act 1978 (which relates to the service of documents by post) in its application to that subsection, the proper address of any person on whom a document is to be served by virtue of this Act shall be his last known address except that—

(*a*) in the case of service on a body corporate or its secretary or clerk, it shall be the address of the registered or principal office of the body corporate;

(*b*) in the case of service on a partnership or a partner or a person having the control or management of a partnership business, it shall be the principal office of the partnership;

and for the purposes of this subsection the principal office of a company registered outside the United Kingdom or of a partnership carrying on business outside the United Kingdom is its principal office within the United Kingdom.

(3) The Secretary of State may by regulations make provision for the manner in which any information is to be given to any person under any provision of Part IV of this Act.

(4) Without prejudice to the generality of subsection (3) above regulations made by the Secretary of State may prescribe the person, or manner of determining

the person, who is to be treated for the purposes of section 28(2) or 30 above as the person from whom any goods were purchased or seized where the goods were purchased or seized from a vending machine.

(5) The power to make regulations under subsection (3) or (4) above shall be exercisable by statutory instrument subject to annulment in pursuance of a resolution of either House of Parliament and shall include power—

(a) to make different provision for different cases; and
(b) to make such supplemental, consequential and transitional provision as the Secretary of State considers appropriate.

45. Interpretation

(1) In this Act, except in so far as the context otherwise requires—

'aircraft' includes gliders, balloons and hovercraft;

'business' includes a trade or profession and the activities of a professional or trade association or of a local authority or other public authority;

'conditional sale agreement', 'credit-sale agreement' and 'hire-purchase agreement' have the same meanings as in the Consumer Credit Act 1974 but as if in the definitions in that Act 'goods' had the same meaning as in this Act;

'contravention' includes a failure to comply and cognate expressions shall be construed accordingly;

'enforcement authority' means the Secretary of State, any other Minister of the Crown in charge of a Government department, any such department and any authority, council or other person on whom functions under this Act are conferred by or under section 27 above;

'gas' has the same meaning as in Part I of the Gas Act 1986;

'goods' includes substances, growing crops and things comprised in land by virtue of being attached to it and any ship, aircraft or vehicle;

'information' includes accounts, estimates and returns;

'magistrates' court', in relation to Northern Ireland, means a court of summary jurisdiction;

'mark' and 'trade mark' have the same meanings as in the Trade Marks Act 1938;

'modifications' includes additions, alterations and omissions, and cognate expressions shall be construed accordingly;

'motor vehicle' has the same meaning as in the Road Traffic Act 1972;

'notice' means a notice in writing;

'notice to warn' means a notice under section 13(1)(b) above;

'officer', in relation to an enforcement authority, means a person authorised in writing to assist the authority in carrying out its functions under or for the purposes of the enforcement of any of the safety provisions or of any of the provisions made by or under Part III of this Act;

Consumer Protection Act 1987

'personal injury' includes any disease and any other impairment of a person's physical or mental condition;

'premises' includes any place and any ship, aircraft or vehicle;

'prohibition notice' means a notice under section 13(1)(*a*) above;

'records' includes any books or documents and any records in non-documentary form;

'safety provision' means the general safety requirement in section 10 above or any provision of safety regulations, a prohibition notice or a suspension notice;

'safety regulations' means regulations under section 11 above;

'ship' includes any boat and any other description of vessel used in navigation;

'subordinate legislation' has the same meaning as in the Interpretation Act 1978;

'substance' means any natural or artificial substance, whether in solid, liquid or gaseous form or in the form of a vapour, and includes substances that are comprised in or mixed with other goods;

'supply' and cognate expressions shall be construed in accordance with section 46 below;

'suspension notice' means a notice under section 14 above.

(2) Except in so far as the context otherwise requires, references in this Act to a contravention of a safety provision shall, in relation to any goods, include references to anything which would constitute such a contravention if the goods were supplied to any person.

(3) References in this Act to any goods in relation to which any safety provision has been or may have been contravened shall include references to any goods which it is not reasonably practicable to separate from any such goods.

(4) Section 68(2) of the Trade Marks Act 1938 (construction of references to use of a mark) shall apply for the purposes of this Act as it applies for the purposes of that Act.

(5) In Scotland, any reference in this Act to things comprised in land by virtue of being attached to it is a reference to moveables which have become heritable by accession to heritable property.

46. Meaning of 'supply'

(1) Subject to the following provisions of this section, references in this Act to supplying goods shall be construed as references to doing any of the following, whether as principal or agent, that is to say—

(*a*) selling, hiring out or lending the goods;
(*b*) entering into a hire-purchase agreement to furnish the goods;
(*c*) the performance of any contract for work and materials to furnish the goods;
(*d*) providing the goods in exchange for any consideration (including trading stamps) other than money;
(*e*) providing the goods in or in connection with the performance of any statutory function; or

(*f*) giving the goods as a prize or otherwise making a gift of the goods;

and, in relation to gas or water, those references shall be construed as including references to providing the service by which the gas or water is made available for use.

(2) For the purposes of any reference in this Act to supplying goods, where a person ('the ostensible supplier') supplies goods to another person ('the customer') under a hire-purchase agreement, conditional sale agreement or credit-sale agreement or under an agreement for the hiring of goods (other than a hire-purchase agreement) and the ostensible supplier—

  (*a*) carries on the business of financing the provision of goods for others by means of such agreements; and
  (*b*) in the course of that business acquired his interest in the goods supplied to the customer as a means of financing the provision of them for the customer by a further person ('the effective supplier'),

the effective supplier and not the ostensible supplier shall be treated as supplying the goods to the customer.

(3) Subject to subsection (4) below, the performance of any contract by the erection of any building or structure on any land or by the carrying out of any other building works shall be treated for the purposes of this Act as a supply of goods in so far as, but only in so far as, it involves the provision of any goods to any person by means of their incorporation into the building, structure or works.

(4) Except for the purposes of, and in relation to, notices to warn or any provision made by or under Part III of this Act, references in this Act to supplying goods shall not include references to supplying goods comprised in land where the supply is effected by the creation or disposal of an interest in the land.

(5) Except in Part I of this Act references in this Act to a person's supplying goods shall be confined to references to that person's supplying goods in the course of a business of his, but for the purposes of this subsection it shall be immaterial whether the business is a business of dealing in the goods.

(6) For the purposes of subsection (5) above goods shall not be treated as supplied in the course of a business if they are supplied, in pursuance of an obligation arising under or in connection with the insurance of the goods, to the person with whom they were insured.

(7) Except for the purposes of, and in relation to, prohibition notices or suspension notices, references in Parts II to IV of this Act to supplying goods shall not include—

  (*a*) references to supplying goods where the person supplied carries on a business of buying goods of the same description as those goods and repairing or reconditioning them;
  (*b*) references to supplying goods by a sale of articles as scrap (that is to say, for the value of materials included in the articles rather than for the value of the articles themselves).

(8) Where any goods have at any time been supplied by being hired out or lent to any person, neither a continuation or renewal of the hire or loan (whether on the same or different terms) nor any transaction for the transfer after that time of any interest in the goods to the person to whom they were hired or

lent shall be treated for the purposes of this Act as a further supply of the goods to that person.

(9) A ship, aircraft or motor vehicle shall not be treated for the purposes of this Act as supplied to any person by reason only that services consisting in the carriage of goods or passengers in that ship, aircraft or vehicle, or in its use for any other purpose, are provided to that person in pursuance of an agreement relating to the use of the ship, aircraft or vehicle for a particular period or for particular voyages, flights or journeys.

47. Savings for certain privileges

(1) Nothing in this Act shall be taken as requiring any person to produce any records if he would be entitled to refuse to produce those records in any proceedings in any court on the grounds that they are the subject of legal professional privilege or, in Scotland, that they contain a confidential communication made by or to an advocate or solicitor in that capacity, or as authorising any person to take possession of any records which are in the possession of a person who would be so entitled.

(2) Nothing in this Act shall be construed as requiring a person to answer any question or give any information if to do so would incriminate that person or that person's spouse.

48. Minor and consequential amendments and repeals

(1) The enactments mentioned in Schedule 4 to this Act shall have effect subject to the amendments specified in that Schedule (being minor amendments and amendments consequential on the provisions of this Act).

(2) The following Acts shall cease to have effect, that is to say—

(*a*) the Trade Descriptions Act 1972; and
(*b*) the Fabrics (Misdescription) Act 1913.

(3) The enactments mentioned in Schedule 5 to this Act are hereby repealed to the extent specified in the third column of that Schedule.

49. Northern Ireland

(1) This Act shall extend to Northern Ireland with the exception of—

(*a*) the provisions of Parts I and III;
(*b*) any provision amending or repealing an enactment which does not so extend; and
(*c*) any other provision so far as it has effect for the purposes of, or in relation to, a provision falling within paragraph (*a*) or (*b*) above.

(2) Subject to any Order in Council made by virtue of subsection (1)(*a*) of section 3 of the Northern Ireland Constitution Act 1973, consumer safety shall not be a transferred matter for the purposes of that Act but shall for the purposes of subsection (2) of that section be treated as specified in Schedule 3 to that Act.

(3) An Order in Council under paragraph 1(1)(*b*) of Schedule 1 to the Northern Ireland Act 1974 (exercise of legislative functions for Northern Ireland) which states that it is made only for purposes corresponding to any of the provisions of this Act mentioned in subsections (1)(*a*) to (*c*) above—

(a) shall not be subject to paragraph 1(4) and (5) of that Schedule (affirmative resolution procedure and procedure in cases of urgency); but

(b) shall be subject to annulment in pursuance of a resolution of either House of Parliament.

50. Short title, commencement and transitional provision

(1) This Act may be cited as the Consumer Protection Act 1987.

(2) This Act shall come into force on such day as the Secretary of State may by order made by statutory instrument appoint, and different days may be so appointed for different provisions or for different purposes.

(3) The Secretary of State shall not make an order under subsection (2) above bringing into force the repeal of the Trade Descriptions Act 1972, a repeal of any provision of that Act or a repeal of that Act or of any provision of it for any purposes, unless a draft of the order has been laid before, and approved by a resolution of, each House of Parliament.

(4) An order under subsection (2) above bringing a provision into force may contain such transitional provision in connection with the coming into force of that provision as the Secretary of State considers appropriate.

(5) Without prejudice to the generality of the power conferred by subsection (4) above, the Secretary of State may by order provide for any regulations made under the Consumer Protection Act 1961 or the Consumer Protection Act (Northern Ireland) 1965 to have effect as if made under section 11 above and for any such regulations to have effect with such modifications as he considers appropriate for that purpose.

(6) The power of the Secretary of State by order to make such provision as is mentioned in subsection (5) above, shall, in so far as it is not exercised by an order under subsection (2) above, be exercisable by statutory instrument subject to annulment in pursuance of a resolution of either House of Parliament.

(7) Nothing in this Act or in any order under subsection (2) above shall make any person liable by virtue of Part I of this Act for any damage caused wholly or partly by a defect in a product which was supplied to any person by its producer before the coming into force of Part I of this Act.

(8) Expressions used in subsection (7) above and in Part I of this Act have the same meanings in that subsection as in that Part.

SCHEDULES

Schedule 1

Limitation of Actions Under Part I

Part I

England and Wales

1. After section 11 of the Limitation Act 1980 (actions in respect of personal injuries) there shall be inserted the following section—

Actions in respect of defective products

11A.—(1) This section shall apply to an action for damages by virtue of any provision of Part I of the Consumer Protection Act 1987.

(2) None of the time-limits given in the preceding provisions of this Act shall apply to an action to which this section applies.

(3) An action to which this section applies shall not be brought after the expiration of the period of ten years from the relevant time, within the meaning of section 4 of the said Act of 1987; and this subsection shall operate to extinguish a right of action and shall do so whether or not that right of action had accrued, or time under the following provisions of this Act had begun to run, at the end of the said period of ten years.

(4) Subject to subsection (5) below, an action to which this section applies in which the damages claimed by the plaintiff consist of or include damages in respect of personal injuries to the plaintiff or any other person or loss of or damage to any property, shall not be brought after the expiration of the period of three years from whichever is the later of—

(*a*) the date on which the cause of action accrued; and
(*b*) the date of knowledge of the injured person or, in the case of loss of or damage to property, the date of knowledge of the plaintiff or (if earlier) of any person in whom his cause of action was previously vested.

(5) If in a case where the damages claimed by the plaintiff consist of or include damages in respect of personal injuries to the plaintiff or any other person the injured person died before the expiration of the period mentioned in subsection (4) above, that subsection shall have effect as respects the cause of action surviving for the benefit of his estate by virtue of section 1 of the Law Reform (Miscellaneous Provisions) Act 1934 as if for the reference to that period there were substituted a reference to the period of three years from whichever is the later of—

(*a*) the date of death; and
(*b*) the date of the personal representative's knowledge.

(6) For the purposes of this section 'personal representative' includes any person who is or has been a personal representative of the deceased, including an executor who has not proved the will (whether or not he has renounced probate) but not anyone appointed only as a special personal representative in relation to settled land; and regard shall be had to any knowledge acquired by any such person while a personal representative or previously.

(7) If there is more than one personal representative and their dates of knowledge are different, subsection (5)(*b*) above shall be read as referring to the earliest of those dates.

(8) Expressions used in this section or section 14 of this Act and in Part I of the Consumer Protection Act 1987 have the same meanings in this section or that section as in that Part; and section 1(1) of that Act (Part I to be construed as enacted for the purpose of complying with the product liability Directive) shall apply for the purpose of construing this section and the following provisions of this Act so far as they relate to an action by virtue of any provision of that Part as it applies for the purpose of construing that Part.

2. In section 12(1) of the said Act of 1980 (actions under the Fatal Accidents Act 1976), after the words 'section 11' there shall be inserted the words 'or 11A'.

3. In section 14 of the said Act of 1980 (definition of date of knowledge), in subsection (1), at the beginning there shall be inserted the words 'Subject to subsection (1A) below,' and after that subsection there shall be inserted the following subsection—

(1A) In section 11A of this Act and in section 12 of this Act so far as that section applies to an action by virtue of section 6(1)(*a*) of the Consumer Protection Act 1987 (death caused by defective product) references to a person's date of knowledge are references to the date on which he first had knowledge of the following facts—

- (*a*) such facts about the damage caused by the defect as would lead a reasonable person who had suffered such damage to consider it sufficiently serious to justify his instituting proceedings for damages against a defendant who did not dispute liability and was able to satisfy a judgment; and
- (*b*) that the damage was wholly or partly attributable to the facts and circumstances alleged to constitute the defect; and
- (*c*) the identity of the defendant;

but, in determining the date on which a person first had such knowledge there shall be disregarded both the extent (if any) of that person's knowledge on any date of whether particular facts or circumstances would or would not, as a matter of law, constitute a defect and, in a case relating to loss of or damage to property, any knowledge which that person had on a date on which he had no right of action by virtue of Part I of that Act in respect of the loss or damage.

4. In section 28 of the said Act of 1980 (extension of limitation period in case of disability), after subsection (6) there shall be inserted the following subsection—

(7) If the action is one to which section 11A of this Act applies or one by virtue of section 6(1)(*a*) of the Consumer Protection Act 1987 (death caused by defective product), subsection (1) above—

- (*a*) shall not apply to the time-limit prescribed by subsection (3) of the said section 11A or to that time-limit as applied by virtue of section 12(1) of this Act; and
- (*b*) in relation to any other time-limit prescribed by this Act shall have effect as if for the words 'six years' there were substituted the words 'three years'.

5. In section 32 of the said Act of 1980 (postponement of limitation period in case of fraud, concealment or mistake)—

- (*a*) in subsection (1), for the words 'subsection (3)' there shall be substituted the words 'subsections (3) and (4A)'; and
- (*b*) after subsection (4) there shall be inserted the following subsection—

(4A) Subsection (1) above shall not apply in relation to the time-limit prescribed by section 11A(3) of this Act or in relation to that time-limit as applied by virtue of section 12(1) of this Act.

6. In section 33 of the said Act of 1980 (discretionary exclusion of time-limit)—

Consumer Protection Act 1987

(*a*) in subsection (1), after the words 'section 11' there shall be inserted the words 'or 11A';
(*b*) after the said subsection (1) there shall be inserted the following subsection—

(1A) The court shall not under this section disapply—

(*a*) subsection (3) of section 11A; or
(*b*) where the damages claimed by the plaintiff are confined to damages for loss of or damage to any property, any other provision in its application to an action by virtue of Part I of the Consumer Protection Act 1987.;
(*c*) in subsections (2) and (4), after the words 'section 11' there shall be inserted the words 'or subsection (4) of section 11A';
(*d*) in subsection (3)(*b*), after the words 'section 11' there shall be inserted the words ', by section 11A'; and
(*e*) in subsection (8), after the words 'section 11' there shall be inserted the words 'or 11A'.

PART II

SCOTLAND

7. The Prescription and Limitation (Scotland) Act 1973 shall be amended as follows.

8. In section 7(2), after the words 'not being an obligation' there shall be inserted the words 'to which section 22A of this Act applies or an obligation'.

9. In Part II, before section 17, there shall be inserted the following section—

Part II not to extend to product liability

16A.—This Part of this Act does not apply to any action to which section 22B or 22C of this Act applies.

10. After section 22, there shall be inserted the following new Part—

PART IIA

PRESCRIPTION OF OBLIGATIONS AND LIMITATION OF ACTIONS UNDER PART I OF THE CONSUMER PROTECTION ACT 1987

Prescription of Obligations

22A. Ten years' prescription of obligations

(1) An obligation arising from liability under section 2 of the 1987 Act (to make reparation for damage caused wholly or partly by a defect in a product) shall be extinguished if a period of 10 years has expired from the relevant time, unless a relevant claim was made within that period and has not been finally disposed of, and no such obligation shall come into existence after the expiration of the said period.

(2) If, at the expiration of the period of 10 years mentioned in subsection (1) above, a relevant claim has been made but has not been finally disposed of, the obligation to which the claim relates shall be extinguished when the claim is finally disposed of.

(3) In this section—

(a) a decision disposing of the claim has been made against which no appeal is competent;
(b) an appeal against such a decision is competent with leave, and the time-limit for leave has expired and no application has been made or leave has been refused;
(c) leave to appeal against such a decision is granted or is not required, and no appeal is made within the time-limit for appeal; or
(d) the claim is abandoned;

a claim is finally disposed of when 'relevant claim' in relation to an obligation means a claim made by or on behalf of the creditor for implement or part implement of the obligation, being a claim made—

(a) in appropriate proceedings within the meaning of section 4(2) of this Act; or
(b) by the presentation of, or the concurring in, a petition for sequestration or by the submission of a claim under section 22 or 48 of the Bankruptcy (Scotland) Act 1985; or
(c) by the presentation of, or the concurring in, a petition for the winding-up of a company or by the submission of a claim in a liquidation in accordance with the rules made under section 411 of the Insolvency Act 1986;

'relevant time' has the meaning given in section 4(2) of the 1987 Act.

(4) Where a relevant claim is made in an arbitration, and the nature of the claim has been stated in a preliminary notice (within the meaning of section 4(4) of this Act) relating to that arbitration, the date when the notice is served shall be taken for those purposes to be the date of the making of the claim.

Limitation of actions

22B. 3 year limitation of actions

(1) This section shall apply to an action to enforce an obligation arising from liability under section 2 of the 1987 Act (to make reparation for damage caused wholly or partly by a defect in a product), except where section 22C of this Act applies.

(2) Subject to subsection (4) below, an action to which this section applies shall not be competent unless it is commenced within the period of 3 years after the earliest date on which the person seeking to bring (or a person who could at an earlier date have brought) the action was aware, or on which, in the opinion of the court, it was reasonably practicable for him in all the circumstances to become aware, of all the facts mentioned in subsection (3) below.

(3) The facts referred to in subsection (2) above are—

(a) that there was a defect in a product;
(b) that the damage was caused or partly caused by the defect;
(c) that the damage was sufficiently serious to justify the pursuer (or other person referred to in subsection (2) above) in bringing an action to which this section applies on the assumption that the defender did not dispute liability and was able to satisfy a decree;

(*d*) that the defender was a person liable for the damage under the said section 2.

(4) In the computation of the period of 3 years mentioned in subsection (2) above, there shall be disregarded any period during which the person seeking to bring the action was under legal disability by reason of nonage or unsoundness of mind.

(5) The facts mentioned in subsection (3) above do not include knowledge of whether particular facts and circumstances would or would not, as a matter of law, result in liability for damage under the said section 2.

(6) Where a person would be entitled, but for this section, to bring an action for reparation other than one in which the damages claimed are confined to damages for loss of or damage to property, the court may, if it seems to it equitable to do so, allow him to bring the action notwithstanding this section.

22C. Actions under the 1987 Act where death has resulted from personal injuries

(1) This section shall apply to an action to enforce an obligation arising from liability under section 2 of the 1987 Act (to make reparation for damage caused wholly or partly by a defect in a product) where a person has died from personal injuries and the damages claimed include damages for those personal injuries or that death.

(2) Subject to subsection (4) below, an action to which this section applies shall not be competent unless it is commenced within the period of 3 years after the later of—

(*a*) the date of death of the injured person;
(*b*) the earliest date on which the person seeking to make (or a person who could at an earlier date have made) the claim was aware, or on which, in the opinion of the court, it was reasonably practicable for him in all the circumstances to become aware—
  (i) that there was a defect in the product;
  (ii) that the injuries of the deceased were caused (or partly caused) by the defect; and
  (iii) that the defender was a person liable for the damage under the said section 2.

(3) Where the person seeking to make the claim is a relative of the deceased, there shall be disregarded in the computation of the period mentioned in subsection (2) above any period during which that relative was under legal disability by reason of nonage or unsoundness of mind.

(4) Where an action to which section 22B of this Act applies has not been brought within the period mentioned in subsection (2) of that section and the person subsequently dies in consequence of his injuries, an action to which this section applies shall not be competent in respect of those injuries or that death.

(5) Where a person would be entitled, but for this section, to bring an action for reparation other than one in which the damages claimed are confined to damages for loss of or damage to property, the court may, if it seems to it equitable to do so, allow him to bring the action notwithstanding this section.

(6) In this section 'relative' has the same meaning as in the Damages (Scotland) Act 1976.

(7) For the purposes of subsection (2)(*b*) above there shall be disregarded knowledge of whether particular facts and circumstances would or would not, as a matter of law, result in liability for damage under the said section 2.

Supplementary

22D. Interpretation of this Part

(1) Expressions used in this Part and in Part I of the 1987 Act shall have the same meanings in this Part as in the said Part I.

(2) For the purposes of section 1(1) of the 1987 Act, this Part shall have effect and be construed as if it were contained in Part I of that Act.

(3) In this Part, 'the 1987 Act' means the Consumer Protection Act 1987.

11. Section 23 shall cease to have effect, but for the avoidance of doubt it is declared that the amendments in Part II of Schedule 4 shall continue to have effect.

12. In paragraph 2 of Schedule 1, after sub-paragraph (*gg*) there shall be inserted the following sub-paragraph—

(*ggg*) to any obligation arising from liability under section 2 of the Consumer Protection Act 1987 (to make reparation for damage caused wholly or partly by a defect in a product);.

SCHEDULE 2

PROHIBITION NOTICES AND NOTICES TO WARN

PART I

PROHIBITION NOTICES

1. A prohibition notice in respect of any goods shall—

(*a*) state that the Secretary of State considers that the goods are unsafe;
(*b*) set out the reasons why the Secretary of State considers that the goods are unsafe;
(*c*) specify the day on which the notice is to come into force; and
(*d*) state that the trader may at any time make representations in writing to the Secretary of State for the purpose of establishing that the goods are safe.

2. (1) If representations in writing about a prohibition notice are made by the trader to the Secretary of State, it shall be the duty of the Secretary of State to consider whether to revoke the notice and—

(*a*) if he decides to revoke it, to do so;
(*b*) in any other case, to appoint a person to consider those representations, any further representations made (whether in writing or orally) by the trader about the notice and the statements of any witnesses examined under this Part of this Schedule.

(2) Where the Secretary of State has appointed a person to consider representations about a prohibition notice, he shall serve a notification on the trader which—

(*a*) states that the trader may make oral representations to the appointed person for the purpose of establishing that the goods to which the notice relates are safe; and

(b) specifies the place and time at which the oral representations may be made.

(3) The time specified in a notification served under sub-paragraph (2) above shall not be before the end of the period of twenty-one days beginning with the day on which the notification is served, unless the trader otherwise agrees.

(4) A person on whom a notification has been served under sub-paragraph (2) above or his representative may, at the place and time specified in the notification—

(a) make oral representations to the appointed person for the purpose of establishing that the goods in question are safe; and
(b) call and examine witnesses in connection with the representations.

3. (1) Where representations in writing about a prohibition notice are made by the trader to the Secretary of State at any time after a person has been appointed to consider representations about that notice, then, whether or not the appointed person has made a report to the Secretary of State, the following provisions of this paragraph shall apply instead of paragraph 2 above.

(2) The Secretary of State shall, before the end of the period of one month beginning with the day on which he receives the representations, serve a notification on the trader which states—

(a) that the Secretary of State has decided to revoke the notice, has decided to vary it or, as the case may be, has decided neither to revoke nor to vary it; or
(b) that, a person having been appointed to consider representations about the notice, the trader may, at a place and time specified in the notification, make oral representations to the appointed person for the purpose of establishing that the goods to which the notice relates are safe.

(3) The time specified in a notification served for the purposes of sub-paragraph (2)(b) above shall not be before the end of the period of twenty-one days beginning with the day on which the notification is served, unless the trader otherwise agrees or the time is the time already specified for the purposes of paragraph 2(2)(b) above.

(4) A person on whom a notification has been served for the purposes of sub-paragraph (2)(b) above or his representative may, at the place and time specified in the notification—

(a) make oral representations to the appointed person for the purpose of establishing that the goods in question are safe; and
(b) call and examine witnesses in connection with the representations.

4. (1) Where a person is appointed to consider representations about a prohibition notice, it shall be his duty to consider—

(a) any written representations made by the trader about the notice, other than those in respect of which a notification is served under paragraph 3(2)(a) above;
(b) any oral representations made under paragraph 2(4) or 3(4) above; and

(*c*) any statements made by witnesses in connection with the oral representations,

and, after considering any matters under this paragraph, to make a report (including recommendations) to the Secretary of State about the matters considered by him and the notice.

(2) It shall be the duty of the Secretary of State to consider any report made to him under sub-paragraph (1) above and, after considering the report, to inform the trader of his decision with respect to the prohibition notice to which the report relates.

5. (1) The Secretary of State may revoke or vary a prohibition notice by serving on the trader a notification stating that the notice is revoked or, as the case may be, is varied as specified in the notification.

(2) The Secretary of State shall not vary a prohibition notice so as to make the effect of the notice more restrictive for the trader.

(3) Without prejudice to the power conferred by section 13(2) of this Act, the service of a notification under sub-paragraph (1) above shall be sufficient to satisfy the requirement of paragraph 4(2) above that the trader shall be informed of the Secretary of State's decision.

PART II

Notices to Warn

6. (1) If the Secretary of State proposes to serve a notice to warn on any person in respect of any goods, the Secretary of State, before he serves the notice, shall serve on that person a notification which—

(*a*) contains a draft of the proposed notice;
(*b*) states that the Secretary of State proposes to serve a notice in the form of the draft on that person;
(*c*) states that the Secretary of State considers that the goods described in the draft are unsafe;
(*d*) sets out the reasons why the Secretary of State considers that those goods are unsafe; and
(*e*) states that that person may make representations to the Secretary of State for the purpose of establishing that the goods are safe if, before the end of the period of fourteen days beginning with the day on which the notification is served, he informs the Secretary of State—
   (i) of his intention to make representations; and
   (ii) whether the representations will be made only in writing or both in writing and orally.

(2) Where the Secretary of State has served a notification containing a draft of a proposed notice to warn on any person, he shall not serve a notice to warn on that person in respect of the goods to which the proposed notice relates unless—

(*a*) the period of fourteen days beginning with the day on which the notification was served expires without the Secretary of State being informed as mentioned in sub-paragraph (1)(*e*) above;
(*b*) the period of twenty-eight days beginning with that day expires without

any written representations being made by that person to the Secretary of State about the proposed notice; or

(c) the Secretary of State has considered a report about the proposed notice by a person appointed under paragraph 7(1) below.

7. (1) Where a person on whom a notification containing a draft of a proposed notice to warn has been served—

(a) informs the Secretary of State as mentioned in paragraph 6(1)(e) above before the end of the period of fourteen days beginning with the day on which the notification was served; and

(b) makes written representations to the Secretary of State about the proposed notice before the end of the period of twenty-eight days beginning with that day,

the Secretary of State shall appoint a person to consider those representations, any further representations made by that person about the draft notice and the statements of any witnesses examined under this Part of this Schedule.

(2) Where—

(a) the Secretary of State has appointed a person to consider representations about a proposed notice to warn; and

(b) the person whose representations are to be considered has informed the Secretary of State for the purposes of paragraph 6(1)(e) above that the representations he intends to make will include oral representations,

the Secretary of State shall inform the person intending to make the representations of the place and time at which oral representations may be made to the appointed person.

(3) Where a person on whom a notification containing a draft of a proposed notice to warn has been served is informed of a time for the purposes of sub-paragraph (2) above, that time shall not be—

(a) before the end of the period of twenty-eight days beginning with the day on which the notification was served; or

(b) before the end of the period of seven days beginning with the day on which that person is informed of the time.

(4) A person who has been informed of a place and time for the purposes of sub-paragraph (2) above or his representative may, at that place and time—

(a) make oral representations to the appointed person for the purpose of establishing that the goods to which the proposed notice relates are safe; and

(b) call and examine witnesses in connection with the representations.

8. (1) Where a person is appointed to consider representations about a proposed notice to warn, it shall be his duty to consider—

(a) any written representations made by the person on whom it is proposed to serve the notice; and

(b) in a case where a place and time has been appointed under paragraph 7(2) above for oral representations to be made by that person or his representative, any representations so made and any statements made by witnesses in connection with those representations, and, after considering those matters, to make a report (including recommendations) to the Secretary of State about the matters considered by him and the proposal to serve the notice.

(2) It shall be the duty of the Secretary of State to consider any report made to him under sub-paragraph (1) above and, after considering the report, to inform the person on whom it was proposed that a notice to warn should be served of his decision with respect to the proposal.

(3) If at any time after serving a notification on a person under paragraph 6 above the Secretary of State decides not to serve on that person either the proposed notice to warn or that notice with modifications, the Secretary of State shall inform that person of the decision; and nothing done for the purposes of any of the preceding provisions of this Part of this Schedule before that person was so informed shall—

(a) entitle the Secretary of State subsequently to serve the proposed notice or that notice with modifications; or
(b) require the Secretary of State, or any person appointed to consider representations about the proposed notice, subsequently to do anything in respect of, or in consequence of, any such representations.

(4) Where a notification containing a draft of a proposed notice to warn is served on a person in respect of any goods, a notice to warn served on him in consequence of a decision made under sub-paragraph (2) above shall either be in the form of the draft or shall be less onerous than the draft.

9. The Secretary of State may revoke a notice to warn by serving on the person on whom the notice was served a notification stating that the notice is revoked.

PART III
General

10. (1) Where in a notification served on any person under this Schedule the Secretary of State has appointed a time for the making of oral representations or the examination of witnesses, he may, by giving that person such notification as the Secretary of State considers appropriate, change that time to a later time or appoint further times at which further representations may be made or the examination of witnesses may be continued; and paragraphs 2(4), 3(4) and 7(4) above shall have effect accordingly.

(2) For the purposes of this Schedule the Secretary of State may appoint a person (instead of the appointed person) to consider any representations or statements, if the person originally appointed, or last appointed under this sub-paragraph, to consider those representations or statements has died or appears to the Secretary of State to be otherwise unable to act.

11. In this Schedule—

'the appointed person' in relation to a prohibition notice or a proposal to serve a notice to warn, means the person for the time being appointed under this Schedule to consider representations about the notice or, as the case may be, about the proposed notice;

'notification' means a notification in writing;

'trader', in relation to a prohibition notice, means the person on whom the notice is or was served.

* * *

Schedules 3, 4, 5 (which deal with amendments and repeals) are omitted

Consumer Arbitration Agreements Act 1988
Chapter 21

ARRANGEMENT OF SECTIONS

England, Wales and Northern Ireland

Section
1. Arbitration agreements.
2. Exclusions.
3. Contracting 'as a consumer'.
4. Power of court to disapply section 1 where no detriment to consumer.
5. Orders adding to the causes of action to which section 1 applies.

Scotland

6. Arbitration agreements: Scotland.
7. Power of court to disapply section 6 where no detriment to consumer.
8. Construction of sections 6 and 7.

Supplementary

9. Short title, commencement, interpretation and extent.

An Act to extend to consumers certain rights as regards agreements to refer future differences to arbitration and for purposes connected therewith.

[28th June 1988]

England, Wales and Northern Ireland

1. Arbitration agreements

(1) Where a person (referred to in section 4 below as 'the consumer') enters into a contract as a consumer, an agreement that future differences arising between parties to the contract are to be referred to arbitration cannot be enforced against him in respect of any cause of action so arising to which this section applies except—

   (a) with his written consent signified after the differences in question have arisen; or
   (b) where he has submitted to arbitration in pursuance of the agreement, whether in respect of those or any other differences; or
   (c) where the court makes an order under section 4 below in respect of that cause of action.

(2) This section applies to a cause of action—

   (a) if proceedings in respect of it would be within the jurisdiction of a county court; or
   (b) if it satisfies such other conditions as may be prescribed for the purposes of this paragraph in an order under section 5 below.

(3) Neither section 4(1) of the Arbitration Act 1950 nor section 4 of the Arbitration Act (Northern Ireland) 1937 (which provide for the staying of court

proceedings where an arbitration agreement is in force) shall apply to an arbitration agreement to the extent that it cannot be enforced by virtue of this section.

2. Exclusions

Section 1 above does not affect—

(a) the enforcement of an arbitration agreement to which section 1 of the Arbitration Act 1975 applies, that is, an arbitration agreement other than a domestic arbitration agreement within the meaning of that section;

(b) the resolution of differences arising under any contract so far as it is, by virtue of section 1(2) of, and Schedule 1 to, the Unfair Contract Terms Act 1977 ('the Act of 1977'), excluded from the operation of section 2, 3, 4 or 7 of that Act.

3. Contracting 'as a consumer'

(1) For the purposes of section 1 above a person enters into a contract 'as a consumer' if—

(a) he neither makes the contract in the course of a business nor holds himself out as doing so; and

(b) the other party makes the contract in the course of a business; and

(c) in the case of a contract governed by the law of sale of goods or hire-purchase, or by section 7 of the Act of 1977, the goods passing under or in pursuance of the contract are of a type ordinarily supplied for private use or consumption;

but on a sale by auction or by competitive tender the buyer is not in any circumstances to be regarded as entering into the contract as a consumer.

(2) In subsection (1) above—

'business' includes a profession and the activities of any Government department, Northern Ireland department or local or public authority; and

'goods' has the same meaning as in the Sale of Goods Act 1979.

(3) It is for those claiming that a person entering into a contract otherwise than as a consumer to show that he did so.

4. Power of court to disapply section 1 where no detriment to consumer

(1) The High Court or a county court may, on an application made after the differences in question have arisen, order that a cause of action to which this section applies shall be treated as one which section 1 above does not apply.

(2) Before making an order under this section the court must be satisfied that it is not detrimental to the interests of the consumer for the differences in question to be referred to arbitration in pursuance of the arbitration agreement instead of being determined by proceedings before a court.

(3) In determining for the purposes of subsection (2) above whether a reference to arbitration is or is not detrimental to the interests of the consumer, the court shall have regard to all factors appearing to be relevant, including, in particular the availability of legal aid and the relative amount of any expense which may result to him—

(*a*) if the differences in question are referred to arbitration in pursuance of the arbitration agreement; and

(*b*) if they are determined by proceedings before a court.

(4) This section applies to a cause of action—

(*a*) if proceedings in respect of it would be within the jurisdiction of a county court and would not fall within the small claims limit; or

(*b*) if it satisfies the conditions referred to in section 1(2)(*b*) above and the order under section 5 below prescribing the conditions in question provides for this section to apply to causes of action which satisfy them.

(5) For the purposes of subsection (4)(*a*) above proceedings 'fall within the small claims limit'—

(*a*) in England and Wales, if in a county court they would stand referred to arbitration (without any order of the court) under rules made by virtue of section 64(1)(*a*) of the County Courts Act 1984;

(*b*) in Northern Ireland, if in a county court the action would be dealt with by way of arbitration by a circuit registrar by virtue of Article 30(3) of the County Courts (Northern Ireland) Order 1980.

(6) Where the consumer submits to arbitration in consequence of an order under this section, he shall not be regarded for the purposes of section 1(1)(*b*) above as submitting to arbitration in pursuance of the agreement there mentioned.

5. Orders adding to the causes of action to which section 1 applies

(1) Orders under this section may prescribe the conditions referred to in section 1(2)(*b*) above; and any such order may provide that section 4 above shall apply to a cause of action which satisfies the conditions so prescribed.

(2) Orders under this section may make different provisions for different cases and for different purposes.

(3) The power to make orders under this section for England and Wales shall be exercisable by statutory instrument made by the Secretary of State with the concurrence of the Lord Chancellor; but no such order shall be made unless a draft of it has been laid before, and approved by resolution of, each House of Parliament.

(4) The power to make orders under this section for Northern Ireland shall be exercisable by the Department of Economic Development for Northern Ireland with the concurrence of the Lord Chancellor; and any such order—

(*a*) shall be a statutory rule for the purposes of the Statutory Rules (Northern Ireland) Order 1979; and

(*b*) shall be subject to affirmative resolution, within the meaning of section 41(4) of the Interpretation Act (Northern Ireland) 1954.

Scotland

6. Arbitration agreements: Scotland

(1) In the case of a consumer contract to which, by virtue of subsections (2) to (4) of section 15 of the Act of 1977 (scope of Part II of that Act), sections 16 to 18 of that Act apply, an agreement to refer future differences arising out of the contract to arbitration cannot, if it is a domestic arbitration agreement,

be enforced against the consumer in respect of a relevant difference so arising except—

(*a*) with his written consent given after that difference has arisen; or
(*b*) where, subject to subsection (2) below, he has submitted to arbitration in pursuance of the agreement (whether or not the arbitration was in respect of that difference); or
(*c*) by virtue of an order under section 7 below in respect of that difference.

(2) In determining for the purposes of subsection (1)(b) above whether the consumer has submitted to arbitration, any arbitration which takes place in consequence of an order of the court under section 7 below shall be disregarded.

7. Power of court to disapply section 6 where no detriment to consumer

(1) Subject to subsection (4) below, the Court of Session or the sheriff ('the court') may, on an application made after a relevant difference has arisen, order that section 6 above shall not apply as respects that difference.

(2) No such order shall be made unless the court is satisfied that it would not be detrimental to the interests of the consumer were the difference to be referred to arbitration in pursuance of the arbitration agreement.

(3) In determining for the purposes of subsection (2) above whether there would be any detriment to the consumer's interests, the court shall have regard to all factors appearing to be relevant, including, in particular, the availability of legal aid and the relative amounts of any expenses which he might incur—

(*a*) if the difference is referred to arbitration; and
(*b*) if it is determined by proceedings before a court.

(4) No order shall be made under subsection (1) above where, if (disregarding the arbitration agreement) the difference were to be resolved by civil proceedings in the sheriff court, the form of summary cause process to be used for the purposes of those proceedings would be that of a small claim.

8. Construction of sections 6 and 7

(1) In sections 6 and 7 above 'consumer' and 'consumer contract' have the meanings assigned to those expressions by section 25(1) of the Act of 1977 and 'domestic arbitration agreement' has the same meaning as in section 1 of the Arbitration Act 1975.

(2) For the purposes of sections 6 and 7 above a difference is 'relevant' where, if (disregarding the arbitration agreement) it were to be resolved by civil proceedings in the sheriff court—

(*a*) the form of process to be used for the purposes of those proceedings would be that of a summary cause; or
(*b*) the proceedings would come within such description of proceedings as may, by order, be specified by the Secretary of State for the purposes of this paragraph.

(3) The power to make an order under paragraph (*b*) of subsection (2) above shall be exercisable by statutory instrument made with the concurrence of the Lord Advocate; but no order shall be so made unless a draft has been laid before, and approved by resolution of, each House of Parliament.

Supplementary

9. Short title, commencement, interpretation and extent

(1) This Act may be cited as the Consumer Arbitration Agreements Act 1988.

(2) This Act shall have effect in relation to contracts made on or after such day as the Secretary of State may by order made by statutory instrument appoint; and different days may be so appointed for different provisions and different purposes.

(3) In this Act 'the Act of 1977' means the Unfair Contract Terms Act 1977.

(4) Sections 1 to 5 above do not extend to Scotland, sections 6 to 8 extend to Scotland only, and this Act, apart from sections 6 to 8, extends to Northern Ireland.

The Mail Order Transactions (Information) Order 1976

(S.I. 1976 No. 1812)

Whereas the Director General of Fair Trading made a reference, to which section 17 of the Fair Trading Act 1973 applies, to the Consumer Protection Advisory Committee:

And whereas a report on that reference has been made by that Committee to the Secretary of State, and pursuant to section 83 of that Act the report has been laid before Parliament:

And whereas the report states that the Committee agree with the proposal set out in paragraph 5 of the Schedule to the reference:

And whereas a draft of this Order has been approved by a resolution of each House of Parliament:

Now, therefore, the Secretary of State, in exercise of his powers under section 22 of the Fair Trading Act 1973, hereby makes the following Order:—

1. This Order may be cited as the Mail Order Transactions (Information) Order 1976 and shall come into operation on 1st January 1977.

2. The Interpretation Act [1978] shall apply for the interpretation of this Order as it applies for the interpretation of an Act of Parliament.

3. (1) A communication to which this Article applies is an advertisement, circular, catalogue or other communication which fulfils the following conditions, that is to say—

　(i) it describes goods;
　(ii) it contains an invitation (express or implied) to persons to order goods of that description by post, and the invitation is not expressly limited to persons who are not consumers;
　(iii) it states, or from its terms it is reasonable to infer, that a payment is to be made before the goods are dispatched;
　(iv) it is not an advertisement made by way of a sound or television broadcast or an exhibition of a film.

(2) Subject to paragraph (3) below, a person shall not, in the course of a business, publish, distribute or furnish or cause to be published, distributed or furnished a communication to which this Article applies unless the communication contains in legible characters the true name or registered business name of the person carrying on the business in the course of which orders sent by post pursuant to the invitation contained in that communication are to be fulfilled and the address at which that business is managed.

(3) Nothing in paragraph (2) above shall require any address of a body corporate to be given in a document which is required to comply—

The Mail Order Transactions (Information) Order 1976

(*a*) with subsection (7) of section 9 of the European Communities Act 1972 or with that subsection as extended by virtue of subsection (8) of that section; or

(*b*) with Article 7 of the Companies (European Communities) Order (Northern Ireland) 1972, or with that Article as extended by virtue of Article 8 thereof,

and which mentions the address of the registered office of the body corporate in compliance therewith.

(4) In this Acticle—

'true name' means, in the case of an individual, his true surname with or without the addition of christian names or forenames or the initials thereof and, in the case of a body corporate, its corporate name; and

'registered business name' means a name registered under the Registration of Business Names Act 1916.

Consumer Protection
The Consumer Transactions (Restrictions on Statements) Order 1976
(S.I. 1976 No. 1813)

Laid before Parliament in draft

Made - - -   1st November 1976

Coming into Operation in accordance with the provisions of Article I

Whereas the Director General of Fair Trading made a reference, to which section 17 of the Fair Trading Act 1973 applies, to the Consumer Protection Advisory Committee:

And whereas a report on that reference has been made by that Committee to the Secretary of State, and pursuant to section 83 of that Act the report has been laid before Parliament:

And whereas the report states that the Committee would agree with the proposals set out in the reference if the proposals were modified in the manner specified in the report:

And whereas a draft of this Order has been approved by a resolution of each House of Parliament:

Now, therefore, the Secretary of State, in exercise of his powers under section 22 of the Fair Trading Act 1973, hereby makes the following Order:—

1. This Order may be cited as the Consumer Transactions (Restrictions on Statements) Order 1976, and shall come into operation as respects—

   (*a*) this Article, Article 2 and Article 3(*a*), at the expiry of the period of 1 month beginning with the date on which this Order is made;
   (*b*) the remainder of Article 3, at the expiry of the period of 12 months beginning with that date; and
   (*c*) the remainder of this Order, at the expiry of the period of 2 years beginning with that date.

2. (1) In this Order—

   'advertisement' includes a catalogue and a circular;

   'consumer' means a person acquiring goods otherwise than in the course of a business but does not include a person who holds himself out as acquiring them in the course of a business;

   'consumer transaction' means—

   (*a*) [a consumer sale, that is a sale of goods (other than an excepted sale) by a seller where the goods—
      (i) are of a type ordinarily bought for private use or consumption, and
      (ii) are sold to a person who does not buy or hold himself out as buying them in the course of a business.

The Consumer Transactions (Restrictions on Statements) Order 1976

For the purposes of this paragraph an excepted sale is a sale by auction, a sale by competitive tender and a sale arising by virtue of a contract for the international sale of goods as originally defined in section 62(1) of the Sale of Goods Act 1893 as amended by the Supply of Goods (Implied Terms) Act 1973;

(b) a hire-purchase agreement (within the meaning of section 189(1) of the Consumer Credit Act 1974) where the owner makes the agreement in the course of a business and the goods to which the agreement relates—
  (i) are of a type ordinarily supplied for private use or consumption, and
  (ii) are hired to a person who does not hire or hold himself out as hiring them in the course of a business;]

(c) an agreement for the redemption of trading stamps under a trading stamp scheme within section 10(1) of the Trading Stamps Act 1964 or, as the case may be, within section 9 of the Trading Stamps Act (Northern Ireland) 1965;

'container' includes any form of packaging of goods whether by way of wholly or partly enclosing the goods or by way of attaching the goods to, or winding the goods round, some other article, and in particular includes a wrapper or confining band;

'statutory rights' means the rights arising by virtue of sections 13 to 15 of the Sale of Goods Act 1893 as amended by the Act of 1973, sections 9 to 11 of the Act of 1973, or section 4(1)(c) of the Trading Stamps Act 1964 or section 4(1)(c) of the Trading Stamps Act (Northern Ireland) 1965 both as amended by the Act of 1973.

(2) The Interpretation Act 1889 shall apply for the interpretation of this Order as it applies for the interpretation of an Act of Parliament.

[*In the definition of 'consumer transaction', paragraphs (a) and (b) were substituted by the Consumer Transactions (Restrictions on Statements) (Amendment) Order 1978 (S.I. 1978 No. 127).*]

3. A person shall not, in the course of a business—

(a) display, at any place where consumer transactions are effected (whether wholly or partly), a notice containing a statement which purports to apply, in relation to consumer transactions effected there, a term which would—
  (i) [be void by virtue of section 6 or 20 of the Unfair Contract Terms Act 1977,] or
  (ii) be inconsistent with a warranty (in Scotland a stipulation) implied by section 4(1)(c) of the Trading Stamps Act 1964 or section 4(1)(c) of the Trading Stamps Act (Northern Ireland) 1965 both as amended by the Act of 1973,

  if applied to some or all such consumer transactions;

(b) publish or cause to be published any advertisement which is intended to induce persons to enter into consumer transactions and which contains a statement purporting to apply in relation to such consumer transactions such a term as is mentioned in paragraph (a)(i) or (ii), being a term which would be void by virtue of, or as the case may be, inconsistent

The Consumer Transactions (Restrictions on Statements) Order 1976

with, the provisions so mentioned if applied to some or all of those transactions;

(c) supply to a consumer pursuant to a consumer transaction goods bearing, or goods in a container bearing, a statement which is a term of that consumer transaction and which is void by virtue of, or inconsistent with, the said provisions, or if it were a term of that transaction, would be so void or inconsistent;

(d) furnish to a consumer in connection with the carrying out of a consumer transaction or to a person likely, as a consumer, to enter into such a transaction, a document which includes a statement which is a term of that transaction and is void or inconsistent as aforesaid, or, if it were a term of that transaction, or were to become a term of a prospective transaction, would be so void or inconsistent.

[*Sub-paragraph (i) of Article 3(a) was substituted by the Consumer Transactions (Restrictions on Statements) (Amendment) Order 1978 (S.I. 1978 No. 127).*]

4. A person shall not in the course of a business—

(i) supply to a consumer pursuant to a consumer transaction goods bearing, or goods in a container bearing, a statement about the rights that the consumer has against that person or about the obligations to the consumer accepted by that person in relation to the goods (whether legally enforceable or not), being rights or obligations that arise if the goods are defective or are not fit for a purpose or do not correspond with a description.

(ii) furnish to a consumer in connection with the carrying out of a consumer transaction or to a person likely, as a consumer, to enter into such a transaction with him or through his agency a document containing a statement about such rights and obligations,

unless there is in close proximity to any such statement another statement which is clear and conspicuous and to the effect that the first-mentioned statement does not or will not affect the statutory rights of a consumer.

5. (1) This Article applies to goods which are supplied in the course of a business by one person ('the supplier') to another where, at the time of the supply, the goods were intended by the supplier to be, or might reasonably be expected by him to be, the subject of a subsequent consumer transaction.

(2) A supplier shall not—

(a) supply goods to which this Article applies if the goods bear, or are in a container bearing, a statement which sets out or describes or limits obligations (whether legally enforceable or not) accepted or to be accepted by him in relation to the goods; or

(b) furnish a document in relation to the goods which contains such a statement,

unless there is in close proximity to any such statement another statement which is clear and conspicuous and to the effect that the first-mentioned statement does not or will not affect the statutory rights of a consumer.

(3) A person does not contravene paragraph (2) above—

(i) in a case to which sub-paragraph (a) of that paragraph applies, unless the goods have become the subject of a consumer transaction;

(ii) in a case to which sub-paragraph (b) applies, unless the document has been furnished to a consumer in relation to goods which were the subject of a consumer transaction, or to a person likely to become a consumer pursuant to such a transaction; or

(iii) by virtue of any statement if before the date on which this Article comes into operation the document containing, or the goods or container bearing, the statement has ceased to be in his possession.

The Business Advertisements (Disclosure) Order 1977
(S.I. 1977 No. 1918)

Whereas the Director General of Fair Trading made a reference, to which section 17 of the Fair Trading Act 1973 applies, to the Consumer Protection Advisory Committee:

And whereas a report on that reference has been made by that Committee to the Secretary of State, and pursuant to section 83 of that Act the report has been laid before Parliament:

And whereas the report states that the Committee would agree with the proposals set out in the Schedule to the reference if the proposals were modified in the manner specified in the report:

And whereas a draft of this order has been approved by a resolution of each House of Parliament:

Now, therefore, the Secretary of State, in exercise of his powers under section 22 of the Fair Trading Act 1973, hereby makes the following Order:—

1. (1) This Order may be cited as the Business Advertisements (Disclosure) Order 1977 and shall come into operation on 1st January 1978.

(2) The Interpretation Act [1978] shall apply for the interpretation of this Order as it applies for the interpretation of an Act of Parliament.

2. (1) Subject to paragraphs (2) and (3) below, a person who is seeking to sell goods that are being sold in the course of a business shall not publish or cause to be published an advertisement—

(*a*) which indicates that the goods are for sale, and
(*b*) which is likely to induce consumers to buy the goods,

unless it is reasonably clear whether from the contents of the advertisement, its format or size, the place or manner of its publication or otherwise that the goods are to be sold in the course of a business.

(2) Paragraph (1) applies whether the person who is seeking to sell the goods is acting on his own behalf or that of another, and where he is acting as agent, whether he is acting in the course of a business carried on by him or not; but the reference in that paragraph to a business does not include any business carried on by the agent.

(3) Paragraph (1) above shall not apply in relation to advertisements—

(*a*) which are concerned only with sales by auction or competitive tender, or
(*b*) which are concerned only with the sale of flowers, fruit or vegetables, eggs or dead animals, fish or birds, gathered, produced or taken by the person seeking to sell the goods.

Consumer Protection

The Consumer Protection (Cancellation of Contracts Concluded away from Business Premises) Regulations 1987

(S.I. 1987 No. 2117)

Made – – – – *7 December 1987*
Laid before Parliament *December 1987*
Coming into force *1 July 1988*

The Secretary of State, being a Minister designated for the purposes of section 2(2) of the European Communities Act 1972 in relation to matters of consumer protection in respect of contracts negotiated away from business premises of the trader, in exercise of the powers conferred on him by that section and of all other powers enabling him in that behalf, hereby makes the following Regulations:

1. Citation and commencement

These Regulations may be cited as the Consumer Protection (Cancellation of Contracts Concluded away from Business Premises) Regulations 1987 and shall come into force on 1st July 1988.

2. Interpretation

(1) In these Regulations—
'business' includes a trade or profession;

'consumer' means a person, other than a body corporate, who, in making a contract to which these Regulations apply, is acting for purposes which can be regarded as outside his business;

'goods' has the meaning given by section 61(1) of the Sale of Goods Act 1979;

'land mortgage' includes any security charged on land and in relation to Scotland includes any heritable security;

'notice of cancellation' has the meaning given by regulation 4(5) below;

'security' in relation to a contract means a mortgage, charge, pledge, bond, debenture, indemnity, guarantee, bill, note or other right provided by the consumer, or at his request (express or implied), to secure the carrying out of his obligations under the contract;

'signed' has the same meaning as in the Consumer Credit Act 1974; and

'trader' means a person who, in making a contract to which these Regulations apply, is acting for the purposes of his business, and anyone acting in the name or on behalf of such a person.

(2) In Scotland any provision in these Regulations requiring a document to be signed shall be complied with by a body corporate if the document is properly executed in accordance with the law of Scotland.

The Consumer Protection Regulations 1987

64. Contracts to which the Regulations apply

(1) The Regulations apply to a contract, other than an excepted contract for the supply by a trader of goods or services to a consumer which is made—

(*a*) during an unsolicited visit by a trader—
  (i) to the consumer's home or to the home of another person; or
  (ii) to the consumer's place of work;
(*b*) during a visit by a trader as mentioned in paragraph (*a*)(i) or (ii) above at the express request of the consumer where the goods or services to which the contract relates are other than those concerning which the consumer requested the visit of the trader, provided that when the visit was requested the consumer did not know, or could not reasonably have known, that the supply of those other goods or services formed part of the trader's business activities;
(*c*) after an offer was made by the consumer in respect of the supply by a trader of the goods or services in the circumstances mentioned in paragraph (*a*) or (*b*) above or (*d*) below; or
(*d*) during an excursion organised by the trader away from premises on which he is carrying on any business (whether on a permanent or temporary basis).

(2) For the purposes of this regulation an excepted contract means

(*a*) any contract—
  (i) for the sale or other disposition of land, or for a lease or land mortgage;
  (ii) to finance the purchase of land;
  (iii) for a bridging loan in connection with the purchase of land; or
  (iv) for the construction or extension of a building or other erection on land:
     Provided that these Regulations shall apply to a contract for the supply of goods and their incorporation in any land or a contract for the repair or improvement of a building or other erection on land, where the contract is not financed by a loan secured by a land mortgage;
(*b*) any contract for the supply of food, drink or other goods intended for current consumption by use in the household and supplied by regular roundsmen;
(*c*) any contract for the supply of goods or services which satisfies all the following conditions, namely—
  (i) terms of the contract are contained in a trader's catalogue which is readily available to the consumer to read in the absence of the trader or his representative before the conclusion of the contract;
  (ii) the parties to the contract intend that there shall be maintained continuity of contact between the trader or his representative and the consumer in relation to the transaction in question or any subsequent transaction; and
  (iii) both the catalogue and the contract contain or are accompanied by a prominent notice indicating that the consumer has a right to return to the trader or his representative goods supplied to him within the period of not less than 7 days from the day on which the goods are received by the consumer and otherwise to cancel the contract within that period without the consumer

The Consumer Protection Regulations 1987

incurring any liability, other than any liability which may arise from the failure of the consumer to take reasonable care of the goods while they are in his possession;

(d) contracts of insurance to which the Insurance Companies Act 1982 applies;

(e) investment agreements within the meaning of the Financial Services Act 1986, and agreements for the making of deposits within the meaning of the Banking Act 1987 in respect of which Regulations have been made for regulating the making of unsolicited calls under section 34 of that Act;

(f) any contract not falling within sub-paragraph (g) below under which the total payments to be made by the consumer do not exceed £35; and

(g) any contract under which credit within the meaning of the Consumer Credit Act 1974 is provided not exceeding £35 other than a hire-purchase or conditional sale agreement.

(3) In this regulation 'unsolicited visit' means a visit by a trader, whether or not he is the trader who supplies the goods or services, which does not take place at the express request of the consumer and includes a visit which takes place after a trader telephones the consumer (otherwise than at his express request) indicating expressly or by implication that he is willing to visit the consumer.

4. Cancellation of Contract

(1) No contract to which these Regulations apply shall be enforceable against the consumer unless the trader has delivered to the consumer notice in writing in accordance with paragraphs (3) and (4) below indicating the right of the consumer to cancel the contract within the period of 7 days mentioned in paragraph (5) below containing both the information set out in Part I of the Schedule to these Regulations and a Cancellation Form in the form set out in Part II of the Schedule and completed in accordance with the footnotes.

(2) Paragraph (1) above does not apply to a cancellable agreement within the meaning of the Consumer Credit Act 1974 or to an agreement which may be cancelled by the consumer in accordance with terms of the agreement conferring upon him similar rights as if the agreement were such a cancellable agreement.

(3) The information to be contained in the notice under paragraph (1) above shall be easily legible and if incorporated in the contract or other document shall be afforded no less prominence than that given to any other information in the document apart from the heading to the document and the names of the parties to the contract and any information inserted in handwriting.

(4) The notice shall be dated and delivered to the consumer—

(a) in the cases mentioned in regulation 3(1)(a), (b) and (d) above, at the time of the making of the contract; and

(b) in the case mentioned in regulation 3(1)(c) above, at the time of the making of the offer by the consumer.

(5) If within the period of 7 days following the making of the contract the consumer serves a notice in writing (a 'notice of cancellation') on the trader or any other person specified in a notice referred to in paragraph (1) above as a person to whom notice of cancellation may be given which, however expressed and whether or not conforming to the cancellation form set out in Part II of

The Consumer Protection Regulations 1987

the Schedule to these Regulations, indicates the intention of the consumer to cancel the contract, the notice of cancellation shall operate to cancel the contract.

(6) Except as otherwise provided under these Regulations, a contract cancelled under paragraph (5) above shall be treated as if it had never been entered into by the consumer.

(7) Notwithstanding anything in section 7 of the Interpretation Act 1978, a notice of cancellation sent by post by a consumer shall be deemed to have been served at the time of posting, whether or not it is actually received.

5. Recovery of money paid by consumer

(1) Subject to regulation 7(2) below, on the cancellation of a contract under regulation 4 above, any sum paid by or on behalf of the consumer under or in contemplation of the contract shall become repayable.

(2) If under the terms of the cancelled contract the consumer or any person on his behalf is in possession of any goods, he shall have a lien on them for any sum repayable to him under paragraph (1) above.

(3) Where any security has been provided in relation to the cancelled contract, the security, so far as it is so provided, shall be treated as never having had effect and any property lodged with the trader solely for the purposes of the security as so provided shall be returned by him forthwith.

6. Repayment of credit

(1) Notwithstanding the cancellation of a contract under regulation 4 above under which credit is provided, the contract shall continue in force so far as it relates to repayment of credit and payment of interest.

(2) If, following the cancellation of the contract, the consumer repays the whole or a portion of the credit—

- (*a*) before the expiry of one month following service of the notice of cancellation, or
- (*b*) in the case of a credit repayable by instalments, before the date on which the first instalment is due,

no interest shall be payable on the amount repaid.

(3) If the whole of a credit repayable by instalments is not repaid on or before the date specified in paragraph (2)(*b*) above, the consumer shall not be liable to repay any of the credit except on receipt of a request in writing signed by the trader stating the amounts of the remaining instalments (recalculated by the trader as nearly as may be in accordance with the contract and without extending the repayment period), but excluding any sum other than principal and interest.

(4) Repayment of a credit, or payment of interest, under a cancelled contract shall be treated as duly made if it is made to any person on whom, under regulation 4(5) above, a notice of cancellation could have been served.

(5) Where any security has been provided in relation to the contract, the duty imposed on the consumer by this regulation shall not be enforceable before the trader has discharged any duty imposed on him by regulation 5(3) above.

The Consumer Protection Regulations 1987

[(6) In this regulation, the following expressions have the meanings hereby assigned to them:—

'cash' includes money in any form;

'credit' means a cash loan and any facility enabling the consumer to overdraw on a current account;

'current account' means an account under which the customer may, by means of cheques or similar orders payable to himself or to any other person, obtain or have the use of money held or made available by the person with whom the account is kept and which records alterations in the financial relationship between the said person and the customer; and

'repayment', in relation to credit, means the repayment of money—

(a) paid to a consumer before the cancellation of the contract; or
(b) to the extent that he has overdrawn on his current account before the cancellation.]

[*The words in square brackets were inserted, with effect from 1 July 1988, by the Consumer Protection (Cancellation of Contracts Concluded away from Business Premises) (Amendment) Regulations 1988 (S.I. 1988 No. 958).*]

7. Return of goods by consumer after cancellation

(1) Subject to paragraph (2) below, a consumer who has before cancelling a contract under regulation 4 above acquired possession of any goods by virtue of the contract shall be under a duty, subject to any lien, on the cancellation to restore the goods to the trader in accordance with this regulation, and meanwhile to retain possession of the goods and take reasonable care of them.

(2) The consumer shall not be under a duty to restore—

(i) perishable goods;
(ii) goods which by their nature are consumed by use and which, before the cancellation, were so consumed;
(iii) goods supplied to meet an emergency; or
(iv) goods which, before the cancellation, had become incorporated in any land or thing not comprised in the cancelled contract,

but he shall be under a duty to pay in accordance with the cancelled contract for the supply of the goods and for the provision of any services in connection with the supply of the goods before the cancellation.

(3) The consumer shall not be under any duty to deliver the goods except at his own premises and in pursuance of a request in writing signed by the trader and served on the consumer either before, or at the time when, the goods are collected from those premises.

(4) If the consumer—

(i) delivers the goods (whether at his own premises or elsewhere) to any person on whom, under regulation 4(5) above, a notice of cancellation could have been served; or
(ii) sends the goods at his own expense to such a person,

he shall be discharged from any duty to retain possession of the goods or restore them to the trader.

(5) Where the consumer delivers the goods as mentioned in paragraph (4)(i) above, his obligation to take care of the goods shall cease; and if he sends the goods as mentioned in paragraph (4)(ii) above, he shall be under a duty to take reasonable care to see that they are received by the trader and not damaged in transit, but in other respects his duty to take care of the goods shall cease.

(6) Where, at any time during the period of 21 days following the cancellation, the consumer receives such a request as is mentioned in paragraph (3) above and unreasonably refuses or unreasonably fails to comply with it, his duty to retain possession and take reasonable care of the goods shall continue until he delivers or sends the goods as mentioned in paragraph (4) above, but if within that period he does not receive such a request his duty to take reasonable care of the goods shall cease at the end of that period.

(7) Where any security has been provided in relation to the cancelled contract, the duty imposed on the consumer to restore goods by this regulation shall not be enforceable before the trader has discharged any duty imposed on him by regulation 5(3) above.

(8) Breach of a duty imposed by this regulation on a consumer is actionable as a breach of statutory duty.

8. Goods given in part-exchange

(1) This regulation applies on the cancellation of a contract under regulation 4 above where the trader agreed to take goods in part-exchange (the 'part-exchange goods') and those goods have been delivered to him.

(2) Unless, before the end of the period of ten days beginning with the date of cancellation, the part-exchange goods are returned to the consumer in a condition substantially as good as when they were delivered to the trader, the consumer shall be entitled to recover from the trader a sum equal to the part-exchange allowance.

(3) During the period of ten days beginning with the date of cancellation, the consumer, if he is in possession of goods to which the cancelled contract relates, shall have a lien on them for—

  (a) delivery of the part-exchange goods in a condition substantially as good as when they were delivered to the trader; or
  (b) a sum equal to the part-exchange allowance;

and if the lien continues to the end of that period it shall thereafter subsist only as a lien for a sum equal to the part-exchange allowance.

(4) In this regulation the part-exchange allowance means the sum agreed as such in the cancelled contract, or if not such sum was agreed, such sum as it would have been reasonable to allow in respect of the part-exchange goods if no notice of cancellation had been served.

9. Amendment of the Consumer Credit Act 1974

(*This regulation amends section 74(2) of the Consumer Credit Act 1974. The amendment is included in that section above.*)

10. No contracting-out

(1) A term contained in a contract to which these Regulations apply is void if, and to the extent that, it is inconsistent with a provision for the protection of the consumer contained in these Regulations.

(2) Where a provision of these Regulations specifies the duty or liability of the consumer in certain circumstances a term contained in a contract to which these Regulations apply is inconsistent with that provision if it purports to impose, directly or indirectly, an additional duty or liability on him in those circumstances.

11. Service of documents

(1) A document to be served under these Regulations on a person may be so served—

- (*a*) by delivering it to him, or by sending it by post to him, or by leaving it with him, at his proper address addressed to him by name;
- (*b*) if the person is a body corporate, by serving it in accordance with paragraph (*a*) above on the secretary or clerk of that body; or
- (*c*) if the person is a partnership, by serving it in accordance with paragraph (*a*) above on a partner or on a person having the control or management of the partnership business.

(2) For the purposes of these Regulations, a document sent by post to, or left at, the address last known to the server of the document as the address of a person shall be treated as sent by post to, or left at, his proper address.

SCHEDULE   Regulation 4(i)

PART I

(information to be contained in notice of cancellation rights)

1. The name of the trader.

2. The trader's reference number, code or other details to enable the contract or offer to be identified.

3. A statement that the consumer has a right to cancel the contract if he wishes and that this right can be exercised by sending or taking a written notice of cancellation to the person mentioned in paragraph 4 within the period of 7 days following the making of the contract.

4. The name and address of a person to whom notice of cancellation may be given.

5. A statement that the consumer can use the cancellation form provided if he wishes.

PART II

(cancellation form to be included in notice of cancellation rights)

(Complete, detach and return this form *ONLY IF YOU WISH TO CANCEL THE CONTRACT.*)

The Consumer Protection Regulations 1987

To: 1

I/We* hereby give notice that I/we* wish to cancel my/our* contract

      2

Signed

Date

*Delete as appropriate

Notes:

1. Trader to insert name and address of person to whom notice may be given.

2. Trader to insert reference number, code or other details to enable the contract or offer to be identified. He may also insert the name and address of the consumer.

The Control of Misleading Advertisements Regulations 1988

Consumer Protection
The Control of Misleading Advertisements Regulations 1988
(S.I. 1988 No. 915)

Made – – – 23 May 1988
Coming into force 20 June 1988

Whereas the Secretary of State is a Minister designed for the purposes of section 2(2) of the European Communities Act 1972 in relation to measures relating to the control of advertising:

And whereas a draft of these Regulations has been approved by a resolution of each House of Parliament pursuant to section 2(2) of and paragraph 2(2) of Schedule 2 to that Act:

Now, therefore, the Secretary of State in exercise of the powers conferred on him by section 2(2) of that Act and of all other powers enabling him in that behalf hereby makes the following Regulations:

1. Citation and commencement

These Regulations may be cited as the Control of Misleading Advertisements Regulations 1988 and shall come into force on 20 June 1988.

2. Interpretation

(1) In these Regulations—

'advertisement' means any form of representation which is made in connection with a trade, business, craft or profession in order to promote the supply or transfer of goods or services, immoveable property, rights or obligations;

'broadcast advertisement' means any advertisement included or proposed to be included in any programme or teletext transmission broadcast by the IBA and includes any advertisement included or proposed to be included in a licensed service by the reception and immediate re-transmission of broadcasts made by the IBA;

'Cable Authority' means the authority mentioned in section 1(1) of the Cable and Broadcasting Act 1984;

'court', in relation to England and Wales and Northern Ireland, means the High Court, and, in relation to Scotland, the Court of Session;

'Director' means the Director General of Fair Trading;

'IBA' means the Independent Broadcasting Authority mentioned in section 1(1) of the Broadcasting Act 1981;

'licensable service' has the meaning given by section 2(2) of the Cable and Broadcasting Act 1984;

'licensed service' means a licensable service in respect of which the Cable

Authority has granted a licence pursuant to section 4 of the Cable and Broadcasting Act 1984;

'publication' in relation to an advertisement means the dissemination of that advertisement whether to an individual person or a number of persons and whether orally or in writing or in any other way whatsoever, and 'publish' shall be construed accordingly.

(2) For the purposes of these Regulations an advertisement is misleading if in any way, including its presentation, it deceives or is likely to deceive the persons to whom it is addressed or whom it reaches and if, by reason of its deceptive nautre, it is likely to affect their economic behaviour or, for those reasons, injures or is likely to injure a competitor of the person whose interests the advertisement seeks to promote.

(3) In the application of these Regulations to Scotland for references to an injunction or an interlocutory injunction there shall be substituted references to an interdict or an interim interdict respectively.

3. Application

(1) These Regulations do not apply to—

(*a*) the following advertisements issued or caused to be issued by or on behalf of an authorised person or appointed representative, that is to say—
   (i) investment advertisements; and
   (ii) any other advertisements in respect of investment business,

(*b*) advertisements of a description referred to in section 58(1)(*d*) of the Financial Services Act 1986, except where any such advertisements consist of or any part of the matters referred to in section 58(1)(*d*)(ii) of that Act as being required or permitted to be published by an approved exchange under Part V of that Act.

(2) In this regulation 'appointed representative', 'approved exchange', 'authorised person', 'exempted person', 'investment advertisement' and 'investment business' have the same meanings as in the Financial Services Act 1986.

4. Complaints to the Director

(1) Subject to paragraphs (2) and (3) below, it shall be the duty of the Director to consider any complaint made to him that an advertisement is misleading, unless the complaint appears to the Director to be frivolous or vexatious.

(2) The Director shall not consider any complaint which these Regulations require or would require, leaving aside any question as to the frivolous or vexatious nature of the complaint, the IBA or the Cable Authority to consider.

(3) Before considering any complaint under paragraph (1) above the Director may require the person making the complaint to satisfy him that—

(*a*) there have been invoked in relation to the same or substantially the same complaint about the advertisement in question such established means of dealing with such complaints as the Director may consider appropriate, having regard to all the circumstances of the particular case;

The Control of Misleading Advertisements Regulations 1988

(b) a reasonable opportunity has been allowed for those means to deal with the complaint in question; and
(c) those means have not dealt with the complaint adequately.

(4) In exercising the powers conferred on him by these Regulations the Director shall have regard to—

(a) all the interests involved and in particular the public interest; and
(b) the desirability of encouraging the control, by self-regulatory bodies, of advertisements.

5. Applications to the Court by the Director

(1) If, having considered a complaint about an advertisement pursuant to regulation 4(1) above, he considers that the advertisement is misleading, the Director may, if he thinks it appropriate to do so, bring proceedings for an injunction (in which proceedings he may also apply for an interlocutory injunction) against any person appearing to him to be concerned or likely to be concerned with the publication of the advertisement.

(2) The Director shall give reasons for his decisions to apply or not to apply, as the case may be, for an injunction in relation to any complaint which these Regulations require him to consider.

6. Functions of the Court

(1) The court on an application by the Director may grant an injunction on such terms as it may think fit but (except where it grants an interlocutory injunction) only if the court is satisfied that the advertisement to which the application relates is misleading. Before granting an injunction the court shall have regard to all the interests involved and in particular the public interest.

(2) An injunction may relate not only to a particular advertisement but to any advertisement in similar terms or likely to convey a similar impression.

(3) In considering an aplication for an injunction the court may, whether or not on the application of any party to the proceedings, require any person appearing to the court to be responsible for the publication of the advertisement to which the application relates to furnish the court with evidence of the accuracy of any factual claim made in the advertisement. The court shall not make such a requirement unless it appears to the court to be appropriate in the circumstances of the particular case, having regard to the legitimate interests of the person who would be the subject of or affected by the requirement and of any other person concerned with the advertisement.

(4) If such evidence is not furnished to it following a requirement made by it under paragraph (3) above or if it considers such evidence inadequate, the court may decline to consider the factual claim mentioned in that paragraph accurate.

(5) The court shall not refuse to grant an injunction for lack of evidence that—

(a) the publication of the advertisement in question has given rise to loss or damage to any person; or
(b) the person responsible for the advertisement intended it to be misleading or failed to exercise proper care to prevent its being misleading.

The Control of Misleading Advertisements Regulations 1988

(6) An injunction may prohibit the publication or the continued or further publication of an advertisement.

7. Powers of the Director to obtain and disclose information and disclosure of information generally

(1) For the purpose of facilitating the exercise by him of any functions conferred on him by these Regulations, the Director may, by notice in writing signed by him or on his behalf, require any person to furnish to him such information as may be specified or described in the notice or to produce to him any documents so specified or described.

(2) A notice under paragraph (1) above may—

(*a*) specify the way in which and the time within which it is to be complied with; and
(*b*) be varied or revoked by a subsequent notice.

(3) Nothing in this regulation compels the production or furnishing by any person of a document or of information which he would in an action in a court be entitled to refuse to produce or furnish on grounds of legal professional privilege, or, in Scotland, on the grounds of confidentiality as between client and professional legal adviser.

(4) If a person makes default in complying with a notice under paragraph (1) above the court may, on the application of the Director, make such order as the court thinks fit for requiring the default to be made good, and any such order may provide that all the costs or expenses of an incidental to the application shall be borne by the person in default or by any officers of a company or other association who are responsible for its default.

(5) Subject to any provision to the contrary made by or under any enactment, where the Director considers it appropriate to do so for the purpose of controlling misleading advertisements, he may refer to any person any complaint (including any related documentation) about an advertisement or disclose to any person any information (whether or not obtained by means of the exercise of the power conferred by paragraph (1) above).

(6) For the purpose of enabling information obtained under certain enactments to be used for facilitating the performance of functions under these Regulations, the following amendments shall be made in provisions respecting disclosure of information, that is to say—

(*There then follows a list, here omitted, of amendments of various statutes.*)

(7) Subject to paragraph (5) above, any person who knowingly discloses, otherwise than for the purposes of any legal proceedings or of a report of such proceedings or the investigation of any criminal offence, any information obtained by means of the exercise of the power conferred by paragraph (1) above without the consent either of the person to whom the information relates, or, if the information relates to a business, the consent of the person for the time being carrying on that business, shall be guilty of an offence and liable on summary conviction to imprisonment for a term not exceeding 3 months or to a fine not exceeding £2,000 or to both.

(8) The Director may arrange for the disseminaton in such form and manner as he considers appropriate of such information and advice concerning the

The Control of Misleading Advertisements Regulations 1988

operation of these Regulations as may appear to him to be expedient to give to the public and to all persons likely to be affected by these Regulations.

8. Complaints to the IBA

(1) It shall be the duty of the IBA to consider any complaint made to it that a broadcast advertisement is misleading, unless the complaint appears to the IBA to be frivolous or vexatious.

(2) The IBA shall give reasons for its decision.

(3) In exercising the powers conferred on it by these regulations the IBA shall have regard to all the interests involved and in particular the public interest.

9. Control by the IBA of misleading advertisements

(1) If, having considered a complaint about a broadcast advertisement pursuant to regulation 8(1) above, it considers that the advertisement is misleading, the IBA may, if it thinks it appropriate to do so, refuse to broadcast the advertisement.

(2) The IBA may require any person appearing to it to be responsible for a broadcast advertisement which the IBA believes may be misleading to furnish it with evidence as to the accuracy of any factual claim made in the advertisement. In deciding whether not to make such a requirement the IBA shall have regard to the legitimate interests of any person who would be the subject of or affected by the requirement.

(3) If such evidence is not furnished to it following a requirement made by it under paragraph (2) above or if it considers such evidence inadequate, the IBA may consider the factual claim inaccurate.

10. Complaints to the Cable Authority

(1) Subject to paragraph (2) below, it shall be the duty of the Cable Authority to consider any complaint made to it that any advertisement included or proposed to be included in a licensed service is misleading, unless the complaint appears to the Authority to be frivolous or vexatious.

(2) The Cable Authjority shall not consider any complaint about an advertisement included or proposed to be included in a licensed service by the reception and immediate retransmission of broadcasts made by the IBA or the British Broadcasting Corporation.

(3) In exercising the powers conferred on it by these Regulations the Cable Authority shall have regard to all the interests involved and in particular the public interest.

11. Control by the Cable Authority of misleading advertisements

(1) If, having considered a complaint about an advertisement pursuant to regulation 10(1) above, it considers that the advertisement is misleading, the Authority may, if it thinks it appropriate to do so, exercise the power conferred on it by section 15(1) of the Cable and Broadcasting Act 1984 (power to give directions) in relation to the advertisement.

(2) The Authority shall give reasons for its decision to give or not to give, as the cast may be, a direction in accordance with paragraph (1) above in any particular case.

The Control of Misleading Advertisements Regulations 1988

(3) The Authority may require any person appearing to it to be responsible for an advertisement which the Authority believes may be misleading to furnish it with evidence as to the accuracy of any factual claim made in the advertisement. In deciding whether or not to make such a requirement the Authority shall have regard to the legitimate interests of any person who would be the subject of or affected by the requirement.

(4) If such evidence is not furnished to it following a requirement made by it under paragraph (3) above or if it considers such evidence inadequate, the Authority may consider the factual claim inaccurate.